This list is continued inside the back cover.

Congratulations!

As a student purchasing *Personal Finance,* you are entitled to prepaid access to the book's Companion Web site!

The Web Site Includes:

* The entire text online, including up-to-date live Web links and a search feature.
* 30-question interactive chapter quizzes and mini-case problems to help you assess your grasp of material.
* An online career center that will guide you through decisions regarding career selection and job searching.

The duration of your subscription is 6 months.

To Activate your Prepaid Subscription

1. Point your Web browser to http://www.aw.com/madura
2. Click on "Student Resources"
3. Select the "Register" link
4. Enter your preassigned Access Code, exactly as it appears below

ACCESS CODE: WSDM-AGREE-REBEL-DYFED-CANTO-JUTES

5. Select "Submit"
6. Complete the online registration form to establish your personal User ID and Password
7. Once your personal User ID and Password are confirmed, you can begin using the *Personal Finance* Companion Web site!

This Access Code can only be used once to establish a subscription. This subscription to the *Personal Finance* Companion Web site is valid for six months upon activation, and is not transferable.

If you did not purchase this product new and in a shrink-wrapped package, this Access Code may not be valid.

Personal Finance

The Addison-Wesley Series in Finance

Personal Finance

Jeff Madura
Florida Atlantic University

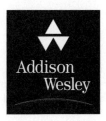

Addison
Wesley

Boston San Francisco New York
London Toronto Sydney Tokyo Singapore Madrid
Mexico City Munich Paris Cape Town Hong Kong Montreal

Acquisitions Editor: Donna Battista
Development Editor: Rebecca Ferris
Senior Production Supervisor: Juliet Silveri
Publishing Services: Lachina Publishing Services
Cover and Text Designer: Leslie Haimes
Design Supervisor: Regina Hagen
Marketing Manager: Adrienne D'Ambrosio
Manufacturing Supervisor: Hugh Crawford
Media Producer: Jennifer Pelland
Supplements Editor: Meredith Gertz

Library of Congress Cataloging-in-Publication

Madura, Jeff.
    Personal finance / Jeff Madura.
        p. cm.
    Includes index.
    ISBN 0-201-70364-5
    1. Finance, Personal. I. Title.

HG179 .M252 2001
332.024--dc21   2001034331

1 2 3 4 5 6 7 8 9 10—RNT—04030201

Brief Contents

Detailed Contents

PART 2   MANAGING YOUR LIQUIDITY

PART 3   PERSONAL FINANCING

PART 4   PERSONAL INVESTING

PART 5   PROTECTING YOUR WEALTH

PART 6   SYNTHESIS OF FINANCIAL PLANNING

Preface

Why should you study personal finance? Actually, a better question might be "Why wouldn't you study personal finance?" Few courses in any subject area have personal finance's potential to profoundly shape your future. Mastering the key concepts will enable you to enhance your personal wealth by building a financial plan that will guide your decisions today and in years to come. For many students, this course will be their only exposure to the field of personal finance. For this reason, *Personal Finance* focuses on the concepts, decision-making tools, and applications of financial planning.

The Internet—in particular, the wide number of personal finance–related sites—has changed the nature of the course. The traditional approach to personal finance was descriptive and focused on rote memorization of definitions and procedures. Yet today's students rarely make any decisions of import without consulting information retrieved from the Internet. Consequently, it is imperative that a personal finance text focus on the key decisions and logic underlying financial planning. Students will then be equipped with the knowledge to interpret the information they obtain online regarding changes in income tax laws, health insurance provisions, retirement programs, and the like.

The book is intended for courses in Personal Finance, Personal Financial Planning, Personal Investing, and Consumer Economics offered by universities, junior colleges, and continuing education programs. No prior knowledge in the subject area is assumed.

DESIGNED TO FORM A FINANCIAL PLAN

The first chapter establishes the text's organization by introducing the key components of a financial plan. The text is organized into parts keyed to the components of a comprehensive financial plan:

1. Budgeting and tax planning,

2. Managing liquidity,

3. Financing large purchases,

4. Investing money,

5. Protecting wealth.

DECISION-MAKING FOCUS

All the information presented in this book is geared toward equipping students with the expertise they need to make informed financial decisions. Each chapter establishes a foundation for the decisions that form the basis of a financial plan. When students complete each chapter, they are therefore prepared to complete the related financial plan subsection.

TAX RELIEF ACT OF 2001

Personal Finance provides complete and current coverage of all the major financial planning areas. Extra attention is devoted to explaining provisions of the Tax Relief Act of 2001 and its impact on marginal tax brackets, tax credits, estate taxes, and 401(k) and individual retirement account contribution limits.

EMPHASIS ON INVESTING

Today's students are more interested in personal investing than ever before. The emergence of online trading companies like E-trade and the ups and downs of the NASDAQ and other stock market indexes have caught students' attention. An emphasis on investing also has pedagogical value, as many of the components of a financial plan require a background in investing. To make effective investment decisions, students must be able to recognize how both the potential return and the risk vary among investments. For these reasons, investment concepts are woven throughout the text and form the focus of six full chapters, including one dedicated to mutual funds.

MATH-FRIENDLY PRESENTATION

The quantitative side of financial planning intimidates many students. *Personal Finance* demystifies the mathematics of personal finance. Formulas and calculations are explained in the text and then illustrated in examples. Every time value of money calculation includes a mock keypad to coach students in the use of financial calculators. Students are referred to Web sites with online calculators whenever pertinent. The Financial Planning Problems and In-text Study Guide provide students with ample opportunity to practice applying math-based concepts.

CAPSTONE CHAPTER

Chapter 20 synthesizes all the parts of the text to highlight the interrelationships among the components of a financial plan. A completed plan for Stephanie Spratt, who is featured in examples throughout the text, underscores that financial planning is an ongoing process that involves tradeoffs.

TEXT ORGANIZATION

Each of the five parts of this text covers one specific component of the financial plan. Part 1, Tools for Financial Planning, describes budgeting, which focuses on how cash inflows are allocated to saving, spending, and taxes. The next component is liquidity management (Part 2) because you must have adequate liquidity before financing or investing. Once your budget plan and your liquidity are in order, you are in a position to plan your financing (Part 3) for major new purchases such as a car or home. Next, you can consider investment alternatives such as stocks, bonds, and mutual funds (Part 4). Finally, your financial plan protects the wealth you have accumulated through effective insurance planning, retirement planning, and estate planning (Part 5).

CHAPTER PEDAGOGY

This text focuses on the key concepts that facilitate decision making in personal finance. The book's outstanding pedagogy, highlighted with an attractive four-color design, captures student interest and aids comprehension.

CHAPTER INTRODUCTION The opening of each chapter demonstrates how the key objectives in that chapter affect your wealth; a diagram illustrates the impact of related decisions on your net worth.

LEARNING OBJECTIVES Corresponding to the main headings in each chapter, the list of learning objectives guides student study.

MARGINAL GLOSSARY Throughout the text, key terms and their definitions appear in the text margin where they are first introduced.

EXPLANATION BY EXAMPLE Practical examples applying concepts in realistic scenarios throughout chapters help cement student understanding. Examples are especially effective in explaining mathematically based concepts. Many concepts are reinforced through a running example of Stephanie Spratt, a recent college graduate working in the Internet sales department of a firm. Students are commonly faced with dilemmas similar to those faced by Stephanie such as how to control recreational spending or whether to buy or lease a car. The Stephanie Spratt examples provide continuity and show how personal finance decisions in the early chapters have an effect on others in the later chapters. Near the end of each chapter, Stephanie builds a piece of her financial plan based on her analysis in the chapter examples.

FINANCIAL PLANNING ONLINE In recognition of the Internet's ability to facilitate every aspect of financial planning, Financial Planning Online inserts in every chapter direct students to pertinent online resources. Each insert includes a full-color screenshot of the specified Web site along with the URL and a detailed description of the resource offered. Many of these features direct students to calculator-based sites that perform custom analyses based on student input for things such as estimating tax liability or determining whether buying or renting a home is more appropriate. Other online applications involve quotations of bank deposit rates, homeowner's insurance policies, car loan rates, stock price quotations, mortgage rates, data available on stocks, mutual funds, and bonds, and financial news used to make investing decisions. The Financial Planning Online links are available in up-to-date form on the text Web site, **http://www.aw.com/madura.**

CHAPTER-ENDING PEDAGOGY

SUMMARY In paragraph form, the Summary presents the key points of the chapter to aid student study.

INTEGRATING THE KEY CONCEPTS Following the Summary is a section called Integrating the Key Concepts that emphasizes the relationship among chapter topics and the five components of a financial plan.

REVIEW QUESTIONS Review Questions test students' understanding by requiring them to compare and contrast concepts, interpret financial quotations, and understand how financial data can be used to make personal finance decisions.

FINANCIAL PLANNING PROBLEMS Financial Planning Problems require students to demonstrate knowledge of mathematically based concepts to perform computations (such as calculating tax liability, returns from a stock investment, and financing costs on a 15-year versus a 30-year fixed-rate mortgage) in order to make well-informed personal finance decisions.

FINANCIAL PLANNING ONLINE EXERCISES To provide practice in using the Internet for financial planning purposes, each chapter includes Financial Planning Online Exercises. For example, students are asked to obtain mortgage rate quotations, stock price quotations, financial ratios, life insurance premium quotations, and interest rate data. These exercises illustrate the type of information that is available online and ensure that students know how to obtain, critically evaluate, and use that information to make personal finance decisions.

BUILDING YOUR OWN FINANCIAL PLAN This case feature guides students through the process of developing their own financial plan. At the end of each chapter, students complete a portion of the financial plan. By the end of the course, students will have completed a financial plan that they can continue implementing beyond the school term. The financial plans will vary according to the students' unique financial situations. Those students who are not working are instructed to develop a plan for when they graduate (based on the income level that they expect at that time). Students who have already begun their careers should build their financial plan based on their prevailing financial situation.

Excel-based software templates are provided on a CD-ROM packaged with the text to aid in calculations and to prompt students through the key steps in the financial decision-making process. At the end of the semester, the software allows students to print out an overall financial plan consisting of the decisions they made in each chapter and the final versions of their personal goals, personal balance sheet, and personal cash flow statement. The software also allows for easy modifications. For example, in the retirement planning chapter (18), students can refer to the personal balance sheet they created in Chapter 2 and revise their cash outflows to allocate more or less to their 401(k) plan. For decisions that require time value of money analysis, the software prompts students for input and then performs the calculation. A Financial Planning Workbook is also provided with each text so that students who prefer to work with pen in hand can create their own financial plan throughout the semester.

THE SAMPSONS—A CONTINUING CASE This case feature challenges students to build a financial plan for a family based on information provided about their background and financial situation. The parents of two children, Dave and Sharon Sampson have made few plans to date regarding their financial future and are eager to start saving toward a new car, their children's college education, and their retirement. Students apply chapter concepts to counsel the Sampsons.

This case can be completed individually or by teams of students. In addition to specific questions that guide students to build the financial plan, a communication question encourages students to present their financial plan for the Sampsons in class.

Templates related to the Sampson family case are provided on the CD-ROM packaged with the text to aid in calculations and provide an easy way of inputting responses to the case questions. Students who prefer a workbook to a CD-ROM can use the Financial Planning Workbook shrink-wrapped with the text.

IN-TEXT STUDY GUIDE To enable students to gauge their knowledge of the chapter's key concepts, the In-text Study Guide includes numerous true-false and multiple-choice questions. Answers are provided in Appendix B.

PART-ENDING PEDAGOGY

BRAD BROOKS: A CONTINUING CASE A financial planning case at the end of each part challenges students to build a financial plan for Brad Brooks based on his background and financial situation. Brad has expensive tastes—as evidenced by his soaring credit card balance—and needs assistance in gaining control over his finances.

This case can be completed individually or by teams of students. In addition to specific questions that guide students to develop Brad's financial plan, a communication question encourages students to present their financial plan for Brad Brooks in class.

Templates related to the Brad Brooks case are provided on the CD-ROM packaged with the text to aid in calculations and provide an easy way of inputting responses to the case questions. Students who prefer a workbook to a CD-ROM can use the Financial Planning Workbook shrink-wrapped with the text.

SUPPORT PACKAGE

The following supplementary materials are available to help busy instructors teach more effectively and to allow busy students to learn more efficiently.

INSTRUCTOR RESOURCES

INSTRUCTOR'S MANUAL Prepared by Marilynn Skinner, Central Georgia Technical College, this comprehensive manual pulls together a wide variety of teaching tools so that instructors can use the text easily and effectively. Each chapter contains an overview of key topics, teaching tips, and detailed answers and solutions to the Review Questions, Financial Planning Problems, and Sampson family case questions. Each part concludes with answers to the Brad Brooks case questions. Instructions for setting up a fantasy stock market game are also provided, along with related student assignments. In addition, the Instructor's Manual features a guide to the 12 *Right on the Money* videos that are available to qualified adopters.

TEST BANK Authored by Carol Wysocki, Columbia Basin College, the Test Bank contains 50 questions per chapter in multiple-choice and short-essay format that can be used for quick test preparation.

INSTRUCTOR'S RESOURCE DISK Fully compatible with the Windows and Macintosh operating systems, this CD-ROM provides a number of resources.

- *PowerPoint Lecture Presentation* Authored by Barbara Rice, Florida College, this useful tool provides slides illustrating key points and exhibits as well as Web site information from the text in lecture note format. The slides can be easily converted to transparencies or viewed electronically in the classroom. Many slides have Excel spreadsheets embedded in them so that instructors can manipulate spreadsheets in the classroom with ease.

- *Computerized Test Bank* The easy-to-use testing software (Test-Gen EQ with QuizMaster-EQ for Windows and Macintosh) is a valuable test preparation tool that allows instructors to view, edit, and add questions.

- *Instructor's Manual and Test Bank* For added convenience, the Instructor's Resource Disk also includes Microsoft Word files for the entire contents of the Instructor's Manual and Test Bank.

VIDEOS A series of twelve videos from the PBS series *Right on the Money*™ hosted by award-winning journalist and financial expert Chris Farrell is available to qualified adopters of the text. An insightful journey through the world of personal finance, the half-hour segments take viewers on the road and around the country to learn valuable lessons through the personal experiences of people working through financial issues. The program is produced by TPT, Twin Cities Public Television, St. Paul/Minneapolis, with the exclusive national sponsorship of ING/ReliaStar, Inc. In its first three seasons, *Right on the Money* has been carried on more than 130 public television stations and seen by millions of viewers. The following episodes are available from Addison-Wesley: Buying or Leasing a Car; Money Where You Work; Credit Cards: Getting out of Debt; Managing Your Student Loans; Mutual Fund Basics; Personal Finance in College; Internet Investing; Credit Report Repairs; Your Bank Account; Protecting Your Financial Privacy; Buying or Renting a Home; and Picking Single Stocks.

Please contact your local Addison-Wesley sales representative for details. For information on the *Right on the Money* series, point your browser to **http://www.rightonthemoney.org.** This comprehensive, interactive Web site complements the series and includes many useful financial resources, tips, suggested readings, and links.

Wall Street Journal Edition

Order *The Wall Street Journal* Edition of this text and your students will receive a 10-week subscription to *The Wall Street Journal* and access to

The Wall Street Journal Online Edition. And for adopting *The Wall Street Journal* Edition, professors will receive a complimentary full-year subscription to *The Wall Street Journal* and access to *The Wall Street Journal* Online Edition at WSJ.com. Please contact your Addison-Wesley sales representative for details.

STUDENT SUPPORT

FINANCIAL PLANNING WORKBOOK AND CD-ROM. As mentioned in the description of the case features, each new copy of the textbook is packaged with a Financial Planning Workbook and CD-ROM to aid students in completing the Building Your Own Financial Plan exercises, the Sampson family continuing case, and the Brad Brooks continuing case. The templates on the CD-ROM are designed to run in Excel 97, Excel 2000, and Excel XP.

COMPANION WEB SITE. Available at **http://www.aw.com/madura,** the Web site provides online access to innovative teaching and learning tools, including:

- 30-question chapter quizzes with tutorial feedback, as well as two mini-case problems per chapter.

- Complete e-book version of the text, which allows for easy navigation to the Financial Planning Online resources and quick searches for key terms.

- An online career center that guides students through decisions regarding career selection and job searching.

- Up-to-date links to the Financial Planning Online features and Financial Planning Online Exercises.

The Companion Web site system includes an online syllabus builder that allows instructors to create a calendar of assignments for each class and to track students' quiz performance with an electronic gradebook.

In addition to the Companion Web site, the Web content is available in CourseCompass, and BlackBoard versions. CourseCompass™ is a nationally hosted, dynamic, interactive online course management system powered by BlackBoard, leaders in the development of Internet-based learning tools. This easy-to-use and customizable program enables professors to tailor content and functionality to meet individual course needs. To see a demo, visit **www.coursecompass.com.** Please contact your local sales representative for more information on obtaining Web content in these various formats.

ACKNOWLEDGMENTS

Addison-Wesley sought the advice of a great many excellent reviewers, all of whom strongly influenced the organization, substance, and approach of this book. The following individuals provided extremely useful evaluations:

Tim Alzheimer, *Montana State University, Bozeman*

Albert L. Auxier, *University of Tennessee, Knoxville*

H. David Barr, *Blinn College*

John Blaylock, *Northeast Community College*

Lyle Bowlin, *University of Northern Iowa*

Margaret A. Camp, *University of Nebraska, Kearney*

Steven L. Christian, *Jackson Community College*

Richard L. Craig, *Western State College*

Sidney W. Eckert, *Appalachian State University*

Thomas M. Finnicum, *Oklahoma State University, Oklahoma City*

Joseph F. Fowler, *Florida Community College*

Garry Grau, *Northeast State Technical Community College*

Joseph D. Greene, *Augusta State University*

Joyce Griffin, *Kansas City Kansas Community College*

Reynolds Griffith, *Stephen F. Austin State University*

Donald G. Hardwick, *Lexington Community College*

Celia Ray Hayhoe, *University of Kentucky*

Jeannne Hilton, *University of Nevada, Reno*

David R. Hoffman, *Arizona State University*

Marilynn E. Hood, *Texas A&M University*

Samira Hussein, *Johnson County Community College*

Roger Ignatius, *Husson College*

Debora C. Johnson, *Southeastern Louisiana University*

Ronald R. Jordan, *New Mexico State University*

Raymond Kerlagon, *Webster University*

Judith Mae King, *Western Carolina University*

Dave Kraemer, *Maysville Community College*

Edward Krohn, *Miami-Dade Community College, Kendall Campus*

Andrew H. Lawrence, *Delgado Community College*

Lauren Leach, *Northwest Missouri State University*

Catherine H. LoCascio, *Niagara County Community College*

Robert A. Lutz, *University of Utah*

Willard Machen, *Amarillo College*

Ken Mark, *Kansas City Kansas Community College*

Geofrey Mills, *University of Northern Iowa*

Dianne R. Morrison, *University of Wisconsin*

David W. Murphy, *Madisonville Community College*

David Oliver, *Edison Community College*

Armand Picou, *University of Central Arkansas*

Barbara Rice, *Florida College*

Julia Sampson, *Malone College*

Nick Sarantakes, *Austin Community College*

Elizabeth Scull, *University of South Carolina*

Marilynn K. Skinner, *Central Georgia Technical College*

Sally Wells, *Columbia College*

Tony Wingler, *University of North Carolina at Greensboro*

Michael J. Woodworth, *Purdue University*

Myrna Wulfson, *SUNY Rockland Community College*

Carol Wysocki, *Columbia Basin College*

Robert S. Young, *Salt Lake Community College*

Special acknowledgment is due to several individuals whose contributions to this project and expertise are great assets: to Steven L. Christian of Jackson Community College for writing the Building Your Own Financial Plan and Brad Brooks case features; to Roger Ignatius of Husson College for writing the Financial Planning Online Exercises; to Barbara Rice of Florida College for preparing the PowerPoint Lecture Note Presentation; to Oliver Schnusenberg of St. Joseph's University for writing the In-Text Study Guide questions; to Marilynn K. Skinner of Central Georgia Technical College for writing the Review Questions and Financial Planning Problems and authoring the Instructor's Manual; to Michael J. Woodworth for his skilled work as an accuracy checker; and to Carol Wysocki of Columbia Basin College for writing the Test Bank.

I wish to acknowledge the help and support of many people associated with Addison-Wesley who made this textbook possible. First and foremost, the contributions of Rebecca Ferris, development editor, were invaluable. Her thorough editing of multiple manuscript drafts and analyses of reviewer feedback were instrumental in shaping the text. I also wish to thank Donna Battista, finance editor, for her persistence and support. The efforts of

Adrienne D'Ambrosio, marketing manager, Jennifer Pelland, media producer, and Meredith Gertz, supplements editor, are also noteworthy.

I greatly appreciated the copyediting by Pat Lewis. Other contributors in the production process whose commitment to quality benefited the project are Juliet Silveri, senior production supervisor, Regina Hagen, senior designer, and Lorne Franklin, project manager at Lachina Publishing Services.

Finally, I wish to thank my wife, Mary, and my parents for their moral support.

Chapter 1

Overview of a Financial Plan

The personal financial planning process enables you to develop a personal financial plan. You should develop a financial plan whether you are unemployed, work for a company, or run your own company. Full-time students can benefit from a financial plan because it can help them control their spending and therefore improve their financial position over time. Even students who are borrowing funds to finance their education can benefit because a financial plan can help them limit their spending and therefore reduce the amount of debt that they accumulate over time.

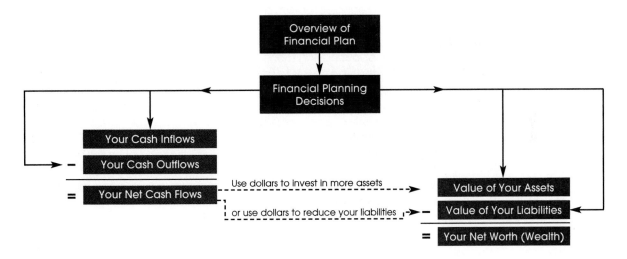

The objectives of this chapter are to:

- introduce the subject of personal finance,
- identify the key components of a financial plan, and
- outline the steps involved in developing your financial plan.

HOW YOU BENEFIT FROM AN UNDERSTANDING OF PERSONAL FINANCE

personal finance
The process of planning your spending, financing, and investing so as to optimize your financial situation.

personal financial plan
A plan that specifies your financial goals and describes the spending, financing, and investing plans that are intended to achieve those goals.

Personal finance (also referred to as **personal financial planning**) is the process of planning your spending, financing, and investing so as to optimize your financial situation. A **personal financial plan** specifies your financial goals and describes the spending, financing, and investing plans that are intended to achieve those goals. An understanding of personal finance is beneficial to you in the following ways:

- **Make Your Own Financial Decisions.** First, an understanding of personal finance enables you to make informed decisions about your financial situation. Each of your spending decisions has an **opportunity cost,** which represents what you give up as a result of that decision. By spending money for a specific purpose, you forgo alternative ways that

1

opportunity cost
What you give up as a result of a decision.

you could have spent the money and also forgo saving the money for a future purpose. For example, if your decision to use your cell phone costs $100 per month, you have forgone the possibility of using that money to buy concert tickets or to save for a new car. Informed financial decisions can increase the amount of money that you accumulate over time, and therefore can give you more flexibility to purchase the products and services you want in the future. To grasp how important financial planning can be, consider the following example.

Example

Stephanie Spratt graduated from college last year with a degree in marketing. She was hired by the Internet sales department of a firm at an annual salary of $38,000. She is excited about having money from her salary to spend. Yet she realizes that she needs to save or invest some of her income. The more she spends for enjoyment today, the less she saves and invests, and therefore the less wealth she will have for spending in the future. Thus, she plans to save a portion of every paycheck so that she can invest money to build her wealth over time. If she saves $5,000 per year for each of the next 10 years and earns an 8 percent return on that money, she will accumulate savings of about $75,000 in 10 years. By establishing a financial plan to limit her spending today, Stephanie can increase her wealth and therefore her potential spending in the future.

- **Judge the Advice of Financial Advisers.** The personal financial planning process will enable you to make informed decisions about your spending, saving, financing, and investing. Nevertheless, you may prefer to rely on advice from various types of financial advisers who specialize in consulting with individuals. An understanding of personal finance allows you to judge the guidance of financial advisers and to determine whether their advice is in your best interest (or in their best interest).

Example

You want to invest $10,000 of your savings. A financial adviser guarantees that your investment will increase in value by 20 percent (or by $2,000) this year, but he will charge you 4 percent of the investment ($400) for his advice. If you have a background in personal finance, you would know that no investment can be guaranteed to increase in value by 20 percent in one year. Therefore, you would realize that you should not trust this financial adviser. You could either hire a more reputable financial adviser or review investment recommendations made by financial advisers on the Internet (often for free).

- **Become a Financial Adviser.** An understanding of personal finance may interest you in pursuing a career as a financial adviser. Financial advis-

1.1   Financial Planning Online: Should You Pursue a Career in Financial Planning?

Go to:
http://www.careers-in-finance.com/fpfacts.htm

This Web site provides:
updated information on job positions in financial planning. Go to this site to review the full array of jobs available in this field.

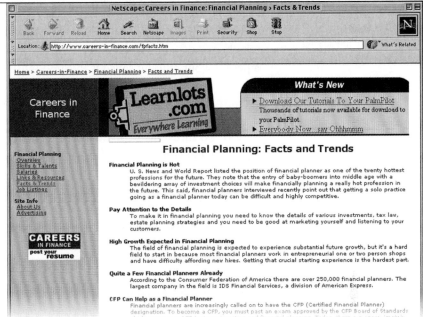

ers are in demand because many people lack an understanding of personal finance or are not interested in making their own financial decisions. Investment advisers, insurance specialists, and financial planners are just a few of the many careers that involve advising individuals about their financial situation. A single course in personal finance is insufficient to start a career as a financial adviser, but it may allow you to determine whether you want to take additional courses to obtain the necessary qualifications.

COMPONENTS OF A FINANCIAL PLAN

A complete financial plan contains your personal finance decisions related to five key components:

1. Budgeting and tax planning.

2. Managing your liquidity.

3. Financing your large purchases.

4. Investing your money.

5. Protecting your wealth (insurance and retirement plans).

These five components are very different; decisions concerning each are captured in separate plans that, taken together, form your overall financial plan. Each component is briefly described in turn.

A Plan for Budgeting and Tax Planning

budget planning (budgeting)
The process of forecasting future expenses and savings.

Budget planning (also referred to as **budgeting**) is the process of forecasting future expenses and savings. That is, it requires you to decide whether to spend or save money. If you receive a given level of income over a period, your amount saved is the amount that you do not spend. The relationship between income received, spending, and saving is illustrated in Exhibit 1.1. Some individuals are "big spenders": they focus their budget decision on how to spend most or all of their income and therefore have little or no money left for saving. Others are "big savers": they set a savings goal and consider spending their income received only after allocating a portion of it toward saving. Budgeting can help you estimate how much of your income will be required to cover monthly expenses so that you can set a goal for saving each month.

The first step in budget planning is to evaluate your current financial position by assessing your income, your expenses, your **assets** (what you own), and your **liabilities** (debt, or what you owe). Your **net worth** is the value of what you own minus the value of what you owe. You can measure your wealth by your net worth. As you save money, you increase your assets and therefore increase your net worth. Budget planning enables you to build your net worth by setting aside part of your income to either invest in additional assets or reduce your liabilities.

assets
What you own.

liabilities
What you owe; your debt.

net worth
The value of what you own minus the value of what you owe.

Your budget is influenced by your income, which in turn is influenced by your education and career decisions. Individuals who pursue higher levels of education tend to have smaller budgets during the education years. After obtaining their degrees, however, they typically are able to obtain jobs that pay higher salaries and therefore have larger budgets.

Exhibit 1.1   How a Budget Plan Affects Savings

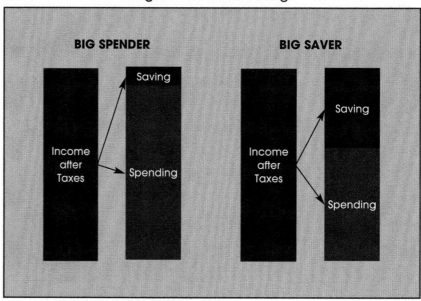

A key part of budgeting is estimating the typical expenses that you will incur each month. If you underestimate expenses, you will not achieve your savings goals. Achieving a higher level of future wealth requires you to sacrifice by keeping spending at a lower level today.

Many financial decisions are affected by tax laws, as some forms of income are taxed at a higher rate than others. By understanding how your alternative financial choices would be affected by taxes, you can make financial decisions that have the most favorable effect on your cash flows. Budgeting and tax planning are discussed in Part 1 because they can be used when making decisions about all other parts of your financial plan.

A Plan to Manage Your Liquidity

liquidity
Access to funds to cover any short-term cash deficiencies.

money management
Decisions regarding how much money to retain in a liquid form and how to allocate the funds among short-term investment instruments.

credit management
Decisions regarding how much credit to obtain to support your spending and which sources of credit to use.

Purchasing products or services each day requires sufficient funds to cover these expenses. Expenses can range from your morning cup of coffee to major car repairs. You need to have **liquidity,** or access to funds to cover any short-term cash deficiencies. You can enhance your liquidity by using money management and credit management.

Money management involves decisions regarding how much money to retain in a liquid form and how to allocate the funds among short-term investment instruments. If you do not have access to money to cover cash deficiencies, you may have insufficient liquidity. That is, you have the assets to cover your expenses, but the money is not easily accessible. Finding an effective liquidity level involves deciding how to invest your money so that you can earn a return, but also have easy access to cash if needed. At times, you may be unable to avoid cash deficiencies because of unanticipated expenses.

Credit management involves decisions about how much credit to obtain to support your spending and which sources of credit to use. Credit is commonly used to cover both large and small expenses when you are short on cash, so it enhances your liquidity. Credit should be used only when necessary, however, as it represents borrowed funds that you will need to pay back with interest (and the interest expenses may be very high). The use of money management and credit management to manage your liquidity is illustrated in Exhibit 1.2.

Exhibit 1.2   Managing Your Liquidity

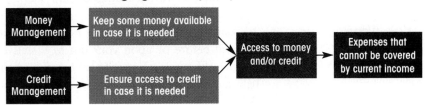

Exhibit 1.3   Financing Process

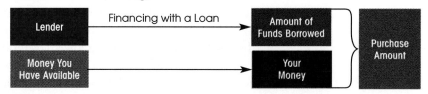

A Plan for Financing

Loans are typically needed to finance large expenditures, such as the payment of college tuition or the purchase of a car or a home. The amount of financing needed is the difference between the amount of the purchase and the amount of money you have available, as illustrated in Exhibit 1.3. Managing loans includes determining how much you can afford to borrow, deciding on the maturity (length of time) of the loan, and selecting a loan that charges a competitive low interest rate.

A Plan for Investing

Any funds that you have beyond what you need to maintain liquidity should be invested to provide you with a return on your investment. Because these funds normally are not used to satisfy your liquidity needs, they can be invested with the primary objective of earning a high return. Potential investments include stocks, bonds, mutual funds, and real estate. You must determine how much of your funds you wish to allocate toward investments and what types of investments you wish to consider. Most investments are subject to **risk** (uncertainty surrounding their potential return), however, so you need to manage them so that your risk is limited to a level you find tolerable.

risk
Uncertainty surrounding the potential return on an investment.

A Plan for Protecting Your Wealth

Protecting your wealth requires insurance planning, retirement planning, and estate planning. **Insurance planning** involves determining the types and amount of insurance that you need to protect your wealth. Insurance protects your wealth by protecting assets that you own, limiting your exposure to potential liabilities, or protecting your income.

insurance planning
Determining the types and amount of insurance needed to protect your wealth.

Retirement planning involves determining how much money you should set aside each year for retirement and how you should invest those funds. Retirement planning must begin well before you retire so that you can accumulate sufficient money to invest and use after you retire. Money contributed to various kinds of retirement plans is protected from taxes until it is withdrawn from the retirement account.

retirement planning
Determining how much money should be set aside each year for retirement and how those funds should be invested.

Estate planning is the act of planning how your wealth will be distributed before or upon your death. Effective estate planning can protect your wealth against unnecessary taxes, and ensure that your wealth is distributed to your family in the manner that you desire.

estate planning
Determining how your wealth will be distributed before or upon your death.

Exhibit 1.4 Components of Your Financial Plan

Protecting Your Wealth (Part 5)

Personal Investing (Part 4)

Personal Financing (Part 3)

Liquidity Management (Part 2)

Tools for Financial Planning (Part 1)

Wealth

How the Text Organization Relates to the Financial Plan's Components

Each of the first five parts of this text covers one specific component of the financial plan. The relationship among the components of the financial plan is illustrated in Exhibit 1.4. Part 1 (Tools for Financial Planning) describes budgeting, which focuses on how cash received (from income or other sources) is allocated to saving, spending, and taxes. Budget planning serves as the foundation of the financial plan, as it is your base for making personal financial decisions.

The next component is liquidity management (Part 2) because you must have adequate liquidity before financing or investing. Once your budget plan and your liquidity are in order, you are in a position to plan

1.2 Financial Planning Online: Skills Needed for Financial Planning

Go to:
http://www.careers-in-finance.com/fpskill.htm

This Web site provides:
information about the skills needed to perform well in a financial planning career. You will have a chance to develop some of these skills while taking a course in personal finance.

Netscape: Careers in Finance: Financial Planning > Skills and Talents Requirements

Back Forward Reload Home Search Netscape Images Print Security Shop Stop

Location: http://www.careers-in-finance.com/fpskill.htm

What's Related

Home > Careers-in-Finance > Financial Planning > Skills & Talents

Careers in Finance

Habitat for Humanity International FREE Letters click here

Financial Planning: Skills and Talents

Financial Planning
Overview
Skills & Talents
Salaries
Links & Resources
Facts & Trends
Job Listings

Site Info
About Us
Advertising

CAREERS IN FINANCE post your resume

The financial planning sector is booming and offers a variety of career options. This field deals with the largest markets of any kind in the world and call on the following skills:

Key Skill Area	Requirement
People skills:	High
Sales skills:	Medium
Communication skills:	High
Analytical skills:	Medium
Ability to synthesize:	High
Creative ability:	Medium
Initiative:	Medium
Work hours:	25-65/week

Commentary

Can Invest Directly or Indirectly
Money managers either directly make investments or help others by providing investment advice. If they are in the first business they are usually called portfolio managers. If they are in the second, they are generally called financial planners.

A Variety of Compensation Approaches Available for Planners
Financial planners can be compensated on a flat per-hour fee basis, a

your financing (Part 3) for major purchases such as a new car or a home. Next, you can consider investment alternatives such as stocks, bonds, and mutual funds (Part 4). Finally, your financial plan (Part 5) protects the wealth you have accumulated through effective insurance planning, retirement planning, and estate planning.

A proper financial plan enhances your net worth and therefore enhances your wealth. In each of the first five parts of the text, you will have the opportunity to develop a component of your financial plan. At the end of each chapter, the Building Your Own Financial Plan exercise offers you guidance on the key decisions that you can make after reading that chapter. You can use the Excel-based software on the CD-ROM available with your text to evaluate your options and make decisions. By completing the Building Your Own Financial Plan exercises, you will have a complete financial plan for yourself at the end of the school term. Exhibit 1.5 lists examples of the decisions you will make for each component.

Exhibit 1.5   Examples of Decisions Made in Each Component of a Financial Plan

A Plan for:	Types of Decisions
1. Managing your budget	What expenses should you anticipate?
	How much money should you attempt to save each month?
	How long will you take to save enough money to make a specific purchase?
	How long will you take to pay off a specific loan?
2. Managing your liquidity	How much money should you maintain in your checking account?
	How much money should you maintain in your savings account?
	Should you use credit cards as a means of borrowing money?
3. Financing	How much money can you borrow to purchase a car?
	Should you borrow money to purchase a car, or should you lease a car?
	How much money can you borrow to purchase a home?
	What type of mortgage loan should you obtain to finance the purchase of a house?
4. Investing	How much money should you allocate toward investments?
	What types of investments should you consider?
	How much risk can you tolerate when investing your money?
5. Protecting your wealth	What type of insurance do you need?
	How much insurance do you need?
	How much money will you need for retirement?
	How much money must you save each year so that you can retire in a specific year?
	How will you allocate your estate among your heirs?

How the Components Relate to Your Cash Flows. Exhibit 1.6 illustrates the typical types of cash inflows (cash that you receive) and cash outflows (cash that you spend). This exhibit also shows how each component of the financial plan reflects decisions on how to obtain or use cash. You receive cash inflows in the form of income from your employer and use some of that cash to spend on products and services. Budgeting (Part 1) focuses on the relationship between your income and your spending. Liquidity management (Part 2) focuses on depositing excess cash or obtaining credit if you are short on cash. Financing (Part 3) focuses on obtaining cash to support your large purchases. Investing (Part 4) focuses on using some of your cash to build your wealth. You can protect your wealth (Part 5) by using some of your cash to purchase insurance and to invest in your retirement.

If you need more cash inflows beyond your income, you may decide to rely on savings that you have already accumulated or obtain loans from creditors. If your income exceeds the amount that you wish to spend, you can use the excess funds to make more investments or to repay some or all of the principal on existing loans. Thus, your investment decisions can serve as a source of funds (selling your investments) or a way of using additional funds (making additional investments). Your financing decisions can serve as a source of funds (obtaining additional loans) or a use of funds (repaying existing loans). The introduction to each chapter describes how the financial decisions discussed in that chapter can affect your cash flows.

Exhibit 1.6   How Financial Planning Affects Your Cash Flows

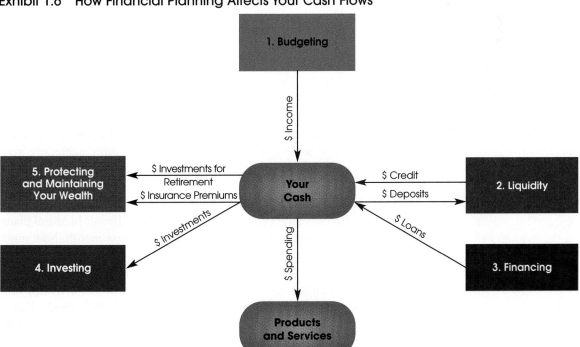

DEVELOPING THE FINANCIAL PLAN

Six steps are involved in developing each component of your financial plan.

Step 1. Establish Your Financial Goals

First, you must determine your financial goals.

Types of Goals. You can specify your goals in the form of purchases that you wish to make someday. These goals in turn influence the amount of money that you will need to make those purchases. Common goals are to live in a better apartment, to purchase a new car, to purchase a home, to take a vacation, and to pay the college tuition for yourself or family members. Your goals may also be specified in the form of an amount of wealth that you hope to have someday, such as a goal to have $200,000 in wealth by age 40. You do not have to identify specific expenditures before establishing a goal of attaining a specific level of wealth. You may simply want to accumulate a specific amount of savings over time so that you can afford to do whatever you want in the future. You may also want to accumulate savings so that you can help other family members or contribute to a worthy cause.

Use Realistic Goals. You need to be realistic about your goals so that you can have a strong likelihood of achieving them. A financial plan that requires you to save almost all of your income is useless if you are unable or unwilling to follow that plan. When this overly ambitious plan fails, you may become discouraged and lose interest in planning. By reducing the level of wealth you wish to attain to a realistic level, you will be able to develop a more viable plan.

Timing of Goals. Financial goals can be distinguished as short term (within the next year), intermediate term (typically between one and five years), or long term (beyond five years). For example, a short-term financial goal may be to accumulate enough money to purchase a car within six months. An intermediate-term goal would be to pay off a school loan in the next three years. A long-term goal would be to save enough money so that you can maintain your lifestyle and retire in 20 years. The more aggressive your goals, the more ambitious your financial plan will need to be.

Step 2. Consider Your Current Financial Position

People in different financial positions will develop different financial plans. Your decisions about how much money to spend next month, how much money to place in your savings account, how often to use your credit card, and how to invest your money depend on your financial position. A person with little debt and many assets will clearly make different decisions than a person with mounting debt and few assets. And a single individual without dependents will have different financial means than a married couple with children, even if the individual and the couple have the same income. The appropriate plan also varies with one's age and wealth. If you are 20 years old with zero funds in your bank account, your financial plan would be different than if you are 65 years old and have saved much of your income over the last 40 years.

Your financial position is highly influenced by your career decision. If you become a social worker, you will be in a different financial position than if you choose to work as an electrical engineer. As a social worker, you will need to save a much higher proportion of your income to achieve the same level of savings that you could achieve as an electrical engineer. People should not automatically pursue the career that provides the highest income, but should recognize that their career choices affect their income, which affects their potential for spending money and saving money.

Step 3. Identify and Evaluate Alternative Plans That Could Achieve Your Goals

Third, you must identify and evaluate the alternative financial plans that could achieve your financial goals (specified in Step 1), given your financial position (determined in Step 2). For example, to accumulate a substantial amount of money in 10 years, you could decide either to save a large portion of your income over those years or to invest your initial savings in an investment that may grow in value over time. The first plan is a more conservative approach, but requires you to save money consistently over time. The second plan does not require as much discipline, because it is relying on the initial investment to grow substantially over time. However, the second plan is more likely to fail, because there is risk related to whether the value of the initial investment will increase as expected.

Step 4. Select and Implement the Best Plan for Achieving Your Goals

Next, you need to select the plan that will be most effective in achieving your goals. This involves an analysis of the alternative plans that are available to you. Individuals in the same financial position with the same financial goals may decide on different financial plans to achieve their goals. For example, you may be willing to save a specific amount of money every month to achieve a particular level of wealth in 10 years. Another individual may prefer to make some risky investments today (rather than save money every month) in order to achieve the same level of wealth in 10 years. The type of plans you select to achieve your financial goals is influenced by your willingness to take risk and your self-discipline.

Step 5. Evaluate Your Financial Plan

After you develop and implement each component of your financial plan, you must monitor your progress to ensure that the plan is working as you intended. The financial plan should not be stored away, but should be easily accessible so that you can evaluate it over time.

Step 6. Revise Your Financial Plan

If you find that you are unable or unwilling to follow the financial plan that you developed, you need to revise the plan to make it more realistic. Of course, your financial goals may have to be reduced as well if you are unable to maintain the plan for achieving a particular level of wealth.

As time passes, your financial position will change, especially upon specific events such as graduating college, marriage, a career change, or the birth of a child. As your financial condition changes, your financial goals may change as well. Financial plans need to be revised to reflect such changes in your means and priorities.

The steps in developing a financial plan are summarized in Exhibit 1.7. To see how the steps can be applied, consider the following example.

Example

Stephanie Spratt just started her career and wants to develop a financial plan. At this point she develops an overview of her current financial position, establishes her goals, and develops a plan for how she might achieve those goals, as shown in Exhibit 1.8.

Key financial planning decisions that relate to Stephanie's financial plan will be summarized at the end of each chapter. Your financial planning decisions will differ from Stephanie's or anyone else's. Nevertheless, the process of building the financial plan is the same. You need to establish goals, assess the alternative methods for achieving your goals, and decide on a financial plan that can achieve your goals.

HOW THE INTERNET FACILITATES FINANCIAL PLANNING

The Internet facilitates every aspect of financial planning. It provides information on all parts of the financial plan, from budgeting, managing liquidity, and financing to investing, insurance, and retirement planning. For example, you can easily access quotations on:

- bank deposit rates,
- prices of cars and homes in your area,
- financing rates on car loans, other personal loans, and home loans,
- prices of stocks and many other types of investments, and
- insurance premiums.

Exhibit 1.7   Summary of Steps Used to Develop a Financial Plan

1. Establish your financial goals.

   - What are your short-term financial goals?

   - What are your intermediate-term financial goals?

   - What are your long-term financial goals?

2. Consider your current financial position.

   - How much money do you have in savings?

   - What is the value of your investments?

   - What is your net worth?

3. Identify and evaluate alternative plans that could achieve your goals.

   - Given your goals and existing financial position described in the previous steps, how can you obtain the necessary funds to achieve your financial goals?

   - Will you need to reduce your spending to save more money each month?

   - Will you need to make investments that generate a higher rate of return?

4. Select and implement the best plan for achieving your goals.

   - What are the advantages and disadvantages of each alternative plan that could be used to achieve your goals?

5. Evaluate your financial plan.

   - Is your financial plan working properly? That is, will it enable you to achieve your financial goals?

6. Revise your financial plan.

   - Have your financial goals changed?

   - Should parts of the financial plan be revised in order to increase the chance of achieving your financial goals? (If so, identify the parts that should be changed, and determine how they should be revised.)

Exhibit 1.8   Overview of Stephanie Spratt's Financial Plan

Step 1. Current Financial Position: I have very little savings at this time and own an old car. My income, which is about $30,000 a year after taxes, should increase over time.

Step 2. Financial Goals: I would like to:

- buy a new car within a year,
- buy a home within two years,
- make investments that will allow my wealth to grow over time, and
- build a large amount of savings for retirement in 20 to 40 years.

Step 3. Plans to Achieve the Goals: Since my current financial position does not provide me with sufficient funds to achieve these financial goals, I need to develop a financial plan for achieving these goals.

One possible plan would be to save enough money until I could purchase the car and home with cash. With this plan, however, I would not have sufficient savings to purchase a home for many years. An alternative is to save enough money to make a down payment on the car and home and to obtain financing to cover the rest of the cost. This alternative plan allows me to allocate some of my income toward investments.

My financing decisions will determine the type of car and home that I will purchase and the amount of funds I will have left to make other investments so that I can build my wealth over time.

Step 4. Selecting and Implementing the Best Plan: Financing the purchase of a car and a home is a more appropriate plan for me. I will prepare a budget so that over time I can accumulate savings that will be used to make a down payment on a new car. Then, I will attempt to accumulate savings to make a down payment on a new home. I need to make sure that I can afford financing payments on any money that I borrow.

Step 5. Evaluating the Plan: Once I establish a budget, I will monitor it over time to determine whether I am achieving the desired amount of savings each month.

Step 6. Revising the Plan: If I cannot save as much money as I desire, I may have to delay my plans for purchasing a car and a home until I can accumulate enough funds to make the down payments. If I am able to exceed my savings goal, I may be able to purchase the car and the home sooner than I had originally expected.

All of these can be used in making financial decisions. A decision of whether to spend money on a new stereo or save the money is dependent on how much you can earn from depositing the money. A decision of whether to purchase a new car depends on the prices of new cars and financing rates on car loans. A decision of whether to purchase a home depends on the prices of homes and financing rates on home loans. A decision of whether to invest in stocks is influenced by the prevailing prices of stocks. A decision of where to purchase insurance may be influenced by the prevailing insurance premiums quoted by different insurance agencies. All of these financial decisions require knowledge of prevailing prices or interest rates, which are literally at your fingertips on the Internet.

The Internet also provides updated information on all parts of the financial plan, such as:

- current tax rates and rules that can be used for tax planning,

- recent performances of various types of investments, and

- new retirement plan rules that can be used for retirement planning.

Furthermore, some Web sites offer online calculators that can be used for a variety of financial planning decisions, such as:

- estimating your taxes,

- determining how your savings will grow over time, and

- determining whether buying or leasing a car is more appropriate.

1.3   Financial Planning Online: Financial Planning Tools for You

Go to:

http://finance.yahoo.com/

This Web site provides:

much information and many tools that can be used for all aspects of financial planning, including tax rates, bank deposit rates, loan rates, credit card information, mortgage rates, and quotations and analysis of stocks, bonds, mutual funds, and insurance policies. It also provides information for creating retirement plans and wills. This Web site will be used to complement the discussion of most of the topics in this text.

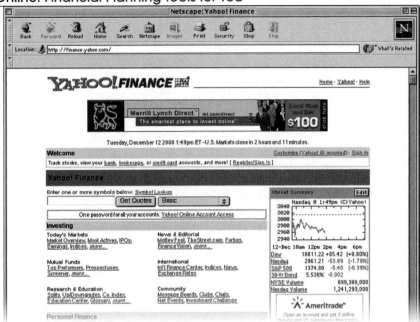

Thus, you can make more informed financial decisions with the Internet because of easy access to the updated information on all parts of the financial plan.

Financial Planning Online

Special features in each chapter called Financial Planning Online illustrate how the Internet facilitates the creation of the various parts of the financial plan. An example of one appears on page 7. Financial Planning Online exercises are also provided at the end of each chapter so that you can practice using the Internet for financial planning purposes. It is inevitable that some of the URLs in this text will change. All of them are updated on the text's Web site for easy navigation.

SUMMARY

Personal financial planning is the process of planning your spending, financing, and investing so as to optimize your financial situation. Your financial planning decisions allow you to develop a financial plan, which involves a set of decisions on how you plan to manage your spending, financing, and investments.

A financial plan has five components: (1) budgeting, (2) managing your liquidity, (3) financing large purchases, (4) investing, and (5) protecting your wealth.

The financial planning process involves six steps: (1) establish your financial goals, (2) consider your current financial position, (3) identify and evaluate alternative plans that could achieve your goals, (4) select and implement the best plan for achieving your financial goals, (5) evaluate the financial plan over time to ensure that you are meeting your goals, and (6) revise the financial plan when necessary.

Integrating the Key Concepts

All of the components of the financial plan are related. In general, the financial planning tools (such as budgeting and tax planning) are used for the financial planning decisions discussed in the following parts. For example, your budget (discussed in Part 1) determines how much money you can set aside to maintain liquidity (Part 2) or to invest in long-term investments (Part 4). The other components of the financial plan are also related. The way you obtain funds to finance large purchases such as a car or a home (discussed in Part 3) is dependent on whether you sell any of your existing investments (discussed in Part 4) to obtain all or a portion of the funds needed. Your need for insurance (discussed in Part 5) is dependent on the types of assets you own (e.g., a car or a home) and is also influenced by the amount of funds that you accumulate from your investment decisions (Part 4). Your ability to save for retirement each month (discussed in Part 5) is dependent on the amount of funds you need to pay off any existing credit balance (discussed in Part 2) or loans (discussed in Part 3).

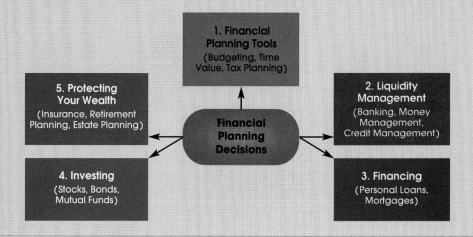

REVIEW QUESTIONS

1. Define personal financial planning. What types of decisions does it involve?

2. What is opportunity cost? What might be some of the opportunity costs of spending $10 per week on the lottery?

3. What are some of the ways you can benefit from an understanding of financial planning?

4. What are the five key components of a financial plan?

5. Define budget planning. What elements must be assessed?

6. How is your net worth calculated? Why is it important?

7. What factors influence income? Why is an accurate estimate of expenses important? How do tax laws affect the budgeting process?

8. What is liquidity? What two factors are considered in managing liquidity? How are they used?

9. What factors are considered in managing financing?

10. What is the primary objective of investing? What else must be considered? What potential investment vehicles are available?

11. What are the three elements of planning to protect your wealth? Define each element.

12. How does each element of financial planning affect your cash flows?

13. What are the six steps in developing a financial plan?

14. How do your financial goals fit into your financial plan? Why should goals be realistic? What are three time frames for goals? Give an example of a goal for each time frame.

15. Name some factors that might affect your current financial position.

16. How do your goals and current financial position affect your creation of alternative financial plans?

17. Once your financial plan has been implemented, what is the next step? Why is it important?

18. Why might you need to revise your financial plan?

19. List some information available on the Internet that might be useful for financial planning. Describe one way you might use some of this information for financial planning purposes.

FINANCIAL PLANNING PROBLEMS

1. Julia brings home $1,600 per month after taxes. Julia's rent is $350 per month, her utilities are $100 per month, and her car payment is $250 per month. Julia is currently paying $200 per month to her orthodontist for her braces. If Julia's groceries cost $50 per week and she estimates her other expenses to be $150 per month, how much will she have left each month to put toward savings to reach her financial goals?

2. Julia (see above) is considering trading in her car for a new one. Her new car payment will be $325 per month, and her insurance cost will increase by $60 per month. Julia determines that her other car-related expenses (gas, oil) will stay about the same. What is the opportunity cost of Julia purchasing the new car?

3. Robert has $3,000 in assets, a finance company loan for $500, and an outstanding credit card balance of $135. Robert's monthly cash inflows are $2,000, and he has monthly expenses of $1,650. What is Robert's net worth?

4. At the beginning of the year, Arianne had a net worth of $5,000. During the year she set aside $100 per month from her paycheck for savings and borrowed $500 from her cousin that she must pay back in January next year. What was her net worth at the end of the year?

5. Anna has just received a gift of $500 for her graduation. If she uses the money to purchase a stereo, how will her net worth be affected? If she invests the $500 at 10 percent interest per year, what will it be worth in one year?

FINANCIAL PLANNING ONLINE EXERCISES

1. Go to the Web site http://www.careers-in-finance. com/fpskill.htm.
   a. What are the most important skills needed to perform the job of a financial planner? Which skills are your strengths, and which are your weaknesses?
   b. How can you obtain the skills you lack?
   c. Review the job listings in your area and the information on salaries. Is a career as a financial planner appealing to you? Why or why not?

2. The purpose of this exercise is to familiarize you with the wide variety of personal finance resources on the Yahoo! Web site. Go to http://finance.yahoo.com/?u.

  a. Go to the Taxes heading in the Personal Finance section and click on Tax Center, then Refund Estimator. Calculate the payroll withholding tax per paycheck for each of the following, assuming the standard deduction, 26 pay periods, and zero tax credits:

   i. A single person earning $45,000 per year.

   ii. A couple filing a joint return with earnings of $70,000 per year. Assume two deductions and a single wage earner.

  b. Use the Back option in your browser to return to http://finance.yahoo.com/?u. Choose Banking Center in the Banking and Bills section and click on Calculators. In the Credit Line section, click on "How Large a Line of Credit Can I Obtain?" Assuming the appraised value of your home is $125,000 and your mortgage is $75,000, find the maximum line of credit you can obtain based on the loan-to-value ratio. Change the value of the home and the mortgage to $100,000 and $70,000, respectively, and check the line of credit you can obtain.

  c. Use the Back option in your browser to return to http://finance.yahoo.com/?u. Under the heading Loans, go to Auto Loans and click on Rates. Find the current rates for your region. Compare your rates with those in another region of the country. Why are the rates different?

  d. Use the Back option in your browser to return to the Auto Loan Center. Click on Calculators, then choose the Loan Payment Calculator. What is the monthly payment for a 48-month loan of $10,000 at both the lowest rate and the highest rate in your region? Use the Sales Tax rate in your state or assume 6 percent. Assume zero down payment and no trade-in or rebates.

Building Your Own Financial Plan

These end-of-chapter experiential exercises are designed to enable you to create a working lifelong financial plan. Like all plans, your personal plan will require periodic review and revision. Each end-of-chapter Building Your Own Financial Plan exercise will include suggestions as to how often each element should be reviewed and/or revised.

 In this first exercise, you should review your current financial situation; if you are a full-time student, base your review on what you anticipate your financial situation will be upon your graduation. After carefully reviewing your current or anticipated financial situation, create three to five short-term goals and the same number of intermediate-term and long-term goals. Enter your goals by hand in the templates provided in the *Financial Planning Workbook* or electronically using the CD-ROM shrink-wrapped with your text.

Your short-term goals should be goals that you can realistically accomplish in one year. They may include, but are not limited to, paying off credit card balances, beginning a 401(k) or other retirement-type savings program, or getting your cash inflows and outflows in balance.

Your intermediate-term goals are goals that you should realistically be able to accomplish in one to five years. They may include, but are not limited to, purchasing a new vehicle, paying off school loans, or paying for a wedding.

Long-term goals will take longer than five years to realistically accomplish. They may include, but are not limited to, purchasing a home, taking a major trip (such as a summer in Europe), or saving sufficient funds to retire at a predetermined age.

The goals that you develop are a first draft and may be added to or modified as you proceed through this course. Do not feel that what you are creating here is in any way cast in stone, as this course is designed to provide you with information and insight that will help you make informed decisions about your financial future. As you gain experience in financial planning, new goals may emerge, and existing goals may change. Once you have completed your financial plan and have established your goals, you should review them on an annual basis or whenever a significant change occurs in your life (e.g., marriage, birth of a child, or a significant change in employment circumstances).

The Sampsons—A Continuing Case

Dave and Sharon Sampson are 30 years old and have two children, who are 5 and 6 years old. Since marrying seven years ago, the Sampsons have relied on Dave's salary, which is currently $48,000 per year. They have not been able to save any money, as Dave's income is just enough to cover their mortgage loan payment and their other expenses.

Dave and Sharon feel they need to take control of their finances. Now that both children are in school, they have decided that Sharon will look into getting a job with mother's hours. She was just hired for a part-time position at a local department store for a salary of $12,000 per year. Dave and Sharon are excited by the prospect of having additional cash inflows—they now feel they have the leeway to start working toward their financial goals.

The Sampsons own a home valued at about $100,000, and their mortgage is $90,000. They have a credit card balance of $2,000. Although they own two cars and do not have any car loans, Sharon's car is old and will need to be replaced soon. Sharon would really like to purchase a new car within the next year; she hopes to save $500 each month until she has accumulated savings of $5,000 to use for a down payment.

The Sampsons are especially concerned about how they will pay for their children's college education. Sharon plans to save an additional $300 each month that will be set aside for this purpose.

The Sampsons know they also need to save for their retirement over time. Yet they do not have a plan right now to achieve that goal because they are focused on saving for a new car and their children's education.

The Sampsons have decided to develop a financial plan. They realize that by formally identifying their main goals, they will be able to implement and monitor their plans over time. At the end of every chapter, you will help the Sampsons develop their financial plan using the key concepts presented in the chapter.

Help the Sampsons summarize their current financial position, their goals, and their plans for achieving their goals by filling out the templates provided in the *Financial Planning Workbook* or on the CD-ROM shrink-wrapped with your text.

IN-TEXT STUDY GUIDE

True/False:
1. Personal finance (financial planning) is the process of planning your spending, financing, and investing so as to optimize your financial situation.

2. You should develop a financial plan only if you are employed or run your own company.

3. Although an understanding of personal finance is useful, it does not enable you to assess the guidance of financial advisers.

4. A single course in personal finance is sufficient to start a career as a financial adviser, as it allows you to determine whether you want to take other related courses.

5. Your net worth is the value of what you own minus the value of what you owe.

6. Any funds that you have beyond what you need to remain liquid should be invested to provide you with a return on your investment.

7. You should manage your investments so as to maximize your risk and return.

8. Financial plans rarely differ across individuals, even if every individual is in a different financial position.

9. There are normally several alternative financial plans that may achieve your financial goals.

10. One way that the Internet facilitates financial planning is by providing quotations that can be used when making financial decisions.

11. Budget planning is the process of forecasting future expenses and savings.

Multiple Choice:

1. The _____ specifies the financial decisions that result from your personal financial planning.
   a. personal finance objective
   b. personal budget
   c. personal financial plan
   d. none of the above

2. Which of the following is the least likely way that you may benefit from having an understanding of personal finance?
   a. becoming the president of a large national bank
   b. making your own financial decisions
   c. assessing the advice of financial advisers
   d. becoming a financial adviser

3. A(n) _____ represents what you give up as a result of making an alternative decision.
   a. liquidity need
   b. opportunity cost
   c. purchase price
   d. financing cost

4. A _____ is not a key component of a complete financial plan.
   a. budget plan
   b. plan to manage your liquidity
   c. plan for financing (managing your credit and loans)
   d. plan for working at a major brokerage firm

5. Your _____ is (are) the value of what you own minus the value of what you owe.
   a. net worth
   b. net assets
   c. net liabilities
   d. budget

6. _____ is access to funds to cover any short-term cash deficiencies.
   a. Money management
   b. Liquidity
   c. Credit management
   d. Cash management

7. Having a _____ level of future wealth (from more savings) requires you to sacrifice by having a _____ level of spending today.
   a. higher; higher
   b. lower; lower
   c. higher; lower
   d. none of the above

8. Which of the following is not a credit management decision?
   a. financing your house with a mortgage
   b. using credit cards to pay your utility bills
   c. investing money in a bank deposit
   d. obtaining a bank loan to purchase a boat

9. The management of your loans would include
   a. determining how much you can afford to borrow.
   b. determining the maturity (length of time) of the loan.
   c. selecting a loan that charges a competitive low interest rate.
   d. all of the above

10. _____ planning involves determining how much you should set aside each year for retirement and how you should invest those funds in the short term.
    a. Retirement
    b. Estate
    c. Tax
    d. None of the above

11. Which of the following is not a type of decision made to protect and build your wealth?
    a. how much insurance you need
    b. how much money to spend on stereo equipment
    c. how much money you will need for retirement
    d. how much money you must save per year so that you can retire in a specific year

12. Which of the following is not a type of decision made to manage your liquidity?
    a. how much money you should maintain in your checking account
    b. how much money you should maintain in your savings account
    c. how much money you can borrow to spend on a car
    d. whether you should use credit cards as a means of borrowing money

13. If your income exceeds the amount that you wish to spend, you should _____ your investments or _____ loans.
    a. reduce; repay existing
    b. reduce; obtain more
    c. increase; repay existing
    d. increase; obtain more

14. Which of the following is not a step in developing the financial plan?
    a. Establish your financial goals.
    b. Identify alternative plans that could achieve your goals.
    c. Evaluate your financial plan.
    d. All of the above are steps in developing the financial plan.

15. The financial plan of a person in a different financial position than yourself would be
    a. different from your financial plan.
    b. the same as your financial plan.
    c. different from or the same as your financial plan, depending on the person's financial goals.
    d. none of the above

16. An appropriate financial plan will probably not be influenced by one's
    a. age.
    b. wealth.
    c. career decision.
    d. An appropriate financial plan will probably be influenced by all of the above.

17. When selecting the financial plan that will best enable you to achieve your goals, you
    a. do not need to conduct an analysis of the alternative solutions that are available.
    b. may choose a different financial plan than an individual in the same financial position.
    c. should choose the same financial plan as an individual in the same financial position and with the same financial goals.
    d. none of the above

18. Which of the following is true regarding the revision of your financial plan?
    a. Your financial goals may have to be reduced if you are unable to maintain the plan for achieving a particular level of wealth.
    b. You need to revise the plan to make it more realistic even if you are able and willing to follow the plan that you developed.
    c. You need to revise the plan even if your financial condition is unchanged.
    d. Financial plans need not be revised to reflect changes in your financial position or your goals.

19. Which of the following probably would not be asked when considering your financial position?
    a. How much money do you have in savings?
    b. What is the value of your investments?
    c. What are your intermediate-term financial goals?
    d. What is your net worth?

20. The Internet facilitates financial planning by providing
    a. information on all parts of the financial plan, such as budgeting, managing liquidity, financing, investing, insurance, and retirement planning.
    b. quotations that can be used when making financial decisions.
    c. updated information on the recent performance of various types of investments.
    d. all of the above

21. If you give something up as a result of making a decision, you are incurring a(n)
    a. net cost.
    b. opportunity cost.
    c. liquidity problem.
    d. none of the above

PART 1

Tools for Financial Planning

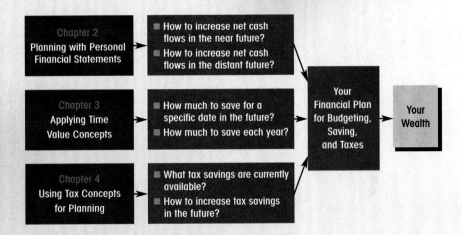

The chapters in this part introduce the key tools used to make financial planning decisions. Chapter 2 describes the personal financial statements that help monitor your spending and guide your budgeting decisions. Chapter 3 illustrates how you can use time value of money concepts to make decisions about saving. Chapter 4 explains how to use tax concepts to assess and minimize your tax liability. Your budget, saving, and tax plans all influence your cash flows and wealth.

Chapter 2

Planning with Personal Financial Statements

Personal financial statements summarize your financial position and cash flows. The two most widely used personal financial statements are the personal cash flow statement and the personal balance sheet. Proper use of these financial statements can enhance your wealth by helping you limit your spending and increase the amount you save each month.

The objectives of this chapter are to:

- explain how to create your personal cash flow statement,
- identify the factors that affect your cash flows,
- show how to create a budget based on your forecasted cash flows,
- describe how to create your personal balance sheet, and
- explain how your net cash flows are related to your personal balance sheet (and therefore affect your wealth).

PERSONAL CASH FLOW STATEMENT

personal cash flow statement
A financial statement that measures a person's cash inflows and cash outflows.

As mentioned in Chapter 1, budgeting is the process of forecasting future expenses and savings. When budgeting, a helpful first step is to create a **personal cash flow statement,** which measures your cash inflows and cash outflows. This comparison of your cash inflows and outflows allows you to determine the amount of cash that you can allocate toward savings or other purposes. It also allows you to monitor how you spend money over time.

Cash Inflows

The main source of cash inflows for people who are working is their salary, but there can be other important sources of income. Deposits in various types of savings accounts can generate cash inflows in the form of interest income. Some stocks also generate dividend income on a quarterly basis.

2.1   Financial Planning Online: Paying Your Bills Online

Go to:
http://moneycentral.msn.com

Click on:
Banking and Bills, then Pay
Bills Online

This Web site provides:
an illustration of how you can
pay your bills online.

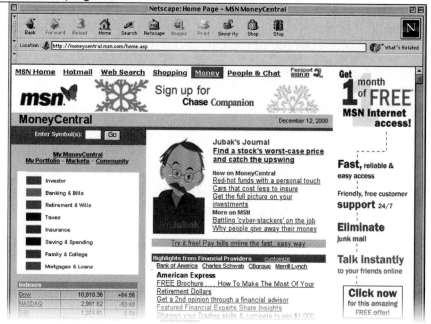

Cash Outflows

Cash outflows represent all of your expenses. Expenses are both large (for example, monthly rent) and small (for example, dry cleaning costs). It is not necessary to document every expenditure, but you should track how most of your money is spent. Recording the type of transaction in your checkbook when you write a check helps identify how your money was spent. Using a credit card for your purchases also provides a written record of your transactions.

Creating a Personal Cash Flow Statement

You can create a personal cash flow statement by recording how you received cash over a given period and how you used cash for expenses.

Example

Stephanie Spratt always limited her spending in college but never established a personal cash flow statement. Now that she has begun her career and is earning a salary, she wants to monitor her spending on a monthly basis. She decides to create a personal cash flow statement for the last month.

Stephanie's Monthly Cash Inflows. Stephanie's present salary is about $3,170 per month ($38,000 annually) before taxes. For budgeting purposes, she is interested in the cash inflow she receives from her employer after taxes.

About $670 per month of her salary goes to taxes, so her disposable (after-tax) income is:

Monthly Salary	$3,170
−Monthly Taxes	−$670
Monthly Cash Inflow	$2,500.

Stephanie then considers other potential sources of cash inflows. She does not receive any dividend income from stock. Since she currently does not have any money deposited in an account that pays interest, she does not earn any income from interest payments. Thus, her entire monthly cash inflows come from her paycheck. She inserts the monthly cash inflow of $2,500 at the top of her personal cash flow statement.

Stephanie's Monthly Cash Outflows. Stephanie looks in her checkbook register to determine how she spent her money last month. Her household payments for the month were as follows:

- $600 for her rent.
- $50 for cable TV.
- $60 for electricity and water.
- $60 for telephone expenses.
- $300 for groceries.
- $130 for a health care plan provided by her employer (this expense is deducted directly from her pay).

Stephanie next reviews several credit card bills to estimate her other typical expenses on a monthly basis:

- About $100 for clothing.
- About $200 for car expenses (insurance, maintenance, and gas).
- About $600 for recreation (including restaurants and a health club membership).

Stephanie uses this cash outflow information to complete her personal cash flow statement, as shown in Exhibit 2.1. Her total cash outflows were $2,100 last month.

Stephanie's Net Cash Flows. Monthly cash inflows and outflows can be compared by estimating **net cash flows,** which are equal to the cash inflows minus the cash outflows. Stephanie estimates her net cash flows to determine how easily she covers her expenses and how much excess cash she has to allocate to savings or other purposes. Her net cash flows during the last month were:

net cash flows
Cash inflows minus cash outflows.

$$\text{Net Cash Flows} = \text{Cash Inflows} - \text{Cash Outflows}$$
$$= \$2,500 \quad - \$2,100$$
$$= \$400.$$

Stephanie enters this information at the bottom of her personal cash flow statement.

Exhibit 2.1   Personal Cash Flow Statement for Stephanie Spratt

Cash Inflows	Last Month
Disposable (after-tax) income	$2,500
Interest on deposits	0
Dividend payments	0
Total Cash Inflows	**$2,500**
Cash Outflows	**Last Month**
Rent	$600
Cable TV	50
Electricity and water	60
Telephone	60
Groceries	300
Health care insurance and expenses	130
Clothing	100
Car expenses (insurance, maintenance, and gas)	200
Recreation	600
Total Cash Outflows	**$2,100**
Net Cash Flows	**+ $400**

FACTORS THAT AFFECT CASH FLOWS

To enhance your wealth, you want to maximize your (or your household's) net cash flows, which involves maximizing cash inflows and minimizing cash outflows. Your cash inflows and outflows are dependent on various factors, as will be described next.

Factors Affecting Cash Inflows

Because your income is the primary source of your cash inflows, these inflows are highly influenced by factors that affect your income level. The key factors to consider are the stage in your career path and your job skills.

Stage in Your Career Path. The stage you have reached in your career path influences cash inflows because it affects your income level. Cash inflows are relatively low for people who are in college or just starting a career (like Stephanie Spratt). They tend to increase as you gain job experience and progress within your chosen career.

Your career stage is closely related to your place in the life cycle. Younger people tend to be at early stages in their respective careers, whereas older people tend to have more work experience and are thus further along the career path. It follows that cash inflows tend to be lower for younger individuals and much higher for individuals in their 50s who are at the peak of their career path.

There are many exceptions to this tendency, however. Some older people switch careers and therefore may be set back on their career path. Other individuals who switch careers from a low-demand industry to a high-demand industry may actually earn higher incomes. Many women put their careers on hold for several years to raise children and then resume their professional lives.

The final stage in the life cycle that we will consider is retirement. The cash flows that come from a salary are discontinued at the time of retirement. After retirement, individuals rely on Social Security payments and interest or dividends earned on investments as an alternative source of income. Consequently, retired individuals' cash inflows tend to be smaller than when they were working. The manner in which age commonly affects cash inflows is summarized in Exhibit 2.2. Notice that there are three distinct phases. Your retirement cash inflows will be derived from income provided by your existing investments and from your retirement plan.

Type of Job. The income that people earn also varies with the type of job they have. Jobs that require specialized skills tend to pay much higher salaries than those that do not require any special skills or that require skills that can be obtained very quickly and easily. The income level associated with

Exhibit 2.2   How Your Cash Inflows Are Related to Your Age

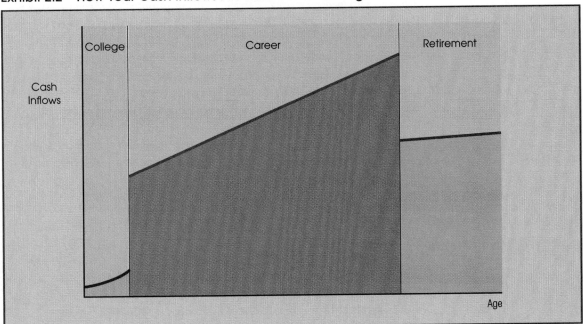

specific skills is also affected by the demand for those skills. The demand for people with a nursing license has been very high in recent years, so hospitals have been forced to pay high salaries to outbid other hospitals for nurses. Conversely, the demand for people with a history or an English literature degree is low because more students major in these areas than there are jobs.

Number of Income Earners in Your Household. If you are the sole income earner, the income (and therefore the cash inflows) of your household will typically be less than if there is a second income earner. Many households now have two income earners, a trend that has substantially increased the cash flows to these households.

Factors Affecting Cash Outflows

The key factors that affect cash outflows are a person's family status, age, and personal consumption behavior.

Size of Family. A person who is supporting a family will normally incur more expenses than a single person without dependents. The more family members, the greater the amount of spending, and the greater the amount of cash outflows.

Age. As people get older, they tend to spend more money on expensive houses, cars, and vacations. This adjustment in spending may result from the increase in their income (cash inflows) over time as they progress along their career path.

Personal Consumption Behavior. People's consumption behavior varies substantially. At one extreme are people who spend their entire paycheck within a few days of receiving it, regardless of the size of the paycheck. Although this behavior is understandable for people who have low incomes, it is also a common practice for some people who have very large incomes—perhaps because they do not understand the importance of saving for the future. At the other extreme are "big savers" who minimize their spending and focus on saving for the future.

Most people's consumption behavior is affected by their income. For example, a married couple tends to spend more money when both the husband and wife are working full-time.

CREATING A BUDGET

The next step in the budgeting process is an extension of the personal cash flow statement. You can forecast net cash flows by forecasting the cash inflows and outflows for each item on the personal cash flow statement. A

budget
A cash flow statement that is based on forecasted cash flows for a future time period.

cash flow statement that is based on forecasted cash flows for a future time period is referred to as a **budget**. Firms maintain budgets to anticipate a surplus or deficiency in funds. Individuals can use budgets for the same purpose. For example, you may develop a budget to determine whether your cash inflows will be sufficient to cover your cash outflows. If you expect your cash inflows to exceed your cash outflows, you can also use the budget to determine the amount of excess cash that you will have available to invest in additional assets.

Example

Stephanie Spratt wants to determine whether she will have sufficient cash inflows to cover all of her cash outflows during this month. She uses the personal cash flow statement she developed last month as a base for forecasting this month's cash flows. However, she adjusts that statement for the following additional expenses that she anticipates this month:

1. Total health care expenses will be $430 this month, due to a minor health care procedure she received recently that is not covered by her insurance.

2. Car maintenance expenses will be $500 this month, primarily due to her plan to purchase new tires for her car.

Stephanie revises her personal cash flow statement from last month to reflect the expected changes this month, as shown in Exhibit 2.3. The numbers in boldface type show the revised cash flows as a result of the unusual circumstances for this month.

The main effects of the unusual circumstances on Stephanie's expected cash flows for this month are summarized in Exhibit 2.4. Notice that the expected cash outflows for this month are $2,700, or $600 higher than the cash outflows in a typical month. In this month, the expected net cash flows are:

$$\text{Expected Net Cash Flows} = \text{Expected Cash Inflows} - \text{Expected Cash Outflows}$$
$$= \$2,500 \qquad - \$2,700$$
$$= -\$200.$$

The budgeting process has alerted Stephanie to this $200 cash shortage.

Anticipating Cash Shortages

In a month with a large amount of unexpected expenses, you may not have sufficient cash inflows to cover your expected cash outflows. If the cash shortage is small, you would likely withdraw funds from your checking account to make up the difference. If you expect a major deficiency for a future month, however, you might not have sufficient funds available to cover it. The budget can warn you of such a problem well in advance so

Exhibit 2.3   Stephanie Spratt's Revised Personal Cash Flow Statement

Cash Inflows	Actual Amounts Last Month	Expected Amounts This Month
Disposable (after-tax) income	$2,500	$2,500
Interest on deposits	0	0
Dividend payments	0	0
Total Cash Inflows	$2,500	$2,500
Cash Outflows	**Actual Amounts Last Month**	**Expected Amounts This Month**
Rent	$600	$600
Cable TV	50	50
Electricity and water	60	60
Telephone	60	60
Groceries	300	300
Health care insurance and expenses	130	**430**
Clothing	100	100
Car expenses (insurance, maintenance, and gas)	200	**500**
Recreation	600	600
Total Cash Outflows	**$2,100**	**$2,700**
Net Cash Flows	**+$400**	**−$200**

Exhibit 2.4   Summary of Stephanie Spratt's Revised Cash Flows

	Last Month's Cash Flow Situation	Unusual Cash Flows Expected This Month	This Month's Cash Flow Situation
Cash inflows	$2,500	$ 0	$2,500
Cash outflows	$2,100	$600	$2,700
Net cash flows	$ 400	−$600	−$ 200

that you can determine how to cover the deficiency. You should set aside funds in a savings account that can serve as an emergency fund in the event that you experience a cash shortage.

Assessing the Accuracy of the Budget

It is useful to periodically compare your actual cash flows over a recent period (such as last month) to the forecasted cash flows in your budget. This comparison indicates whether your forecasts are on target or inaccu-

"It's no use darling - I can't afford you anymore."

rate. Many individuals tend to be overly optimistic about their cash flow forecasts: they overestimate their cash inflows and underestimate their cash outflows; as a result, their net cash flows are less than expected. By detecting such forecasting errors, you can take steps to improve your budgeting. You may decide to limit your spending to stay within your budgeted cash outflows. Or you may choose not to adjust your spending habits, but increase your forecast of cash outflows to reflect reality. By budgeting accurately, you are more likely to detect any future cash flow shortages and therefore can prepare in advance for any deficiencies.

Example

Recall that Stephanie Spratt forecasted cash flows to create a budget for this coming month. Now it is the end of the month, so she can assess whether her forecasts were accurate. Her forecasted cash flows are shown in the second column of Exhibit 2.5. She compares the actual cash flows (third column) to her forecast and calculates the difference between them (shown in the fourth column). This difference between columns two and three is referred to as the forecasting error; a positive difference means that the actual cash flow level was less than forecasted, while a negative difference means that the actual cash flow level exceeded the forecast.

Reviewing the fourth column of Exhibit 2.5, Stephanie notices that total cash outflows were $100 more than expected. Her net cash flows were −$300 (a deficiency of $300), which is worse than the expected level of −$200. Stephanie assesses the individual cash outflows to determine where she underestimated. Although grocery expenses were slightly lower than expected, her clothing and recreation expenses were higher than she anticipated. Stephanie must next determine whether those expenses were abnormally high this month or are likely to be at that level in the future. She decides that the expenses were abnormally high in this month only, so she believes that her budgeted cash flows should be reasonably accurate in most months.

Forecasting Net Cash Flows over Several Months

To forecast your cash flows for several months ahead, you can follow the same process as for forecasting one month ahead. Whenever particular types of cash flows are expected to be normal, they can be forecasted from previous months when the levels were normal. Adjustments can be made to account for any cash flows that are expected to be unusual in a specific

Exhibit 2.5   Comparison of Stephanie Spratt's Budgeted and Actual Cash Flows for This Month

Cash Inflows	Expected Amounts (forecasted at the beginning of the month)	Actual Amounts (determined at the end of the month)	Forecasting Error
Disposable (after-tax) income	$2,500	$2,500	$0
Interest on deposits	0	0	0
Dividend payments	0	0	0
Total Cash Inflows	**$2,500**	**$2,500**	**$0**
Cash Outflows	Expected Amounts	Actual Amounts	Forecasting Error
Rent	$600	$600	$0
Cable TV	50	50	0
Electricity and water	60	60	0
Telephone	60	60	0
Groceries	300	280	+20
Health care insurance and expenses	430	430	0
Clothing	100	170	−70
Car expenses (insurance, maintenance, and gas)	500	500	0
Recreation	600	650	−50
Total Cash Outflows	**$2,700**	**$2,800**	**−$100**
Net Cash Flows	**−$200**	**−$300**	**−$100**

month in the future. (For example, around the winter holidays you can expect to spend more on gifts and recreation.)

Expenses such as health care, car repairs, and household repairs often occur unexpectedly. Although such expenses are not always predictable, you should budget for them periodically. You should assume that you will likely incur some unexpected expenses for health care as well as for repairs on a car or on household items over the course of several months. Thus, your budget may not be perfectly accurate in any specific month, but it will be reasonably accurate over time. If you do not account for such possible expenses over time, you will likely experience lower net cash flows than expected over time.

Creating an Annual Budget

If you are curious about how much money you may be able to save in the next year, you can extend your budget out for longer periods. You should first create an annual budget and then adjust it to reflect anticipated large changes in your cash flows.

Example

Stephanie Spratt believes her budget for last month (except for the unusual health care and car expenses) is typical for her. She wants to extend it to forecast the amount of money that she might be able to save over the next year. Her cash inflows are predictable because she already knows her salary for the year. Some of the monthly cash outflows (such as rent and the cable bill) in her monthly budget are also relatively certain because they are stable from one month to another. To forecast these types of cash outflows, she simply multiplies the monthly amount by 12 (for each month of the year) to derive an estimate of the annual expenses, as shown in the third column of Exhibit 2.6.

Some other items vary from month to month, but she thinks that last month's budgeted amount is a reasonable estimate for the next 12 months. The estimate may be too high in some months and too low in other months, but she should achieve a reasonable estimate over the entire set of 12 months. Over the next 12 months, Stephanie expects net cash flows of $4,800. Therefore, she sets a goal of saving $4,800, which she can place in a bank account or invest in stocks.

Improving the Budget

As time passes, you should review your budget to determine whether you are progressing toward the financial goals that you established. If you decide that you want to increase your savings so that you can more easily achieve your financial goals, you should identify the components within the budget that you can change to improve your budget over time.

Example

Recall that Stephanie Spratt earns a salary of $2,500 per month after taxes. She typically expects to spend about $2,100 and invest the remaining $400 in assets (such as bank accounts or stocks). She would like to save a substantial amount of money so that she can purchase a new car and a home someday, so she considers how she might increase her net cash flows.

Stephanie assesses her personal income statement to determine whether she can increase her cash inflows or reduce her cash outflows. First, she focuses on cash inflows. She would like to generate more cash inflows than $2,500, but she is already paid well, given her skills and experience. She considers pursuing a part-time job on weekends, but does not want to use her limited free time to work. Therefore, she realizes that given her present situation and preferences, she will not be able to increase her monthly cash inflows. Thus, she must focus on reducing her monthly cash outflows. In other words, she needs to reduce her monthly spending so that she can save more than $400 per month.

Exhibit 2.6   Annual Budget for Stephanie Spratt

Cash Inflows	Typical Month	This Year's Cash Flows (equal to the typical monthly cash flows × 12)
Disposable (after-tax) income	$2,500	$30,000
Interest on deposits	0	0
Dividend payments	0	0
Total Cash Inflows	**$2,500**	**$30,000**

Cash Outflows	Typical Month	This Year's Cash Flows
Rent	$600	$7,200
Cable TV	50	600
Electricity and water	60	720
Telephone	60	720
Groceries	300	3,600
Health care insurance and expenses	130	1,560
Clothing	100	1,200
Car expenses (insurance, maintenance, and gas)	200	2,400
Recreation	600	7,200
Total Cash Outflows	**$2,100**	**$25,200**
Net Cash Flows	**+$400**	**$4,800** (difference between cash inflows and outflows)

Stephanie reviews the summary of cash outflows on her budget to determine how she can reduce spending. Of the $2,100 that she spends per month, about $1,500 is spent on what she considers necessities (such as her rent and utilities). The remainder of the cash outflows (about $600) is spent on recreation; Stephanie realizes that any major reduction in spending will have to be in this category of cash outflows.

Stephanie looks more closely at her spending for recreation purposes. Most of this spending is on her health club membership and on eating at restaurants. She does not want to give up those forms of recreation, but she recognizes that she can scale back her spending while still enjoying these activities. Specifically, she observes that her health club is upscale and overpriced. She can save about $60 per month by going to a different health club that offers essentially the same services. She also decides to reduce her spending at restaurants by about $40 per month. By revis-

2.2 Financial Planning Online: The Impact of Your Reduced Spending

Go to:
http://www.financenter.com/
products/analyzers/budget.fcs

Click on:
"What's it worth to reduce my spending?"

This Web site provides:
an estimate of the savings that you can accumulate over time if you can reduce your spending on one or more of your monthly expenses. Doing so can help you improve your budget situation.

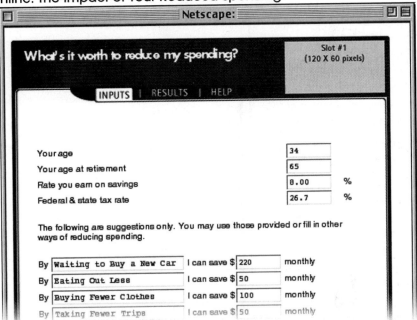

ing her spending behavior in these ways, she can reduce her cash out-flows by $100 per month, as summarized here:

	Previous Cash Flow Situation	Planned Cash Flow Situation
Monthly cash inflows	$2,500	$2,500
Monthly cash outflows	$2,100	$2,000
Monthly net cash flows	$400	$500
Yearly net cash flows	$4,800	$6,000

This reduction in spending will increase net cash flows from the present level of about $400 per month to a new level of $500 per month. Over the course of a year, her net cash flows will now be $6,000. Although Stephanie had hoped to find a solution that would improve her personal cash flow statement more substantially, she believes this is a good start. Most importantly, her budget is realistic.

PERSONAL BALANCE SHEET

The next step in the budgeting process is to create a personal balance sheet. A budget tracks your cash flows over a given period of time, whereas a personal balance sheet provides an overall snapshot of your wealth. The

2.3   Financial Planning Online: Budgeting Advice for You

Go to:
http://www.financenter.com/
products/analyzers/budget.fcs

Click on:
"How much am I spending?"

This Web site provides:
a comparison of your actual
budget versus your desired
budget (based on your income
and spending habits) and
shows how you could improve
your budget.

		Netscape:		
How much am I spending?				**Slot #1** (120 X 60 pixels)
	INPUTS | RESULTS | HELP			

	Current spending	Desired spending
Home payment	$ 900	$ 500
Home maintenance	$ 50	$ 50
Utilities	$ 160	$ 130
Auto payments	$ 300	$ 300
Auto expenses	$ 300	$ 200
Insurance payments	$ 250	$ 150
Child care	$ 300	$ 300
Alimony	$ 0	$ 0
Education	$ 150	$ 150
Food	$ 260	$ 180

personal balance sheet
A summary of your assets
(what you own), your liabilities
(what you owe), and your net
worth (assets minus liabilities).

personal balance sheet summarizes your **assets** (what you own), your **liabilities** (what you owe), and your **net worth** (assets minus liabilities). Therefore, it reflects your financial position at a specific point in time.

Assets

The assets on a balance sheet can be classified as liquid assets, household assets, and investments.

liquid assets
Financial assets that can be
easily sold without a loss in
value.

Liquid Assets. Liquid assets are financial assets that can be easily sold without a loss in value. They are especially useful for covering upcoming expenses. Some of the more common liquid assets are cash, checking accounts, and savings accounts. Cash is handy to cover small purchases, while a checking account is convenient for larger purchases. Savings accounts are desirable because they pay interest on the money that is deposited. For example, if your savings account offers an interest rate of 4 percent, you earn annual interest of $4 for every $100 deposited in your account. The management of liquid assets is necessary to cover day-to-day transactions and is discussed in Part 2.

household assets
Items normally owned by a
household, such as a home, a
car, and furniture.

Household Assets. Household assets include items normally owned by a household, such as a home, a car, and furniture. The financial planning involved in purchasing large household assets is discussed in Part 3. These items tend to make up a larger proportion of a person's total assets than the liquid assets.

When creating a personal balance sheet, you need to assess the values of your household assets. The market value of an asset is the amount you would receive if you sold the asset today. For example, if you purchased a car last year for $20,000, the car may have a market value of $14,000 today, meaning that you could sell it to someone else for $14,000. The market values of cars can easily be obtained from various sources on the Internet, such as http://kbb.com/. Although establishing the precise market value of some assets such as a house may be difficult, you can use recent selling prices of other similar houses nearby to obtain a reasonable estimate.

Investments. Some of the more common investments are in debt securities, stocks, and rental property.

bonds
Certificates issued by borrowers to raise funds.

Bonds are certificates issued by borrowers (typically, firms and government agencies) to raise funds. When you purchase a $1,000 bond that was just issued, you provide a $1,000 loan to the issuer of the bond. You earn interest while you hold the bond for a specified period. (Bonds are the subject of Chapter 13.)

stocks
Certificates representing partial ownership of a firm.

Stocks are certificates representing partial ownership of a firm. Firms issue stock to obtain funding for various purposes, such as purchasing new machinery or building new facilities. Many firms have millions of shareholders who own shares of the firm's stock.

The investors who purchase stock are referred to as shareholders or stockholders. You may consider purchasing particular stocks if you have excess funds. You can sell some of your stock holdings when you need funds. Retired investors tend to hold a large amount of stocks.

The market value of stocks changes daily. The prevailing market value of a stock can be found at many Web sites, including http://finance.yahoo.com/?u. Investors who purchase stock can earn a return on their investment if the stock's value increases over time. They can also earn a return if the firm pays dividends to its shareholders.

Investments such as stocks normally are not considered liquid assets because they can result in a loss in value if they have to be sold suddenly. Stocks are commonly viewed as a long-term investment and therefore are not used to cover day-to-day expenses. (Stocks will be discussed in detail in Chapters 10 through 12.)

mutual funds
Investment companies that sell shares to individuals and invest the proceeds in investment instruments such as bonds or stocks.

Mutual funds sell shares to individuals and invest the proceeds in an overall portfolio of investment instruments such as bonds or stocks. They are managed by portfolio managers who decide what securities to purchase so that the individual investors do not have to make the investment decisions themselves. The minimum investment varies depending on the particular fund, but it is usually between $500 and $3,000. The value of the shares of any mutual fund can be found in periodicals such as the *Wall Street Journal* or on various Web sites. More information on mutual funds is provided in Chapter 14.

real estate
Rental property and land.

rental property
Housing or commercial property that is rented out to others.

Real estate includes holdings in rental property and land. **Rental property** is housing or commercial property that is rented out to others. Some individuals purchase a second home and rent it out to generate additional income every year. Others purchase apartment complexes for the same reason. Some individuals purchase land as an investment because the value of land may increase over time.

Liabilities

Liabilities represent debt (what you owe) and can be segmented into current liabilities and long-term liabilities.

current liabilities
Debt that will be paid within a year.

Current Liabilities. **Current liabilities** are debt that you will pay off in the near future (within a year). The most common example of a current liability is a credit card balance that will be paid off in the near future. Credit card companies send the user a monthly bill that itemizes all the purchases made in the previous month. If your balance is paid in full upon receipt of the bill, no interest is charged on the balance. Thus, your balance is paid off and the liability is eliminated until the next month when you receive the next monthly bill.

long-term liabilities
Debt that will be paid over a period longer than one year.

Long-Term Liabilities. **Long-term liabilities** are debt that will be paid over a period beyond one year. A common long-term liability of students is a student loan, which reflects debt that a student must pay back to a lender over time after graduation. This liability requires you to pay an interest expense periodically. Once you pay off this loan, you eliminate this liability and do not have to pay any more interest expenses. In general, it is desirable to limit your liabilities so that you can limit the amount of interest owed.

Other common examples of long-term liabilities are a car loan and a mortgage (housing) loan. Car loans typically have a maturity of between 3 and 5 years, while mortgages typically have a maturity of 15 or 30 years. Both types of loans can be paid off before their maturity.

Net Worth

Your net worth is the difference between the value of your assets (what you own) and the value of your liabilities (what you owe):

Net Worth = Value of Total Assets − Value of Total Liabilities

In other words, if you sold enough of your assets to pay off all of your liabilities, your net worth would be the amount of assets you would have remaining. Your net worth is a measure of your wealth because it represents what you own after deducting any money that you owe. If your liabilities exceed your assets, your net worth is negative.

Creating a Personal Balance Sheet

You should create a personal balance sheet to determine your net worth. Update it periodically to monitor how your wealth changes over time.

Example

Stephanie Spratt wants to determine her net worth. She can do so by creating a personal balance sheet that identifies her assets and her liabilities. Her net worth can be determined as the value of her assets minus the value of her liabilities.

Stephanie's Assets. Stephanie owns:

- $500 in cash.
- $3,500 in her checking account.
- Furniture in her apartment that is worth about $1,000.
- A car that is worth about $1,000.
- 100 shares of stock that she just purchased for $3,000 ($30 per share). This stock does not pay dividends.

Stephanie uses this information to complete the top of her personal balance sheet, shown in Exhibit 2.7. She classifies each item that she owns as a liquid asset, a household asset, or an investment asset.

Stephanie's Liabilities. Stephanie owes $2,000 on her credit card; she will pay off this debt soon. She does not have any other liabilities at this time. She lists the one liability on her personal balance sheet under "Current Liabilities" because she will pay off the debt soon. Since she has no long-term liabilities at this time, her total liabilities are $2,000.

Stephanie's Net Worth. Finally, Stephanie determines her net worth as the difference between her total assets and total liabilities. Notice from her personal balance sheet that her total assets are valued at $9,000, while her total liabilities are valued at $2,000. Thus, her net worth is:

$$\text{Net Worth} = \text{Total Assets} - \text{Total Liabilities}$$
$$= \$9,000 - \$2,000$$
$$= \$7,000.$$

Changes in the Personal Balance Sheet

If you earn new income this month but spend all of it on products or services that are not considered personal assets, you will not increase your assets and therefore will not increase your net worth. For example, if you spend all of your income on rent, food, and concert tickets, there is no adjustment to your personal balance sheet. Conversely, if you invest in assets over time, your personal balance sheet will change. Nevertheless, your net worth will not increase unless the value of your assets increases by more than your liabilities increase.

Exhibit 2.7   Stephanie Spratt's Personal Balance Sheet

Assets

Liquid Assets

Cash	$500
Checking account	3,500
Savings account	0
Total liquid assets	$4,000

Household Assets

Home	$0
Car	1,000
Furniture	1,000
Total household assets	$2,000

Investment Assets

Stocks	$3,000
Total investment assets	$3,000
Total Assets	**$9,000**

Liabilities and Net Worth

Current Liabilities

Credit card balance	$2,000
Total current liabilities	$2,000

Long-Term Liabilities

Mortgage	$0
Car loan	0
Total long-term liabilities	$0
Total Liabilities	**$2,000**
Net Worth	**$7,000**

Example

Stephanie Spratt is considering purchasing a new car for $20,000. To make the purchase, she would:

- trade in her existing car, which has a market value of about $1,000,

- write a check for $3,000 as a down payment on the car, and

- obtain a five-year loan for $16,000 to cover the remaining amount owed to the car dealer.

Her personal balance sheet would be affected as shown in Exhibit 2.8 and explained next.

Change in Stephanie's Assets. Stephanie's assets would change as follows:

- Her car would now have a market value of $20,000 instead of $1,000.

- Her checking account balance would be reduced from $3,500 to $500.

Thus, her total assets would increase by $16,000 (her new car would be valued at $19,000 more than her old one, but her checking account would be reduced by $3,000).

Change in Stephanie's Liabilities. Stephanie's liabilities would also change:

- She would now have a long-term liability of $16,000 as a result of the car loan.

Therefore, her total liabilities would increase by $16,000 if she purchases the car.

Change in Stephanie's Net Worth. If Stephanie purchases the car, her net worth would be:

$$\text{Net Worth} = \text{Total Assets} - \text{Total liabilities}$$
$$= \$25,000 \quad - \$18,000$$
$$= \$7,000.$$

Stephanie's net worth would remain unchanged as a result of buying the car because her total assets and total liabilities would increase by the same amount. This illustrates that your purchase of additional assets does not necessarily increase your wealth.

Stephanie's Decision. By assessing her revised personal balance sheet, Stephanie now understands that the purchase of a new car will not increase her net worth. She decides not to purchase the car at this time. Still, she is concerned that her old car will require high maintenance in the future, so she decides that she will likely buy a car in a few months once she improves her financial position.

Analysis of the Personal Balance Sheet

The budgeting process helps you monitor your cash flows and evaluate your net worth. In addition, by analyzing some financial characteristics within your personal balance sheet or cash flow statement, you can monitor your level of liquidity, your amount of debt, and your ability to save.

Liquidity. Recall that liquidity represents your access to funds to cover any short-term cash deficiencies. You need to monitor your liquidity over time

Exhibit 2.8   Stephanie's Personal Balance Sheet If She Purchases a New Car

Assets

	Present Situation	If She Purchases a New Car
Liquid Assets		
Cash	$500	$500
Checking account	3,500	500
Savings account	0	0
Total liquid assets	$4,000	$1,000
Household Assets		
Home	$0	$0
Car	1,000	20,000
Furniture	1,000	1,000
Total household assets	$2,000	$21,000
Investment Assets		
Stocks	$3,000	$3,000
Total investment assets	$3,000	$3,000
Total Assets	**$9,000**	**$25,000**

Liabilities and Net Worth

Current Liabilities		
Credit card balance	$2,000	$2,000
Total current liabilities	$2,000	$2,000
Long-Term Liabilities		
Mortgage	$0	$0
Car loan	0	16,000
Total long-term liabilities	$0	$16,000
Total Liabilities	**$2,000**	**$18,000**
Net Worth	$7,000	$ 7,000

to ensure that you have sufficient funds when they are needed. Your liquidity can be measured by the *liquidity ratio*, which is measured as:

$$\text{Liquidity Ratio} = \text{Liquid Assets/Current Liabilities}$$

A high liquidity ratio implies a higher degree of liquidity.

Example

Based on the information in her personal balance sheet shown in Exhibit 2.7, Stephanie decides to measure her liquidity:

Liquidity Ratio = Liquid Assets/Current Liabilities

= $4,000/$2,000

= 2.0.

Stephanie's liquidity ratio of 2.0 means that for every dollar of current liabilities, she has $2 of liquid assets. This means that she has more than enough funds available to cover her current liabilities, so she is maintaining sufficient liquidity to cover her current liabilities. A current ratio of less than 1.0 would mean that Stephanie's liquid assets were not sufficient to cover her current liabilities. Under these conditions, Stephanie would need to boost her liquidity.

Debt Level. You also need to monitor your debt level to ensure that it does not become so high that you are unable to cover your debt payments. A debt level of $20,000 would not be a serious problem for a person with assets of $100,000, but it could be quite serious for someone with hardly any assets. Thus, your debt level should be measured relative to your assets, as shown here:

Debt-to-Asset Ratio = Total Liabilities/Total Assets

A high debt ratio reflects an excessive amount of debt and should be reduced over time to avoid any debt repayment problems. Individuals in this position should review their cash flows so as to maximize inflows and minimize outflows.

Example

Based on her personal balance sheet, Stephanie calculates her debt-to-asset ratio as:

Debt-to-Asset Ratio = Total Liabilities/Total Assets

= $2,000/$9,000

= 22.22%.

This 22.22 percent debt level is not overwhelming. Even if Stephanie lost her job, she could still cover her debt by selling some of her existing assets.

Savings Rate. To determine the proportion of disposable income that you save, you can measure your savings over a particular period in comparison to your disposable income using the following formula:

Savings Rate = Savings during the Period/
Disposable Income during the Period

Example

Based on her cash flow statement, Stephanie earns $2,500 in a particular month and typically has net cash flows of $400 that she allocates to savings or investments. Thus, she calculates her typical saving rate per month as:

Savings Rate = Savings during the Period/Disposable Income during the Period
= $400/$2,500
= 16%.

Thus, Stephanie saves 16 percent of her disposable income.

RELATIONSHIP BETWEEN CASH FLOWS AND WEALTH

The relationship between the personal cash flow statement and the personal balance sheet is shown in Exhibit 2.9. This relationship is important because it explains how you build wealth (net worth) over time. If you use net cash flows to invest in more assets, you increase the value of your assets without increasing your liabilities. Therefore, you increase your net worth. You can also increase your net worth by using net cash flows to reduce your liabilities.

The point is that you build wealth by using part of your income to invest in more assets or to reduce your debt. So, the more of your income that you allocate to investing in assets or to reducing your debt, the greater will be the increase in your net worth.

Your net worth can change even if your net cash flows are zero. For example, if the market value of your car declines over time, the value of this asset is reduced. Thus, your net worth will decline. Conversely, if the value of a stock that you own increases, the value of your assets will rise, and your net worth will increase.

Increase Cash Flows to Increase Your Wealth

Because your net cash flows are key to increasing your wealth, you should recognize the ways in which you can increase your net cash flows. First,

Exhibit 2.9   How Net Cash Flows Can Be Used to Increase Net Worth

Your cash inflows are primarily affected by your stage in your career path and your type of job. Your cash outflows are influenced by your family status, age, and personal consumption behavior. If you develop specialized skills, you may be able to obtain a job position that increases your cash inflows. If you limit your consumption, you can limit your spending and therefore reduce your cash outflows. Either of these actions will increase net cash flows and thus allow you to increase your wealth.

You can forecast net cash flows (and therefore anticipate cash deficiencies) by creating a budget, which is based on forecasted cash inflows and outflows for an upcoming period.

You can also assess the accuracy of your cash flow forecasts by comparing the cash flows that actually occur over a period to the forecasted level. A budget can be created for monthly periods or for longer periods such as a year.

The personal balance sheet measures the value of your assets, your liabilities, and your net worth. The assets can be categorized into liquid assets, household assets, and investments. Liabilities can be categorized as current or long-term liabilities. The difference between total assets and total liabilities is net worth, which is a measure of your wealth.

The net cash flows on the personal cash flow statement are related to the net worth on the personal balance sheet. When you have positive net cash flows over a period, you can invest that amount in additional assets, which results in an increase in your net worth (or your wealth). Alternatively, you may use the net cash flows to pay off liabilities, which also increases your wealth.

Integrating the Key Concepts

Budgeting is a starting point for developing your financial plan. Before you can look for ways to improve your cash flows, you need to recognize how you spend or save your money. Your budget decisions dictate your level of spending and saving and therefore affect the other parts of the financial plan. The amount you save affects your liquidity (Part 2), the amount of financing necessary (Part 3), the amount of funds that you can invest (Part 4), and the level of wealth that you need to protect through insurance, retirement planning, and estate planning (Part 5).

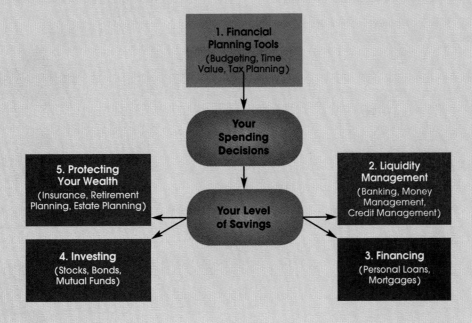

REVIEW QUESTIONS

1. What two personal financial statements are most important to personal financial planning?

2. Define cash inflows and cash outflows and identify some sources of each. How are net cash flows determined?

3. In general, how can you revise your cash flows to maximize your wealth?

4. Identify some factors that affect cash inflows.

5. Identify some factors that affect cash outflows.

6. What is a budget? How is it used? How can a budget help when you are anticipating cash shortages?

7. How do you assess the accuracy of your budget? How can finding forecasting errors improve your budget?

8. How should unexpected expenses be handled in the budget? How might these expenses affect the budget for a specific month? Over time?

9. Describe the process of creating an annual budget.

10. Suppose you want to improve your budget and increase your savings. What should you do?

11. What is a personal balance sheet?

12. Name three classifications of assets. Briefly define and give an example of each.

13. What are bonds? What are stocks? What are mutual funds? Describe how each of these provides a return on your investment.

14. Describe some ways real estate might provide a return on an investment.

15. What are liabilities? Differentiate between current liabilities and long-term liabilities.

16. Why is net worth a measure of wealth?

17. How does your net worth increase? Will the purchase of additional assets always increase your net worth? Why or why not?

18. What three financial characteristics may be monitored by analyzing your personal balance sheet?

19. What is the liquidity ratio? What does it indicate? How is the debt-to-asset ratio calculated? What does a high debt ratio indicate? How is your savings rate determined?

20. Describe how wealth is built over time. How do your personal cash flow statement and your personal balance sheet assist in this process?

FINANCIAL PLANNING PROBLEMS

1. Angela earns $2,170 per month before taxes in her full-time job and $900 in her part-time job. About $650 per month is needed to pay taxes. What is Angela's disposable income?

2. Angela (from problem 1) inspects her checkbook and her credit card bills and determines that she has the following monthly expenses:

Rent	$500
Cable TV	30
Electricity	100
Water	25
Telephone	40
Groceries	400
Car expenses	350
Health insurance	200
Clothing and personal items	175
Recreation	300

   What is Angela's net cash flow?

3. Angela makes a budget based on her personal cash flow statement. In two months, she must pay $375 for tags and taxes on her car. How will this payment affect her cash flow for that month? Suggest ways Angela might handle this situation.

4. From the information in the above questions, how much can Angela expect to save in the next 12 months?

5. Angela analyzes her personal budget and decides that she can reduce her recreational spending by $50 per month. How much will that increase her annual savings? What will her annual savings be now?

6. If Angela is saving $350 per month, what is her savings rate (i.e., savings as a percentage of disposable income)?

7. Billy and Millie have the following assets:

	Fair Market Value
Home	$85,000
Cars	22,000
Furniture	14,000
Stocks	10,000
Savings account	5,000
Checking account	1,200
Bonds	15,000
Cash	150
Mutual funds	7,000
Land	19,000

What is the value of their liquid assets? What is the value of their household assets? What is the value of their investments?

8. Billy and Millie have the following liabilities:

Mortgage	$43,500
Car loan	2,750
Credit card balance	165
Student loans	15,000
Furniture note (6 months)	1,200

What are their current liabilities? What are their long-term liabilities? What is their net worth?

9. Billy and Millie would like to trade in one of their cars with a fair market value of $7,000 for a new one with a fair market value of $21,500. The dealer will take their car and provide a $15,000 loan for the new car. If they make this deal, what will be the effect on their net worth?

10. What is Billy and Millie's liquidity ratio? What is their debt-to-asset ratio? Comment on each ratio.

FINANCIAL PLANNING ONLINE EXERCISES

Go to http://www.financenter.com/products/analyzers/budget.fcs and click on "What's it worth to reduce my spending?"

1. You can input various expenses that can be reduced and determine the savings that will accrue over time. Input your age, your age at retirement, 2 percent for the rate you can earn on savings, and 25 percent and 6 percent for the federal and state tax rates, respectively.
   a. If you waited to buy a car, you could, perhaps, save $220 monthly. Enter this information and go to the Results page to find out what this savings would amount to at retirement.
   b. If you ate out less, you could save, say, $150 monthly. Enter this information and go to the Results page to find out what this adds up to by retirement.
   c. If you went to fewer movies and reduced expenses by $50 monthly, how much extra could you save by retirement? Enter this information and go to the Results page to find out the impact.
   d. If you paid off credit card balances and reduced interest costs by $100 monthly, how much could you accumulate by retirement? Enter this information and go to the Results page to find out.
   e. If you took all these measures to reduce your spending, what is the total savings you could accrue at retirement? To find out, look at the bottom section on the Results page.

Go to http://www.financenter.com/products/analyzers/budget.fcs and click on "How much am I spending?"

1. Do you want to know how your spending habits affect your future wealth? Using this information, you can fine-tune your budget.
   a. Enter an actual home payment or rent of $600 per month and a desired amount of $550. Click on the Results tab to determine the impact of this difference on future wealth. You can also view the impact graphically by clicking on the Graph tab.
   b. Enter an actual expense for utilities of $350 per month and your desired amount of $250. Click on the Results tab, and you can calculate the effect on future wealth. You can also view the impact graphically by clicking on the Graph tab.
   c. Enter an actual expense for food of $600 monthly and a desired amount of $500. Click on the Results tab, and you can determine the financial consequences in figures. You can also view the results graphically by clicking on the Graph tab.
   d. Enter actual entertainment expenses of $250 monthly and a desired amount of $175. Click on the Results tab to determine the financial impact on future wealth. You can also view the results graphically by clicking on the Graph tab.

Building Your Own Financial Plan

Two major components of any good personal financial plan are a personal cash flow statement and a balance sheet. Again, if you are a full-time student, prepare your cash flow statement based upon your anticipated cash flow at graduation.

 In preparing your personal balance sheet and cash flow statement, use the template provided in the *Financial Planning Workbook* and CD-ROM to assist you. In most cases, you will not have all of the cash inflows and outflows or assets and liabilities listed on the template.

When preparing your personal balance sheet, a discussion with your parents might disclose assets that should be included, such as the cash surrender value of insurance policies or trust funds. For your liabilities, be sure to include any educational loans even if they are not payable until after graduation and/or may be repaid by rendering prescribed services (e.g., teaching in a low-income school district).

When preparing your personal cash flow statement, break down all expenses into the frequency in which you are/will be paid. For example, if your car insurance is $700 per year and you are paid monthly, divide the $700 by 12. If you are paid biweekly, divide the $700 by 26.

Personal cash flow statements should be set up based upon the frequency of your pay. In this way, each time you are paid, you can distribute your paycheck to the appropriate cash outflow categories.

If, after preparing your personal cash flow statement, you have an excess of cash outflows over cash inflows, you should review in detail each cash outflow to determine its necessity and whether it can realistically be reduced in order to balance your cash inflows and outflows. Using Web sites like http://www.financenter.com/products/analyzers/budget.fcs (click on "What's it worth to reduce my spending?"), you can also estimate the savings that you can accumulate over time by reducing your cash outflows.

Personal financial statements should be reviewed annually or whenever you experience a change that affects your cash inflows such as getting a raise, obtaining a new job, marrying, or getting divorced.

After completing your personal cash flow statement and balance sheet on the template pro-
vided, return to the goals you prepared in Chapter 1 and make any necessary revisions indicated by your personal cash flow statement and balance sheet.

The Sampsons—A Continuing Case

 The Sampsons realize that the first step toward achieving their financial goals is to create a budget capturing their monthly cash inflows and outflows. Dave and Sharon's combined income is now about $4,000 per month after taxes. With the new cash inflows from Sharon's paycheck, the Sampsons have started spending more on various afterschool programs for their children such as soccer leagues, tennis lessons, and the like. In Chapter 1, they resolved to save a total of $800 per month for a new car and for their children's education.

Reviewing their checking account statement from last month, Dave and Sharon identify the following monthly household payments:

- $900 for the mortgage payment ($700 loan payment plus home insurance and property taxes).
- $60 for cable TV.
- $80 for electricity and water.
- $70 for telephone expenses.
- $500 for groceries.
- $160 for a health care plan provided by Dave's employer (this expense is deducted directly from Dave's salary).

The Sampsons also review several credit card bills to estimate their other typical expenses on a monthly basis:

- About $200 for clothing.
- About $300 for car expenses (insurance, maintenance, and gas).
- About $100 for school expenses.
- About $1,000 for recreation and programs for the children.

To determine their net worth, the Sampsons also assess their assets and liabilities, which include the following:

- $300 in cash.
- $1,700 in their checking account.
- Home valued at $100,000.
- Furniture worth about $3,000.
- Sharon's car, which needs to be replaced soon, is worth about $1,000. Dave's car is worth approximately $8,000.

- They owe $90,000 on their home mortgage and about $2,000 on their credit cards.

1. Using the above information, prepare a personal cash flow statement for the Sampsons.

2. Based on their personal cash flow statement, will the Sampsons be able to meet their savings goals? If not, how do you recommend that they revise their personal cash flow statement in order to achieve their savings goals?

3. Prepare a personal balance sheet for the Sampsons.

4. What is the Sampsons' net worth? Based on the personal cash flow statement that you prepared in question 1, do you expect that their net worth will increase or decrease in the future? Why?

IN-TEXT STUDY GUIDE

True/False:

1. The two most popular personal financial statements are the personal cash flow statement and the personal income statement.

2. A person's stage in a career path is closely related to that person's stage in the life cycle.

3. People's consumption behavior rarely varies.

4. You can forecast net cash flows by forecasting the assets and liabilities for each item on the personal balance sheet.

5. If a small cash shortage occurs when there are unexpected expenses, you would likely withdraw funds from your checking account to make up the difference.

6. It is useful to periodically compare your actual cash flow statement over a recent period (such as last month) to your forecasted cash flows over that period to determine whether your forecasts are reasonable.

7. The difference between actual and forecasted cash flows is referred to as the absolute liability error.

8. In general, whenever particular types of cash flows are expected to be normal, they can be forecasted from previous months in which the level was normal.

9. The ability to increase your net worth depends on the factors that affect your cash inflows and cash outflows.

10. Household assets are financial assets that can be easily sold without a loss in value.

11. The market value of stocks usually does not change on a daily basis.

12. The more of your income that you allocate to investing in assets or to reducing your debt, the greater will be the increase in your net worth.

13. Real estate includes rental property and land.

Multiple Choice:

1. When constructing a budget, it is helpful to use a personal cash flow statement, which measures a person's _____ and _____.
   a. assets; liabilities
   b. cash inflows; cash outflows
   c. revenues; expenses
   d. none of the above

The following information refers to questions 2 through 4.

Bill Peters receives a present salary of about $4,300 per month before taxes. Bill pays $1,200 in monthly taxes. His monthly rent totals $1,000, and he incurs other monthly household payments as follows:

- $40 for cable TV.
- $30 for electricity and water.
- $80 for telephone expenses.
- $200 for groceries.
- $30 for charitable contributions.
- $50 for a health care plan.

Bill's other typical monthly expenses are listed below:

- $50 for clothing.
- $400 for car expenses (monthly payment, insurance, maintenance, and gas)
- $500 for recreation (movies, restaurants, etc.).

2. Based on the above information, Bill Peters's after-tax disposable income is
   a. $3,100.
   b. $2,100
   c. $1,670.
   d. $720.

3. Bill Peters's net cash flow is
   a. $3,100.
   b. $2,100.
   c. $1,670.
   d. $720.

4. Now assume that Bill Peters relies on the above information to forecast his cash flows in future months. Further assume that he anticipates paying an additional $1,000 this month for major repairs on his car. Based on this information, Bill's expected net cash flow next month is
   a. −$280.
   b. $670.
   c. $1,100.
   d. $2,100.

5. _____ is not a key factor affecting your cash inflows.
   a. Your stage in your career path
   b. Your job skills
   c. Your personal consumption behavior
   d. All of the above are key factors affecting your cash inflows.

6. Job opportunities for which there is a _____ demand probably pay _____ salaries.
   a. high; low
   b. low; low
   c. low; high
   d. none of the above

7. Which of the following is not true regarding budgets?
   a. A cash flow statement that is based on forecasted cash flows for a future time period is referred to as a budget.
   b. Firms use budgets to anticipate any deficiencies in funds.
   c. Individuals can use budgets to anticipate any deficiencies in funds.
   d. All of the above are true regarding budgets.

8. Many individuals tend to _____ their cash inflows and _____ their cash outflows.
   a. underestimate; overestimate
   b. overestimate; underestimate
   c. accurately estimate; underestimate
   d. overestimate; accurately estimate

9. A _____ difference between actual cash flows and forecasted cash flows means that the actual cash flow level _____ the forecast.
   a. positive; was less than
   b. negative; exceeded
   c. positive; exceeded
   d. none of the above

10. Peter Hennings forecasted his expected cash flows for this month using his cash flows from last month. Last month, net cash flows were −$100, and Peter's total cash outflows this month were $50 less than expected. Everything else being equal, what is Peter's net cash flow this month?
    a. −$50
    b. −$150
    c. −$100
    d. $50

11. If you do not budget for unexpected expenses in a given month, you will likely experience _____ net cash flows than expected over time.
    a. lower
    b. higher
    c. the same
    d. none of the above

12. Jenny Santana is developing an annual budget based only on her monthly cash flows. In a typical month, Jenny experiences cash inflows of $2,200 and cash outflows of $1,500. Based on this information, Jenny's net cash flow in the annual budget is
    a. $700.
    b. $7,700.
    c. $9,100.
    d. $8,400.

13. The personal _____ summarizes your assets (what you own), your liabilities (what you owe), and your net worth (assets minus liabilities).
    a. income statement
    b. balance sheet
    c. statement of cash flows
    d. statement of retained earnings

14. _____ assets include items normally owned by a household, such as a home, a car, and furniture.
    a. Liquid
    b. Investment
    c. Household
    d. None of the above

15. _____ is (are) certificates issued by borrowers (typically, firms and government agencies) to obtain long-term funds.
    a. Bonds
    b. Stocks
    c. Commercial paper
    d. None of the above

16. Which of the following is not an example of a long-term liability?
    a. student loan
    b. mortgage
    c. car loan
    d. purchases on credit at a local grocery store

The following information refers to questions 17 and 18.

Sarah Evans has total assets of $10,000, including a car that is currently worth $1,500. Sarah's liabilities total $5,000.

17. Based on this information, Sarah's net worth is
    a. −$5,000.
    b. $5,000.
    c. $10,000.
    d. −$10,000.

18. Now assume that Sarah trades in her old car to purchase a new one that costs $25,000. To do so, she writes a check for $5,000 and finances the remainder of the cost with a five-year loan. Based on this information, Sarah's net worth now is
    a. $30,000.
    b. $28,500.
    c. $5,000.
    d. $23,500.

19. To determine the proportion of disposable income you save, you would probably calculate the
    a. liquidity ratio.
    b. debt-to-asset ratio.
    c. savings rate.
    d. none of the above

20. Everything else being equal, if you use your net cash flows to invest in _____ assets, you _____ your net worth.
    a. fewer; increase
    b. more; increase
    c. more; decrease
    d. none of the above

21. _____ sell shares to individuals and invest the proceeds in investment instruments such as bonds or stocks.
    a. Mutual funds
    b. Budget plans
    c. Financial plans
    d. None of the above

Chapter 3

Applying Time Value Concepts

The concept of the time value of money demonstrates that a dollar received today is worth more than a dollar received tomorrow. This point is crucial to financial planning because the dollar received today can be saved (invested) and earn interest. By using the time value of money to make financial planning decisions, you can increase your future income (cash inflows) and the value of your future assets, thereby enhancing your wealth.

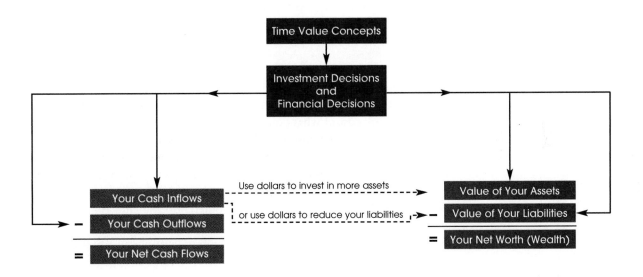

The objectives of this chapter are to:

- estimate the future value of a dollar amount that you save today,
- estimate the present value of a dollar amount that will be received in the future,
- estimate the future value of an annuity, and
- estimate the present value of an annuity.

The time value of money is a powerful principle. In fact, it is so powerful that Albert Einstein stated that it was one of the strongest forces on earth. The time value is especially important for estimating how your money may grow over time.

Example

Assume that your ancestors settled in the American colonies in 1690. At that time, one of them invested $20 in a savings account at a local bank earning 5 percent interest annually. Also assume that this ancestor never informed his family members of this transaction and that the money remained in the account accumulating interest of 5 percent annually until the year 2000, when the bank locates you and informs you of the account. Over this time period, the $20 would have accumulated to $74 million.

As a more realistic example, consider that if you invest just $2,000 in a bank account today that earns 6 percent a year, this investment will be worth about $11,487 in 30 years.

These examples show how the value of money grows over time when you receive a return on your investment. When you spend money, you incur an opportunity cost of what you could have done with that money had you not spent it. In the previous example, if you had spent the $2,000 on a vacation rather than saving the money, you would have incurred an opportunity cost of the other alternative ways that you could have used the money. That is, you can either have a vacation today or have that money accumulate to be worth $34,900 in 30 years (among other possible choices). Whatever decision you make, you will forgo some alternative uses of those funds.

The time value of money is most commonly applied to two types of cash flows: a single dollar amount (also referred to as a lump sum) and an annuity. An **annuity** can be defined as a stream of equal payments that are received or paid at equal intervals in time. For example, your depositing of $50 as new savings in a bank account at the end of every month is an annuity. Your telephone bill is not an annuity, as the payments are not the same each month. This chapter will discuss the time value of money computations related to the future and present value of both lump-sum and annuity cash flows. Calculations are illustrated using both time value tables and a financial calculator.

annuity (or ordinary annuity)
A series of equal cash flow payments that are received or paid at equal intervals in time.

FUTURE VALUE OF A SINGLE DOLLAR AMOUNT

compounding
The process by which money accumulates interest.

The process by which money that you currently hold accumulates interest over time is referred to as **compounding**. In many situations, it is useful to estimate the future value of the amount of money you currently have. For example, you may want to know how much a sum of money will grow to by the time you retire. Or you may want to calculate how much a bank deposit will be worth in five years when you plan to buy a home. Measuring the future value of a sum of money indicates how your present savings could accumulate in the future. It also allows you to determine whether you will be able to afford a new car or a down payment on a home in the future.

To determine the future value of an amount of money you deposit today, you need to know:

- the amount of your deposit (or other investment) today,
- the interest rate to be earned on your deposit, and
- the number of years the money will be invested.

future value interest factor (FVIF)

A factor multiplied by today's savings to determine how the savings will accumulate over time.

The future value is calculated by using a **future value interest factor (FVIF)**, which is a factor multiplied by today's savings to determine how the savings will accumulate over time. It is dependent on the interest rate and the number of years the money is invested. Your deposit today is multiplied by the *FVIF* to determine the future value of the deposit.

Using the Future Value Table

Exhibit 3.1 shows the *FVIF* for various interest rates (*i*) and time periods (*n*). Each column in Exhibit 3.1 lists an interest rate, while each row lists a possible time period. By reviewing any column of Exhibit 3.1, you will notice that as the number of years increases, the *FVIF* becomes higher. This means that the longer the time period in which your money is invested at a set rate of return, the more your money will grow.

Reviewing any row of Exhibit 3.1, notice that as the interest rate increases, the *FVIF* becomes higher. This means that the higher the rate of return, the more your money will grow over a given time period.

Example

John Espe wants to know how much money he will have in five years if he invests $5,000 now and earns an annual return of 9 percent. The present value of his money (*PV*) is the amount invested, or $5,000. The *FVIF* for an interest rate of 9 percent and a time period of five years is 1.539 (look down the column 9%, and across the row for 5 years). Thus, the future value (*FV*) of the $5,000 in five years will be:

$$FV = PV \times FVIF_{i,n}$$
$$FV = PV \times FVIF_{9\%,5}$$
$$= \$5,000 \times 1.539$$
$$= \$7,695.$$

Using a Financial Calculator

A variety of financial calculators are available for purchase. These calculators greatly simplify time value calculations as the following example shows.

Exhibit 3.1   Future Value of $1 (*FVIF*)

Year	1%	2%	3%	4%	5%	6%	7%	8%	9%
1	1.010	1.020	1.030	1.040	1.050	1.060	1.070	1.080	1.090
2	1.020	1.040	1.061	1.082	1.102	1.124	1.145	1.166	1.188
3	1.030	1.061	1.093	1.125	1.158	1.191	1.225	1.260	1.295
4	1.041	1.082	1.126	1.170	1.216	1.262	1.311	1.360	1.412
5	1.051	1.104	1.159	1.217	1.276	1.338	1.403	1.469	1.539
6	1.062	1.126	1.194	1.265	1.340	1.419	1.501	1.587	1.677
7	1.072	1.149	1.230	1.316	1.407	1.504	1.606	1.714	1.828
8	1.083	1.172	1.267	1.369	1.477	1.594	1.718	1.851	1.993
9	1.094	1.195	1.305	1.423	1.551	1.689	1.838	1.999	2.172
10	1.105	1.219	1.344	1.480	1.629	1.791	1.967	2.159	2.367
11	1.116	1.243	1.384	1.539	1.710	1.898	2.105	2.332	2.580
12	1.127	1.268	1.426	1.601	1.796	2.012	2.252	2.518	2.813
13	1.138	1.294	1.469	1.665	1.886	2.113	2.410	2.720	3.066
14	1.149	1.319	1.513	1.732	1.980	2.261	2.579	2.937	3.342
15	1.161	1.346	1.558	1.801	2.079	2.397	2.759	3.172	3.642
16	1.173	1.373	1.605	1.873	2.183	2.540	2.952	3.426	3.970
17	1.184	1.400	1.653	1.948	2.292	2.693	3.159	3.700	4.328
18	1.196	1.428	1.702	2.026	2.407	2.854	3.380	3.996	4.717
19	1.208	1.457	1.754	2.107	2.527	3.026	3.617	4.316	5.142
20	1.220	1.486	1.806	2.191	2.653	3.207	3.870	4.661	5.604
25	1.282	1.641	2.094	2.666	3.386	4.292	5.427	6.848	8.623
30	1.348	1.811	2.427	3.243	4.322	5.743	7.612	10.063	13.268

Example

Brian Clapton has $5,687 to invest in the stock market today. Brian likes to invest for the long term and plans to choose his stocks carefully. He will invest his money for 12 years in certain stocks on which he expects a return of 10 percent annually. Although financial calculators can vary slightly in their setup, most would require inputs as shown at the right.

Where:

N = number of periods

I = interest rate

Exhibit 3.1 (continued)

10%	12%	14%	15%	16%	18%	20%	25%	30%
1.100	1.120	1.140	1.150	1.160	1.180	1.200	1.250	1.300
1.210	1.254	1.300	1.322	1.346	1.392	1.440	1.563	1.690
1.331	1.405	1.482	1.521	1.561	1.643	1.728	1.953	2.197
1.464	1.574	1.689	1.749	1.811	1.939	2.074	2.441	2.856
1.611	1.762	1.925	2.011	2.100	2.288	2.488	3.052	3.713
1.772	1.974	2.195	2.313	2.436	2.700	2.986	3.815	4.827
1.949	2.211	2.502	2.660	2.826	3.185	3.583	4.768	6.276
2.144	2.476	2.853	3.059	3.278	3.759	4.300	5.960	8.157
2.358	2.773	3.252	3.518	3.803	4.435	5.160	7.451	10.604
2.594	3.106	3.707	4.046	4.411	5.234	6.192	9.313	13.786
2.853	3.479	4.226	4.652	5.117	6.176	7.430	11.642	17.922
3.138	3.896	4.818	5.350	5.936	7.288	8.916	14.552	23.298
3.452	4.363	5.492	6.153	6.886	8.599	10.699	18.190	30.288
3.797	4.887	6.261	7.076	7.988	10.147	12.839	22.737	39.374
4.177	5.474	7.138	8.137	9.266	11.974	15.407	28.422	51.186
4.595	6.130	8.137	9.358	10.748	14.129	18.488	35.527	66.542
5.054	6.866	9.276	10.761	12.468	16.672	22.186	44.409	86.504
5.560	7.690	10.575	12.375	14.463	19.673	26.623	55.511	112.46
6.116	8.613	12.056	14.232	16.777	23.214	31.948	69.389	146.19
6.728	9.646	13.743	16.367	19.461	27.393	38.338	86.736	190.05
10.835	17.000	26.462	32.919	40.874	62.669	95.396	264.70	705.64
17.449	29.960	50.950	66.212	85.850	143.371	237.376	807.79	2620.00

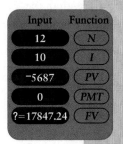

Input	Function
12	N
10	I
⁻5687	PV
0	PMT
?=17847.24	FV

PV = present value, which is the initial amount deposited

PMT = payment, which is not applicable in this problem

FV = future value of the deposit you make today, which is computed by the calculator

The PV is a negative number here, reflecting the outflow of cash to make the investment. The calculator computes the future value to be $17,848.24, which indicates that Brian will have $17,848.24 in his brokerage account in 12 years if he achieves a return of 10 percent annually on his $5,687 investment.

Use a financial calculator to determine the future value of $10,000 invested at 9 percent for five years. (This is the previous example used for the FVIF table.) Your answer should be $7,695. Any difference in answers using the FVIF table versus using a financial calculator is due to rounding.

PRESENT VALUE OF A DOLLAR AMOUNT

discounting
The process of obtaining present values.

In many situations, you will want to know how much money you must deposit or invest today to accumulate a specified amount of money at a future point in time. The process of obtaining present values is referred to as **discounting**. Suppose that you want to have $20,000 for a down payment on a house in three years. You want to know how much money you need to invest today to achieve $20,000 in three years. That is, you want to know the present value of $20,000 that will be received in three years, based on some interest rate that you could earn over that period.

To determine the present value of an amount of money received in the future, you need to know:

■ the amount of money to be received in the future,

■ the interest rate to be earned on your deposit, and

■ the number of years the money will be invested.

present value interest factor (PVIF)
A factor multiplied by a future value to determine the present value of that amount.

The present value can be calculated by using a **present value interest factor (PVIF)**, which is a factor multiplied by the future value to determine the present value of that amount. It is dependent on the interest rate and the number of years the money is invested.

Using the Present Value Table

Exhibit 3.2 shows the PVIF for various interest rates (i) and time periods (n). Each column in Exhibit 3.2 lists an interest rate, while each row lists a time period.

Reviewing any column of Exhibit 3.2, you will notice that the PVIF is lower as the number of years increases. This means that less money is needed to achieve a specific future value when the money is invested for a greater number of years.

Reviewing any row of Exhibit 3.2, you will notice that the PVIF is lower as the interest rate increases. This means that less money is needed to achieve a specific future value when you earn a higher rate of return.

Example

You would like to accumulate $50,000 in five years by making a single investment today. You believe you can achieve a return from your investment of 8 percent annually. What is the dollar amount that you need to invest today to achieve your goal?

The PVIF in this example is .681 (look down the column 8% and across the row for 5 years). Using the present value table, the present value (PV) is:

Exhibit 3.2   Present Value of $1 (*PVIF*)

Year	1%	2%	3%	4%	5%	6%	7%	8%	9%	10%
1	.990	.980	.971	.962	.952	.943	.935	.926	.917	.909
2	.980	.961	.943	.925	.907	.890	.873	.857	.842	.826
3	.971	.942	.915	.889	.864	.840	.816	.794	.772	.751
4	.961	.924	.888	.855	.823	.792	.763	.735	.708	.683
5	.951	.906	.863	.822	.784	.747	.713	.681	.650	.621
6	.942	.888	.837	.790	.746	.705	.666	.630	.596	.564
7	.933	.871	.813	.760	.711	.665	.623	.583	.547	.513
8	.923	.853	.789	.731	.677	.627	.582	.540	.502	.467
9	.914	.837	.766	.703	.645	.592	.544	.500	.460	.424
10	.905	.820	.744	.676	.614	.558	.508	.463	.422	.386
11	.896	.804	.722	.650	.585	.527	.475	.429	.388	.350
12	.887	.788	.701	.625	.557	.497	.444	.397	.356	.319
13	.879	.773	.681	.601	.530	.469	.415	.368	.326	.290
14	.870	.758	.661	.577	.505	.442	.388	.340	.299	.263
15	.861	.743	.642	.555	.481	.417	.362	.315	.275	.239
16	.853	.728	.623	.534	.458	.394	.339	.292	.252	.218
17	.844	.714	.605	.513	.436	.391	.317	.270	.231	.198
18	.836	.700	.587	.494	.416	.350	.296	.250	.212	.180
19	.828	.686	.570	.475	.396	.331	.276	.232	.194	.164
20	.820	.673	.554	.456	.377	.312	.258	.215	.178	.149
25	.780	.610	.478	.375	.295	.233	.184	.146	.116	.092
30	.742	.552	.412	.308	.231	.174	.131	.099	.075	.057

(continues)

$$PV = FV \times PVIF_{i,n}$$
$$PV = FV \times PVIF_{8\%,5}$$
$$= \$50,000 \times 0.681$$
$$= \$34,050.$$

Thus, you need to invest $34,050 today to have $50,000 in five years if you expect an annual return of 8 percent.

Exhibit 3.2   *(continued)*

Year	12%	14%	15%	16%	18%	20%	25%	30%
1	.893	.877	.870	.862	.847	.833	.800	.769
2	.797	.769	.756	.743	.718	.694	.640	.592
3	.712	.675	.658	.641	.609	.579	.512	.455
4	.636	.592	.572	.552	.516	.482	.410	.350
5	.567	.519	.497	.476	.437	.402	.328	.269
6	.507	.456	.432	.410	.370	.335	.262	.207
7	.452	.400	.376	.354	.314	.279	.210	.159
8	.404	.351	.327	.305	.266	.233	.168	.123
9	.361	.308	.284	.263	.225	.194	.134	.094
10	.322	.270	.247	.227	.191	.162	.107	.073
11	.287	.237	.215	.195	.162	.135	.086	.056
12	.257	.208	.187	.168	.137	.112	.069	.043
13	.229	.182	.163	.145	.116	.093	.055	.033
14	.205	.160	.141	.125	.099	.078	.044	.025
15	.183	.140	.123	.108	.084	.065	.035	.020
16	.163	.123	.107	.093	.071	.054	.028	.015
17	.146	.108	.093	.080	.060	.045	.023	.012
18	.130	.095	.081	.069	.051	.038	.018	.009
19	.116	.083	.070	.060	.043	.031	.014	.007
20	.104	.073	.061	.051	.037	.026	.012	.005
25	.059	.038	.030	.024	.016	.010	.004	.001
30	.033	.020	.015	.012	.007	.004	.001	.000

Using a Financial Calculator

Using a financial calculator, present values can be obtained quickly by inputting all known variables and solving for the one unknown variable.

Example

Loretta Callahan would like to accumulate $500,000 by the time she retires in 20 years. If she can earn an 8.61 percent return annually, how much must she invest today to have $500,000 in 20 years? Since the unknown variable is the present value (*PV*), the calculator input will be:

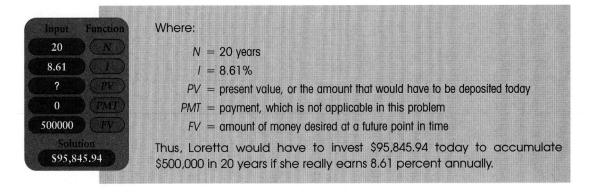

Where:

N = 20 years

I = 8.61%

PV = present value, or the amount that would have to be deposited today

PMT = payment, which is not applicable in this problem

FV = amount of money desired at a future point in time

Thus, Loretta would have to invest $95,845.94 today to accumulate $500,000 in 20 years if she really earns 8.61 percent annually.

Use a financial calculator to determine the present value of a single sum by calculating the present value of $50,000 in five years if the money is invested at an interest rate of 8 percent. This is the example used earlier to illustrate the present value tables. Your answer should be $34,029.16.

FUTURE VALUE OF AN ANNUITY

annuity due
A series of equal cash flow payments that occur at the beginning of each period.

timelines
Diagrams that show payments received or paid over time.

As noted earlier, an annuity (also called an ordinary annuity) is a series of equal cash flow payments that occur at the end of each period. An alternative to an ordinary annuity is an **annuity due,** which is a series of equal cash flow payments that occur at the beginning of each period. Thus, an annuity due differs from an ordinary annuity in that the payments occur at the beginning instead of the end of the period.

The best way to illustrate the future value of an ordinary annuity is through the use of **timelines,** which show the payments received or paid over time.

Example

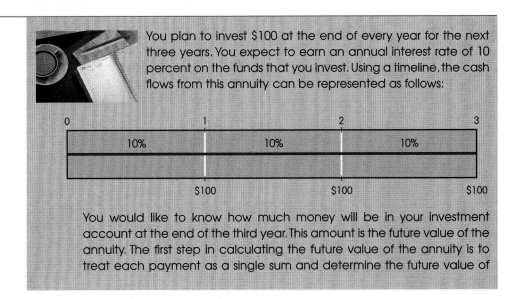

You plan to invest $100 at the end of every year for the next three years. You expect to earn an annual interest rate of 10 percent on the funds that you invest. Using a timeline, the cash flows from this annuity can be represented as follows:

You would like to know how much money will be in your investment account at the end of the third year. This amount is the future value of the annuity. The first step in calculating the future value of the annuity is to treat each payment as a single sum and determine the future value of each payment individually. Next, add up the individual future values to obtain the future value of the annuity.

Since the first payment will be invested from the end of year 1 to the end of year 3, it will be invested for two years. Since the second payment will be invested from the end of year 2 to the end of year 3, it will be invested for one year. The third payment is made at the end of year 3, the point in time at which we want to determine the future value of the annuity. Hence, the third-year payment will not accumulate any interest. Using the future value in Exhibit 3.1 to obtain the future value interest factor for two years and 10 percent ($FVIF_{10\%,2} = 1.21$) and the future value interest factor for one year and 10 percent ($FVIF_{10\%,1} = 1.10$), the future value of your annuity can be determined as follows:

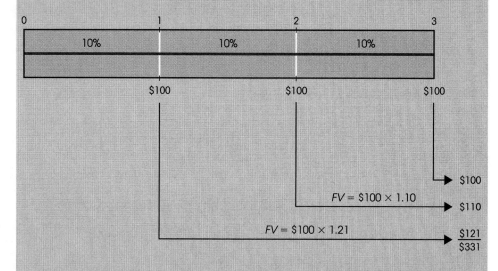

Adding up the individual future values leads to the conclusion that the future value of this annuity is $331 (i.e., you will have $331 in your account at the end of the third year). Notice that $300 of the $331 represents the three $100 payments. Thus, the remaining $31 of the $331 is the combined interest you earned on the three payments.

Using the Future Value Annuity Table

future value interest factor for an annuity (FVIFA)

A factor multiplied by the periodic savings level (annuity) to determine how the savings will accumulate over time.

Computing the future value of an annuity by looking up each individual single-sum future value interest factor (*FVIF*) is rather tedious. Consequently, Exhibit 3.3 lists the factors for various interest rates and periods (years). These factors are referred to as **future value interest factors for an annuity (FVIFA$_{i,n}$)**, where *i* is the periodic interest rate and *n* is the number of payments in the annuity. The annuity payment (*PMT*) can be multiplied by the *FVIFA* to determine the future value of the annuity (*FVA* = *PMT* × *FVIFA*). Each column in Exhibit 3.3 lists an interest rate, while each row lists the period of concern.

3.1   Financial Planning Online: Estimating the Future Value of Your Savings

Go to:

http://moneycentral.msn.com/
investor/calcs/n_savapp/
main.asp

Click on:

Savings Calculator

This Web site provides:

an estimate of the future value of
your savings, based on your
initial balance, the amount
saved per period, the interest
rate, and the number of periods.

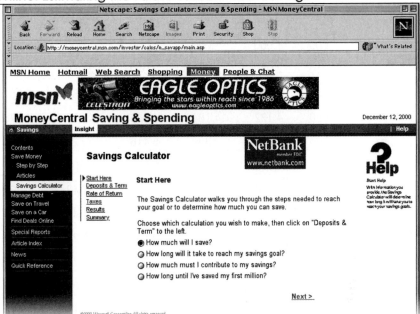

Example

Assume that you have won the lottery and will receive $150,000
at the end of every year for the next 20 years. As soon as you
receive the payments, you will invest them at your bank at an
interest rate of 7 percent annually. How much will be in your
account at the end of 20 years (assuming you do not make
any withdrawals)?

To find the answer, you must determine the future value of an annuity. (The
stream of cash flows is in the form of an annuity since the payments are
equal and equally spaced in time.) Using Exhibit 3.3 to determine the
factor, look in the $i = 7\%$ column and the $n = 20$ periods row. Exhibit 3.3
shows that this factor is 40.995.

The next step is to determine the future value of your lottery annuity:

$$FVA = PMT \times FVIFA_{i,n}$$
$$= PMT \times FVIFA_{7,20}$$
$$= \$150,000 \times 40.995$$
$$= \$6,149,250.$$

Thus, after 20 years, you will have $6,149,250 if you invest all your lottery
payments in an account earning an interest rate of 7 percent.

Exhibit 3.3   Future Value of a $1 Ordinary Annuity (*FVIFA*)

Year	1%	2%	3%	4%	5%	6%	7%	8%
1	1.000	1.000	1.000	1.000	1.000	1.000	1.000	1.000
2	2.010	2.020	2.030	2.040	2.050	2.060	2.070	2.080
3	3.030	3.060	3.091	3.122	3.152	3.184	3.215	3.246
4	4.060	4.122	4.184	4.246	4.310	4.375	4.440	4.506
5	5.101	5.204	5.309	5.416	5.526	5.637	5.751	5.867
6	6.152	6.308	6.468	6.633	6.802	6.975	7.153	7.336
7	7.214	7.434	7.662	7.898	8.142	8.394	8.654	8.923
8	8.286	8.583	8.892	9.214	9.549	9.897	10.260	10.637
9	9.369	9.755	10.159	10.583	11.027	11.491	11.978	12.488
10	10.462	10.950	11.464	12.006	12.578	13.181	13.816	14.487
11	11.567	12.169	12.808	13.486	14.207	14.972	15.784	16.645
12	12.683	13.412	14.192	15.026	15.917	16.870	17.888	18.977
13	13.809	14.680	15.618	16.627	17.713	18.882	20.141	21.495
14	14.947	15.974	17.086	18.292	19.599	21.015	22.550	24.215
15	16.097	17.293	18.599	20.024	21.579	23.276	25.129	27.152
16	17.258	18.639	20.157	21.825	23.657	25.673	27.888	30.324
17	18.430	20.012	21.762	23.698	25.840	28.213	30.840	33.750
18	19.615	21.412	23.414	25.645	28.132	30.906	33.999	37.450
19	20.811	22.841	25.117	27.671	30.539	33.760	37.379	41.466
20	22.019	24.297	26.870	29.778	33.066	36.786	40.995	45.762
25	28.243	32.030	36.459	41.646	47.727	54.865	63.249	73.106
30	34.785	40.568	47.575	56.805	66.439	79.058	94.461	113.283

As an exercise, use the future value annuity table to determine the future value of five $172 payments, received at the end of every year, and earning an interest rate of 14 percent. Your answer should be $1,137.

Using a Financial Calculator to Determine the Future Value of an Annuity

Using a financial calculator to determine the future value of an annuity is similar to using the calculator to determine the future value of a single dollar amount. As before, the known variables must be input in order to solve for the unknown variable.

The following example illustrates the use of a financial calculator to determine the future value of an annuity.

Exhibit 3.3 (continued)

9%	10%	12%	14%	16%	18%	20%	25%	30%
1.000	1.000	1.000	1.000	1.000	1.000	1.000	1.000	1.000
2.090	2.100	2.120	2.140	2.160	2.180	2.200	2.250	2.300
3.278	3.310	3.374	3.440	3.506	3.572	3.640	3.813	3.990
4.573	4.641	4.779	4.921	5.066	5.215	5.368	5.766	6.187
5.985	6.105	6.353	6.610	6.877	7.154	7.442	8.207	9.043
7.523	7.716	8.115	8.536	8.977	9.442	9.930	11.259	12.756
9.200	9.487	10.089	10.730	11.414	12.142	12.916	15.073	17.583
11.028	11.436	12.300	13.233	14.240	15.327	16.499	19.842	23.858
13.021	13.579	14.776	16.085	17.518	19.086	20.799	25.802	32.015
15.193	15.937	17.549	19.337	21.321	23.521	25.959	33.253	42.619
17.560	18.531	20.655	23.044	25.733	28.755	32.150	42.566	56.405
20.141	21.384	24.133	27.271	30.850	34.931	39.580	54.208	74.327
22.953	24.523	28.029	32.089	36.786	42.219	48.497	68.760	97.625
26.019	27.975	32.393	37.581	43.672	50.818	59.196	86.949	127.91
29.361	31.772	37.280	43.842	51.660	60.965	72.035	109.69	167.29
33.003	35.950	42.753	50.980	60.925	72.939	87.442	138.11	218.47
36.974	40.545	48.884	59.118	71.673	87.068	105.931	173.64	285.01
41.301	45.599	55.750	68.394	84.141	103.740	128.117	218.05	371.52
46.018	51.159	63.440	78.969	98.603	123.414	154.740	273.56	483.97
51.160	57.275	72.052	91.025	115.380	146.628	186.688	342.95	630.17
84.701	98.347	133.334	181.871	249.214	342.603	471.981	1054.80	2348.80
136.308	164.494	241.333	356.787	530.312	790.948	1181.882	3227.20	8730.00

Example

You have instructed your employer to deduct $80 from your paycheck every month and automatically invest the money at an annual interest rate of 5 percent. You intend to use this money for your retirement in 30 years. How much will be in the account at that time?

This problem differs from the problems we have seen so far, in that the payments are received on a monthly (not annual) basis. You would like to obtain the future value of the annuity and consequently need the number

Input	Function
360	*N*
0.417	*I*
0	*PV*
80	*PMT*
? = 66630	*FV*
Solution	
$66,630.00	

of periods, the periodic interest rate, the present value, and the payment. Because there are 12 months in a year, there are 30 × 12 = 360 periods. Furthermore, since the annual interest rate is 5 percent, the monthly interest rate is 5/12 = 0.417 percent. Also, note that to determine the future value of an annuity, most financial calculators require an input of 0 for the present value. The payment in this problem is 80.

The input for the financial calculator would be as shown at the left.

Thus, you will have $66,630 when you retire in 30 years as a result of your monthly investment.

PRESENT VALUE OF AN ANNUITY

Just as the future value of an annuity can be obtained by compounding the individual cash flows of the annuity and then adding them up, the present value of an annuity can be obtained by discounting the individual cash flows of the annuity and adding them up.

Referring to our earlier example of an ordinary annuity with three $100 payments and an interest rate of 10 percent, we can graphically illustrate the process as follows:

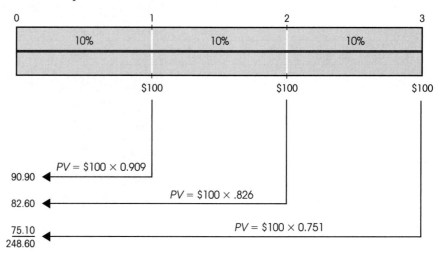

present value interest factor for an annuity (PVIFA)

A factor multiplied by a periodic savings level (annuity) to determine the present value of the annuity.

Adding up the individual present values leads to the conclusion that the present value of this annuity is $248.60. Therefore, three $100 payments received at the end of each of the next three years are worth $248.60 to you today if you can invest your money at an interest rate of 10 percent.

Using the Present Value Annuity Table

Exhibit 3.4 shows the **present value interest factors for an annuity (PVIFA$_{i,n}$)** for various interest rates (i) and time periods (n) in the annuity. Each column in Exhibit 3.4 lists an interest rate, while each row lists a time period.

Exhibit 3.4   Present Value of $1 Ordinary Annuity (*PVIFA*)

Year	1%	2%	3%	4%	5%	6%	7%	8%	9%	10%	12%
1	0.990	0.980	0.971	0.962	0.952	0.943	0.935	0.926	0.917	0.909	0.893
2	1.970	1.942	1.913	1.886	1.859	1.833	1.808	1.783	1.759	1.736	1.690
3	2.941	2.884	2.829	2.775	2.723	2.673	2.624	2.577	2.531	2.487	2.402
4	3.902	3.808	3.717	3.630	3.546	3.465	3.387	3.312	3.240	3.170	3.037
5	4.853	4.713	4.580	4.452	4.329	4.212	4.100	3.993	3.890	3.791	3.605
6	5.795	5.601	5.417	5.242	5.076	4.917	4.767	4.623	4.486	4.355	4.111
7	6.728	6.472	6.230	6.002	5.786	5.582	5.389	5.206	5.033	4.868	4.564
8	7.652	7.325	7.020	6.733	6.463	6.210	5.971	5.747	5.535	5.335	4.968
9	8.566	8.162	7.786	7.435	7.108	6.802	6.515	6.247	5.995	5.759	5.328
10	9.471	8.983	8.530	8.111	7.722	7.360	7.024	6.710	6.418	6.145	5.650
11	10.368	9.787	9.253	8.760	8.306	7.887	7.499	7.139	6.805	6.495	5.938
12	11.255	10.575	9.954	9.385	8.863	8.384	7.943	7.536	7.161	6.814	6.194
13	12.134	11.348	10.635	9.986	9.394	8.853	8.358	7.904	7.487	7.103	6.424
14	13.004	12.106	11.296	10.563	9.899	9.295	8.745	8.244	7.786	7.367	6.628
15	13.865	12.849	11.938	11.118	10.380	9.712	9.108	8.559	8.061	7.606	6.811
16	14.718	13.578	12.561	11.652	10.838	10.106	9.447	8.851	8.313	7.824	6.974
17	15.562	14.292	13.166	12.166	11.274	10.477	9.763	9.122	8.544	8.022	7.120
18	16.398	14.992	13.754	12.659	11.690	10.828	10.059	9.372	8.756	8.201	7.250
19	17.226	15.678	14.324	13.134	12.085	11.158	10.336	9.604	8.950	8.365	7.366
20	18.046	16.351	14.877	13.590	12.462	11.470	10.594	9.818	9.129	8.514	7.469
25	22.023	19.523	17.413	15.622	14.094	12.783	11.654	10.675	9.823	9.077	7.843
30	25.808	22.397	19.600	17.292	15.372	13.765	12.409	11.258	10.274	9.427	8.055

(continues)

Example

You have just won the lottery. As a result of your luck, you will receive $82,000 at the end of every year for the next 25 years. Now, a financial firm offers you a lump sum of $700,000 in return for these payments. If you can invest your money at an annual interest rate of 9 percent, should you accept the offer?

This problem requires you to determine the present value of the lottery annuity. If the present value of the annuity is higher than the amount

Exhibit 3.4   *(continued)*

Year	14%	16%	18%	20%	25%	30%
1	0.877	0.862	0.847	0.833	.800	.769
2	1.647	1.605	1.566	1.528	1.440	1.361
3	2.322	2.246	2.174	2.106	1.952	1.816
4	2.914	2.798	2.690	2.589	2.362	2.166
5	3.433	3.274	3.127	2.991	2.689	2.436
6	3.889	3.685	3.498	3.326	2.951	2.643
7	4.288	4.039	3.812	3.605	3.161	2.802
8	4.639	4.344	4.078	3.837	3.329	2.925
9	4.946	4.607	4.303	4.031	3.463	3.019
10	5.216	4.833	4.494	4.193	3.571	3.092
11	5.453	5.029	4.656	4.327	3.656	3.147
12	5.660	5.197	4.793	4.439	3.725	3.190
13	5.842	5.342	4.910	4.533	3.780	3.223
14	6.002	5.468	5.008	4.611	3.824	3.249
15	6.142	5.575	5.092	4.675	3.859	3.268
16	6.265	5.668	5.162	4.730	3.887	3.283
17	6.373	5.749	5.222	4.775	3.910	3.295
18	6.467	5.818	5.273	4.812	3.928	3.304
19	6.550	5.877	5.316	4.843	3.942	3.311
20	6.623	5.929	5.353	4.870	3.954	3.316
25	6.873	6.097	5.467	4.948	3.985	3.329
30	7.003	6.177	5.517	4.979	3.995	3.332

offered by the financial firm, you should reject the offer. Using Exhibit 3.4 to determine the factor, we look in the $i = 9\%$ row and the $n = 25$ periods column. Exhibit 3.4 shows that this factor is 9.823.

The next step is to determine the present value of the annuity:

$$PVA = PMT \times PVIFA_{i,n}$$
$$= PMT \times PVIFA_{9,25}$$
$$= \$82,000 \times 9.823$$
$$= \$805,486.$$

Thus, the 25 payments of $82,000 each are worth $805,486 to you today if you can invest your money at an interest rate of 9 percent. Consequently, you should reject the financial firm's offer to purchase your future lottery payments for $700,000.

As an exercise, use the present value annuity table to determine the present value of eight $54 payments, received at the end of every year and earning an interest rate of 14 percent. Your answer should be $250.50, which means that the eight payments have a present value of $250.50.

Using a Financial Calculator to Determine the Present Value of an Annuity

Determining the present value of an annuity with a financial calculator is similar to using the calculator to determine the present value of a single-sum payment. Again, the known variables are input in order to solve for the unknown variable.

Example

A recent retiree, Dave Buzz receives his $600 pension monthly. He will receive this pension for 20 years. If Dave can invest his funds at an interest rate of 10 percent, he should be indifferent between receiving this pension and a lump-sum payment today of what amount?

This problem requires us to determine the present value of the pension annuity. Because there are 20 × 12 = 240 months in 20 years, n = 240. The monthly (periodic) interest rate is 10/12 = 0.833 percent. Thus, i = 0.833. Using these inputs with a financial calculator, we obtain the inputs shown to the left.

The present value is $62,192. Thus, if Dave is offered a lump sum of $62,192 today, he should accept it if he can invest his funds at an interest rate of 10 percent.

Input	Function
240	N
0.833	I
?	PV
600	PMT
0	FV
Solution	
$62,192.00	

USING TIME VALUE TO ESTIMATE SAVINGS

Now that you understand the various time value calculations, you can apply them when financial planning. The key time value tools for building your financial plan are estimating the future value of annual savings and determining the amount of annual savings necessary to achieve a specific amount of savings in the future. Recognizing how much savings you can accumulate over time can motivate you to save money every month.

Estimating the Future Value from Savings

The future value of an annuity is especially useful when determining how much money you will have saved by a future point in time if you periodically save a specific amount of money every year. You can apply this process when you are saving for a large purchase (such as a down payment on a home) in the near future or even for your retirement in the distant future.

Example

Stephanie Spratt believes that she may be able to save about $5,000 per year. She wants to know how much she will have in 30 years if she earns 6 percent annual interest on her investment. The annuity in this example is $5,000. The future value annuity factor based on a 30-year period and a 6 percent interest rate is 79.058. Thus, the future value is:

$5,000 × 79.058 = $395,290.

If Stephanie could earn a higher return on her funds, the future value annuity factor would be higher, and the future value of her savings would also be higher. If she could earn 7 percent instead of 6 percent on her savings, the future value annuity factor would be 94.461, and the future value would be:

$5,000 × 94.461 = $472,305.

3.2 Financial Planning Online: How Long Will It Take to Achieve Your Savings Goal?

Go to:
http://moneycentral.msn.com/
investor/calcs/n_savapp/main.
asp

Click on:
Savings Calculator

This Web site provides:
an estimate of how much you
must save per period to achieve
your savings goal, based on
your initial balance, the number
of periods in which you will
save, and the interest rate.

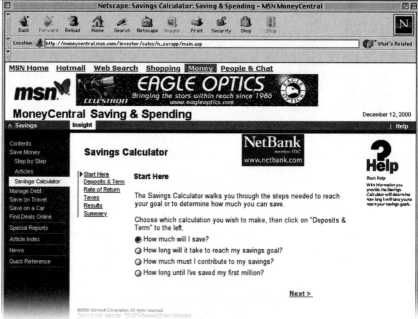

Estimating the Annual Savings That Will Achieve a Future Amount

The future value of annuity tables are also useful for determining how much money you need to save each year to achieve a specific amount of savings at a designated future point in time. Thus, you can estimate the size of the annuity that is necessary to achieve a specific future value of savings that you desire. Because $FVA = PMT \times FVIFA$, the terms can be rearranged to solve for the annuity:

$$FVA/FVIFA = PMT.$$

Example

Stephanie Spratt now wants to know how much money she must save every year to achieve $600,000 in 30 years, based on a 7 percent interest rate. In this example, the future value is $600,000, and the future value interest factor is 94.461. The unknown variable is the annuity.

$PMT = FVA/FVIFA$

$\quad = \$600,000/94.461$

$\quad = \$6,352.$

Thus, Stephanie would need to invest $6,352 each year to accumulate $600,000 in 30 years.

Exhibit 3.5 shows how the time value tools can be used to develop a financial plan for Stephanie Spratt. Stephanie developed a tentative plan to save $5,000 per year. After applying the time value tools, however, she recognizes that she could accumulate $600,000 in 30 years by saving $6,352 per year. She decides to strive for this higher level of annual savings. Because she realizes that this goal is ambitious, she sets a minimum goal of saving $5,000 per year.

HOW A SAVINGS PLAN FITS WITHIN YOUR FINANCIAL PLAN

The key savings decisions for building your financial plan are:

1. How much should I attempt to accumulate in savings for a future point in time?

2. How much should I attempt to save every month or every year?

These decisions require an understanding of the time value of money. Exhibit 3.5 shows how these savings decisions apply to Stephanie Spratt's financial plan.

Exhibit 3.5 How Time Value of Money Decisions Fit Within Stephanie Spratt's Financial Plan

Goals for a Savings Plan

1. <u>Attempt to determine how much savings I will accumulate by various future points in time.</u>
2. <u>Determine how much I need to save each year to ensure a comfortable living upon retirement.</u>

Analysis

Present Situation:

Expected Savings per Year = <u>$5,000</u>

Expected Annual Rate of Return = <u>6% or 7%</u>

Estimated Amount of Savings to Be Accumulated:

Savings Accumulated over:	Assume Annual Return = 6%	Assume Annual Return = 7%
5 years	$28,185	$28,753
10 years	65,905	69,080
15 years	116,380	125,645
20 years	183,930	204,975
25 years	274,325	316,245
30 years	395,290	472,305

Annual Savings Needed to Achieve a Specific Savings Goal:

Savings Goal = <u>$80,000 in 10 years, $200,000 in 20 years, $500,000 in 30 years</u>

Expected Annual Rate of Return = <u>6% or 7%</u>

Savings Goal	Assume Annual Return = 6%	Assume Annual Return = 7%
$80,000 in 10 years	$6,069	$5,790
$200,000 in 20 years	5,437	4,879
$500,000 in 30 years	6,324	5,293

<u>To achieve a savings goal of $80,000 in 10 years, I would need to save $6,069 per year (assuming an annual return of 6 percent on my money). To achieve a goal of $200,000 in 20 years, I would need to save $5,437 per year (assuming a 6 percent annual return).</u>

Decisions

Decision on My Savings Goal in the Future:

If I can save $5,000 a year, I should accumulate $28,185 in 5 years and $65,905 in 10 years. These estimates are based on an assumed annual return of 6 percent. If my annual return is higher, I should accumulate even more than that. The estimated savings for longer time periods are much higher.

A comparison of the third column with the second column in the table shows how much more savings I could accumulate if I can earn an annual return of 7 percent instead of 6 percent.

Decision on My Savings Goal per Year:

Although my initial plan was to develop a budget for saving about $5,000 a year, I will try to save more so that I can achieve my savings goals. I will use a minimum savings goal of $5,000, but will try to save about $6,000 per year.

DISCUSSION QUESTIONS

1. How would Stephanie's savings decisions be different if she were a single mother of two children?

2. How would Stephanie's savings decisions be affected if she were 35 years old? If she were 50 years old?

SUMMARY

You can estimate the future value of a single dollar amount to determine the future value of a bank deposit or a fund established for retirement. It is determined by estimating the compounded interest that is generated by the initial amount. The future value can be determined by using a future value table or a financial calculator.

You can estimate the present value of a single dollar amount so that you know what a future payment would be worth if you had it today. The present value of a single dollar amount to be received in the future is determined by discounting the future value. The present value of a future amount to be received can be determined by using a present value table or a financial calculator.

You can estimate the future value of an annuity so that you can determine how much a stream of payments will be worth at a specific time in the future. This involves determining the future value of every single dollar amount contained within the annuity, which is easily estimated by using a future value annuity table or a financial calculator.

You can estimate the present value of an annuity so that you can determine how much a stream of future payments is worth today. This involves determining the present value of every single dollar amount contained within the annuity, which is easily estimated by using a present value annuity table or a financial calculator.

Integrating the Key Concepts

Time value tools can be applied to all parts of your financial plan. When you borrow money for liquidity reasons or to finance your use of credit cards, the amount of debt grows over time if it is not paid off. When you save money for liquidity reasons or for investment purposes, your money will grow over time if you earn a positive return. The time value tools are especially useful for retirement planning, because they allow you to estimate the future value of retirement funds if you follow a particular savings pattern over time.

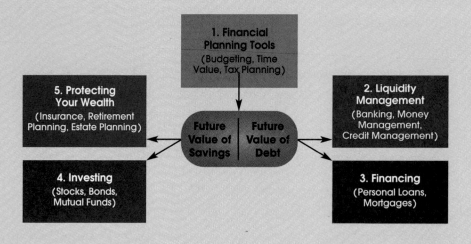

REVIEW QUESTIONS

1. What is meant by the time value of money? How is it related to opportunity costs?

2. To what types of cash flows can the time value of money concepts be applied?

3. What is an annuity?

4. Define compounding. How is it used in financial planning?

5. What two methods can be used to calculate future values?

6. What is the formula for determining the future value of a single sum when using the future value interest factor table? What information must be known in order to find the correct future value interest factor?

7. What is discounting?

8. Describe some instances when you might want to determine the present value of an amount.

In questions 9 through 12, indicate whether you would use the table for determining the future value of a single sum (*FVIF*), the present value of a single sum (*PVIF*), the future value of an annuity (*FVIFA*), or the present value of an annuity (*PVIFA*).

9. You want to know how much you must deposit today to have $5,000 in five years.

10. You plan to contribute $300 per month to your company's retirement plan and want to know how much you will have at retirement.

11. You received $500 as a gift for graduation, and you want to know how much it will be worth in three years if you deposit it in a savings account.

12. You must decide between accepting a lump-sum settlement and annual payments.

13. What formula is used to determine the present value of an annuity? How might this formula be put to use?

14. What formula would you use to determine how much you would need to save each month to have a specific amount at a specific time in the future?

15. In determining the future value of an annuity to be invested monthly over a five-year period, what number of periods should you use?

FINANCIAL PLANNING PROBLEMS

1. Rodney received $1,000 in cash as graduation gifts from various relatives. He wants to invest it in a certificate of deposit (CD) so that he will have a down payment on a car when he graduates from college in five years. His bank will pay 6 percent for the five-year CD. How much will Rodney have to put down on his car?

2. Michelle is attending college and has a part-time job. Once she finishes college, Michelle would like to relocate to a metropolitan area. She wants to build her savings so that she'll have a "nest egg" to start her off. Michelle works out her budget and decides she can afford to set aside $50 per month for savings. Her bank will pay her 3 percent on her savings account. What will Michelle's balance be in five years?

3. Twins Jessica and Joshua, both 25, graduated from college and began working in the family restaurant business. The first year Jessica began putting $2,000 in an individual retirement account and contributed to it for the next 10 years. After 10 years she made no further contributions until she retired at age 65. Joshua did not start making contributions to his individual retirement account until he was 35, but he continued making contributions of $2,000 each year until he was 65. Assuming that both Jessica and Joshua receive 10 percent interest per year, how much will Jessica have at retirement? How much did she contribute in total? How much will Joshua have at retirement? How much did he contribute in total?

4. Becky wants to have $2,000 in spending money to take on a trip to Disney World in three years. How much must she deposit now in a savings account that pays 5 percent to have the money she needs in three years?

5. Amy and Vince want to save $7,000 so that they can take a trip to Europe in four years. How much must they save each month to have the money they need if they can get 8 percent on their savings?

6. Judith has just become eligible to participate in her company's retirement plan. Her company does not match contributions, but the plan does average an annual return of 12 percent. Judith is 40 and plans to work to age 65. If she contributes $200 per month, how much will she have in her retirement plan at retirement?

7. Stacey would like to have $1 million available to her at retirement. Her investments have an average annual return of 11 percent. If she makes contributions of $300 per month, will she reach her goal when she retires in 30 years?

8. Ronnie would like to give his new grandson a gift of $10,000 on his eighteenth birthday. Ronnie can get 7 percent interest on a certificate of deposit. How much must he deposit now in order to achieve his goal?

9. Sandra wants to deposit $100 each year for her son on his birthday. If she places it in a savings account that pays 5 percent, what amount will be in the account in 20 years?

10. Earl wants to know how much he will have available to spend on his trip to Belize in three years if he deposits $3,000 today at an interest rate of 9 percent.

11. Jesse has just learned that she won $1 million in her state lottery. She has the choice of receiving a lump-sum payment of $312,950 or $50,000 per year for the next 20 years. Jesse can invest the lump sum at 8 percent, or she can invest the annual payments at 6 percent. Which should she choose for the greatest return after 20 years?

12. Winners of the Georgia Lotto drawing are given the choice of receiving the winning amount divided equally over 20 years or as a lump-sum cash option amount. The cash option amount is determined by discounting the winning amount at 7 percent over 20 years. This week the lottery is worth $6 million to a single winner. What would the cash option payout be?

13. Lucy spends $10 per week on lottery tickets. If she takes the same amount that she spends on lottery tickets in a year and invests it each year

for the next five years at 10 percent, how much will she have in five years?

14. John can take his $1,000 income tax refund and invest it in a 36-month certificate of deposit at 7 percent, or he can use the $1,000 to purchase a stereo system and put $30 a month in a bank savings account that will pay him 7 percent interest. Which choice will give him the higher return?

15. How much will you have in 36 months if you invest $75 a month at 10 percent interest?

FINANCIAL PLANNING ONLINE EXERCISES

Go to http://www.teachmefinance.com and click on "time value of money."

1. Review the information on Present Value and Future Value and the examples. What is the relationship between Present Value and Future Value?

2. Use the Back option on your browser to go to the previous page. Click on Annuities. Review the information and examples.

3. Use the Back option to go to the previous page and click on Perpetuities. Read the information and the examples. What are perpetuities?

4. Use the Back option on your browser to go to the previous page. Click on the Future Value of an Uneven Cash Flow. Review the information and the illustration.

Go to http://www.savedaily.com/learningcenter/timevaluemoney.asp.

1. Click on Save Daily and Reap the Rewards under Personal Finance. Read the information on compounding and the value of saving daily. How does compounding affect retirement savings?

2. Use the Back option on your browser to go to the previous page. Under Investing, click on the Time Value of Money. Review the information on the time value of money. How does the time value of money affect saving and borrowing?

3. Use the Back option on your browser to go to the previous page. Under Financial Planning Concepts, click on What is Financial Planning? Review the information. Why is financial planning a valuable tool?

4. Use the Back option on your browser to go to the previous page. Under Financial Planning Concepts, click on What are the Benefits of Financial Planning? Read the information and assess the benefits of financial planning to reach your goals. What are the most significant benefits of financial planning?

Building Your Own Financial Plan

Based on the goals that you established in Chapter 1 and the personal cash flow statement that you created in Chapter 2, you are now ready to begin determining how to go about achieving many of your goals. Most financial goals are achieved by some sort of savings/investing plan.

Using the present and future value tools that you learned in this chapter combined with the information provided by your personal cash flow statement, make some computations as to how long it will take to accomplish your intermediate- and long-term goals. For example, if you wish to save $1 million for your retirement at age

55, look at the effect that different interest rates and different annual amounts saved will have on your ability to achieve this goal.

For each goal, make three calculations using an interest rate that you now believe you can earn on your invested savings and one higher and one lower than that rate. If you find that none of the interest rates selected allows you to accumulate sufficient funds to meet your goal, revise the interest rates higher and/or rework your cash flow statement in a way that will allow you to increase your savings. Use the template provided for this chapter in the *Financial Planning Workbook* and on the CD-ROM to perform the calculations and enter your results. The online calculators in the Financial Planning Online features in this chapter may also aid your calculations.

In later chapters, we will explore different savings/investing mediums and the rates of return that can be realistically anticipated from each. For now, just play some "what-ifs" as to rates of return earned on various investments for each goal.

For intermediate- and long-term goals, a review of this kind should be done on an annual basis, although long-term goals may require a somewhat less frequent review.

The Sampsons—A Continuing Case

Recall that Dave and Sharon Sampson established a plan to save $300 per month (or $3,600 per year) for their children's education. Their oldest child is 6 years old and will begin college in 12 years. They will invest the $300 in a savings account that they expect will earn interest of about 5 percent a year over the next 12 years. The Sampsons wonder how much additional money they would accumulate if they could earn 7 percent a year on the savings account instead of 5 percent. Finally, they wonder how their savings would accumulate if they could save $400 per month (or $4,800 per year) instead of $300 per month.

1. Help the Sampsons determine how much they will have for the children's education by calculating how much $3,600 in annual savings will accumulate to if they earn interest of (a) 5 percent and (b) 7 percent. Next, determine how much $4,800 in annual savings will accumulate to if they earn interest of (a) 5 percent and (b) 7 percent.

2. What is the impact of the higher interest rate of 7 percent on the Sampsons' accumulated savings?

3. What is the impact of the higher savings of $4,800 on their accumulated savings?

4. If the Sampsons set a goal to save $70,000 for their children's college education in 12 years, how would you determine the yearly savings necessary to achieve this goal? How much would they have to save by the end of each year to achieve this goal, assuming a 5 percent annual interest rate?

IN-TEXT STUDY GUIDE

True/False:

1. The time value of money implies that a dollar received tomorrow is worth more than a dollar received today.

2. The process of obtaining future values is referred to as discounting.

3. To determine the present value of a future sum, it is necessary to know the interest rate to be earned on your deposit.

4. An annuity in which the cash flows occur at the end of the period is known as an annuity due.

5. The future value of an annuity is especially useful when attempting to determine how much money you will have saved by a future point in time if you periodically save a specific amount of money every year.

6. A stream of cash flows that begins with a payment of $100, which then grows by 5 percent every year, is an example of an annuity.

7. The future value interest factor (FVIF) is dependent on the interest rate and the number of years the money is invested.

8. You are interested in computing the present value of $2,000 to be received in two years. The interest rate is 12 percent, compounded quarterly. You would need to use eight periods and an interest rate of 48 percent in your present value calculations.

9. The present value of an annuity can be obtained by discounting the individual cash flows of the annuity and adding them up.

10. The time value of money is especially important for estimating how your money may grow over time.

Multiple Choice:
Questions 8, 12, and 18 require a financial calculator.

1. The time value of money implies that a dollar received today is worth _____ a dollar received tomorrow.
   a. less than
   b. more than
   c. the same as
   d. none of the above

2. Which of the following is not an example of an annuity?
   a. mortgage payments
   b. car payments
   c. telephone bills
   d. $100 received today, $100 received next year, $100 received in two years

3. The process of obtaining future values is referred to as
   a. compounding.
   b. discounting.
   c. annuitizing.
   d. none of the above

4. You do not need to know the _____ to determine the future value of a lump sum.
   a. present value
   b. annuity payment
   c. interest rate to be earned
   d. number of years the money is invested

5. Assume that you invest $5,000 today at an interest rate of 10 percent for four years. What is the future value of the $5,000?
   a. $7,401.22
   b. $7,387.28
   c. $7,200.00
   d. $7,320.50

6. The present value interest factor (PVIF) does not depend on the
   a. interest rate.
   b. number of years.
   c. present value.
   d. The PVIF depends on all of the above.

7. When you graduate from college in four years, you would like to have $30,000 to make a down payment on a house. Assuming you can earn a return of 9 percent annually, you have to invest _____ today to realize your goal.
   a. $15,055.99
   b. $25,156.84
   c. $21,252.76
   d. $27,471.90

8. Jeff Bloom is 23 years old and wants to retire when he is 45. Jeff believes that $1 million will be sufficient for his retirement. If Jeff can earn an interest rate of 7 percent annually, he has to invest _____ today to have the $1 million when he is 45 years old.
   a. $226,000
   b. $141,000
   c. $450,000
   d. $610,000

9. In an ordinary annuity, payments are made or received _____ of each period.
   a. at the end
   b. in the middle
   c. at the beginning
   d. none of the above

The following information refers to questions 10 through 12.

Bettina Brown has just won the lottery. As a result, she will receive $20,000 at the end of every year for the next 30 years. She invests these payments at an interest rate of 10 percent as soon as she receives them.

10. How much money will be in Bettina's account at the end of 30 years (assuming no withdrawals are made from the account)?
    a. $348,988.05
    b. $7,071,674.36
    c. $3,289,880.45
    d. none of the above

11. If Bettina could earn an interest rate of 8 percent, the present value of her lottery winning would be
    a. $201,253.14.
    b. $225,155.67.
    c. $2,265,664.22.
    d. $1,987,546.47.

12. Now assume Bettina is instead offered an option to receive $10,000 at the end of every year for the next 60 years. If Bettina can invest her money at an interest rate of 8 percent, this alternative option is worth _____ to her now, and she should _____ this option.
    a. $1,012,570.64; choose
    b. $1,012,570.64; not choose
    c. $123,765.52; choose
    d. $123,765.52; not choose

The following information refers to questions 13 through 15.

Nicholas Tage just received a settlement from his insurance company. The insurance company offers him two options: receive a one-time payment of $300,000 today (Option 1) or receive $30,000 at the end of each quarter for the next three years (Option 2).

13. Assuming Nicholas can invest his money at a quarterly interest rate of 2 percent, the present value of Option 2 is
    a. $317,260.24.
    b. $226,082.34.
    c. $75,545.10.
    d. $38,047.25.

14. Based on your answer to question 13, Nicholas should
    a. accept Option 1.
    b. accept Option 2.
    c. be indifferent between Options 1 and 2.
    d. none of the above

15. Assuming that Nicholas chooses Option 2, how much will be in his account after three years if he invests every payment immediately at a quarterly interest rate of 2 percent?
    a. $317,260.24
    b. $226,082.34
    c. $569,313.79
    d. $402,362.69

16. If you invest $2,500 for three years at an interest rate of 12 percent, compounded monthly, you will have _____ at the end of the three years.
    a. $3,512.32
    b. $2,575.75
    c. $3,576.92
    d. none of the above

17. Given a positive interest rate, the future value of a given sum will always be _____ the present value of the sum.
    a. less than
    b. greater than
    c. equal to
    d. less than or equal to

18. As a result of a lawsuit settlement, you will receive $5,000 per year for the next 10 years. If you deposit these payments immediately into an account paying an interest rate of 6.5 percent, how much is the annuity worth to you today?
    a. $35,944.15
    b. $23,089.76
    c. $9,385.69
    d. none of the above

19. The _____ the interest rate, the _____ the present value.
    a. higher; higher
    b. higher; lower
    c. lower; lower
    d. none of the above

20. Peter Barnes would like to save $50,000 to buy a boat in five years. If Peter can invest his money at an interest rate of 11 percent compounded annually, he would have to deposit _____ today.
    a. $29,233.96
    b. $85,516.97
    c. $29,672.57
    d. none of the above

Chapter 4

Using Tax Concepts for Planning

A substantial portion of the income you receive from your salary and from your investments is subject to income taxes. The higher your income, the more taxes you pay, and the less money you have to spend or save. By understanding how your income is taxed, you can make decisions that may reduce your taxes, increase your after-tax cash flows, and therefore enhance your wealth.

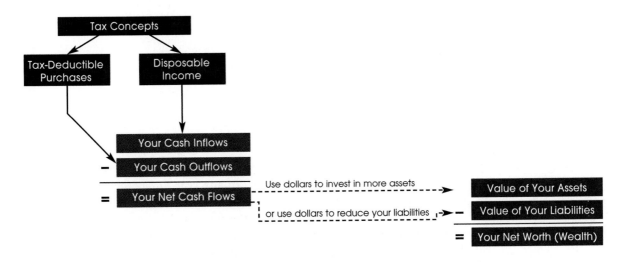

The objectives of this chapter are to:

- explain how to determine your tax filing status,
- explain how to calculate your gross income,
- demonstrate how deductions and exemptions can be used,
- explain how to determine your taxable income, tax liability, and refund or additional taxes owed, and
- provide a comprehensive example that demonstrates how to fill out a tax form and determine your tax liability.

BACKGROUND ON TAXES

Financial planning involves spending and investment decisions that affect your income. Some examples include your decision to:

- take a second job so that you can enhance your wealth,
- purchase a home that will be financed with a mortgage,
- invest in stocks or bonds, and
- contribute a portion of your salary to your retirement account.

All of these decisions affect the amount of taxes you pay and therefore affect your wealth. Individuals pay taxes at the federal, state, and local levels.

4.1 Financial Planning Online: Internal Revenue Service

Go to:
http://www.irs.gov

This Web site provides:
information about tax rates, guidelines, and deadlines.

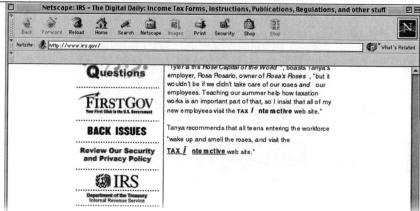

The purpose of taxes is to finance government activities. On average, Americans earn enough by May 10 of any year to pay their federal, state, and local taxes. The federal tax system is administered by a branch of the U.S. Treasury Department called the Internal Revenue Service (IRS). In 2001, the largest reduction in federal taxes since 1981 was legislated in a tax package championed by President Bush. This new legislation calls for sweeping changes over the next 10 years. This chapter covers the basic federal income tax process. (Later chapters will also refer to the tax implications of specific planning decisions.)

Social Security and Medicare Taxes

FICA (Federal Insurance Contributions Act) taxes
Taxes paid to fund the Social Security System and Medicare.

Medicare
A government health insurance program that covers people over age 65 and provides payments to health care providers in the case of illness.

Your wages are subject to **FICA (Federal Insurance Contributions Act) taxes** that fund the Social Security System and Medicare. Your employer withholds FICA taxes from your wages in each paycheck. The Social Security System uses the funds to make payments to you upon retirement (subject to age and other requirements). **Medicare** is a government health insurance program that covers people over age 65 and provides payments to health care providers in the case of illness. The Social Security taxes are equal to 6.20 percent of your salary up to a maximum level (the level was $80,400 in the year 2001 and changes over time). There is no Social Security tax on income beyond this maximum level. The Medicare taxes are 1.45 percent of your salary, regardless of the salary amount. Your employer pays the same amount of FICA and Medicare taxes on your behalf.

Example

Stephanie Spratt earned a salary of $38,000 this year. She is subject to total FICA taxes of 7.65 percent—6.20 percent for Social Security and 1.45 percent for Medicare. Thus, her Social Security taxes and Medicare taxes are:

	Social Security Tax	Medicare Tax
Tax rate	6.2% (up to a maximum of $80,400)	1.45%
Tax amount	.062 × $38,000 = $2,356	.0145 × $38,000 = $551

Her total FICA taxes are $2,907 (computed as $2,356 + $551).

The taxes described above also apply if you are self-employed. However, self-employed persons serve not only as the employee but also as the employer. Their FICA taxes are equal to 15.3 percent, which represents the 7.65 percent FICA tax paid by the employee plus the 7.65 percent FICA tax paid by the employer. The Social Security tax rate is again capped at the maximum limit, while the Medicare tax rate applies to the entire earnings. One-half of the FICA taxes paid by self-employed people is tax-deductible (i.e., half can be deducted from income when determining the federal income tax).

Personal Income Taxes

personal income taxes
Taxes imposed on income earned.

Your income is also subject to **personal income taxes**, which are taxes imposed on income you earn. Any year that you earn income, you must file a completed Form 1040, which determines whether a sufficient amount of taxes was already withheld from your paycheck, whether you still owe some taxes, or whether the government owes you a refund. If you still owe some taxes, you should include a check for the taxes owed along with your completed Form 1040.

Form 1040EZ, the simplest tax form to use, is an appropriate alternative to Form 1040 in some cases. Generally, this form is used by individuals whose filing status is either single or married filing jointly, who have no dependents, and whose taxable income is less than $50,000. The deadline for filing with the IRS is April 15 following the tax year, plus any extensions. Tax forms can be downloaded from several Web sites, including Yahoo! Several software programs, including TurboTax, MacInTax, and Quicken, are also available to help you prepare your return. An example of Form 1040 is shown in Exhibit 4.1. Refer to this form as you read through the chapter.

Tax Relief Act of 2001

In the summer of 2001, Congress passed the Economic Growth and Tax Relief Reconciliation Act of 2001 (more commonly referred to as the Tax Relief Act of 2001). Provisions of the new $1.35 trillion tax package specifying lower tax rates will be phased in gradually from 2001 until the bill expires in 2010. This law does not change the process or forms used for computing taxes; instead, it impacts various adjustments made to determine your personal income taxes. As the process to determine your personal taxes is described in this chapter, pertinent tax provisions that are

Exhibit 4.1 Form 1040

Form **1040** Department of the Treasury—Internal Revenue Service
U.S. Individual Income Tax Return **2000** (99) IRS Use Only—Do not write or staple in this space.

For the year Jan. 1–Dec. 31, 2000, or other tax year beginning ____ , 2000, ending ____ , 20 ____ | OMB No. 1545-0074

Label

(See instructions on page 19.)

Use the IRS label. Otherwise, please print or type.

L A B E L H E R E

Your first name and initial | Last name | Your social security number

If a joint return, spouse's first name and initial | Last name | Spouse's social security number

Home address (number and street). If you have a P.O. box, see page 19. | Apt. no.

City, town or post office, state, and ZIP code. If you have a foreign address, see page 19.

▲ **Important!** ▲
You **must** enter your SSN(s) above.

Presidential Election Campaign (See page 19.) ▶

Note. Checking "Yes" will not change your tax or reduce your refund.
Do you, or your spouse if filing a joint return, want $3 to go to this fund? . . . ▶

You: ☐ Yes ☐ No Spouse: ☐ Yes ☐ No

Filing Status

Check only one box.

1 ☐ Single
2 ☐ Married filing joint return (even if only one had income)
3 ☐ Married filing separate return. Enter spouse's social security no. above and full name here. ▶ _____
4 ☐ Head of household (with qualifying person). (See page 19.) If the qualifying person is a child but not your dependent, enter this child's name here. ▶ _____
5 ☐ Qualifying widow(er) with dependent child (year spouse died ▶ ____). (See page 19.)

Exemptions

If more than six dependents, see page 20.

6a ☐ **Yourself.** If your parent (or someone else) can claim you as a dependent on his or her tax return, **do not** check box 6a
b ☐ **Spouse** . . . .
c **Dependents:**

(1) First name Last name	(2) Dependent's social security number	(3) Dependent's relationship to you	(4) ✓ if qualifying child for child tax credit (see page 20)
			☐
			☐
			☐
			☐
			☐
			☐

No. of boxes checked on 6a and 6b ____

No. of your children on 6c who:
• lived with you
• did not live with you due to divorce or separation (see page 20)

Dependents on 6c not entered above

Add numbers entered on lines above ▶ ☐

d Total number of exemptions claimed . . . .

Income

Attach Forms W-2 and W-2G here. Also attach Form(s) 1099-R if tax was withheld.

If you did not get a W-2, see page 21.

Enclose, but do not attach, any payment. Also, please use Form 1040-V.

7 Wages, salaries, tips, etc. Attach Form(s) W-2 . . . . | **7**
8a **Taxable** interest. Attach Schedule B if required . . . . | **8a**
b **Tax-exempt** interest. **Do not** include on line 8a . . . | **8b** ____
9 Ordinary dividends. Attach Schedule B if required . . . . | **9**
10 Taxable refunds, credits, or offsets of state and local income taxes (see page 22) . . | **10**
11 Alimony received . . . . | **11**
12 Business income or (loss). Attach Schedule C or C-EZ . . . . | **12**
13 Capital gain or (loss). Attach Schedule D if required. If not required, check here ▶ ☐ | **13**
14 Other gains or (losses). Attach Form 4797 . . . . | **14**
15a Total IRA distributions . | **15a** ____ | b Taxable amount (see page 23) | **15b**
16a Total pensions and annuities | **16a** ____ | b Taxable amount (see page 23) | **16b**
17 Rental real estate, royalties, partnerships, S corporations, trusts, etc. Attach Schedule E | **17**
18 Farm income or (loss). Attach Schedule F . . . . | **18**
19 Unemployment compensation . . . . | **19**
20a Social security benefits . | **20a** ____ | b Taxable amount (see page 25) | **20b**
21 Other income. List type and amount (see page 25) _____ | **21**
22 Add the amounts in the far right column for lines 7 through 21. This is your **total income** ▶ | **22**

Adjusted Gross Income

23 IRA deduction (see page 27) . . . . | **23**
24 Student loan interest deduction (see page 27) . . . . | **24**
25 Medical savings account deduction. Attach Form 8853 . | **25**
26 Moving expenses. Attach Form 3903 . . . . | **26**
27 One-half of self-employment tax. Attach Schedule SE . | **27**
28 Self-employed health insurance deduction (see page 29) | **28**
29 Self-employed SEP, SIMPLE, and qualified plans . . | **29**
30 Penalty on early withdrawal of savings . . . . . . | **30**
31a Alimony paid b Recipient's SSN ▶ _____ | **31a**
32 Add lines 23 through 31a . . . . | **32**
33 Subtract line 32 from line 22. This is your **adjusted gross income** . . . . . ▶ | **33**

For Disclosure, Privacy Act, and Paperwork Reduction Act Notice, see page 56.   Cat. No. 11320B   Form **1040** (2000)

Exhibit 4.1 *(continued)*

Tax and Credits

34	Amount from line 33 (adjusted gross income)		**34**
35a	Check if: ☐ **You** were 65 or older, ☐ Blind; ☐ **Spouse** was 65 or older, ☐ Blind. Add the number of boxes checked above and enter the total here . . . ▶ **35a**		
b	If you are married filing separately and your spouse itemizes deductions, or you were a dual-status alien, see page 31 and check here . . . . . ▶ **35b** ☐		

Standard Deduction for Most People

Single: $4,400

Head of household: $6,450

Married filing jointly or Qualifying widow(er): $7,350

Married filing separately: $3,675

36	Enter your **itemized deductions** from Schedule A, line 28, **or standard deduction** shown on the left. **But** see page 31 to find your standard deduction if you checked any box on line 35a or 35b **or** if someone can claim you as a dependent		**36**
37	Subtract line 36 from line 34		**37**
38	If line 34 is $96,700 or less, multiply $2,800 by the total number of exemptions claimed on line 6d. If line 34 is over $96,700, see the worksheet on page 32 for the amount to enter .		**38**
39	**Taxable income.** Subtract line 38 from line 37. If line 38 is more than line 37, enter -0-		**39**
40	**Tax** (see page 32). Check if any tax is from **a** ☐ Form(s) 8814 **b** ☐ Form 4972 . . .		**40**
41	Alternative minimum tax. Attach Form 6251		**41**
42	Add lines 40 and 41 . . . . ▶		**42**
43	Foreign tax credit. Attach Form 1116 if required	**43**	
44	Credit for child and dependent care expenses. Attach Form 2441	**44**	
45	Credit for the elderly or the disabled. Attach Schedule R .	**45**	
46	Education credits. Attach Form 8863	**46**	
47	Child tax credit (see page 36)	**47**	
48	Adoption credit. Attach Form 8839	**48**	
49	Other. Check if from **a** ☐ Form 3800 **b** ☐ Form 8396 **c** ☐ Form 8801 **d** ☐ Form (specify) _____	**49**	
50	Add lines 43 through 49. These are your **total credits**		**50**
51	Subtract line 50 from line 42. If line 50 is more than line 42, enter -0- . . . . . ▶		**51**

Other Taxes

52	Self-employment tax. Attach Schedule SE	**52**
53	Social security and Medicare tax on tip income not reported to employer. Attach Form 4137	**53**
54	Tax on IRAs, other retirement plans, and MSAs. Attach Form 5329 if required	**54**
55	Advance earned income credit payments from Form(s) W-2	**55**
56	Household employment taxes. Attach Schedule H	**56**
57	Add lines 51 through 56. This is your **total tax** . . . . ▶	**57**

Payments

If you have a qualifying child, attach Schedule EIC.

58	Federal income tax withheld from Forms W-2 and 1099 . .	**58**	
59	2000 estimated tax payments and amount applied from 1999 return	**59**	
60a	**Earned income credit (EIC)**	**60a**	
b	Nontaxable earned income: amount . . ▶ _____ and type ▶		
61	Excess social security and RRTA tax withheld (see page 50)	**61**	
62	Additional child tax credit. Attach Form 8812	**62**	
63	Amount paid with request for extension to file (see page 50)	**63**	
64	Other payments. Check if from **a** ☐ Form 2439 **b** ☐ Form 4136	**64**	
65	Add lines 58, 59, 60a, and 61 through 64. These are your **total payments** . . . . ▶		**65**

Refund

Have it directly deposited! See page 50 and fill in 67b, 67c, and 67d.

66	If line 65 is more than line 57, subtract line 57 from line 65. This is the amount you **overpaid**		**66**
67a	Amount of line 66 you want **refunded to you** . . . . ▶		**67a**
▶ **b**	Routing number	▶ **c** Type: ☐ Checking ☐ Savings	
▶ **d**	Account number		
68	Amount of line 66 you want **applied to your 2001 estimated tax** . ▶	**68**	

Amount You Owe

69	If line 57 is more than line 65, subtract line 65 from line 57. This is the **amount you owe**. For details on how to pay, see page 51 . . . . ▶	**69**
70	Estimated tax penalty. Also include on line 69 . .	**70**

Sign Here

Joint return? See page 19.

Keep a copy for your records.

Under penalties of perjury, I declare that I have examined this return and accompanying schedules and statements, and to the best of my knowledge and belief, they are true, correct, and complete. Declaration of preparer (other than taxpayer) is based on all information of which preparer has any knowledge.

Your signature	Date	Your occupation	Daytime phone number ( )
Spouse's signature. If a joint return, **both** must sign.	Date	Spouse's occupation	May the IRS discuss this return with the preparer shown below (see page 52)? ☐ **Yes** ☐ **No**

Paid Preparer's Use Only

Preparer's signature ▶	Date	Check if self-employed ☐	Preparer's SSN or PTIN
Firm's name (or yours if self-employed), address, and ZIP code ▶		EIN	
		Phone no. ( )	

being gradually phased in are identified. (Changes that affect retirement and estate planning will be discussed in Chapters 18 and 19.)

Notice from Exhibit 4.1 that determining taxes requires you to address:

- Filing status
- Gross income
- Adjusted gross income
- Exemptions
- Itemized deductions
- Standard deduction
- Taxable income (adjusted gross income)
- Tax credits
- Capital gains and losses

Each of these topics is covered in this chapter, so that you will be equipped to fill out Form 1040 to determine your taxes. As the tax concepts are explained, a continuing example is provided for Stephanie Spratt, who has a relatively simple tax situation. Near the end of the chapter, a more complex example is provided showing taxes for a family.

FILING STATUS

Each year, taxpayers must specify a filing status when submitting their income tax return. The alternatives are:

- single,
- married filing joint return,
- married filing separate return,
- head of household, and
- qualifying widow(er) with dependent child.

Married people can combine their incomes and file a joint return, or each can file a separate tax return. The "head of household" status can be selected by single people who have at least one dependent in their household. The tax rates applied when using this status may be more favorable than when filing under the "single" status. If you are a qualifying widow(er) with a dependent child, you are entitled to use the joint tax rates for two years following the death of your spouse, assuming that you do not remarry, have a child for whom you can claim an exemption, and pay more than half the cost of maintaining your residence.

GROSS INCOME

gross income
All reportable income from any source, including salary, interest income, dividend income, and capital gains received during the tax year.

To calculate your federal income tax, first determine your gross income. **Gross income** consists of all reportable income from any source. It includes your salary, interest income, dividend income, and capital gains received during the tax year. It also includes income from your own business, as well as from tips, prizes and awards, rental property, and scholarships that exceed tuition fees and book costs. Some types of income are not taxed, including health and casualty insurance reimbursements, child support payments received, reimbursements of moving expenses and other expenses by an employer, veteran's benefits, and welfare benefits.

Wages and Salaries

If you work full-time, your main source of gross income is probably your salary. Wages and salaries, along with any bonuses, are subject to federal income taxes. Contributions made to an employer retirement plan are often made with pre-tax dollars and thus reduce your gross income. Consequently, they are not subject to immediate taxation. Contributions to your employer-sponsored retirement account, whether made by you or your employer, are not subject to income taxes until those funds are withdrawn from the account. Many employees take advantage of their employer-sponsored retirement plan to reduce their current income taxes and obtain tax-deferred growth of their retirement fund.

Interest Income

interest income
Interest earned from investments in various types of savings accounts at financial institutions, from investments in debt securities such as Treasury bonds, or from providing loans to other individuals.

Individuals can earn **interest income** from investments in various types of savings accounts at financial institutions. They can also earn interest income from investing in debt securities such as Treasury bonds that pay interest periodically or from providing loans to other individuals. Note that interest income earned from investments in municipal bonds issued by state and local government agencies is normally exempt from federal taxation. Any tax-exempt interest income is not included when determining taxes.

Dividend Income

dividend income
Income received in the form of dividends paid on shares of stock or mutual funds.

Individual taxpayers can earn **dividend income** by investing in stocks or mutual funds. Some firms pay dividends to their shareholders on a quarterly basis. Other firms elect not to pay dividends to their shareholders and instead reinvest all of their earnings to finance their existing operations. This can benefit shareholders because a firm's share price is more likely to appreciate over time if the firm reinvests all of its earnings.

The worksheet for adding up your interest income and dividend income—Schedule B of Form 1040—is shown in Exhibit 4.2.

Capital Gains

Individuals commonly purchase securities (also called financial assets) such as stocks or debt instruments (such as bonds) that are issued by firms to raise

Exhibit 4.2 Schedule B of Form 1040

OMB No. 1545-0074   Page **2**

Name(s) shown on Form 1040. Do not enter name and social security number if shown on other side.

Your social security number

Schedule B—Interest and Ordinary Dividends

Attachment
Sequence No. **08**

Note. If you had over $400 in taxable interest, you must also complete Part III.

Part I **Interest** (See page B-1 and the instructions for Form 1040, line 8a.)	**1** List name of payer. If any interest is from a seller-financed mortgage and the buyer used the property as a personal residence, see page B-1 and list this interest first. Also, show that buyer's social security number and address ▶	**Amount**

Note. If you received a Form 1099-INT, Form 1099-OID, or substitute statement from a brokerage firm, list the firm's name as the payer and enter the total interest shown on that form.

		1	
2	Add the amounts on line 1	**2**	
3	Excludable interest on series EE and I U.S. savings bonds issued after 1989 from Form 8815, line 14. You **must** attach Form 8815	**3**	
4	Subtract line 3 from line 2. Enter the result here and on Form 1040, line 8a ▶	**4**	

Note. If you had over $400 in ordinary dividends, you must also complete Part III.

Part II **Ordinary** **Dividends** (See page B-1 and the instructions for Form 1040, line 9.)	**5** List name of payer. Include only ordinary dividends. If you received any capital gain distributions, see the instructions for Form 1040, line 13 ▶	**Amount**

Note. If you received a Form 1099-DIV or substitute statement from a brokerage firm, list the firm's name as the payer and enter the ordinary dividends shown on that form.

		5	
6	Add the amounts on line 5. Enter the total here and on Form 1040, line 9 . ▶	**6**	

Part III **Foreign** **Accounts** **and Trusts** (See page B-2.)	You must complete this part if you **(a)** had over $400 of interest or ordinary dividends; **(b)** had a foreign account; or **(c)** received a distribution from, or were a grantor of, or a transferor to, a foreign trust.	**Yes**	**No**
	7a At any time during 2000, did you have an interest in or a signature or other authority over a financial account in a foreign country, such as a bank account, securities account, or other financial account? See page B-2 for exceptions and filing requirements for Form TD F 90-22.1		
	b If "Yes," enter the name of the foreign country ▶		
	8 During 2000, did you receive a distribution from, or were you the grantor of, or transferor to, a foreign trust? If "Yes," you may have to file Form 3520. See page B-2		

For Paperwork Reduction Act Notice, see Form 1040 instructions.

Schedule B (Form 1040) 2000

 Printed on recycled paper

4.2   Financial Planning Online: Updated Capital Gain Tax Rates

Go to:

http://taxes.yahoo.com/
buystock/index.html

This Web site provides:
capital gain tax rates and
implications for various investments.

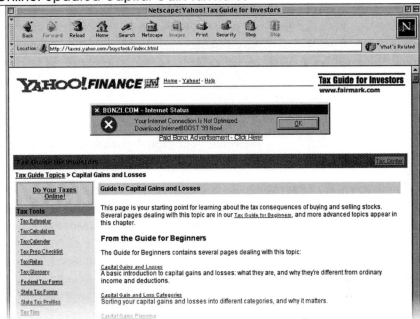

capital gain

Income earned when an asset
is sold at a higher price than
was paid for the asset.

capital loss

A loss that results from selling
an asset at a lower price than
was paid for the asset.

short-term capital gain

A gain on assets that were
held less than 12 months.

long-term capital gain

A gain on assets that were
held for 12 months or longer.

capital gains tax

The tax that is paid on a gain
earned as a result of selling an
asset for more than the purchase price.

capital. They also invest in other income-producing assets, such as rental properties. When individuals sell these types of assets at a higher price than they paid, they earn a **capital gain.** If they sell the assets for a lower price than they paid, they sustain a **capital loss.**

A **short-term capital gain** is a gain on assets that were held less than 12 months. A **long-term capital gain** is a gain on assets that were held for 12 months or longer. This distinction is important because it affects the **capital gains tax** (the tax that is paid on capital gains). Net short-term gains and long-term gains are reported in the section on gross income.

The capital gains tax is a maximum of 20 percent of the long-term capital gain and is even lower for individuals in very low ordinary income tax brackets. For example, an individual in the 15 percent tax bracket will pay a 10 percent capital gains tax. The tax benefits are larger for individuals in the higher tax brackets. An individual in the 36 percent tax bracket will pay only a 20 percent tax on long-term capital gains.

Example

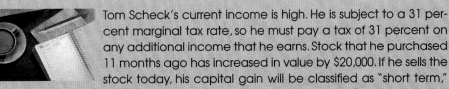

Tom Scheck's current income is high. He is subject to a 31 percent marginal tax rate, so he must pay a tax of 31 percent on
any additional income that he earns. Stock that he purchased
11 months ago has increased in value by $20,000. If he sells the
stock today, his capital gain will be classified as "short term,"
and he will pay a tax rate of 31 percent on that gain, or $6,200. If he holds
the stock for another month, his capital gain will be classified as "long

term," therefore subjecting it to a 20 percent maximum tax rate. If the value of the stock is the same in a month, his tax on the long-term gain will be $4,000. Thus, holding the stock for one more month cuts Tom's taxes by $2,200.

Use the worksheet labeled Schedule D of Form 1040 for individuals to determine your capital gains taxes. This worksheet is shown in Exhibit 4.3.

Determining Gross Income

Gross income is determined by adding up your salary, interest income, dividend income, and capital gains.

Example

Stephanie Spratt earned a salary of $38,000 over the most recent year. She earned no income from interest, dividends, or short-term capital gains. Her gross income over the year is:

Salary	$38,000
+Interest Income	0
+Dividend Income	0
+Capital Gain	0
=Gross Income	$38,000

Adjusted Gross Income

adjusted gross income
Adjusts gross income for contributions to IRAs, alimony payments, interest paid on student loans, and other special circumstances.

Your **adjusted gross income** is calculated by adjusting your gross income for contributions to individual retirement accounts (IRAs), alimony payments, interest paid on student loans, and other special circumstances. If you do not have any special adjustments, your adjusted gross income is the same as your gross income.

Example

Stephanie Spratt did not contribute any of her salary to an IRA this year. She also does not qualify for any other special adjustments to her gross income. Therefore, her adjusted gross income is $38,000, the same as her gross income.

Exhibit 4.3   Schedule D of Form 1040

SCHEDULE D (Form 1040) Department of the Treasury Internal Revenue Service (99)	**Capital Gains and Losses** ▶ Attach to Form 1040. ▶ See Instructions for Schedule D (Form 1040). ▶ Use Schedule D-1 for more space to list transactions for lines 1 and 8.	OMB No. 1545-0074 20**00** Attachment Sequence No. **12**

Name(s) shown on Form 1040   **Your social security number**

Part I   Short-Term Capital Gains and Losses—Assets Held One Year or Less

(a) Description of property (Example: 100 sh. XYZ Co.)	(b) Date acquired (Mo., day, yr.)	(c) Date sold (Mo., day, yr.)	(d) Sales price (see page D-6)	(e) Cost or other basis (see page D-6)	(f) Gain or (loss) Subtract (e) from (d)	
1						

2 Enter your short-term totals, if any, from Schedule D-1, line 2 . . . . | **2** |

3 Total short-term sales price amounts. Add column (d) of lines 1 and 2 . . . . . | **3** |

4 Short-term gain from Form 6252 and short-term gain or (loss) from Forms 4684, 6781, and 8824 | **4** |

5 Net short-term gain or (loss) from partnerships, S corporations, estates, and trusts from Schedule(s) K-1 | **5** |

6 Short-term capital loss carryover. Enter the amount, if any, from line 8 of your 1999 Capital Loss Carryover Worksheet . . . . | **6** ( )

7 **Net short-term capital gain or (loss).** Combine column (f) of lines 1 through 6 ▶ | **7** |

Part II   Long-Term Capital Gains and Losses—Assets Held More Than One Year

(a) Description of property (Example: 100 sh. XYZ Co.)	(b) Date acquired (Mo., day, yr.)	(c) Date sold (Mo., day, yr.)	(d) Sales price (see page D-6)	(e) Cost or other basis (see page D-6)	(f) Gain or (loss) Subtract (e) from (d)	(g) 28% rate gain or (loss) ★ (see instr. below)
8						

9 Enter your long-term totals, if any, from Schedule D-1, line 9 . . . . | **9** |

10 Total long-term sales price amounts. Add column (d) of lines 8 and 9 . . . . . | **10** |

11 Gain from Form 4797, Part I; long-term gain from Forms 2439 and 6252; and long-term gain or (loss) from Forms 4684, 6781, and 8824 . . . . | **11** |

12 Net long-term gain or (loss) from partnerships, S corporations, estates, and trusts from Schedule(s) K-1. . . . . . | **12** |

13 Capital gain distributions. See page D-1 . . . . | **13** |

14 Long-term capital loss carryover. Enter in both columns (f) and (g) the amount, if any, from line 13 of your 1999 Capital Loss Carryover Worksheet . . . . . . | **14** ( ) ( )

15 Combine column (g) of lines 8 through 14 . . . . | **15** |

16 **Net long-term capital gain or (loss).** Combine column (f) of lines 8 through 14 ▶ | **16** |
Next: Go to Part III on the back.

*
28% rate gain or loss includes **all** "collectibles gains and losses" (as defined on page D-6) and up to 50% of the eligible gain on qualified small business stock (see page D-4).

For Paperwork Reduction Act Notice, see Form 1040 instructions.   Cat. No. 11338H   **Schedule D (Form 1040) 2000**

(continued)

Exhibit 4.3 *(continued)*

Part III	Summary of Parts I and II

17 Combine lines 7 and 16. If a loss, go to line 18. If a gain, enter the gain on Form 1040, line 13 · · · · **17**

    Next: Complete Form 1040 through line 39. Then, go to **Part IV** to figure your tax if:

      • Both lines 16 and 17 are gains **and**

      • Form 1040, line 39, is more than zero.

      Otherwise, **stop here.**

18 If line 17 is a loss, enter here and as a (loss) on Form 1040, line 13, the **smaller** of these losses:

      • The loss on line 17 **or**

      • ($3,000) or, if married filing separately, ($1,500) . . . . **18** (   )

    Next: Skip **Part IV** below. Instead, complete Form 1040 through line 37. Then, complete the **Capital Loss Carryover Worksheet** on page D-6 if:

      • The loss on line 17 exceeds the loss on line 18 **or**

      • Form 1040, line 37, is a loss.

Part IV	Tax Computation Using Maximum Capital Gains Rates

19 Enter your taxable income from Form 1040, line 39 . . . . **19**

20 Enter the **smaller** of line 16 or line 17 of Schedule D **20**

21 If you are filing Form 4952, enter the amount from Form 4952, line 4e **21**

22 Subtract line 21 from line 20. If zero or less, enter -0- **22**

23 Combine lines 7 and 15. If zero or less, enter -0- **23**

24 Enter the **smaller** of line 15 or line 23, but not less than zero . . . **24**

25 Enter your unrecaptured section 1250 gain, if any, from line 17 of the worksheet on page D-8 . . . . **25**

26 Add lines 24 and 25 . . . . **26**

27 Subtract line 26 from line 22. If zero or less, enter -0- **27**

28 Subtract line 27 from line 19. If zero or less, enter -0- **28**

29 Enter the **smaller** of:

    • The amount on line 19 **or**

    • $26,250 if single; $43,850 if married filing jointly or qualifying widow(er); $21,925 if married filing separately; or $35,150 if head of household   } **29**

30 Enter the **smaller** of line 28 or line 29 . . . . **30**

31 Subtract line 22 from line 19. If zero or less, enter -0- **31**

32 Enter the **larger** of line 30 or line 31 . . . . ▶ **32**

33 Figure the tax on the amount on line 32. Use the Tax Table or Tax Rate Schedules, whichever applies **33**

    Note. If the amounts on lines 29 and 30 are the same, skip lines 34 through 37 and go to line 38.

34 Enter the amount from line 29 . . . . **34**

35 Enter the amount from line 30 . . . . **35**

36 Subtract line 35 from line 34 . . . . ▶ **36**

37 Multiply line 36 by 10% (.10) **37**

    Note. If the amounts on lines 19 and 29 are the same, skip lines 38 through 51 and go to line 52.

38 Enter the **smaller** of line 19 or line 27 . . . . **38**

39 Enter the amount from line 36 . . . . **39**

40 Subtract line 39 from line 38 . . . . ▶ **40**

41 Multiply line 40 by 20% (.20) **41**

    Note. If line 26 is zero or blank, skip lines 42 through 51 and go to line 52.

42 Enter the **smaller** of line 22 or line 25 . . . . **42**

43 Add lines 22 and 32 . . . . **43**

44 Enter the amount from line 19 . . . . . **44**

45 Subtract line 44 from line 43. If zero or less, enter -0- **45**

46 Subtract line 45 from line 42. If zero or less, enter -0- . . . . ▶ **46**

47 Multiply line 46 by 25% (.25) **47**

    Note. If line 24 is zero or blank, skip lines 48 through 51 and go to line 52.

48 Enter the amount from line 19 . . . . **48**

49 Add lines 32, 36, 40, and 46 . . . . **49**

50 Subtract line 49 from line 48 . . . . **50**

51 Multiply line 50 by 28% (.28) **51**

52 Add lines 33, 37, 41, 47, and 51 . . . . **52**

53 Figure the tax on the amount on line 19. Use the Tax Table or Tax Rate Schedules, whichever applies **53**

54 **Tax on all taxable income (including capital gains).** Enter the **smaller** of line 52 or line 53 here and on Form 1040, line 40. . . . . **54**

Schedule D (Form 1040) 2000

DEDUCTIONS AND EXEMPTIONS

You may be able to claim deductions and exemptions, which reduce the amount of your gross income subject to taxation.

Standard Deduction

standard deduction
A fixed amount that can be deducted from adjusted gross income to determine taxable income.

marriage penalty
Term used to describe the fact that many two-income married people pay more in taxes than if they were single.

The **standard deduction** is a fixed amount deducted from adjusted gross income to determine taxable income. The amount of the standard deduction is not affected by the amount of income you earned during the year; instead it varies according to your filing status and whether you are over age 65. Each year, the IRS adjusts the amount of the standard deduction to keep pace with inflation. The Tax Relief Act of 2001 addresses the so-called **marriage penalty** in the tax code that causes many two-income married people to pay more in taxes than if they were single. Starting in 2005, the standard deduction for married couples will be gradually increased until it covers twice the income level for single individuals in 2009. Exhibit 4.4 lists the standard deduction amounts for the 2000 tax year. The additional deductions in the last column of Exhibit 4.4 are applied to each qualifying spouse (taxpayer), regardless of whether that person files a joint or separate return, and blind taxpayers.

Example

Stephanie Spratt's tax filing status is single. Therefore, she can take a standard deduction of $4,400 from her adjusted gross income. Alternatively, she can itemize her deductions (as explained next). She will take the standard deduction unless her itemized deductions exceed the standard deduction.

Itemized Deductions

itemized deductions
Specific expenses that can be deducted to reduce taxable income.

Itemized deductions are specific expenses that can be deducted to reduce taxable income. Taxpayers itemize their deductions on the tax form so that they can subtract these deductions from their adjusted gross income to determine their taxable income.

Taxpayers typically work through the process of itemizing their deductions and then compare the total dollar value to the standard deduction that

Exhibit 4.4 Standard Deduction Amounts for the 2000 Tax Year

Status	Under Age 65	Additional Standard Deduction (over age 65 or blind)
Married, filing jointly	$7,350	$850
Head of household	6,450	1,150
Single individual	4,400	1,150
Married, filing separately	3,675	850

4.3   Financial Planning Online: Updated State Income Tax Rates

Go to:
http://taxes.yahoo.com/
statereport.html

This Web site provides:
income tax rates and information on personal exemptions for each state.

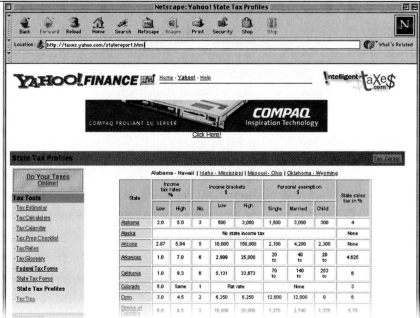

State	Income tax rates %		Income brackets $			Personal exemption $			State sales tax in %
	Low	High	No.	Low	High	Single	Married	Child	
Alabama	2.0	5.0	3	500	3,000	1,500	3,000	300	4
Alaska	No state income tax								None
Arizona	2.87	5.04	5	10,000	150,000	2,100	4,200	2,300	None
Arkansas	1.0	7.0	6	2,999	25,000	20 to	40 to	20 to	4.625
California	1.0	9.3	6	5,131	33,673	70 to	140 to	253 to	6
Colorado	5.0	Same	1	Flat rate		None			3
Conn.	3.0	4.5	2	6,250	6,250	12,000	12,000	0	6
District of Columbia	6.0	9.5	3	10,000	20,000	1,370	2,740	1,370	5.75

they are allowed. The larger the amount of deductions, the lower will be the taxable income on which taxes are assessed. Thus, a taxpayer will choose to itemize if doing so results in lower taxable income than the standard deduction. Otherwise, the taxpayer will use the standard deduction. Several of the more common itemized deductions are explained below.

interest expense
Interest paid on borrowed money.

Interest Expense. When people borrow funds to purchase a home, they pay **interest expense,** or interest on the money that they borrowed. The annual interest payments made on such a loan are an itemized deduction. Interest payments on student loans are an itemized deduction subject to income limits. The Tax Relief Act of 2001 increased the income ranges, making the deduction more widely available. Interest payments made on car loans or personal loans, annual credit card fees, and loan fees are not tax-deductible.

state income tax
An income tax imposed by some states on people who receive income from employers in that state.

State Taxes. Many states impose a **state income tax** (between 3 and 10 percent) on people who receive income from employers in that state. These state taxes can be deducted as an itemized deduction.

real estate tax
A tax imposed on a home or other real estate in the county where the property is located.

Real Estate Taxes. Owners of homes or other real estate are subject to **real estate taxes** imposed by the county where the property is located. These real estate taxes can be deducted as an itemized deduction.

Medical Expenses. People who incur a large amount of unreimbursed medical expenses may deduct the following expenses:

- I SUPPOSE YOU HAVE THE RECEIPTS TO QUALIFY YOUR DEDUCTIONS?

www.cartoonstock.com

1. Amounts paid for prevention, diagnosis, or alleviation of physical or mental defects or illness.

2. Amounts paid to affect any structure or function of the body.

3. Expenses for transportation primarily for and essential to medical care.

4. Accident and health insurance premiums (such as for health care and prescription drugs).

People with medical expenses that exceed 7.5 percent of adjusted gross income may deduct that excess amount as an itemized deduction. This deduction is specifically for people who incur an unusually high level of medical expenses in a particular year.

Charitable Gifts. People who make charitable gifts to qualified organizations (such as the Humane Society) can deduct their contribution as an itemized deduction.

Other Expenses. It may be possible to deduct a portion of losses due to casualties or theft and major job-related expenses that are not reimbursed by employers. However, these expenses are deductible only if they are substantial, as they must be in excess of specified minimum levels (based on a percentage of adjusted gross income). Note that qualified higher education expenses (other than room and board) may also be deducted.

Summary of Deductible Expenses. Taxpayers sum all of their various deductions to determine whether to itemize or use the standard deduction.

Example

Stephanie Spratt does not own a home; therefore, she pays no interest expense on a mortgage and pays no real estate taxes. She does not pay state income taxes in her state of Texas. She made charitable contributions amounting to $200. Her total eligible itemized deductions are:

Deductions	
Interest Expense	$0
State Income Taxes	0
Real Estate Taxes	0
Unreimbursed Medical	0
Charity	200
Total	$200

> If Stephanie decides to take the standard deduction, she can deduct $4,400 from her gross income instead of the itemized deductions described above. Since the standard deduction far exceeds her itemized deductions of $200, she decides to take the standard deduction.

The worksheet for itemized deductions is Schedule A of Form 1040 for individuals. An example of Schedule A is shown in Exhibit 4.5.

Exemptions

exemption
An amount that can be deducted for each person who is supported by the income reported on a tax return.

An **exemption** is permitted for each person who is supported by the income reported on a tax return. For example, children in a household are claimed as exemptions by their parents on tax forms. Exemptions reduce taxable income even if the taxpayer decides to take the standard deduction rather than itemizing. A personal exemption can be claimed for the person filing a tax return, for a spouse, and for each dependent. Each year the amount of the exemption is adjusted for inflation. In the 2000 calendar year, each personal exemption was $2,800. The total amount of exemptions is deducted from gross income to determine taxable income.

Example

Stephanie Spratt is single and has no children living in her household. She can claim one exemption for herself, which allows her to deduct $2,800 from her adjusted gross income.

TAXABLE INCOME AND TAXES

Before calculating the taxes that you owe, you need to determine your taxable income, as explained next.

taxable income
Adjusted gross income less deductions and exemptions.

Taxable Income

Taxable income is equal to adjusted gross income less deductions and exemptions.

Example

Recall that Stephanie Spratt's adjusted gross income is $38,000, her standard deduction is $4,400, and her exemptions are $2,800. Therefore, her taxable income for the year is:

Adjusted Gross Income	$38,000
− Deductions	4,400
− Exemptions	2,800
= Taxable Income	$30,800

Exhibit 4.5 Schedule A of Form 1040

SCHEDULES A&B (Form 1040) Department of the Treasury Internal Revenue Service (99)	**Schedule A—Itemized Deductions** (Schedule B is on back) ▶ **Attach to Form 1040.** ▶ **See Instructions for Schedules A and B (Form 1040).**	OMB No. 1545-0074 2000 Attachment Sequence No. **07**

Name(s) shown on Form 1040 — Your social security number

Medical and Dental Expenses		**Caution.** Do not include expenses reimbursed or paid by others.		
	1	Medical and dental expenses (see page A-2)	1	
	2	Enter amount from Form 1040, line 34. 2		
	3	Multiply line 2 above by 7.5% (.075)	3	
	4	Subtract line 3 from line 1. If line 3 is more than line 1, enter -0-		4
Taxes You Paid (See page A-2.)	5	State and local income taxes	5	
	6	Real estate taxes (see page A-2)	6	
	7	Personal property taxes	7	
	8	Other taxes. List type and amount ▶	8	
	9	Add lines 5 through 8		9
Interest You Paid (See page A-3.) **Note.** Personal interest is not deductible.	10	Home mortgage interest and points reported to you on Form 1098	10	
	11	Home mortgage interest not reported to you on Form 1098. If paid to the person from whom you bought the home, see page A-3 and show that person's name, identifying no., and address ▶	11	
	12	Points not reported to you on Form 1098. See page A-3 for special rules	12	
	13	Investment interest. Attach Form 4952 if required. (See page A-3.)	13	
	14	Add lines 10 through 13		14
Gifts to Charity If you made a gift and got a benefit for it, see page A-4.	15	Gifts by cash or check. If you made any gift of $250 or more, see page A-4	15	
	16	Other than by cash or check. If any gift of $250 or more, see page A-4. You **must** attach Form 8283 if over $500	16	
	17	Carryover from prior year	17	
	18	Add lines 15 through 17		18
Casualty and Theft Losses	19	Casualty or theft loss(es). Attach Form 4684. (See page A-5.)		19
Job Expenses and Most Other Miscellaneous Deductions (See page A-5 for expenses to deduct here.)	20	Unreimbursed employee expenses—job travel, union dues, job education, etc. You **must** attach Form 2106 or 2106-EZ if required. (See page A-5.) ▶	20	
	21	Tax preparation fees	21	
	22	Other expenses—investment, safe deposit box, etc. List type and amount ▶..................	22	
	23	Add lines 20 through 22	23	
	24	Enter amount from Form 1040, line 34. 24		
	25	Multiply line 24 above by 2% (.02)	25	
	26	Subtract line 25 from line 23. If line 25 is more than line 23, enter -0-		26
Other Miscellaneous Deductions	27	Other—from list on page A-6. List type and amount ▶		27
Total Itemized Deductions	28	Is Form 1040, line 34, over $128,950 (over $64,475 if married filing separately)? ☐ **No.** Your deduction is not limited. Add the amounts in the far right column for lines 4 through 27. Also, enter this amount on Form 1040, line 36. ☐ **Yes.** Your deduction may be limited. See page A-6 for the amount to enter.	▶	28

For Paperwork Reduction Act Notice, see Form 1040 instructions.   Cat. No. 11330X   Schedule A (Form 1040) 2000

101

Taxes

progressive
A term used to characterize a tax system where a positive relationship exists between an individual's income level and that person's tax rate.

Once you know what your taxable income is, you can use a table such as Exhibit 4.6 to determine the taxes that you owe. Taxes are dependent not only on your taxable income, but also on your filing status. Exhibit 4.6 shows the tax schedules for different filing statuses for the 2000 tax year. Notice that the income tax system in the United States is **progressive**. That

Exhibit 4.6   Individual Tax Rates for the Year 2000

If Your Taxable Income Is	You Pay This Amount on the Base of the Bracket	Plus This Percentage on the Excess over the Base
Panel A. Single Individuals		
Up to $26,250	$0	15.0%
$26,250–$63,550	$3,937.50	28.0%
$63,550–$132,600	$14,381.50	31.0%
$132,600–$288,350	$35,787.00	36.0%
Over $288,350	$91,857.00	39.6%
Panel B. Married Couples Filing Jointly or Qualifying Widow(er)		
Up to $43,850	$0	15.0%
$43,850–$105,950	$6,577.50	28.0%
$105,950–$161,450	$23,965.50	31.0%
$161,450–$288,350	$41,170.50	36.0%
Over $288,350	$86,854.50	39.6%
Panel C. Married Couples Filing Separately		
Up to $21,925	$0	15.0%
$21,925–$52,975	$3,228.75	28.0%
$52,975–$80,725	$11,982.75	31.0%
$80,725–$144,175	$20,585.25	36.0%
Over $144,175	$43,427.25	39.6%
Panel D. Head of Household		
Up to $35,150	$0	15.0%
$35,150–$90,800	$5,272.50	28.0%
$90,800–$147,050	$20,854.50	31.0%
$147,050–$288,350	$38,292.00	36.0%
Over $288,350	$89,160.00	39.6%

is, the higher an individual's income, the higher the percentage of that income paid in taxes.

The Tax Relief Act of 2001 created a new 10 percent tax bracket that applies to the first $6,000 of income for single individuals and $12,000 of income for married couples filing jointly in 2001. The income ranges will increase over time. In addition, the income tax rates above 15 percent will be gradually reduced so that by 2006, the 28% tax rate will fall to 25%, the 31% tax rate will fall to 28%, the 36% tax rate will fall to 33%, and the 39.6% tax rate will fall to 35%. Furthermore, as mentioned earlier, the income level subject to the 15 percent tax rate for the married filing jointly category will be increased to address the marriage penalty.

Determining Your Tax Liability. To determine your tax liability, simply refer to your filing status and follow the instructions at the top of the columns of the tax schedule. Converting the instructions into formula form gives the following equation for the tax liability:

$$\text{Tax Liability} = \text{Tax on Base} + [\text{Percentage on Excess over the Base} \times (\text{Taxable Income} - \text{Base})]$$

Example

Stephanie Spratt's taxable income is $30,800. Her filing status is single.

Stephanie uses the following steps to determine her taxes:

- Her income falls within the second bracket in Panel A, from $26,250 to $63,550.

- The base of that bracket is $26,250. The tax on the base is $3,937.50, as shown in the second column of Panel A.

- The tax rate applied to the excess income over the base is 28 percent, as shown in the third column of Panel A. This means that Stephanie's **marginal tax bracket** is 28 percent, so any additional (marginal) income that she earns is subject to a 28 percent tax.

- Stephanie's excess income over the base is $4,550 (computed as $30,800 − $26,250). Thus, the tax on the excess over the base is $1,274 (computed as $4,550 × 28%).

In summary, her tax liability is:

Tax Liability = Tax on Base + [Percentage on Excess over the Base × (Taxable Income − Base)]

= $3,937.50 + [28% × ($30,800 − $26,250)]

= $3,937.50 + [28% × ($4,550)]

= $3,937.50 + $1,274

= $5,211.50.

marginal tax bracket
The tax rate imposed on any additional (marginal) income earned.

This tax liability represents about 14 percent of her income. However, recall that she also paid $2,907 in FICA taxes. Thus, Stephanie's total taxes are $8,118.50 (calculated as $5,211.50 + $2,907).

Tax Credits

tax credits
Amounts that offset taxes; the full amount of the tax credit is subtracted from taxes owed.

You may be able to reduce your tax liability if you are eligible for tax credits. **Tax credits** offset taxes, as the full amount of the tax credit is subtracted from taxes owed: A tax credit of $1,000 will reduce your taxes by $1,000. Compare this result with the effect of a $1,000 deduction. The deduction reduces your taxable income by $1,000, but reduces your taxes by only a proportion of that amount. For this reason, a dollar's worth of tax credits is more valuable than a dollar's worth of deductions.

child tax credit
A tax credit ($500) allowed for each child in a household who is less than 17 years old (reduced or eliminated for households in high-income brackets).

Child Credits. A **child tax credit** is a tax credit allowed for each child in a household who is less than 17 years old. As a result of the Tax Relief Act of 2001, the child tax credit is $600 as of 2001, and will be gradually increased until it reaches $1,000 in 2010. The child tax credit is not available to households above certain income levels. A key provision of the child tax credit is that it is available as a refund to low-income workers who owe no income tax.

4.4   Financial Planning Online: Updated Income Tax Rates

Go to:
http://taxes.yahoo.com/rates.html

This Web site provides:
updated income tax rates for each filing status and for various income tax brackets.

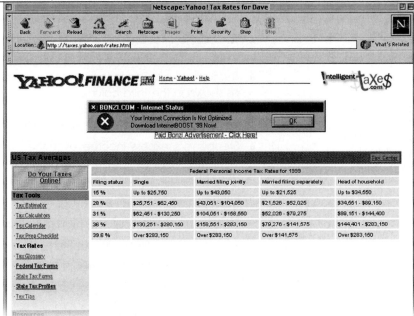

Filing status	Single	Married filing jointly	Married filing separately	Head of household
15 %	Up to $25,750	Up to $43,050	Up to $21,525	Up to $34,550
28 %	$25,751 - $62,450	$43,051 - $104,050	$21,526 - $52,025	$34,551 - $89,150
31 %	$62,451 - $130,250	$104,051 - $158,550	$52,026 - $79,275	$89,151 - $144,400
36 %	$130,251 - $280,150	$158,551 - $283,150	$79,276 - $141,575	$144,401 - $283,150
39.6 %	Over $283,150	Over $283,150	Over $141,575	Over $283,150

college expense credits
Tax credits for parents who incur college expenses, based on the amount of financial support they provide.

College Expense Credits. Some **college expense credits** are also allowed. Parents receive a tax credit equal to $1,000 for the first $1,000 that they provide to each dependent for college expenses in each of the first two years of college. They also receive a 50 percent tax credit on the next $1,000 spent on college (or up to $500) for each child in each of the first two years of college. Thus, if you pay $1,800 in the first or second year of college, you receive a tax credit of $1,400 (computed as a $1,000 credit for the first $1,000 paid and a 50 percent credit on the additional $800 paid). Self-supporting students can use the tax credits to reduce their own taxes. There are limits (increased by the Tax Relief Act of 2001) imposed on the amount of expense credits allowed. Furthermore, the tax credit for college expenses is reduced or eliminated for taxpayers with high income levels.

As a result of the Tax Relief Act of 2001, education savings accounts (previously called Education IRAs) allow tax-free contributions of $2,000 (the previous limit was $500 per year). State and private universities can also offer prepaid tuition programs with tax benefits.

earned income credit
A special credit for taxpayers who earn low incomes; can reduce the amount of taxes owed.

Earned Income Credit. The **earned income credit** is a special credit for tax-payers who earn low incomes. To qualify, you must work, have earned income, and have investment income of less than $2,350. Adjusted gross income must be less than $10,380 for taxpayers without a qualifying child, less than $27,143 for those with one qualifying child, and less than $31,152 for those with more than one qualifying child. The credit reduces the amount of taxes owed, if any.

Other Tax Credits. Other tax credits may also be available. For example, there are tax credits for child care and adoptions. The tax credit amount is dependent on the expenses incurred and income limits.

COMPREHENSIVE TAX EXAMPLE

A comprehensive example is provided here to reinforce your understanding of the tax concepts discussed in this chapter. Ken Hein's compensation from his employer was $44,000 in 2000. He also had $1,500 of interest income and $2,500 of dividend income this year. He contributed $4,000 toward his employer-sponsored retirement account. Ken incurred various deductible expenses that will be mentioned shortly. He also had a short-term capital gain of $2,000 and a long-term capital gain of $1,000 this year.

Ken's contribution to his employer-sponsored retirement plan does not count as salary for federal income tax purposes. However, he will still pay FICA taxes on that amount. Ken's FICA taxes, personal income taxes, and capital gain taxes are determined here.

Ken's FICA Taxes

The FICA taxes on Ken Hein's $44,000 salary are as follows:

	Social Security Tax	Medicare Tax
Tax rate	6.2% (up to a salary of $80,400)	1.45%
Tax amount	.062 × $44,000 = $2,728	.0145 × $44,000 = $638

Thus, Ken's total FICA taxes are $2,728 + $638 = $3,366.

Ken's Personal Taxes

Ken's personal taxes are determined by computing his gross income, his adjusted gross income, his deductions, and his exemptions.

Gross Income. Ken's gross income is:

Salary (after retirement contribution)	$40,000
+ Interest Income	1,500
+ Dividend Income	2,500
+ Long-Term Capital Gain	1,000
+ Short-Term Capital Gain	2,000
= Gross Income	$47,000

Adjusted Gross Income. Ken does not have any special adjustments, so his adjusted gross income is the same as his gross income ($47,000).

Standard Deduction. Ken Hein is married and files his tax return jointly; he is under age 65. Per Exhibit 4.4, his standard deduction is $7,350, which he can deduct from his adjusted gross income to determine his taxable income. Alternatively, he can itemize deductions instead of using the standard deduction. He will choose the option that minimizes his tax liability.

Itemized Deductions. Ken's itemized deductions for this year include $7,000 of mortgage interest, $2,000 in state income taxes, and $3,000 of real estate taxes. In addition, Ken incurred medical expenses of $8,450. Since his adjusted gross income is $47,000, the first $3,525 (computed as .075 × $47,000) of his medical expenses are not deductible. Since his medical expenses exceed 7.5 percent of his adjusted gross income by $4,925, he can deduct $4,925 of medical expenses as an itemized deduction.

Medical Expenses	$8,450
Amount That Is Not Deductible	− 3,525 (computed as .075 × $47,000)
Amount That Is Deductible	$4,925

Ken contributed $1,000 to a local animal shelter. Therefore, he can deduct $1,000 as an itemized deduction.

Total Deductions. Ken Hein's deductions from his adjusted gross income are summarized here:

Deductions	
Interest Expense	$7,000
State Income Taxes	2,000
Real Estate Taxes	3,000
Medical	4,925
Charity	1,000
Total	$17,925

Ken Hein can deduct $17,925 as a result of his itemized deductions, versus only $7,350 if he uses the standard deduction. Thus, he is better off itemizing than taking the standard deduction.

Exemptions. Ken Hein has a wife and an 18-year-old daughter that he supports in his household. He can claim his personal exemption and one exemption each for his wife and daughter. Thus, the total amount of exemptions he can claim for the 2000 tax year is:

Personal Exemption	$2,800
Exemptions for Wife and One Dependent (2 × $2,800)	$5,600
Total	$8,400

Taxable Income. Recall that Ken Hein's adjusted gross income is $47,000, his itemized deductions amount to $17,925, and his exemptions amount to $8,400. Thus, Ken Hein's taxable income is determined as:

Adjusted Gross Income		$47,000
Deductions	$17,925	
Exemptions	8,400	
Total	$26,325	
Taxable Income		$20,675

Therefore, Ken's taxable income is $20,675. This includes a $1,000 long-term capital gain, which will be discussed in the next section. The following calculations apply to the taxable income, excluding the long-term capital gain, or $20,675 − $1,000 = $19,675. Ken's filing status is "married, filing jointly." Thus, his applicable tax rates are in Panel B of Exhibit 4.6.

Ken uses the following steps to determine his taxes:

- His income falls within the first bracket in Panel B, from $0 to $43,850.

- The base of that bracket is $0.

- The tax rate applied to the excess income over the base is 15 percent, as shown in the third column of Panel B.

- Ken's excess income over the base is $19,675 − $0 = $19,675. Thus, the tax on the excess over the base is 15 percent of $19,675, or $2,951.25.

In summary, his tax liability prior to adding his capital gains tax is:

$$
\begin{aligned}
\text{Tax Liability} &= \text{Tax on Base} + [\text{Percentage on Excess over the Base} \times \\
&\quad (\text{Taxable Income} - \text{Base})] \\
&= \$0 + [15\% \times (\$19,675 - \$0)] \\
&= \$0 + [15\% \times (\$19,675)] \\
&= \$0 + \$2,951.25 \\
&= \$2,951.25.
\end{aligned}
$$

If Ken's taxable income had exceeded $43,850, there would have been a tax on the base plus the applicable tax rate on the excess over the base. To illustrate, suppose Ken's taxable income is $52,750. Panel B of Exhibit 4.6 shows that his base income is $43,850, the tax on his base income is $6,577.50 (see the second column), and the tax rate on his excess income over the base income is 28 percent (see the third column). Thus, his tax liability would have been:

4.5   Financial Planning Online: Estimating Your Taxes

Go to:
http://taxes.yahoo.com/
estimator

This Web site provides:
an estimate of your tax liability for the year and the tax refund that you will receive (if you already paid in more taxes than your tax liability), based on your income, filing status, exemptions, and deductions.

$$
\begin{aligned}
\text{Tax Liability} &= \text{Tax on Base} + [\text{Percentage on Excess over the Base} \times \\
&\quad (\text{Taxable Income} - \text{Base})] \\
&= \$6{,}577.50 + [28\% \times (\$52{,}750 - \$43{,}850] \\
&= \$6{,}577.50 + [28\% \times (\$8{,}900)] \\
&= \$6{,}577.50 + \$2{,}492 \\
&= \$9{,}069.50.
\end{aligned}
$$

Ken's tax liability in this example is much higher than in the previous example because of his higher taxable income. Ken could also use tax tables to determine his tax liability based on his level of taxable income.

Ken's Capital Gain Tax

Recall that Ken had a long-term capital gain of $1,000. Reviewing Exhibit 4.3, based on his taxable income of $20,675, he is subject to a long-term capital gain tax rate of 10 percent (note that the tax rate can be as high as 20 percent for some individuals). Ken's long-term capital gain tax is:

$$
\begin{aligned}
\text{Capital Gain Tax} &= \text{Long-Term Capital Gain} \times \text{Long-Term Capital} \\
&\quad \text{Gain Tax Rate} \\
&= \$1{,}000 \times .10 \\
&= \$100
\end{aligned}
$$

Ken's total tax liability is therefore $3,051.25 ($2,951.25 as computed on the $19,675 + $100 on the long-term capital gain).

HOW TAX PLANNING FITS WITHIN YOUR FINANCIAL PLAN

The key tax planning decisions for building your financial plan are:

1. What tax savings are currently available to you?

2. How can you increase your tax savings in the future?

The key tax concepts for building your financial plan are recognizing different deductions and exemptions as you plan your future. These deductions and exemptions will enable you to reduce your taxes and therefore increase your net cash flows. An example of how the tax concepts apply to Stephanie Spratt's financial plan is provided in Exhibit 4.7.

Since individuals who earn a high level of income can be exposed to very high tax rates, they should consider ways to reduce their tax liability. Some of the most useful strategies to reduce taxes are having a mortgage (because interest payments are tax-deductible), investing in retirement accounts that offer tax advantages, investing in stocks that pay no dividends, and investing in municipal bonds whose interest is exempt from federal taxes. These strategies are discussed in more detail later in the text.

Exhibit 4.7   Application of Tax Concepts to Stephanie Spratt's Financial Plan

Goals for Tax Planning

1. Reduce taxable income (thereby reducing taxes paid) to the extent allowable by the IRS.
2. Reduce taxes paid by deferring income.

Analysis

Present Situation:

Annual Salary = $38,000

Federal Income Taxes = $5,211.50

Taxes (excluding FICA) as a Percentage of Salary = 13.72%

Reduce Taxes by:	Comment
Increasing deductions?	The only qualified deduction I had was for a charitable contribution of $200, so this is not an option for me this year.
Reducing gross income?	I did not contribute any portion of my income to an individual retirement account or a qualified retirement plan; therefore, this option is not available.
Total tax savings?	$0 per year

Long-Term Tax Plan:

Reduce Taxes by:	Comment
Increasing deductions?	If I purchase a home, the interest expense on my mortgage loan, as well as the real estate taxes I will pay, both qualify as itemized deductions. These deductions will likely be higher than the standard deduction to which I would be entitled. I can therefore reduce my taxable income and taxes paid.
Reducing gross income?	I can also consider a contribution to an IRA or to my employer's qualified pension plan. If I can afford to contribute $2000 of my salary to either the IRA or the qualified plan, I will reduce my gross income and defer taxes paid on that portion of my income.
Tax savings (computed below)	$1,008

To compute my estimated tax savings, I will compare the taxes paid under my current situation to what I would pay if I bought a home and paid $6,000 in interest and real estate taxes and contributed $2,000 to an IRA.

Category	Current Situation	Long-Term Plan
Gross Income	$38,000	$38,000
− IRA contribution	0	2,000
= Adjusted gross income	38,000	36,000
− Deductions	4,400	6,000
− Exemptions	2,800	2,800
= Taxable income	30,800	27,200
Tax liability (based on applying tax rates to the taxable income)	5,211.50	4,203.50

Total Tax Savings = $1,008 per year

Decisions

Decisions Regarding Tax Savings for This Year:

I currently qualify for no tax savings.

Decisions Regarding Tax Savings in the Future:

I can improve my cash flows over time by taking advantage of tax deductions. If I buy a home, the interest that I would pay on the mortgage loan, as well as the real estate taxes I would be assessed, is tax-deductible. The purchase of a home would likely increase my monthly cash outflows, but I would benefit from deducting the interest payments and real estate taxes as itemized deductions, thereby reducing my taxable income.

I could also benefit from contributing a portion of my income to an IRA or qualified retirement plan, since contributions can usually be made before federal income taxes are assessed. This strategy would allow me to defer some taxes, while also setting aside some funds for retirement.

As my income increases, my tax bracket may increase. I need to maximize my potential tax savings to limit the taxes I will pay. I should contribute the maximum allowable amount to my retirement plan (without compromising my cash budget) so that I can take full advantage of the related tax savings. Also, I hope to buy a home in the future. The interest I will pay on a mortgage loan for this home will be high, but I will enjoy tax savings, while also building equity in my home.

If I get married someday, our joint income would likely be subject to a higher income tax rate than my present income. However, we would likely be able to take advantage of tax savings by purchasing a home and making additional contributions to IRAs or qualified retirement plans.

DISCUSSION QUESTIONS

1. How would Stephanie's tax planning decisions be different if she were a single mother of two children?

2. How would Stephanie's tax planning decisions be affected if she were 35 years old? If she were 50 years old?

SUMMARY

The first step in filing a federal income tax return is to determine your filing status. You may have a choice, and the status chosen can affect the taxes that you owe. Gross income consists primarily of your salary, interest income, dividend income from investments in stocks, and capital gains. A short-term capital gain is realized on an asset held for a period of less than one year and is counted as ordinary income. A long-term capital gain is subject to a capital gain tax, which is generally lower than a person's ordinary income tax rate.

Your adjusted gross income is calculated by adjusting gross income for any contributions to an individual retirement account (IRA) and for some other special circumstances. The adjusted gross income must be determined because it is used to determine eligibility for personal exemptions, itemized deductions, and IRA contributions.

Deductions and exemptions are relevant because they are subtracted from adjusted gross income before determining your taxes. Thus, they can reduce the amount of taxes owed. Deductions include interest expenses incurred from holding a mortgage, state income taxes, real estate taxes, unreimbursed medical expenses, charitable contributions, and some other expenses. Exemptions are allowed for persons supported by the income reported on a tax return. You can elect to use a standard deduction instead of itemized deductions if doing so provides you with higher tax benefits.

Your taxable income is determined by subtracting the total value of your deductions and exemptions from your adjusted gross income. Your tax liability is dependent on your taxable income, and the tax rate applied is dependent upon your filing status and income level. The Tax Relief Act of 2001 will impact many tax provisions, including marginal brackets, over the next several years.

The comprehensive example illustrates how your income tax is reduced if you have various deductions that you can itemize or if you have exemptions.

Integrating the Key Concepts

Tax planning can be applied to all parts of your financial plan. It is useful for financing decisions because some types of financing result in interest expenses that are tax-deductible. It is used when making investment decisions because the income earned on some types of investments is exempt from taxes, and long-term capital gains are subject to lower tax rates than short-term capital gains. Tax planning is especially useful for retirement planning because most retirement plans offer some type of tax advantage. It is even useful for estate planning because some estates are subject to no or low taxes if they are properly organized.

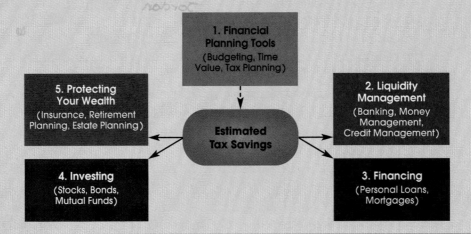

REVIEW QUESTIONS

1. Why is it important to understand the tax consequences of your financial decisions?

2. What are FICA taxes? Describe the two portions of FICA and explain what they pay for. Who pays FICA?

3. What happens to FICA taxes for those who are self-employed?

4. Who may file Form 1040EZ? What tax form do most other individual taxpayers file?

5. Name the five filing statuses. Briefly describe how your filing status is determined. What parts of the tax form are affected by your filing status?

6. What is gross income? List some types of income that would be included in gross income. What are some types of payments that you might receive that would *not* be included in gross income?

7. What are capital gains? When is a capital gain considered short-term? Long-term?

8. How is adjusted gross income determined?

9. What is the standard deduction based on? List some items to be considered for itemized deductions.

10. What is an exemption? How many exemptions may a taxpayer claim?

11. How is taxable income calculated?

12. What is meant by a progressive tax system? What is a marginal tax rate?

13. What is the difference between a tax deduction and a tax credit? Which is more valuable?

14. List some common types of tax credits.

15. Which of the following would be included in gross income?

Salary	Prizes
Business income	Tips
Veteran's benefits	Welfare benefits
Alimony	Dividend income
Child support	

16. Distinguish between interest income and dividend income.

17. List the four classifications of medical expenses. Are your total allowable medical expenses deductible?

18. What is the difference between the tax consequences for short-term and long-term capital gains?

19. What form is used as a worksheet for determining itemized deductions?

20. What is the purpose of income tax? Who administers the federal tax system?

FINANCIAL PLANNING PROBLEMS

1. Janet makes $450 per week. How much can she expect to be withheld from her check for Social Security tax? Medicare tax? Total FICA taxes?

2. Avery makes $27,000 per year. How much can he expect to contribute to FICA taxes this year? How much will his employer contribute?

3. Nolan is self-employed as a carpenter. He made $42,000 last year. How much did he contribute to FICA taxes last year?

4. ~~Larry~~ Stephen is in a 15 percent marginal tax bracket. ~~Last year~~ 2015 he sold stock that he had held for nine months for a gain of $1,900. How much tax must he pay on this capital gain? How much would the tax be if he had held the stock for 13 months?

5. Stuart is in a ~~28~~ 25 percent tax bracket. Recently, he sold stock that he had held longer than a year for a gain of $20,000. How much tax will Stuart pay on this gain?

6. ~~Jim~~ Jordan sold a stock that he held for 11 months at a capital gain of $10,000. He is in the ~~28~~ 25% percent marginal tax bracket. How much will he be taxed on his gain?

7. Teresa and Marvin are married and file a joint return. The standard deduction for their filing status is $7,350. They have the following itemized deductions:

Medical bills above the 7.5% limit	$400
Interest expense	3,500
State income taxes	1,500
Miscellaneous deductions	250

Should Teresa and Marvin itemize their deductions or use the standard deduction?

8. Martha's adjusted gross income is $24,200. She has $1,800 in unreimbursed medical expenses. How much in medical expenses can Martha claim as an itemized deduction?

9. Jerry's adjusted gross income is $16,700. Jerry has $1,800 in unreimbursed medical expenses. How much can Jerry claim as an itemized deduction?

10. Nick Peters is married and has three children in college. His wife is a homemaker. Nick has adjusted gross income of $37,400. If Nick's standard deduction is $7,350, his itemized deductions are $11,200, and he gets an exemption of $2,800 per dependent, what is his taxable income?

11. Using the information in problem 10, if Nick's itemized deductions increase by $2,000, how will his taxable income be impacted?

12. Martin has a marginal tax rate of 28 percent. He suddenly realizes that he neglected to include a $1,000 tax deduction. How will this oversight affect his taxes?

13. If Martin from problem 12 had forgotten a $1,000 tax credit (instead of a $1,000 tax deduction), how would his taxes be affected?

14. Tracy is single and earns $37,000 a year. Tracy is gathering information for her current year's tax return and has the following items:

Unreimbursed medical expenses	$3,000
State income tax	1,850
Interest expense (first mortgage)	3,040
Interest expense (second mortgage)	1,200
Real estate tax	700
Interest expense—car loan	550
Interest expense—credit card	125
Gifts to charity	300

How much may Tracy claim as itemized deductions?

15. Using the information in problem 14, if Tracy's standard deduction is $4,400 and her exemption is $2,800, what is her taxable income?

FINANCIAL PLANNING ONLINE EXERCISES

Go to http://taxes.yahoo.com. Click on Refund Estimator.

1. Using the Refund Estimator for the current year, input the following information and calculate the estimated taxes:

Filing status:	Single
Exemptions:	Yourself
Income:	$50,000
Adjustments:	IRA contribution $2,000
Deductions:	Standard deduction
Credits:	Zero
Other taxes:	Zero

2. Estimate the taxes using all the above information except the $2,000 IRA contribution.

3. You can input your personal tax information to estimate your taxes. Calculate your taxes with and without the IRA contribution to assess the impact of IRA contributions on taxes.

4. Use the Back option to go back to http://taxes.yahoo.com. Click on Tax Prep Checklist and view the data. What documents do you need to prepare a tax return?

Go to http://taxes.yahoo.com. Scroll down to the Tax Tips section.

1. Under Charitable Contributions, review the recommendations. How can you use this information to save on taxes?

2. Under Education, look up the allowable credits and deductions for educational expenses. What information could you use in preparing your tax return?

3. Click on Retirement Planning and read the tips for saving on taxes while saving for retirement. How can you use this information to lower your taxes?

4. Use the Back option to go back to http://taxes.yahoo.com. Click on Tax Calendar and review the important tax dates for the current year's Tax Return. Can you make use of this information in your tax planning?

Building Your Own Financial Plan

By properly managing your tax situation, you can not only significantly improve your annual cash flow situation but also enhance your ability to achieve your goals in a timely fashion.

First, explore ways in which you can utilize various tax advantage devices such as 401(k)s, IRAs, and employer matches to not only reduce your current tax liability, but also achieve future financial goals. Web sites like http://www.dtonline.com also provide helpful tips for reducing your tax liability. List the tax advantage options that may prove beneficial in reaching your goals established in Chapter 1 on the template provided for this chapter in the *Financial Planning Workbook* and on the CD-ROM. Undoubtedly, you will find that the long-term goals have the most options. The template will be modified as you proceed through this course and become aware of other tax advantage options.

This exercise should help you develop a portion of your financial plan while giving you some insights into what employee benefits you should look for from a prospective employer. Talk to friends and relatives and find out how they utilize tax advantage devices to reduce their taxes and achieve financial goals.

 Another crucial element of proper tax management is the selection of an appropriate tax preparer. Your options vary from doing your own tax return to engaging the services of a certified public accountant. When you begin your search for a tax preparer, you will find some questions in the template for this chapter that should aid your selection.

Once you have selected a tax preparer whom you trust, it is really not necessary to periodically review this decision. You should, however, remember that as your personal financial situation becomes more complex (e.g., you have a home, you itemize, your portfolio grows to include international stocks), you may need a tax preparer with more advanced skills. Be sure that the skills of your tax preparer are a match for the sophistication level of your personal financial situation.

The Sampsons—A Continuing Case

 Dave and Sharon Sampson want to determine their taxes for the year 2000. Dave will earn $48,000 this year, while Sharon's earnings from her part-time job will be $12,000. Neither Dave nor Sharon contributes to a retirement plan at this time. Recall that they have two children. The Sampsons will pay $6,300 in home mortgage interest and $1,200 in real estate taxes, and they will make charitable contributions of $600 for the year.

Help the Sampsons estimate their federal taxes for this year by filling in the template provided in the *Financial Planning Workbook* and on the CD-ROM shrink-wrapped with your text. (An updated template is available at www.aw.com/madura.)

IN-TEXT STUDY GUIDE

True/False:

1. By understanding how your income may be taxed, you can make decisions that reduce your taxes, enhance your after-tax cash flows, and therefore enhance your wealth.

2. FICA is a government health insurance program that provides health insurance for people over age 65 and provides payments in the case of illness.

3. An employer must match the Medicare taxes that each of its employees pays.

4. Married people can combine their incomes and file a joint return, or each can file a separate tax return.

5. Gross income includes all income from any sources.

6. Interest income earned from investments in bonds issued by the federal government is normally exempt from federal taxation.

7. A standard deduction is an amount to be deducted to determine your FICA tax.

8. Itemized deductions are specific expenses that can be deducted to reduce taxable income.

9. A marginal tax rate of 30 percent means that all previous income has been taxed at a 30 percent tax rate.

10. The U.S. tax system is progressive, meaning that higher incomes are taxed at higher tax rates.

11. If you are a qualifying widow(er) with a dependent child, you are entitled to use the joint tax rates for two years following the death of your spouse, assuming that you remarried.

12. Contributions to your employer-sponsored retirement account, whether made by you or your employer, are not subject to income taxes until those funds are withdrawn from the retirement account.

Multiple Choice:

1. Which of the following will not affect the amount of taxes you pay?
   a. taking a third job to enhance your wealth
   b. purchasing a home that will be financed with a mortgage
   c. contributing a portion of your salary to your retirement account
   d. All of the above will affect the amount of taxes you pay.

2. _____ uses its funds to make payments to you upon retirement (subject to age and other requirements).
   a. FICA
   b. The Social Security System
   c. Medicare
   d. None of the above

The following information refers to questions 3 and 4.

Billy Benson earned a salary of $52,000 this year.

3. Billy will pay FICA taxes for Social Security in the amount of
   a. $3,224.
   b. $32,240.
   c. $754.
   d. $7,540.

4. Billy will pay FICA taxes (excluding the employer's contribution) for Medicare in the amount of
   a. $3,224.
   b. $32,240.
   c. $754.
   d. $7,540.

5. Self-employed individuals pay FICA taxes at a rate of
   a. 7.65 percent.
   b. 1.45 percent.
   c. 15.30 percent.
   d. 2.90 percent.

6. _____ is not a filing status.
   a. Single
   b. Married filing separate returns
   c. Qualifying widow(er) with independent child
   d. Head of household

7. Individuals can earn _____ income from investments in various types of savings accounts at financial institutions.
   a. interest
   b. dividend
   c. wage
   d. option

8. Oliver Ontario purchased stock 13 months ago. Since then, the stock has increased in value by $35,000. Oliver is in the 28 percent tax bracket. If Oliver sells the stock today, he will pay a capital gain tax of
   a. $9,800.
   b. $7,000.
   c. $3,500.
   d. none of the above

The following information refers to questions 9 and 10.

Humphrey Porter earned a salary of $70,000 this year. Additionally, Humphrey had $1,000 in interest income, $2,000 in dividend income, and a short-term capital gain of $5,000.

9. Humphrey's gross income for the year 2000 is
   a. $72,000.
   b. $75,000.
   c. $78,000.
   d. $76,000.

10. Assume Humphrey filed as head of household this year. If he took the standard deduction and had a personal exemption and an exemption for one dependent, his taxable income for the year 2000 is
   a. $70,950.
   b. $68,900.
   c. $68,200.
   d. $65,950.

11. _____ are specific expenses that can be deducted to reduce taxable income.
   a. Standard deductions
   b. Itemized deductions
   c. Exemptions
   d. Adjusted expenses

12. Which of the following is not a typical type of itemized deduction?
   a. interest expenses on a car loan
   b. real estate taxes imposed by the county where the real estate is located
   c. medical expenses incurred to affect any structure or function of the body
   d. charitable gifts to certain qualified organizations

13. Melanie incurred interest expenses of $8,000 on a mortgage loan during this year. Furthermore, she incurred state income taxes of $1,000. She also contributed $500 to the American Cancer Society. Based on this information, Melanie's itemized deductions for this tax year are
   a. $1,500.
   b. $9,000.
   c. $8,000.
   d. $9,500.

14. Ron Bamberg had an adjusted gross income of $90,000 for one year. In that year, his deductions and exemptions totalled $8,100. Ron's taxable income for the year was
   a. $83,930.
   b. $81,900.
   c. $82,950.
   d. $87,250.

15. Mira had taxable income of $150,000. Bob had taxable income of $30,000. Mira's marginal tax rate is _____ Bob's.
   a. the same as
   b. lower than
   c. higher than
   d. none of the above

16. A(n) _____ does not represent an itemized deduction.
   a. child tax credit
   b. interest expense
   c. state tax
   d. real estate tax

17. The _____ is a special credit for taxpayers who earn low incomes.
   a. child tax credit
   b. Medicare credit
   c. earned income credit
   d. college expense credit

18. Lance Cage is a married individual filing separately. Lance is 68 years old. The amount of standard deductions Lance qualifies for is
   a. $3,600.
   b. $4,525.
   c. $7,200.
   d. $4,300.

The following information refers to questions 19 and 20.

Frank Shaeffer earned a salary totaling $80,000.

19. Frank's Social Security taxes are
   a. $1,160.00.
   b. $4,960.00.
   c. $4,501.20.
   d. $6,120.00.

20. Frank's total FICA taxes (excluding the employer's contribution) are
   a. $6,120.00.
   b. $5,661.20.
   c. $5,553.90.
   d. none of the above

21. _____ reduce taxable income even if the taxpayer does not itemize.
   a. Exemptions
   b. Capital gains
   c. Standard deductions
   d. None of the above

Part 1: Brad Brooks—A Continuing Case

Your childhood friend, Brad Brooks, has asked you to help him gain control of his personal finances. Single and thirty years old, Brad is employed as a salesperson for a technology company. His annual salary is $48,000. He claims no exemptions (he enjoys the big refund check in May), and after Social Security, Medicare, and federal, state, and local income taxes, his monthly take-home pay is $2,743. Brad has recently moved from his comfortable two-bedroom apartment with rent of $600 per month to a condo that rents for $1,000 per month. The condo is in a plush property owner's association with two golf courses, a lake, and an activity center. You review his other monthly expenses and find the following:

Renter's insurance	$20
Car payment (balance on car loan $10,000; book value of car $11,000)	500
Utilities (gas, electric, cable)	100
Cell phone (personal calls)	250
House phone	30
Food (consumed at home)	200
Clothes	100
Car expenses (gas, insurance, maintenance)	250
Entertainment (dining out, golf, weekend trips)	400

Brad is surprised at how much money he spends on clothes and entertainment. He uses his credit cards for these purchases (the balance is $8,000 and climbing) and has little trouble making the required monthly payments. He would, however, like to see the balance go down and eventually pay it off completely.

Brad's other goal is to save $4,000 a year so that he can retire in 20 years. He would like to start saving in five years as he does not think the delay will affect the final amount of retirement savings he will accumulate.

Brad currently has about $4,000 in his checking account and $200 in his savings account (the balance necessary to receive fee-free checking). He has furniture valued at $1,500 and owns

$1,300 of tech stocks, which he believes have the potential to make him rich.

To assist your friend in gaining control of his personal finances, you decide to do the following:

1. a. Prepare personal financial statements for Brad, including a personal cash flow statement and personal balance sheet.

   b. Based on these statements, make specific recommendations to Brad as to what he needs to do to achieve his goals of paying off his credit card balance and saving for retirement.

   c. What additional goals could you recommend to Brad for both the short and the long term?

2. Consider Brad's goal to retire in 20 years by saving $4,000 per year starting five years from now.

   a. Based on your analysis of Brad's cash flow and your recommendations, is saving $4,000 per year a realistic goal? If not, what other goal would you advise?

   b. In order for Brad to know what his $4,000 per year will accumulate to in 20 years, what additional assumption (or piece of information) must he make (or have)?

   c. Assuming that Brad invests the $4,000 per year for 20 years in something that will return 12 percent, how much will he have at that time?

   d. How much will it cost Brad to wait five years to start investing? How much additional funds will Brad have to save each year to end up with the same amount that he would have if he started saving now instead of five years from now? (Again assume a 12 percent annual return.)

3. Develop three or four suggestions that could help Brad reduce his income tax exposure. List the pros and cons of each.

4. Would any of your recommendations in questions 1 through 3 change if Brad were 45? If he were 60? Why or why not?

5. Prepare a written or oral report on your findings and recommendations to Brad.

PART 2

Managing Your Liquidity

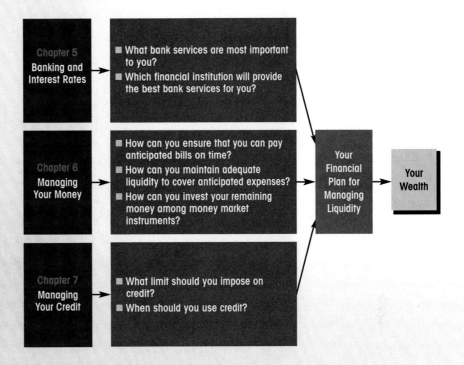

Chapter 5 Banking and Interest Rates	■ What bank services are most important to you? ■ Which financial institution will provide the best bank services for you?		
Chapter 6 Managing Your Money	■ How can you ensure that you can pay anticipated bills on time? ■ How can you maintain adequate liquidity to cover anticipated expenses? ■ How can you invest your remaining money among money market instruments?	Your Financial Plan for Managing Liquidity	Your Wealth
Chapter 7 Managing Your Credit	■ What limit should you impose on credit? ■ When should you use credit?		

The chapters in this part explain the key decisions you can make to ensure adequate liquidity. Chapter 5 describes how to select a local financial institution to facilitate your banking needs. Chapter 6 details how you can manage your money to prepare for future expenses. Chapter 7 explains how you can access credit as an additional source of liquidity. Your selection of a financial institution, money management, and credit management will influence your liquidity and therefore affect your cash flows and wealth.

Chapter 5

Banking and Interest Rates

Commercial banks and other financial institutions provide various financial services. In particular, they allow you to deposit funds in interest-earning accounts and provide loans if you need to borrow money. When you invest funds in interest-bearing accounts, the return you earn from your investment is dependent on the level of interest rates at that time. Similarly, the rate of interest you pay when borrowing money is dependent on the current level of interest rates. Therefore, an understanding of interest rates will help you make investment decisions that improve your interest income (cash inflows) and financing decisions that minimize your interest expenses (cash outflows), thereby increasing your wealth.

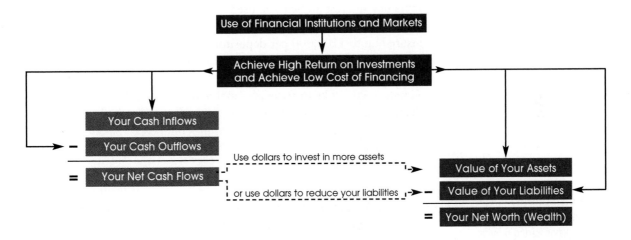

The objectives of this chapter are to:

- describe the functions of financial institutions,
- identify the components of interest rates, and
- outline the term structure of interest rates.

TYPES OF FINANCIAL INSTITUTIONS

Individuals rely on financial institutions when they wish to invest or borrow funds. The major types of financial institutions used by individuals are classified as depository institutions and nondepository institutions.

Depository Institutions

depository institutions
Financial institutions that accept deposits (that are insured up to a maximum level) from individuals and provide loans.

Depository institutions are financial institutions that offer traditional checking and savings accounts for individuals or firms and also provide loans. They pay interest on savings deposits and charge interest on loans. The interest rate charged on loans exceeds the interest rate paid on deposits. The institutions use the difference to cover other expenses and to achieve some earnings for their stockholders.

Depository institutions are skilled in assessing the ability of prospective borrowers to repay loans. This is a critical part of their business, since the interest from loans is a key source of their revenue.

There are three types of depository institutions: commercial banks, savings institutions, and credit unions.

commercial banks
Financial institutions that accept deposits and use the funds to provide commercial (business) and personal loans.

Commercial Banks. **Commercial banks** are financial institutions that accept deposits in checking and savings accounts and use the funds to provide commercial (business) and personal loans. The checking accounts normally do not pay interest. The savings accounts pay interest, while certain other accounts pay interest and can be used to write checks. These accounts are described in more detail in the next chapter. Deposits at commercial banks are insured up to $100,000 per depositor by the Federal Deposit Insurance Corporation (FDIC), a government-owned insurance agency that ensures the safety of bank deposits.

Commercial banks provide personal loans to individuals who wish to purchase a car or other products. They also offer mortgage loans to individuals who wish to purchase a home. Some commercial banks own other types of financial institutions (such as those described next) that provide additional services to individuals.

savings institutions (or thrift institutions)
Financial institutions that accept deposits and provide mortgage and personal loans to individuals.

Savings Institutions. **Savings institutions** (also referred to as thrift institutions) accept deposits and provide mortgage and personal loans to individuals. They differ from commercial banks in that they tend to focus more on providing mortgage loans to individuals and less on providing commercial loans. They typically offer the same types of checking and savings deposits as banks, and these deposits are also insured up to $100,000 per depositor by the FDIC.

credit unions
Nonprofit depository institutions that serve members who have a common affiliation (such as the same employer or the same community).

Credit Unions. **Credit unions** are nonprofit depository institutions that serve members who have a common affiliation (such as the same employer or the same community). Credit unions have been created to serve the employees of specific hospitals, universities, and even some corporations. They offer their members deposit accounts that are similar to the accounts offered by commercial banks and savings institutions; the accounts are insured by the National Credit Union Share Insurance Fund (NCUSIF) for up to $100,000 per member. Credit unions also provide mortgage and personal loans to their members.

nondepository institutions
Financial institutions that do not offer federally insured deposit accounts, but provide various other financial services.

Nondepository Institutions

Nondepository institutions are financial institutions that provide various financial services, but their deposits are not federally insured. The main types of nondepository institutions that serve individuals are finance companies, securities firms, insurance companies, and investment companies.

finance companies
Nondepository institutions that specialize in providing personal loans to individuals.

Finance Companies. Finance companies specialize in providing personal loans to individuals. These loans may be used for various purposes such as purchasing a car or other products or adding a room to a home. Finance companies tend to charge relatively high rates on loans because they lend to individuals who are perceived to have a higher risk of defaulting on the loans. When the economy weakens, borrowers may have more difficulty repaying loans, causing finance companies to be subject to even higher levels of loan defaults.

securities firms
Nondepository institutions that facilitate the purchase or sale of securities by firms or individuals by providing investment banking services and brokerage services.

Securities Firms. Securities firms facilitate the purchase or sale of securities (such as stocks or bonds) by firms or individuals by offering investment banking services and brokerage services. Investment banking services include: (1) placing securities that are issued by firms, meaning that the securities firm finds investors who wish to purchase those securities; (2) advising firms regarding the sale of securities, which involves determining the price at which the securities may be sold and the amount of securities that should be sold; and (3) advising firms that are considering mergers about the valuation of a firm, the potential benefits of being acquired or of acquiring another firm, and the financing necessary for the merger to occur.

In addition to offering investment banking services, securities firms also provide brokerage services, which facilitate the trading of existing securities. That is, the firms execute trades of securities for their customers. One customer may desire to sell a specific stock while another may want to buy that stock. Brokerage firms make a market for stocks and bonds by matching up willing buyers and sellers.

insurance companies
Nondepository institutions that provide insurance to protect individuals or firms against possible adverse events.

Insurance Companies. Insurance companies sell insurance to protect individuals or firms against possible adverse events. Specifically, life insurance companies provide insurance in the event of a person's death. Property and casualty companies provide insurance against damage to property, including automobiles and homes. Health insurance companies insure against specific types of health care costs. Insurance serves a crucial function for individuals because it compensates them (or their beneficiaries) in the event of adverse conditions that could otherwise ruin their financial situation. Chapters 16 and 17 discuss insurance options in detail.

investment companies
Nondepository institutions that sell shares to individuals and use the proceeds to invest in securities to create mutual funds.

Investment Companies. Investment companies use money provided by individuals to invest in securities to create mutual funds. The minimum amount an individual can invest in a mutual fund is typically between $500 and $3,000. Since the money received by individuals is pooled and invested in a portfolio of securities, an individual who invests in a mutual fund is part-owner of that portfolio. Thus, mutual funds provide a means by which investors with only a small amount of money can invest in a portfolio of securities. More than 6,000 mutual funds are available to individual investors. More details on mutual funds are provided in Chapter 14.

Exhibit 5.1   How a Financial Conglomerate Serves Individuals

FINANCIAL CONGLOMERATE

Bank Subsidiary	→	Accepts Deposits
		Provides Personal Loans
		Offers Credit Cards

| Securities Subsidiary | → | Provides Brokerage Services |
| | | Offers Mutual Funds |

| Insurance Subsidiary | → | Provides Insurance Services |

Financial Conglomerates

financial conglomerates
Financial institutions that offer a diverse set of financial services to individuals or firms.

Financial conglomerates offer a diverse set of financial services to individuals or firms. Examples of financial conglomerates include Citigroup, Bank of America, and Merrill Lynch. A financial conglomerate may not only accept deposits and provide personal loans, but may also offer credit cards. It may have a brokerage subsidiary that can execute stock transactions for individuals. It may also have an insurance subsidiary that offers insurance services. It may even have an investment company subsidiary that offers mutual funds containing stocks or bonds. Exhibit 5.1 shows the types of services offered by a typical financial conglomerate. By offering all types of financial services, the financial conglomerate may serve as a one-stop shop where individuals can conduct all of their financial services.

ADDITIONAL SERVICES FINANCIAL INSTITUTIONS OFFER

In addition to accepting deposits and providing personal loans, securities services, and insurance services, financial institutions provide many other services. These may include credit card financing, debit cards, safety deposit boxes, access to automated teller machines, cashier's checks, money orders, and traveler's checks.

Credit Card Financing

Individuals use credit cards to purchase products and services on credit. At the end of each billing cycle, you receive a bill for the credit you used over that period. MasterCard and Visa credit cards allow you to finance your purchases over time through various financial institutions. Thus, if you are able to pay only the minimum balance on your card, the financial institution will finance the outstanding balance and charge you interest over time for the credit that it provides to you.

Debit Cards

debit card
A card that is used to make purchases that are charged against an existing checking account.

A **debit card** is used to make purchases that are charged against an existing checking account. If you use a debit card to pay $100 for a car repair, your checking account balance is reduced by $100. Thus, using a debit card has the same result as writing a check from your checking account. Many financial institutions offer debit cards for individuals who find using a debit card more convenient than carrying their checkbook with them. In addition, some merchants will accept a debit card but not a check because they are concerned that the check may bounce.

A debit card differs from a credit card in that it does not provide credit. With a debit card, individuals cannot spend more than they have in their checking account. Those who like the convenience of a credit card, but do not want to spend more than they can afford may view this feature favorably.

Safety Deposit Boxes

safety deposit box
A box at a financial institution where a customer can store valuable documents, certificates, jewelry, or other items.

Many financial institutions offer access to a **safety deposit box**, where a customer can store valuable documents, certificates, jewelry, or other items. Customers are charged an annual fee for access to a safety deposit box.

Automated Teller Machines (ATMs)

automated teller machines (ATMs)
Machines where individuals can deposit and withdraw funds any time of the day.

Bank customers are likely to deposit and withdraw funds at an **automated teller machine (ATM)** by using their ATM card and entering their personal identification number (PIN). Located in numerous convenient locations, these machines allow customers access to their funds 24 hours a day, any day of the year. Some financial institutions have ATMs throughout the United States and in foreign countries. Individuals can usually use ATMs from financial institutions other than their own, but may be charged a service fee, such as $1 per transaction.

Cashier's Checks

cashier's check
A check that is written on behalf of a person to a specific payee and will be charged against a financial institution's account.

A **cashier's check** is a check that is written on behalf of a person to a specific payee and will be charged against a financial institution's account. It is especially useful when the payee is concerned that a personal check may bounce.

Example

You wish to buy a used car for $2,000 from Rod Simpkins, who is concerned that you may not have sufficient funds in your account. So you go to Lakeside Bank, where you have your checking account, and request that Lakeside write a cashier's check for $2,000 to Rod Simpkins. After verifying your account balance, the bank complies with your request and reduces your checking account balance by $2,000. It will likely charge you a small fee such as $10 or $15 for this service. Rod accepts the cashier's check from you because he knows that this check is backed by Lakeside Bank and will not bounce.

Money Orders

A **money order** is a check that is written on behalf of a person and will be charged against an institution's account. The U.S. Post Office and some financial institutions provide this service.

money order
A check that is written on behalf of a person and will be charged against a nonfinancial institution's account.

traveler's check
A check that is written on behalf of an individual and will be charged against a large well-known financial institution or credit card sponsor's account.

While on your spring break vacation, you run out of money. You call your friend Dawn Madden, who does not have a checking account. She has some cash that she could send you, but she fears that the cash could be lost (or stolen) in the mail. She brings $100 in cash to a U.S. Post Office and requests that the post office write a money order to you. The post office charges a fee for this service. When you receive the money order in the mail, you cash it at a nearby bank or post office.

Traveler's Checks

A **traveler's check** is a check that is written on behalf of an individual and will be charged against a large well-known financial institution or credit card sponsor's account. It is similar to a cashier's check, except that no payee is designated on the check. Traveler's checks are accepted around the world. If they are lost or stolen, the issuer will usually replace them without charge.

You are planning a road trip across the United States and are not sure that you will find ATMs in some remote towns. Although you will need $1,200 to cover all of your expenses, you want to carry only $200 in cash. So you go to your local bank and request $1,000 in traveler's checks. You pay $1,000 and receive 10 traveler's checks, each worth $100. You are asked to sign the top portion of each of the 10 checks. Your bank also charges you a fee of $1 per $100 of traveler's checks, or a total of $10 (the fee varies among financial institutions).

SELECTING A FINANCIAL INSTITUTION

Your choice of a financial institution should be based on convenience, deposit rates and deposit insurance, and fees.

- **Convenience.** You should be able to deposit and withdraw funds easily, which means the financial institution should be located close to where you live or work. You may also benefit if it has ATMs in convenient locations. In addition, a financial institution should offer most or all of the services you might need. Some financial institutions offer Internet banking, which allows you to keep track of your deposit accounts and even apply for loans online.

5.1   Financial Planning Online: Reviews of Online Banks

Go to:
http://www.gomez.com

Click on:
Finance, then Banks

This Web site provides:
reviews and ratings of various online banks, as well as descriptions of services offered.

■ **Deposit Rates and Insurance.** The interest rates offered on deposits vary among financial institutions. You should comparison shop by checking the rates on the types of deposits that you might make. Financial institutions also vary on the minimum required balance. A lower minimum balance on savings accounts is preferable because it gives you more flexibility if you do not want to tie up your funds. Make sure that any deposits are insured by the FDIC or NCUSIF.

5.2 Financial Planning Online: Financial Institutions That Can Serve Your Needs

Go to:

http://dir.yahoo.com/business_
and_economy/finance_and_
investment/banking/

This Web site provides:
information about individual
financial institutions (including
Internet banks), such as the
services they offer and the
interest rates they pay on
deposits or charge on loans.

- **Fees.** Many financial institutions charge fees for various services. Determine any fees for writing checks or using ATMs. Avoid financial institutions that charge high fees on services you need, even if the institutions offer relatively high rates on deposits.

INTEREST RATES ON DEPOSITS AND LOANS

Thus far, this chapter has focused on financial institutions and their services, such as accepting deposits and providing loans. The return you receive from your deposits in a financial institution and the cost of borrowing money from a financial institution are dependent on the interest rates. Therefore, your cash inflows and outflows are affected by the interest rates existing at the time of your transactions with the institution.

certificate of deposit (CD)
An instrument that is issued by a depository institution and specifies a minimum investment, an interest rate, and a maturity.

Most depository institutions issue **certificates of deposit (CDs)**, which specify a minimum investment, an interest rate, and a maturity. For example, a bank may require a $500 minimum investment on all the CDs it offers. The maturities may include one month, three months, six months, one year, and five years. The money invested in a particular CD cannot be withdrawn until the maturity date, or it will be subject to a penalty for early withdrawal.

The interest rate offered may vary among maturities. Interest rates on CDs are commonly stated on an annualized basis so that they can be compared among deposits. An annual interest rate of 6 percent on your deposit means that at the end of one year, you will receive interest equal to 6 percent of the amount that you originally deposited.

Risk-Free Rate

risk-free rate
A return on an investment that is guaranteed for a specified period.

A **risk-free rate** is a return on an investment that is guaranteed for a specified period. As an example, at a commercial bank you can invest in a CD with a maturity that matches your desired investment horizon. When you invest in a CD that has a maturity of one year, you are guaranteed the interest rate offered on that CD. Even if the bank goes bankrupt, the CD is insured by the federal government, so you will receive your deposit back at the time of maturity with the interest you are owed.

Risk Premium

Rather than investing in risk-free deposits that are backed by the federal government, you could invest in deposits of some financial firms that offer a higher interest rate. These deposits are sometimes called certificates, but should not be confused with the CDs that are backed by government insurance. These certificates are subject to default risk, meaning that you may receive a lower return than you expected if the firm goes bankrupt.

If you have accumulated only a small amount of savings, you should maintain all of your savings in a financial institution where deposits are guaranteed by the government. It is not worthwhile to strive for a higher return because you could lose a portion or all of your savings.

If you have a substantial amount of money, however, you may consider investing a portion of it in riskier deposits or certificates, but you should expect to be compensated for the risk. Your potential return should contain a **risk premium**, or an additional return beyond the risk-free rate that you could earn from a deposit guaranteed by the government. The higher the potential default risk of an investment, the higher the risk premium that you should expect.

risk premium
An additional return beyond the risk-free rate that can be earned from a deposit guaranteed by the government.

If a particular risky deposit is supposed to offer a specific return (R) over a period and you know the risk-free rate (R_f) offered on a deposit backed by the government, you can determine the risk premium (RP) offered on the risky deposit:

$$RP = R - R_f$$

Example

Today, your local commercial bank is offering a one-year CD with an interest rate of 6 percent, so the existing one-year risk-free rate is 6 percent. You notice that Metallica Financial Company offers an interest rate of 10 percent on one-year certificates. The risk premium offered by this certificate is:

$$
\begin{aligned}
RP &= R - R_f \\
&= 10\% - 6\% \\
&= 4\%.
\end{aligned}
$$

You need to decide whether receiving the extra 4 percentage points in the annual return is worth the default risk. As you have a moderate amount of savings accumulated, you determine that the risk is not worth taking.

5.3   Financial Planning Online: Current Interest Rate Quotations

Go to:
http://www.bloomberg.com/
markets/rates.html

This Web site provides:
updated quotations on key
interest rates and charts showing recent movements in these
rates. It also illustrates how
bank deposit rates and loan
rates have changed over time.

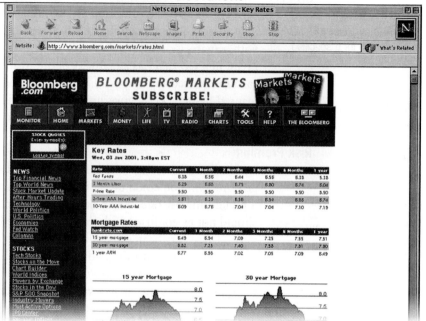

Loan Rate

Financial institutions obtain much of their funds by accepting deposits from individuals. They use the money to provide loans to other individuals and firms. In this way, by depositing funds, investors provide credit to financial markets. Financial institutions must charge a higher interest rate on the loans than they pay on the deposits so that they can have sufficient funds to pay their employees and earn a profit. Therefore, to borrow funds, you normally must pay a higher interest rate on the loan than the prevailing rate offered on deposits. The annual interest rate on loans to individuals is often 3 to 7 percentage points above the annual rate offered on deposits. For example, if the prevailing annual interest rate on various deposits is 6 percent, the prevailing annual interest rate on loans to individuals may be 9 to 13 percent.

The interest rate a financial institution charges for a loan may vary among individuals. Higher rates of interest are charged on loans that are exposed to higher default risk. So, individuals with poor credit histories or low incomes will likely be charged higher interest rates.

Impact of Changes in Interest Rates

As time passes, the general level of interest rates changes (as explained in detail in the chapter appendix). When interest rates rise, individuals who make deposits will earn a higher rate of interest, while individuals who need to borrow funds will have to pay a higher rate. You can find the current levels of interest rates on the Internet.

Comparing Interest Rates and Risk

When considering investments that have different degrees of risk, the proper choice depends on your risk tolerance. If you plan to use all of your invested funds for necessities one year from now, you may need to avoid risk completely. In this case, you should choose a risk-free investment because other investments could be worth less in one year than they are worth today. However, you will receive a relatively low rate of interest on your investment.

If you will need only a portion of your initial investment at the time the investment matures, you may be willing to take some risk. In this case, you may prefer an investment that offers a higher interest rate than the risk-free rate, but is exposed to the possibility of a loss. You can afford to take some risk, since you would still have sufficient funds to pay for your necessities even if the investment results in a loss. However, you should still consider a risky investment only if the risk premium on the investment compensates you for the risk.

No single choice is optimal for all investors, as the proper choice varies with the investor's situation and willingness to tolerate risk. Some individuals are more willing to accept risk than others. But even those individuals who are more risk tolerant should avoid risk in specific situations. If they know that they will need all of their money to pay for necessities in the near future, they should select investments that will not decline over their planned investment horizon. Thus, the investment decision is based on your risk tolerance, which in turn is influenced by your financial situation.

Example

Stephanie Spratt plans to invest $2,000. She will use these funds in one year as part of a down payment if she purchases a home. She is considering the following alternatives for investing the $2,000 over the next year:

1. A bank CD that offers a return of 6 percent (the risk-free rate) over the next year and is backed by government insurance.

2. An investment in a deposit at a financial firm that offers an interest rate of 9 percent this year but is not backed by a government guarantee.

Stephanie evaluates her possible investments. The 6 percent return from investing in the CD would result in an accumulated amount of:

Accumulated Amount = Initial Investment × (1 + Return)

$$= \$2,000 \times (1 + .06)$$

$$= \$2,120.$$

The accumulated amount if Stephanie invests in the risky deposit is:

Accumulated Amount = Initial Investment × (1 + Return)

$$= \$2,000 \times (1 + .09)$$

$$= \$2,180.$$

Comparing the two accumulated amounts, Stephanie sees that she would earn an extra $60 from the risky deposit if the firm performs well over the next year. There is a risk that the return from the risky deposit could be poorer, however. If the risky deposit pays her only what she originally invested, she would earn zero interest. If the firm goes bankrupt, it might not have any funds at all to pay her. Although the chances that this firm will go bankrupt are low, Stephanie decides that the possibility of losing her entire investment is not worth the extra $60 in interest. She decides to invest in the bank CD.

TERM STRUCTURE OF INTEREST RATES

term structure of interest rates
The relationship between the maturities of risk-free debt securities and the annualized yields offered on those securities.

Investors who consider investing in bank deposits or other debt securities must determine the maturity at which they wish to invest. When investors provide credit to financial markets, the relationship between the maturity of an investment and the interest rate on the investment is referred to as the **term structure of interest rates.** The term structure is often based on rates of return (or yields) offered by Treasury securities (which are debt securities issued by the U.S. Treasury) with different maturities. The rates of CDs and Treasury securities with a specific maturity are very similar at a given point in time, so this term structure looks very similar to one that would be derived from deposit rates of financial institutions. An understanding of the term structure is important to investors and borrowers because it provides them with the risk-free interest rates that they could earn for various maturities.

Example

You are considering depositing $500 in a financial institution. You do not expect to need the funds for at least three years. The first step when considering possible investment maturities is to assess the term structure of interest rates so that you know the interest rate quoted for each maturity. The institution's rates as of today are shown in Exhibit 5.2.

The relationship between the maturities and annualized yields in Exhibit 5.2 is graphed in Exhibit 5.3. The term structure shown here for one specific point in time illustrates that annualized interest rates are higher on investments with longer terms to maturity. Thus, the longer the investment horizon you choose, the higher the annualized interest rate you receive.

You must also consider how long you plan to invest the funds (three years). You should not invest in a deposit that has a longer term to maturity than the time when you will need the funds because you will be subject to a penalty if you withdraw the funds before that date.

Exhibit 5.2   Annualized Deposit Rates Offered on Deposits with Various Maturities

Maturity	Annualized Deposit Rate (%)
1 month	4.0
3 months	4.3
6 months	4.7
1 year	5.0
2 years	5.2
3 years	5.4
4 years	5.5
5 years	5.7
10 years	6.0

Exhibit 5.3   Comparison of Interest Rates among Deposits

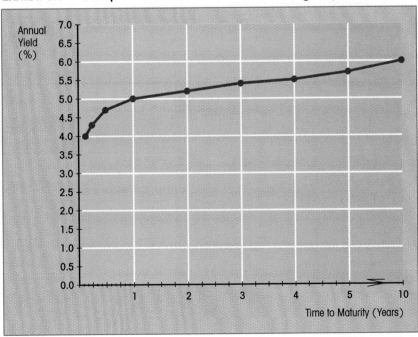

Exhibit 5.4   Treasury Security Yields

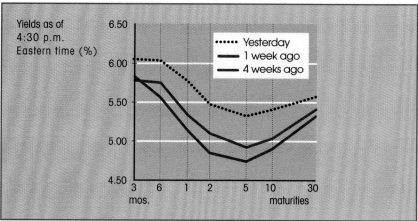

Yields as of 4:30 p.m. Eastern time (%)

- ····· Yesterday
- — 1 week ago
- — 4 weeks ago

(Maturities: 3, 6 mos. | 1, 2, 5, 10, 30 maturities)

Illustration of Shifts in the Yield Curve

The yield curve derived from annualized Treasury security yields appears every day in the *Wall Street Journal,* as shown in Exhibit 5.4. The current day's yield curve is compared to the curve that existed one week ago and four weeks ago. This allows you to easily see how the returns from investing in debt securities with different maturities have changed over time.

5.4   Financial Planning Online: Updated Treasury Yields

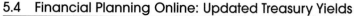

Go to:
http://www.bloomberg.com

Click on:
U.S. Treasuries

This Web site provides:
yields of Treasury securities with various maturities. This information is useful for determining how your return from investing funds in Treasury securities or bank deposits could vary with the maturity you choose.

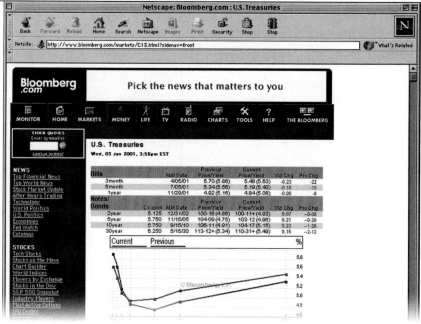

HOW BANKING SERVICES FIT WITHIN YOUR FINANCIAL PLAN

The key banking decisions for your financial plan are:

1. What banking service characteristics are most important to you?

2. What financial institution provides the best banking service characteristics for you?

Interest rates will play a role in your decisions because you can compare rates among financial institutions to determine where you would earn the highest return on your deposits or pay the lowest rate on your loans. By making proper banking decisions, you can ensure that you receive the banking services that you need to conduct your financial transactions. As an example, Exhibit 5.5 shows how banking service decisions apply to Stephanie Spratt's financial plan.

Exhibit 5.5   How Banking Services Fit within Stephanie Spratt's Financial Plan

Goals for Banking Services

1. Identify the most important banking services.
2. Determine which financial institution will provide me with the best banking services.

Analysis

Characteristic	How It Affects Me
Interest rate offered on deposits	This will affect the amount of interest income I earn on deposits.
Interest rate charged on mortgages	I could use the same financial institution if I buy a home in the future.
Interest rate charged on personal loans	I could use the same financial institution if I obtain a personal loan in the future.
Fees charged for checking services	I will be writing many checks, so fees are important.
Location	The ideal financial institution would have a branch near my apartment building and near where I work.
Online services available	This would make my banking more convenient.
ATMs	Check locations for convenience and whether any fees are charged for using ATMs.

Decisions

Decision regarding Important Characteristics of a Financial Institution:

The most important banking service for me is the checking account because I will write many checks every month. I prefer a bank that does not charge fees for check writing. I also value convenience, which I measure by the location of the financial institution's branches, and its online services. I would prefer a financial institution that offers reasonable rates on its deposit accounts, but convenience is more important to me than the deposit rate.

Decision regarding the Optimal Financial Institution:

After screening financial institutions according to my criteria, I found three financial institutions that are desirable. I selected Quality Savings, Inc., because it does not charge for check writing, has branches in convenient locations, and offers online banking. It also pays relatively high interest rates on its deposits and charges relatively low interest rates (compared to other financial institutions) on its loans. I may consider obtaining a mortgage there someday if I buy a home, as its mortgage rate was comparable to those of other financial institutions.

DISCUSSION QUESTIONS

1. How would Stephanie's banking service decisions be different if she were a single mother of two children?

2. How would Stephanie's banking service decisions be affected if she were 35 years old? If she were 50 years old?

SUMMARY

Depository institutions (commercial banks, savings institutions, and credit unions) accept deposits and provide loans. Nondepository institutions include insurance companies (which provide insurance), securities firms (which provide brokerage and other services), and investment companies (which offer mutual funds). Financial conglomerates offer a wide variety of these financial services so that individuals can obtain all their financial services from a single firm.

An interest rate is composed of the risk-free rate and the risk premium. The risk-free rate is the rate of interest paid on an investment that has no risk over a specific investment period (such as a bank deposit backed by government insurance).

Risky investments offer a return that exceeds the risk-free rate. The risk premium is the additional amount above the risk-free rate that risky investments offer. The higher an investment's risk, the higher the risk premium it must offer to entice investors.

The term structure of interest rates is the relationship between interest rates and maturities. It is measured by the yield curve, which shows the interest rate offered at each maturity level. The yield curve is typically upward sloping, meaning that the annualized interest rate is higher for debt securities with longer terms to maturity.

Integrating the Key Concepts

Your selection of a financial institution is important for various parts of your financial plan. A financial institution can serve your liquidity needs (Part 2) by offering a source for your deposits. In addition, a financial institution may also satisfy your financing needs (Part 3) by providing a personal loan or a mortgage loan so that you can purchase a car or a home. It may be able to advise you on your investments (Part 4) or even sell you the types of investments that you desire. It may also be able to offer you a retirement account (Part 5).

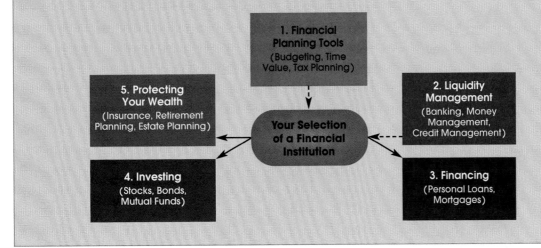

Interest Rates: How They Are Determined and Why They Change

Given the potential impact of a change in the risk-free interest rate on investor returns and on the financing charges on borrowed funds, you should closely monitor changes in the risk-free interest rate over time. The following discussion provides a framework that not only enables you to understand why interest rates change, but also allows you to anticipate potential changes in interest rates, which may affect some of your investment and financing decisions.

HOW THE RISK-FREE INTEREST RATE IS DETERMINED

The risk-free interest rate on borrowed funds is determined by the total (or aggregate) supply of funds provided by all investors and the total (or aggregate) demand for funds by all borrowers. This can be most easily understood by imagining that there is a single commercial bank that accepts deposits from any investors who have funds that they wish to invest and channels the funds as loans to all borrowers who need funds.

The interest rate on debt represents the cost of using debt (credit) for the borrower and the reward for providing credit for the creditor. The interest rate at a given point in time is dependent on the interaction between the amount that savers are willing to save and the amount that borrowers wish to borrow. To understand how the interest rate on credit is determined, assume that the students in your class represent the entire set of borrowers and creditors in financial markets. The savers will serve as creditors by providing their funds to the borrowers. Assume that the students in the first three rows are planning to save some money, while the students in the last three rows will need to borrow money. Also assume that there is no chance that the borrowers will default on the loans that they obtain.

Aggregate Supply of Funds

The amount that the savers in the first three rows will accumulate is dependent on the interest rate that they can obtain on their funds. If you could survey them about how much they are willing to save, you would be able to create a supply curve like that shown in Exhibit 5A.1, which reflects the aggregate amount of funds that will be supplied to the market at various possible interest rates.

For a relatively low annual interest rate (such as 2 percent), the aggregate supply of funds is also low because investors do not receive much of a reward. If the nominal interest rate is 6 percent, however, the aggregate supply of funds is higher because the reward to investors is higher. If the nominal interest rate is 11 percent, the aggregate supply of funds is even higher. The supply curve (labeled S_1) in Exhibit 5A.1 illustrates that the aggregate supply of funds provided by investors is positively related to the interest rate offered to investors who are willing to supply the funds at a given point in time.

Aggregate Demand for Funds

The amount that the borrowers in your classroom will borrow is dependent on the interest rate that they will have to pay on those funds. If you could survey them about how much they are willing to borrow, you would be able to create a demand curve like that shown in Exhibit 5A.1, which reflects the aggregate amount of funds that will be demanded by borrowers at various possible interest rates.

For a relatively low annual interest rate (such as 2 percent), the aggregate demand for funds is very high because the cost of borrowing is so low. When the interest rate is 6 percent, the aggregate demand for funds is lower

Exhibit 5A.1   How an Equilibrium Interest Rate Is Determined

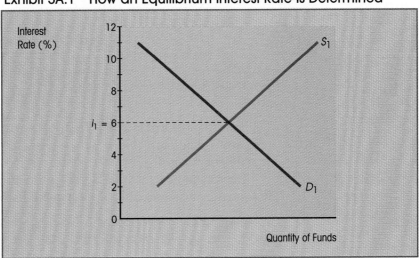

because the cost of borrowing is higher. When the interest rate is even higher, such as 11 percent, the aggregate demand for funds is even lower.

Combining Supply and Demand

In Exhibit 5A.1, the intersection between the supply curve (S_1) and the demand curve (D_1) for funds results in an equilibrium interest rate of 6 percent, at which the quantity of funds supplied is equal to the quantity of funds demanded. At an interest rate above 6 percent in Exhibit 5A.1, the quantity of funds supplied will exceed the quantity of funds demanded at that point in time, and there will be a surplus of funds, so some of the funds will not be used. Conversely, at an interest rate below 6 percent in Exhibit 5A.1, the quantity of funds supplied will not be sufficient to accommodate the demand for funds. The equilibrium interest rate at a given point in time equates the aggregate supply and demand for funds.

WHY INTEREST RATES CHANGE

A change in the risk-free interest rate causes other interest rates to change. Therefore, understanding why the risk-free interest rate changes allows you to understand why other interest rates change. Because the equilibrium interest rate is influenced by the interaction between the supply curve and the demand curve for funds, a shift in either or both of these curves will cause a shift in the interest rate.

Shift in the Supply Curve

Any factors that cause a change in the supply of funds available will shift the supply curve and affect the equilibrium interest rate.

Example

Assume that the students in the first row have incurred some unexpected expenses and can no longer save funds. If you were able to redo your survey, you would find that the aggregate supply schedule has shifted inward, as shown in Exhibit 5A.2. This means that at any possible interest rate, less funds are supplied to the market. The inward shift in the supply curve forces the equilibrium interest rate to increase.

If the students had increased (instead of reduced) their savings, the supply curve would have shifted outward, and the equilibrium interest rate would have declined.

The common factors that cause a shift in the supply curve are a shift in savings by investors and a shift in monetary policy, as described next.

Shift in Savings by Investors. Since investors supply funds, any change in their saving behavior will affect the aggregate supply of funds available and the interest rate.

Exhibit 5A.2   Impact of an Inward Shift in the Supply Schedule

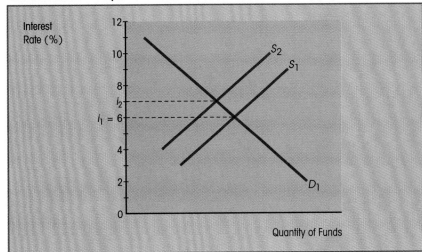

Example

 Assume that investors receive a tax break this year and suddenly have more disposable income than they expected. They may increase their savings, which means they will supply a larger amount of funds to the financial markets. They will provide a larger supply of savings at any existing interest rate level, which causes an outward shift in the supply curve.

money supply
Demand deposits (checking accounts) and currency held by the public.

Shift in Monetary Policy. The **money supply** consists of demand deposits (checking accounts) and currency held by the public. Some definitions of the money supply include other types of bank deposits as well. The money supply is commonly used by investors as an indicator of the amount of funds that financial institutions can provide to consumers or businesses as loans.

The U.S. money supply is controlled by the Federal Reserve System (called "the Fed"), which is the central bank of the United States. The act of controlling the money supply is referred to as **monetary policy**. The Fed's monetary policy affects the money supply, which can influence interest rates. Thus, the Fed can affect the value of firms by influencing interest rate movements. Whether the Fed can continuously control interest rates over a long period of time as a result of a specific monetary policy is subject to debate. However, the Fed can definitely push interest rates to a specific desired level over a short-term period, and this can affect financing costs for firms or individuals.

monetary policy
The actions taken by the Federal Reserve to control the money supply.

The Federal Reserve Bank has funds that are not deposited in any commercial bank or other financial institution. The Fed most commonly conducts monetary policy through **open market operations**, which involve

open market operations
The Fed's buying and selling of Treasury securities.

5.5   Financial Planning Online: Fed's Upcoming Meetings

Go to:

http://www.bloomberg.com/
bbn/fedwatch.html

This Web site provides:
updated information about the
Fed's recent actions and
upcoming meetings, as well as
forecasts of future policy decisions and the potential impact
of these decisions. You can
use this information to anticipate how the values of your
securities may be affected by
possible Fed policy actions.

buying or selling Treasury securities (debt securities issued by the Treasury).
The Fed can either use some of its funds to buy Treasury securities in the
secondary market, or it can sell to investors some of its holdings of Treasury securities that it previously purchased in the secondary market. By
affecting the account balances maintained by investors, these transactions
affect the level of the money supply and therefore interest rates.

When the Fed wishes to reduce interest rates, it increases the amount
of funds at commercial banks by using some of its reserves to purchase
Treasury securities held by investors. Investors suddenly have more cash
than they did before, which may cause them to increase their savings. The
amount of funds supplied to the market at any possible interest rate
increases, causing the supply curve to shift outward. The increase in the
supply of funds available places downward pressure on the equilibrium
interest rate. Consequently, interest rates decline in response to the Fed's
monetary policy.

When the Fed wishes to increase interest rates, it sells to investors some
of the Treasury securities that it had previously purchased. The payments
made by investors to the Fed for these transactions reduce the amount of
funds that investors have for savings. The reduction in the supply of funds
available at commercial banks reduces the amount of funds that banks can
lend, and causes interest rates to increase.

Shift in the Demand Curve

Any factors that cause a change in the demand for funds available will shift the demand curve and affect the equilibrium interest rate.

Example

Assume that the students in one row suddenly need to borrow more funds than they initially anticipated. These students are now more willing to borrow funds at each possible interest rate. Thus, the aggregate demand curve shifts out, as shown in Exhibit 5A.3. This means that at any possible interest rate, more funds are demanded by borrowers. The outward shift in the demand curve will force the equilibrium interest rate to increase.

If the students in the example had reduced (instead of increased) the amount they wished to borrow, the demand curve would have shifted inward, and the equilibrium interest rate would have declined.

Any factors that cause a change in the demand for funds will shift the demand curve and affect the equilibrium interest rate. The key factors that affect the aggregate demand for funds are shifts in government demand for funds, shifts in business demand for funds, and shifts in the household demand for funds, which are described next.

Shift in the Government Demand for Funds. The U.S. government frequently borrows substantial amounts of funds. Any shift in the government's borrowing behavior can affect the aggregate demand for funds and affect the equilibrium interest rate.

Exhibit 5A.3   Impact of an Outward Shift in the Demand Schedule

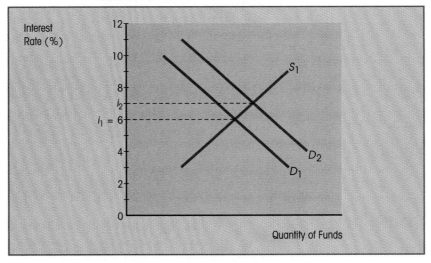

Example

Assume the U.S. government suddenly needs to borrow more funds than it normally borrows. The total amount of funds demanded will now be larger at any possible interest rate level, causing the demand curve to shift outward. This shift results in a shortage of funds at the original equilibrium interest rate and places upward pressure on the interest rate.

If the government had reduced (instead of increased) the amount that it borrows, the opposite effects would have occurred. The demand curve would have shifted inward, resulting in a surplus of funds at the original interest rate and ultimately in a lower interest rate.

Shift in the Business Demand for Funds. Firms are also common borrowers of funds. When economic conditions change, businesses review their spending plans and adjust their demand for funds. This shift in demand affects the interest rate.

Example

Assume that businesses have just become more optimistic about the economy and expect an increase in consumer demand for the products they produce. Consequently, they are more willing to expand and must borrow more funds to support their expansion. Their actions result in an increase in the aggregate demand for funds (an outward shift in the demand curve), similar to the effect of increased government borrowing. The shift results in a higher equilibrium interest rate.

If the businesses had suddenly expected a weaker (instead of a stronger) economy, the opposite effects would occur. Firms tend to reduce their expansion plans when they expect a weak economy. Therefore, they reduce the amount of funds borrowed. This decreases the aggregate demand for funds (an inward shift in the demand curve) and results in a lower equilibrium interest rate.

Shift in the Household Demand for Funds. Households commonly borrow funds to purchase new homes, automobiles, and other products. The amount that they wish to borrow can change in response to economic conditions.

Example

Assume that households suddenly expect that inflation (the degree to which prices rise) will be higher than initially expected. They may increase their spending so that they can purchase specific products such as a car or a home now before prices rise. The increased spending means that households will also increase their borrowing because they commonly use borrowed funds to pay for these products. Thus, the increase in expected inflation causes an increase in the aggregate demand for funds, which results in a higher equilibrium interest rate.

Combining the Factors

Some economic conditions can affect more than one factor. For example, an increase in expected inflation can reduce the aggregate supply of saving because it encourages savers to spend now before prices increase further. In this case, both forces place upward pressure on the equilibrium interest rate.

Factors sometimes change in ways that result in opposing forces on the equilibrium interest rate. For example, the government may need to borrow additional funds, which places upward pressure on interest rates, while the Fed increases the money supply (which can place downward pressure on interest rates). Under these conditions, interest rates can move in either direction, depending on which force is more dominant.

REVIEW QUESTIONS

1. Compare and contrast the three types of depository institutions.

2. List the four types of nondepository financial institutions and describe the role of each.

3. What is a financial conglomerate? List some services financial conglomerates provide.

4. What is the difference between a debit card and a credit card?

5. Name the special services that banks provide. How might you make use of them?

6. Steve just received his first paycheck and wants to open a checking account. There are five banks in his hometown. What should Steve consider when choosing a bank?

7. When making banking decisions, why should you be concerned about current interest rates?

8. What is a risk-free rate? Give an example of an investment with a risk-free rate. Why is there no risk?

9. What is a risk premium? Who might take advantage of it?

10. How is the risk premium calculated?

11. Where do financial institutions obtain funds for making loans? How are the interest rates for loans determined? Are the interest rates the same for all borrowers? Why or why not?

12. What effect would a general change in current interest rates have on you as a depositor or borrower?

13. In considering investments with different degrees of risk, what two factors will influence an investor's decision? What situation should all investors avoid? Why?

14. What is meant by the "term structure of interest rates"? Why is this concept important to an investor?

Questions 15 through 20 are based on the chapter appendix.

15. How is the risk-free interest rate on borrowed funds determined? What affects the aggregate supply and demand for funds? What is the equilibrium rate?

16. In relation to supply and demand, what causes interest rates to change?

17. What are two causes of shifts in the money supply curve? What is monetary policy? What organization controls monetary policy in the United States?

18. Describe the most common method the Federal Reserve uses to affect the money supply.

19. Briefly discuss the three key factors that would cause a shift in the demand for funds and a change in the equilibrium interest rate.

20. How might expectations of higher inflation affect the household demand for funds?

FINANCIAL PLANNING PROBLEMS

Refer to the following chart when answering problems 1 through 4:

	Hillsboro Bank	First National	South Trust Bank	Sun Coast Bank
ATM charges:				
Home bank	Free	Free	Free	Free
Other bank	4 free, then $1 per use	$1.25	$1.25	$1.25
Checking:				
Minimum deposit	$100	$25	$1	$1
Minimum balance to avoid fees	0	0	$500	0
Monthly fees	$6	$7	$11	$2.50
Check-writing charges	12 free, then 75 cents per check	7 free, then 75 cents per check	Unlimited	Each check 25 cents

1. Stuart wants to open a checking account with a $100 deposit. Stuart believes he will write 15 checks per month and use other banks' ATMs eight times a month. He will not be able to maintain a minimum balance. Which bank should Stuart choose?

2. Julie wants to open a bank account with $75. Julie estimates that she will write 20 checks per

month and use her ATM card at the home bank. She will not maintain a large balance. Which bank should Julie choose?

3. Veronica plans to open a checking account with her $1,200 tax refund check. She believes she can maintain a $500 minimum balance. Also, she estimates that she will write 10 checks per month and will use other bank's ATMs as many as 15 times per month. Which bank should Veronica choose?

4. Randy, a student, has $500 to deposit in a new checking account. Randy knows he will not be able to maintain a minimum balance. He will not use an ATM card, but will write a large number of checks. Randy is trying to choose between the unlimited check writing offered by South Trust and the low per check fee offered by Sun Coast. How many checks would Randy have to write each month for the account at South Trust to be the better option?

5. Casey has $1,000 to invest in a certificate of deposit. Her local bank offers her 6.5 percent on a 12-month FDIC-insured CD. A nonfinancial institution offers her 9.2 percent on a 12-month CD. What is Casey's risk premium? What else must she consider?

FINANCIAL PLANNING ONLINE EXERCISES

Go to http://dir.yahoo.com/business_and_economy/finance_and_investment/banking/. Click on the Internet Banking category. Then click on Gomez Internet Banking Scorecard.

1. According to the scorecard, what is the best online bank? Compare banks on the list based on the criteria used to make this determination such as ease of use, overall cost, and on-site resources among others.

2. This Web page includes a feature that allows you to compare online banks. Choose two banks from the pull-down menus to compare on criteria that you value.

3. Referring to the advice in the "Which Bank is the Best for Me?" section, choose the online bank that would best meet your needs. Why is this the case?

4. Do you have a question about online banks? If so, there is a feature on this page where you can ask it.

Use the Back option on your browser to go to http://dir.yahoo.com/business_and_economy/finance_and_investment/banking/internet_banking/. Click on Xolia.com. Then click on Online Broker.

1. In the Resource Center under the heading Education, click on "Online Investing: The Basics" and review the information.

2. Use the Back option on your browser and go to the menu page. Click on "Risks of Online Investing" under the heading "Test Your Knowledge." Review the information and list the risks of investing online. What can you do if you are defrauded?

3. Use the Back option on your browser and go to the menu page. Click on "How to Open an Account." Read the information. How long does it take to set up an account? Are there minimum balance requirements?

4. Use the Back option on your browser and go to the menu page. Click on "How to Make Your First Trade" and review the information. What are the important steps in making a trade?

Building Your Own Financial Plan

A variety of financial institutions are available to meet your banking, savings, and checking needs. Each institution offers a variety of services and products at varying costs. On the template for this chapter in the *Financial Planning* *Workbook* and on the CD-ROM, list the various services in order of their importance to you with "10" being the most important and "1" the least. Then visit five financial institutions in person or via the Internet to gather information (try to include at least one commercial bank, one savings and loan, and one credit union in your group of five). For each of the 10 services listed, rate the institutions from "5" as the best for that service to "1" as the worst for that service of the group. Enter your scores on the template and multiply each institution's score by the priority you put on that service. Total the scores to determine which of the five institutions will best meet your needs.

The Sampsons—A Continuing Case

 Recall that the Sampsons have resolved to save a total of $800 per month. Dave and Sharon notice that their local bank offers the certificates of deposit listed below; they now need to determine which CDs will best suit their savings goals. Each CD requires a minimum investment of $300. Recall that the Sampsons are saving for a down payment on a new car that they will purchase within a year. They are also saving for their children's college education, which begins 12 years from now.

Maturity	Annualized Interest Rate (%)
1 month	4.0
3 months	4.2
6 months	4.6
1 year	5.0
3 years	5.2
5 years	5.4
7 years	5.5
10 years	6.0

1. Advise the Sampsons on the maturity to select when investing their savings in a CD for a down payment on a new car. What are the advantages or disadvantages of the relatively short-term maturities versus the longer-term maturities?

2. Advise the Sampsons on the maturity to select when investing their savings for their children's education. Describe any advantages or disadvantages of the relatively short-term maturities versus the longer–term maturities.

3. If you thought that interest rates were going to rise in the next few months, how might this affect the advice that you give the Sampsons?

IN-TEXT STUDY GUIDE

True/False:

1. When you have funds to invest, the return that you earn from your investment may be dependent on the level of interest rates in the financial markets at that time.

2. Credit unions are financial institutions that accept deposits and use the funds to provide commercial (business) loans to entities with a good credit rating.

3. A debit card is used to make purchases that are charged against an existing credit card.

4. A cashier's check is a check that is written on behalf of a person to a specific payee and will be charged against a financial institution's account.

5. A traveler's check is similar to a cashier's check, except that no payee is designated on the check.

6. A certificate of deposit (CD) represents partial ownership of a firm.

7. The rate of interest paid on a CD is often referred to as the risk-free interest rate because there is no risk surrounding the rate of return.

8. A one-year bank loan has an interest rate that is below its one-year CD rate.

9. For a relatively high annual interest rate, the aggregate supply of funds should be low.

10. The term structure of interest rates refers to the relationship between the maturity of an investment and the interest rate on the investment.

11. Finance companies tend to charge relatively low loan rates because they provide loans to some firms and individuals that are perceived to exhibit higher risk (of defaulting on the loans received).

Multiple Choice:

1. _____ are not a type of depository institution.
   a. Commercial banks
   b. Securities firms
   c. Savings institutions
   d. Credit unions

2. Deposits at financial institutions are insured up to _____ per depositor by the Federal Deposit Insurance Corporation (FDIC).
   a. $50,000
   b. $80,000
   c. $100,000
   d. $150,000

3. _____ are financial institutions that accept deposits and provide mortgage and personal loans to individuals.
   a. Commercial banks
   b. Securities firms
   c. Savings institutions
   d. Credit unions

4. _____ facilitate the purchase or sale of securities by firms or individuals.
   a. Securities firms
   b. Finance companies
   c. Insurance companies
   d. Investment companies

5. A _____ is a check written on behalf of a person to a specific payee that is charged against a financial institution's account.
   a. cashier's check
   b. certified order
   c. CD
   d. NOW account

6. The _____ rate may be used as a measure of a risk-free rate.
   a. mortgage
   b. stock
   c. primary
   d. CD

7. Currently, a one-year CD rate offers an interest rate of 4.5 percent. Brown Company offers an interest rate of 8.0 percent. Based on this information, the risk premium offered by Brown is
   a. 4.5 percent.
   b. 8.0 percent.
   c. 3.5 percent.
   d. 12.5 percent.

8. The _____ the risk that the lender will not be repaid on a loan provided to you, the _____ the risk premium that you would have to pay with respect to the prevailing risk-free rate.
   a. higher; higher
   b. lower; higher
   c. higher; lower
   d. Answers (b) and (c) are correct.

9. For a relatively _____ annual interest rate (such as 2 percent), the aggregate demand for funds should be very _____.
   a. low; low
   b. high; high
   c. low; high
   d. Answers (a) and (b) are correct.

10. Last month, the annualized risk-free interest rate for a three-year maturity was 4.63 percent. If you had financed a computer purchase last month, you would have been charged a risk premium of 4.50 percent. Based on this information, the interest rate on the loan to purchase the computer is
    a. 4.63 percent.
    b. 8.00 percent.
    c. 4.50 percent.
    d. 9.13 percent.

The following information refers to questions 11 through 13.

Olga Sorsa would like to invest $1,500. She is considering two investment alternatives. The first alternative is a Treasury bill that would guarantee her a return of 5 percent over the next year. The second alternative is a corporate bond that will provide a 4 percent return over the next year under unfavorable conditions, or an 8 percent return over the next year under favorable conditions.

11. What is the accumulated amount after one year if Olga invests in the Treasury bill?
    a. $1,500
    b. $1,575
    c. $75
    d. $1,620

12. What is the accumulated amount of the corporate bond after one year under unfavorable conditions?
    a. $1,575
    b. $1,620
    c. $1,560
    d. $1,500

13. What is the accumulated amount of the corporate bond after one year under favorable conditions?
    a. $1,575
    b. $1,620
    c. $1,560
    d. $1,500

14. The risk premium offered by an investment is _____ to the degree of risk exhibited by that investment.
    a. positively related
    b. negatively related
    c. unrelated
    d. none of the above

15. The relationship between the maturity of an investment and the interest rate on the investment is referred to as the
    a. equilibrium interest rate.
    b. Phillips curve.
    c. term structure of interest rates.
    d. none of the above

16. The _____ the investment horizon chosen, the _____ the annualized interest rate that can usually be locked in at this time.
    a. longer; lower
    b. shorter; higher
    c. longer; higher
    d. a and b are correct

17. _____ sell shares to individuals and use the proceeds to invest in securities to create mutual funds.
    a. Securities firms
    b. Finance companies
    c. Insurance companies
    d. Investment companies

18. The annual interest rate on loans offered to individuals is often _____ percentage points above the annual interest rate offered on deposits.
    a. 1 to 2
    b. 2 to 20
    c. 3 to 7
    d. 5 to 15

Questions 19 through 21 refer to Appendix 5A.

19. Which of the following is not a common factor that causes a shift in the demand for funds?
    a. a shift in savings behavior
    b. a shift in the government demand for funds
    c. a shift in the business demand for funds
    d. All of the above are common factors that cause a shift in the demand curve.

20. When the Federal Reserve wishes to _____ interest rates, it _____ the amount of funds at commercial banks.
    a. reduce; reduces
    b. increase; increases
    c. reduce; increases
    d. Answers (a) and (b) are correct.

21. If the Federal Reserve buys or sells Treasury securities to affect the money supply, it uses
    a. reserves at commercial banks.
    b. open market operations.
    c. discount rate adjustments.
    d. federal funds rate adjustments.

Managing Your Money

Proper money management decisions ensure that you will have sufficient funds to cover any expected and unexpected expenses, therefore minimizing your financing costs from using credit. In addition, effective money management can enhance your interest income (cash inflows) generated by your short-term investments. In these ways, proper money management will increase your wealth.

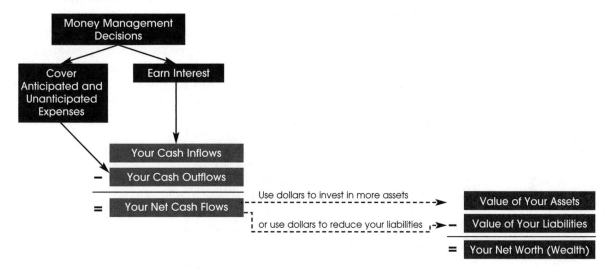

The objectives of this chapter are to:

- provide a background on money management,
- describe the most popular money market investments,
- identify the risk associated with money market investments, and
- explain how to manage the risk of your money market investments.

BACKGROUND ON MONEY MANAGEMENT

money management
A series of decisions made over a short-term period regarding cash inflows and outflows.

Money management involves a series of decisions you make over a short-term period regarding your cash inflows and outflows. It is separate from decisions on investing funds for a long-term period (such as several years) or borrowing funds for a long-term period. Instead, it focuses on maintaining short-term investments to achieve both liquidity and an adequate return on your investments, as explained next.

Liquidity

liquidity
Your ability to cover any cash deficiencies that you may experience.

As discussed in Chapter 1, **liquidity** refers to your ability to cover any short-term cash deficiencies. Recall that the personal cash flow statement determines the amount of excess or deficient funds that an individual will have at the end of a period, such as one month from now. Money management is related to the personal cash flow statement because it determines how to use excess funds or allocate excess cash inflows, or how to obtain funds if your cash inflows are insufficient. You should maintain a sufficient amount of funds in liquid assets such as a checking account or savings account to draw on when your cash outflows exceed your cash inflows. In this way, you maintain adequate liquidity.

Some individuals rely on a credit card (to be discussed in detail in Chapter 7) as a source of liquidity rather than maintaining liquid investments. Many credit cards provide temporary free financing from the time you make purchases until the date when your payment is due. If you have insufficient funds to pay the entire credit card balance when the bill is due, you may pay only a portion of your balance and finance the rest of the payment. The interest rate is usually quite high, commonly ranging from 12 to 20 percent. Maintaining liquid assets that you can easily access when you need funds allows you to avoid using credit and paying excessive finance charges.

Example

 Stephanie Spratt's cash inflows are $2,500 per month after taxes. Her cash outflows are normally about $2,100 per month, leaving her with $400 in cash each month. This month she expects that she will have an extra expense of $600; therefore, her cash outflows will exceed her cash inflows by $200. She needs a convenient source of funds to cover the extra expense.

Liquidity is necessary because there will likely be periods when your cash inflows are not adequate to cover your cash outflows. Maintaining an excessive amount of liquid funds entails an opportunity cost. A portion of those funds could have been invested in less liquid assets that are expected to generate a higher return. The relationship between the proportion of your funds invested in liquid assets and the potential return on your invested funds is shown in Exhibit 6.1. In general, the more liquid an investment,

Exhibit 6.1   Relationship between Your Liquidity and the Return on Your Funds

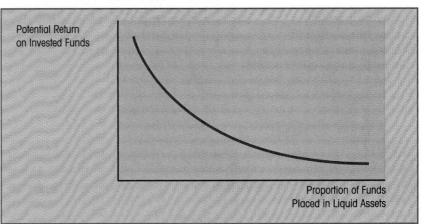

6.1   Financial Planning Online: Estimating the Future Value of Your Savings

Go to:
http://www.financenter.com/
products/analyzers/savings.fcs

Click on:
"How much will my savings be
worth?"

This Web site provides:
estimates of what your savings
will be worth in the future and
even graphs the growth in your
savings over time.

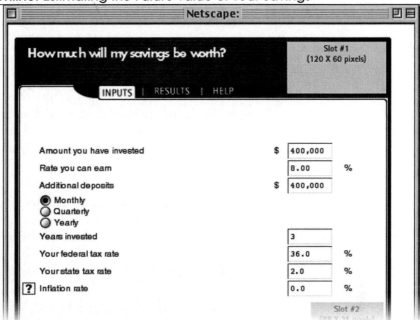

the lower its return, so you forgo higher returns when maintaining a high
degree of liquidity.

Adequate Return

When you maintain short-term investments, you should strive to achieve
the highest possible return. The return on your short-term investments is
dependent on the prevailing risk-free rate and the level of risk you are willing to tolerate. Some assets that satisfy your liquidity needs may not necessarily achieve the return that you expect. For example, you could maintain
a large amount of cash in your wallet as a source of liquidity, but it would
earn a zero rate of return. Conversely, some investments may provide an
adequate return, but are not liquid. To achieve both liquidity and an adequate return, you should consider investing in multiple money market
investments with varied returns and levels of liquidity.

MONEY MARKET INVESTMENTS

When individuals have short-term funds, they commonly invest them in the
following money market investments:

- Checking account

- NOW account

- Savings deposit

- Certificate of deposit

- Money market deposit account (MMDA)
- Treasury bills
- Money market fund
- Asset management account

All of these investments except Treasury bills and money market funds are offered by depository institutions and are insured for up to $100,000 in the event of default by the institution. Each of these investments is described in turn, with attention given to their liquidity and typical return.

Checking Account

Individuals deposit sufficient funds in a checking account (also called demand deposit account) at a depository institution to write checks or use their debit card to pay for various products and services. Most people maintain a traditional checking account because it allows an unlimited number of checks to be written, as long as there is a sufficient amount of funds in the account. It also provides a convenient way for you to keep a record of how you are spending your money, which is especially valuable for budgeting purposes. A checking account is a very liquid investment because you can access the funds (by withdrawing funds or writing checks) at any time.

overdraft protection
An arrangement that protects a customer who writes a check for an amount that exceeds the checking account balance; it is a short-term loan from the depository institution where the checking account is maintained.

Overdraft Protection. Some depository institutions offer **overdraft protection,** which protects a customer who writes a check for an amount that exceeds the checking account balance. The protection is essentially a short-term loan. For example, if a customer writes a check for $300 but has a checking account balance of only $100, the depository institution will provide overdraft protection by making a loan of $200 to the customer to make up the difference. Without overdraft protection, checks written against an insufficient account balance bounce, meaning that they are not honored by the depository institution. In addition, a customer who writes a check that bounces may be charged a penalty fee by the financial institution. Customers who make use of overdraft protection usually incur a cost in the form of a high interest rate charged on the loan.

stop payment
A financial institution's notice that it will not honor a check if someone tries to cash it; usually occurs in response to a request by the writer of the check.

Stop Payment. If you write a check but believe that it was lost and never received by the payee, you may request that the financial institution **stop payment**, which means that the institution will not honor the check if someone tries to cash it. In some cases, a customer may even stop payment to prevent the recipient from cashing a check. For example, if you write a check to pay for home repairs, but the job is not completed, you may decide to stop payment on the check. Normally, a fee is charged for a stop payment service.

Fees. Depository institutions may charge a monthly fee such as $15 per month for providing checking services unless the depositor maintains a minimum balance in the checking account or a minimum aggregate balance in other accounts at that institution. Some financial institutions charge a fee

"Your pot o' gold is doing nothing for you sitting at the end of the rainbow. At the very least, you should put it in a no—risk interest-bearing account."

per check written instead of a monthly fee. The specific fee structure and the rules for waiving the fee vary among financial institutions, so you should compare fees before you decide where to set up your checking account.

No Interest. A disadvantage of investing funds in a checking account is that the funds do not earn any interest. For this reason, you should keep only enough funds in your checking account to cover anticipated expenses and a small excess amount in case unanticipated expenses arise. You should not deposit more funds in your checking account than you think you may need, because you can earn interest by investing in other money market investments.

NOW Account

NOW (negotiable order of withdrawal) account

A type of deposit offered by depository institutions that provides checking services and pays interest.

Another deposit offered by depository institutions is a **negotiable order of withdrawal (NOW) account.** An advantage of a NOW account over a traditional checking account is that it pays interest, although the interest is relatively low compared with many other bank deposits. The depositor is required to maintain a minimum balance in a NOW account, so the account is not as liquid as a traditional checking account.

Example

Stephanie Spratt has a checking account with no minimum balance; she is considering opening a NOW account that requires a minimum balance of $500 and offers an interest rate of 3 percent. She has an extra $800 in her checking account that she could transfer to the NOW account. How much interest would she earn over one year in the NOW account?

Interest Earned = Deposit Amount × Interest Rate

= $800 × .03

= $24.

Stephanie would earn $24 in annual interest from the NOW account, versus zero interest from her traditional checking account. She would need to maintain the $500 minimum balance in the NOW account, whereas she has the use of all of the funds in her checking account. She decides to leave the funds in the checking account, as the extra liquidity is worth more to her than the $24 she could earn from the NOW account.

Savings Deposit

Traditional savings accounts offered by a depository institution pay a higher interest rate on deposits than that offered on a NOW account. In addition, funds can normally be withdrawn from a savings account at any time. A savings account does not provide checking services. It is less liquid than a checking account or a NOW account because you have to go to the institution or to an ATM to access funds, which is less convenient than writing a check. The interest rate offered on savings deposits varies among depository institutions. Many institutions quote their rates on their Web sites.

Example

Stephanie Spratt wants to determine the amount of interest that she would earn over one year if she deposits $1,000 in a savings account that pays 4 percent interest.

Interest Earned = Deposit Amount × Interest Rate
                = $1,000 × .04
                = $40.

Although the interest income is attractive, she cannot write checks on a savings account. As she expects to need the funds in her checking account to pay bills in the near future, she decides not to switch those funds to a savings account at this time.

Certificate of Deposit

As mentioned in Chapter 5, a certificate of deposit (CD) offered by a depository institution specifies a minimum amount that must be invested, a maturity date on which the deposit matures, and an annualized interest rate. Common maturity dates of CDs are one month, three months, six months, one year, three years, and five years. CDs can be purchased by both firms and individuals. CDs that have small denominations (such as $10,000 or less) are sometimes referred to as **retail CDs** because they are more attractive to individuals than to firms.

retail CDs
Certificates of deposit that have small denominations (such as $10,000 or less).

Return. Depository institutions offer higher interest rates on CDs than on savings deposits. The higher return is compensation for being willing to maintain the investment until maturity. Interest rates are quoted on an annualized (yearly) basis. The interest to be generated by your investment in a CD is based on the annualized interest rate and the amount of time until maturity. The interest rates offered on CDs vary among depository institutions.

Example

A three-month (90-day) CD offers an annualized interest rate of 6 percent and requires a $5,000 minimum deposit. You want to determine the amount of interest you would earn if you invested $5,000 in the CD. Since the interest rate is annualized, you will receive only a fraction of the 6 percent rate because your investment is for a fraction of the year:

Interest Earned = Deposit Amount × Interest Rate × Adjustment for Investment Period

$$= \$5{,}000 \times .06 \times \frac{90}{365}$$

This process can be more easily understood by noting that the interest rate is applied for only 90 days, whereas the annual interest rate reflects 365 days. The interest rate that applies to your 90-day investment is for about one-fourth (90/365) of the year, so the applicable interest rate is:

Interest Rate $= .06 \times \dfrac{90}{365}$

$$= .0148 \text{ or } 1.48\%.$$

The 1.48 percent represents the actual return on your investment.

Now the interest can be determined by simply applying this return to the deposit amount:

Interest Earned = Deposit Amount × Interest Rate

$$= \$5{,}000 \times .0148$$

$$= \$73.97.$$

Liquidity. A penalty is imposed for early withdrawal from CDs, so these deposits are less liquid than funds deposited in a savings account. You should consider a CD only if you are certain that you will not need the funds until after it matures. You may decide to invest some of your funds in a CD and other funds in more liquid assets.

Choice among CD Maturities. CDs with longer terms to maturity typically offer higher annualized interest rates. However, CDs with longer maturities tie up your funds for a longer period of time and are therefore less liquid. Your choice of a maturity for a CD may depend on your need for liquidity. For example, if you know that you may need your funds in four months, you could invest in a three-month CD and then place the funds in a more liquid asset (such as your checking account or savings account) when the CD matures. If you do not expect to need the funds for one year, you may consider a one-year CD.

Money Market Deposit Account (MMDA)

money market deposit account (MMDA)
A deposit offered by a depository institution that requires a minimum balance, has no maturity date, pays interest, and allows a limited number of checks to be written each month.

A **money market deposit account (MMDA)** is a deposit account offered by a depository institution that requires a minimum balance to be maintained, has no maturity date, pays interest, and allows a limited number of checks to be written each month. The specific details vary among financial institutions. For example, an account might require that a minimum balance of $2,500 be maintained over the month and charge a $15 per month fee in any month when the minimum balance falls below that level.

An MMDA differs from a NOW account in that it provides only limited checking services while paying a higher interest rate than that offered on NOW accounts. Many individuals maintain a checking account or NOW

6.2   Financial Planning Online: Deposit Rates Offered by Banks

Go to:

http://www.bankrate.com/brm/rate/dep_home.asp

This Web site provides:

information on the highest interest rates offered on deposits by banks across the United States as well as in your specific city.

account to cover most of their day-to-day transactions and an MMDA to capitalize on the higher interest rate. Thus, they may maintain a larger amount of funds in the MMDA and use this account to write a large check for an unexpected expense. The MMDA is not as liquid as a checking account because it limits the amount of checks that can be written.

Treasury Bills

Treasury securities

Debt securities issued by the U.S. Treasury.

As mentioned in Chapter 5, **Treasury securities** are debt securities issued by the U.S. Treasury. When the U.S. government needs to spend more money than it has received in taxes, it borrows funds by issuing Treasury securities. Individuals can purchase Treasury securities through a brokerage firm. Treasury securities are offered with various maturities, such as three months, six months, one year, 10 years, and 30 years. For money management purposes, individuals tend to focus on **Treasury bills (T-bills)**, which are Treasury securities that will mature in one year or less. T-bills are available with a minimum value at maturity (called the par value) of $10,000 and are denominated in multiples of $5,000 above that minimum.

Treasury bills (T-bills)

Treasury securities with maturities of one year or less.

Return. Treasury bills are purchased at a discount from par value. If you invest in a T-bill and hold it until maturity, you earn a capital gain, which is the difference between the par value of the T-bill at maturity and the amount you paid for the T-bill. Your return on the T-bill is the capital gain as a percentage of your initial investment.

Example

You pay $9,400 to purchase a T-bill that has a par value of $10,000 and a one-year maturity. When the T-bill matures, you receive $10,000. The return on your T-bill is:

$$\text{Return on T-Bill} = \frac{\$10,000 - \$9,400}{\$9,400}$$

$$= 6.38\%.$$

When measuring returns on investments, most individuals annualize the returns so that they can compare returns on various investments with different maturities. An investment over a one-month period will likely generate a smaller dollar amount of return than a one-year investment. To compare the one-month and one-year investments, you need to determine the annualized yield (or percentage return) on each investment.

For an investment that lasts three months (one-fourth of a year), its return is multiplied by 4 to determine the annualized return. For an investment that lasts six months (one-half of a year), its return is multiplied by 2 to determine the annualized return. The most precise method of annualizing a return is to multiply the return by $365/N$, where N is the number of days the investment existed.

Example

You pay $9,700 to purchase a T-bill with a par value of $10,000 and a maturity of 182 days. The annualized return on your T-bill is:

$$\text{Return on T-Bill} = \frac{\$10,000 - \$9,700}{\$9,700} \times \frac{365}{182}$$

$$= 6.20\%.$$

secondary market
A market where existing securities such as Treasury bills can be purchased or sold.

Secondary Market. There is a **secondary market** for T-bills where they can be sold before their maturity with the help of a brokerage firm. This secondary market not only allows investors to sell T-bills before maturity, but also allows individuals to purchase T-bills that were previously owned by someone else. The return on a T-bill is usually slightly lower than the return on a CD with the same maturity, but T-bills are more liquid because they have a secondary market, whereas CDs must be held until maturity. If you sell a T-bill in the secondary market, your capital gain is the difference between what you sold the T-bill for and what you paid for the T-bill. Your return is this capital gain as a percentage of your initial investment.

Example

You purchase a T-bill for $9,700 and sell the T-bill in the secondary market 60 days later for a price of $9,820. Your annualized return is:

$$\text{Return on T-Bill} = \frac{\$9,820 - \$9,700}{\$9,700} \times \frac{365}{60}$$

$$= 7.53\%.$$

Quotations. The prices of various T-bills and the returns they offer investors who hold them until maturity are quoted in financial newspapers and on the Internet.

Money Market Funds (MMFs)

money market funds (MMFs)
Accounts that pool money provided by individuals and invest in securities that have a short-term maturity, such as one year or less.

commercial paper
Short-term debt securities issued by large corporations that typically offer a slightly higher return than Treasury bills.

Money market funds (MMFs) pool money provided by individuals to invest in securities that have a short-term maturity, such as one year or less. In fact, the average time remaining to maturity of debt securities held in an MMF is typically less than 90 days. Many MMFs invest in short-term Treasury securities or in wholesale CDs (in denominations of $100,000 or more). Investors can invest in MMFs by sending a check for the amount they wish to have invested for them. Some MMFs invest mainly in **commercial paper,** which consists of short-term debt securities issued by large corporations. Commercial paper typically generates a slightly higher interest rate than T-bills. Money market funds are not insured, but most of them invest in very safe investments and have a very low risk of default.

MMFs offer some liquidity in that individuals can write a limited number of checks on their accounts each month. Often the checks must exceed a minimum amount (such as $250). Individuals may use the checking account associated with an MMF to cover large expenditures, while maintaining a regular checking account to cover smaller purchases. Many individuals invest in an MMF so that they can earn interest until the money is needed. Some MMFs are linked with other accounts so that the money can earn interest until it is transferred to another account. Specifically, many brokerage accounts allow investors to place any unused funds in an MMF until the funds are used to purchase stock.

Example

Assume that you set up an account with $9,000 to purchase stock at a brokerage firm on May 1. On that day, you purchase 100 shares of a stock priced at $50. To cover the purchase, the brokerage firm withdraws $5,000 (computed as $50 × 100 shares) from your account. You still have $4,000 that you have not used, which is placed in a specific MMF account at the brokerage firm. This MMF offers the same limited check-writing services as other MMFs. The money will sit in that account until you use it to purchase stock or write checks against the account. Assuming that the interest rate earned on the MMF is 6 percent annually (.5 percent per month), and you do not purchase any more stock until June 1, you will earn interest on that account over the month when the funds were not used:

Amount Invested in MMF $\times$ Interest Rate per Month = Interest Earned in 1 Month

$$\$4,000 \times .005 = \$20.$$

Therefore, the MMF account balance increases by $20 to $4,020 because the funds earned interest. Any unused balance will continue to earn interest until you use it to purchase stock or write checks against the account.

Money Market Fund Quotations. Every Thursday the *Wall Street Journal* publishes the yields provided by various money market funds, as shown in Exhibit 6.2. The first column lists the name of the MMF; the second column, the average maturity of the investments of that fund; the third column, the annualized yield generated by the fund; and the fourth column, the size of the fund (measured in millions of dollars). As an example, the Harbor fund is highlighted in Exhibit 6.2. This fund's investments have a time to

Exhibit 6.2   Weekly Money Market Fund Yields

FUND	AVG. MAT.	7 DAY YIELD	ASSETS	FUND	AVG. MAT.	7 DAY YIELD	ASSETS	FUND	AVG. MAT.	7 DAY YIELD	ASSETS
FidTryCR	22	4.69	1085	FlexInst	60	5.78	80	GnGovB p	69	4.88	592
59WallStTreas	58	4.96	274	FlexFd	60	5.60	209	GnMuB p	37	2.69	402
59WallStMM	55	5.20	1563	Fortis A	50	4.77	203	GnMMkt	87	5.22	1036
FInvTrUSGvt	60	5.48	325	ForumDACI	42	5.58	62	GSILFdl	46	5.22	6337
FInvTrUSTrs	9	5.31	72	FrmDACISS	42	5.33	56	GSILGvl	22	5.29	215
FinSqFed	45	5.41	12720	Forum DAG Obl	15	5.45	51	GSILMMI	39	5.38	2969
FinSq Gov	40	5.51	3972	ForumDAGI	34	5.27	37	GSILTrsOblgl	9	5.12	817
FinSq POF	43	5.61	17901	ForumDAGO ISS	15	5.20	48	GSILPOI	26	5.22	902
FinSqTrsy	42	5.25	885	ForumDAT Obl	37	5.28	156	GSILTrsInstl	45	4.96	542
FinSq TOF	8	5.36	4457	FrnklFT	64	5.55	1305	GlenGovtCash	43	5.39	591
FinSq MMF	45	5.60	9483	FrkMnyC	64	4.85	62	GovTxMgSS	47	5.18	2273
FITPrMonMktl	23	5.51	138	FrklFTGS f	34	5.13	58	GovOb IS	35	5.51	6008
FstAmGvObD	34	5.08	414	FrkFdl bf	34	4.78	138	GovOb SS	35	5.26	3300
FstAmGvObY	34	5.23	969	FreedomCshMgmt	36	5.04	3418	GovTxMgIS	47	5.43	1718
FstAmTrObD	19	4.95	3853	FreedomGovt	34	4.97	662	GrtHallGv	57	5.17	335
FstAmGvObA p	34	4.93	491	FremntMM	52	5.48	747	GreatHallInstPr	44	5.42	509
FstAmPrObA	40	5.04	5222	FrkMny	64	5.32	2579	GrtHallPr	46	5.11	5571
FstAmPrObY	40	5.38	7126	GEInstMM	25	5.25	34	GrdCMA	20	4.76	460
FstAmPrObD	40	5.23	611	GEMnyMktA	25	5.28	281	GrdCsFd	19	5.03	414
FstAmTrObA p	19	4.85	58	GabelliUST	51	4.99	757	HSBC Csh	48	5.28	187
FstAmTrObY	19	5.10	2228	GalaxyGvRes p	58	4.65	255	HSBC Gvt	13	5.07	20
FirstCshRsvl	48	5.62	40	GalaxyGvR	54	5.05	341	HSBCInvMM A	27	5.15	471
FirstCshRsvlll	48	5.37	205	GalaxyGvTr	54	5.22	552	HSBCInvMM D	27	5.30	546
FtlnvCs	70	5.21	192	GalaxyInUSTr	37	5.32	4647	HSBCInvMM Y	27	5.55	479
First Muni	36	3.68	65	GalaxyInstMM	44	5.33	550	HSBCInvUSMM A	11	4.94	1027
FstOmahaGv	60	5.13	294	GalaxyMM R	54	5.01	3250	HSBCInvUSMM D	11	5.09	620
First USGv	41	5.48	101	GalaxyMM T	54	5.17	2260	HSBC USTrea	9	4.69	65
FirstMerGv	48	5.09	234	GalaxyMMBKB	54	4.99	114	HnHrzTScInstSwp	26	4.44	401
FsrInstMn	39	5.32	3622	GalaxyPRes p	55	4.64	4810	HnHrzTrSecTr	26	4.69	1734
FirstrMM	40	4.89	864	GalaxyTrBKB	43	4.90	208	Harbor	81	5.68	132
FsrTreasA	54	4.75	2514	GalaxTrR	43	4.91	594	HarrisCashC	31	5.66	3031
FsrTreasl	54	4.60	2494	GalaxyTrsTr	43	5.05	702	HTInsgtGvN p	44	5.25	315
FirstrUSGov	52	4.89	14	GnGvSec	69	5.12	619	HarrisGovtC	44	5.60	277
FlagCashResA	44	5.19	13	GeneralB p	87	4.99	3783	HarrisMMktN	31	5.31	1378

maturity of 81 days, on average. It provided an annualized yield of 5.68 percent to its investors over the last week. It has $132 million in assets.

Asset Management Account

asset management account
An account that combines deposit accounts with a brokerage account and provides a single consolidated statement.

An **asset management account** combines deposit accounts with a brokerage account that is used to buy or sell stocks. The advantage of an asset management account is that it provides a single consolidated statement showing the ending balances and activity of all the accounts. Asset management accounts are available at some depository institutions and brokerage services. The financial institutions that offer these accounts require that the sum of all the accounts in the asset management account exceed some minimum amount, such as $15,000. One of the special benefits that may be offered to individuals who maintain an asset management account is a so-called sweep account that sweeps any unused balance in the checking account into the money market account at the end of the day. Thus, any unused balance remains available for writing checks and earns interest in the meantime.

Comparison of Money Market Investments

The various money market investments are compared in Exhibit 6.3. In general, there is a tradeoff between the expected return on the investment and the degree of liquidity or size of the investment. Money market investments that offer a higher return tend to have less liquidity.

The relationship between the returns and the liquidity of money market investments is illustrated graphically in Exhibit 6.4. Checking accounts offer the most liquidity but provide no return. At the other extreme, a one-year CD provides the highest return but has less liquidity than the other money market instruments.

Exhibit 6.3   Comparison of Money Market Investments

Money Market Investment	Advantages	Disadvantages
Checking account	Very liquid	No interest
Now account	Very liquid	Low interest rate; minimum balance required
MMDA	Liquid	Low interest rate
Savings account	Liquid	Low interest rate
Certificate of deposit (CD)	Relatively high interest rate	Less liquid
Treasury bill	Relatively high interest rate	High minimum purchase
Money market fund (MMF)	Liquid	Not as liquid as checking or NOW accounts
Asset management account	Convenient	High minimum balance required

Exhibit 6.4   Comparison of the Liquidity and Returns of Money Market Instruments

Return

● One-Year CD

  ● Three-Month CD

    ● Three-Month T-bill

      ● Savings Account

        ● MMDA

          ● NOW Account

                    Checking Account

                                    Liquidity

RISK OF MONEY MARKET INVESTMENTS

When investors consider investing short-term funds in various money market instruments, they must recognize their exposure to risk, or the uncertainty surrounding the potential return. Money market investments are vulnerable to three types of risk: (1) credit risk, (2) interest rate risk, and (3) liquidity risk. Each of these types of risk can cause uncertainty about the potential return to be earned from a particular investment.

6.3   Financial Planning Online: Impact of Different Deposit Rates on Your Wealth

Go to:
http://www.financenter.com/
products/analyzers/savings.fcs

Click on:
"How much difference will the rate make?"

This Web site provides:
estimates of the future savings that you will accumulate over time at different deposit rates. These estimates illustrate the additional savings you will accumulate by depositing your money in a financial institution that pays a higher interest rate.

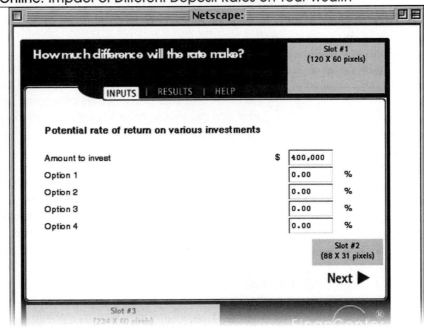

Credit Risk

credit risk (or default risk)
The risk that a borrower may not repay on a timely basis.

When you invest in money market securities, you may be exposed to **credit risk** (also referred to as **default risk**), which is the risk that the borrower will not repay on a timely basis. The borrower may make late payments or may even default on the credit; in that event, you will receive only a portion (or none) of the money you invested.

Many money market investments are insulated from credit risk. For example, deposits at commercial banks and savings institutions are insured up to $100,000 by the Federal Deposit Insurance Corporation (FDIC). Treasury securities are backed by the federal government. Some MMFs are exposed to credit risk, because they invest in large deposits of financial institutions that are insured only up to $100,000 and in short-term securities issued by firms.

Interest Rate Risk

interest rate risk
The risk that the value of an investment could decline as a result of a change in interest rates.

Interest rate risk is the risk that the value of an investment could decline as a result of a change in interest rates.

Example

Assume that you purchase a one-year T-bill that offers you a return of 5 percent over the next year. Three months after you purchase the Treasury security, interest rates rise. Now you are disappointed that you locked in this investment at 5 percent because other investments (including existing T-bills) are now offering an annualized return of about 6 percent for investors who hold the security until maturity. You can sell your T-bill in the secondary market, but you realize that investors will pay a relatively low price for it because they can buy new securities that offer an annualized return of 6 percent. This explains why the value of a debt security decreases in response to an increase in interest rates.

If you do not want to sell your T-bill for a discounted price, you can simply hold on to it until it matures. However, the return on your investment over the entire one-year period will be only 5 percent even though T-bills issued after you purchased your security are offering higher returns. Neither of your two options is desirable.

Investors who wish to limit their exposure to interest rate risk can invest in debt securities that have shorter maturities. If you had held a three-month security instead of a one-year security in the previous example, you could have redeemed your security at maturity after three months and reinvested your money at the prevailing higher interest rate.

Liquidity Risk

Recall that liquidity represents your ability to cover any short-term cash deficiencies. To be liquid, an investment should be easily converted to cash. Some

liquidity risk
The potential loss that could occur as a result of converting an investment into cash.

investments are subject to a loss when they are converted to cash. **Liquidity risk** is the potential loss that could occur as a result of converting an investment to cash. For example, a retail CD has liquidity risk because it cannot be sold in the secondary market. You would suffer a penalty if you tried to redeem it before maturity at the financial institution where you invested in the CD.

The liquidity risk of an investment is influenced by the activity in its secondary market. If a particular debt security has a strong secondary market, it can usually be sold quickly and at less of a discount than a debt security with an inactive secondary market. For example, you can easily sell a T-bill in a secondary market, which is why T-bills are more liquid than CDs.

RISK MANAGEMENT OF MONEY MARKET INVESTMENTS

Risk management of money market investments involves (1) assessing the risk exhibited by the investments and (2) using your assessment of risk and your unique financial situation to determine the optimal allocation of your short-term funds among money market investments.

Risk Assessment of Money Market Investments

Individuals must consider the risk-return tradeoff before making investment decisions. The money market securities described in this chapter tend to be insulated from credit risk because they are insured or backed by the government. Treasury securities and small bank deposits are largely free from credit risk. One exception is an investment in MMFs that invest in commercial paper. If the commercial paper held by a particular MMF defaults, the return generated by the MMF will be adversely affected, and so will the return to investors who invested in that MMF.

As mentioned earlier, money market investments that have shorter maturities have less interest rate risk. In addition, investments in MMFs tend to have the least liquidity risk, especially when their investments focus on securities that will mature within the next month. Treasury securities that will mature in the next month or so also have very little liquidity risk.

Securities that are exposed to risk have to offer higher yields than less risky investments to attract funds from investors. In other words, the prospect of a higher return compensates investors for taking on a higher level of risk. Investors can earn a higher return by investing in MMFs that hold investments subject to credit risk (such as commercial paper). The yields are also higher for securities that are particularly vulnerable to interest rate risk. Recall that debt securities with shorter maturities offer lower annualized yields. A three-month debt security typically offers a slightly lower annualized yield than a one-year security. However, the debt securities with longer maturities have more exposure to interest rate risk.

Yields are also higher for securities that are more exposed to liquidity risk. A retail CD must offer a slightly higher yield than a Treasury security with the same maturity because the Treasury security is more liquid.

Determining the Optimal Allocation of Money Market Investments

In general, your money management should be guided by the following steps:

1. Anticipate your upcoming bills, and ensure that you have sufficient funds in your checking account.

2. Estimate the additional funds that you might need in the near future, and consider investing them in an investment that offers sufficient liquidity (such as an MMF). You may even keep a little extra in reserve here for unanticipated expenses.

3. Use the remaining funds in a manner that will earn you a higher return, within your level of risk tolerance.

The optimal allocation for you will likely be different from the optimal allocation for another individual. An individual whose future net cash flows will be far short of upcoming expenses will need to keep a relatively large proportion of funds in a liquid investment (such as a checking account or a NOW account). Another person who has sufficient cash flows to cover expenses will not need much liquidity. The difference is illustrated in Exhibit 6.5. Even though the two individuals have the same level of net cash flows, one person must maintain more liquidity than the other because of the upcoming expenses.

Your decision on how to invest your short-term funds (after determining how much money to maintain in your checking account) should account for your willingness to tolerate risk. If you want to minimize all forms of risk, you may simply consider investing all of your funds in an MMF that always focuses on Treasury securities maturing within a month or less. However, you will likely improve on the yield if you are willing to accept

Exhibit 6.5   How Liquidity Is Affected by Anticipated Expenses

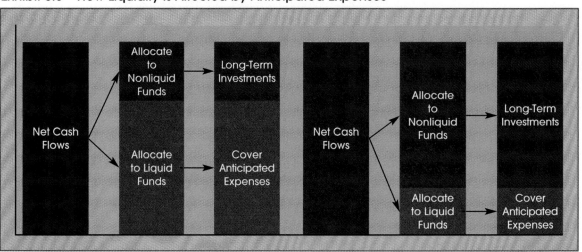

some degree of risk. For example, if you know that you will not need your funds for at least six months and do not expect interest rates to rise substantially over that period, you might consider investing your funds in a six-month retail CD. A compromise would be to invest a portion of your short-term funds in the six-month retail CD and the remaining funds in the MMF that focuses on Treasury securities. The CD offers you a higher expected return (although less liquidity), while the MMF offers you liquidity in case you need funds immediately.

Example

 Stephanie Spratt has $2,000 available to allocate to money market investments. She knows that she will need $400 to cover several small bills in the next week and may also need $600 in a month or so to pay for repairs on her car engine. She does not expect to need the other funds for at least six months. Her financial institution offers the following annualized yields on various money market instruments:

	Annualized Yield (%)
Checking account	0
NOW account ($500 minimum balance)	2.0
Savings deposit	3.0
MMDA ($2,500 minimum balance)	4.0
MMF ($300 minimum balance)	4.0
Three-month CD	4.5
Six-month CD	5.2
One-year CD	6.0

Stephanie's existing checking account has a balance close to zero. She also has an MMF with a balance of $300, which she must maintain to meet the minimum balance. She will first focus on meeting her liquidity needs and then decide how to invest the remaining funds that are not needed to cover possible expenses. She decides to allocate $400 to her checking account so that she can write several checks to cover her upcoming bills. It is not worthwhile to invest these funds elsewhere as she will need the funds soon, and the checking account is the only investment that will allow her to write several small checks.

She knows that she might need another $600 in the near future for car repairs, but wants to earn as high a return as possible until she needs the money. She immediately eliminates the MMDA from consideration because it would require a minimum balance of $2,500. She decides to invest the $600 in her MMF. She can write a check from this account to cover the car repairs; meanwhile, the funds invested in the MMF will earn 4 percent interest on an annualized basis.

Stephanie now has $1,000 remaining to allocate and anticipates that she will not need the money for at least six months. She does not consider investing the $1,000 in a one-year CD, even though it offers a relatively high interest rate, because she may need the funds in six months. She decides to invest the $1,000 in a six-month CD, so that she can earn a relatively high return.

If Stephanie had excess funds that she would not need for a few years, she would consider investing the residual in other investments (such as stocks) that offer a higher potential return. The potential return and risk of these other investments are discussed in Part 4.

HOW MONEY MANAGEMENT FITS WITHIN YOUR FINANCIAL PLAN

The following are the key money management decisions that should be included in your financial plan:

1. How can you ensure that you can pay your anticipated bills on time?

2. How can you maintain adequate liquidity in case you incur unanticipated expenses?

3. How should you invest any remaining funds among money market investments?

By making proper decisions, you can avoid using credit and can maximize the return on your liquid assets. As an example, Exhibit 6.6 shows how money market decisions apply to Stephanie Spratt's financial plan.

Exhibit 6.6   How Money Management Fits within Stephanie Spratt's Financial Plan

Goals for Money Management

1. Maintain sufficient liquidity to ensure that all anticipated bills are paid on time.
2. Maintain sufficient liquidity in case I incur unanticipated expenses.
3. Invest any excess funds in deposits that offer the highest return while ensuring adequate liquidity.

Analysis

	Amount	Payment Method
Monthly cash inflows	$2,500	Direct deposited into checking account.
Typical monthly expenses	1,400	Write checks to pay these bills.
Other expenses for clothing or recreation	700	Use credit cards and then pay the credit card balance by check once a month.

Decisions

Decision on How to Ensure Adequate Liquidity to Cover Anticipated Expenses:

The two paychecks I receive each month amounting to $2,500 after taxes are direct deposited into my checking account. I can use this account to cover the $1,400 in anticipated bills each month. I can also use this account to write a check for the monthly credit card bill. I will attempt to leave about $400 extra in the checking account because my expenses may vary from month to month.

Decision on How to Ensure Liquidity to Cover Unanticipated Expenses:

I will also attempt to maintain about $2,500 in a money market fund or a money market deposit account in case I need additional funds. I can earn interest on this money while ensuring liquidity.

Decision on How to Invest Remaining Funds so as to Achieve the Highest Return While Enhancing Liquidity:

As I accumulate additional savings, I will invest in certificates of deposit with short terms to maturity (such as one month). This money will not be as liquid as the MMF or MMDA, but it will be accessible when the CD matures. The interest rate on the CD will be higher than the interest I can earn on my MMF or MMDA.

DISCUSSION QUESTIONS

1. How would Stephanie's money management decisions be different if she were a single mother of two children?

2. How would Stephanie's money management decisions be affected if she were 35 years old? If she were 50 years old?

SUMMARY

Money management involves the selection of short-term investments that satisfy your liquidity needs and also provide you with an adequate return on your investment. It is challenging because the short-term investments that offer relatively high returns tend to have less liquidity.

Popular short-term investments considered for money management include checking accounts, NOW accounts, savings accounts, CDs, MMDAs, Treasury bills, money market funds, and asset management accounts. Checking accounts and NOW accounts offer the most liquidity. CDs and T-bills offer the highest return.

The risks related to money market investments are credit (default) risk, interest rate risk, and liquidity risk. The money market investments offered by depository institutions are insured and insulate you from the risk that the institution could default. Investments in T-bills have no default risk because they are backed by the federal government. Money market securities tend to have a low level of default risk because they have short-term maturities. They also have relatively low liquidity risk because of the short-term maturities of their assets.

When applying money management, you should first anticipate your expenses in the next month and maintain enough funds in your checking account to cover those expenses. In addition, you should estimate the potential level of unanticipated expenses (such as possible car repairs) and maintain enough funds in a short-term investment such as a money market fund to cover these expenses. Finally, invest the remaining funds to earn a high return within your level of risk tolerance.

Integrating the Key Concepts

Your money management decisions determine your level of liquidity and also affect other parts of your financial plan. If your money market investments have a high degree of liquidity, you have more funds that you can use. The amount of liquidity that you maintain is partly determined by your budgeting decisions (Part 1) because you will need more liquidity if your cash outflows are expected to exceed your cash inflows.

The decision to maintain a high degree of liquidity can affect your financing decisions (Part 3) because the more of your cash that you can use, the less you will need to rely on loans. Your money management will also affect your investment decisions (Part 4) because you can focus on investments that are not liquid if you already have sufficient liquidity from your money market investments.

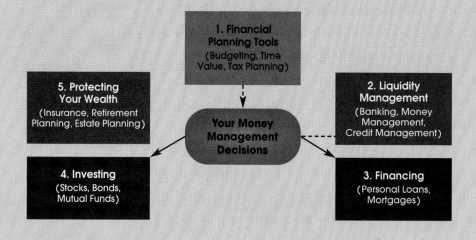

REVIEW QUESTIONS

1. Define money management. How does it differ from long-term investment of funds or long-term borrowing?

2. What is liquidity? How is your personal cash flow statement used to help manage your liquidity? How does money management relate to the cash flow statement?

3. Name some ways an individual might handle a cash flow deficiency. Which way would be preferable? Why? What is the opportunity cost of having excessive amounts of liquid funds?

4. What two factors affect the return on short-term investments? What is the relationship between liquidity and return?

5. Why do individuals use checking accounts? What is the disadvantage of having funds in a checking account? Explain overdraft protection and stop payment orders. Are all bank fee structures the same?

6. What is a NOW account? How is it different from a regular checking account? How does a savings account compare with a NOW account?

7. What terms does a financial institution specify for certificates of deposit? Why are rates on CDs higher than those on savings accounts? What is the opportunity cost of higher rates on CDs? What factor would most affect your choice of maturity date on a CD?

8. How does a money market deposit account (MMDA) differ from a NOW account? When might a depositor use an MMDA?

9. What are Treasury securities? What is a T-bill? How is it denominated? How do you earn a return on a T-bill? How is the return calculated?

10. Compare the interest rates offered on T-bills and CDs. Which type of investment is more liquid? Why?

11. What are money market funds (MMFs)? What types of securities do they invest in? What is commercial paper? Are MMFs risky investments? Are they liquid?

12. What is an asset management account? Discuss the advantages of such an account as well as its requirements.

13. Compare the various money market investments with respect to return and liquidity. Give examples.

14. Name and describe the three types of risk to which money market investments are vulnerable.

15. Compare the money market investments described in this chapter in terms of their vulnerability to credit risk, interest rate risk, and liquidity risk. What is the risk-return tradeoff for these investments?

16. What steps should you take to determine the best allocation of your money market investments? What factors should you consider?

FINANCIAL PLANNING PROBLEMS

1. Teresa has just opened a NOW account that pays 3.5 percent interest. If she maintains a minimum balance of $500 for the next 12 months, how much interest will she earn?

2. Nancy is depositing $2,500 in a six-month CD that pays 4.25 percent interest. How much interest will she accrue if she holds the CD until maturity?

3. Travis has invested $3,000 in a three-month CD at 4 percent. How much will Travis have to reinvest when the CD matures?

4. Teddy has invested $10,000 in an 18-month CD that pays 6.25 percent. How much interest will Teddy receive at maturity? (Hint: Remember to compound.)

5. Troy paid $9,600 to purchase a T-bill with a face value of $10,000. What is Troy's return if he holds the T-bill to maturity?

6. Davis has $20,000 excess cash to invest. He can purchase a $20,000 T-bill for $19,400 or two $10,000 T-bills for $9,600 each. Which will give him the better return?

7. Stacy purchased a $40,000 T-bill for $38,400. A few months later, Stacy sold the T-bill for $39,000. What was Stacy's return on the T-bill?

8. Brenda purchased a $30,000, 90-day T-bill for $29,550. What will Brenda's return be when the T-bill matures? What will her annualized rate be?

9. On June 1, Amy deposited $4,000 in an MMDA that pays 5 percent interest. On October 31, Amy invested $2,000 in a three-month CD that pays 6 percent. At the end of the year, how much interest will Amy have earned, assuming she hasn't taken anything out of the money market deposit account?

10. Thomas can invest $10,000 by purchasing a 1-year T-bill for $9,275, or he can place the $10,000 in a 12-month CD paying 8 percent. Which will give the higher return? In addition to return, what else must Thomas consider when making his investment decision?

FINANCIAL PLANNING ONLINE EXERCISES

Go to http://www.financenter.com/products/analyzers/savings.fcs, and click on "How much will my savings be worth?" Using this site, you can find the answer to the question, "How Much Will My Savings Be Worth?"

1. By inputting an investment amount, the monthly deposit, the return, the period of investment, the tax rate, and the inflation rate, you can calculate the value of your investment. Input $5,000 as the initial investment, $100 for the monthly deposit, 6 percent for the return, 25 percent for the federal tax rate, 6 percent for the state tax rate, 3 percent for the inflation rate, and 20 years for the period invested. Click on "Results." How much will your investment be worth in 20 years, both with and without taxes? Click on the Graphs option to view the results graphically.

2. Click on the input tab to go back to the input page. Change the monthly deposit to $300. How much will your investment be worth in 20 years?

3. Click on the input tab to go back to the input page. Change the period of investment to 30 years. How much more money will you be able to accumulate in 30 years as opposed to 20?

4. Change the rate you can earn on your investment from 6 to 8 percent and evaluate the results and graph.

Go to http://www.financenter.com/products/analyzers/budget.fcs, and click on "How much am I spending?"

1. To determine how much you need to save for a major purchase, input $8,000 as the amount you need, $1,000 as what you will invest now, a $200 monthly deposit, 36 months for the savings period, 6 percent return, 25 percent federal tax rate, and 6 percent state tax rate. Will your investing plan allow you to achieve your goal? If not, how should you revise your plan? Click on Graphs to view the results graphically.

2. Click on the input tab to go back to the input page. To accumulate $15,000 for a down payment on a house, you plan to save $150 per month over a five-year period at an 8 percent return. Will your plan work? If not, how should you revise it?

3. So, you want to be a millionaire. Use the same calculator to determine how to accumulate $1 million to use for your retirement with an initial investment of $25,000, monthly investment of $750, and a 7 percent return over a 30-year period. Will your plan work? If not, what adjustments can you make?

Building Your Own Financial Plan

Money market investments provide vehicles to assist you in accomplishing your short-term financial goals. Refer back to the three to five short-term goals you established in Chapter 1. For each goal, rate the importance (high, medium, or low) of the following items:

1. Liquidity

2. Risk

3. Fees/minimum balance

4. Return

Now, rank each of the money market investments as good, fair, or poor with respect to how they meet your four goals. For example, a checking account might be ranked good for liquidity, fair for risk, and poor for fees and return. Once you have established the priority of your goals and ranked the money market investments, select the money market investment that will best help you achieve each short-term goal.

 Enter the information on the template for this chapter in the *Financial Planning Workbook* and on the CD-ROM.

Note: You may find it necessary to revisit some of the financial institutions involved in your Chapter 5 analysis to gather the information necessary to select the most appropriate money market investment for each short-term goal.

The Sampsons—A Continuing Case

 Recall from Chapter 2 that the Sampsons currently have about $300 in cash and $1,700 in their checking account. This amount should be enough to cover upcoming bills. Every month they attempt to maintain just the minimum amount of liquid assets. They have just started to save money and will deposit the savings in the bank CD they chose in Chapter 5. This money, which is earmarked for a down payment on a car and for their children's education, will be tied up for the maturity of the CD. Therefore, these savings are not a source of liquidity. Review the Sampsons' recent cash flow statement and their personal balance sheet, and offer them advice on how they can improve their liquidity situation.

The Sampson's Personal Cash Flow Statement

Cash Inflows (Monthly)	**$4,000**
Cash Outflows (Monthly)	
Rent	$900
Cable TV	60
Electricity and water	80
Telephone	70
Groceries	500
Health care insurance and expenses	160
Clothing	300
Car expenses (insurance, maintenance, and gas)	400
School expenses	100
Recreation	700
Total Cash Outflows	**$3,270**
Net Cash Flows (Monthly)	**+$730**

The Sampson's Personal Balance Sheet

Assets

Liquid Assets	
Cash	$300
Checking account	1,700
Savings account	0
Total liquid assets	**$2,000**

Household Assets	
Home	$130,000
Cars	9,000
Furniture	3,000
Total household assets	**$142,000**

Investment Assets	
Stocks	0
Total investment assets	0

Total Assets	**$144,000**

Liabilities and Net Worth

	Current Liabilities
Credit card balance	$2,000
Total current liabilities	$2,000
	Long-Term Liabilities
Mortgage	100,000
Car loan	0
Total long-term liabilities	$100,000
Total Liabilities	**$102,000**
Net Worth	**$42,000**

1. Based on the cash flow statement and personal balance sheet, do the Sampsons have adequate liquidity? If not, what level of savings should they maintain for liquidity purposes?

2. Advise the Sampsons on money market investments they should consider to provide them with adequate liquidity.

IN-TEXT STUDY GUIDE

True/False:

1. Money management involves a series of decisions you make over a long-term period regarding your cash inflows and outflows.

2. Money management is related to the cash budget because it determines how you use excess funds or obtain funds if your cash outflows exceed your cash inflows.

3. Liquidity is an individual's ability to cover any cash deficiencies that he may experience.

4. Some depository institutions allow for overdraft protection, which protects a customer who writes a check for an amount that exceeds the CD balance.

5. An advantage of a NOW account over a traditional checking account is that it pays interest, although the interest is relatively low compared with many other investments.

6. A traditional savings account offered by a depository institution pays an interest rate on deposits that is lower than that offered on a NOW account.

7. Common maturity dates of retail CDs are 7 years, 10 years, and 20 years.

8. Certificates of deposit are highly liquid.

9. An MMDA differs from a NOW account in that it provides only limited checking services while paying a higher interest rate than that offered on NOW accounts.

10. Interest rate risk is the risk that the value of an investment could decline as a result of a change in interest rates.

11. Although liquidity is necessary, an opportunity cost is incurred when maintaining an excessive amount of liquid funds.

Multiple Choice:

1. Individuals with short-term funds would probably not invest them in
   a. checking accounts.
   b. corporate bonds.
   c. NOW accounts.
   d. CDs

2. Peter Udal just transferred $1,300 to a NOW account that offers an interest rate of 2.5 percent. Over one year, Peter will earn interest of
   a. $39.00.
   b. $25.00.
   c. $32.50.
   d. none of the above

3. You just placed $3,200 in a one-month (31-day) CD that offers an annualized interest rate of 5.7 percent. When the CD matures, you will receive _____ in interest.
   a. $15.49
   b. $182.40
   c. $14.52
   d. $45.48

4. When the U.S. government wants to spend more money than it receives in taxes, it can obtain additional funds by _____ Treasury securities.
   a. buying
   b. selling
   c. buying or selling
   d. none of the above

5. _____ is the risk that a borrower will not repay on a timely basis.
   a. Credit (default) risk
   b. Interest rate risk
   c. Liquidity risk
   d. None of the above

6. Which of the following money market investments is probably the least liquid?
   a. checking account
   b. NOW account
   c. money market funds
   d. CDs

7. Treasury bills are purchased at a(n) _____ par value.
   a. premium relative to
   b. discount relative to
   c. amount equal to
   d. none of the above

8. Walter Lemmon just paid $9,500 to purchase a one-year Treasury bill with a par value of $10,000. The return on Walter's T-bill will be
   a. 5.26 percent.
   b. 5.00 percent.
   c. 10.00 percent.
   d. None of the above

The following information refers to questions 9 and 10.

You just paid $9,650 to purchase a Treasury bill with a par value of $10,000 and a maturity of 182 days.

9. The annualized return on the T-bill is
   a. 3.63 percent.
   b. 7.02 percent.
   c. 7.27 percent.
   d. 3.50 percent.

10. If you hold the T-bill for 90 days and then sell it in the secondary market for $9,870, your annualized return is
    a. 7.02 percent.
    b. 7.27 percent.
    c. 4.57 percent.
    d. 9.25 percent.

11. Short-term debt instruments issued by large corporations are called
    a. money market deposit accounts (MMDAs).
    b. commercial paper.
    c. money market funds (MMFs).
    d. CDs.

12. Which of the following is the least liquid?
    a. checking account
    b. corporate bonds
    c. NOW account
    d. money market fund

13. _____ is the potential loss that could occur as a result of converting an investment to cash.
    a. Credit (default) risk
    b. Interest rate risk
    c. Liquidity risk
    d. None of the above

14. In general, money market securities that have _____ maturities have _____ interest rate risk.
    a. longer; less
    b. shorter; more
    c. shorter; less
    d. Answers (a) and (b) are correct.

15. Generally, yields are _____ for securities that are exposed to _____ liquidity risk.
    a. higher; more
    b. higher; less
    c. lower; more
    d. none of the above

The following information refers to questions 16 and 17.

You just paid $9,875 to purchase a Treasury bill with a par value of $10,000 and a maturity of 91 days.

16. The annualized return on the T-bill is
    a. 1.25 percent.
    b. 4.95 percent.
    c. 1.27 percent.
    d. 5.08 percent.

17. Assuming you hold the T-bill for 45 days and then sell it in the secondary market for $9,950, your annualized return is
    a. 6.16 percent.
    b. 6.08 percent.
    c. 7.50 percent.
    d. 7.59 percent.

18. _____ is not a money market investment.
    a. A checking account
    b. A Treasury bill
    c. A common stock
    d. A money market fund

19. A _____ offered by a depository institution specifies a minimum amount that must be
invested, a maturity date on which the deposit
matures, and an annualized interest rate.
   a. NOW account
   b. certificate of deposit
   c. savings account
   d. money market deposit account

20. If you want to cash in a CD without being
charged by your bank, you can
   a. cash it in two months before maturity.
   b. wait until it matures.
   c. write checks against the CD account.
   d. none of the above

Chapter 7

Managing Your Credit

The ability to obtain credit and use it properly is a key to personal finance. Credit enables you to purchase products and services before you have the funds to pay for them. Proper use of credit can minimize your finance costs and therefore reduce your future cash outflows. In this way, proper decisions on how to use credit will enhance your wealth.

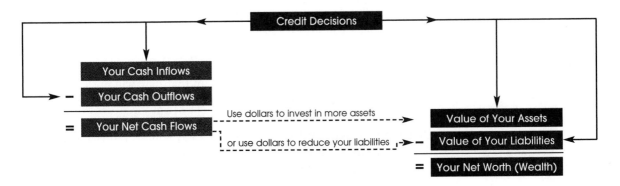

The objectives of this chapter are to:

- provide a background on credit,
- explain the key characteristics of credit cards, and
- offer tips on using credit cards.

BACKGROUND ON CREDIT

credit
Funds provided by a creditor to a borrower that will be repaid by the borrower in the future with interest.

Credit represents funds a creditor provides to a borrower that the borrower will repay in the future with interest. The funds borrowed are sometimes referred to as the principal, so repayment of credit may be segmented into interest and principal payments. Credit is frequently extended to borrowers as a loan with set terms such as the amount of credit provided and the maturity date when the credit will be repaid. For most types of loans, interest payments are made periodically (such as every quarter or year), and the principal payment is made at the maturity date, when the loan is to be terminated. This chapter focuses on the use of credit (which is often extended through credit cards), while other types of loans for large purchases such as a car or home are discussed in the next two chapters.

Advantages of Using Credit

Individuals borrow funds when the dollar amount of their purchases exceeds the amount of their available cash. Many individuals use borrowed funds to purchase a home or car or to pay their tuition fees, while others use credit (such as a credit card) for convenience when making day-to-day purchases.

Disadvantages of Using Credit

There can be a high cost to using credit. If you borrow too much money, you may have difficulty making your credit card payments in the future. It is easier to obtain credit than to pay it back. And having a credit line can tempt you to make impulse purchases that you cannot afford. If you are unable to repay the credit you receive, you may not be able to obtain credit again or will have to pay a very high interest rate to obtain it. Your ability to save money will also be reduced if you have large credit payments, as illustrated in Exhibit 7.1.

Warren Buffett, a successful billionaire investor, recently offered financial advice to some students. He told them that they will not make financial progress if they are borrowing money at 18 percent (a typical interest rate on credit cards). In recent years, more than 1 million people in the United States have filed for bankruptcy each year. A primary reason for these bankruptcies is that the individuals obtained more credit than they could repay. Even if obtaining credit at a high interest rate does not cause personal bankruptcy, it limits the potential increase in personal wealth.

Establish a Credit History

You receive credit when you use utilities such as water, electric power, and telephone services. The utility company extends credit by providing a service, and you are billed at the end of a period (such as one month). Thus, utility companies provide a form of short-term credit. To obtain this credit, you normally must make an initial deposit at the time the account is created. When you have accounts with utility companies, you develop a credit

Exhibit 7.1   Impact of Credit Payments on Saving

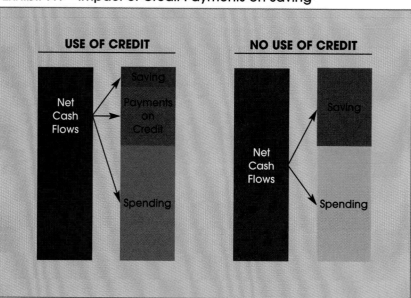

7.1   Financial Planning Online: Personal Credit Counseling

Go to:
http://banking.yahoo.com

Click on:
Credit Counseling

This Web site provides:
links to credit counseling services for individuals who need help in managing credit.

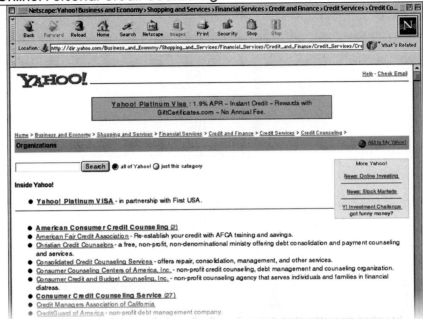

history over time that documents how timely you pay your bills. You can establish a favorable credit history by paying your utility bills before the due date. Doing so indicates to potential creditors that you may also repay other credit provided to you in a timely manner.

Impact of the Interest Rate on Credit Payments

simple interest rate
The percentage of credit that must be paid as interest on an annual basis.

When you borrow funds, you are charged an interest rate. The **simple interest rate** is the percentage of the credit that you must pay as interest on an annual basis.

Example

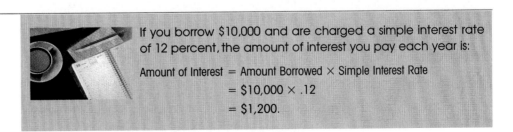

If you borrow $10,000 and are charged a simple interest rate of 12 percent, the amount of interest you pay each year is:

Amount of Interest = Amount Borrowed × Simple Interest Rate
= $10,000 × .12
= $1,200.

Exhibit 7.2 shows the amount of interest you would pay per year on a $10,000 loan at various simple interest rates, as well as the total amount of interest that would be paid over a four-year period. Notice how much larger

Exhibit 7.2 How Interest Payments Are Influenced by Interest Rates

Simple Interest Rate	Simple Interest Payment per Year	Total Simple Interest Payments over Four Years
6%	$600	$2,400
8	800	3,200
10	1,000	4,000
12	1,200	4,800
14	1,400	5,600
16	1,600	6,400
18	1,800	7,200
20	2,000	8,000

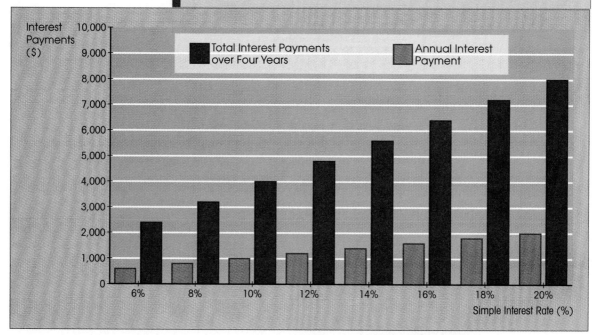

annual percentage rate (APR)

The simple interest rate including any fees charged by the creditor.

the interest payments are when you pay a higher interest rate. When obtaining credit, it is important to seek out the lowest interest rate possible.

The **annual percentage rate (APR)** on credit is the simple interest rate after including any fees (such as an application processing fee) imposed by the creditor. The APR is useful because it allows you to easily compare financing costs among various possible creditors.

CREDIT CARDS

The easiest way to establish credit is to apply for a credit card. There is no shortage of credit card companies eager to extend you credit in today's society. A credit card allows you to purchase products on credit wherever that card is honored. You receive a statement once a month that identifies the purchases you made with the credit card during that period. Normally, credit cards are not used for very large expenditures such as cars or homes, but they are very convenient for smaller purchases, such as meals at restaurants, gasoline, clothing, car repairs, and even groceries. In particular, credit cards offer three advantages. First, you can purchase products and services without carrying a large amount of cash or a checkbook. Second, you obtain free financing until the credit card statement arrives. Third, you receive a monthly statement that contains a consolidated list of the purchases you made with the credit card, which enables you to keep track of your spending. In some cases, you receive an annual statement as well, detailing expenses by category, which can be useful in preparing your income tax return.

Applying for a Credit Card

When you apply for a credit card, potential creditors obtain information from you, from credit bureaus, and about the economy so that they can assess your ability to repay credit.

Personal Information. When you apply for credit, you are asked to complete an application that typically requests the following information:

- Cash inflows: What is your monthly income?

- Cash outflows: How much do you spend per month?

- Credit history: Have you borrowed funds in the past? Did you repay any previous loans in a timely manner?

- Capital: Do you have any funds in the form of savings or stocks that can be used if necessary to cover future debt payments?

- Collateral: Do you have any assets that can be used as collateral to secure the borrowed funds? (If you could not repay your debt, you could sell these assets to obtain the funds needed to repay the loans.)

Creditors generally prefer that you have a high level of cash inflows, a low level of cash outflows, a large amount of capital and collateral, and a good credit history. Nevertheless, they commonly extend credit to individuals who do not have all of these attributes. For example, although creditors recognize that college students may not earn much income, they may still provide a limited amount of credit if they believe that the students are likely to repay it. Some creditors may also extend credit at higher interest rates to individuals who have a higher risk of defaulting.

P. Steiner

"An invitation to the gold card . . ."

Credit Check. Creditors typically obtain a credit report from a credit bureau to see if you have a history of late payments, existing unpaid bills, and other credit problems. Historical credit problems normally remain on a credit bureau's report for seven years. If you claim bankruptcy because you are unable to pay your bills, this information normally remains on a credit bureau's report for 10 years.

You can check to make sure that a credit bureau has accurate information about you by requesting an online report from a credit bureau, such as Equifax Credit Information Services (www.equifax.com) or Experian (www.experian.com). Each credit bureau has its own method of checking and reporting information, although all credit bureaus offer reports that indicate your ability to make payments on time. If you find any errors in your credit history, you can contact the bureaus to request that they be corrected. You are entitled to receive the name of any credit agency whose credit report prevents you from obtaining credit.

In addition to information about the applicant, creditors also consider existing economic conditions when they evaluate credit applications. If eco-

7.2   Financial Planning Online: Your Credit Card Report

Go to:
http://loan.yahoo.com/c/index.html

This Web site provides:
a credit report that assesses your creditworthiness. The report is available to you online for a small fee.

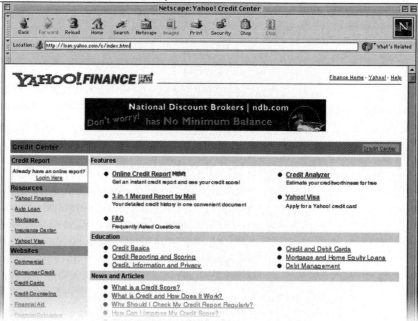

nomic conditions weaken, and you lose your job, you may be unable to repay your loan. Thus, creditors are less willing to extend credit when the economy is weak.

Types of Credit Cards

The most popular credit cards are MasterCard, Visa, and American Express. MasterCard and Visa allow your payments to be financed, but American Express requires that the balance be paid in full each month. These three types of cards are especially convenient because they are accepted by so many merchants. The merchants honor credit cards because they recognize that many consumers will make purchases only if they can use their credit cards. A credit card company receives a percentage (commonly between 2 and 4 percent) of the payments made to merchants with its credit card. For example, when you use your MasterCard to pay for a $100 car repair at a Shell Oil station, Shell will pay MasterCard a percentage, perhaps $3.

Many financial institutions issue MasterCard and Visa credit cards to individuals. Each financial institution makes its own arrangements with credit card companies to do the billing and financing when necessary. The institution provides financing if individuals using the card that it issued choose not to pay their balance in full when they receive a billing statement. The financial institutions benefit by providing financing because they typically earn a high rate of interest on the credit extended. Some universities and charitable organizations also issue MasterCard and Visa credit cards and also provide financing if needed.

retail (or proprietary) credit card

A credit card that is honored only by a specific retail establishment.

Retail Credit Cards. An alternative to MasterCard, Visa, and American Express credit cards is a **retail** (or **proprietary**) **credit card** that is issued for use at a specific retail establishment. For example, many retail stores (such as J.C. Penney and Macy's) and gas stations (such as Shell Oil and Exxon Mobil) issue their own credit card. If you use a Shell Oil credit card to pay for gas at a Shell station, Shell does not have to pay a small percentage of the proceeds to MasterCard or any other credit card company. You can usually obtain an application for a proprietary card when you are paying for products or services. You may be given instant credit when you complete the application. With most retail credit cards, you can pay a small portion of the balance owed each month, which means that the merchant finances your purchase. The interest rate you are charged when financing with retail credit cards is normally 18 percent or higher.

One disadvantage of a proprietary credit card is that it limits your purchases to a single merchant. You may find that the limit is an advantage if you are trying to restrict your use of credit so that you do not spend beyond your means. For example, you could use a Shell credit card to pay for gasoline and car repairs, but not to buy CDs, clothing, and many other products. Another disadvantage is that using many proprietary cards means you will have several credit card bills to pay each month; using one card for all purchases allows you to write only one check to cover all the credit card payments.

Credit Limit

Credit card companies set a credit limit, which specifies the maximum amount of credit allowed. The credit limit varies among individuals. It may be a relatively small amount (such as $300) for individuals who have a low income. The credit limit can usually be increased for individuals who prove that they are creditworthy by paying their credit card bills on time. Some credit card companies may allow a large limit (such as $10,000 or more) to households that have made their credit payments on a consistent basis and have higher incomes.

Annual Fee

Many credit card companies charge an annual fee, such as $50 or $70, for the privilege of using their card. The fee is sometimes waived for individuals who use their credit cards frequently and pay their credit card bills in a timely manner.

Incentives to Use the Card

Some credit card companies offer a bonus to cardholders. For example, they may award a point toward a free trip on an airline for every dollar spent. After accumulating 20,000 points, you receive a coupon for a free flight anywhere in the United States. Thus, if you spend $20,000 over the year on purchases and use this particular credit card for all of them, you will accumulate enough points by the end of the year to earn a free round-trip on a designated airline to any destination in the United States. Some airlines issue their own credit cards, which provide similar benefits.

Prestige Cards

prestige cards
Credit cards, such as gold cards or platinum cards, issued by a financial institution to individuals who have an exceptional credit standing.

Financial institutions may issue **prestige cards** to individuals who have an exceptional credit standing. These cards, sometimes referred to as gold cards or platinum cards, provide extra benefits to cardholders. For example, the card may provide insurance on rental cars and special warranties on purchases. Many cardholders receive an upgrade to a gold card or platinum card after they prove that they are creditworthy by making their payments on time.

Grace Period

Credit cards typically allow a grace period in which you are not charged any interest on your purchases. The grace period is usually about 20 days from the time the credit card statement is "closed" (any purchases after that date are put on the next month's bill) and the time the bill is due. The credit card issuer essentially provides you with free credit from the time you made the purchase until the bill is due.

7.3   Financial Planning Online: Estimating Your Future Credit Card Payments

Go to:

http://www.financenter.com/
products/analyzers/card.fcs

Click on:

"How important is the interest rate?"

This Web site provides:

estimates of your future credit card payments based on your credit card balance and the interest rate that you are charged.

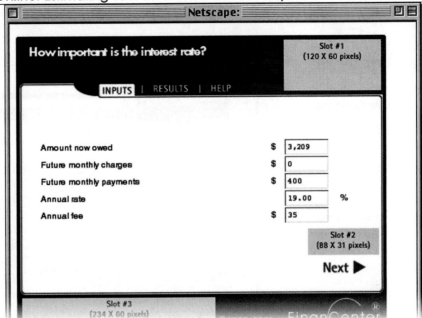

How important is the interest rate?   Slot #1
                                                      (120 X 60 pixels)

INPUTS | RESULTS | HELP

Amount now owed	$	3,209
Future monthly charges	$	0
Future monthly payments	$	400
Annual rate		19.00 %
Annual fee	$	35

Slot #2
(88 X 31 pixels)

Next ▶

Slot #3
(234 X 60 pixels)

Example

On June 1, Stephanie Spratt paid a car repair bill of $200 with her credit card. The closing date for that month's billing statement is June 30, and the bill is due around July 20. In this case, Stephanie receives about 50 days of free credit. On June 20, she purchased some clothing with her credit card. For that purchase, which is also on the billing statement, she receives about 30 days of free credit. On July 10, she purchased concert tickets with her credit card. This purchase occurs after the closing date of the billing statement and therefore will be listed on the next billing statement, which is due on about August 20. For this purchase, credit is extended for about 40 days.

Cash Advances

Many credit cards also allow cash advances. You can obtain cash advances at automated teller machines (ATMs). Since a cash advance represents credit extended by the sponsoring financial institution, interest is charged on this transaction. A transaction fee of 1 or 2 percent of the advance may also be charged. Credit card companies also provide checks that you can use to make purchases that cannot be made by credit card. The interest rate applied to cash advances is often higher than the interest rate charged on credit extended for specific credit card purchases. The interest rate is applied at the time of the cash advance; the grace period that applies to

7.4 Financial Planning Online: Reviews of Credit Card Issuers

Go to:
http://www.gomez.com

Click on:
Finance, then Credit Cards

This Web site provides:
reviews and ratings of various credit card issuers and describes features offered by each credit card.

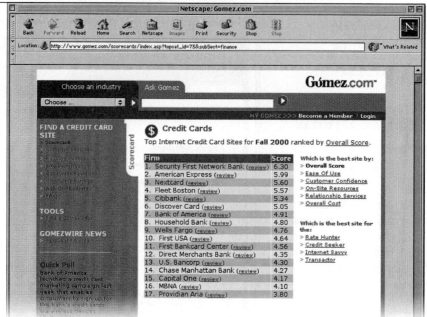

purchases with a credit card does not apply to cash advances. So, although cash advances are convenient, they can also be extremely costly.

Interest Rate

Some individuals use credit cards as a means of financing their purchases. That is, they pay only a portion of the credit card bill at the end of the month, and the sponsoring financial institution covers the remainder. This process reflects an extension of credit from the financial institution to the individual. An interest rate is applied to the credit that has been extended. The interest rate charged on credit is commonly between 15 and 20 percent on an annualized basis and does not vary much over time. Although financing is convenient for individuals who are short of funds, it is expensive and should be avoided if possible.

Many credit cards advertise a very low "teaser" interest rate, which is normally applicable for the first three or six months. Some people transfer their balances from one credit card to another as soon as the period of low interest rates has ended. The issuer of the first credit card may charge a fee when transferring the balance to a new credit card with the low teaser rate.

The finance charge is usually determined using either the previous balance method, the average daily balance method, or the adjusted balance method, which are described in the appendix to this chapter. For all methods, most purchases after the statement closing date are not considered when determining the finance charge because of the grace period. These purchases will appear on your next monthly statement. The finance charge applies only to balances that were not paid in full before their due date in the current billing period.

Credit Card Statement

Individuals typically receive a credit card bill at the end of their billing cycle. This bill lists all the purchases that were made with that credit card (an example is illustrated in Exhibit 7.3) during that period, as well as any balance carried over from the previous statement.

A credit card statement includes the following information:

- Previous balance: The amount carried over from the previous credit card statement.

- Purchases: The amount of credit used this month to make purchases.

- Cash advances: The amount of credit used this month by writing checks against the credit card account or making ATM withdrawals.

- Payments: The payments that you made to the sponsoring financial institution this billing cycle.

- Finance charge: The finance charge that is applied to any credit that exceeds the grace period or to any cash advances.

- New balance: The amount that you owe the financial institution as of now.

- Minimum payment: The minimum amount that you must pay.

The credit card statement details why your new balance differs from the balance shown on your statement in the previous month. The difference between the previous balance and the new balance results from any new purchases, cash advances, or finance charges, which increase your balance, versus any payments, which reduce your balance. The statement also shows the method of calculating finance charges.

Exhibit 7.3   Example of a Credit Card Purchase

Example

Suppose you have a credit card balance of $700 because of purchases you made last month that you did not pay off. During that billing period, you send in $200 to pay off part of your outstanding balance. You also use the credit card for $100 of new purchases. Since you relied on the sponsoring financial institution to pay $500 of last month's bill, you owe a finance charge. Assuming the institution imposes a finance charge of 1.5 percent per month and uses the adjusted balance method to determine the finance charge (which results in a finance charge of $7.50 as described in the chapter appendix), your credit card statement is as follows:

Previous Balance	$700.00
+ New Purchases	100.00
+ Cash Advances	0
− Payments	200.00
+ Finance Charges	7.50
= New Balance	$607.50

If you had paid the full amount of the previous balance ($700) during the billing period, the statement would have been as follows:

Previous Balance	$700
+ New Purchases	100
+ Cash Advances	0
− Payments	700
+ Finance Charges	0
= New Balance	$100

Thus, if you had paid $700 instead of $200, you would not have borrowed from the sponsoring financial institution and would not have incurred a finance charge. The new balance at the end of this billing period would simply be the amount of purchases that occurred over this period.

When you receive your account statement, you should always scrutinize it for errors. There may be a math error, a double charge for a purchase, or an incorrect amount on a purchase. Under consumer protection laws, you have the right to dispute possible errors.

Comparing Credit Cards

Some individuals have numerous credit cards, which can complicate record keeping and increase the probability of losing one or more credit cards. You can consolidate your bills by using just one credit card to cover your purchases. If you decide to use only one credit card, the following criteria will help you determine which card is most desirable.

Acceptance by Merchants. Some credit cards are more widely accepted than others. MasterCard and Visa are accepted by more merchants than other credit cards. You should make sure that your card is accepted by the types of merchants where you typically make your purchases.

Annual Fee. If you shop around, you may be able to find a credit card that does not charge an annual fee.

Interest Rate. The interest rate you are charged when you do not pay the entire credit card balance on time varies among financial institutions that provide financing on credit cards. This factor is especially relevant if you expect that you will rely on the financial institution to cover your balance in some periods.

As mentioned earlier, some credit cards offer a "teaser rate," which is substantially lower than the normal interest rate charged on borrowed funds. The teaser rate is used to entice you to apply for that card. Be aware, however, that this rate is likely to be available only for a short time before the normal interest rate is charged.

Maximum Limit. Some credit cards allow a higher maximum limit on monthly purchases than others. A very high maximum may not be necessary, and may tempt you to spend excessively. Make sure that the maximum limit is high enough to cover any necessary monthly purchases, but not so high that it encourages you to spend beyond what you can afford.

7.5 Financial Planning Online: The Best Credit Card for You

Go to:
http://www.bankrate.com/brm/rate/cc_home.asp

This Web site provides:
links to help you get the best overall credit card rate, the lowest introductory rate, frequent flier credit cards, and other special features.

TIPS ON USING CREDIT CARDS

Since you are likely to have one or more credit cards, consider the following tips to enjoy their use without incurring excessive costs.

Use a Credit Card Only If You Can Cover the Bill

Treat a credit card as a means of convenience, not a source of funds. Use a credit card only if you will have the cash to cover the payment when you receive your credit card statement. The use of this self-imposed credit limit is illustrated in Exhibit 7.4. The difference between your expected cash inflows and your expenses paid by check (such as rent) or by cash is the maximum amount of credit that you can use and still ensure full payment of the credit card balance. If you use less credit than this maximum amount, you will have some money left over for savings or investing.

Impose a Tight Credit Limit

As explained above, you can impose your own credit limit equal to any excess funds that you have so that you can pay the credit card bill in full when it is due. This strategy does not force you to set aside any savings. You may consider imposing a tighter credit limit as part of your budgeting process so that you can save a specific amount every month. This limit is illustrated in Exhibit 7.5. You determine the maximum amount of credit you will use each month only after accounting for all spending to be paid by check or cash, as well as a specified amount of saving.

Exhibit 7.4   Self-Imposed Credit Limit Based on Monthly
                    Cash Inflows

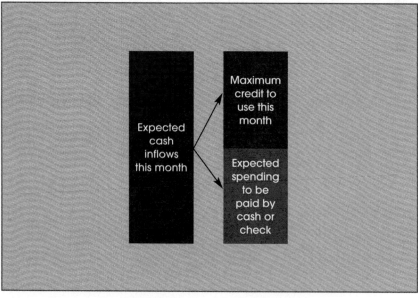

Exhibit 7.5   Self-Imposed Credit Limit Based on Monthly Cash Inflows and a Monthly Savings Goal

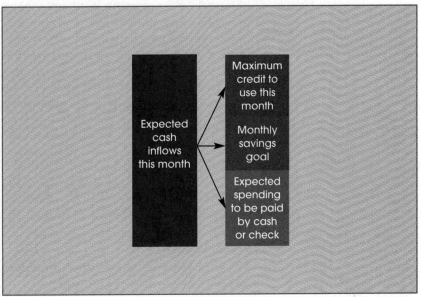

Pay Credit Card Bills before Investing Money

When you finance credit card balances, your cost of financing will normally be much higher than the return you are receiving on any money market investments that you hold. You should always pay off any balance on credit cards before you invest funds anywhere else.

Example

Stephanie Spratt just received a credit card bill for $700. The sponsoring financial institution charges a 20 percent annual interest rate on the outstanding balance. Stephanie has sufficient funds in her checking account to pay the credit card bill, but she is considering financing her payment. If she pays $100 toward the credit card bill and finances the remaining $600 for one year, she will incur interest expenses of:

Interest = Loan Amount × Interest Rate

= $600 × .20

= $120.

She could use the $600 to invest in savings rather than pay off her credit card bill. After one year, the $600 in a savings account will accumulate to $618 based on a 3 percent annual interest rate, as shown here:

Interest Earned on Deposit = Initial Deposit × Interest Rate

= $600 × .03

= 18.

Her interest owed on the credit card loan ($120) exceeds the interest earned on the deposit ($18) in one year by $102. Stephanie decides that she would be better off using her cash to pay off the credit card bill immediately. By using her money to cover the credit card bill, she gives up the opportunity to earn 3 percent on that money, but she also avoids the 20 percent rate charged on the credit card loan. Thus, her wealth is $102 higher as a result of using funds to pay off the credit card bill rather than investing in a bank deposit. Although she could have used the funds to invest in a high-risk investment that might achieve a greater return, paying off the credit card guarantees that she can avoid a 20 percent financing rate.

In general, you should always attempt to avoid credit cards when you have the money to cover the purchases instead. The likely return that you might earn from investing your money is usually less than the financing rate that you will be charged when you delay paying your credit card bills in full. Debit cards are a good alternative to credit cards because they offer the same convenience of not holding cash.

Some individuals use their money to invest in risky investments (such as stocks) rather than pay off their credit card bills. They apparently believe that their return from the investments will be higher than the cost of financing. Although some investments have generated large returns in specific years, it is difficult to earn returns that consistently exceed the high costs of

7.6   Financial Planning Online: Pay Off Your Debt or Invest in Savings?

Go to:
http://www.financenter.com/
products/analyzers/budget.fcs

Click on:
"Should I pay off debt or invest in savings?"

This Web site provides:
a recommendation of whether you should use your money to pay off your existing debt or invest in savings, based on information about your existing debt and the interest rate available on deposits.

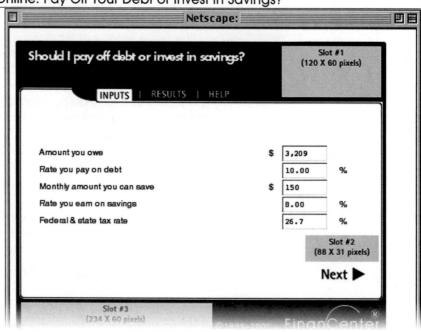

7.7   Financial Planning Online: Estimating the Time Necessary to Pay Off Your Balance

Go to:
http://www.financenter.com/
products/analyzers/budget.fcs

Click on:
"What will it take to pay off my
balance?"

This Web site provides:
an estimate of the number of
monthly payments that you
need to make to pay off your
credit card balance, based on
your existing balance, the
amount you can pay per
month, and the interest rate
you pay on your balance.

Netscape:		
What will it take to pay off my balance?		Slot #1 (120 X 60 pixels)

INPUTS | RESULTS | HELP

Amount now owed	$	3,209
Future monthly charges	$	12
Future monthly payments	$	350
Desired months to pay off		0
Annual fee	$	35
Annual rate		19.00 %

Future rate change
◉ None
○ An increase of `1.00` % per year
○ A decrease of `1.00` % per year

Slot #2

financing with credit cards. If the thrill of a good return on your investment makes you think about delaying your credit card payment, consider the following logic. When you use money to pay your credit card bill immediately, you are preventing a charge of about 20 percent interest. Therefore, you have effectively increased your savings by 20 percent by using these funds to pay off the credit card debt.

Use Savings If Necessary to Pay the Credit Card Bill on Time

If your recent cash inflows are not sufficient to cover the credit card bill, you should pull funds from savings (if there is no penalty for withdrawal) to cover the payment.

If You Cannot Avoid Credit Card Debt, Pay It Off before Other Debt

If you cannot pay off your credit card balance in full each month with income or with savings, at least pay off this balance as soon as possible. The interest rate charged on this debt is likely to be higher than interest rates on other loans. If you have other debt outstanding, you should pay off credit card debt first (assuming that the credit card debt has a higher interest rate). Even if you cannot pay your bill in full, you should still attempt to pay as much as possible so that you can minimize finance charges.

If possible, you may even consider taking out a home equity loan (discussed in the next chapter) to pay any credit card bills so that you can avoid the high interest expenses. This strategy makes sense only if your credit card debt is substantial (such as several thousand dollars), and the interest rate on the home equity loan is less than that on your credit card.

HOW CREDIT MANAGEMENT FITS WITHIN YOUR FINANCIAL PLAN

The following are the key credit management decisions that should be included within your financial plan:

1. What limit should you impose on your credit card?

2. When should you use credit?

By making proper decisions, you can avoid using credit and can maximize the return on your liquid assets. As an example, Exhibit 7.6 shows how credit decisions apply to Stephanie Spratt's financial plan.

Exhibit 7.6   How Credit Management Fits within Stephanie Spratt's Financial Plan

Goals for Managing Credit

1. Set my own limit on credit card purchases to ensure that I will always be able to pay off the credit balance in the same month.
2. Set a policy to avoid incurring high interest expenses on credit cards.

Analysis

Monthly Cash Inflows	$2,500
− Typical Monthly Expenses (paid by checks)	−1,400
= Amount of Funds Available	1,100

Liquid Assets	Balance	Annualized Interest Rate (%)
Cash	$100	0
Checking account balance	800	0
Money market fund	400	3.0
One-month CD	1,200	4.3
Credit card balance	600	20.0

Decisions

Decision on Credit Limit:

Given that I have $1,100 each month left from my salary after paying typical expenses (by check), I have $1,100 remaining that can be used for credit card purchases if necessary. I will impose a maximum limit of $1,100 on my credit card spending. As my income rises over time, I may consider increasing my credit limit, but only up to some level that I can afford to pay off immediately when I receive the bill.

Decision on Paying Off Credit Balances:

Given the interest rates that I can earn on deposit accounts versus the interest rate I would pay on a credit card balance, I will always pay off my credit card balance, even if I must withdraw funds from my deposit accounts to do so.

DISCUSSION QUESTIONS

1. How would Stephanie's credit management decisions be different if she were a single mother of two children?

2. How would Stephanie's credit management decisions be affected if she were 35 years old? If she were 50 years old?

SUMMARY

An advantage of using credit is that it enables you to obtain products and services that you cannot afford otherwise. A disadvantage of credit is that it is easier to obtain it than to pay it back. Some individuals use too much credit and are unable to make their credit payments, which may prevent them from obtaining credit in the future. When individuals apply for credit, they provide information about their cash inflows (income), cash outflows (spending habits), and collateral.

Credit cards are distinguished by whether the sponsor is Visa, MasterCard, American Express, a proprietary merchant (such as J.C. Penney), or some other sponsor. They are also distinguished by the credit limit, the annual fee, the interest rate charged on credit not paid by the due date, and whether they provide cash advances.

Credit cards should be used with discipline. You should impose your own credit limits rather than spend up to the limit granted by the card. You should attempt to avoid financing costs, either by using income to cover the amount due or by withdrawing money from savings if necessary.

Integrating the Key Concepts

Your credit decisions affect not only your liquidity level, but also other parts of your financial plan. If you have borrowed a large amount of funds through credit cards, you will be more restricted on additional financing (Part 3) because lenders are less willing to lend you funds if you already have substantial debt. Lenders may also be less willing to lend funds if you have a large amount of credit open in your name, even if you have not used the credit.

Your credit decisions will also affect your investment decisions (Part 4) because you would probably be better off avoiding investments until you pay off any credit card balances. Alternatively, you may need to sell some of your investments to obtain sufficient cash to pay off any credit card balances.

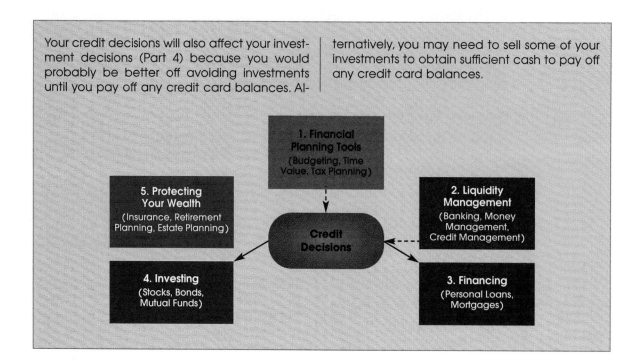

Finance Payment Methods

This appendix explains the methods that financial institutions use to calculate finance charges on outstanding credit card balances. The following three methods are commonly used:

- **Previous Balance Method.** Under the previous balance method, interest is charged on the balance at the beginning of the new billing period. This method is the least favorable of the three to the cardholder because finance charges are applied even if part of the outstanding balance is paid off during the billing period.

- **Average Daily Balance Method.** The most frequently used method is the average daily balance method. For each day in the billing period, the credit card company takes your beginning balance at the start of the day and then subtracts any payments made by you on that day in order to determine the balance at the end of the day. Then, it determines the average daily balance at the end of the day for every day in the billing period. This method takes into account the time when you pay off any part of the outstanding balance. Thus, if you pay off part of the outstanding balance during the billing period, your finance charges will be lower under this method than under the previous balance method.

- **Adjusted Balance Method.** Under the adjusted balance method, interest is charged based on the balance at the end of the new billing period. This method is most favorable for you because it applies finance charges only to the outstanding balance that was not paid off during the billing period.

The following example illustrates the three methods for determining finance charges.

Example

 Assume that as of June 10, you have an outstanding credit card balance of $700 from purchases made over the last month. The new billing period begins on June 11. Assume that your outstanding balance for the first 15 days of this new billing period (from June 11 to June 25) is $700. Then, on June 25, the financial institution receives a payment of $200 from you, reducing the balance to $500. This is the balance for the remaining 15 days of the billing period.

- **Previous Balance Method.** Under this method, you will be subject to a finance charge that is calculated by applying the monthly interest rate to the $700 outstanding at the beginning of the new billing period. Using a monthly interest rate of 1.5 percent, your finance charge is:

$$\$700 \times .015 = \$10.50.$$

- **Average Daily Balance Method.** Under this method, the monthly interest rate is applied to the average daily balance. Since your daily balance was $700 over the first 15 days and $500 over the last 15 days, your average daily balance was $600 over the 30-day billing period. Using a monthly interest rate of 1.5 percent, your finance charge is:

$$\$600 \times .015 = \$9.00.$$

- **Adjusted Balance Method.** Under this method, you will be subject to a finance charge that is calculated by applying the monthly interest rate to the $500 outstanding at the end of the new billing period. Using a monthly interest rate of 1.5 percent, your finance charge is:

$$\$500 \times .015 = \$7.50.$$

Notice from this example that the finance charge is lower if the credit card company uses the adjusted balance method. Individuals who frequently have financing charges can save a substantial amount of money over time by relying on a credit card that uses this method. The best way to reduce financing charges, however, is still to pay the entire credit card bill before the due date every month.

REVIEW QUESTIONS

1. What is credit? What are its advantages and disadvantages?

2. How does the interest rate affect your credit payments? What is meant by simple interest? What is the APR, and what is it used for?

3. How does paying your utility bills help you establish credit? How can you use utility bills to develop a credit history?

4. What are three advantages of using a credit card? Can you think of any disadvantages?

5. What information will you need to supply when applying for credit? What kinds of attributes are creditors looking for? Must you have all these attributes to get credit?

6. Aside from the information you supply, what information do creditors obtain from credit bureaus? How long do credit problems stay on your record? How should errors on your credit report be handled? What other factors may influence the decision to grant you credit?

7. Describe the differences between a credit card like MasterCard or Visa and a retail or proprietary card. How do MasterCard and Visa generate revenue? What is the biggest disadvantage of a proprietary card?

8. What is a credit limit? How can you increase your credit limit?

9. How might you eliminate the annual fees that are charged by some credit cards?

10. Discuss how credit cards offer incentives to use the cards. How else might credit card companies reward cardholders with excellent credit ratings?

11. What is a grace period? How can you use it to your advantage?

12. When is a finance charge applied to credit purchases? What are teaser rates? What is the common range of interest rates on credit cards?

13. What is a cash advance? How are they commonly obtained? Discuss interest rates and grace periods with regard to cash advances.

14. List some items that appear on the credit card statement. What accounts for the difference between your previous balance and your new balance?

15. In comparing credit cards, what things might you consider?

16. List five tips for using credit cards wisely.

17. Should you view credit cards as a source of funds? Why or why not? Why should you self-impose a tight credit limit?

18. Why is paying the credit card balance in full so important? What should you do if you can't avoid credit card debt? Explain.

19. What credit management decisions should be included in your financial plan?

20. Discuss some ways that charging large amounts on your credit cards might affect your overall financial planning.

FINANCIAL PLANNING PROBLEMS

1. Donald is comparing credit cards. He has narrowed his choice to two cards that may meet his needs. Card A has an APR of 21 percent. Card B has an APR of only 14 percent, but also charges a $25 annual fee. Donald feels he will not pay off his balance each month, but will carry a balance forward of about $400 each month. Which credit card should he choose?

2. Paul's credit card closes on the 9th of the month, and his payment is due on the 30th. If Paul purchases a stereo for $300 on June 12, how many interest-free days will he have? When will he have to pay for the stereo in full in order to avoid finance charges?

3. Chrissy currently has a credit card that charges 15 percent interest. She usually carries a balance of about $500. Chrissy has received an offer for a new credit card with a teaser rate of 3 percent for the first three months; after that, the rate goes to 19.5 percent. What will her total annual interest be with her current card? What will her interest be the first year if she switches? Should she switch?

4. Margie has had a tough month. First, she had dental work that cost $700. Next, she had her car transmission rebuilt, which cost $1,400. She put both of these unexpected expenses on her credit card. If she does not pay her credit card balance when due, she will be charged 15 percent interest. Margie has $15,000 in a money market account that pays 5 percent interest. How much interest would she pay (annualized) if she does not pay off her credit card balance? How much interest will she lose if she writes the check out of her money market account? Should she write the check?

5. Troy has a credit card that charges 18 percent on outstanding balances and on cash advances. Last month Troy left a balance on his credit card of $200. This month Troy took out a cash advance of $150 and made $325 in purchases. Troy made a payment of $220. What will the total of Troy's new balance be on his next credit card statement, taking into account finance charges?

FINANCIAL PLANNING ONLINE EXERCISES

Go to http://banking.yahoo.com.

1. Click on "Rates." Check the rates on savings deposits, personal loans, auto loans, and 30-year mortgages. What are the best rates for each category?

2. Use the Back option on your browser to go back to the previous page. Click on "Basics of Banking," then "Advantages, disadvantages of debit cards."

For what particular uses would a debit card be best suited?

3. Use the Back option on your browser to go back to the previous page. Under Checking, click on "Direct Deposits." What are the advantages to a customer and the bank of using a direct deposit?

4. Use the Back option on your browser to go back to the previous page. Under "Credit Cards," click on "Credit Card Fraud." What steps can you take to avoid becoming a victim of credit card fraud?

Go to http://www.financenter.com/products/analyzers/card.fcs and click on "How important is the interest rate?"

1. Input $2,000 as the amount owed on your credit card, $150 future monthly charges, $350 future monthly payments, 19 percent annual interest rate, and zero as the annual fee. Click on "Results" and view the graph by clicking on Graphs.

2. Click on the input tab to go back to the previous page. Change the annual interest rate to 7 percent. How do the time to pay off the debt and the total interest expenses change?

3. Click on the input tab to go back to the previous page. Increase the future monthly payments to $450 and determine the effect on interest expense and the time to pay off the debt. Click on "Results" and then Graphs.

4. Click on the input tab to go back to the previous page. By reducing future monthly charges to $200, how do you alter the interest expense and the time to pay off the debt?

Building Your Own Financial Plan

Credit is one of the most useful and dangerous elements of a personal financial plan. Properly used and managed, it can enable you to improve and maximize your cash flows. Improperly used, it can provide no end of trouble and aggravation. This exercise will assist you in reviewing and planning your credit management.

In the first part of the exercise, you will determine whether your credit history is being properly and accurately reported in the credit reports that banks and other lending institutions use to evaluate your creditworthiness. All consumers should obtain a copy of their credit report at least once a year. Upon obtaining your credit report, review the contents carefully to determine that they are accurate and complete. You can obtain your credit report on the Internet at *www.transunion.com* or *www.credit base.com*. Both provide reasonably priced reports that are easily obtained online, via telephone, or by mail. Report any inaccuracies to the credit bureaus.

Next, go to the MSN homepage, click on the tab entitled "Money," and then click on "Saving and Spending." When the Saving and Spending page comes up, go to the section entitled

"More Tools" on the left. Click on the debt evaluator in this section and follow the instructions to determine your overall creditworthiness. Use either actual data or your projected data upon graduation.

The last part of this exercise is designed to help you evaluate the many credit cards (Visa and MasterCard) that are currently on the market. The template provided with this chapter in the *Financial Planning Workbook* and on the CD-ROM will assist you in this process.

The Sampsons—A Continuing Case

Recall that the Sampsons have been carrying a balance of about $2,000 on their credit card for several months. They have been paying the minimum amount due and using any excess net cash flows to implement their new savings plan for a new car and their children's college education. To date, they have saved $2,000; they are currently earning 5 percent on the savings. Meanwhile, their credit card is charging them 18 percent. Dave and Sharon want to evaluate the return they are receiving from their savings versus the interest expenses they are accruing on their credit card.

1. Compare the amount of interest that the Sampsons are earning on their savings and paying on their credit card debt by filling out the following table:

	Focus on Savings	Focus on Paying Off Credit Balance
Interest rate earned on savings	5%	5%
Interest rate paid on credit	18%	18%
Savings balance	____	____
Credit balance	____	____
Annual interest paid on credit	____	____
Annual interest earned on savings	____	____

2. Advise the Sampsons on whether they should continue making minimum payments on their credit card or use money from their savings to pay off the credit balance.

3. Explain how the Sampsons' credit card decisions are related to their budget.

IN-TEXT STUDY GUIDE

True/False:

1. Credit represents funds provided by a borrower to a creditor that will be repaid by the creditor in the future with interest.

2. The simple interest rate is the percentage of the credit that you must pay as interest on an annual basis.

3. The simple interest rate quoted on credit represents the interest rate charged including all fees (such as an application fee) imposed by the creditor.

4. In a sense, utility companies provide a form of short-term credit to their customers.

5. The easiest way to establish credit is to apply for a credit card.

6. Credit card companies commonly extend credit to individuals with low incomes, such as college students.

7. All credit bureaus utilize the same method of checking and reporting information.

8. Regarding the grace period, the credit card user essentially provides the credit card issuer with free credit from the time the user makes the purchase until the user must pay the bill.

9. If part of a credit card balance is paid off during the billing period, the previous balance method results in the lowest finance charges.

10. The interest rate you are charged when you do not pay the entire amount of the credit card bill on time varies among financial institutions that provide financing on credit cards.

11. The difference between your expected cash inflows and your expenses paid by check (such as rent) or by cash is the minimum amount of credit that you can use in order to ensure full payment of the credit card balance.

Multiple Choice:

The following information refers to questions 1 and 2.

Robert Roy just borrowed $45,000. Robert is charged a simple interest rate of 11 percent.

1. Robert will pay _____ in interest each year.
   a. $4,090.90
   b. $4,950.00
   c. $5,500.00
   d. $4,500.00

2. If the loan lasts for five years, the total interest Robert will pay over the five years is
   a. $24,750.00.
   b. $20,454.50.
   c. $22,500.00.
   d. $19,800.00.

3. Which of the following is not a disadvantage of using credit?
   a. Borrowing enables you to obtain products or services now that you could not afford if you had to pay with cash.
   b. Some individuals may not realize the cost involved in using credit.
   c. If individuals are unable to repay the credit that they received, they may not be able to obtain credit again.
   d. It is difficult to make financial progress if you are borrowing at an 18 percent interest rate.

4. Which of the following statements is not true with respect to credit cards?
   a. They are very convenient for many types of purchases.
   b. They provide you with free financing until the due date on the credit card statement.
   c. The monthly statement provides you with a consolidated list of the purchases you made with the credit card, which enables you to keep track of how you are spending your money.
   d. All of the above statements are true with respect to credit cards.

5. When applying for a credit card, you will probably not be asked for information regarding
   a. your cash inflows and outflows.
   b. your credit history.
   c. the number of children you have.
   d. your capital.

6. Credit card companies receive _____ percent of the payment made to the merchant when their credit cards are used.
   a. 1 to 2
   b. 2 to 4
   c. 4 to 6
   d. 6 to 8

7. Which of the following is not one of the most popular credit cards?
   a. Carte Blanche
   b. American Express
   c. MasterCard
   d. Visa

8. A _____ credit card is honored by only one merchant.
   a. progressive
   b. possessive
   c. proprietary
   d. wholesale

9. Which of the following is not a method of determining the finance charges on a credit card?
   a. previous balance method
   b. average daily balance method
   c. adjusted balance method
   d. All of the above are methods of determining the finance charges on a credit card.

10. The _____ method charges interest based on the balance at the beginning of the new billing period.
    a. previous balance
    b. average daily balance
    c. adjusted balance
    d. new cycle

11. The _____ method charges interest based on the balance at the end of the new billing period.
    a. previous balance
    b. average daily balance
    c. adjusted balance
    d. new cycle

The following information refers to questions 12 through 15.

As of July 14, Chris Boyle has an outstanding credit card balance of $2,100 from purchases made over the last month. The new billing period begins on July 15. After 15 days, on July 30, Chris makes a payment of $1,000, reducing his balance to $1,100. This was the credit card balance for the remaining 15 days of the billing period. The monthly finance charge is 1.5 percent.

12. Using the previous balance method, Chris's finance charge is
    a. $31.50.
    b. $24.00.
    c. $16.50.
    d. $15.00.

13. Using the average daily balance method, Chris's finance charge is
    a. $31.50.
    b. $24.00.
    c. $16.50.
    d. $15.00.

14. Using the adjusted balance method, Chris's finance charge is
    a. $31.50.
    b. $24.00.
    c. $16.50.
    d. $15.00.

15. If Chris had charged $500 of new purchases this billing period, his finance charge under the adjusted balance method would be
    a. $31.50.
    b. $24.00.
    c. $16.50.
    d. $15.00.

16. Which of the following is not shown on a credit card statement?
    a. the previous balance
    b. purchases
    c. the minimum amount due
    d. the most recent credit rating

17. Assume you owe $1,000 on your credit card. You currently have sufficient funds to pay off this entire amount, but decide instead to invest $1,000 in a savings account earning 4 percent interest annually. After one year, what is the difference between the amount owed on the credit card and the interest earned on the $1,000 in your savings account, assuming a finance charge of 20 percent annually on the credit card?
    a. $200
    b. $160
    c. $40
    d. none of the above

18. _____ represents funds provided by a creditor to a borrower that will be repaid by the borrower in the future with interest.
    a. Credit
    b. Debit
    c. Adjustment
    d. None of the above

19. The _____ quoted on credit represents the simple interest rate charged after including any fees imposed by the creditor.
    a. effective annual rate (EAR)
    b. annual percentage rate (APR)
    c. money market rate (MMR)
    d. debit card rate (DCR)

20. The credit limit on a credit card
    a. is the same for all borrowers.
    b. specifies a minimum amount of credit that is allowed.
    c. may be a relatively small amount for individuals who have a low income.
    d. usually cannot be increased for any individual.

21. The ability to save money is _____ when credit payments are _____.
    a. reduced; small
    b. reduced; large
    c. increased; large
    d. None of the above

Part 2: Brad Brooks—A Continuing Case

Brad Brooks is pleased with your assistance in preparing his personal financial statements and your suggestions for improving his personal financial situation. He has called you for guidance on questions that have come to mind after reviewing the information you have given him to date.

First, he wants to know what bank and brokerage firm he should move his accounts to. He is mostly interested in ones that will assist him in making investment and money management decisions. He finds savings accounts boring and has no desire to have one because the interest rate is so low.

Brad is also concerned about his liquidity. His credit card (a bank card with a $35 annual fee and 18 percent interest rate) is nearing its credit limit of $10,000. He is reluctant to sell his stocks to get cash to pay off the credit balance; he thinks they could double in value over the next five years, and he does not want to repurchase them at a high price a year or so down the road.

Brad is also questioning whether to pay off his credit card. He can easily afford the $200 monthly payment and can see no reason to pay off the balance.

1. Assuming that you could convince Brad to maintain checking, savings, and retirement accounts, discuss the pros and cons of various types of financial institutions where Brad could maintain his

    a. checking account.

    b. savings account.

    c. retirement account.

    Be sure to comment on Brad's idea to find financial institutions that can give him advice on his financial decisions.

2. If Brad's stocks double in value over the next five years, what annual return would he realize? (Hint: Use the future value table.) Based on his projected annualized return, would it be advisable to sell the stocks to pay off his credit card? Should Brad consider shopping for a new credit card?

3. How would you address Brad's reluctance to pay off his credit card balance? Show him what he could earn in five years if he paid it off and invested the interest saved at 6 percent.

4. Would your advice change if Brad were

    a. 45 years old?

    b. 60 years old?

5. Prepare a written or oral report on your findings and recommendations for Brad.

PART 3

Personal Financing

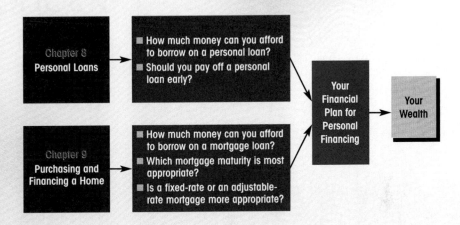

The chapters in this part explain how you can use credit to obtain funds to support your spending. Chapter 8 describes the process of obtaining a personal loan and the types of decisions that are made when considering a personal loan. Chapter 9 describes the process of obtaining a mortgage and the types of decisions that are made when considering a mortgage loan. Your decisions regarding whether to borrow, how much to borrow, and how to borrow will affect your cash flows and wealth.

Chapter

Personal Loans

As mentioned in the previous chapter, your ability to obtain credit and to use it effectively is central to your financial well-being. This chapter focuses on your use of personal loans to finance large purchases. Proper decisions on whether to obtain a personal loan, which source to use for a personal loan, how much to borrow, and what terms to arrange can enhance your wealth.

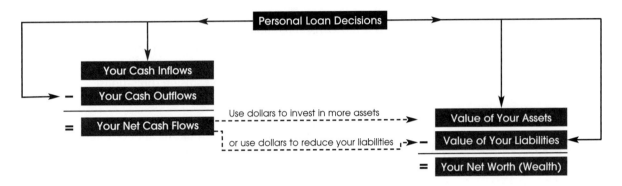

The objectives of this chapter are to:

- provide a background on personal loans,

- describe the types of interest rates that are charged on personal loans,

- describe home equity loans,

- describe car loans, and

- explain how to decide between financing the purchase of a car and leasing a car.

BACKGROUND ON PERSONAL LOANS

Individuals commonly obtain a personal loan to finance a large purchase, such as a car. A personal loan is different from access to credit (from a credit card) in that it is normally used to finance one large purchase and has a specific repayment schedule. The loan is provided at the time of your purchase and is used along with your cash down payment to cover the entire purchase price. You can pay off the personal loan on an installment basis, for example, by making a payment each month for the next 48 months.

Before obtaining a personal loan, you should identify possible sources of financing and evaluate the possible loan terms.

Sources of Loans

The most common source of financing is a personal loan from a financial institution. Commercial banks, savings institutions, finance companies, and credit unions all provide personal loans. Some finance companies are subsidiaries of automobile manufacturers that finance purchases of cars. For example, GMAC Financial Services is a finance company that is owned by General Motors. Savings institutions are the primary lenders to individuals who need mortgage loans, the subject of Chapter 9.

An alternative source of financing is one or more family members or friends. If they trust that you will repay the loan on time and in full, they may be willing to provide you with a loan that earns the same interest rate as their savings account. You could also offer to pay an interest rate on the loan that is a few percentage points above the savings rate. By borrowing funds from family and friends, you can often get a more favorable rate than financial institutions offer. The loan agreement should be in writing and signed by all parties to avoid any possible misinterpretations.

The Personal Loan Process

The personal loan process involves submitting the application, negotiating the loan contract, and negotiating the interest rate. A sample loan application is shown in Exhibit 8.1.

Exhibit 8.1   An Example of a Loan Application

Application Process. When applying for a loan, prospective borrowers need to provide information from their personal balance sheet and personal cash flow statement to document their ability to repay the loan.

- **Personal Balance Sheet.** Recall from Chapter 2 that your financial condition is partially measured by a personal balance sheet. The personal balance sheet indicates your assets, liabilities, and net worth at a specific point in time. The assets are relevant because they may serve as possible collateral to back a loan. The liabilities are relevant because they represent your existing debts.

- **Personal Cash Flow Statement.** Your financial condition is also represented by your personal cash flow statement, as discussed in Chapter 2. This statement indicates your cash inflows and cash outflows and therefore suggests how much free cash flow you have on a periodic basis. Lenders use this cash flow information to determine whether you qualify for a loan and, if so, the maximum size of the loan that you deserve. An individual with existing loans or credit card debt may have insufficient cash flows to cover the payments on any additional loans.

  The key component of the personal cash flow statement of most prospective borrowers is their income. Lenders require income documentation, such as a Form W-2, which indicates annual earnings, or pay stubs, which indicate the recent salary.

loan contract
A contract that specifies the terms of a loan, as agreed to by the borrower and the lender.

Loan Contract. If the lender approves your loan application, it will work with you to develop a **loan contract,** which specifies the terms of the loan, as agreed to by the borrower and the lender. Specifically, the loan contract identifies the amount of the loan, interest rate, repayment schedule, maturity, and collateral.

- **Amount of the Loan.** The amount of the loan is based on how much the lender believes you can pay back in the future. You should attempt to borrow only the amount of funds that you will need because you will be charged interest on the entire amount that you borrow.

- **Interest Rate.** The interest rate is critical because it determines the cost incurred on a personal loan. It must be specified in a loan contract. More information about interest rates is provided in a later section.

amortized
To repay the principal of a loan (the original amount loaned out) through a series of equal payments. A loan repaid in this manner is said to be amortized.

- **Loan Repayment Schedule.** Personal loans are usually **amortized,** which means that the principal (original amount loaned out) is repaid through a series of equal payments. Each loan repayment includes both interest owed and a portion of the principal. As more of the principal is paid down, the amount of interest is reduced, and a larger portion of the payment is used to repay principal.

maturity
In respect to a loan, the life or duration of the loan.

- **Maturity.** A loan contract specifies the **maturity,** or life of the loan. A longer maturity for a loan results in lower monthly payments and therefore makes it easier to cover the payments each month. For example, the monthly

"A high-five isn't binding, sir. You still have to sign a loan agreement."

www.cartoonstock.com

payment on a five-year loan for $16,000 may be $100 less than the payment on a four-year loan for the same amount. With the five-year loan, however, you are in debt for an additional year, and you pay more interest over the life of the loan than you would on the four-year loan. In general, you should select a maturity on personal loans that is as short as possible, as long as you allow yourself sufficient liquidity. If you have extra funds during the time you have a loan, you should consider paying off the loan early for two reasons. First, you can reduce the total amount of interest by paying off the loan early. Second, you will be able to save the money that you would otherwise have used to make the loan payments.

collateral
Assets of a borrower that back a secured loan in the event that the borrower defaults.

- **Collateral.** A loan agreement also describes the **collateral,** or assets of the borrower (if any) that back the loan in the event that the borrower defaults. When a loan is used to purchase a specific asset, that asset is commonly used as collateral. For example, if your purchase of a boat is partly financed, the boat would serve as collateral. That is, the lender could repossess the boat if you were unable to make the loan payments. Some loans are backed by assets other than those purchased with the loan. For example, a boat loan could be backed by stocks that you own.

8.1 Financial Planning Online: Loan Request Online

Go to:
http://www.lendingtree.com

This Web site provides:
a set of questions that you can answer to specify the type of loan that you desire. You will then receive up to four loan offers from various financial institutions within the next business day.

secured loan
A loan that is backed or secured by collateral.

unsecured loan
A loan that is not backed by collateral.

A loan that is backed or secured by collateral is referred to as a **secured loan**; a loan that is not backed by collateral is an **unsecured loan.** In general, you will receive more favorable terms (such as a lower interest rate) on a secured loan because the lender has less to lose in the event that the loan is not repaid.

INTEREST RATES ON PERSONAL LOANS

The three most common types of interest rates financial institutions use to measure the interest due on personal loans are the annual percentage rate, simple interest, and add-on interest.

Annual Percentage Rate

annual percentage rate (APR)
A rate that measures the finance expenses (including interest and other expenses) on a loan on an annualized basis.

As a result of the Truth-in-Lending Act (1969), lenders are required to specify a standardized loan rate with directly comparable interest expenses over the life of the loan. This makes it easier for individuals to compare loans offered by different lenders and select the best loan. The **annual percentage rate (APR)** measures the finance expenses (including interest and all other expenses) on a loan on an annualized basis.

Example

Assume that you have a choice of borrowing $2,000 over the next year from Bank A, Bank B, or Bank C. Bank A offers an interest rate of 10 percent on its loan. Bank B offers an interest rate of 8 percent, but also charges a fee of $100 at the time the loan is granted. Bank C offers an interest rate of 6 percent, but charges a loan fee of $200 at the time the loan is granted. Exhibit 8.2 shows the APRs.

In this example, Bank A offers the lowest APR for a one-year loan. Even though its interest rate is higher, its total financing costs are lower than those charged by the other banks because it does not have any fees. Thus, the APR on its loan is equal to the interest rate charged on the loan. In contrast, the APRs on the loans provided by Banks B and C are much higher than the interest rate charged on their loans because of the fees.

Exhibit 8.2   Measurement of the Annual Percentage Rate

	Interest Expenses	Other Finance Expenses	Total Finance Expenses	Number of Years	Average Annual Finance Expenses	Annual Percentage Rate (APR)*
Bank A	$200	0	$200	1	$200	$200/$2,000 = 10%
Bank B	160	$100	260	1	260	$260/$2,000 = 13%
Bank C	120	200	320	1	320	$320/$2,000 = 16%

*The APR is calculated by dividing the average annual finance expenses by the average annual loan balance.

Simple Interest

simple interest

Interest on a loan computed as a percentage of the existing loan amount (or principal).

Simple interest is the interest computed as a percentage of the existing loan amount (or principal). It is measured using the principal, the interest rate applied to the principal, and the loan's time to maturity (in years). The loan repayment schedule is easily determined by a computer or a calculator or even on various Web sites. If you input the loan amount, the interest rate, and the loan maturity, the loan repayment schedule will provide you with the following information:

1. The monthly payment.

2. The amount of each monthly payment applied to pay interest.

3. The amount of each monthly payment applied to pay down the loan principal.

4. The outstanding loan balance that remains after each monthly payment.

The size of the monthly payment is dependent on the size of the loan, the interest rate, and the maturity. The larger the loan amount, the larger the monthly payment. The higher the interest rate, the larger the monthly payment. For a given loan amount and interest rate, the longer the period over which the loan is repaid (e.g., 36 months versus 24 months), the smaller the monthly payment. As mentioned earlier, however, the longer the maturity, the more you will pay in interest expenses.

Example

 You obtain a loan of $2,000 that is based on the simple interest method with an annual interest rate of 12 percent (1 percent per month) and 12 equal monthly payments. Given this information, a computer generates the loan repayment schedule in Exhibit 8.3. Notice at the top of the exhibit that each monthly payment is $177.70. Each payment consists of an interest payment and a portion that goes to repay the loan principal. At the end of the first month, the interest owed on $2,000 based on a monthly interest rate of 1 percent is:

Interest Owed = Outstanding Loan Balance × Interest Rate

$$= \$2{,}000 \times .01$$
$$= \$20.$$

Since the total payment is $177.70, and the interest payment is $20, the remainder ($157.70) is applied to pay down the principal. The outstanding loan balance after one month is:

Outstanding Loan Balance = Previous Balance − Principal Payment

$$= \$2{,}000 - \$157.70$$
$$= \$1{,}842.30.$$

Exhibit 8.3   Example of Loan Repayment Schedule: One-Year Loan, 12 Percent Interest Rate (Monthly Payment = $177.70)

Month	Interest Payment	Payment of Principal	Outstanding Loan Balance
			$2,000.00
1	$20.00	$157.70	1,842.30
2	18.42	159.27	1,683.03
3	16.83	160.87	1,522.16
4	15.22	162.48	1,359.68
5	13.60	164.10	1,195.58
6	11.96	165.74	1,029.84
7	10.30	167.40	862.44
8	8.62	169.07	693.37
9	6.93	170.76	522.61
10	5.23	172.47	350.13
11	3.50	174.20	175.94
12	1.76	175.94	0

At the end of the second month, the interest rate of 1 percent is applied to the outstanding balance to determine the interest payment:

Interest Owed = $1,842.30 × .01
= $18.42.

This same process is followed to determine the amount of interest that is paid each month. The remainder of each payment is applied to pay off the principal. As each month passes, the outstanding loan balance is reduced, so the interest payment in the following month is reduced. The total monthly payment remains the same for all months, so the principal payment increases over time.

add-on interest method
A method of determining the monthly payment on a loan; involves calculating the interest that must be paid on the loan amount, adding the interest and loan principal together, and dividing by the number of payments.

Add-On Interest

With the **add-on interest method,** the amount of the monthly payment is determined by calculating the interest that must be paid on the loan amount, adding the interest and loan principal together, and dividing by the number of payments.

Example

Reconsider the example in which you receive a loan of $2,000 to be repaid over one year, but assume that you are charged 12 percent interest based on the add-on method. You would first determine the amount of interest that is owed by applying the annual interest rate to the loan amount:

Interest Owed = $2,000 × .12
          = $240.

Next, determine the total payment owed by adding the interest to the loan amount:

Total Payment = $2,000 + $240
          = $2,240.

Finally, divide the total payment by the number of monthly payments:

Monthly payment = $2,240/12
          = $186.67.

Notice that your monthly payment with the add-on method is about $9 per month more than your payment with the simple interest method. Even though the same interest rate is used for both methods, the add-on method is more costly. The reason is that the interest payment is not reduced over time as you pay off the loan.

HOME EQUITY LOAN

home equity loan
A loan where the equity in a home serves as collateral for the loan.

One of the most popular types of loans obtained by individuals is a **home equity loan,** which allows homeowners to borrow against the equity in their home. The home serves as collateral to back the loan. The borrowed funds can be used for any purpose, including a vacation, tuition payments, or health care expenses.

equity of a home
The market value of a home minus the debt owed on the home.

The **equity of a home** is determined by subtracting the amount owed on the home from its market value. Thus, if a home has a market value of $100,000 and the homeowner has a mortgage loan (discussed in the next chapter) with a balance of $60,000 remaining, the equity value is $40,000. A home equity loan essentially provides you with a line of credit. That is, it allows you to borrow the amount that you need up to a specific credit limit. You pay interest only on the amount of funds that you borrow. You can typically pay the interest owed per month on the amount you borrow and then pay the principal at a specified maturity date. You may also be allowed to pay off the principal at any point prior to maturity and still have access to the funds if you need them in the future.

Credit Limit on a Home Equity Loan

Financial institutions provide home equity loans of up to 80 percent of the value of the equity in a home. The actual limit depends on how equity is defined.

Limit Based on Equity Invested. Some financial institutions set a credit limit based on the amount of equity that you have invested in a home.

Example

Assume that you own a home worth $100,000 that you purchased four years ago. You initially made a down payment of $20,000 and took out an $80,000 mortgage. Every month, you make a mortgage payment, which is applied to the interest on the mortgage loan and the principal (or equity) of the home. Over the last four years, your mortgage payments have paid $10,000 in equity. Thus, you have invested $30,000 in the home, including your $20,000 down payment at the time you purchased it. Assuming that the home's market value has not changed, a creditor may be willing to provide you with a home equity loan of 70 percent based on the amount of equity you have invested in the home.

Maximum Amount of Credit Provided = Amount of Equity in Home × .70

= $30,000 × .70

= $21,000.

If you default on a home equity loan, the lender can claim your home, use a portion of the proceeds to pay off the mortgage, and use the remainder to cover your home equity loan. If the market price of the home declines, the equity that you invested is reduced. For this reason, lenders do not like to lend the full amount of the equity when extending a home equity loan.

Limit Based on the Market Value of Equity. Financial institutions also define equity based on the market value of your equity, which is the market value of the home minus the mortgage balance (amount still owed on the home). When the market value of a home rises, they may be willing to provide more credit than if the market value remains the same.

Example

Use the information in the previous example, except now assume that the market value of your home has risen from $100,000 to $120,000 since you purchased it. Recall that you paid off $10,000 of the $80,000 mortgage loan, so your mortgage balance is $70,000. The market value of the equity in the home is:

Market Value of Equity in Home = Market Value of Home − Mortgage Balance

= $120,000 − $70,000

= $50,000.

The market value of the equity is $50,000, while the amount of equity that you invested in the home is $30,000. The difference between these two amounts is the $20,000 increase in the value of the home since you purchased it. The credit limit based on the market value of the equity is:

$$\text{Maximum Amount of Credit Provided} = \text{Market Value of Equity in Home} \times .70$$
$$= \$50,000 \times .70$$
$$= \$35,000.$$

Interest Rate

A home equity loan typically uses a variable interest rate that is tied to a specified interest rate index that changes periodically (such as every six months). The loan contract specifies how the interest rate will be determined. For example, it may be set equal to the average deposit rates across financial institutions within a particular district plus 3 percentage points. Because the home serves as collateral for a home equity loan, the lender faces less risk than with an unsecured loan. Therefore, the interest rate is lower on a home equity loan.

Tax-Deductible Interest. Interest that is paid on a home equity loan of up to $100,000 is tax-deductible. Borrowers can therefore reduce their taxes by using a home equity loan instead of other types of loans or credit cards.

Example

 You borrow $10,000 with a home equity loan. If you pay $1,000 in interest on the home equity loan in a particular year, you can deduct this amount from your taxable income. Assuming your marginal income tax rate is 28 percent, your tax savings in that year are:

$$\text{Tax Savings in One Year from Home Equity Loan} = \text{Amount of Interest Paid}$$
$$\times \text{Marginal Tax Rate}$$
$$= \$1,000 \times .28$$
$$= \$280.$$

Thus, when you use a home equity loan, you not only benefit from a relatively low interest rate, but you also generate a tax savings.

CAR LOANS

Another common type of loan obtained by individuals is a car loan. When you decide to obtain a car, you must select the car, negotiate the price, and determine whether to finance the purchase of the car or lease the car.

Selecting the Car

Although the selection of a car is largely based on your personal preferences, the following financial criteria should also be considered.

Price. Stay within your budget. Avoid purchasing a car that will require you to obtain a second job or establish an unrealistic monthly budget to afford the car payments.

8.2 Financial Planning Online: Prices of New Cars

Go to:
http://autos.yahoo.com/new-cars/

This Web site provides:
estimates of what you should pay for any new car, based on the car's features and options that you specify.

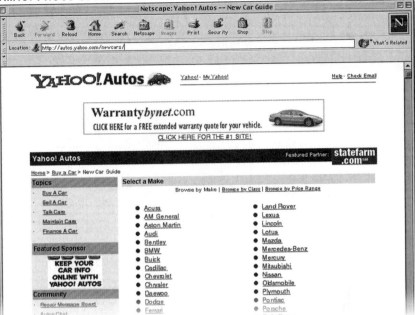

Insurance. Some cars are subject to significantly higher insurance costs because they are more difficult to repair after accidents, are higher priced, or are common theft targets. Obtain insurance estimates on any car that you might purchase before making the purchase.

Resale Value. Some cars have a much higher resale value than others. For example, you can expect that an Acura will have a higher resale value than a Hyundai. Although you cannot perfectly predict the future resale value of a car, you can look at today's resale value of similar cars that were sold years ago. Numerous sites on the Internet, such as www.edmunds.com, provide the market values of used cars, which can be used to determine the resale value as a proportion of the original sales price.

Repair Expenses. Some cars are subject to much higher repair bills than others. To compare potential repair expenses, review *Consumer Reports* magazine, which commonly estimates the typical repair expenses for various cars.

Financing Rate. If you plan to finance your car purchase through the car dealer, you should compare financing rates among dealers. One dealer may charge a lower price for the car but charge higher financing costs for the loan. Other dealers may offer an unusually low financing rate, but charge a higher price on the car. When financing through a car dealer, beware of a dealer markup, in which the dealer arranges the loan and then marks up the lender's interest rate without disclosing the markup to the customer. For example, a dealer may obtain financing for your car at 10 percent, but charge

8.3   Financial Planning Online: Trade-in and Retail Values of Used Cars

Go to:

http://www.kbb.com/

This Web site provides:
trade-in and retail values for a used car, based on the condition of the car, its age, and other characteristics that you specify.

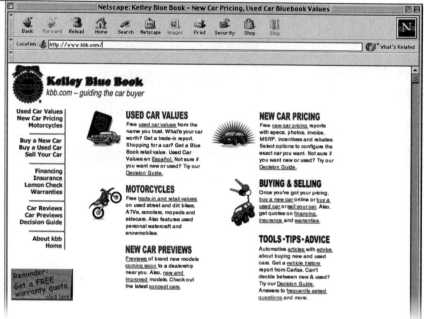

you 12 percent. Many individuals prefer to obtain financing from a financial institution so that they have a choice of several lenders. If you obtain financing from a financial institution rather than the dealer, you can easily compare financing rates of various financial institutions on the Internet.

In some cases, you may wish to determine how much you can borrow before you decide which car to purchase because your purchase decision depends on how much you can borrow. You can use auto loan Internet sites to estimate the maximum amount you can borrow, based on financial information you provide.

Example

Stephanie Spratt has been working full-time for about a year and has saved enough money to afford a down payment on a new car. She considers which car to buy based on the following criteria:

- **Price.** Stephanie's favorite cars are priced in the $35,000 to $45,000 range, but she does not want to borrow such a large amount of money. She hopes to buy a home within a few years (which will require another loan) and therefore wants to limit the amount she borrows now.

  Next, Stephanie reviews her current assets to determine her down payment amount. She can sell her existing car for $1,000. She has accumulated about $4,000 in savings, which she would like to maintain for

8.4   Financial Planning Online: Car Loan Interest Rate Quotation

Go to:
http://loan.yahoo.com/a/

Click on:
Quote Estimator

This Web site provides:
a car loan interest rate quotation based on your desired car, the amount you need to borrow, and the term of the loan.

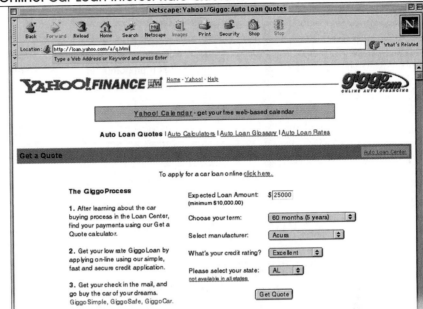

liquidity. She also still has her stock, which is worth about $3,000 at this time. She would prefer to keep her stock rather than sell it. She decides to use the $1,000 from the sale of her used car to make the down payment.

Stephanie wants to borrow no more than $17,000 to buy a car, so she considers cars in the $16,000 to $20,000 price range. She identifies eight cars that are within that range, but she does not like three of them and therefore focuses on the remaining five cars. Next, she obtains more detailed information on the prices of the five cars online.

■ **Resale Value, Repair Expenses, and Insurance.** Stephanie also uses the Internet to obtain ratings on the resale value, repair expenses, and insurance rates for each of the five cars. She recognizes that some dealers attempt to attract customers by offering unusually low financing rates, but then price the car higher to offset the low financing rate. She prefers to avoid these types of dealers, so she plans to obtain her financing from a car-financing Web site. She inputs information about her salary and loan history and is able to quickly determine the financing rate she would pay.

Using the Internet, Stephanie easily obtains the information shown in Exhibit 8.4. Car A has a relatively low resale value after two years. Car D has relatively high repair expenses and service maintenance. Cars A and C have relatively high insurance rates. Therefore, she eliminates Cars A, C, and D. She will choose between Cars B and E.

Exhibit 8.4   Stephanie Spratt's Car Analysis

Car	Expected Resale Value after Two Years (as a proportion of original sales price)	Repair Expenses and Service Maintenance	Insurance
A	Low	Moderate	High
B	Moderate	Low	Low
C	Moderate	Moderate	High
D	Moderate	High	Moderate
E	Moderate	Low	Moderate

Negotiating the Price

When shopping for a car, you have a choice between dealers that negotiate and dealers that offer one set price for a specific car to all customers. Any dealer that negotiates will purposely price its cars well above the price for which it is willing to sell the car. These car dealers expect you to negotiate. In fact, their strategy is to make you think that you got a great deal as a result of the negotiations. If any customer is naïve enough to pay the full price, the car dealer earns a much larger profit at the customer's expense.

8.5   Financial Planning Online: Prevailing Car Loan Interest Rates

Go to:
http://biz.yahoo.com/b/r/a.html

This Web site provides:
average car loan interest rates across the United States and in various states, which provide a useful benchmark for you to consider before obtaining a car loan.

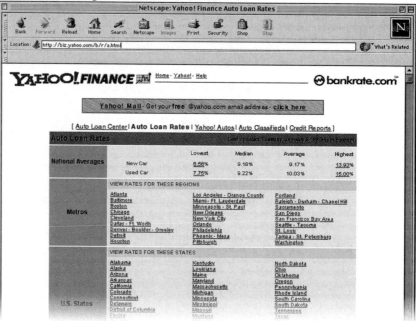

The salespeople are trained to act as if they are almost giving the car away to the customer by reducing the price by 5 to 20 percent. During the negotiations, they will say that they must discuss the price you offer with the sales manager. They already know the price at which they can sell the car to you, but this creates the appearance that they are pleading with the sales manager. Their discussions with the manager normally occur where you can watch as they go through their act.

During the negotiations, the dealer may offer you "free" rustproofing, a CD system, floor mats, or other features. These features are usually priced very high to make you believe you are getting a good deal.

If you are trading a car in, some dealers will pay a relatively high price for your trade-in, but charge a high price for the new car. For example, they may pay you $500 more than your used car is worth, but then charge you at least $500 more than they would have charged for the new car if you did not have a car to trade in. For this reason, you should attempt to negotiate the price on the new car first, before even mentioning that you have a car to trade in.

If you decide to purchase a car from such a dealer, many of the salespeople will congratulate you as if you had just won the lottery. This is also part of their strategy to make you feel that you got a great deal.

Recently, many car dealerships have been created that do not haggle on the price. Buying a car from these dealers is not only stress-free but far less time-consuming. They set one price for a car, so you do not have to prepare for a negotiating battle. Some of these car dealerships still negotiate, however, so before you buy the car, you should make sure the price is no higher than that quoted by other dealers.

The lesson is that some car dealers attempt to make a higher profit from customers who are not well informed about the price that they should pay for a car. One way to avoid being taken when purchasing a car is to become informed. Shop around and make sure that you know the typical sales price for your car. You can obtain this information from *Consumer Reports* and other consumer magazines. Some Web sites will provide you with a quote based on the car model and features you want. You can do all of your shopping from your computer without going to a dealer and may even be able to order the car online with the features you want.

Example

Stephanie has decided to use the Internet to shop for her car. Several Web sites state the price for each of the two new cars she is considering (Cars B and E from the previous example). She reviews specific details about each car, including which car has more value relative to its price, the options, available colors, and when the car can be delivered. She believes that while Car B is cheaper, its value will depreciate more quickly than Car E's. In addition, she can get the exact options and color she desires for Car E, and it can be delivered soon. She is almost ready to purchase Car E, which is priced at $18,000 including taxes. But first, she wants to consider the financing costs per month and whether to lease the car rather than purchase it.

Financing Decisions

If you consider purchasing a new car and plan to finance the purchase, you should estimate the dollar amount of the monthly payment. By evaluating your typical monthly cash inflows and outflows, you can determine whether you can afford to make the required payments to finance the car. You should conduct the estimate before shopping for a car so that you know how much you can afford. The more money needed to cover the car payments, the less you can add to your savings or other investments.

Example

Stephanie Spratt wants to compare her monthly car payments if she borrows $15,000 versus $17,000 to buy a car. She must also decide whether to repay the loan over three years, four years, or five years. The larger the down payment she makes, the less she will need to borrow. However, she wants to retain some of her savings to maintain liquidity and to use for a future down payment on a house.

Stephanie goes to a car-financing Web site where she is asked to input the approximate amount she will borrow. The Web site then provides the interest rate that is available and shows the payments that she would have to make under each alternative loan amount and repayment period, as shown in Exhibit 8.5. The interest rate of 7.6 percent at the top of the exhibit is a fixed rate that Stephanie can lock in at this time for the loan period. The possible loan amounts are shown at the top of the columns, while each row shows a different loan repayment period.

Notice how the payment changes if Stephanie extends the loan period. If she borrows $17,000, her payment would be $530 for a three-year loan, $412 for a four-year loan, or $341 for a five-year loan. She can lower her payment by extending the loan period.

Alternatively, she can lower her monthly payments by reducing her loan amount from $17,000 to $15,000. Notice that if she takes out a four-year loan for $15,000, her monthly payment is less than if she borrows $17,000.

Stephanie selects the $17,000 loan with a four-year term, which results in a monthly payment of $412. The four-year term is preferable because the monthly loan payment for a three-year term is higher than she wants to pay. Since the purchase price of the car is $18,000, she will use the proceeds from selling her old car to cover the $1,000 down payment.

Exhibit 8.5   Stephanie's Possible Monthly Loan Payments (Assume Interest Rate = 7.6 Percent)

Loan Maturity	Loan Amount	
	$15,000	$17,000
36 months (3 years)	$467	$530
48 months (4 years)	363	412
60 months (5 years)	301	341

PURCHASE VERSUS LEASE DECISION

A popular alternative to buying a car is leasing one. An advantage of leasing is that you do not need a substantial down payment. In addition, you return the car to the car dealer at the end of the lease period, so you do not need to worry about finding a buyer for the car.

Leasing a car also has disadvantages. Since you do not own the car, you have no equity investment in it, even though the car still has value. You are also responsible for maintenance costs while you are leasing it. Keep in mind that you will be charged for any damage to the car over the lease period.

8.6   Financial Planning Online: Estimating Your Monthly Loan Payments

Go to:
http://loan.yahoo.com/a/
autocalc.html

Click on:
Loan Payment Calculator

This Web site provides:
estimates of your monthly loan payments based on the interest rate and maturity of the loan that you specify.

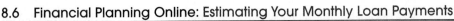

8.7 Financial Planning Online: What Is the Optimal Loan Maturity?

Go to:
http://www.financenter.com/
products/analyzers/auto.fcs

Click on:
"What term of loan should I
choose?"

This Web site provides:
a comparison of what your car
loan payments will be depending on whether you obtain a
loan with a relatively short
maturity or a loan with a
longer term to maturity.

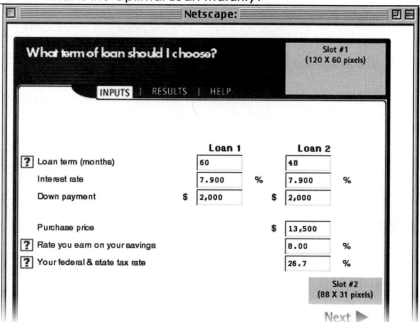

Some car dealers impose additional charges beyond the monthly lease payments. You will be charged if you drive more than the maximum number of miles specified in the lease agreement. You may be assessed a fee if you decide to end the lease before the period specified in the contract. You may also have to purchase more car insurance than you already have. Some of these charges may be hidden within the lease agreement. Thousands of customers have filed legal claims, alleging that they were not informed of all possible charges when leasing a car. If you ever seriously consider leasing, make sure that you read and understand the entire lease agreement.

Example

Stephanie Spratt now wonders if she should lease the car she selected, rather than purchasing it for $18,000. If she purchases the car, she can invest $1,000 as a down payment today, and the remaining $17,000 will be financed by a car loan. She will pay $412 per month over four years to cover the financing. She expects that the car will be worth $10,000 at the end of four years. By purchasing instead of leasing, she forgoes interest that she could have earned from investing the $1,000 down payment over the next four years. If she invests the funds in a bank, she would earn 4 percent annually after considering taxes paid on the interest.

Alternatively, she could lease the same car for $300 per month over the four-year period. The lease would require an $800 security deposit, which she would receive back at the end of the four-year period. However, she would forgo interest she could have earned if she had invested the $800 instead. And, at the end of a lease, she would have no equity and no car.

Stephanie's comparison of the cost of purchasing versus leasing is shown in Exhibit 8.6. Stephanie estimates the total cost of purchasing the car to be $10,936 while the total cost of leasing is $14,528. Therefore, she decides to purchase the car.

The decision to purchase versus lease a car is highly dependent on the estimated market value of the car at the end of the lease period. If the expected value of the car in the previous example were $6,000 instead of $10,000 after four years, the total cost of purchasing the car would have been $4,000 more. Substitute $6,000 for $10,000 in Exhibit 8.6 and recalculate the cost of purchasing to verify this. With an expected market value of $6,000, the total cost of purchasing the car would have been higher than the total cost of leasing, so leasing would have been preferable. When comparing leasing and purchasing costs, remember that some dealers may impose additional charges for leasing, such as a charge for driving more than the maximum miles allowed. You need to include any of these expenses in your estimate of the leasing expenses.

8.8 Financial Planning Online: Should You Lease or Buy?

Go to:
http://loan.yahoo.com/a/autocalc.html

Click on:
Lease Payment Calculator

This Web site provides:
a comparison of the cost of leasing versus purchasing a car, based on the value and other information about your desired car.

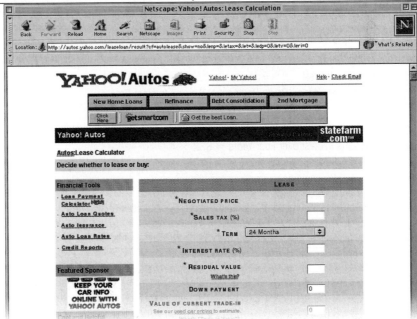

Exhibit 8.6   Stephanie's Comparison of the Cost of Purchasing versus Leasing

Cost of Purchasing the Car

	Cost
1. Down payment	$1,000

2. Down payment of $1,000 results in foregone interest income:

Foregone Interest
Income per Year = Down Payment × Annual Interest Rate
= $1,000 × .04
= $40

Foregone Interest over Four Years = $40 × 4 = $160	160

3. Total monthly payments are:

Total Monthly Payments = Monthly Payment × Number of Months
= $412 × 48
= $19,776

	19,776
Total	$20,936
Minus: Expected amount to be received when car is sold in four years	−10,000
Total cost	$10,936

Cost of Leasing the Car for Four Years

	Cost

1. Security deposit of $800 results in foregone interest income
(although she will receive her deposit back in four years):

Foregone Interest
Income per Year = Down Payment × Annual Interest Rate
= $800 × .04
= $32

Foregone Interest over Four Years = $32 × 4 = $128	$128

2. Total monthly payments are:

Total Monthly Payments = Monthly Payment × Number of Months
= $300 × 48
= $14,400

	14,400
Total cost	$14,528

STUDENT LOANS

student loan
A loan provided to finance part of the expenses a student incurs while pursuing a degree.

Another popular type of loan obtained by individuals is a **student loan,** which is a loan provided to finance a portion of the expenses a student incurs while pursuing a degree. One of the best sources of information about student loans is your school's financial aid office. Some student loans are provided directly to the student, while others are provided to the student's parents.

The lender may be the federal government or one of many financial institutions that participate in student loan programs. Student loans are typically provided at interest rates subsidized by the government to encourage students to pursue degrees. The repayment schedule is typically deferred, so students do not begin to repay the loans until they have completed their degrees and entered the workforce. The interest is tax-deductible up to a maximum of $2,500, which reduces the financing costs even more. The tax benefits are phased out for individuals who are in high tax brackets.

HOW PERSONAL LOANS FIT WITHIN YOUR FINANCIAL PLAN

The following are the key personal loan decisions that should be included within your financial plan:

1. How much money can you afford to borrow on a personal loan?

2. If you obtain a personal loan, should you pay it off early?

By making proper decisions, you can avoid accumulating an excessive amount of debt. Exhibit 8.7 provides an example of how personal loan decisions apply to Stephanie Spratt's financial plan. The exhibit shows how Stephanie reviews her typical monthly cash flows to determine whether she can cover her monthly loan payments.

Exhibit 8.7   How Personal Loan Management Fits within Stephanie Spratt's Financial Plan

Goals for Personal Financing

1. Limit the amount of financing to a level and maturity that I can pay back on a timely basis.
2. For any personal loan, I will consider paying off the loan balance as soon as possible.

Analysis

Monthly Cash Inflows	$2,500
− Typical Monthly Expenses	1,400
− Monthly Car Loan Payment	412
= Amount of Funds Available	$688

Decisions

Decision on Affording a Personal Loan:

The financing of my new car requires a payment of $412 per month. This leaves me with $688 per month after paying typical monthly expenses. I can afford to make the payments. I will not need additional personal loans for any other purpose.

Decision on Paying Off Personal Loan Balances:

The car loan has an interest rate of 7.6 percent. I expect that my stock investment will earn a higher rate of return than this interest rate. Once I have accumulated more savings, however, I will seriously consider using my savings and invested funds to pay off the balance of the loan early.

DISCUSSION QUESTIONS

1. How would Stephanie's personal loan decisions be different if she were a single mother of two children?

2. How would Stephanie's personal loan decisions be affected if she were 35 years old? If she were 50 years old?

SUMMARY

When applying for a personal loan, you need to disclose your personal balance sheet and cash flow statement so that the lender can evaluate your ability to repay a loan. A loan contract specifies the amount of the loan, interest rate, maturity, and collateral.

The common types of interest rates charged on personal loans are the annual percentage rate (APR), simple interest, and add-on interest. The APR measures the interest and other expenses as a percentage of the loan amount on an annualized basis. Simple interest measures the interest as a percentage of the existing loan amount. Add-on interest calculates interest on the loan amount, adds the interest and principal, and divides by the number of payments.

A home equity loan commonly has more favorable terms than other personal loans. It has a relatively low interest rate because of the collateral (the home) that backs the loan. In addition, the interest paid on a home equity loan is tax-deductible up to a limit.

Your decision to purchase a car may require financing. You can reduce your monthly payments on the car loan if you make a higher down payment, but doing this may reduce your liquidity. Alternatively, you can reduce your monthly payments by extending the loan period.

The decision of whether to purchase a car with a car loan or lease a car requires an estimation of the total cost of each alternative. The total cost of purchasing a car consists of the down payment, the forgone interest income from the down payment, and the total monthly loan payments. The total cost of leasing consists of the forgone interest income from the security deposit and the total monthly lease payments.

Integrating the Key Concepts

Your personal loan decisions not only determine how much money you can spend, but also affect other parts of your financial plan. Your decision to obtain a personal loan can affect your liquidity management (Part 2) because an existing personal loan may reduce the amount of credit you can obtain with credit cards. A personal loan also places some pressure on your liquidity needs because you will need to ensure sufficient funds to cover your monthly loan payment. Personal loans can also affect your investment decisions (Part 4) because it may be wise

to avoid investments until the personal loan is paid off. Once you have a personal loan, the decision to invest makes sense only if the return on the investment will exceed the interest rate on the personal loan. Otherwise, you would benefit from using your money to pay off the loan rather than make investments. If your personal loan decision results in the purchase of a new car, you will also have to obtain insurance (Part 5) because you will need to protect the value of the car and be insured against any liability resulting from the car.

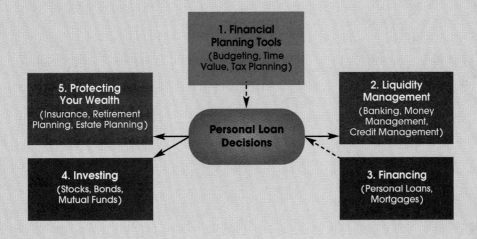

REVIEW QUESTIONS

1. List some possible sources of personal loans. Which source may be able to give you a more favorable interest rate? What precaution should be taken with this type of loan?

2. Name the parts of the personal loan process.

3. What does it mean to say that a loan is amortized? Discuss the relationship of principal and interest as more loan payments are made.

4. What information must borrowers supply to lenders in the loan application process? Why is this information important to lenders?

5. What information is included in a loan contract? How is the amount of the loan determined?

6. Explain how collateral works. Do all loans have collateral? What is the relationship between collateral and interest rates?

7. How does the maturity of a loan affect the monthly payments? How should you select the maturity?

8. What is the purpose of the annual percentage rate measurement? Why would lenders with the same interest rates report different APRs?

9. What is simple interest? What information is needed to compute it? What information will a loan repayment schedule yield?

10. How are payments calculated under the add-on interest method?

11. Why are loan payments under the simple interest method usually lower than loan payments under the add-on interest method?

12. What is home equity? Describe how a home equity loan works.

13. Financial institutions provide home equity loans of up to 80 percent of the value of the equity in the home. Discuss the two ways financial institutions might define equity to set credit limits. What happens if you default on a home equity loan?

14. How are interest rates calculated for home equity loans? Why do borrowers prefer home equity loans to other loans?

15. How can borrowers enjoy tax savings by using a home equity loan? How is this tax savings computed?

16. List the steps in buying a car. What financial criteria should be considered? Discuss each briefly.

17. How can the Internet aid in car buying?

18. Describe some techniques that car salespeople might use in negotiating the price of the car. What should you be aware of at "no-haggle" dealerships?

19. Cars may be purchased or leased. What would be the first step in financing a purchase? Aside from the interest rate, what two things will have the largest impact on the size of your monthly payment?

20. What are the advantages of leasing? Disadvantages? Give some advice for someone considering leasing.

FINANCIAL PLANNING PROBLEMS

1. Tony needs to borrow $1,000 for the next year. Bank South can give him the loan at 9 percent. SunCoast Bank can give him the loan at 7 percent, but charges a $50 loan origination fee. First National will give him the loan at 6 percent with a $25 loan origination fee. Determine the total interest and fees Tony will be charged in each case. Which loan should Tony choose?

2. Beth has just borrowed $5,000 on a four-year loan at 8 percent interest. Complete the amortization table below for the first five months of the loan.

3. What if Beth had made the same loan as an add-on interest loan? How would her payments differ? Why is there a difference?

4. Tracy is borrowing $8,000 on a six-year, 11 percent, add-on interest loan. What will Tracy's payments be?

5. Mary and Marty are interested in obtaining a home equity loan. Their house was purchased five years ago for $125,000 and now has a market value of $156,000. Originally, Mary and Marty paid $25,000 down on the house and took out a $100,000 mortgage. The current balance on their mortgage is $72,000. The bank uses 70 percent of

Payment Number	Beginning Balance	Payment Amount	Applied to Interest	Applied to Principal	New Balance
1	$5,000.00	$102	$33.33	$68.67	$4,931.33
2	__a__	102	32.88	__b__	4,862.21
3	4,862.21	__c__	__d__	69.59	4,792.62
4	4,792.62	102	__e__	70.05	__f__
5	4,722.57	102	31.48	__g__	__h__

equity in determining the credit limit. What will their credit limit be if the bank bases their credit limit on equity invested and will loan them 70 percent of the equity?

6. What will Mary and Marty's credit limit be if the bank uses the market value of equity to determine their credit limit and will loan them 70 percent of the equity?

7. Mary and Marty decide to borrow $30,000 on a home equity line of credit. The interest rate for the loan is 6.75 percent for the entire year, and they take out the loan on May 1. Mary and Marty are in the 36 percent tax bracket. What will be their tax savings for the first year?

8. Noel is considering using his $20,000 home equity line of credit to purchase a new car. Noel has a 15 percent marginal tax rate. If he pays $1,400 in interest on his home equity loan in the first year, what will his tax savings be?

9. Sharon is considering the purchase of a car. After making the down payment, she will finance $15,500. Sharon is offered three maturities. On a four-year loan, Sharon will pay $371.17 per month. On a five-year loan, Sharon's monthly payments will be $306.99, and on a six-year loan, they will be $264.26. Sharon rejects the four-year loan, as it is not within her budget. How much interest will Sharon pay over the life of the loan on the five-year loan? On the six-year loan? Which should she choose?

10. If Sharon had been able to afford the four-year loan, how much interest would she have saved compared to the five-year loan?

FINANCIAL PLANNING ONLINE EXERCISES

Go to http://www.kbb.com.

1. Click on "Used Car Values" and then click on "Retail." Select 1995 and then Ford. Click on "Taurus" and then on "4-Door GL Sedan." Choose V6 engine type, automatic transmission. Then input mileage of 30,000 miles and your zip code. You will be given the price of this car at retail.

2. Use the Back option on your browser to go back to the previous page. This time, choose "Trade-in" and enter the same information. What is the trade-in price? How does it differ from the retail price?

3. Go to http://www.kbb.com. Click on "New Car Previews." Click on "2001 Ford Escape" to obtain information about this new car.

4. Use the Back option on your browser to go back to the previous page. Click on a new car that interests you. You will find useful information about the new model.

Go to http://loan.yahoo.com/a/autocalc.html.

1. In the Auto Loan Calculators section, click on "Loan vs. Lease Calculator." Input $12,000 price, 6 percent sales tax, 48-month term of loan and lease, 8 percent interest rate, $6,000 residual value at end of lease, and $3,500 down payment or trade-in and rebates. How do monthly payments for borrowing and leasing and the total cost under each option compare?

2. Use the Back option on your browser to go back to the previous page. Choose a shorter-term lease of 36 months. With the shorter maturity, what is the change in the lease payments and the total cost of leasing?

3. Go to http://www.financenter.com/products/analyzers/auto.fcs and click on "How much should I put down for a vehicle?" to determine how large a down payment to make on a car. Input the proposed down payment as $3,000 under Loan 1 and as $4,000 under Loan 2. Specify a purchase price of $12,000, loan term of 48 months, interest rate of 8 percent, rate earned on savings as 2 percent, and a federal income tax rate of 36 percent. Which option will cost more? Why?

Building Your Own Financial Plan

Loans to finance purchases such as automobiles and homes may be obtained from a variety of sources, each of which has advantages and disadvantages. For example, automobile purchases may be financed through the dealer, a local bank, a credit union, or a finance company. In this exercise, you will review all loans that you currently have or anticipate having upon graduation and identify as many sources of these loans as possible. You will then evaluate the advantages and disadvantages of each source to assist you in determining where to best meet your various borrowing needs. You will likely be able to find the necessary information about loan terms on the financial institutions' Web sites. The template provided with this chapter in the *Financial Planning Workbook* and on the CD-ROM will assist you in the evaluation process.

Whether or not you are in need of a car at the moment, take the time to compare the cost of buying versus leasing using the second template for this chapter.

The Sampsons—A Continuing Case

 After about 10 months of saving $500 a month, the Sampsons have achieved their goal of saving $5,000 that they will use as a down payment on a new car. (They have also been saving an additional $300 per month over the last year for their children's college education.) Sharon's new car is priced at $25,000 plus 5 percent sales tax. She will receive a $1,000 trade-in credit on her existing car and will make a $5,000 down payment on the new car. The Sampsons would like to allocate a maximum of $500 per month to the loan payments on Sharon's new car. The annual interest rate on a car loan is currently 7 percent. They would prefer to have a relatively short loan maturity, but cannot afford a monthly payment higher than $500.

1. Advise the Sampsons on possible loan maturities. Go to http://loan.yahoo. com/a/auto-calc.html and click on "Loan Payment Calculator." Input information to determine the possible monthly car payments for a three-year (36-month) payment period, a four-year (48-month) payment period, and a five-year (60-month) period. Enter the results in the following table.

	Three-Year (36-month) Period	Four-Year (48-month) Period	Five-Year (60-month) Period
Interest rate	7%	7%	7%
Monthly interest payment			
Total finance payments			
Total payments including the down payment and trade-in			

2. What are the tradeoffs among the three alternative loan maturities?

3. Based on the information on finance payments that you retrieved from the loan payment Web site, advise the Sampsons on the best loan maturity for their needs.

IN-TEXT STUDY GUIDE

True/False:

1. Before obtaining a personal loan, you should recognize the possible sources of financing and the various loan characteristics.

2. Commercial banks are the primary lenders to individuals who need mortgage loans when purchasing homes.

3. Lenders are required to specify a standardized loan rate with directly comparable interest expenses to loans from different lenders over the life of the loan.

4. Simple interest is the interest computed as a percentage of the existing loan amount (or principal).

5. The size of the monthly payment is independent of the number of payments to be made on the loan.

6. With the add-on interest method, the amount of the monthly payment is determined by calculating the interest that must be paid on the loan amount and dividing the total interest by the number of payments.

7. A home equity loan allows homeowners to borrow against the equity in their home.

8. Any car dealer who negotiates will purposely price a car well above the price at which he is willing to sell the car.

9. A disadvantage of leasing is that you need a substantial down payment.

10. When a loan is used to purchase a specific asset, that asset is commonly used as collateral.

Multiple Choice:

1. When applying for a loan, borrowers will probably need to provide information regarding their
   a. personal balance sheet.
   b. personal cash flow statement.
   c. assets.
   d. Borrowers probably need to provide information regarding all of the above.

2. A loan contract typically does not specify
   a. the amount of the loan.
   b. collateral.
   c. age of the borrower.
   d. the maturity of the loan.

3. A _____ maturity for a loan results in _____ monthly payments.
   a. shorter; lower
   b. longer; lower
   c. longer; higher
   d. Answers (a) and (c) are correct.

4. _____ is not a common type of interest rate used on personal loans.
   a. The effective annual rate
   b. The annual percentage rate
   c. Simple interest
   d. Add-on interest

5. _____ measures the finance expenses (including interest and other expenses) on a loan on an annualized basis.
   a. The effective annual rate
   b. The annual percentage rate
   c. Simple interest
   d. Add-on interest

The following information applies to questions 6 through 8.

Bill Wadley has a choice of borrowing $5,000 over the next year from either Bank A, Bank B, or Bank C. Bank A offers an interest rate of 12 percent on its loan. Bank B offers an interest rate of only 6 percent, but charges $150 at the time the loan is granted. Bank C offers an interest rate of 8 percent, but charges $100 at the time the loan is granted.

6. Based on this information, Bank B has an annual percentage rate of _____ percent.
   a. 6
   b. 8
   c. 9
   d. 12

7. Based on this information, Bank C has an annual percentage rate of _____ percent.
   a. 6
   b. 8
   c. 9
   d. 10

8. Based on this information, the most attractive interest rate is offered by
   a. Bank A.
   b. Bank B.
   c. Bank C.
   d. none of the above

The following information applies to questions 9 through 12.

You have just been granted a loan of $3,500 that is based on the simple interest method. The loan has an annual interest rate of 10 percent and requires you to make 12 equal monthly payments of $307.71 each.

9. How much of the payment in the first month represents the interest payment?
   a. $307.71
   b. $35.00
   c. $30.77
   d. $29.17

10. What is the outstanding loan balance after you make the first payment?
    a. $3,500.00
    b. $3,470.83
    c. $3,221.46
    d. $3,227.29

11. What amount of the payment in the second month represents payment of interest?
    a. $29.17
    b. $26.85
    c. $28.92
    d. $26.89

12. Assume instead that the loan described above is based on the add-on interest method. Your monthly payment would be
    a. $307.71.
    b. $320.83.
    c. $326.67.
    d. none of the above

13. In general, monthly payments determined using the add-on interest method are _____ monthly payments determined using the simple interest method.
    a. lower than
    b. higher than
    c. equal to
    d. none of the above

14. In determining the credit limit on a home equity loan, which of the following methods is not commonly used?
    a. limit based on equity invested
    b. limit based on the market value of equity
    c. limit based on total assets owned
    d. All of the above methods are commonly used to determine the credit limit on a home equity loan.

The following information applies to questions 15 and 16.

Five years ago, you purchased a $150,000 home. Your initial down payment was $30,000, and you financed the remainder with a mortgage. Your mortgage payments over the last five years total $15,000. Your home is currently worth $175,000.

15. Using the limit based on equity invested method and assuming the lender allows you to borrow 70 percent of the value of the equity in the home, the maximum amount of a home equity loan you are eligible for is
    a. $31,500.
    b. $105,000.
    c. $49,000.
    d. $38,500.

16. Using the limit based on the market value of equity and assuming the lender allows you to borrow 70 percent of the value of the equity in the home, the maximum amount of a home equity loan you are eligible for is
    a. $31,500.
    b. $105,000.
    c. $49,000.
    d. $38,500.

17. You borrowed $20,000 with a home equity loan to buy a new car. You paid $2,000 in interest on the home equity loan last year. If your marginal income tax rate is 28 percent, your tax savings last year were
    a. $0.
    b. $2,000.
    c. $500.
    d. $560.

18. When planning to purchase a car, you should consider
    a. the price of the car.
    b. the insurance on the car.
    c. the resale value of the car.
    d. You should consider all of the above.

19. Which of the following is not a disadvantage of leasing?
    a. You must worry about finding a buyer for the car at the end of the lease period.
    b. You have no equity investment in the car.
    c. You may be charged if you drive more than a maximum number of miles specified in the original lease agreement.
    d. You may have to purchase more car insurance than you already have.

20. From a cost perspective, it is always more advantageous to
    a. purchase a car.
    b. lease a car.
    c. use a car rental.
    d. none of the above

Chapter 9

Purchasing and Financing a Home

One of the most important personal financial decisions is the purchasing and financing of a home due to the long-term and costly nature of the investment. Your decision on how much to spend and how to finance the purchase of a home will affect your cash outflows on a monthly basis for many years. Your decision of which home to purchase will affect your gain (or loss) when you sell the home and will influence the value of your assets over time. In these ways, the home-buying decision will affect your wealth.

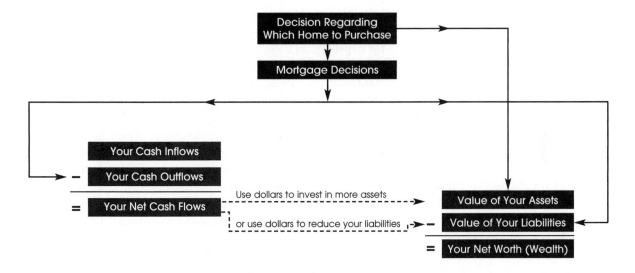

The objectives of this chapter are to:

- explain how to select a home to purchase,

- explain how to conduct a valuation of a home,

- describe the transaction costs of purchasing a home,

- identify the characteristics of a fixed-rate mortgage,

- describe the characteristics of an adjustable-rate mortgage,

- show how to compare the costs of purchasing versus renting a home, and

- explain the mortgage refinancing decision.

SELECTING A HOME

Buying a home may be the single biggest investment you will ever make, so the decision should be taken very seriously. You should carefully consider several factors. You should evaluate the homes for sale in your target area to determine the typical price range and features. Once you decide on a realistic price range and identify a specific home that you desire, you can compare the cost of buying that home to the cost of renting. In this way, you can weigh the extra cost of owning a home against the benefits of home ownership.

An alternative to purchasing a house is to purchase a condominium. In a condominium, individuals own units of a housing complex, but jointly own the surrounding land and common areas (such as parking lots) and amenities (such as a swimming pool). The benefits of a condominium are somewhat different from those of a house. Whereas a house is detached, units in a condominium are typically attached, so there is less privacy. Condominium expenses are shared among unit owners, while the owners of a house pay for expenses on their own. Nevertheless, the factors to be considered when selecting or financing a house are also relevant when purchasing a condominium. Thus, the following discussion will use *home* rather than *house* to indicate that it also applies to a condominium.

You may consider advice from a real estate broker when you assess homes, decide whether to buy a home, or determine which home to purchase. Yet you should not rely completely on the advice of real estate brokers because they have a vested interest: they earn a commission only if you purchase a home through them. You should consider their input, but make decisions that meet your needs and preferences. A good real estate broker will ask you about your preferences and suggest appropriate homes.

When selecting a home, you should first determine how much money you can afford to pay per month for a mortgage based on your budget. This process will remove homes from consideration that are too expensive. Second, you should use various criteria to evaluate the homes that you are still considering.

How Much Can You Afford?

Most individuals pay for a home with a down payment (perhaps 10 to 20 percent of the purchase price) and obtain a mortgage loan to finance the rest. You will pay monthly mortgage payments over the life of the loan. The lenders that provide mortgage loans determine how much money they will lend you based on your financial situation and credit history. Various Web sites can estimate the maximum value of a home you can afford based on your financial situation (such as your income and your net worth).

Affordable Down Payment. You can determine your maximum down payment by estimating the market value of your assets that you are willing to convert to cash today for the purpose of making a down payment and paying for transaction costs (such as closing costs) when obtaining a mortgage. You should also maintain some funds for liquidity purposes to cover unanticipated bills. In addition, you may own some investments or other assets that you prefer not to sell.

9.1   Financial Planning Online: How Much Money Can You Borrow?

Go to:
http://www.financenter.com/
products/analyzers/home.fcs

Click on:
"How much can I borrow?"

This Web site provides:
an estimate of how much
money you could borrow to
finance a home, based on
your income and other financial information.

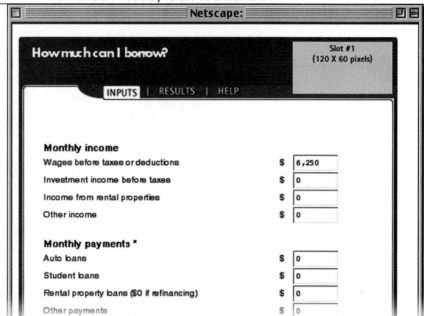

Affordable Monthly Mortgage Payments. How large a mortgage payment can you afford? Refer to your cash flow statement to determine how much net cash flow you have to make a mortgage payment. Recognize that if you purchase a house, you will no longer have a rent payment, so that money can be used as part of the mortgage payment. You should also be aware, however, that owning a home entails some expenses (such as property taxes, homeowner's insurance, and home repairs) that will occur periodically. You should not plan to purchase a home that will absorb all your current excess cash inflows. The larger your mortgage payments, the less you can add to your savings or other investments.

Example

Stephanie Spratt just received an unexpected bonus and a promotion from her employer. After assessing her financial situation, she decides that she may want to purchase a home in the near future. She now has about $15,000 in liquid assets that she is willing to use toward a down payment or transaction costs associated with the purchase of a home. She evaluates her personal cash flows. Since she would no longer need to pay rent for her apartment, she can afford to allocate $900 a month to monthly mortgage payments. She begins to look at homes for sale in the range of $70,000 to $85,000. Once she identifies a home that she may want to purchase, she will obtain estimates of the required down payment, the transaction costs, and the mortgage payment.

"I think there's been some sort of mistake
- I still owe my soul to the mortgage company."

www.cartoonstock.com

Criteria Used to Select a Home

The most important factors to consider when selecting a home are identified here:

- **Price.** Stay within your budget. Avoid purchasing a home that you cannot afford. Although your favorite may have ample space and a large yard, it may not be worth the stress of struggling to make the mortgage payments.

- **Convenient Location.** Focus on homes in a convenient area so that you can minimize commuting time to work or travel time to other activities. You may save 10 or more hours of travel time a week.

- **Maintenance.** Some homes built by well-known construction companies have lower repair bills than others. In addition, newer homes tend to need fewer repairs than older homes. A home with a large yard requires more maintenance.

  A unique characteristic of condominiums is that all people who live in the condominium complex share common areas, such as a swimming pool or tennis court. The residents normally pay a fixed monthly fee to cover the costs of maintaining the common areas. In addition, they may be assessed an extra fee to maintain the structure of the condominium, such as a new roof or other repairs.

- **School System.** If you have children, the reputation of the school system is very important. Even if you do not have children, the resale value of your house benefits from a good school system.

- **Insurance.** When you own a home, you need to purchase homeowner's insurance, which covers the home in case of burglary or damage. The cost of home insurance varies among homes. It is higher for more expensive

9.2 Financial Planning Online: Recent Sales Prices of Nearby Homes

Go to:
http://realestate.yahoo.com/real estate/homevalues/

This Web site provides:
sales prices of homes on a street in a city that you specify over a recent period that you specify. It can also provide a list of homes in the city you specify that sold within a certain price range.

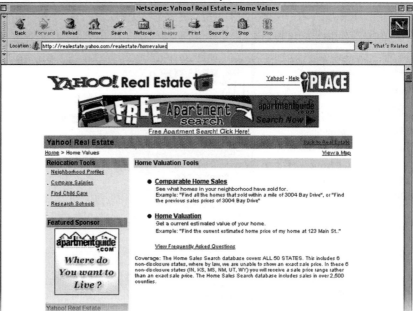

homes and for homes in high-risk areas (such as flood zones) because it costs the insurer more to replace parts of the home that are damaged.

- **Taxes.** Taxes are imposed on homes to pay for local services, such as the local school system and the local park system. Taxes vary substantially among locations. Annual property taxes are often between 1 and 2 percent of the market value of the home. Thus, the tax on a $100,000 home is typically between $1,000 and $2,000 per year. Property taxes are tax-deductible if you itemize deductions on your income tax form. You can deduct them from your income when determining your federal income tax.

- **Homeowner's Association.** Some homes are connected with homeowner's associations, which set guidelines for the homes and may even assess fees that are used to hire security guards or to maintain common grounds within the area. The monthly fees charged by some homeowner's associations are very high and should be considered when buying a home.

- **Resale Value.** The resale value of a home is highly dependent on its location. Most homes with similar features within a specific subdivision or neighborhood are in the same range. Although home prices in a given subdivision tend to increase at a similar rate, the general rate of increase can vary substantially among subdivisions. For example, homes in a subdivision within walking distance of a school may be worth more than comparable houses several miles from the school.

9.3   Financial Planning Online: Listing of Homes Nearby for Sale

Go to:
http://www.realtor.com

This Web site provides:
a listing of homes for sale in an area that you specify and homes in the price and size range that you specify.

You cannot perfectly predict the future resale value of a home, but you can evaluate today's resale value of similar homes in that location that were sold years ago. Information about home prices is provided on numerous Web sites. Be aware, however, that the rate of increase in home prices in previous years does not necessarily serve as a good predictor of the future, so there is some uncertainty about the future value.

Keep in mind that when you use a realtor to sell a home (as most people do), you will pay the realtor a commission that is usually about 6 percent of the selling price. Thus, if you resell your home for $100,000, you will probably pay a commission of about $6,000 and therefore receive $94,000. The buyer of a home does not pay commissions.

- **Personal Preferences.** In addition to the general criteria described above, you will have your own personal preferences regarding such features as the number of bedrooms, size of the kitchen, and size of the yard.

VALUATION OF A HOME

You should use the criteria described previously to screen your list of desirable homes so that you can spend time analyzing the advantages and disadvantages of three or four particular homes. You will probably find some homes that meet all your criteria, but are simply overpriced and therefore should not be purchased.

Market Analysis

market analysis
An estimate of the price of a home based on the prices of similar homes in the area.

You can conduct a **market analysis,** in which you estimate the price of a home based on the prices of similar homes in the area. The market value can be estimated by multiplying the number of square feet in a home by the average price per square foot of similar homes in the area. A real estate broker or appraiser may also provide you with a valuation.

Example

Stephanie Spratt finds the selling prices of three other homes in the same area, with a similar lot size, and about the same age as the home that she wants to purchase. The purchase prices are shown in the second column of Exhibit 9.1.

She recognizes that the homes in an area vary in price due to their size. She determines the price per square foot by dividing each home's price by the square feet, as shown in the third column. Then she determines that the average price per square foot of the three homes is $64, as shown at the bottom of the exhibit.

Since the home that Stephanie wants to purchase has 1,300 square feet, she estimates its market value to be:

Market Value of Home = Average Price per Square Foot × Square Feet of Home

$$= \$64 \times 1{,}300$$
$$= \$83{,}200.$$

She estimates the price of this home at $83,200. Although she will consider other factors, this initial analysis gives her some insight into what the home is worth. For example, the real estate broker told her that the owner of the home has already moved and wants to sell it quickly. Stephanie considers making an offer of $80,000, but she first needs to determine the costs that she will incur as a result of purchasing the home.

Exhibit 9.1   Using a Market Analysis to Purchase a Home

House Size	Price	Price per Square Foot
1. 1,200 square feet	$78,000	$78,000/1,200 = $65
2. 1,300 square feet	$87,100	$87,100/1,300 = $67
3. 1,100 square feet	$66,000	$66,000/1,100 = $60
Average price per square foot = ($65 + $67 + $60)/3 = $64		

Effects on Business Activity and Zoning Laws

The value of a home is also dependent on the demand for homes in that area or subdivision, which can vary in response to business activity or zoning laws.

Business Activity Nearby. Homeowners typically attempt to live close to their workplaces, so they can minimize their commuting time to work. When a large firm moves into an area, people hired for jobs at that firm search for homes nearby. As a result, demand for homes in the area increases, and home prices may rise as well.

Conversely, when a large firm closes its facilities, home prices in that area may decline as homeowners who worked there attempt to sell their homes. The large supply of homes for sale relative to demand may cause homeowners to lower their price in order to find a willing buyer.

Zoning Laws. Locations are zoned for industrial use or residential use. When zoning laws for a location change, its desirability may be affected. Homes near areas that have just been zoned for industrial use become less desirable. Therefore, the demand for homes in these areas may decline, causing prices of homes to decline as well.

Zoning laws also change for school systems. The value of a subdivision can change substantially in response to a change in the public schools that the resident children would attend. Proximity to schools can increase home values, while increased distance from schools often lowers home values.

Obtaining a Second Opinion on Your Valuation

If your valuation leads you to believe that a particular home is undervalued, you may want to get a second opinion before you try to purchase that home. If you are using a real estate broker to help you find a home, that broker may conduct a valuation of the home and offer suggestions about the price that you should be willing to offer. Be aware, however, although brokers are experienced at valuing homes, some brokers provide a valuation that is intended to serve the seller rather than the buyer. That is, they may overestimate the value, so that potential buyers are convinced that the home is worth buying. In this way, the brokers can ensure that a home is sold and that they receive a commission. Although many real estate brokers are honest and will provide an unbiased estimate, you should always conduct your own valuation and carefully assess the broker's valuation process.

Negotiating a Price

Once you have finished your valuation and are convinced that you should buy a particular home, you need to negotiate a price with the seller of the home by making an offer. Some homes are initially priced above the price that the seller will accept. As with any investment, you want to make sure that you do not pay more than you have to for a home.

You may consider the advice of your real estate broker on the offer that you should make. Most sellers are willing to accept less than their original asking price. Once you decide on an offering price, you can submit an offer in the form of a contract to buy the home, which must be approved by the seller. Your real estate broker takes the contract to the seller and serves as the intermediary between you and the seller during the negotiation process.

The seller may accept your offer, reject it, or suggest that you revise it. If the asking price is $100,000, and you offer $90,000, the seller may reject that offer but indicate a willingness to accept an offer of, say, $96,000. Then the decision reverts back to you. You can agree, reject that offer, or revise the contract again. For example, you may counter by offering $94,000. The contract can go back and forth until the buyer and seller either come to an agreement or decide that it is no longer worthwhile to pursue a possible agreement. The contract stipulates not only the price, but also other conditions that are requested by the buyer, such as repairs to be completed by the seller and the date when the buyer will be able to move into the home.

TRANSACTION COSTS OF PURCHASING A HOME

Once you have determined a price range that you can afford, screened your list of homes that you desire, and started the offer process, you should begin applying for a mortgage from a financial institution. The loan application process requires that you summarize your financial condition, including your income, your assets, and your liabilities. You will need to provide proof of income, such as recent paycheck stubs and bank statements. The lender will check your financial condition by contacting your employer to verify that you are still employed and to learn your present salary.

In addition to applying for a mortgage, you will need to plan to cover the transaction costs of purchasing the home. These include the down payment and closing costs.

Down Payment

When you purchase a home, you use your money to make a down payment and pay the remaining amount owed with financing. Your down payment represents your equity investment in the home.

For a conventional mortgage, a lender typically requires a down payment of 10 to 20 percent of the home's selling price. The lender expects you to cover a portion of the purchase price with your own money because the home serves as collateral to back the loan. The lending institution bears the risk that you may possibly default on the loan. If you are unable to make your mortgage payments, the lender can take ownership of the home and sell it to obtain the funds that you owe.

If the home's value declines over time, however, a creditor may not obtain all the funds that it initially lent. Thus, your down payment provides a cushion in case the value of the home declines. Because of your down payment, the lender could sell the home for less than the original purchase price and still recover all of the mortgage loan.

With government-backed loans, a traditional lender extends the loan, but the government insures it in the event of default. Government-backed mortgages may require lower down payments and may even specify lower interest rates than conventional mortgages. Government-backed mortgages are often backed by the Federal Housing Administration (FHA) or the Veterans Administration (VA). To qualify for federally insured mortgages, borrowers must satisfy various requirements imposed by the guarantors. The FHA loans enable low- or middle-income individuals to obtain mortgage financing. The VA loans are extended to military veterans. Both FHA and VA loans are assumable in the event that the homeowner who initially qualified for the mortgage loan decides to sell the home.

Closing Costs

A borrower incurs various fees in the mortgage loan application process. These fees are often referred to as closing costs. The most important fees are identified here.

Loan Application Fee. When applying for a mortgage loan, you may be charged an application fee by the lender. The fee typically ranges from $100 to $500.

points
A fee charged by the lender when a mortgage loan is provided; stated as a percentage of the purchase price.

Points. At the time a mortgage loan is provided, lenders often charge a fee that is commonly referred to as **points**. Points are stated as a percentage of the purchase price. Many lenders charge between 1 and 2 percent of the mortgage loan. If you are charged 2 points when you obtain a mortgage in the amount of $100,000, a fee of $2,000 (computed as 2% × 100,000) is charged at the time the loan is granted. Points are tax-deductible, so the expense can be deducted from your income when determining your taxable income.

Loan Origination Fee. Lenders may also charge a loan origination fee, which is usually 1 percent of the mortgage amount. If you are charged a 1 percent origination fee on a $100,000 mortgage, the fee is $1,000 (computed as 1% × $100,000). Many lenders allow homeowners to select among different fee structures. Thus, you may be able to pay a lower loan origination fee if you accept a slightly higher interest rate. Some lenders may not charge an origination fee, but instead charge a higher interest rate on the mortgage.

Appraisal Fee. Lenders wish to extend a mortgage loan that is less than the market value of the home. If you are unable to make your monthly payments, the financial institution can sell the home to recoup the mortgage loan that it provided. An appraisal is used to estimate the market value of the home and thus protects the financial institution's interests. The fee for the appraisal commonly ranges between $200 and $500.

Title Search and Insurance. An agreement to purchase a home from a current owner (as opposed to a new home from a developer) typically involves various transaction costs for a title search and insurance. A title search is conducted by the mortgage company to ensure that the home or property is owned by the seller. Title insurance provides you with protection in the event that persons other than the seller show evidence that they hold the actual deed of ownership to the property. It also protects you in the event that there are other liabilities attached to the home that were not discovered during the title search.

Example

Recall that Stephanie Spratt is considering making an offer of $80,000 on a house. She wants to determine what her transaction costs would be. She is planning to make a down payment of $8,000 and borrow $72,000. She called York Financial Institution for information on obtaining a mortgage loan. She learned that if she applied for a $72,000 mortgage, York would charge the following:

- 1 point
- 1 percent origination fee
- $300 for an appraisal
- $200 application fee
- $400 for a title search and title insurance
- $200 for other fees

Thus, the total closing costs would be:

Points	(1% × $72,000)	$720
Origination Fee	(1% × $72,000)	720
Appraisal Fee		300
Application Fee		200
Title Search and Insurance		400
Other Fees		200
Total		$2,540

Thus, Stephanie will need a down payment of $8,000 and $2,540 in closing costs to purchase the home.

Both the closing costs and the down payment are due after the offer for the home has been accepted at the time of the closing. During the closing, the title for the home is transferred to the buyer, the seller is paid in full, and the buyer takes possession of the home.

CHARACTERISTICS OF A FIXED-RATE MORTGAGE

fixed-rate mortgage
A mortgage in which a fixed interest rate is specified until maturity.

A mortgage loan is most likely the biggest loan you will ever obtain in your lifetime. The terms for mortgages vary. You will need to decide whether to obtain a fixed-rate or adjustable-rate mortgage and what the maturity of the mortgage should be. Traditionally, mortgages had a fixed interest rate and a maturity of 30 years. A **fixed-rate mortgage** specifies a fixed interest rate

9.4   Financial Planning Online: Will You Qualify for a Mortgage?

Go to:
http://loan.yahoo.com/m/

Click on:
Pre-Qualify for a Mortgage

This Web site provides:
an opinion about whether you will be approved for your desired mortgage loan. It requires your input on the purchase price of the home you plan to purchase, along with your income and other financial information.

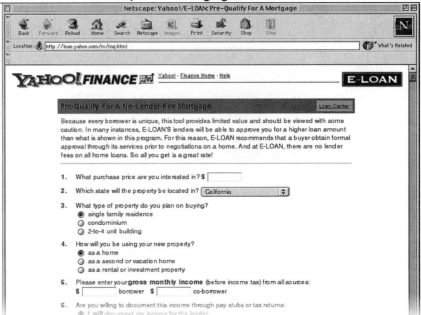

9.5   Financial Planning Online: Average Mortgage Rates

Go to:
http://biz.yahoo.com/b/r/m.html

This Web site provides:
national averages for mortgage rates, as well as average mortgage rates for specific regions and states.

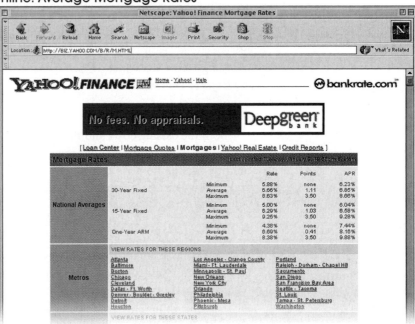

that is constant for the life of the mortgage. When homeowners expect that interest rates will rise over time, they tend to prefer fixed-rate mortgages because their interest payments will be sheltered from the rising market interest rates. Many other types of mortgages are available, but the traditional fixed-rate 30-year mortgage is still popular. You can access various Web sites to obtain a general summary of prevailing mortgage rates, but rates vary among financial institutions. If you sell a home before the mortgage is paid off, you can use a portion of the proceeds from selling the home to pay off the mortgage. Alternatively, it may be possible for the buyer to assume your mortgage under some conditions.

Amortization Table

Your monthly mortgage payment for a fixed-rate mortgage is based on an amortization schedule. This schedule discloses the monthly payment that you will make, based on a specific mortgage amount, a fixed interest rate level, and a maturity.

Allocation of the Mortgage Payment. Each monthly mortgage payment represents a partial equity payment that pays a portion of the principal of the loan and an interest payment.

Example

Stephanie Spratt decides to review mortgage Web sites to estimate her monthly mortgage payments. One Web site asks her to input the mortgage amount she desires and the interest rate that she expects to pay on a 30-year mortgage. She inputs $72,000 as the amount and 8 percent as the interest rate. The Web site then provides her with an amortization schedule, which is summarized in Exhibit 9.2. This exhibit shows how her mortgage payments would be allocated to paying off principal versus interest. Notice how the initial payments are allocated mostly to interest, with a relatively small amount used to pay off the principal. For example, for month 2, $49 of her payment is applied to the principal, while $479 goes to pay the interest expense. Initially, when the amount of principal is large, most of her payment is needed to cover the interest owed. As time passes, the proportion of the payment allocated to equity increases. Notice that by month 360, $525 of the payment is applied to principal and $3 to interest.

Notice, too, that her balance after 100 months is $65,163. This means that over a period of more than eight years, Stephanie would pay off less than $7,000 of the equity in her home, or less than 10 percent of the original mortgage amount. After 200 months (two-thirds of the life of the 30-year mortgage), her mortgage balance would be almost $52,000, which means she would have paid off about $20,000 of the $72,000 mortgage.

Exhibit 9.2   Amortization Schedule for a 30-Year (360-Month) Fixed-Rate Mortgage for $72,000 at an 8 Percent Interest Rate

Month	Payment	Principal	Interest	Balance
1	$528	$48	$480	$71,952
2	528	49	479	71,903
10	528	51	477	71,502
•				
•				
•				
25	528	57	472	70,691
•				
•				
•				
49	528	66	462	69,211
•				
•				
•				
100	528	93	435	65,163
•				
•				
•				
200	528	181	347	51,877
•				
•				
•				
360	528	525	3	0

Note: Numbers are rounded to the nearest dollar.

The amount of Stephanie's annual mortgage payments that would be allocated to paying off the principal is shown in Exhibit 9.3. In the first year, she would pay off only $601 of the principal, while the rest of her mortgage payments ($5,738) in the first year would be used to pay interest. This information is very surprising to Stephanie, so she reviews the mortgage situation further to determine if it is possible to build equity more quickly.

Exhibit 9.3   Allocation of Principal versus Interest Paid per Year on a $72,000 Mortgage

Year	Principal Paid in That Year	Interest Paid in That Year
1	$601	$5,738
2	651	5,688
3	705	5,634
4	764	5,576
6	896	5,444
8	1,051	5,289
10	1,233	5,107
12	1,446	4,894
15	1,836	4,503
17	2,154	4,186
20	2,736	3,603
22	3,209	3,131
24	3,764	2,576
26	4,415	1,925
28	5,178	1,161
30	6,073	266

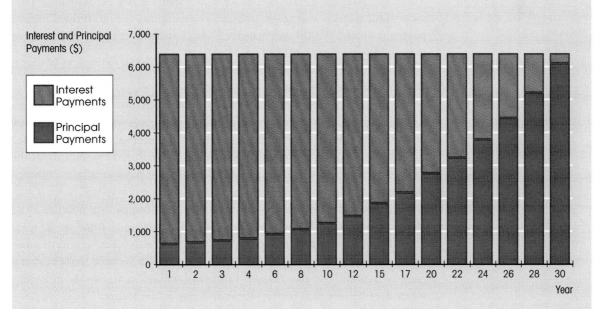

9.6   Financial Planning Online: Amortization Schedule

Go to:
http://loan.yahoo.com/m/
mortcalc.html

Click on:
Amortization Calculator

This Web site provides:
an amortization schedule
based on the interest rate and
mortgage term you input. Mortgage payments are shown on
an annual basis (or a monthly
basis if you wish). The
monthly payment is segmented
into the portion used to pay
interest and the portion used to
pay down the loan principal.

Impact of the Mortgage Amount on the Monthly Payment

The larger the mortgage amount, the larger your monthly payments will
be for a given interest rate and maturity. Exhibit 9.4 shows the monthly
payment based on a 30-year mortgage and an 8 percent interest rate for
different mortgage amounts. Notice how much higher the mortgage payment is for a larger mortgage amount. For example, the monthly mortgage
payment for a $90,000 mortgage is $660, while the monthly payment for
a $100,000 mortgage is $734.

Impact of the Interest Rate on the Monthly Payment

Given the large amount of funds that you may borrow to finance a home,
you should make every effort to obtain a mortgage loan that has a low
interest rate. The lower the interest rate on the mortgage, the smaller the
monthly mortgage payment. A slight increase (such as 0.5 percent) in the
interest rate can increase your monthly mortgage payments by a substantial amount.

In the last decade, the 15-year mortgage has become very popular as an
alternative to the 30-year mortgage. The interest rate charged on 15-year
and 30-year fixed-rate mortgages is typically related to other long-term interest rates (such as the 30-year Treasury bond rate) at the time that the mortgage is created. For this reason, homeowners seek a fixed-rate mortgage
when they believe that interest rates will rise in the future.

Exhibit 9.4   Monthly Mortgage Payments Based on Different Mortgage Amounts (30-Year Fixed-Rate Mortgage; Interest Rate = 8 Percent)

Mortgage Amount	Monthly Mortgage Payment
$60,000	$440
70,000	513
80,000	587
90,000	660
100,000	734
110,000	807
120,000	880

Impact of the Mortgage Maturity on the Monthly Payment

The maturity of the mortgage indicates how long you will take to complete your financing payments and pay off the mortgage. At that point, you own the home outright. The advantage of a 15-year mortgage is that you will have paid off your mortgage after 15 years, whereas a 30-year mortgage requires payments for an additional 15 years. Monthly payments on a 15-year mortgage are typically higher, but you pay less interest over the life of the loan and build equity at a faster pace.

9.7   Financial Planning Online: Should You Obtain a 15-Year or a 30-Year Mortgage?

Go to:
http://www.financenter.com/products/analyzers/home.fcs

Click on:
"Which is better: 15 or 30 year term?"

This Web site provides:
a comparison of payments that you would make on a 15-year versus a 30-year mortgage on a particular home. It also estimates the amount of additional payments you would make with a 30-year mortgage rather than a 15-year mortgage.

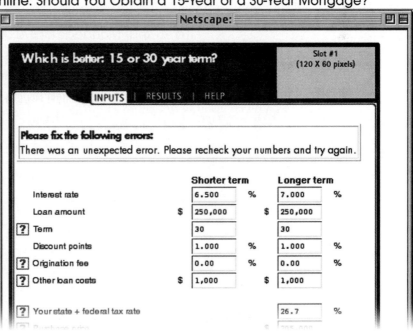

The advantage of a 30-year mortgage is that you have smaller monthly payments for a given mortgage loan amount than you would for a 15-year mortgage. Thus, the monthly payments may be more affordable, and you may have more liquidity.

Estimating the Monthly Mortgage Payment

You can use mortgage loan Web sites to obtain estimates of your monthly payments based on a specific mortgage amount and maturity.

Example

Stephanie Spratt wants to estimate her monthly mortgage payment on a $72,000 fixed-rate mortgage, based on several interest rate scenarios for 15- and 30-year maturities, as shown in Exhibit 9.5. At an interest rate of 7 percent, the monthly payment on the 30-year mortgage would be $479. At an interest rate of 9 percent, the monthly payment on the 30-year mortgage would be $579, or $100 more. Next, Stephanie evaluates the payments for a 15-year term. She believes she can obtain a loan at an 8 percent interest rate on either maturity, so she focuses on the difference in monthly payments pertaining to that rate.

Although the monthly payment is more for the 15-year mortgage, the difference is not as large as Stephanie expected. Given the interest rate of 8 percent, the 15-year mortgage requires a monthly payment of $688, which is $160 more than the $528 payment on the 30-year mortgage. This is the obvious disadvantage of a 15-year mortgage.

Exhibit 9.5   Comparison of Monthly Payments for a 30-Year versus a 15-Year Mortgage of $72,000 Based on Different Interest Rates

| Interest Rate | Monthly Payment on a: | |
	30-Year Mortgage	15-Year Mortgage
7.0%	$479	$647
7.5	503	667
8.0	528	688
8.5	554	709
9.0	579	730
9.5	605	752
10.0	632	774

Note: Payments are rounded to the nearest dollar.

The advantage is that she would pay down the mortgage sooner, meaning that she would more quickly accumulate a larger equity investment in the house. To gain more insight on this advantage, she reviews a Web site to compare the remaining loan balance for each of the two mortgage maturities on a year-by-year basis. This comparison is summarized in Exhibit 9.6. Notice that after six years, she would still owe $67,554 on the 30-year mortgage, versus $52,852 (almost $15,000 less) on the 15-year mortgage. After 10 years, she would owe almost $30,000 more on the 30-year mortgage than on the 15-year mortgage. After 15 years, she would still owe about $55,000 on the 30-year mortgage, while the 15-year mortgage would be paid off.

The Web site also shows the total payments over the life of the mortgage for both types of mortgages if the mortgage is not paid off until maturity.

Exhibit 9.6 Comparison of Mortgage Balance for a 15-Year versus a 30-Year Mortgage (Initial Mortgage Amount = $72,000; Interest Rate = 8 Percent)

End of Year	Balance on 30-Year Mortgage	Balance on 15-Year Mortgage
1	$71,399	$69,410
2	70,747	66,604
3	70,042	63,566
4	69,278	60,275
5	68,450	56,712
6	67,554	52,852
7	66,583	48,672
8	65,533	44,146
9	64,395	39,244
10	63,162	33,934
11	61,826	28,185
12	60,381	21,957
13	58,815	15,213
14	57,119	7,910
15	55,283	0

Note: Balances are rounded to the nearest dollar.

9.8   Financial Planning Online: Estimating Your Monthly Mortgage Payment

Go to:
http://loan.yahoo.com/m/
mortcalc.html

Click on:
Payment Calculator

This Web site provides:
an estimate of your monthly
mortgage payment based on
the amount of your mortgage
loan, the interest rate, and the
maturity.

	30-Year Mortgage	15-Year Mortgage
Total Principal Payments	$72,000	$72,000
Total Interest Payments	118,192	51,852
Total Payments	$190,192	$123,852

Stephanie would pay about $66,000 more in interest with the 30-year mortgage than with the 15-year mortgage. The total interest payments on the 30-year mortgage are much larger than the total principal payments that would be made over the life of the mortgage.

Weighing the advantages of the 15-year mortgage against the disadvantage of paying the extra $160 per month, Stephanie decides she prefers the 15-year mortgage. Even if she decides to sell this home before she pays off the 15-year mortgage, she will have paid down a larger amount of the mortgage. Since she will have a larger equity investment (from paying off more of the principal) with the 15-year mortgage, she will increase her net worth to a greater degree.

adjustable-rate mortgage (ARM)
A mortgage where the interest owed changes in response to movements in a specific market-determined interest rate.

CHARACTERISTICS OF AN ADJUSTABLE-RATE MORTGAGE

An alternative to a fixed-rate mortgage is an **adjustable-rate mortgage (ARM),** in which the interest owed changes in response to movements in a specific market-determined interest rate. An ARM is sometimes referred to as a variable-rate mortgage. ARMs represent about one-fourth of all home mortgages. Like a fixed-rate mortgage, an ARM can be obtained for a 15-year or a 30-year maturity. ARMs have various characteristics that must be stated in the mortgage contract.

Initial Rate

Many ARMs specify a relatively low initial mortgage rate over the first year or so. This initial rate is beneficial to homeowners in that it results in a low monthly mortgage payment over the first year. Homeowners should recognize, however, that this rate is only temporary, as the mortgage rate will be adjusted.

Interest Rate Index

The initial mortgage rate will be adjusted after a period (such as one year) in line with a specified interest rate index. The interest rate index to which the mortgage rate is tied must be included in the mortgage contract. Many ARMs use a rate that is tied to the average cost of deposits of financial institutions. For example, the interest rate charged on an ARM might be set at 3 percentage points above that benchmark. Thus, if the benchmark is 4 percent in a given year, the ARM will apply an interest rate of 7 percent (computed as 4% + 3%). If the interest rate index has risen to 5 percent by the time of the next mortgage rate adjustment, the new mortgage rate will be 8 percent (computed as 5% + 3%).

Frequency of Rate Adjustments

The mortgage contract also specifies how frequently the mortgage rate will be adjusted. Many ARMs specify that the rate will be adjusted once a year. Thus, the mortgage rate is set based on the specified interest rate index and then remains the same for the next 12 months. This means that the monthly payments will be constant for the next 12 months. At the end of the 12-month period, the mortgage rate is revised based on the prevailing interest rate index and is held constant for the following 12 months.

Some mortgages allow for less frequent adjustments, such as every three years or every five years. Others allow a single adjustment at the end of the fifth year, and the adjusted rate is then held constant over the next 25 years of a 30-year mortgage.

Other ARMs offer the following alternatives:

- An interest rate that adjusts every five years.

- An interest rate that is fixed for the first three years, but converts to an ARM (and adjusts annually) after three years.

- An interest rate that is fixed for the first five years, but converts to an ARM (and adjusts annually) after five years.

- An interest rate that adjusts for the first five years and then is fixed (based on an interest rate index at that time) for the next 25 years.

With so many alternatives available, you can easily find a mortgage that fits your preferences. For example, if you expect that interest rates will decline consistently over time, you may prefer an ARM that is adjusted every year. If your expectations are correct, your mortgage rate will decline over time with the decline in market interest rates. It is difficult to accurately forecast the direction of interest rates, however, which means that your future mortgage payments are uncertain.

Caps on Adjustable-Rate Mortgages

caps

Maximum and minimum fluctuations in the interest rate on an adjustable-rate mortgage.

The mortgage contract also typically specifies **caps,** or a maximum and minimum fluctuation in the interest rate. For example, an ARM may have a cap of 2 percent per year, which prevents the mortgage rate from being adjusted upward by more than 2 percentage points from its existing level in each year. Assume the market interest rate increases by 3 percentage points from one year to the next. Without a cap, the mortgage rate on the ARM would increase by 3 percentage points. With a 2 percent cap, however, only an increase of 2 percentage points is allowed in that year. This cap is useful because it limits the potential increase in the mortgage payments that may result from an increase in interest rates.

In addition to a cap on the annual increase in the mortgage rate, there is usually a lifetime cap, which represents the maximum amount of the increase in the mortgage rate over the life of the mortgage. A lifetime cap of 5 percent is commonly used. Thus, if an ARM has an initial mortgage rate of 7 percent and a 5 percent cap, the maximum mortgage rate over the life of the mortgage would be 12 percent.

Financing with a Fixed- versus an Adjustable-Rate Mortgage

Your decision to use a fixed- versus an adjustable-rate mortgage to finance the purchase of a home is dependent on your expectations of future interest rates. The primary advantage of an ARM is that the initial interest rate is lower than that of a fixed-rate mortgage. Yet, if interest rates rise, you may end up paying a higher interest rate on your mortgage than if you had obtained a fixed-rate mortgage.

Example

Stephanie Spratt has already determined that if she finances with a 15-year fixed-rate mortgage, she would pay an 8 percent interest rate. Alternatively, she could obtain an adjustable-rate mortgage that specifies an initial rate of 6 percent, with the interest rate adjusted each year to an index reflecting the average cost of bank funds plus 3 percentage points. Assuming the index rate is 5 percent next year, the rate applied to her mortgage would be 8 percent for the following year.

Stephanie notices that financial experts have predicted an increase in interest rates in the near future. She is uncomfortable with the uncertainty

9.9 Financial Planning Online: Should You Obtain a Fixed- or an Adjustable-Rate Mortgage?

Go to:
http://www.financenter.com/
products/analyzers/home.fcs

Click on:
"Which is better: fixed or
adjustable?"

This Web site provides:
a comparison of payments that
you would make on a fixed-
rate versus an adjustable-rate
mortgage. It can be used to
determine which type of mortgage is more desirable.

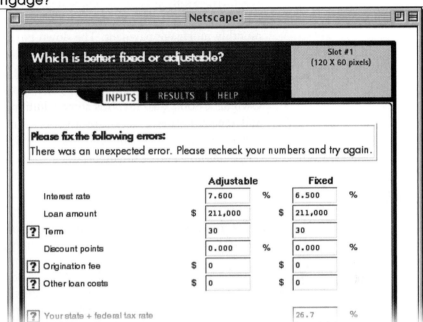

surrounding her mortgage rate and therefore surrounding her mortgage payment. Although the ARM would result in a lower mortgage payment in the first year, it would result in a higher mortgage payment in the following years if interest rates increase. Thus, Stephanie decides to choose a fixed-rate mortgage instead of the ARM.

DECISION TO OWN A HOME VERSUS RENT

When considering the purchase (and therefore ownership) of a home, you should compare the cost of purchasing a home with the cost of renting. People attribute different advantages and disadvantages to owning a home versus renting because preferences are subjective. Some individuals value the privacy of a home, while others value the flexibility of an apartment, which allows them to move without much cost or difficulty. The financial assessment of owning a home versus renting can be performed in an objective manner. Once the financial assessment is conducted, personal preferences can also be considered.

Estimating the Total Cost of Renting and Owning

The main cost of renting a home is the monthly rent payment. There is also an opportunity cost of tying up funds in a security deposit. Those funds could have been invested if you did not need to provide the security deposit. Another possible cost of renting is the purchase of renter's insurance.

The primary costs of purchasing a home are the down payment and the monthly mortgage payment. The down payment has an opportunity cost because the funds could have been invested to earn interest if they were not tied up in the purchase of the home. Closing costs are incurred at the time the home is purchased, although a portion of these costs is tax-deductible. Owning a home also involves some additional costs, such as maintenance and repair. Property taxes are assessed annually as a percentage of the home's value. Homeowner's insurance is paid annually and is primarily based on the value of the home.

Example

Stephanie Spratt has found a home she desires and has obtained financing. Before making a final decision, she wants to compare the cost of the home to the cost of remaining in her apartment. Although she would prefer a home, she wants to determine how much more expensive the home is compared to the apartment. If she purchases the home, she expects to live in it for at least three years. Therefore, she decides to compare the cost of owning a home to the cost of renting over the next three years, so that she can determine whether the advantages of living in a home merit the extra cost. First, Stephanie calculates the cost of renting:

- **Cost of Rent.** Her estimated cost of renting is shown in the top panel of Exhibit 9.7. Her rent is currently $600 per month, so her annual rent is $7,200 (computed as $600 × 12). She does not expect a rent increase over the next three years and therefore estimates her cost of renting over this period to be $7,200 × 3 = $21,600. (If she had expected an increase in rent, she would have simply added the extra cost to the estimated rent over the next three years.)

- **Cost of Renter's Insurance.** She does not have renter's insurance at this time, as the value of her household assets is low.

- **Opportunity Cost of Security Deposit.** She provided a security deposit of $1,000 to the apartment complex. While she expects to get this deposit back when she stops renting, there is an opportunity cost associated with it. She could have invested those funds in a tax-free money market fund earning 4 percent annually, which would have generated annual interest of $40 (computed as $1,000 × .04). The opportunity cost over three years is three times the annual cost, or $120.

- **Total Cost of Renting.** Stephanie estimates the total cost of renting as $7,240 per year and $21,720 over the next three years, as shown in Exhibit 9.7.

Exhibit 9.7 Comparing the Total Cost of Renting versus Buying a Home over a Three-Year Period

Cost of Renting

	Amount per Year	Total over Next Three Years
Rent ($600 per month)	$7,200	$21,600
Renter's insurance	0	0
Opportunity cost of security deposit	40	120
Total cost of renting	$7,240	$21,720

Cost of Purchasing

	Amount per Year	Total over Next Three Years
Mortgage payment ($688 per month)	$8,256	$24,768
Down payment	8,000	8,000 (first year only)
Opportunity cost of down payment	320	960
Property taxes	1,000	3,000
Home insurance	600	1,800
Closing costs	2,540	2,540 (first year only)
Maintenance costs	1,000	3,000
Total costs before tax benefits		$44,068
Tax savings on:		
Interest Payments		$4,480
Property Taxes	280	840
Points	202	202 (first year only)
Total tax savings		$5,522
Equity investment		$16,434
Increase in home value		0
Value of equity		$16,434
Cost of purchasing home over three years		$22,112

Stephanie determines the total cost of purchasing a home by adding up expenses, subtracting any tax savings, and subtracting the value of the equity:

- **Mortgage Payment.** The primary cost of buying a home is the mortgage payment, which she expects to be $688 per month or $8,256 per year (not including payments for property taxes or house insurance).

- **Down Payment.** Stephanie would make a down payment of $8,000 to buy the home.

- **Opportunity Cost of the Down Payment.** An opportunity cost is associated with the down payment. If Stephanie did not buy a house, she could have invested the $8,000 in a tax-free security and earned 4 percent per year. Therefore, the annual opportunity cost (what she could have earned if she invested the funds) is $320 (computed as $8,000 × .04).

- **Property Taxes.** Property taxes are another annual expense. Stephanie assumes that the annual property tax will be $1,000 based on last year's property tax paid by the current owner of the home.

- **Home Insurance.** Insurance on this home will cost $600 per year (this estimate is based on the home insurance premium paid by the current owner of the home).

- **Closing Costs.** In addition, the closing costs (transaction costs) associated with buying a home must be included, although those costs are incurred only in the first year for a mortgage and do not apply in the remaining years of the mortgage life. The closing costs are estimated to be $2,540, as shown earlier.

- **Maintenance Costs.** Stephanie expects maintenance costs on the home to be $1,000 per year.

- **Utilities.** She will pay for utilities such as water and electricity and will incur a cable TV bill if she buys the home. She already incurs those costs while renting an apartment, so she does not need to include them in her analysis.

- **Tax Savings.** Stephanie must also consider the tax savings that a home provides. Since the home mortgage interest is tax-deductible, she estimates that her taxes will be reduced by 28 percent of the amount by which her taxable income is reduced. The amount of mortgage interest changes every year, and therefore so does her tax savings from interest expenses. She can estimate her interest expenses over three years by using an amortization table based on her mortgage amount, mortgage maturity, and mortgage rate. She estimates that her interest expense over the next three years will be about $16,000. Her tax savings over the three years will therefore be:

Tax Savings = Interest × Applicable Tax Rate
$$= \$16,000 \times .28$$
$$= \$4,480.$$

Stephanie will also generate tax savings from property taxes because they are tax-deductible. Given an annual property tax of $1,000, she estimates her annual tax savings to be:

Tax Savings = Annual Property Tax × Applicable Tax Rate

= $1,000 × .28

= $280.

Assuming property taxes do not change, this $280 tax savings is the same for each year, so the tax savings over three years would be $840 (computed as $280 × 3).

Stephanie will also generate a tax savings in the first year on the points she paid as part of the closing costs, because the cost of points is tax-deductible. Assuming that the cost of points is $720, she estimates this tax savings as:

Tax Savings = Cost of Points × Applicable Tax Rate

= $720 × .28

= $202.

- **Value of the Equity Investment.** Another advantage of owning a home is that Stephanie will have an equity investment in it. Her down payment will be $8,000, and she will pay about $8,434 in principal on her mortgage over the three-year period. The value of this equity investment could be higher in three years if the market value of the home increases. If Stephanie assumes that the home's value will not change, the value of the equity investment will be $16,434 (computed as $8,000 + $8,434).

- **Total Cost of Purchasing a Home.** The total cost of purchasing a home is determined by adding up all the expenses, subtracting the tax savings, and then subtracting the equity investment. As shown in Exhibit 9.7, Stephanie estimates that the total cost of purchasing the home over the three-year period will be $22,112.

The total cost of purchasing a home is close to the total cost of renting over a three-year period. When she sells the home, however, she will likely incur a commission cost of 6 percent of the selling price, or approximately $5,000. Stephanie concludes that she will buy a home rather than continue to rent her apartment for the following reasons. First, she would rather live in a home than an apartment. Second, she believes that the value of the home will increase over time. If the home increases in value by about 2 percent a year over the three-year period, the value of her equity investment will increase by about $5,000. This increase would cover the commission from selling the home in three years. Furthermore, if she decides not to sell the home, she will not incur a commission cost.

Now that Stephanie has decided that she wants to purchase a home and can afford it, she submits her offer of $80,000, which is accepted by the seller.

9.10   Financial Planning Online: Should You Rent or Buy?

Go to:
http://loan.yahoo.com/m/

Click on:
Calculators

Click on:
Rent Vs Own

This Web site provides:
a recommendation on whether you should buy a home, based on your rent versus the expenses of the home you are considering.

SPECIAL TYPES OF MORTGAGES

In some cases, prospective buyers do not qualify for a traditional fixed-rate mortgage or an adjustable-rate mortgage. Some special types of mortgages are available that can make a home more affordable.

Graduated Payment Mortgage

graduated payment mortgage
A mortgage where the payments are low in the early years and then rise to a higher level over time.

A **graduated payment mortgage** sets relatively low monthly mortgage payments when the mortgage is first created and then gradually increases the payments over the first five or so years. The payments level off after that time. This type of mortgage may be useful for someone whose income will increase over time, since the mortgage payments will increase as the homeowner's income increases. A graduated payment mortgage would not be desirable for people who are not certain that their income will rise.

Balloon Payment Mortgage

balloon payment mortgage
A mortgage where the monthly payments are relatively low, but one large payment is required after a specified period to pay off the mortgage loan.

A **balloon payment mortgage** sets relatively low monthly payments and then requires one large payment (called a balloon payment) after a specified period (such as five years) to pay off the remainder of the mortgage loan. A balloon payment mortgage is sometimes offered by the seller of a home to the buyer, especially when the buyer cannot afford to make large monthly payments and does not qualify for a more traditional mortgage. In this situation, the seller might provide a mortgage for five years. The expectation is that the buyer's income will rise, enabling the buyer to obtain a traditional mortgage from a financial institution before the end of the five-year period. Then, the buyer will have enough cash to make the balloon payment to the seller.

MORTGAGE REFINANCING

mortgage refinancing
Paying off an existing mortgage with a new mortgage that has a lower interest rate.

Mortgage refinancing involves paying off an existing mortgage with a new mortgage that has a lower interest rate. You may use mortgage refinancing to obtain a new mortgage if market interest rates (and therefore mortgage rates) decline. One disadvantage of mortgage refinancing is that you will incur closing costs again. Nevertheless, it may still be advantageous to refinance because the savings on your monthly mortgage payments (even after considering tax effects) may exceed the new closing costs. Mortgage refinancing is more likely to be worthwhile when the prevailing mortgage interest rate is substantially below the interest rate on your existing mortgage. It is also more likely to be worthwhile when you expect to be living in the home for a long time because you will reap greater benefits from the lower monthly mortgage payments that result from refinancing.

Refinancing Analysis

To determine whether you should refinance, you can compare the advantage of monthly savings of interest expenses to the cost of refinancing. If the benefits from reducing your interest expenses exceed the closing costs incurred from refinancing, the refinancing is feasible.

Example

Stephanie Spratt decides that if interest rates decline in the future, she may refinance at the lower interest rate. If interest rates decline to 7 percent a year from now, Stephanie would save about $40 on her monthly mortgage payment by refinancing. Stephanie next needs to determine the potential savings in the monthly interest payments over the time that she expects to remain in the house.

A monthly reduction in interest payments of $40 reflects an annual reduction of $480 (computed as $40 × 12). But because interest on the mortgage is tax-deductible, the reduction in interest payments by $480 interest means that her taxable income would be $480 higher. Since her marginal tax rate is 28 percent, her taxes would increase:

Annual Increase in Taxes = Annual Increase in Taxable Income × Marginal Tax Rate
$$= \$480 \times .28$$
$$= \$134.$$

Her annual savings due to refinancing at a lower interest rate would be:

$480 − $134 = $346.

Assuming that she plans to remain in the house for two more years from the time of refinancing, her total savings would be:

$346 \times 2 = \$692$.

The disadvantage of refinancing is that Stephanie may once again incur the same closing costs ($2,540). Before comparing this cost to the benefits of refinancing, she accounts for the tax savings. Since the points are tax-deductible, she determines the tax savings from these costs:

$$\text{Tax Savings on Points} = \text{Cost of Points} \times \text{Marginal Tax Rate}$$
$$= \$720 \times .28$$
$$= \$202.$$

$$\text{After-tax Closing Costs} = \text{Closing Costs} - \text{Tax Savings}$$
$$= \$2,540 - \$202$$
$$= \$2,338.$$

The after-tax closing costs ($2,338) due to refinancing would exceed the savings on the interest payments ($692) over the next two years. Thus, Stephanie is now aware that if interest rates decrease by 1 percent over the next year, it would not be worthwhile for her to refinance her home.

The advantages of refinancing (lower interest payments) occur each year, while the disadvantage (closing costs) occurs only at the time of refinancing. Therefore, refinancing tends to be more beneficial when a homeowner plans to own the home for a longer period. The savings from a lower interest payment can accumulate over each additional year the mortgage exists.

HOW A MORTGAGE FITS WITHIN YOUR FINANCIAL PLAN

The following are the key mortgage loan decisions that should be included within your financial plan:

1. What mortgage amount can you afford?

2. What maturity should you select?

3. Should you consider a fixed-rate or an adjustable-rate mortgage?

By making proper decisions, you can avoid accumulating an excessive amount of debt. Exhibit 9.8 provides a summary of how Stephanie Spratt's mortgage loan decisions apply to her financial plan.

Exhibit 9.8 How Mortgage Financing Fits within Stephanie's Financial Plan

Goals for Mortgage Financing

1. Limit the amount of mortgage financing to a level that is affordable.
2. Select a short loan maturity if possible, assuming that the payments are affordable.
3. Select the type of mortgage loan (fixed- or adjustable-rate) that is more likely to result in lower interest expenses.

Analysis

	15-Year Mortgage (8% interest rate)	30-Year Mortgage (8% interest rate)
Monthly payment	$688	$528
Total interest payments	$51,852	$118,192
Advantages	Pay off mortgage in half the time of a 30-year mortgage; pay lower interest expenses on the loan	Smaller monthly payment
Difference between mortgage payment and rent payment	$688 − $600 = $88	$528 − $600 = −$72

Decisions

Decision on Affording a Mortgage:

The monthly interest payment on a $72,000 mortgage loan with a 15-year maturity is $688. My rent is $600 per month, so the difference is $88 per month. Since my monthly cash flows (from my salary) exceed my typical monthly expenses (including my car loan payment) and my purchases of clothes by almost $600, I can afford that difference. I will not save as much money as I planned if I buy a home, but I will be building wealth.

Decision on the Mortgage Maturity:

I prefer the 15-year mortgage because I will pay off a larger portion of the principal each year.

Decision on the Type of Mortgage Loan:

I prefer the fixed-rate mortgage because I know with certainty that the monthly payments will not increase. I am worried that interest rates may increase in the future, which would cause interest expenses to be higher on the adjustable-rate mortgage.

DISCUSSION QUESTIONS

1. How would Stephanie's mortgage financing decisions be different if she were a single mother of two children?

2. How would Stephanie's mortgage financing decisions be affected if she were 35 years old? If she were 50 years old?

SUMMARY

When considering the purchase of a home, you should evaluate your financial situation to determine how much you can afford. Some of the key criteria used in the selection process are price, convenience of the location, quality, the school system, and the potential resale value.

You can conduct a valuation of a home with a market analysis. Homes in the same area that were recently sold can be used to determine the average price per square foot. Then this price per square foot can be applied to the square footage of the home you wish to value.

The transaction costs of purchasing a home include the down payment and closing costs. The key closing costs are points and the origination fee.

A fixed-rate mortgage specifies a fixed interest rate to be paid over the life of the mortgage. Since most of the monthly mortgage payment on a 30-year mortgage is allocated to cover the interest expense in the early years, a relatively small amount of principal is paid off in those years. A 15-year fixed-rate mortgage is a popular alternative to the 30-year mortgage. It requires a larger monthly payment, but a larger proportion of the payment is allocated to principal in the early years.

An adjustable-rate mortgage (ARM) ties the interest rate to an interest rate index, so the mortgage interest rate changes over time with the index. Homeowners who expect interest rates to decline in the future are especially likely to choose ARMs.

Before making a final decision to buy a home, you can compare the total cost of owning a home versus renting over a particular period to determine which choice will enhance your financial position more. The total cost of owning a home is estimated by adding up the expenses associated with the home, subtracting the tax savings from owning the home, and subtracting the expected value of the equity of the home at the end of the period.

You may consider mortgage refinancing when quoted interest rates on new mortgages decline. When refinancing, you will incur closing costs. Thus, you should consider refinancing only if the benefits (expected reduction in interest expenses over time) exceed the closing costs.

Integrating the Key Concepts

Your mortgage decision affects your ability to purchase a home, as well as other parts of the financial plan. You will need to maintain more liquidity (Part 2) than before to ensure that you will have sufficient funds each month to make your mortgage payment. You will likely have less funds for investments (Part 4) and may even have to sell some of your investments to have sufficient cash to make a down payment or monthly mortgage payments. Your decision to buy a home means that you will have to obtain insurance (Part 5) to protect the home and be insured against any liability resulting from the home.

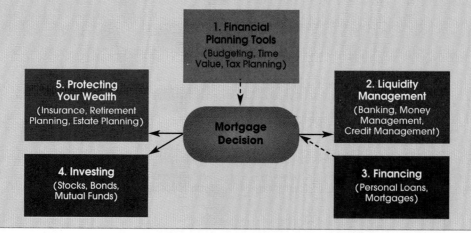

REVIEW QUESTIONS

1. What is your first task when considering buying a home? Why is this step important? How can a real estate broker help you?

2. What are the two financial components you must consider before purchasing a home? Why?

3. What information must be considered when determining an affordable down payment and monthly mortgage payments?

4. List the criteria you should use when selecting a home.

5. Describe how price, convenience of the location, and maintenance affect your home-buying decisions.

6. Why is the reputation of the school system in the area of the home you are buying important?

7. Why do insurance costs and taxes vary among homes?

8. What is the main factor in determining a home's resale value? How can you predict a home's resale value? Who pays commissions when a home is sold?

9. Once you have reduced your list of three or four homes down to one home, what is your next step? Should you offer the price the seller is asking? Describe how you would conduct a market analysis of the home.

10. What drives the change in a home's value? What conditions might cause the demand for homes in an area to rise? Explain.

11. How do lenders protect their interest in a home? Describe two federally backed home loan programs.

12. What are closing costs? List and briefly describe the different closing costs you might incur.

13. Describe the characteristics of a fixed-rate mortgage. Why do certain homeowners prefer a fixed-rate mortgage to an adjustable-rate mortgage?

14. What is an amortization table?

15. List three things that determine the amount of the monthly mortgage payment and explain how they affect the payment.

16. Discuss some of the characteristics of an adjustable-rate mortgage. What will influence your choice of a fixed- or adjustable-rate mortgage?

17. What are the main costs of renting?

18. Describe some of the costs of buying a home. What are the potential tax savings?

19. Describe the features of two special kinds of mortgages.

20. What is mortgage refinancing?

FINANCIAL PLANNING PROBLEMS

1. Dorothy and Matt are ready to purchase their first home. Their current monthly cash inflows are $4,900, and their current monthly cash outflows are $3,650. Their rent makes up $650 of their cash flows. They would like to put 10 percent of their cash inflows in savings and leave another $200 in their checking account for emergencies. How much of a mortgage payment could they manage under these conditions?

2. Dolly and Kenny are ready to make an offer on an 1,800-square-foot house that is priced at $135,000. They investigate other homes on lots of similar size and find the following information:

   - A 2,400-square-foot house sold for $168,000.
   - A 1,500-square-foot house sold for $106,500.
   - A 1,100-square-foot house sold for $79,000.

   What offer should they make on the house?

3. Larry and Laurie have found a home and made a $125,000 offer that has been accepted. Their bank charges a loan origination fee of 1 percent of the loan, points of 1.5 percent, and a 10 percent down payment. Other fees include a $25 loan application fee, a $250 appraisal fee, and $350 for title search and insurance. How much cash will Larry and Laurie need at closing?

4. On a mortgage loan balance of $69,900 with a 6.75 percent interest rate and a monthly payment of $634, how much will be paid on the principal each month?

5. Lloyd and Jean are considering purchasing a home that would require a $75,000 mortgage. The payment on a 30-year mortgage for this amount is $498.97. The payment for a 15-year

maturity is $674.12. How much interest would they save if they can afford the 15-year loan?

6. Teresa rents her apartment for $650 per month, utilities not included. When she moved in, she paid a $700 security deposit using money from her savings account that was paying 3 percent interest. Her renter's insurance costs her $60 per year. How much does it cost Teresa to rent for a year?

7. Eric has found a condominium in an area where he believes he would enjoy living. He would need a $5,000 down payment from his savings and would have to pay 5 percent additional closing costs (or $2,500) to purchase the condo. His monthly payments would be $520 including property taxes and insurance. The condominium's homeowner's association charges maintenance fees of $400 per year. Calculate the cost of Eric's condo during the first year.

8. Eric (from problem 7) paid interest of $4,330 during his first year in the condo. His property taxes were $600, and his insurance was $460. If Eric is in a 28 percent marginal tax rate bracket, what were his tax savings for his first year?

9. Doug and Lynn bought their home three years ago and have a mortgage payment of $601.69. Interest rates have recently fallen, and they can now get payments of $491.31 if they refinance. What would their annual savings be if they refinanced? They are in a 15 percent marginal tax rate bracket.

10. If the cost of refinancing their house is $3,860, how long would Doug and Lynn (from problem 9) have to remain in their home in order to recover the cost?

FINANCIAL PLANNING ONLINE EXERCISES

Go to http://www.financenter.com/products/analyzers/home.fcs and click on "How much can I borrow?"

1. Input $3,000 wages, $500 in other income, $300 in auto loans, $100 for student loans, $125 for other loans, desired interest rate of 9 percent, 15-year loan term, 5 percent down payment, no other debts, $1,000 credit card balance, $1,500 property tax, and $300 property insurance. What are the conservative estimates and aggressive estimates of what you can afford to borrow to finance the purchase of a home?

2. Click on the input tab to go back to the previous page. Change the interest rate to 10 percent. What is the difference in monthly payments on the loan?

3. Click on the input tab to return to the inputs page. Change the loan term to 30 years. What is the difference in monthly payments on the loan?

4. Go to http://loan.yahoo.com/m/. Click on "Pre-Qualify for a Mortgage." Input the requested information to determine if you qualify for a mortgage.

5. Use the Back option on your browser to go back to the previous page. Click on "Recommendations." Input the following information: $100,000 loan amount, $120,000 estimated value of the property, and 28 percent federal tax. The remaining information can be kept at the default settings. What mortgage type is best for your situation?

Go to http://loan.yahoo.com/m/.

1. Click on "Calculators" and go to the "Starting the Loan Process" section. Click on "Am I Better Off Renting?" Values are already input for the monthly rent, price of home, taxes, etc. Find out if renting is better than buying for the scenario presented on the Web site or for your own situation.

2. Use the Back option on your browser to go back to the previous page. Change the amount of monthly rent to $500 and see how that affects the recommendation on buying or renting.

3. Go to http://www.financenter.com/products/analyzers/home.fcs and click on "Which is better: 15 or 30 year term?" Use the values already input for the 15- and 30-year mortgage terms. Obtain a comparison on the monthly payments and the total cost of each option by clicking the "Results" tab. What is the difference between the monthly payments for the two loan options? How much less will the 15-year loan cost over the life of the loan than the 30-year loan?

4. Go to http://loan.yahoo.com/m/mortcalc.html. Click on "Payment Calculator" in the "Yahoo Real Estate" section. Input a $100,000 mortgage amount, 8 percent interest rate, and 30-year term. What are the monthly payments?

5. Next, click on "Amortization Calculator." Input the same information as above without any extra payments for both 15-year and 30-year terms. Compare the total amount of money paid in principal and interest for the two maturities.

Building Your Own Financial Plan

The purchase of a home is the largest expenditure that most individuals will make in their lifetime. For this reason, you should approach this decision with as much information as possible. This exercise will familiarize you with various information sources and will alert you to what you can and cannot expect from a realtor. Most of this exercise will be done on the Internet; enter your results on the template provided with this chapter in the *Financial Planning Workbook* and on the CD-ROM.

First, go to the Web address www.msn.com. After the MSN homepage loads, you will note on the left a list of topics. Click on "House and Home."

Your first task will be to determine the availability of homes in your price range in the area where you wish to live. Under the heading "Find Homes for Sale," enter your price range in the boxes indicated and the zip code of the area where you wish to purchase a house. Click on "go" and a list of houses will appear. Review the list and when you find a home that interests you, click on it for more details. You will be provided with additional information on the house and with a monthly payment worksheet. Compare the required down payment to the amount you established in your goals (if one of your goals was to save for a house) to determine if your estimate is high or low. Also compare the monthly payment indicated with your personal cash flow statement to determine if it is in line with your estimates. You may find it necessary to make some revisions in your goals or personal cash flow statements.

Next, obtain a multiple listing booklet for the area in which you are interested. These can be found in many locations, including grocery stores, barber shops, and, of course, most realtor offices. Using the MSN HomeAdvisor.com page, go to the area marked "How Much Is Your Home Worth?" Enter the street address of a house in the area and the appropriate zip code. Click "go" and on the next page that will come up, click "Don't Know" where appropriate. Compare the price estimate from the MSN Web site to the asking price in the multiple listing book. Do this for several houses, being sure to note the realtor who has the listing on each house. Are you detecting any pattern from certain realtors as to over- or underpricing?

The last exercise involving the MSN Web site will be to familiarize yourself with sources of home mortgage loans. Using the "Get A Loan On-Line" section, type in the dollar amount you anticipate needing to finance your home. Click "go," and you will be provided with a list of lenders, the terms of the loans they are offering, and the interest rates on each loan.

Review the terms for both fixed- and adjustable-rate mortgages. Compare the monthly payments and interest rates for the various loans to find the best mortgage for your situation. Using the template provided for this chapter, create an amortization table for your preferred loan and compare the allocation of principal versus interest paid per year on the loan. Finally, compare the cost of buying a home to renting over a 3-year period to make sure that homeownership is a wise financial decision at this time.

Go to several other search engines, such as Excite and Yahoo!, to find additional information for home buying and financing. You may want to bookmark some of these pages for future reference.

The Sampsons—A Continuing Case

The Sampsons purchased a home last year. They have a 30-year mortgage with a fixed interest rate of 8.6 percent. Their monthly mortgage payment (excluding property taxes and insurance) is about $700 per month. In the last year, interest rates have declined. A 30-year mortgage now has an interest rate of 8 percent. Dave and Sharon want to determine how much they can lower their monthly payments by refinancing. By refinancing, they would incur transaction fees of $1,400 after considering any tax effects.

1. Use a Web site to determine the monthly mortgage payment (excluding property taxes and insurance) on a $90,000 mortgage if the Sampsons obtain a new 30-year mortgage at the 8 percent interest rate. (One Web site that can be used for this purpose is http://loan.yahoo.com/m/mortcalc.html.)

2. The Sampsons expect that they will not move for at least three years. Advise the Sampsons on whether they should refinance their mortgage by comparing the savings of refinancing with the costs.

3. Why might your advice about refinancing change in the future?

IN-TEXT STUDY GUIDE

True/False:

1. When you purchase a home, the entire cost is usually financed with a mortgage.

2. The resale value of a home is highly dependent on its location.

3. The buyer of a home pays a commission to the realtor selling the home.

4. In a market analysis of a home, the price of the home is estimated based on other homes in the area with similar features.

5. Points represent the loan application fee.

6. An adjustable-rate mortgage specifies a fixed interest rate that remains the same for the life of the mortgage loan.

7. Compared to a 15-year mortgage, a 30-year mortgage results in a lower amount of interest paid over the life of the mortgage.

8. Many adjustable-rate mortgages specify a relatively low initial mortgage rate over the first year of the mortgage.

9. A balloon payment mortgage is sometimes offered by the seller of a home to the buyer.

10. When you refinance a mortgage, you will not incur closing costs a second time.

Multiple Choice:

1. Which of the following is not a criterion to consider when selecting a home?
   a. price
   b. location
   c. school system
   d. All of the above are criteria considered when selecting a home.

2. The _____ the cost of a home, the _____ the insurance.
   a. lower; higher
   b. higher; higher
   c. higher; lower
   d. none of the above

3. Annual property taxes are often between _____ percent of the market value of the home.
   a. 1 and 2
   b. 3 and 4
   c. 5 and 6
   d. 7 and 8

4. The demand for homes in an area usually does not change in response to
   a. changes in zoning laws.
   b. changes in the local school system.
   c. changes in building laws.
   d. The demand for homes in an area can change in response to all of the above.

5. Points are usually between _____ percent of the mortgage loan; loan origination fees are usually _____ percent of the mortgage amount provided by the lender.
   a. 1 and 2; 3
   b. 2 and 3; 2
   c. 1 and 2; 1
   d. 2 and 3; 4

The following information applies to questions 6 and 7.

Trevor Hopkins just applied for a $90,000 mortgage from Bank A. Bank A will charge the following:

- 2 points
- 1 percent origination fee
- $250 application fee
- $500 for a title search

6. Trevor's closing costs total
   a. $1,150.
   b. $1,650.
   c. $2,550.
   d. $3,450.

7. Trevor's down payment is 10 percent of the $100,000 cost of the home. Thus, he will need a total of _____ to purchase the home.
   a. $11,150
   b. $11,650
   c. $12,550
   d. $13,450

8. During the early years of a fixed-rate mortgage, a large percentage of the monthly mortgage payment will represent
   a. principal reduction.
   b. interest payments.
   c. a reduction in the home's equity.
   d. none of the above

9. The _____ the interest rate on the mortgage, the _____ the monthly mortgage payment.
   a. higher; larger
   b. lower; larger
   c. higher; smaller
   d. Answers (b) and (c) are correct.

10. When interest rates are expected to rise, home-owners would prefer a(n)
    a. fixed-rate mortgage.
    b. adjustable-rate mortgage.
    c. variable-rate mortgage.
    d. mixed-rate mortgage.

11. Adjustable-rate mortgages represent about _____ percent of all home mortgages.
    a. 60
    b. 50
    c. 25
    d. 10

12. Without exception, adjustable-rate mortgages (ARMs) adjust the mortgage rate every
    a. year.
    b. two years.
    c. three years.
    d. none of the above

13. The primary cost of purchasing a home is
    a. the down payment.
    b. the monthly mortgage payments.
    c. the down payment and the monthly mortgage payments.
    d. the closing costs.

The following information applies to questions 14 through 16.

Oliver Vorth is currently renting an apartment for $1,000 a month. Oliver does not believe that this rent will change in the next four years. At the time Oliver rented the apartment, he left a $500 security deposit. Oliver is thinking about purchasing a $150,000 home requiring a down payment of $20,000 and monthly mortgage payments of $800. Annual property taxes associated with the home would be $1,500. One-time closing costs total $650. Oliver expects to pay maintenance of $1,200 a year for the home. Furthermore, Oliver's total interest payments and property tax payments over the next four years will be approximately $28,000. Oliver is in the 28 percent tax bracket and can invest his funds at an annual interest rate of 5 percent.

14. Including any opportunity costs, what is Oliver's total cost of renting over the next four years?
    a. $12,000
    b. $12,080
    c. $48,000
    d. $48,100

15. What would Oliver's total mortgage payments be over the next four years?
    a. $38,400
    b. $39,050
    c. $58,400
    d. $59,050

16. Including any opportunity costs, Oliver's total cost of purchasing would be
    a. $47,960.
    b. $41,510.
    c. $66,010.
    d. $61,510.

17. A _____ mortgage sets relatively low monthly mortgage payments when the mortgage is first created and then gradually increases the payments over the first few years.
    a. fixed-rate
    b. adjustable-rate
    c. graduated payment
    d. balloon payment

18. A _____ mortgage sets relatively low monthly payments and then requires one large payment after a specified period to pay off the remainder of the mortgage loan.
    a. fixed-rate
    b. adjustable-rate
    c. graduated payment
    d. balloon payment

19. Adjustable-rate mortgages (ARMs) are especially desired by homeowners who expect interest rates to _____ in the future.
    a. increase
    b. decline
    c. remain stable
    d. none of the above

20. When purchasing a home, which of the following costs will you not incur?
    a. down payment
    b. closing costs
    c. realtor's commission
    d. loan application fee

21. _____ mortgages guarantee repayment of the loan to the lender.
    a. Federally insured
    b. Conventional
    c. Graduated payment
    d. Adjustable-rate

Part 3: Brad Brooks—A Continuing Case

 Thanks to your help, Brad Brooks is feeling so good about the state of his personal finances that he decides it is time to celebrate by upgrading his car and housing situations. Brad has stopped using his cell phone for personal calls and has more closely monitored his entertainment expenses. As a result, his monthly cash inflows now exceed his outflows by approximately $350 per month. Brad has found a red SUV—his favorite color. He can get the fully loaded car for $35,000. He still owes $10,000 on his two-year-old sedan (which has 57,000 miles) and has found a buyer who will pay him $15,000 cash. This would enable him to pay off his current car loan and still have $5,000 for a down payment on the SUV, which he would finance for four years at 8 percent. Anticipating your objections to purchasing the SUV, Brad has an alternative plan to lease the SUV for three years. The terms of the lease are $600 per month, 15,000 miles per year (20 cents per mile average charge), and $1,200 due upon signing for the first month's lease payment and security deposit.

Brad also has been given the opportunity to purchase his condo. He knows that he will enjoy tax advantages with ownership and is eager to reduce his tax burden. He can make the purchase with 10 percent down; the total purchase price is $90,000. Closing fees and other loan costs due at closing will total $3,100. The taxes on his condo will be $1,800 per year, his Property Owners' Association (POA) fee is $70 per month, and his insurance will increase by $360 a year.

1. Refer to Brad's personal cash flow statement that you developed in Part 1. Recompute his expenses to determine if Brad can afford to:

   a. purchase the new car.

   b. lease the new car.

   c. purchase his condo.

   d. purchase both the car and the condo.

   e. lease the car and purchase the condo.

2. What are the advantages and disadvantages to Brad of leasing rather than purchasing a car?

3. Based on the information you provided, Brad decides not to buy the condo at this time. How can he save the necessary funds to purchase a condo or house in the future? Be specific in your recommendations.

4. How would your advice to Brad differ if he were:

   a. 45 years old?

   b. 60 years old?

5. Prepare a written or oral report on your findings and recommendations to Brad.

PART 4

Personal Investing

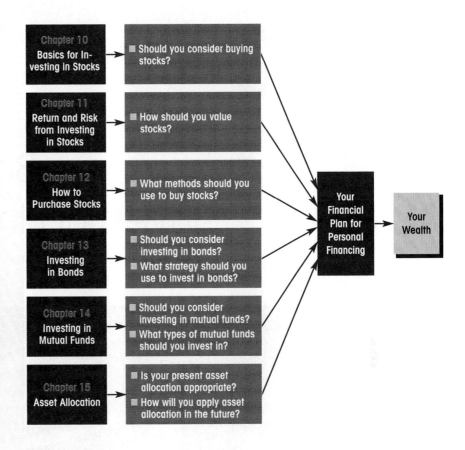

Chapter 10 Basics for Investing in Stocks	■ Should you consider buying stocks?
Chapter 11 Return and Risk from Investing in Stocks	■ How should you value stocks?
Chapter 12 How to Purchase Stocks	■ What methods should you use to buy stocks?
Chapter 13 Investing in Bonds	■ Should you consider investing in bonds? ■ What strategy should you use to invest in bonds?
Chapter 14 Investing in Mutual Funds	■ Should you consider investing in mutual funds? ■ What types of mutual funds should you invest in?
Chapter 15 Asset Allocation	■ Is your present asset allocation appropriate? ■ How will you apply asset allocation in the future?

Your Financial Plan for Personal Financing → Your Wealth

The chapters in this part explain the various types of investments that are available, how to value investments, and how to determine which investments to select. Chapters 10, 11, and 12 focus on decisions regarding investing in stock, while Chapter 13 highlights investing in bonds. Chapter 14 on mutual funds explains the advantages and disadvantages of investing in a portfolio of securities rather than individual stocks and bonds. Chapter 15 shows the importance of allocating your money across various types of investments. Your decisions regarding whether to invest, how much to invest, and how to invest will affect your cash flows and wealth.

Chapter 10

Basics for Investing in Stocks

Investing is an important part of financial planning. Before selecting a particular investment, you need to set investment goals and determine how much money you can invest. There are many different types of investments that you can consider. One of the most popular types of investments is stock, which is the focus of this chapter and the next two chapters.

You may consider investing in stocks to earn a high return, therefore increasing your wealth. Before investing in stocks, you should understand how to assess their potential return, risk, and sensitivity to economic and industry conditions. Your ability to analyze stocks in this manner can enhance your dividend income (cash inflows) generated by your investments in stock and can increase the value of your assets (stock holdings) over time. Therefore, an understanding of stock analysis basics can enhance your wealth.

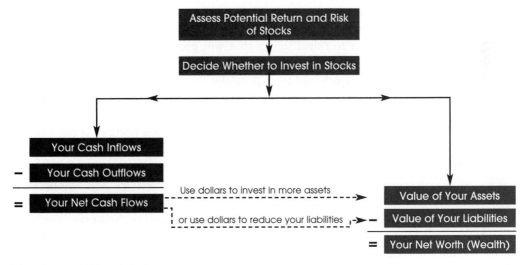

The objectives of this chapter are to:

- provide a background on stocks,
- explain stock returns,
- identify the risks of investing in stocks,
- identify the functions of stock exchanges, and
- explain how to interpret stock price quotations.

BACKGROUND ON STOCKS

stocks
Certificates that represent partial ownership of a firm.

As defined in Chapter 2, **stocks** are certificates that represent partial ownership of a firm. Firms issue stocks to obtain funds to support their business operations. For example, a firm might use the funds to build a manufacturing plant, implement a marketing program, or purchase machinery. In this way, the issuance of stock enables the firm to expand its operations, thereby generating additional earnings that can be reinvested in the firm. Stock has no maturity date, so the stock can exist forever, although when some corporations have excess cash available, they periodically repurchase some of the stock they issued.

In addition to being beneficial to corporations, stocks are a common investment for investors. When investors purchase a specific stock of any particular firm, they become shareholders of the firm. Investors invest in stock because they believe that they may earn a higher return than if they invested the money in a bank deposit or alternative money market investments. Since many individuals invest a substantial amount of money in stocks, an understanding of stocks is a critical part of personal finance.

Investors can be classified as institutional investors or individual investors. **Institutional investors** are professionals who are responsible for investing the money of a financial institution on behalf of the clients they serve. They attempt to select stocks that will provide a reasonable return on investment. The employees of financial institutions who make investment decisions are referred to as portfolio managers because they manage a portfolio of securities (including stocks). More than half of all trading in financial markets is attributable to institutional investors.

institutional investors
Professionals who are responsible for investing the money of a financial institution on behalf of the clients they serve.

Individual investors commonly invest a portion of the money earned from their jobs. Like institutional investors, they invest in stocks to earn a reasonable return on their investment. In this way, their money can grow by the time they wish to use it to make purchases. The number of individuals involved in investing has increased substantially in the last 20 years, as they have become more interested in managing their own investments.

individual investors
Individuals who invest a portion of their own money earned from their jobs.

Many individual investors hold their stocks for periods beyond one year. In contrast, some individual investors called **day traders** buy stocks and then sell them on the same day. They hope to capitalize on very short-term movements in security prices. In many cases, their investments last for only a few minutes. Many day traders conduct their investing as a career, relying on their returns from investing as their main source of income. This type of investing is very risky because the stock prices of even the best-managed firms periodically decline due to economic and industry conditions. Day trading is not recommended for most investors.

day traders
Individual investors who buy stocks and then sell them on the same day to capitalize on very short-term movements in security prices.

Dividends

As mentioned in Chapter 2, some firms distribute a portion of their earnings as dividends to investors. Other firms elect not to pay dividends and instead reinvest all earnings in the firm. Dividends are normally paid on a quarterly basis. For stocks that pay dividends, the typical amount of dividends paid per year is usually between 1 and 3 percent of the stock's price at the beginning of the year. Firms tend to keep their dividend level at a fixed dollar amount per share, but may increase this amount periodically.

Firms generally prefer not to reduce their dividends, but sometimes have to if they experience low or no profits and therefore do not have sufficient funds to pay their dividends.

Common versus Preferred Stock

common stock
A certificate issued by a firm to raise funds that represents partial ownership in the firm.

preferred stock
A certificate issued by a firm to raise funds that entitles shareholders to first priority (ahead of common stockholders) to receive dividends.

Stock can be classified as common stock or preferred stock. **Common stock** is a certificate issued by a firm to raise funds that represents partial ownership in the firm. Investors who hold common stock normally have the right to vote on issues such as the election of the board of directors, who are responsible for ensuring that the firm's managers serve the interests of its shareholders. **Preferred stock** is a certificate issued by a firm to raise funds that entitles shareholders to first priority (ahead of common stockholders) to receive dividends. Corporations issue common stock more frequently than preferred stock. The price of preferred stock is not as volatile as the price of common stock and does not have as much potential to increase substantially. For this reason, investors who strive for high returns typically invest in common stock. Cautious investors may prefer preferred stock because it is less risky.

Roles of the Primary and Secondary Markets

primary market
A market where newly issued securities are traded.

initial public offering (IPO)
The first offering of a firm's stock to the public.

A **primary market** is a market where newly issued securities are traded. The first offering of a firm's stock to the public is referred to as an **initial public offering (IPO)**. During 1998, the mean increase in price for Internet stocks on the first trading day following the IPO was 84 percent. If you had invested $10,000 in each of these Internet IPOs at the initial price, on average you would have accumulated $8,400 more than your investment in a single day. Some IPOs have generated a return of more than 500 percent in their first day of trading. For example, shares of theglobe.com increased by 606 percent on its first day. On December 9, 1999, an IPO for the firm VA Linux Systems began with an initial price of $30 per share. By the end of that day, the share price was $239.25. Investors who purchased the shares at the offering price had a one-day return on their investment of 698 percent. An investment of $10,000 at the initial price was worth almost $80,000 by the end of the first day. News like this has interested many investors in investing in IPO stocks.

Individual investors do not necessarily have access to these IPOs at the initial price, however. Institutional investors (such as mutual funds or insurance companies with large amounts of money to invest) normally have the first shot at purchasing shares of an IPO. Most individual investors can invest (if there are any shares left) only after the institutional investors have had a chance to purchase shares.

Although some IPOs have generated spectacular returns for investors, many other IPOs have performed poorly. The stock price of 1-800- Flowers. com declined by 41 percent over the four months following its IPO in August 1999, while CareerBuilder's stock price declined by 56 percent over

"Good news! I held my IPO at recess and now I'm the 12th richest man in America."

the seven months following its IPO in June 1999. On average, the long-term return on IPOs is weak compared to typical returns of other stocks in aggregate. Many firms (such as pets.com) that engaged in IPOs have failed within a few years, causing investors to lose all of their investment.

After an IPO, investors who purchased the stock can sell it to other investors in the **secondary market**, where existing stocks are traded. The secondary market is critical, because it enables investors to easily sell their stock holdings to other investors whenever they need funds or expect that the stock price will decrease in the future. The price of a stock changes continuously as a result of changes in the supply of the security for sale by some investors and changes in the demand for that security by other investors in the secondary market. To distinguish between the primary and secondary markets, consider the following example.

secondary market
A market where existing stocks are traded.

10.1 Financial Planning Online: IPOs

Go to:
http://www.ipo.com

This Web site provides:
information about firms that are about to engage in an IPO and also summarizes the performance of recent IPOs.

Example

In April 1996, Yahoo! used the primary market to raise funds for its business by engaging in an IPO. Many investors purchased Yahoo! shares at the time of the IPO. Some shareholders sold their shares sometime after the IPO in the secondary market. These shares were not repurchased by Yahoo! but were simply sold to other investors who wished to purchase Yahoo! stock. Investors who purchased Yahoo! stock at the time of the IPO earned a large gain from selling their shares later, as the price of Yahoo! stock increased over time.

RETURN FROM INVESTING IN STOCKS

Shareholders can earn a return on their investment in two ways. First, they can receive dividends. Second, they can earn a return if the price of the stock increases by the time they sell it. The market value of a firm is based on the number of shares of stock outstanding multiplied by the price of the stock. The price of a share of stock is determined by dividing the market value of the firm by the number of shares of stock outstanding. Thus, a firm that has a market value of $600 million and 10 million shares of stock outstanding has a value per share of:

$$\text{Value of Stock per Share} = \text{Market Value of Firm/Number of Shares Outstanding}$$
$$= \$600,000,000/10,000,000$$
$$= \$60.$$

The market price of a stock is dependent on the number of investors who are willing to purchase the stock (the demand for the stock) and the number of investors who wish to sell their holdings of the stock (the supply of stock for sale). There is no limit to how high a stock's price can rise. The demand for the stock and the supply of stock for sale are influenced by the respective firm's business performance, as measured by its earnings and other characteristics. When the firm performs well, its stock becomes more desirable to investors, who demand more shares of that stock. In addition, investors holding shares of this stock are less willing to sell it. The increase in the demand for the stock and the reduction in the number of shares of stock for sale by investors result in a higher stock price.

Conversely, when a firm performs poorly (has low or negative earnings), its market value declines. The demand for shares of its stock also declines. In addition, some investors who had been holding the stock will decide to sell their shares, thereby increasing the supply of stock for sale and resulting in a lower stock price. The performance of the firm depends on how well it is managed. Investors benefit when they invest in a well-managed firm because the firm's earnings usually will increase, and so will its stock price. Under these conditions, investors will be able to sell the stock in the future at a higher price than they paid for it, which results in a capital gain for them. Conversely, a poorly managed firm may have lower earnings than expected and a low stock price.

Tradeoff between Dividends and Stock Price Appreciation

growth stocks
Stocks representing firms with substantial growth opportunities.

A firm's decision to distribute earnings as dividends, rather than reinvesting all of its earnings to support future growth, may depend on the opportunities that are available to the firm. In general, firms that pay high dividends tend to be older, established firms that have less chance for substantial growth. Conversely, firms that pay low dividends tend to be younger firms that have more growth opportunities. The stocks representing firms with substantial growth opportunities are often referred to as **growth stocks.** An investment in these younger firms offers the prospect of a very large return because they have not reached their potential. At the same time, an investment in these firms is exposed to much higher uncertainty because they are more likely to fail or experience very weak performance than mature firms.

income stocks
Stocks that provide investors with periodic income in the form of large dividends.

The higher the dividend paid by a firm, the lower is its potential stock price appreciation. When a firm distributes a large proportion of its earnings to investors as dividends, it limits its potential growth and the potential degree to which its value (and stock price) may increase. Stocks that provide investors with periodic income in the form of large dividends are referred to as **income stocks.**

Measuring a Stock's Return

Investors commonly estimate recent stock returns to determine how well their stocks have performed. The return on your investment in stocks accounts for any dividends you received as well as the change in the stock's price over your investment period:

$$R = \frac{(P_{t+1} - P_t) + D}{P_t}$$

where R is the return, P_t is the price of the stock at the time of the investment, P_{t+1} is the price of the stock at the end of the investment horizon, and D is the dividends earned over the investment horizon.

Example

You purchased 100 shares of Wax, Inc., stock for $50 per share one year ago. During the year, the firm experienced strong earnings. It paid dividends of $1 per share over the year, and you sold the stock for $58 at the end of the year. Your return on your investment was:

$$R = \frac{(P_{t+1} - P_t) + D}{P_t}$$

$$= \frac{(\$58 - \$50) + \$1}{\$50}$$

$$= .18 \text{ or } 18\%.$$

You are also interested in calculating the dollar amount of your return. The dollar amount of your investment is equal to the number of shares purchased (S) multiplied by the price paid per share (P_t), or:

Dollar Amount of Investment $= S \times P_t$

$$= 100 \times \$50$$

$$= \$5,000.$$

The dollar amount of your dividends is the number of your shares multiplied by the dividend per share (D):

Dollar Amount of Dividends $= S \times D$

$$= 100 \times \$1$$

$$= \$100.$$

The dollar amount received from selling the stock is the number of shares multiplied by the price per share at the time you sold the stock:

Dollar Amount Received from Selling the Stock $= S \times P_{t+1}$

$$= 100 \times \$58$$

$$= \$5,800.$$

The dollar amount of your return is the difference between what you received from dividends and from the sale of the stock and what you paid for the stock, or:

Dollar Amount of Return = (Dollar Amount + Dollar Amount − Dollar Amount
of Dividends   Received from   Paid for the Stock
Selling the Stock)

$$= (\$100 + \$5,800) - \$5,000$$

$$= \$900.$$

The dollar amount of the return is not directly comparable between investments because of differences in the amount invested. A $900 return on a $5,000 investment is much better than a $1,000 return on a $50,000 investment. Therefore, return is most commonly measured on a percentage basis. In our example, the $900 earned from investing in the stock can be measured as a percentage of the investment ($5,000):

Return $= \$900/\$5,000$

$$= .18 \text{ or } 18\%.$$

Note that this is the same as the return computed earlier in the example.

10.2   Financial Planning Online: Estimating the Stock Price Needed to Achieve Your Desired Return

Go to:

http://www.financenter.com/
products/analyzers/stock.fcs

Click on:

"At what price should I sell a
stock to achieve my target rate
of return?"

This Web site provides:

an estimate of the price at
which you need to sell a stock
you own in order to achieve a
return that you specify.

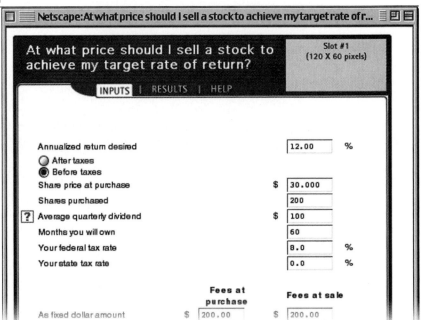

Differential Tax Effects on Returns. Recall from Chapter 4 that dividends received and capital gains resulting from the sale of stocks held one year or less are classified as ordinary income for federal income tax purposes. Capital gains resulting from the sale of stocks held more than one year are subject to a long-term capital gains tax. Given the differences in tax rates applied to short-term and long-term capital gains, some investors may achieve a higher return by investing in stocks and holding them for more than one year.

Example

Continue with the facts of the previous example where you purchased 100 shares of Wax stock, except that instead of selling the stock after one year, you sell the stock after 366 days (one day beyond a year). By holding the stock for one more day, your capital gain shifts from a short-term gain to a long-term gain (taxed at 20 percent). Assume that your marginal tax rate (tax rate charged on any additional ordinary income) is 40 percent. The tax effects of the previous example with the short-term capital gain are shown in the second column of Exhibit 10.1, while the tax effects of the long-term capital gain are shown in the third column. The taxes on dividends are as follows:

Tax on Dividends Received = Amount of Dividend × Marginal Income Tax Rate

= $100 × .40

= $40.

The tax on capital gains depends on whether the gain is short term or long term. The short-term capital gains tax is:

Tax on Short-Term Capital Gain = Amount of Short-Term Capital Gain ×
Marginal Income Tax Rate
= $800 × .40
= $320.

The long-term capital gains tax is:

Tax on Long-Term Capital Gain = Amount of Long-Term Capital Gain ×
Long-Term Capital Gain Tax Rate
= $800 × .20
= $160.

The long-term capital gains tax is $160 lower than the short-term capital gains tax. Thus, your after-tax income from holding the stock one extra day is $160 higher. It is possible to offset a capital gain with a capital loss, as described in the appendix to this chapter.

Exhibit 10.1   Comparing the Tax Effects on Short- and Long-Term Capital Gains

	If Stock Is Held for One Year:	If Stock Is Held for More than One Year:
Dividends	$100	$100
Short-term capital gain	800	0
Long-term capital gain	0	800
Total income	$900	$900
Tax on dividends (40%)	$40	$40
Short-term capital gains tax (40%)	320	0
Long-term capital gains tax (20%)	0	160
Total taxes	$360	$200
After-tax income	$540	$700

How Wealth Is Influenced by Stock Returns

If the value of your stock investments increases, and your liabilities do not increase, your wealth increases. Thus, the degree to which you can accumulate wealth is partially dependent on your stock investment decisions if you choose to invest in stocks. If you save some money during the year and invest it in stocks at the end the year, the future value (FV) of this investment

10.3   Financial Planning Online: Estimating the Return on Your Stock

Go to:
http://www.financenter.com/
products/analyzers/stock.fcs

Click on:
"What is the return on my
stocks if I sell now?"

This Web site provides:
an estimate of the return that
you would earn on your stock
over the period you held it if
you decide to sell the stock
now.

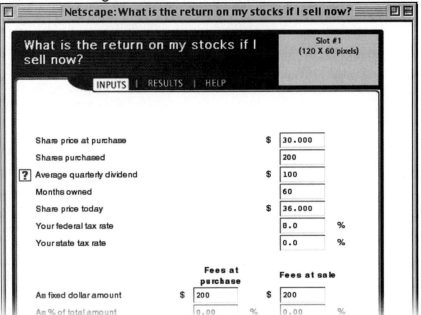

can be measured using the time value of money for the future value interest factors for an annuity as:

$$FV \text{ of Stock Investment} = \text{Investment} \times FVIFA_{i,n}$$

where i is the annual return on the investment and n is the number of years
until the end of the investment period.

Example

Stephanie Spratt has $4,000 that she can use to invest in
stocks. If she earns an annual return of 6 percent on her investment, she determines that the value of those stocks will be
$7,163 in 10 years. If she earns an annual return of 10 percent,
the value of those stocks will be $10,375 in 10 years. If she can
earn an annual return of 20 percent, the value of her investment will be
$24,767 in 10 years. The higher the rate of return, the higher the future
value interest factor of an annuity (*FVIFA*), and the larger the amount of
funds that she will accumulate.

If you can invest a specific amount in the stock market every year, the
future value of these annual investments can be estimated as:

$$FV \text{ of Annual Stock Investments} = \text{Annual Investment} \times FVIFA_{i,n}.$$

Example

Stephanie Spratt believes that she can save $4,000 to invest in stocks at the end of each year for the next 10 years. If she expects to earn 10 percent on her investments, she can use the future value interest factor of an annuity at 10 percent over 10 years, which is 15.937 (see the table on page 608). Based on her annual investment of $4,000 and the future value interest factor of an annuity (FVIFA), she will accumulate:

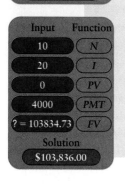

FV of Annual Stock Investments = Annual Investment × $FVIFA_{i,n}$
$$= \$4,000 \times 15.937$$
$$= \$63,748.$$

The input for the financial calculator is as shown at the left.

If Stephanie can earn an annual return of 20 percent on her investments, the FVIFA is 25.959, and the value of her annual investments in 10 years will be:

FV of Annual Stock Investments = Annual Investment × $FVIFA_{i,n}$
$$= \$4,000 \times 25.959$$
$$= \$103,836.$$

The input for the financial calculator is as shown at the left.

Notice how the increase in Stephanie's wealth is sensitive to the rate of return earned on her annual investment. The 20 percent annual return would allow her to accumulate $40,088 more than if she earned only a 10 percent annual return.

The example shows how the performance of your investments can result in significant differences in your future wealth. Thus, an understanding of how to value stocks can enable you to make stock investment decisions that increase your returns and enhance your wealth.

RISK FROM INVESTING IN STOCKS

The value of a firm's stock varies over time with the firm's actual and potential performance. A firm's business performance is influenced by future economic conditions (such as an increase in economic growth), industry conditions (such as an increase in competition), and the firm's specific conditions (such as its business decisions). Because these conditions are uncertain, the firm's future performance is uncertain, and so is the return on the firm's stock.

Stocks of relatively small firms usually have greater potential for growth and a higher return over time. They exhibit more uncertainty, and also are more exposed to the possibility of substantial declines in price than larger stocks. The stock prices of firms that experience very poor performance (weak sales, high expenses, possible failure) may decline substantially over time and could even fall to zero.

Example

You consider purchasing Bizarre.com stock at a price of $60 per share. You expect to earn a return of 14 percent from this investment because analysts predict the firm's sales and earnings will increase. You decide to track the stock's performance for several months. You notice that the firm's revenue and earnings are declining. Due to these adverse conditions, Bizarre.com does not pay its dividend, and its price declines to $48. The return on the stock over this year based on these adverse conditions would be:

$$R = \frac{(P_{t+1} - P_t) + D}{P_t}$$

$$= \frac{(\$48 - \$60) + \$0}{\$60}$$

$$= -.20 \text{ or } -20\%.$$

You expected this stock to provide a 14 percent return, but it declined in value by 20 percent. As this example illustrates, the returns on stocks are uncertain.

The performance of individual stocks varies enormously. For example, in 1999, Family Golf Centers stock experienced a loss of 93 percent. If you had invested $10,000 at the beginning of that year, your investment would have been worth just $700 by the end of the year. Just For Feet stock also experienced a loss of 93 percent over the same period. Compare these losses to the gain of 3,770 percent for Puma Technology stock over the same period, which would have turned your $10,000 investment into $387,000 after one year. Few would have guessed that Puma Technology would perform so well, or that Family Golf Centers and Just For Feet would perform so poorly. These examples illustrate how the potential returns of stocks are subject to much uncertainty. You tend to hear about the stocks that perform extremely well. Yet the prices of many stocks of small companies have become worthless, and the investors in those stocks lost their entire investment. Although it is impossible to accurately predict a stock's return, the potential risk of an investment can be analyzed.

Measuring a Stock's Risk

range of returns
The difference between a stock's highest return and its lowest return over a given period.

Investors measure the risk of stocks to determine the degree of uncertainty surrounding their future returns. The most widely used measures of a stock's risk are its range of returns, its beta, and the standard deviation of its returns.

Range of Returns. By reviewing the monthly returns of a specific stock over a given period (available at various Web sites), you can determine the **range**

of returns, from the smallest (most negative) to the largest return. Compare a stock that has a range of monthly returns from −3 percent to +4 percent over the last year with another stock that has a range of −11 percent to +10 percent. The first stock is less risky because its range of returns is smaller and therefore is more stable. Stocks with a wide range are normally perceived to have more risk because they have a higher probability of experiencing a large decline in price.

beta

A common measure of the risk of a stock that indicates its sensitivity to general market movements.

Beta. The risk of a stock is commonly measured by its **beta,** or its sensitivity to general market movements. Betas of stocks are estimated and reported by various investment services, such as Value Line. A stock that moves in tandem with the overall stock market will have a beta equal to about 1.0. This means that the stock is expected to change by 1 percent in the same direction as the stock market for every 1 percent change in the market.

A stock that moves by a smaller degree than the stock market has a beta of less than 1.0, meaning it moves in the same direction as the stock market but by a smaller degree. If a stock has a beta of .6, its returns are expected to move by only .6 percent for every 1 percent change in the stock market. Stocks with low betas do not perform as well as most other stocks during periods of rising stock prices, but do not decline as much as most other stocks during periods of declining prices.

A stock that moves by a larger degree than the stock market has a beta of more than 1.0. For example, if a stock has a beta of 1.2, its returns are expected to move by 1.2 percent for every 1 percent change in the market. Stocks with high betas perform better than most other stocks during periods of rising stock prices, but perform worse than most during periods of declining prices.

Example

You are considering investing in three different stocks (X, Y, and Z). You review a financial Web site that provides the beta of each stock, as shown in the second column of Exhibit 10.2. Given the beta, you can estimate how each of the three stocks would perform based on the scenarios in column 3 (favorable market conditions) and column 4 (unfavorable market conditions).

Notice that the possible returns of stock Z (the high-beta stock) are more dispersed than those of the other stocks. Its returns are stronger than the others under favorable conditions and weaker than the others under unfavorable conditions. Thus, it has potential for high returns (under favorable conditions), but is also subject to a high degree of risk (very poor returns under unfavorable conditions). If you are willing to tolerate much risk, you would consider investing in stock Z, but if you want to play it safe, you would avoid stock Z.

Exhibit 10.2   How a Stock's Beta Affects Its Expected Returns

	Beta	Stock's Expected Return If Market Return Is 10%	Stock's Expected Return If Market Return is −10%
Stock X	.6	6%	−6%
Stock Y	1.0	10%	−10%
Stock Z	1.3	13%	−13%

A stock's beta can change over time, so it is not possible to predict a stock's return based on a market return with perfect accuracy. Nevertheless, the beta does provide a general indication of how a stock will respond to stock market conditions.

standard deviation

A measure of the degree of volatility in a stock's returns over time.

Standard Deviation of Returns. A third measure of risk is the **standard deviation** of a stock's monthly returns, which measures the degree of volatility in the stock's returns over time. A large standard deviation means that the stock returns deviate substantially from the mean over time. For example, suppose that stock J has a mean monthly return of 1 percent, but a standard deviation of 10 percent. This means that stock J's return commonly deviates from the mean by a large amount. Meanwhile stock K also has a mean monthly return of 1 percent, but a standard deviation of only 3 percent.

10.4   Financial Planning Online: Price Trends of Your Stocks

Go to:
http://finance.yahoo.com/

This Web site provides:
historical price movements for a stock that you specify. Type in the symbol for your stock and then click on "Charts." You can assess the price movements of the stock you specify for today, for the last year, or even for the last five years. You can easily monitor the price of a stock you already own or may purchase in the future.

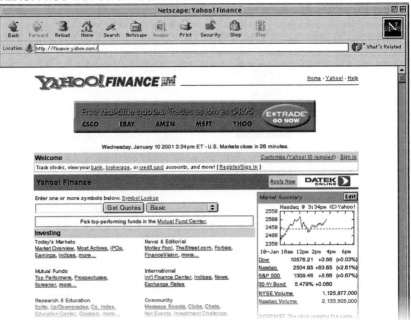

Stock K's monthly returns deviate from its mean return to a smaller degree. The more volatile a stock, the greater the chance that the stock could deviate far from its mean in a given period. Thus, a stock with a high standard deviation is more likely to experience a large gain or a large loss in a given period. The stock's return is subject to greater uncertainty, and for this reason, it is perceived as more risky.

Although the three risk measures differ, they tend to rank the risk levels of stocks somewhat consistently. That is, a very risky stock will normally have a relatively high beta, a wide range of returns, and a high standard deviation of returns.

Limiting Your Risk from Investing in Stocks

The amount of risk that individual investors can tolerate is subjective. They can select investments that are subject to little or no uncertainty, but will earn a relatively low return. At the other extreme, they can select investments that have the potential to earn more than 50 percent in a single year, but also entail much risk. Many other investments are available that are in between these two extremes. Investors who decide to pursue higher potential returns must be willing to accept the higher risk associated with these investments.

You can reduce your risk from investing in stocks in many ways. First, you can focus your investments on stocks of firms that have been successful for many years. Investments in such stocks can still result in a loss, but there is less risk than if you invest in the stock of a small firm that has been in business for only a few years.

Second, you can diversify your investments among many different stocks, thereby reducing your exposure to any particular stock. If you divide your money equally among five stocks, and one stock performs poorly, your exposure is limited. The other stocks should not be adversely affected by the conditions affecting that firm. You could limit your exposure even more by diversifying among several different stocks in different industries.

Even if you diversify your investment among various stocks, you are still exposed to general stock market conditions, as the values of all stocks can decline during periods in which stock market conditions are weak. For this reason, you should consider investing in other investments along with stocks. This will be discussed in more detail in Chapter 15 on asset allocation.

One additional way to limit your risk from investing in stocks is to learn as much as you can about your investments and the stock market in general before making investment decisions. Stay up-to-date with current events, especially financial news. With more knowledge, you can make more prudent investment decisions.

STOCK EXCHANGES

Investors who are considering purchasing stocks must understand how the stock markets work. They need to know about stock exchanges and how to review the list of stocks that are traded on each exchange.

stock exchanges
Facilities that allow investors to purchase or sell existing stocks.

Stock exchanges are facilities that allow investors to purchase or sell existing stocks. They facilitate trading in the secondary market so that investors can sell specific stocks that they previously purchased. An organized securities exchange occupies a physical location where trading occurs. A stock has to be listed on a stock exchange to be traded there, meaning that it must fulfill specific requirements of the exchange; for example, to list its stock, a firm may have to be a minimum size and have a minimum number of shares of stock outstanding. The requirements ensure that there will be an active market for the stock in which shares are commonly traded.

New York Stock Exchange

The most popular organized exchange in the United States is the New York Stock Exchange (NYSE), which handles transactions for more than 3,000 stocks. The transactions are conducted by the traders who own the 1,300 "seats" on the NYSE and are allowed to trade stocks listed on the exchange for themselves or for others. A seat essentially represents a license to trade stocks on the exchange. All 1,300 seats are occupied. A would-be trader can obtain a seat only if someone else is willing to sell it. The price of a seat was about $46,000 in 1990 but about $2.7 million in 2000—an indication of the increased demand for seats. Some traders (called **floor traders**) execute trades to accommodate requests by other investors (such as yourself) while other traders execute trades for themselves.

floor traders
Traders at a stock exchange who execute trades to fulfill orders placed by other investors.

When floor traders execute trades for other investors, they earn a commission in the form of a bid-ask spread, which reflects the difference between the price at which they are willing to buy a stock and the price at which they are willing to sell it. For example, suppose a trader executed an order where one investor bid $20.12 per share to buy a stock while the seller received $20.00 per share. The bid-ask spread of $.12 per share goes to the floor trader. In this example, a trade of 1,000 shares cost $120 because of the bid-ask spread. Some traders, called **specialists**, help to make a market in one or more stocks by taking the position opposite of orders placed by clients. That is, they may be willing to buy the stocks that you want to sell or sell holdings of their stocks that you want to buy.

specialists
Traders who help to make a market in one or more stocks by taking the position opposite of orders placed by clients.

A Typical Stock Transaction on the NYSE. Investors who trade stocks have an account at a brokerage firm (Chapter 12 describes the use of brokerage accounts to purchase stock in more detail). To buy a stock that is listed on the NYSE, they tell their brokerage firm the name of the stock and the number of shares they want to purchase. The brokerage firm sends the message electronically to one of the floor traders at the NYSE, who stands at a specific spot on the trading floor where that stock is traded. The floor trader signals a willingness to buy the shares of that stock and receives a response from another trader there who is trying to sell that stock. The price is negotiated using hand signals. Once the trade is completed, the floor broker at the NYSE sends confirmation to the brokerage firm that the trade has been made, and the brokerage firm informs the investor that the trade has been completed.

Other Stock Exchanges

About 800 stocks are listed on the American Stock Exchange (AMEX). These stocks are generally from smaller firms and are less actively traded than those on the NYSE. There are also some regional securities exchanges located in large U.S. cities. These regional exchanges tend to have less stringent listing requirements and therefore list stocks from smaller firms that may be well known in that specific region. Stocks are traded on the AMEX and the regional stock exchanges in much the same way as on the NYSE.

Over-the-Counter (OTC) Market

over-the-counter (OTC) market
An electronic communications network that allows investors to buy or sell securities.

market-makers
Traders who execute trades on the OTC market and earn commissions in the form of a bid-ask spread.

The **over-the-counter (OTC) market** is an electronic communications network that allows investors to buy or sell securities. It is not a visible facility like the organized exchanges. Trades are communicated through a computer network by **market-makers,** who execute the trades on the OTC, and earn commissions in the form of a bid-ask spread. Whereas trades on stock exchanges are between two traders who are standing next to each other, trades in the OTC market are conducted over a computer network between two dealers sitting in their respective offices, who may be hundreds or thousands of miles apart.

The listing requirements for the OTC market are generally less stringent than those for the NYSE. More than 4,000 stocks are listed on the OTC market. A key part of the OTC market is the Nasdaq, or the National Association of Securities Dealers Automated Quotation system. The Nasdaq provides continual updated market price information on OTC stocks that meet its requirements on size and trading volume. The Nasdaq and the AMEX merged in 1998, although they still perform separate functions.

Electronic Communication Networks (ECNs)

Electronic Communication Networks (ECNs)
Computer systems that match up desired purchases and sales of stocks.

Electronic Communication Networks (ECNs) are computer systems that match up desired purchases and sales of stocks. For example, the ECN receives orders from investors to buy shares of a stock at a specified price and matches them up with orders from investors to sell the stock at that price. A person is not needed to perform the match. ECNs now make up about 30 percent of all trading of Nasdaq stocks. ECNs are becoming very popular because they enable investors to bypass the market-makers who historically facilitated trading of Nasdaq stocks and therefore to avoid the transaction costs (bid-ask spread) charged by the market-makers.

ECNs are also being used to execute some transactions on the NYSE and AMEX. They can match orders any time, so they are especially valuable at night after the exchanges are closed.

At some online brokerage firms, if an order comes in after the stock exchanges are closed (during so-called after-hours trading), the firm will send the order to the ECNs where the trade will be executed. Currently, the one problem with using ECNs at night is that the trading volume may be insufficient. An investor who wants to sell a stock may not be able to find a willing buyer. In that case, the investor would have an easier time selling the stock during normal trading hours. As more investors learn that they can have orders executed at night by some online brokerage firms, the trading volume will increase, and the ECNs will become even more popular.

Foreign Stock Exchanges

Foreign stock exchanges facilitate investments in foreign securities. Most countries have at least one stock exchange where local stocks are traded. Investors in the United States can purchase foreign stocks through their brokerage firm. The U.S. brokerage firm electronically transfers the order to a brokerage firm in the foreign country. The foreign brokerage firm then transfers the order to the local stock exchange to complete the trade. The investor sends a check (in dollars) to the U.S. brokerage firm, which converts the money to a foreign currency and makes the payment. Investors' transaction costs for foreign stock trades are higher than for trades that can be completed on a U.S. exchange. Some foreign stocks are traded on U.S. stock exchanges as **American depository receipts**, which are certificates representing ownership of foreign stocks.

American depository receipts

Certificates representing ownership of foreign stocks.

STOCK QUOTATIONS

Price quotations are readily available for actively traded stocks. The most up-to-date quotes can be obtained electronically via a personal computer. Price information is available from stockbrokers and is widely published by the news media. Popular sources of stock quotations are financial newspapers (such as the *Wall Street Journal*), business sections of many local newspapers, financial news television networks (such as CNBC), and financial Web sites.

Stock quotations provide information about the price of each stock over the previous day or a recent period. An example of stock quotations provided by the *Wall Street Journal* is shown in Exhibit 10.3. Notice that the name of the stock is abbreviated in the third column; the ticker symbol of each stock is beside the name. Investors use the ticker symbol to identify the stock that they want a brokerage firm to buy or sell for their account. The first two columns show the stock's high and low price for the past year. This range indicates how volatile the stock's price has been. Some investors use this range as a simple measure of the firm's risk.

The annual dividends paid by the stock are shown in the fifth column, to the right of the ticker symbol. The dividend yield (annual dividends as a percentage of the stock price) is shown in the sixth column. This represents the annual return that you would receive just from the dividends if you purchased the stock today and if the dividend payments are unchanged.

Exhibit 10.3 Daily Stock Quotations

52 WEEKS HI	LO	STOCK	SYM	DIV	YLD %	PE	VOL 100s	HI	LO	CLOSE	NET CHG
3475	1544	▲FoxEntnGp A	FOX	...		cc	2862	2397	2375	2390	− 017
1763	955	FraGrthFd	FRF	3.91	39.5	...	143	990	980	990	+ 005
20994	5710	FraTelecm	FTE	.95	1.6	...	389	6151	5951	6009	− 196
2525	2006	FrnchsFin	FFA	2.22	10.0	9	1307	2250	2220	2243	+ 036
1119	638	FrnklnCovey	FC	...		dd	221	845	845	845	...
1238	426	FrnklnElcPub	FEP	...		92	89	590	545	550	− 050
893	675	FrnklnMulti	FMI	.67a	7.5	...	26	889	885	889	...
4830	2463	FrnklnRes	BEN	.26f	.6	18	3364	4260	4150	4174	− 093
835	631	FrnklnUnvlTr	FT	.80a	10.0	...	472	810	795	802	+ 002
7013	3688	FredMac	FRE	.68	1.0	19	37566	66	6390	6585	+ 085
5470	4363	FredMac pfK		2.90	5.5	...	2	53	53	53	− 050
2488	2144	FredMacDeb	FWG	1.67	6.8	...	4	2470	2470	2470	+ 006
1313	675	FrptMcCG A	FCXA	...		45	628	1276	1250	1265	− 010
1425	675	FrptMcCG B	FCX	...			9249	1405	1366	1405	+ 005
1638	925	FrptMcCG pfA		1.75	11.8	...	141	1498	1470	1485	− 013
2225	15	FrptMcCG pfB		1.23e	6.2	...	68	2007	1975	1994	− 017
1713	1250	FrptMcCG pfC		1.14e	7.7	...	53	1513	1485	1490	− 023
1275	675	FrptMcCG pfD		3.34e	36.3	...	25	925	9	920	− 005
756	150	FremontGen	FMT	.16	4.4	dd	3829	378	310	360	+ 059
1825	7	FremontGen TOPrS		2.25	15.0	...	193	1524	1380	15	+ 119
3088	2238	FresensMed	FMS	.22	.8	29	259	2720	27	2720	+ 004
1650	1325	FresensMed pf		.18	1.1	...	127	1625	1545	1610	+ 080
994	338	FrshDlMnte	FDP	...		13	213	775	750	775	+ 025
963	331	FriedeGldmn	FGH	...		dd	9824	385	250	271	− 105
1744	550	FrdmnBillRm	FBR	...		17	458	620	605	615	− 011
913	513	FrontrOil	FTO	...		7	2798	885	781	860	− 025
2676	1394	FurnBrndInt	FBN	...		11	3433	2491	2412	2455	− 050

-G-G-G-

52 WEEKS HI	LO	STOCK	SYM	DIV	YLD %	PE	VOL 100s	HI	LO	CLOSE	NET CHG
5050	29	GATX	GMT	1.24f	2.8	13	1689	4448	4310	4372	− 051
1057	650	G&L Rlty	GLR	.50	4.8	dd	26	1038	1029	1035	...
1725	1325	G&L Rlty pfA		2.56	15.2	...	9	1690	1650	1685	− 010
1675	12	G&L Rlty pfB		2.45	15.3	...	6	1620	1605	1605	− 020
3575	119	GC Cos	GCX	...		dd	63	255	250	250	− 001
713	306	GP Strategs	GPX	...		dd	138	429	410	425	+ 015
3719	2356	GPU Inc	GPU	2.18	7.0	16	4157	3110	3049	3099	+ 001
3688	16	Gabelli A	GBL	...		15	76	3015	2980	3003	+ 002

52 WEEKS HI	LO	STOCK	SYM	DIV	YLD %	PE	VOL 100s	HI	LO	CLOSE	NET CHG
3725	2425	▲Hertz	HRZ	.20	.6	11	419	3550	3544	3548	+ 003
sᵥ 6809	2845	HewlettPk	HWP	.32	1.1	18	94911	2939	2802	2885	+ 025
1544	475	Hexcel	HXL	...		...	296	1105	1095	1098	+ 001
1479	881	Hibernia	HIB	.52	3.6	14	4450	1453	1427	1450	+ 001
975	763	HilncoFd	HIO	1.01a	10.9	...	1444	928	920	928	+ 004
634	444	HiYldFd	HYI	.60	9.8	...	82	620	610	612	− 003
681	476	HiYldPlsFd	HYP	.87	14.1	...	384	615	607	615	+ 005
963	681	HighIndsIns	HIC	...		dd	143	819	8	819	+ 004
2719	2013	▲HighwdProp	HIW	2.28	9.2	14	2844	2525	2482	2490	+ 030
23	1619	▲HighwdProp pfB		2.00	9.0	...	11	2226	2205	2210	− 018
23	1650	▲HighwdProp pfD		2.00	9.0	...	34	2255	2224	2224	− 018
4213	2656	▲HilbRogl	HRH	.68	1.8	25	224	3825	3775	3825	+ 025
5638	2875	Hillenbrnd	HB	.84f	1.7	21	1567	5139	5062	5070	− 032
1263	638	Hilton	HLT	.08	.7	16	8666	1090	1060	1071	+ 012
s 6750	1869	HispBrdcst	HSP	...		54	5069	2354	2165	2250	+ 029
14625	8250	Hitachi	HIT	.80	.9	...	496	8792	8705	8775	− 011
1706	969	HollngrInt A	HLR	.55	3.4	65	2092	1640	1622	1630	+ 004
70	3469	HomeDpt	HD	.16	.4	38	79655	4493	4220	4250	− 210
3175	2550	▲HomePropNY	HME	2.28	8.5	18	662	27	2670	2695	+ 016
306	075	HomeBase	HBI	...		dd	6137	250	220	243	− 014
763	350	Hornestake	HM	.02	.4	dd	14087	567	550	582	− 015
2788	1556	HonInd	HNI	.48f	1.9	14	717	2495	2392	2485	+ 050
9075	6450	▲HondaMotor	HMC	.43e	.5	...	480	80	79	79	− 145
5913	3213	Honeywell	HON	.75	1.6	23	96458	4824	4575	4673	− 142
2219	12	▲HoraceMn	HMN	.42	2.5	33	1531	1669	1610	1662	+ 022
2175	1363	HormelFood	HRL	.37f	1.7	18	2053	2154	21	2150	+ 032
27	1021	▲HortonDR	DHI	.20f	.9	8	3244	2295	2238	2280	+ 043
2650	1856	HsptlyProp	HPT	2.80	10.8	12	1530	2623	2575	2595	− 005
2525	18	HsotlyProp pfA		2.38	9.7	...	35	25	2465	2465	− 045
2625	1950	HostMar pfA		2.50	9.7	...	70	2590	2577	2580	− 010
2618	1913	HostMar pfB		2.50	9.6	...	23	2609	2601	2605	− 013
1387	850	HostMar REIT	HMT	1.04f	8.2	dd	10287	1262	1225	1262	+ 018
5181	2950	▲HougtnMif	HTN	.52	1.2	23	1168	4315	4240	4248	− 004
2550	2025	HshldCapI TOPrS		2.06	8.3	...	2	2494	2494	2494	− 006
2575	2294	HshldCapII TOPrS		2.17	8.7	...	52	2505	2490	2490	− 015
2480	1875	HshldCapIV TOPrS		1.81	7.5	...	78	2450	2415	2425	− 005
n 2825	25	HshldCapV TOPrS		2.50	8.9	...	245	28	2785	28	...

10.5 Financial Planning Online: Today's Performance for All Stock Markets

Go to:

http://finance.yahoo.com/m2?u

This Web site provides:

a summary of today's performance for all major stock markets around the world. Click on "Charts" to review the historical movements of any country's stock index, or click on "News" for updated news about a specific market. This Web site allows you to monitor any stock market in which you may want to invest.

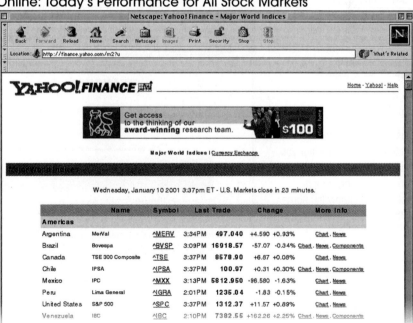

In the seventh column is the price-earnings (PE) ratio, which represents the stock price divided by the firm's earnings per share. Some investors closely monitor the PE ratio when attempting to value stocks, as will be discussed in more detail in Chapter 11.

The remaining information summarizes the trading of the stock on the previous day. The eighth column shows the volume of trading (in 100s). For some widely traded stocks, a million shares may trade per day, while 20,000 or fewer shares may trade per day for smaller stocks.

The ninth and tenth columns show the high ("hi") and low ("lo") price of the stock over the course of the previous day. If you considered purchasing a stock on the previous day, you can monitor the range of prices to determine the lowest and highest possible prices that you might have paid for the stock.

The closing price ("close") is shown in the eleventh column. It serves as a reasonable indicator of the opening price on the following day, but after-hours trading can cause the opening price today to differ from the official closing price yesterday. The last column discloses the net change ("net chg") in price in the stock, which is measured as the change in the closing price from the previous day. Investors review this column to determine how stock prices changed from one day to the next.

Review the stock quotations of Hilton stock, which is highlighted in Exhibit 10.3. Its ticker symbol is HLT. This is the symbol that is used when stock price quotations are disclosed in the financial news. Its price has

10.6   Financial Planning Online: Obtaining Stock Quotations

Go to:
http://finance.yahoo.com/?u

This Web site provides:
quotations on stocks that you identify by their symbol. You can also use the symbol lookup if you know the name of the firm but not the symbol.

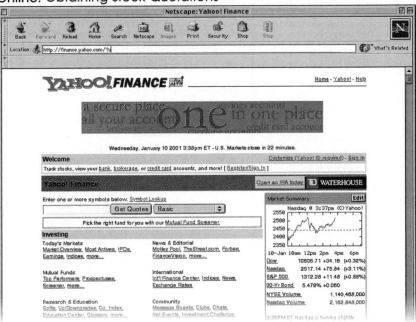

traded between $6.38 and $12.63 over the last 12 months. Its annual dividend is $.08, which represents an annualized yield of .7 percent if you buy the stock at its prevailing quoted price. Its PE ratio is 16, indicating that its stock is currently priced at 16 times its earnings per share. Its volume of trading for the day was 866,600, with its price ranging from a high of $10.90 to a low of $10.60 per share. When the market closed for the day, its price was $10.71, which was up $.12 from the previous day.

HOW STOCKS FIT WITHIN YOUR FINANCIAL PLAN

The following are the key decisions about common stock that should be included within your financial plan:

1. Should you consider buying stock?

2. What methods will you use to value stocks?

3. What methods will you use to invest in stocks?

This chapter has focused on the first of these three decisions, while the other two decisions are discussed in the next two chapters. The decision regarding whether to consider buying common stock is based on your financial position. You must weigh the potential return from investing in stock against the risk. Exhibit 10.4 provides an example of how this decision applies to Stephanie Spratt's financial plan.

Exhibit 10.4   How Stocks Fit within Stephanie Spratt's Financial Plan

---

Goals for Investing in Stock

1. Determine whether to buy stock.
2. Determine how to value stocks when deciding whether to buy them (discussed in Chapter 11).
3. Determine what methods to use for investing in stocks (discussed in Chapter 12).

Analysis

Monthly Cash Inflows	$2,500
− Typical Monthly Expenses	1,488
− Monthly Car Loan Payment	412
= Amount of Funds Available	$600

Decision

Decision on Buying Stock:

Now that I have purchased a car and a home, my cash outflows have increased. My estimate of cash outflows includes my mortgage payment instead of a rent payment. After _paying for my typical monthly expenses (not including recreation), I have $600 left each month. I am not in a financial position to buy stock at this time because I will use some of these funds each month for recreation and will deposit the remaining funds in liquid accounts such as a money market fund. I need to increase my liquidity since I might incur unexpected home repair expenses periodically. Beyond maintaining liquidity, I hope to save enough money to pay off the car loan early. Once I pay off that loan, I will no longer have the $412 car loan payment and can then reconsider whether to invest in stocks. My salary should also increase over time, which will make stocks more affordable._

Stephanie's first concerns should be to maintain adequate liquidity and to ensure that she can make existing loan payments. She already owns 100 shares of one stock, which she can sell if she needs additional funds. Since she recently purchased a car and a home, she does not have a large amount of funds available to invest in stock.

DISCUSSION QUESTIONS

1. How would Stephanie's stock-investing decisions be different if she were a single mother of two children?

2. How would Stephanie's stock investing decisions be affected if she were 35 years old? If she were 50 years old?

SUMMARY

A stock is initially issued as an initial public offering (IPO) in the primary market, but after the IPO it trades in the secondary market. The secondary market enables investors to buy stocks that were previously issued by firms or to sell stocks that they had previously purchased.

Stocks can provide a return to investors in the form of dividends or as capital gains if the stock price increases over the period the stock was held. Dividends are taxed as ordinary income. Short-term capital gains (for a period of one year or less) are also taxed as ordinary income. Long-term capital gains (for a period of more than one year) are subject to a capital gains tax, which is a lower tax rate than the marginal tax rate for most investors. Therefore, most investors can obtain a tax advantage by holding stocks beyond one year.

Stocks are risky because their future returns are uncertain. The return on a stock is influenced by economic conditions, industry conditions, and specific conditions of the firm, all of which are uncertain. The risk of a stock can be measured by its range of returns, its standard deviation of returns, and its beta. Stocks of smaller firms tend to have more risk than those of larger firms.

Stock exchanges facilitate the trading of stocks in the secondary market by matching investors who want to sell a specific stock with other investors who wish to buy that stock. The stocks of very large firms are usually traded on the New York Stock Exchange (NYSE). The over-the-counter (OTC) market facilitates the trading of stocks of smaller firms, in addition to some large firms.

Stock price quotations provide recent stock prices and other trading information, such as the dividend yield (annual dividends divided by the prevailing price), the PE ratio (prevailing stock price divided by the annual earnings per share), volume of shares traded on the previous day, and closing price on the previous day.

Integrating the Key Concepts

Your decisions to invest in stocks can affect your income (dividends and capital gains). Since these decisions can affect your cash inflows over time, they may also affect your liquidity (Part 2). They may also affect the amount of financing you need (Part 3) and your retirement planning (Part 5).

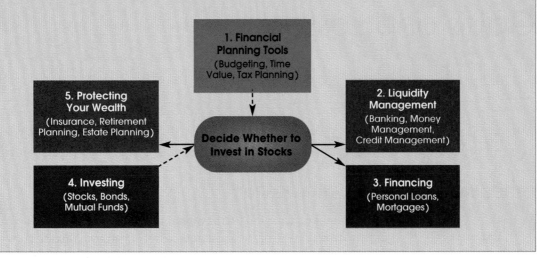

Appendix 10A

Offsetting Capital Gains and Losses

You can offset capital gains and losses when determining your tax effects, as explained next.

OFFSETTING LONG-TERM CAPITAL GAINS

If you experience a long-term capital gain from selling a stock and a long-term capital loss from selling another stock, you owe capital gains taxes on the amount by which the long-term capital gains exceed the long-term capital losses. For example, if your long-term capital gains are $800, and your long-term capital losses are $500, your "net" long-term capital gain is:

$$
\begin{aligned}
\text{Net Long-Term Capital Gain} &= \text{Long-Term Capital Gain} \\
&\quad - \text{Long-Term Capital Loss} \\
&= \$800 - \$500 \\
&= \$300.
\end{aligned}
$$

Applying the 20 percent long-term capital gains tax rate, your tax on the long-term capital gain is:

$$
\begin{aligned}
\text{Long-Term Capital Gains Tax} &= \text{Net Long-Term Capital Gain} \\
&\quad \times \text{Long-Term Capital Gain Tax Rate} \\
&= \$300 \times .20 \\
&= \$60.
\end{aligned}
$$

If the long-term capital losses exceed the long-term capital gains, you will not owe a capital gains tax.

When investors experience a long-term capital gain, they commonly sell stocks to generate a long-term capital loss within the same year so that they can offset part or all of their gain and thereby avoid paying taxes on it. However, a tax law known as the "wash rule" prohibits investors from claiming a capital loss due to selling a stock for tax purposes and then immediately buying that stock back. They must wait 30 days after selling

10.7   Financial Planning Online: Comparing Short-Term versus Long-Term Capital Gains Taxes on Your Stock

Go to:
http://www.financenter.com/
products/analyzers/stock.fcs

Click on:
"Should I wait a year to sell
my stocks?"

This Web site provides:
estimates of the capital gain
taxes that you would pay on
a stock if you hold it less
than 12 months versus
more than 12 months.

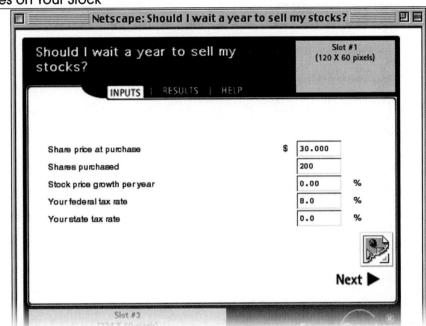

the stock before they can repurchase it. This rule encourages investors to sell only those stocks that they really want to discard, rather than selling a stock just to create a long-term capital loss for tax purposes.

OFFSETTING CAPITAL LOSSES

If you have more long-term capital losses than long-term capital gains, you can deduct up to $3,000 of the capital losses from your ordinary income in any given year. If your net capital losses exceed $3,000, you can either generate more capital gains to offset the losses or carry the excess forward to the next year. For example, if your net capital losses are $5,000 this year, you can take a $3,000 deduction against your ordinary income. The remaining $2,000 can be used in other ways to offset gains. You could sell a stock that will generate a capital gain to offset the net losses before the end of the year. The advantage of this strategy is that the long-term capital gain is offset by your existing losses, so you will not be taxed on that gain. Alternatively, you can carry forward the $2,000 long-term capital loss and apply it to offset $2,000 of your long-term capital gains in the following year.

REVIEW QUESTIONS

1. What steps should you take before selecting a particular investment? Why are stocks a popular investment vehicle? What must you understand before investing in stocks?

2. What are stocks? How are stocks beneficial to corporations? How are they beneficial to investors?

3. Classify the two types of investors. What are day traders?

4. What are dividends? Do all firms pay them?

5. Discuss the differences between common stock and preferred stock.

6. What is a primary market? Discuss initial public offerings. Do all investors have access to IPOs? What is the secondary market?

7. How do shareholders earn returns from investing in stocks? How is the market value of a firm determined? What determines the market price of a stock?

8. What determines if a firm will pay dividends? What are growth stocks? What are income stocks?

9. What is the formula for estimating returns on stocks? Describe each element of the formula. How do you calculate the dollar amount of your returns?

10. Discuss the different tax effects on returns on stock. How may investors achieve a higher return?

11. How can investments in stock increase your wealth? How would you calculate the value of an investment in stock of a single sum over time? How would you calculate the value of an investment in stock of a specific amount over several periods?

12. What three factors influence a firm's performance? Discuss the risk and return of small firms.

13. Why do investors measure risk? Describe the three most widely used methods of measuring risk.

14. Discuss several ways investors can limit their risk.

15. What are stock exchanges? How do they facilitate the trading of stocks?

16. Describe a typical stock transaction at the New York Stock Exchange. What are floor traders? What are specialists? What other exchanges trade stock in a similar manner as the NYSE?

17. Discuss the difference between traditional stock markets like the NYSE and the over-the-counter market. What are Electronic Communication Networks? Why are they becoming popular? What is the disadvantage of ECNs?

18. How might an investor purchase foreign stocks?

19. List several ways investors can obtain price quotations.

20. List and briefly explain the information included in most stock quotations.

21. Briefly discuss the rules for offsetting capital gains and losses. What is the "wash rule"? How can you handle a long-term capital loss? (See the chapter appendix.)

FINANCIAL PLANNING PROBLEMS

1. Joel purchased 100 shares of stock for $20 per share. During the year, he received dividend checks amounting to $150. Joel recently sold his stock for $32 per share. What was Joel's return on his stock?

2. Continuing with question 1, what is the dollar amount of Joel's return?

3. Joel is in a 28 percent tax bracket. What amount of taxes will he pay on his capital gains if he held the stock for less than a year?

4. How much would Joel save in taxes if he held the stock for more than a year?

5. Tammy has $3,500 that she wants to invest in stock. She believes she can earn a 12 percent return. What will be the value of Tammy's investment in 10 years?

6. Dawn decides that she will invest $2,000 each year in stock for the next five years. She believes she can earn a 9 percent return over that time period. How much will Dawn's investment be worth at the end of five years?

7. Floyd wants to invest the $15,000 he received from his grandfather's estate. He wants to use the money to finance his education when he pursues his doctorate in five years. What amount will he have if he earns a 9 percent return? If he receives a 10 percent return? What if he can earn 12 percent?

8. Morris will start investing $1,500 a year in stocks. He feels he can average a 12 percent return. If he follows this plan, how much will he accumulate in 5 years? In 10 years? In 20 years?

9. Thomas purchased 400 shares of stock A for $23 a share and sold them more than a year later for $20 per share. He purchased 500 shares of stock B for $40 per share and sold them for $53 per share after holding them for more than a year. Both of the sales were in the same year. If Thomas is in a 28 percent tax bracket, what will his capital gains tax be for the year? (See the chapter appendix.)

10. This current tax year, Charles sold 500 shares of stock A for $12,000. In addition, he sold 600 shares of stock A for $6,000. Charles had paid $20 per share for all his shares of stock A. What amount of loss will he be able to take against his ordinary income assuming both sales were on stocks held for more than one year. (See the chapter appendix.)

FINANCIAL PLANNING ONLINE EXERCISES

Go to http://www.financenter.com/products/analyzers/ stock.fcs and click on: "Should I wait a year to sell my stocks?"

1. The purpose of this exercise is to estimate the capital gains taxes that you would pay on a stock investment if you hold it for less than 12 months versus 12 months or more. Input the following information in the online calculator: $30 share price at purchase, 200 shares purchased, .75 percent stock price growth per month, 15 percent federal tax rate, and 8 percent state tax rate. Click on "Results." For the two scenarios, what are the capital gains taxes you would pay in dollar and percentage terms? Click the "Help" button to learn the rationale behind these calculations.

2. Click on the input tab to return to the Inputs page. Change the share price at purchase to $50, shares purchased to 500, stock price growth per month to 1.50 percent, federal tax rate to 28 percent, and state tax rate to 8 percent. What are the capital gains taxes for a holding period of less than 12 months versus a holding period of 12 months or more?

3. Why is there a difference in the return between the two holding periods?

4. What effect do the federal and state tax rates have on the returns for each option? What role should taxes play in making investment decisions?

Go to http://www.financenter.com/products/analyzers/ stock.fcs and click on: "At what price should I sell a stock to achieve my target rate of return?"

1. The purpose of this exercise is to estimate the price at which you need to sell a stock you own in order to achieve a return that you specify. On the Inputs page, enter a 12 percent annualized return desired "After Taxes," $30 share price at purchase, 200 shares purchased, $100 average quarterly dividend, 60 months owned, 15 percent federal tax rate, and 8 percent state tax rate. The fees at purchase and sale are fixed dollar amounts of $200 each. Enter zeros for Percent of Total Amount and Dollar Amount per Share. Dividend income is invested elsewhere at a rate of 4 percent. Check the Results page. What is the selling price necessary to achieve your target return? Click on the Graphs tab to view the results graphically. The calculations are explained under the Help tab.

2. Click on the input tab to return to the Inputs page. Change the annualized return desired to 30 percent and check the Results page and graph. What is the selling price necessary to achieve your desired return?

3. Click on the input tab to return to the Inputs page. Change the annualized return desired to 12 percent, federal tax rate to 28 percent, and state tax rate to 8 percent. Check the Results and Graph. At what price must you sell the stock to achieve your target return?

4. What impact does a higher desired return have on the selling price? What impact do federal and state taxes have on the selling price for a desired return?

Building Your Own Financial Plan

Very likely, some of the goals you established in Chapter 1 can best be met through investing in common and preferred stocks. Before taking the plunge of stock investing, however, you need to address a few questions.

The first of these is to determine your risk tolerance. Not all investors have the "stomach" for the uncertainty surrounding returns on common stock investments. On the template provided with this chapter in the *Financial Planning Workbook* and on the CD-ROM, you will find a simple risk tolerance test. Follow the instructions and you will have an indication of your risk tolerance for investing in stocks. This test is not meant to be a "psychologically" based analysis of your risk tolerance. It will, however, give you some good insights into your risk tolerance level.

The next issue to be addressed is how different stocks are suited to different goals. For example,

a growth stock might be desirable if your goal is to build for a retirement that is 30 years away, while a growth and income stock might be better suited to provide the down payment for a house within the next five years. The template for this chapter provides a table for you to articulate your goals and list the appropriate kind of stock. It also provides the opportunity to put down in print your reasoning as to why a particular kind of stock is good in helping to meet a particular goal.

The decision as to what kind of stock is right for a particular goal should be reviewed on an annual basis. The closer a goal comes to fulfillment, the more likely it is that a change in investing strategy will be necessary.

The Sampsons—A Continuing Case

 Recall that the Sampsons recently started saving about $300 per month ($3,600 per year) for their children's college education. They are currently investing this amount in bank CDs each month, but they are now considering investing in stock instead. Dave and Sharon have never owned stock before. They are currently earning an interest rate of 5 percent on their CDs. If they invest in a specific stock from this point on, they will achieve

an annual return ranging from 2 to 9 percent. The stock will generate an annual return of only 2 percent if stock market conditions are weak in the future, but it could generate an annual return of 9 percent if stock market conditions are strong. The Sampsons want to compare the potential returns of investing in stock to the CD.

1. Compare the returns from investing in bank CDs to the possible returns from stock over the next 12 years by filling in the following table:

Savings Accumulated over the Next 12 Years

	CD: Annual Return = 5%	Weak Stock Market Conditions	Strong Stock Market Conditions
Amount invested per year	$3,600	$3,600	$3,600
Annual return	5%	2%	9%
FVIFA ($n = 12$ years)	_____	_____	_____
Value of investments in 12 years	_____	_____	_____

2. Explain to the Sampsons why there is a trade-off when investing in bank CDs versus stock to support their children's future college education.

3. Advise the Sampsons on whether they should invest their money each month in bank CDs, in stocks, or in some combination to save for their children's college education.

IN-TEXT STUDY GUIDE

True/False:

1. Stocks are certificates that represent ownership in corporations.

2. Position traders buy stocks and sell them on the same day.

3. The first offering of a firm's stock to the public is referred to as a seasoned equity offering.

4. Growing companies tend to pay a lot of dividends.

5. Many firms do not pay dividends because they prefer to reinvest all of their profits so that they can expand their businesses.

6. You are allowed to offset capital gains and losses when determining your tax effects. (See the chapter appendix.)

7. The "wash rule" prohibits investors from claiming a capital loss and buying the stock back within 2 years. (See the chapter appendix.)

8. The value of a firm's stock tends to vary over time with its actual and potential performance.

9. The risk of a stock is commonly measured by its beta, or its sensitivity to firm-specific conditions.

10. The listing requirements for the over-the-counter market are less stringent than those for the New York Stock Exchange.

11. Institutional investors are professionals who are responsible for investing the money of a financial institution.

12. American depository receipts are certificates representing ownership of domestic stocks.

Multiple Choice:

1. A corporation issues stock to
   a. distribute its ownership.
   b. obtain funds to support operations.
   c. incur fixed interest charges.
   d. none of the above

2. Corporations issue _____ more frequently than _____.
   a. common stock; bonds
   b. preferred stock; common stock
   c. preferred stock; bonds
   d. common stock; preferred stock

3. After an initial public offering (IPO), investors who hold stock can sell it to other investors in the
   a. primary market.
   b. secondary market.
   c. money market.
   d. bond market.

4. Common stock does not generate a return to shareholders in the form of
   a. interest.
   b. dividends.
   c. stock price appreciation.
   d. Common stock generates a return in the form of all of the above.

5. A firm has a market value of $1 billion. The firm has 20 million shares of stock outstanding. Based on this information, the per-share price of the firm's stock is
   a. $33.33.
   b. $20.00.
   c. $50.00.
   d. none of the above

6. The _____ the amount of dividends paid by a firm, the _____ is its potential stock price appreciation.
   a. larger; higher
   b. smaller; higher
   c. larger; lower
   d. Answers (b) and (c) are correct.

The following information applies to questions 7 through 9.

One year ago, Norbert Wagner purchased 30 shares of Willie, Inc., stock for $20 per share. During the last year, Willie, Inc., experienced strong earnings and paid dividends of $0.50 per share. Norbert just sold the stock for $19 per share.

7. Norbert received total dividends in the amount of
   a. $0.50.
   b. $10.00.
   c. $15.00.
   d. $19.00.

8. Ignoring taxes, Norbert's return from investing in Willie, Inc., was
   a. −2.50 percent.
   b. 2.50 percent.
   c. −2.63 percent.
   d. 7.00 percent.

9. Ignoring taxes, what is Norbert's dollar amount of return?
   a. $15
   b. −$15
   c. $30
   d. $25

The following information applies to questions 10 and 11.

You just sold 50 shares of XYZ Corporation for $65 a share. You purchased the stock for $50 a share. You are in the 28 percent tax bracket.

10. Assuming you held the stock for eight months, you would pay taxes in the amount of _____ on this transaction.
    a. $910
    b. $210
    c. $700
    d. $150

11. Assuming you held the stock for 13 months, you would pay taxes in the amount of _____ on this transaction.
    a. $910
    b. $210
    c. $700
    d. $150

12. You just sold two investments, both of which you held for 15 months. Your capital gain on the first stock totaled $5,000. On the second investment, you incurred a capital loss of $3,500. You are in the 28 percent tax bracket. What is the total capital gains tax you have to pay? (See the chapter appendix.)
    a. $1,000
    b. $700
    c. $300
    d. $420

13. Last year, you incurred long-term capital losses totaling $10,000 and long-term capital gains totaling $5,000. Based on this information, you can deduct _____ from your ordinary income on last year's tax return. (See the chapter appendix.)
    a. $3,000
    b. $4,000
    c. $5,000
    d. $10,000

14. Freddie Miller just invested $5,000 in stocks. He expects an annual return of about 9 percent. In five years, Freddie will have accumulated
    a. $7,693.12.
    b. $7,756.64.
    c. $5,450.00.
    d. none of the above

15. Stocks of _____ firms usually have greater potential for growth and a _____ return over time.
    a. larger; higher
    b. smaller; higher
    c. smaller; lower
    d. larger; lower

16. A stock has a beta of 1.5. The expected market return next year is 15 percent. Thus, the stock's expected return is
    a. 15.0 percent.
    b. 10.0 percent.
    c. 22.5 percent.
    d. none of the above

17. A stock's _____ indicates the difference between its highest return and its lowest return over a given period.
    a. beta
    b. range of returns
    c. standard deviation
    d. variance

18. Conaghan Stock returns have a standard deviation of 2 percent while Scully Stock returns have a standard deviation of 5 percent. Based on this information,
    a. the stocks have no risk
    b. the stocks have the same risk
    c. the risk of Conaghan stock is higher
    d. the risk of Scully stock is higher

19. On the New York Stock Exchange, _____ help to make a market in one or more stocks by taking the position opposite of orders placed by clients.
    a. specialists
    b. floor traders
    c. position traders
    d. market-makers

20. _____ engage in trades desired by other investors on the New York Stock Exchange.
    a. Specialists
    b. Position traders
    c. Floor traders
    d. Market-makers

Chapter 11

Valuation and Analysis of Stocks

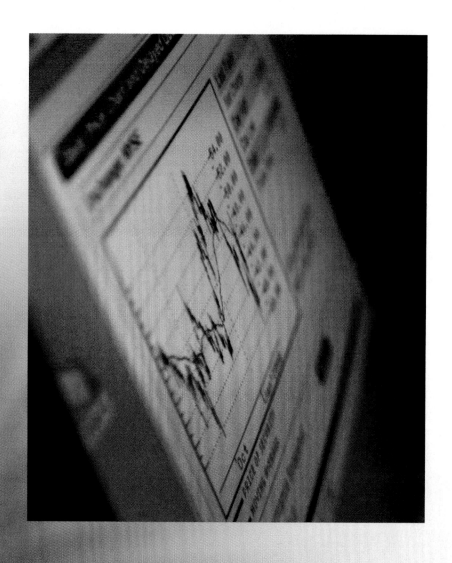

Before investing in stocks, you need to value them to ensure that they are not priced higher than they are worth. Your valuations will also identify stocks that may be undervalued in the market. The stocks that you purchase will influence your dividend income (cash inflows), as well as the value of your assets (stock holdings) in the future. By using the proper methods to value stocks, you can enhance your wealth.

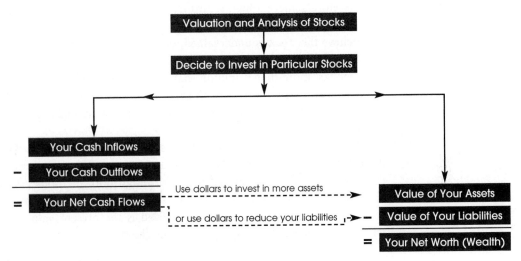

The objectives of this chapter are to:

- explain how to value stocks,
- describe how to conduct an economic analysis of stocks,
- show how to conduct an industry analysis of stocks, and
- illustrate how to conduct an analysis of a firm.

STOCK VALUATION

Individuals estimate the market value of a stock just as they estimate the market value of a car or home. A stock is different from a car or a home, however, in that it does not serve a physical function such as transportation or housing. A stock is simply intended to generate a return on the money invested.

The price of a stock is based on the demand for that stock versus the supply of stock for sale. The demand for shares is determined by the number of investors who wish to purchase shares of the stock. The supply of stock for sale is determined by the number of investors who decide to sell their shares.

The first step in the valuation process is to identify a firm that you think may perform well in the future. By conducting a valuation of this firm's stock, you can determine whether its price is overvalued, undervalued, or on target. You may find that some stocks with much potential are already overvalued (that is, have a market price that exceeds what you determine the stock is worth).

You buy a stock when you think that it is undervalued and that you can therefore achieve a high return from investing in it. Yet your purchase of the stock means that some other investor was willing to sell it. So, while you believe the stock is undervalued, others apparently think it is overvalued. This difference in opinion is what causes a high volume of trading. For some stocks, more than 1 million shares are traded each day as a result of these divergent views of the stock's true value. Therefore, investors who use specific methods to value a stock may be able to achieve higher returns than others.

There is no consensus about the best method for valuing stocks. Two of the more popular methods, the price-earnings method and the price-revenue method, are described here. Although both methods can easily be applied to value a stock, they are subject to limitations that will be addressed. An additional valuation method is the present value method, which is described in the appendix to this chapter.

Price-Earnings (PE) Method

One method for determining the value of a stock is to find the present value of the firm's earnings. The higher the earnings, the more funds the firm has to pay dividends to its shareholders or to reinvest for further expansion (which will ultimately generate additional earnings). The most common method of using earnings to value stocks is the **price-earnings (PE) method,** in which a firm's earnings are multiplied by the mean industry PE ratio. A stock's PE ratio is its stock price per share (P) divided by its annual earnings per share (E):

price-earnings (PE) method

A method of valuing stocks in which a specific firm's earnings per share are multiplied by the mean industry price-earnings (PE) ratio.

$$\text{Price-Earnings (PE) Ratio} = P/E.$$

You can find the PE ratio of any firm in stock quotations in financial newspapers such as the *Wall Street Journal* and on many financial Web sites. A PE ratio of 10 means that the firm's stock price is 10 times the firm's earnings per share.

You can use the PE method to value a firm as follows:

1. Look up the PE ratios of stocks in the firm's industry.

2. Multiply the average industry PE ratio times the firm's earnings per share.

3. Compare your estimated value of the firm's stock to its market value to determine whether the stock is currently undervalued or overvalued.

Example

Stephanie Spratt is impressed with Trail.com, an online clothing firm that focuses on the 18–22 age bracket. The prices of clothes at Trail.com are much lower than at competitors, and the quality is high. Reading about the firm on its Web site and in various financial newspapers, Stephanie has learned that it plans to expand its clothing lines. She thinks that the firm's performance may increase over time. The prevailing price of Trail.com stock is $61 per share.

Stephanie decides to apply the PE method to value Trail.com stock, which has had recent annual earnings of $5 per share. Only three other corporations have very similar businesses to Trail.com and have stock that is traded. Stephanie uses the Stock Quotes section of the Yahoo! Web site to determine the PE ratios of these firms. One firm has a PE ratio of 10, the second firm has a PE ratio of 12, and the third has a PE ratio of 14.

Stephanie derives a value for Trail.com's stock by multiplying its recent annual earnings per share by the average industry PE ratio:

1. Mean PE Ratio of Industry = (10 + 12 + 14)/3
$$= 12.$$

2. Valuation of Stock = Firm's Earnings per Share × Mean Industry PE Ratio
$$= \$5 \times 12$$
$$= \$60.$$

This valuation of $60 is below the prevailing stock price ($61) of Trail.com, indicating that the stock is slightly overvalued. Given this valuation, Stephanie decides not to purchase Trail.com stock at this time.

Deriving an Estimate of Earnings. Because the stock price of a firm is influenced by expected earnings, investors may prefer to use expected earnings rather than past earnings to value a firm and its corresponding industry. Many investors rely on Value Line, the Institutional Brokerage Estimate System (IBES), and other investment services for earnings forecasts for each firm. Some earnings forecasts can be obtained from publications in libraries and also from specific Web sites. If investors expect no change in earnings from last year to this year, last year's earnings can be used.

Limitations of the PE Method. Forecasting earnings is difficult. Therefore, valuations of a stock that are based on expected earnings may be unreliable because the earnings forecast is imprecise.

Even if the forecast of earnings is accurate, there is still a question of the proper PE multiple that should be used to value a stock. The firm that you are valuing may deserve to have a lower PE ratio than other firms, if its future performance is subject to more uncertainty. For example, perhaps the firm is using less advanced technology than its competitors, which could adversely

11.1 Financial Planning Online: PE Ratios

Go to:
http://finance.yahoo.com/?u

This Web site provides:
the PE ratio of a firm you specify. Insert the symbol for the
firm that you are interested in,
and click on "Profile."

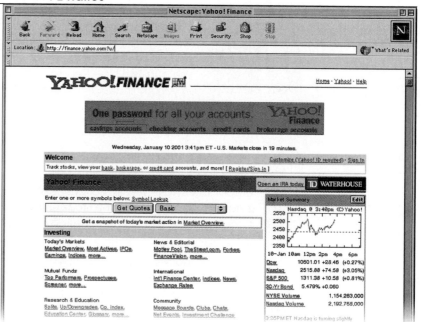

11.2 Financial Planning Online: Earnings Estimates for Valuing Your Stock

Go to:
http://biz.yahoo.com/research/
earncal/today.html

This Web site provides:
recent earnings per share
(EPS) estimates of a firm that
you specify, which you can
use when applying the PE
method of valuing stocks.

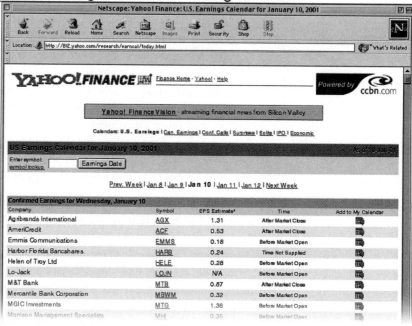

affect its performance in a few years. Consequently, the lower PE ratio may not necessarily mean that the firm's stock is undervalued by the market.

Another limitation of the PE method is that the results will vary with the firms selected to derive a mean industry PE ratio. Should this ratio be derived from the three closest competitors (as in the example)? Or from the 10 closest competitors? For firms that conduct several types of business, it is difficult to determine who the closest competitors are. Thus, investors may apply the wrong industry PE ratio and derive an inaccurate valuation, which may cause them to buy stocks that are not really undervalued.

Price-Revenue (PR) Method

price-revenue (PR) method
A method of valuing stocks in which the revenue per share of a specific firm is multiplied by the mean industry ratio of share price to revenue.

A second common valuation method is the **price-revenue (PR) method**, in which the industry's average ratio of share price to revenue is multiplied by revenue per share for a specific firm. When a firm sells its products, it generates revenue. The higher a firm's revenues, the higher its valuation within a specific industry. Since stock prices reflect expectations of future performance, investors should use recently reported revenues only if they believe the reported revenues represent a reasonable forecast of the future. The PR method is especially popular for valuing firms (such as some Internet firms) that cannot be valued with the PE method because they have negative earnings.

Example

 Stephanie applies the PR method to value Trail.com's stock. A financial Web site discloses that Trail.com has expected revenues of $29 per share and that the other firms in the same industry have a price-to-revenue (PR) ratio of 2.0 on average. Based on this information, Stephanie estimates the value of Trail.com to be:

Valuation of Stock = Expected Revenues of Firm per Share × Mean Industry PR Ratio

$$= \$29 \times 2.0$$
$$= \$58.$$

Since Trail.com stock is currently priced at $61, she decides that the stock is overpriced, so she will not buy it at this time.

Limitations of the PR Method. As with the PE method, the application of the PR method is subject to error if it is based on a set of firms whose operations are not very similar to those of the firm that is being valued. Second, revenues do not indicate how well a firm is managed. If two firms in the same industry have the same revenues, the firm with the lower costs will normally be valued higher. Yet the PR method will give these two firms the same value because this method ignores costs incurred by the firms. For this reason, the PE method may be a more appropriate valuation method. As mentioned,

11.3   Financial Planning Online: Assessing the Financial Condition of Your Stock

Go to:
http://finance.yahoo.com/?u

This Web site provides:
recent valuation ratios of a firm
that you specify. Type in a
stock's symbol, and then click
on "Profile" for this information,
which you may consider when
making investment decisions.

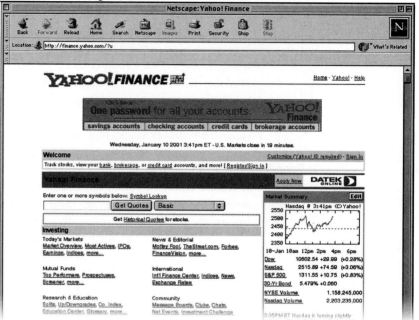

however, the PE method is not useful when the firm being valued or the firms
in the corresponding industry have recently experienced negative earnings.

ECONOMIC ANALYSIS OF STOCKS

When investors consider possible stocks in which to invest, they commonly
focus on the potential performance of the respective firms. In evaluating
these stocks, they consider information pertaining to economic conditions,
industry conditions, and firm-specific conditions.

An economic analysis involves assessing any economic conditions that
can affect a firm's stock price, including economic growth, interest rates,
and inflation. Each of these conditions is discussed in turn.

Economic Growth

economic growth
A measure of growth in a
country's economy over a particular period.

**gross domestic product
(GDP)**
The total market value of all
products and services produced in a country.

In the United States, **economic growth** is the growth in the U.S. economy
over a particular period. It is commonly measured by the amount of production in the United States, or the **gross domestic product (GDP)**, which reflects
the total market value of all products and services produced in the United
States. The production level of products and services is closely related to
the aggregate (overall) demand for products and services. When aggregate
demand by consumers rises, firms produce more products to accommodate
the increased demand. This higher level of production results in more jobs
and higher incomes. Consumers now have more money to spend, which

results in additional aggregate demand for products and services. The firms that provide products and services experience higher sales (revenue) and earnings, and their stock prices may rise.

When economic conditions are weak, the aggregate demand for products and services declines. Firms experience a lower level of sales and earnings, and their stock prices may decline as a result. Some firms impose layoffs because they do not need as many employees. Consumers have less income and therefore have less money to spend. This may cause an additional decline in the aggregate demand for products and services, and firms' stock prices may decrease as well.

The relationship between economic conditions and stock prices is shown in Exhibit 11.1, which shows the return on an index of 500 large U.S. firms from one year to the next. The shaded areas in the exhibit represent recessionary periods, in which U.S. GDP experienced a decline for at least six months. Notice how the stock returns are weak during each recessionary period. In fact, stocks experienced negative returns in each of the four recessionary periods shown in the exhibit.

Some firms are more sensitive to changes in economic conditions than others. Firms that produce products such as cereal and other necessities may not be affected by economic declines because the demand for their products remains somewhat constant regardless of the economy. In contrast, the demand for some other products (such as cars, boats, and houses) tends to fall during periods of slow economic growth. Consequently, the stock price of a cereal producer is not as sensitive to economic conditions as the stock price of a boat manufacturer.

Exhibit 11.1   Impact of Recessionary Periods (shaded) on Stock Returns

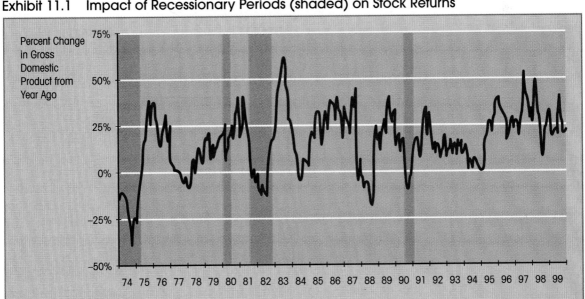

11.4   Financial Planning Online: Upcoming Economic Announcements Related to Stocks

Go to:

http://biz.yahoo.com/c/e.html

This Web site provides:

a list of upcoming announcements about economic conditions (inflation, economic growth, unemployment, etc.) that could affect stock market conditions. You can use this information when considering whether to invest in stocks at a particular point in time.

YAHOO! FINANCE   Home · Yahoo! · Help   BRIEFING.COM®
Live Market Analysis

FREE 2001   Get YOURS today!

Calendars: U.S. Earnings | Can. Earnings | Conf. Calls | Surprises | Splits | IPO | Economic

Economic Calendar   Jan 08 - Jan 12

Last Week   **Next Week**

Date	Time (ET)	Statistic	For	Actual	Briefing Forecast	Market Expects	Prior	Revised From
Jan 08	3:00 pm	Consumer Credit	Nov	$12.9B	$8.0B	$8.0B	$17.3B	$16.7B
Jan 10	10:00 am	Wholesale Inventories	Nov	0.4%	0.3%	0.3%	0.4%	0.3%
Jan 11	8:30 am	Export Prices ex-ag.	Dec	-	NA	NA	-0.1%	-
	8:30 am	Import Prices ex-oil	Dec	-	NA	NA	-0.1%	-
	8:30 am	Initial Claims	01/06	-	375K	370K	375K	-
Jan 12	8:30 am	Core PPI	Dec	-	0.1%	0.1%	0.0%	-
	8:30 am	PPI	Dec	-	-0.1%	0.1%	0.1%	-
	8:30 am	Retail Sales	Dec	-	-0.6%	-0.2%	-0.4%	-
	8:30 am	Retail Sales ex-auto	Dec	-	0.1%	0.2%	0.2%	-

Investors can monitor indicators of economic growth in financial newspapers and business publications. Some of the more popular indicators include personal income levels, the level of employment, and new home sales. Investors also monitor production indexes for aluminum, lumber, and oil.

Fiscal Policy Effects. Given the potential impact of economic growth on stock prices, investors also monitor the U.S. government's **fiscal policy,** or the means by which the government imposes taxes on individuals and corporations and by which it spends its money. When corporate tax rates are increased, the after-tax earnings of corporations are reduced, which means there is less money for shareholders. When individual tax rates are increased, individuals have less money to spend and therefore consume fewer products. The demand for products and services declines as a result, reducing firms' earnings.

fiscal policy

The means by which the U.S. government imposes taxes on individuals and corporations and by which it spends its money.

Interest Rates

Interest rates can affect economic growth and therefore have an indirect impact on stock prices. In general, stocks perform better when interest rates are low because firms can obtain financing at relatively low rates. In addition, firms tend to be more willing to expand when interest rates are low, and their expansions stimulate the economy. When interest rates are low, investors also tend to shift more of their funds into stock because the interest earned on money market securities is relatively low. The general shift into stocks increases the demand for stocks, which places upward pressure on stock prices.

Some stock prices are more sensitive to interest rates than others. Changes in interest rates affect the amount of products and services that can be purchased with borrowed funds. Many consumers rely on borrowed funds to purchase cars or homes. When interest rates rise, monthly loan payments increase, and some consumers can no longer afford some cars and homes. Consequently, when interest rates rise, car manufacturers and homebuilders may experience lower sales and lower earnings, and therefore their stock prices may decline.

Conversely, lower interest rates may enable more consumers to afford cars or homes. Car manufacturers and homebuilders then experience higher earnings, and their stock prices tend to increase as well.

Financial publications often refer to the Federal Reserve Board ("the Fed") when discussing interest rates because the Fed uses monetary policy to influence interest rates. Through its interest rate policies, the Fed affects the amount of spending by consumers with borrowed funds and therefore influences economic growth.

Inflation

inflation
The increase in the general level of prices of products and services over a specified period.

consumer price index (CPI)
A measure of inflation that represents prices of various consumer products, such as groceries, household products, housing, and gasoline.

producer price index (PPI)
A measure of inflation that represents prices of products, such as coal, lumber, and metals, that are used to produce other products.

Stock prices are also affected by **inflation,** or the increase in the general level of prices of products and services over a specified period. One of the most common measures of inflation is the **consumer price index (CPI),** which represents prices of various consumer products, such as groceries, household products, housing, and gasoline. An alternative measure of inflation is the **producer price index (PPI),** which represents prices of products, such as coal, lumber, and metals, that are used to produce other products. Inflation can cause an increase in the prices that firms pay for materials or equipment. The firms may then increase their prices to reflect these higher costs in an attempt to prevent their earnings from declining. The increase in prices, however, may lower the demand for their products, which may in turn reduce earnings. In general, stock prices tend to decrease when inflation is expected to increase.

The main publications providing information about inflation and other economic conditions are listed in Exhibit 11.2. These publications commonly provide historical data for inflation, economic growth, interest rates, and many other economic indicators.

INDUSTRY ANALYSIS OF STOCKS

A firm's stock price is also susceptible to industry conditions. The demand for products or services within an industry may change over time. For example, the popularity of the Internet increased the demand for computers, disks, printers, and Internet guides in the 1990s. Producers of these products initially benefited from the increased demand. However, as other firms notice the increased demand, they often enter an industry. Thus changes in competition are another industry factor that frequently affects sales,

Exhibit 11.2   Sources of Economic Information

Published Sources

- **Federal Reserve Bulletin:** provides data on economic conditions, including interest rates, unemployment rates, inflation rates, and the money supply.

- **Federal Reserve District Bank publications:** provide information on national and regional economic conditions.

- **Survey of Current Business:** provides data on various indicators of economic activity, including national income, production levels, and employment levels.

Online Sources

- **Bloomberg (www.bloomberg.com):** provides reports on interest rates, other economic conditions, and news announcements about various economic indicators.

- **Yahoo! (www.yahoo.com):** provides information and news about economic conditions.

- **Federal Reserve System Web site (www.federalreserve.gov):** provides detailed statistics on economic conditions.

- **Investorlinks Web site (www.investorlinks.com/charts/index.html):** provides forecasts for various economic conditions, including gross domestic product and inflation in the United States.

earnings, and therefore the stock price of a firm. Competition has intensified for many industries as a result of the Internet, which has reduced the costs of marketing and delivering products for some firms.

Industry Indicators

Investors can obtain information about firms and their corresponding industry from various sources, as summarized in Exhibit 11.3. Numerous financial Web sites also provide information on specific industries. For example, Yahoo! offers financial performance information for major firms in any industry.

Another indicator of industry performance is the industry stock index, which measures how the market value of the firms within the industry has changed over a specific period. The prevailing stock index for a particular industry indicates the expectations of investors in general about that industry. Investors can also use industry stock indexes to compare a firm's stock value over a recent period to other stocks in the particular industry. Some industry and sector indexes are provided in the *Wall Street Journal* and on various Web sites. The use of indexes to evaluate stock performance is described in Chapter 12.

Exhibit 11.3 Sources of Industry Information

Published Sources

Although some government publications offer industry information, the most popular sources are provided by the private sector.

- **Value Line Industry Survey:** provides an industry outlook, performance levels of various industries, and financial statistics for firms in each industry over time.

- **Standard and Poor's Industry Survey:** provides statistics used to assess industry conditions.

- **Standard and Poor's Analysts Handbook:** provides financial statistics for various industries over time.

Online Sources

- **Bloomberg (www.bloomberg.com):** identifies industry stock indexes that have experienced substantial changes.

- **Investorlinks Web site (www.investorlinks.com):** contains news articles related to specific industries.

- **Yahoo! (www.yahoo.com):** provides financial news and statistics for each industry.

- **CNBC Web site (www.cnbc.com/news/markets/indgroups.html):** provides stock indexes for various industry sectors.

11.5 Financial Planning Online: Industry Analysis

Go to:
http://biz.yahoo.com/research/indgrp/

This Web site provides:
information on firms in various industries, including last quarter's earnings per share (EPS), this quarter's EPS, and a summary of recommendations by analysts. It allows you to assess a specific industry, including a firm's competitors.

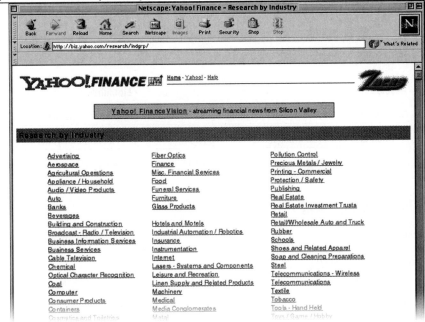

ANALYSIS OF THE FIRM

Beyond economic and industry conditions, firms are also affected by their own decisions. One firm can outperform another in the same industry because its managers make better decisions about how to finance its business, market its products, and manage its employees.

Annual Report

Firms that are publicly traded create an annual report that contains standardized financial information. Specifically, the report includes a letter from the firm's chief executive officer (CEO) summarizing recent performance and expected performance in the future. It also contains financial statements measuring the firm's financial condition that you can examine in the same manner that you evaluate your personal financial statements to determine your financial condition. Many annual reports can be retrieved from the Web sites of the firms of concern. Investors who retrieve annual reports commonly focus on the balance sheet and income statement.

balance sheet
A financial statement that indicates a firm's sources of funds and how it has invested its funds as of a particular point in time.

Balance Sheet. The **balance sheet** of a firm indicates its sources of funds and how it has invested its funds as of a particular point in time. An example of a firm's balance sheet is shown in Exhibit 11.4. It is segmented into two parts: (1) assets and (2) liabilities and shareholder's equity. These two parts of the balance sheet must balance.

The firm's assets indicate how it has invested its funds and what it owns. Assets are often classified as short-term and long-term assets. Short-

Exhibit 11.4   Balance Sheet for Stewart Corporation (numbers are in millions)

Assets		Liabilities and Shareholder's Equity	
Short-term (current) assets		Short-term liabilities	
Cash and marketable securities	$100	Accounts payable	$300
Accounts receivable	400	Short-term debt	0
Inventories	500	**Total short-term liabilities**	**$300**
Total short-term assets	**$1,000**		
Fixed assets	$400	Long-term debt	$200
Less depreciation	−100		
Net fixed assets	$300	Shareholder's equity	800
Total assets	**$1,300**	**Total liabilities and shareholder's equity**	**$1,300**

term assets include cash, securities purchased by the firm, accounts receivable (money owed to the firm for previous sales), and inventories (materials used to produce products, and finished products waiting to be sold). Long-term assets (sometimes called fixed assets) include machinery and buildings purchased by the firm.

The liabilities and shareholder's equity indicate how the firm has obtained its funds. Liabilities represent the amount owed to creditors or suppliers and are classified as short term or long term. Shareholder's equity is the net worth of the firm. It represents the investment in the firm by investors.

income statement
A financial statement that measures a firm's revenues, expenses, and earnings over a particular period of time.

Income Statement. The firm's **income statement** measures its revenues, expenses, and earnings over a particular period of time. It may be reviewed by investors who want to determine how much income (earnings) the firm generated over a particular period or what expenses the firm incurred. An annual report may include an income statement for the year of concern and for the four quarters within that year.

An example of an income statement is shown in Exhibit 11.5. The income statement starts with revenues generated by the firm over the period of concern. Then the cost of goods sold (which includes the cost of materials used in production) is subtracted to derive gross profit. Operating expenses (such as salaries) are subtracted from the gross profit to determine earnings before interest and taxes (also referred to as operating profit). Finally, interest payments and taxes are subtracted to determine the earnings after taxes (also referred to as net profit).

Exhibit 11.5   Income Statement for Stewart Corporation (numbers are in millions)

Revenue	$3,000
Cost of goods sold	1,400
Gross profit	$1,600
Operating expenses	1,130
Earnings before interest and taxes	$470
Interest	20
Earnings before taxes	$450
Taxes	150
Earnings after taxes	$300

Firm-Specific Characteristics

Investors use a firm's balance sheet and income statement to analyze the following characteristics:

- Liquidity
- Financial leverage
- Efficiency
- Profitability

Each of these characteristics is described in turn, and some popular ratios used to measure these characteristics are summarized in Exhibit 11.6 and applied to Stewart Corporation's financial statements.

Exhibit 11.6   Ratios Used to Analyze Stewart Corporation

Measures of Liquidity	Stewart Corporation (numbers in millions)
$\text{Current ratio} = \dfrac{\text{current assets}}{\text{current liabilities}}$	$\text{Current ratio} = \dfrac{\$1,000}{\$300} = 3.33$
Measures of Financial Leverage	
$\text{Debt ratio} = \dfrac{\text{total debt}}{\text{total assets}}$	$\text{Debt radio} = \dfrac{\$200}{\$1,300} = .15$
$\text{Times interest earned ratio} = \dfrac{\text{earnings before interest and taxes}}{\text{interest payments}}$	$\text{Times interest earned ratio} = \dfrac{\$470}{\$20} = 23.5$
Measures of Efficiency	
$\text{Inventory turnover} = \dfrac{\text{cost of goods sold}}{\text{average daily inventory}}$	$\text{Inventory turnover} = \dfrac{\$1,400}{\$500*} = 2.8$
$\text{Average collection period} = \dfrac{\text{average receivables}}{\text{average daily sales}}$	$\text{Average collection period} = \dfrac{\$400}{(\$3,000/365)} = 48.67$
$\text{Asset turnover ratio} = \dfrac{\text{sales}}{\text{average total assets}}$	$\text{Asset turnover ratio} = \dfrac{\$3,000}{\$1,300^\dagger} = 2.31$
Profitability Ratios	
$\text{Net profit margin} = \dfrac{\text{earnings}}{\text{sales}}$	$\text{Net profit margin} = \dfrac{\$300}{\$3,000} = 10\%$
$\text{Return on assets} = \dfrac{\text{earnings}}{\text{assets}}$	$\text{Return on assets} = \dfrac{\$300}{\$1,300} = 23\%$
$\text{Return on equity} = \dfrac{\text{earnings}}{\text{equity}}$	$\text{Return on equity} = \dfrac{\$300}{\$800} = 37.5\%$

*This assumes that the inventory level represents the average level.
†This assumes that the prevailing asset level represents the average level.

current ratio
The ratio of a firm's short-term assets to its short-term liabilities.

financial leverage
A firm's reliance on debt to support its operations.

debt ratio
A measure of financial leverage that measures the proportion of total assets financed with debt.

times interest earned ratio
A measure of financial leverage that measures the ratio of the firm's earnings before interest and taxes to its total interest payments.

inventory turnover
A measure of efficiency; computed as the cost of goods sold divided by average daily inventory.

Liquidity. A firm's assets and liabilities can be assessed to determine its liquidity, or its ability to cover any expenses. A firm has a high degree of liquidity if it has a large amount of assets that can be easily converted to cash and has a relatively small amount of short-term liabilities. You can assess a firm's liquidity by computing its **current ratio,** which is the ratio of its short-term assets to its short-term liabilities. A high ratio relative to the industry norm represents a relatively high degree of liquidity.

Financial Leverage. A firm obtains funds by borrowing funds from suppliers or creditors or by selling shares of its stock (equity) to investors. Many firms prefer to borrow funds rather than issue stock. An excessive amount of stock may spread the shareholder ownership of the firm too thin, placing downward pressure on the stock price. If a firm borrows too much money, however, it may have difficulty making its interest payments on loans. Investors commonly assess a firm's balance sheet to determine its ability to make debt payments. Thus, investors closely monitor the firm's **financial leverage,** or its reliance on debt to support its operations.

A firm's financial leverage can be measured by its **debt ratio,** which measures the proportion of total assets financed with debt. A firm with a high debt ratio relative to the industry norm has a high degree of financial leverage and therefore may have a relatively high risk of default on its future debt payments. Some firms with a relatively high degree of financial leverage can easily cover their debt payments if they generate stable cash inflows over time. The debt ratio focuses just on the firm's level of debt and does not account for its cash flows. Thus, a more appropriate measure of a firm's ability to repay its debt is the **times interest earned ratio,** which measures the ratio of the firm's earnings before interest and taxes to its total interest payments. A high times interest earned ratio (relative to the industry norm) means that the firm should be more capable of covering its debt payments.

Efficiency. The composition of assets can indicate how efficiently a firm uses its funds. If it generates a relatively low level of sales and earnings with a large amount of assets, it is not using its assets efficiently. A firm that invests in assets has to obtain funds to support those assets. The less assets it uses to generate its sales, the less funds it needs to borrow or obtain by issuing stock.

You can use the **inventory turnover** to measure how efficiently a firm manages its inventory. It is calculated as the cost of goods sold divided by average daily inventory. A higher number relative to the industry norm represents relatively high turnover, which is more efficient.

"Remember, the customer always comes first in the billing department."

www.cartoonstock.com

11.6   Financial Planning Online: Determining Industry Norms

Go to:

http://biz.yahoo.com/research/indgrp

This Web site provides:

information on various industry groups and allows you to obtain financial information on firms you specify in any industry. By reviewing financial information for various firms within an industry, you can measure the industry norm.

average collection period

A measure of efficiency; computed as accounts receivable divided by average daily sales.

asset turnover ratio

A measure of efficiency; computed as sales divided by average total assets.

operating profit margin

A firm's operating profit divided by sales.

net profit margin

A measure of profitability that measures net profit as a percentage of sales.

return on assets

A measure of profitability; computed as net profit divided by total assets.

return on equity

A measure of profitability; computed as net profit divided by the owner's investment in the firm (stockholder's equity).

You can use the **average collection period** to determine the average age of accounts receivable. It is measured as accounts receivable divided by average daily sales. A higher number relative to the industry norm means a longer collection period, which is less efficient.

You can use the **asset turnover ratio** to assess how efficiently a firm uses its assets. This ratio is measured as sales divided by average total assets. A higher number relative to the industry norm reflects higher efficiency.

Profitability. You can also use the income statement and balance sheet to assess a firm's profitability. The **operating profit margin** is the operating profit divided by sales, and the **net profit margin** measures net profit as a percentage of sales. The **return on assets** is the net profit divided by total assets. The **return on equity** is measured as net profit divided by the owner's investment in the firm (stockholder's equity). The higher the profitability ratios relative to the industry norm, the higher the firm's profitability.

Other Sources of Information

In addition to annual reports, investors use several other sources of information to research individual firms. Some of the more popular sources are summarized in Exhibit 11.7. The wire services are also a common source of information, which can be found on numerous Internet sites. Although the Internet provides a substantial amount of information, you should be careful when using this information to make your investment decisions. A classic example that offers valuable lessons is the case of Emulex stock. At

Exhibit 11.7   Sources of Firm-Specific Information

Published Sources

- **Value Line Investment Survey:** provides detailed financial information about 1,700 firms including forecasts of each firm's future performance.

- **Standard and Poor's Corporate Records:** provides financial information about each corporation.

- **Moody's Industrial Manual:** provides detailed financial information about each corporation.

- **Moody's OTC Manual:** provides detailed financial information for each firm that is traded on the over-the-counter market.

Online Sources

Many firms provide annual reports on their Web sites. In addition, see:

- **Report Gallery (www.reportgallery.com):** provides annual reports for many firms.

- **Securities and Exchange Commission (SEC) Web site (www.sec.gov):** provides annual reports of many firms.

- **Yahoo! (www.yahoo.com):** provides a stock screener that allows investors to identify stocks that have particular financial characteristics.

9:30 A.M. on August 25, 2000, a press release stated that the earnings of Emulex were lower than expected and that the firm's CEO had resigned. Investors began to dump their shares in response to this news. The news was a surprise not only to investors, but to the CEO of Emulex, as the press release was false. Yet, within an hour, the statement was posted on numerous Web sites, and the stock price of Emulex had declined by 62 percent. The trading of the stock was halted, which allowed time for executives of Emulex to provide information that refuted the press release. When trading resumed, the stock price rose to where it had been before the press release. By the end of the day, various government agencies, including the Federal Bureau of Investigation, were investigating the case.

Within a few days, it was determined that this false press release was created by a junior college student who had previously worked for a company that issued press releases. He created the fictitious information so that he could buy Emulex at a very low price and sell it for a much higher price. By causing the price to decline so much, he generated a capital gain of more than $200,000 within a day from trading Emulex stock. His actions were illegal, however, so he could not keep his gain and was also subject to other severe penalties.

The lesson from this case is to make sure your information is valid before you act on it. Reputable Web sites attempt to validate the information they disclose, but they are unable to completely guard against a hoax like this.

11.7   Financial Planning Online: Financial News about Your Stock

Go to:
http://finance.yahoo.com/?u

This Web site provides:
financial news about any firm
that you specify. Once you type
in the firm's symbol, click on
"News" for a summary of
recent news articles about the
firm. This can help you monitor the activities of a stock that
you may purchase in the future
or that you have already purchased.

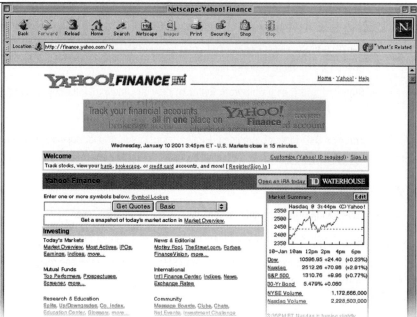

Information Provided by Value Line. Exhibit 11.8 provides an example of the
firm-specific information provided by the Value Line Investment Survey.
Each component of the exhibit discussed here is designated with a letter
code. The name of the firm is shown in the top left corner (a). Along the
top of the page, notice the recent stock price (b), the price-earnings (PE)
ratio (c), the relative PE ratio comparable to other firms in the industry (d),
and the firm's dividend yield, equal to annual dividends divided by the price
per share (e).

Just below the firm's name in the upper left corner are Value Line's ratings of the firm (f). The firm's beta (g), which measures the sensitivity of its
stock price relative to the market, is shown below those ratings. To the
right of the beta is the firm's stock price trend over the last several years (h).
The firm's stock trading volume information (i) appears below the stock
price trend.

In the middle of the page is a spreadsheet that shows the trends of various financial statistics that are identified in the right margin. The top rows
of the spreadsheet (j) show the financial statistics on a per share basis so
that they can be compared with those of other firms.

In the middle of the spreadsheet, you will find the trend of the PE ratio
(k), the relative PE ratio (l), and the dividend yield (m). Also notice the
trends of various profitability ratios, including the net profit margin (n).

The firm's long-term sources of funds are shown in the section called
"capital structure" (o) to the left of the bottom part of the spreadsheet. Just

Exhibit 11.8   An Example from Value Line Investment Survey

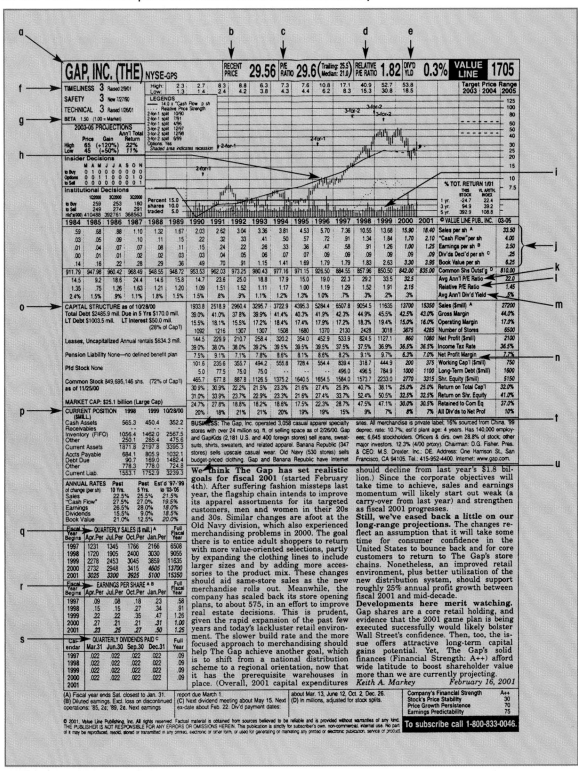

below the capital structure is information (p) that can be used to assess the firm's liquidity. Below that information, you will find quarterly data on sales (q), earnings (r), and dividends (s). A general summary of the firm's business (t) appears below the right portion of the spreadsheet and a general analysis of the business (u) appears below the business summary.

Using Your Stock Analysis to Make Investment Decisions

By conducting an analysis of the economy, the industry, and the firm itself, you can assess a firm's future performance. This process enables you to determine whether to purchase the firm's stock. Exhibit 11.9 summarizes the potential impact of economic, industry, and firm-specific conditions on a firm's stock price.

Exhibit 11.9   Factors That Increase and Decrease the Stock's Price

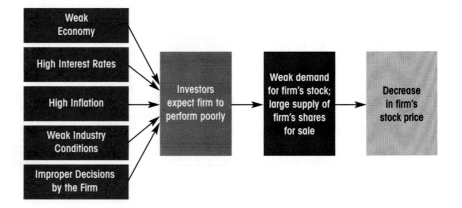

information that was available to investors should have justified higher valuations of those stocks before their prices increased. It is easy to look back and realize that we would have benefited from purchasing shares of Microsoft or Dell Computer or Yahoo! when their stocks first publicly traded. Yet who really knew that these stocks would perform so well at that time? An investor can achieve high returns from a hunch about a specific stock. The concept of market efficiency acknowledges that when you invest in stocks, some of those stocks may outperform the market in general. However, it implies that stock selections by an investor will not consistently beat the market.

HOW STOCK VALUATION FITS WITHIN YOUR FINANCIAL PLAN

Recall the key decisions about stock that should be included within your financial plan:

1. Should you consider buying stock?

2. How should you value stocks when determining whether to buy them?

3. What methods should you use for investing in stocks?

The first decision was discussed in the previous chapter. If you consider buying stock, you need to determine which common stocks are undervalued and deserve to be purchased. This decision requires an analysis of stocks, as discussed in this chapter. Exhibit 11.10 provides an example of how this decision applies to Stephanie Spratt's financial plan. Methods for investing in stock will be discussed in the next chapter.

Stephanie's first concerns should be maintaining adequate liquidity and making her existing loan payments. She is not in a position to buy stock right now (as she concluded in the previous chapter). However, she wants to monitor one stock that she may purchase someday when her financial position improves.

Exhibit 11.10   How Stock Valuation Fits within Stephanie Spratt's Financial Plan

Goals for Investing in Stock

1. Determine if I could benefit from investing in stock (discussed in the previous chapter).
2. If I decide to invest in stock, determine how to value a stock.
3. Determine the method I would use for investing in stocks (discussed in Chapter 12).

Analysis

Method Used to Assess the Value of Trail.com Stock	Opinion
1. Price-earnings (PE) method	Can easily be used to value a stock, but is limited because it assumes that the firm has the same PE ratio as its competitors.
2. Price-revenue (PR) method	Is more appropriate than the PE method when the firm's earnings are negative. However, it is limited because it assumes the firm has the same PR ratio as its competitors.
3. Assessment of economy, industry, and firm	This method provides much valuable information, but it is subjective and does not lead to a precise estimate of the firm's value.

Decision

Decision Regarding How to Value Stocks:

Although all three methods can be used, each has limitations. I plan to use all three methods when valuing a stock. I will consider purchasing a stock only if all three methods indicate that the stock is undervalued. Even under these conditions, I may still consider investing in a stock only if other sources of information (such as financial experts) agree with my views. Until I learn more about stock valuation, I should recognize my limitations and limit the amount of money that I invest in individual stocks.

DISCUSSION QUESTIONS

1. How would Stephanie's stock investing decisions be different if she were a single mother of two children?

2. How would Stephanie's stock investing decisions be affected if she were 35 years old? If she were 50 years old?

SUMMARY

Stocks can be valued using several methods. The price-earnings (PE) method estimates the stock's value by applying the mean industry PE ratio to the firm's recent or expected annual earnings. The price-revenue (PR) method estimates the stock's value by applying the mean industry PR ratio to the firm's revenue per share. The present value method (discussed in the appendix) estimates the present value of future cash flows that the investor expects to receive over the period in which the stock is held.

An economic analysis involves assessing how a stock's price can be affected by economic conditions. The most closely monitored economic factors that can affect stock prices are economic growth, interest rates, and inflation. In general, stocks are favorably affected by economic growth, a decline in interest rates, and a decline in inflation.

An industry analysis involves assessing how a stock's price can be affected by industry conditions. Two closely monitored industry characteristics are consumer preferences within an industry and industry competition. Stocks are favorably affected when the firms recognize shifts in consumer preferences and when the firms face a relatively low degree of competition.

An analysis of a firm involves reviewing the annual report and the financial statements (such as the balance sheet and income statement), along with other financial reports. This analysis includes an assessment of the firm's liquidity, financial leverage, efficiency, and profitability.

Stock market efficiency implies that stock prices reflect all public information. If the stock market is efficient, there are no benefits from trying to use public information to achieve unusually high returns. Many investors, however, believe that the stock market is not efficient and therefore attempt to determine whether a specific stock is undervalued.

Integrating the Key Concepts

Your decision to invest in specific stocks is not only related to your other investment decisions, but also affects other parts of your financial plan. When buying stocks, you should consider your liquidity (Part 2). If your liquidity is limited, you may desire to achieve some degree of liquidity from any stocks you purchase. The stocks of large firms would be most appropriate because they are more liquid than stocks of small firms. That is, they can be sold more easily in the market because there are more potential buyers who are willing to buy well-known stocks.

Before investing in any stocks, you should reassess your financing (Part 3). Compare your expected return on any specific stock you may purchase with the interest rate incurred on any personal loan that you have. Consider paying off any personal loans before you invest in stocks, unless the return on stocks will exceed the interest rate incurred on personal loans. If, after considering liquidity and your financing situation, you still decide to invest in stocks, you need to decide whether the investment should be for your retirement account (Part 5). Your choice of stocks may depend on whether the investment is for your retirement account because those stocks that typically result in more taxes (such as those that pay high dividends) may be more appropriate for a retirement account where the dividend income may be tax-deferred.

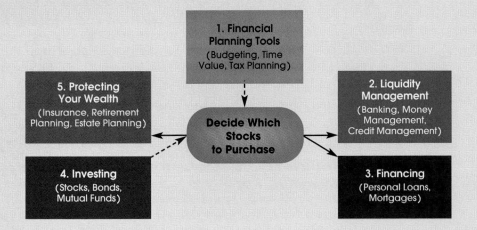

Using the Present Value Method to Value Stocks

present value method
A method of valuing stocks that determines the stock's present value over the period in which you plan to hold it.

In addition to the stock valuation methods described in the chapter, you can also value a stock using the **present value method**. This method involves determining the stock's present value over the period in which you plan to hold the stock, by following these steps:

1. Estimate the future cash flows (dividends and the expected selling price of the stock).

2. Determine the return you would require to invest in the stock.

3. Discount the expected cash flows at your required rate of return, which determines the present value of the stock (and therefore the price that you think the stock is worth today).

After completing these steps, compare the estimated value of the stock to its market value to determine whether the stock is currently undervalued.

Example

Stephanie Spratt considers buying Trail.com stock, which is currently priced at $61 per share. She expects Trail.com stock to pay dividends of $2 per share each year (for simplicity, assume the dividend is paid at the end of each year). She expects the stock to be worth $64 per share at the end of three years when she would sell it. To invest in this stock, she would want a return of 12 percent.

Given the information, the three steps are as follows:

1. The expected cash flows to Stephanie are $2 per share in year 1, $2 per share in year 2, and $66 (computed as $2 + $64) per share in year 3.

2. Since her required rate of return is 12 percent, she discounts any future cash flows by 12 percent to determine the present value of the expected cash flows; the discounting could be computed by using a calculator or by multiplying the expected dividend in each year by its respective present value interest factor.

3. Her valuation of the stock is the present value of the expected future cash flows:

$$\text{Valuation of Stock} = \$2/(1 + .12)^1 + \$2/(1 + .12)^2 + \$66/(1 + .12)^3$$
$$= \$1.78 + \$1.59 + \$46.98$$
$$= \$50.35.$$

Her valuation of this stock is $50.35, while the prevailing market price is $61.00. This means that if Stephanie purchases the stock for that price, and the dividends and future price are as expected, she would not earn the return that she desires (and used to discount the future expected cash flows). Since the prevailing market price is more than this valuation, she believes that the stock price is overvalued.

The most difficult part of this valuation method is estimating the future cash flows. The future price of the stock is difficult to predict. If your estimate of the future stock price is poor, your valuation will be poor as well. If you overestimate the price of the stock at the time you plan to sell it, you will overestimate the value of the stock today. This may cause you to purchase a stock today that will not achieve the return that you expected.

REVIEW QUESTIONS

1. What drives the price of a stock? How do you begin the valuation process for a stock? What are you trying to determine through stock valuation? How does stock valuation factor into the volume of trading on a stock? Which investors may be able to achieve a high rate of return?

2. How is the price-earnings ratio computed? Describe how you can use the PE method to value a firm. How can you derive an estimate of earnings? What are the limitations of using the PE method?

3. When might you use the price-revenue method rather than the PE method? How is PR ratio calculated? What are some limitations of the PR method?

4. When performing an economic analysis of stocks, what three economic factors are most closely watched?

5. Explain how economic growth is measured. How does economic growth affect stock prices? How does the government's fiscal policy affect economic growth?

6. How do interest rates affect economic growth? Why do interest rates affect some stock prices more than others? Who controls interest rates?

7. What is inflation? How is inflation measured? How does inflation affect stock prices?

8. Why is an industry analysis of stocks important? List some sources of information about firms and their industry.

9. Why is it necessary to analyze the firm? What is an annual report? What information does it contain to aid the analysis?

10. What characteristics of a firm do investors analyze by using the balance sheet and the income statement?

11. What is liquidity? How is it measured?

12. What is financial leverage? Discuss two ways to measure financial leverage.

13. What determines the efficiency of a firm? How can efficiency be measured?

14. Where is the information found to determine a firm's profitability? Describe the financial formulas used to measure it.

15. List some additional sources of information about individual firms. Why should you carefully evaluate the information you use?

16. What information is provided by the Value Line Investment Survey?

17. What does the term *efficient market* mean? What is an inefficient market?

18. Describe how an efficient market works.

19. Historically, some stocks that provide very high returns can be identified. Does this mean the market is inefficient? Why or why not?

20. How can investors value a stock using the present value method?*

FINANCIAL PLANNING PROBLEMS

1. Denise has a choice between two stocks. Stock A has a current stock price of $33.50 and earnings per share of $2.23. Stock B has a current stock price of $30.50 and earnings per share of $2.79. Both stocks are in the same industry, and the average PE ratio for the industry is 13. Which stock would be the better choice? Why?

2. Denise decides to use the price-revenue method to value the firms. She determines that the industry PR ratio is 1.5. Stock A is reporting revenues at $20 per share. Stock B is reporting revenues at $22 per share. Which stock is the better choice?

3. Angie is considering adding a stock to her portfolio. She requires a 15 percent return and will hold the stock for 10 years. She expects the stock to pay no dividends, but she expects to be able to sell the stock at the end of 10 years for $150 per share. The current stock price is $38. Should she buy the stock?*

4. Sarah requires a 12 percent return on her investment. She estimates that stock A will continue to pay dividends of $3 per share over the next five years. She projects that in five years she will be able to sell stock A for $90 per share. What is the maximum price she should pay for stock A at this time?*

5. Andy wishes to purchase stock in XYZ Corporation. He needs at least a 10 percent return over the next three years. Dividends on the stock have been steady over the last several years at $1.50

* Question based on chapter appendix.

per share, and Andy expects that will continue. Andy also expects that he will be able to sell the stock in three years at $62.00 a share. The current price is $46.50 per share. Should Andy purchase the stock?*

* Question based on chapter appendix.

FINANCIAL PLANNING ONLINE EXERCISES

Go to http://finance.yahoo.com/?u.

1. In this exercise, you will examine information on the financial condition of a stock. Under "Yahoo! Finance," enter the stock symbol UNM, and click on "Get Quotes." You will get information on UNUM Corporation. Under "More Info," click on "Profiles." Three pages of information will be provided, including a description of the company's businesses, address, recent events, insider purchases and sales, officers of the company, and price and volume information on the stock. How is this information of use to investors?

2. In the "Statistics at a Glance" section, review the Book Value per Share, Earnings per Share, Price/Earnings ratio, Profit Margin, Return on Assets, Return on Equity, Debt/Equity ratio. Are UNUM shares a good investment at the current share price?

3. Use the Back option in your browser to return to http://finance.yahoo.com/?u. Enter the symbol MSFT and click on "Get Quotes" to obtain information on Microsoft. Under "More Info," click on "Profiles." Review the financial ratios. Are Microsoft shares a good investment at the current price? Why or why not?

4. How do Microsoft and UNUM Corporation compare as investments based on the financial information available at this Web site?

Go to http://screen.yahoo.com/stocks.html.

1. This exercise allows you to identify stocks that satisfy your criteria. In the "Stock Screener" under "Industry," choose any; choose 1–2 for Average Analyst Recommendation; choose $10 for Minimum Share Price and $100 for Maximum; for Market Cap, choose Mid Cap; under Price/Earnings Ratio, select 5 for Minimum and >50 for Maximum; for Average Daily Volume, select 100K–500K shares/day; for 1-Yr Estimated Earnings Growth, choose increased 25–50% and for 1-Yr Stock Price Performance, choose increased 25–50%. Click "Find Stocks." What stocks meet the criteria? What are their ticker symbols, PE ratios, returns percentages, prices, and growth rates?

2. Compare two stocks that meet the criteria. Which is the better investment?

3. Use the Back option in your browser to return to http://screen.yahoo.com/stocks.html. Choose "Stock Screener." Under "Industry," select any; for Average Analyst Recommendation, choose 1–2; for Share Price, select $25 for Minimum and $100 for Maximum; for Market Cap, choose Large Cap; for Price/Earnings Ratio, choose 5 for Minimum and >50 for Maximum; for Average Daily Volume, select >1 million shares/day; for 1-Year Estimated Earnings Growth, choose increased 25–50%, and for 1-Year Stock Price Performance, choose increased 25–50%. Click "Find Stocks." What stocks meet the selected criteria?

4. Compare two stocks on this list based on the financial information provided and justify your preference between the two stocks.

Building Your Own Financial Plan

One of the best financial instruments to accomplish many intermediate- and long-term goals is investment in stocks. Investment specialists have said that at any given time there are 20 to 50 stocks that could make someone a millionaire within a short period of time. The secret, of course, is to find just one of those 20 to 50 stocks. In this exercise, you will analyze two or three stocks to determine if they are good investments and, therefore, a suitable means to accomplish some of the intermediate- and long-term goals you established in Chapter 1.

Researching stocks has become much easier, thanks in large part to the Internet. This exercise will be carried out using two Web sites. The first will take you to the Federal Reserve Board Beige Book. The Beige Book will give you insight into what the Federal Reserve Board expects of the economy in the near future. The second Web site will provide you with the necessary information on the company you specify to determine its suitability for your portfolio. The template provided for this chapter in the *Financial Planning Workbook* and on the CD-ROM is structured with a series of questions that will guide your analysis.

When investing in stocks, it is necessary to monitor happenings in the economy and the market. Events may very quickly have a significant impact—favorable or unfavorable—on the price trends of a stock. How frequently you monitor information will depend on market conditions and the volatility of your own individual stocks. Web sites such as http://finance.yahoo.com/?u allow you to easily research financial news about any firm.

The Sampsons—A Continuing Case

 The Sampsons have decided to invest some of their savings in stocks to support their children's future college education. They do not know much about investing in stocks, so they investigate various Web sites that provide information on economic and industry conditions. They learn that the economy is expected to strengthen in the future and that the technology sector is expected to perform particularly well. Dave and Sharon are tempted to invest their entire savings in technology stocks to capitalize on what they have learned.

1. Advise the Sampsons as to whether they should put all of their investments in technology stocks.

2. Should the information the Sampsons read on the Web site affect how they invest in stocks?

IN-TEXT STUDY GUIDE

True/False:

1. The price of a stock is based on the demand for that stock versus the supply of stock for sale.

2. The present value method is definitely the most reliable method of valuing stock.*

3. The most common method of using earnings to value stocks is the price-earnings (PE) method.

4. The price-revenue (PR) ratio is the industry's average ratio of revenue per share to share price.

5. Fiscal policy determines how the U.S. government taxes individuals and corporations and how it spends money.

6. All firms in the economy are equally affected by changes in economic conditions.

7. In general, stock prices tend to increase when inflation is expected to increase.

8. An industry analysis is often necessary because a firm's stock price is also susceptible to industry conditions.

9. The debt ratio focuses on the firm's level of debt and its cash flows.

10. An efficient stock market implies that you and other investors will not be able to correctly identify stocks that are undervalued because stocks are valued properly by the market.

* Question based on chapter appendix.

Multiple Choice:

1. When you buy a stock, you may do so because you think the stock is
   a. fairly priced.
   b. undervalued.
   c. overvalued.
   d. none of the above

2. The _____ method is not commonly used to value stock.
   a. present value
   b. price-earnings
   c. price-revenue
   d. price-dividend

The following information applies to questions 3 and 4.

Billy Bowers is considering purchasing X Corporation stock, which is currently priced at $45 a share. Billy expects to hold the stock for two years and then sell it for $60 per share. X Corporation will pay dividends of $2 per share in each of the next two years. Billy requires a return of 10 percent on X Corporation stock.

3. Based on this information, Billy will receive total cash flows per share in the amount of _____ over the next two years.
   a. $47
   b. $60
   c. $62
   d. $64

4. Based on the present value method, Billy should be willing to pay _____ per share of X Corporation stock.*
   a. $53.06
   b. $52.89
   c. $58.18
   d. $51.24

The following information applies to questions 5 and 6.

Brewer, Inc., operates in the manufacturing industry. The PE ratios of two other firms in the industry are 15 and 20. Brewer's most recent earnings per share were $3.12.

5. Based on this information, a fair valuation of Brewer stock would be _____ per share.
   a. $15.00
   b. $46.80
   c. $62.40
   d. $54.60

6. Brewer Stock is currently trading for $60 per share. Thus, you believe that the stock is
   a. undervalued.
   b. overvalued.
   c. fairly priced.
   d. none of the above

* Question based on chapter appendix.

7. Which of the following is not a disadvantage of the PE method of valuing stock?
   a. It is difficult to forecast earnings.
   b. The results vary with the industry composite used to derive a mean industry PE ratio.
   c. The firm you are valuing may deserve to have a lower PE ratio than other firms.
   d. It is difficult to determine the prevailing price of the stock.

8. When using the PR method to value stock, the _____ a firm's revenues, the _____ the valuation within a specific industry.
   a. higher; lower
   b. lower; higher
   c. lower; lower
   d. Answers (a) and (b) are correct.

9. WHAM.com has expected revenues of $25 per share, and other firms in its industry have a PR ratio of 3.0, on average. Thus, the value of WHAM.com is estimated to be
   a. $25.00.
   b. $8.33.
   c. $75.00.
   d. none of the above

10. Which of the following is not a limitation of the PR method of valuing stock?
    a. It is difficult to estimate future revenues.
    b. Revenues do not indicate how efficient a firm is.
    c. The application of a PR multiple is subject to error if it is derived from firms that do not have very similar operations to the firm that is being valued.
    d. All of the above are limitations of the PR method.

11. When aggregate demand _____, unemployment _____.
    a. increases; increases
    b. decreases; increases
    c. increases; decreases
    d. Answers (b) and (c) are correct.

12. In general, stocks perform _____ when interest rates are _____.
    a. better; high
    b. better; low
    c. poorer; low
    d. none of the above

13. Which of the following is not a direct measure of inflation?
    a. gross domestic product (GDP)
    b. consumer price index (CPI)
    c. producer price index (PPI)
    d. All of the above are direct measures of inflation.

14. A firm's _____ indicates its reliance on debt to support its operations.
    a. efficiency
    b. profitability
    c. liquidity
    d. financial leverage

15. A firm with a _____ debt ratio relative to the industry norm has a _____ degree of financial leverage.
    a. high; low
    b. low; high
    c. high; high
    d. none of the above

16. You would probably not use the _____ to assess a firm's efficiency.
    a. operating profit margin
    b. inventory turnover
    c. asset turnover
    d. average collection period

17. Which of the following is not a measure of profitability?
    a. net profit margin
    b. debt ratio
    c. return on assets
    d. return on equity

18. If a stock market is _____, this implies that stock prices fully reflect information that is available to investors.
    a. perfect
    b. highly leveraged
    c. efficient
    d. systematic

19. The _____ ratio measures the ratio of a firm's earnings before interest and taxes to its total interest payments.
    a. times interest earned
    b. debt
    c. interest
    d. leverage

20. An analysis of a firm involves an assessment of the firm's
    a. liquidity.
    b. financial leverage.
    c. efficiency.
    d. all of the above

Chapter **12**

Buying Stocks

When investing in stocks, you need to formulate an investment strategy to determine which stocks to purchase. Your investing strategy will affect the dividends (cash inflows) provided by your stocks and the value of your assets (stock holdings) over time. Therefore, the proper use of a stock investment strategy will enhance your wealth.

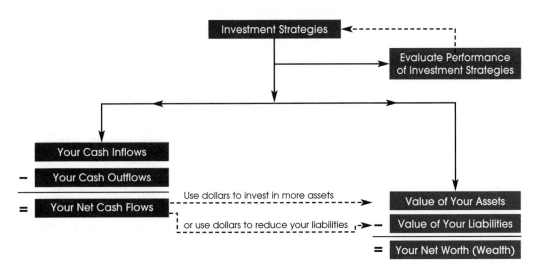

The objectives of this chapter are to:

- describe various methods that can be used when determining which stocks to purchase,

- explain how to execute the purchase or sale of stocks,

- discuss buying stocks on margin, and

- explain how to assess your stock portfolio's performance.

STOCK INVESTMENT STRATEGIES

When deciding which stocks to purchase, investors follow one or more of the following methods:

- Invest based on valuation methods

- Invest in stock mutual funds

- Invest in publicly traded indexes

- Invest based on adviser recommendations

Invest Based on Valuation Methods

You can make your investment decisions based on the valuations you conduct for specific stocks. Recall from Chapter 11 that the valuation of stocks

stock portfolio
The collection of stocks that you own.

can dictate which stocks you should purchase. Your **stock portfolio** is the collection of stocks that you own. As conditions change, valuations change, and you may rearrange your stock portfolio by selling some stocks or buying additional stocks. Investors normally use either fundamental analysis or technical analysis to make their stock investment decisions.

fundamental analysis
Stock valuation based on fundamental characteristics (such as revenue and earnings) of the firm or its sensitivity to economic conditions.

Fundamental Valuation Methods. Many investors value stocks by using **fundamental analysis,** which involves an examination of the fundamental characteristics (such as revenue and earnings) of the firm or its sensitivity to economic conditions. You can use the valuation methods described in the previous chapters to identify stocks that are undervalued. You can also periodically apply these valuation methods to the stocks in your portfolio and sell stocks that you believe are now overvalued.

technical analysis
Stock valuation based on historical price patterns.

Technical Methods. Some investors use **technical analysis,** which is the valuation of stocks based on historical price patterns. For example, an investor might purchase a stock whenever its price rises for two consecutive days, because this trend creates an expectation that the trend will continue. A related example is to sell a stock whenever its price declines for two consecutive days, because this trend creates an expectation that the price will continue to decline.

Many investors strongly believe that they can achieve high returns by using technical analysis. A review of historical prices may show that some patterns have persisted over time. Stock charts showing historical data are widely available on various Web sites, including the Yahoo! Web site. Some investors detect a pattern of price movements for a particular stock prior to a price rise and then purchase that stock the next time the same pattern occurs. Even if a trend has persisted in the past, however, there is no guarantee that it will continue in the future.

Invest in Stock Mutual Funds

Investors who have limited funds and want a diversified stock portfolio, yet do not want to assess many individual stocks, may consider investing in a stock mutual fund. The minimum investment may be as low as $500, and the fund is managed by an experienced portfolio manager. Because a stock mutual fund typically invests in numerous stocks, you can invest in a widely diversified portfolio with a small amount of money. There are thousands of stock mutual funds to choose from. More details about the characteristics and types of mutual funds are provided in Chapter 14.

publicly traded stock indexes
Securities whose values move in tandem with a particular stock index representing a set of stocks.

Invest in Publicly Traded Indexes

Another option for investors who want a diversified portfolio of stocks is to invest in **publicly traded stock indexes,** which are securities whose values move in tandem with a particular stock index representing a set of stocks.

Much research has shown that sophisticated investors (such as well-paid portfolio managers of financial institutions) are unable to achieve returns on their stock portfolios that exceed the average returns among all stocks. Thus, by investing in an index, individual investors can ensure that their performance will match that index.

One of the most popular publicly traded indexes is the Standard & Poor's Depository Receipt (S.P.D.R., also called Spider), which is a basket of stocks that matches the S&P 500 index and is traded on the American Stock Exchange. You can buy Spiders through a broker, just like stocks. When investors expect that the large U.S. stocks represented by the S&P 500 will experience strong performance, they can capitalize on their expectations by purchasing shares of Spiders. The shares trade at one-tenth the S&P 500 value. Thus, when the S&P 500 is valued at 1700, a Spider is valued at $170 per share. If you invest in Spiders at $170 and the S&P 500 index rises to 1800, you will be able to sell the shares for $180 per share. Thus, over your investment horizon, the share price will have increased by about 5.88 percent—the same as the appreciation in the index itself.

Spiders provide investors with a return not only in the form of potential share price appreciation, but also in the form of dividends. They pay dividends in the form of additional shares to the investors. Any expenses incurred by the Spiders from creating the index are deducted from the dividends.

Investors can also invest in other indexes. Diamonds are shares of the Dow Jones Industrial Average (DJIA) index and are measured as one one-hundredth of the DJIA value. Thus, if investors have higher expectations about the 30 companies that make up the Dow than about the 500 firms in the S&P 500, they will choose to invest in Diamonds rather than Spiders. Investors can also invest in specific sector indexes as well as in market indexes. There are publicly traded indexes that represent a variety of specific sectors, including the Internet, energy, technology, and financial sectors. Because an index represents several stocks, the investor achieves some degree of diversification by investing in an index.

Invest Based on Adviser Recommendations

You can easily obtain recommendations from advisers (such as analysts and some brokerage firms) on television and in financial periodicals. Some investors rely on these recommendations to make their investment decisions. Recommendations from advisers have limitations, however. You should ask yourself why these analysts are willing to provide advice on undervalued stocks rather than simply investing in the stocks themselves. Are they willing to invest their own money in the stocks that they recommend?

If a stock is currently priced at $40, should investors listen to an adviser who recommends buying the stock? If they follow this advice, they must believe that this adviser knows more than the other market participants. After all, many other advisers are not recommending this stock.

Some brokerage firms may advise you to frequently buy or sell securities, rather than holding on to your investment portfolio over time. For each transaction, however, you must pay a commission to that brokerage firm. In addition, frequent trading may cause you to hold on to stocks less than one year, so any capital gain is on a "short-term" investment. Thus, the capital gain is treated like ordinary income for federal income tax purposes unless the gain occurs as a result of trading stocks in your retirement account. If your marginal tax rate on ordinary income is higher than 20 percent (the maximum long-term capital gain tax rate), you will be subject to a higher tax rate because you did not hold the stocks for at least one year. Brokerage firms should remind you of this tax effect before suggesting that you sell stocks that you have held for less than one year.

Many studies have shown that the recommendations by advisers do not lead to better performance than the stock market in general. Some advisers have very limited experience in analyzing and valuing securities. Even those who are very experienced will not necessarily be able to help you achieve unusually high performance.

Individuals may still desire to use an adviser to ensure that they invest in securities that reflect their investment objectives. In addition, some individuals may not wish to spend time analyzing stocks and managing their portfolio. These are reasonable motives for hiring an adviser, assuming that the adviser is able to provide you with valuable advice.

Advisers tend to be overly optimistic about stocks. They are generally unwilling to recommend that investors sell stocks because they do not want to offend any firms with which their own investment firm might do business in the future. In 1999, the firm First Call tracked 27,000 recommendations of stocks by analysts, and only 35 of these recommendations were

12.1   Financial Planning Online: Analyst Recommendations

Go to:
http://finance.yahoo.com/?u

This Web site provides:
analyst recommendations about a stock that you specify. To review the recommendations for a stock that you own or may purchase, type in the stock's symbol, and then click on "Research."

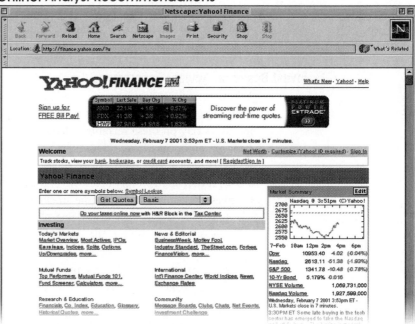

to sell a specific stock. In other words, analysts made about 1 "sell" recommendation for every 770 "buy" recommendations. Analyst recommendations are not necessarily focused on serving the individual investor. Thus, the advice you receive on stocks to buy or sell will not necessarily enhance your wealth.

HOW TO PURCHASE OR SELL STOCKS

discount brokerage firm
A brokerage firm that executes your desired transactions but does not offer investment advice.

full-service brokerage firm
A brokerage firm that offers investment advice and executes transactions.

The market for a stock is created from the flow of orders from investors to buy or sell each stock. Recall from Chapter 10 that the orders to buy a stock are matched with orders to sell that security at a price agreeable to both parties in each transaction. To buy or sell a stock, you establish an account at a brokerage firm. You can choose a discount or full-service brokerage firm. A **discount brokerage firm** executes your desired transactions but does not offer investment advice. A **full-service brokerage firm** offers investment advice and executes transactions.

Full-service brokerage firms tend to charge higher fees for their services than discount brokers. For example, a full-service brokerage firm may charge you between 3 and 8 percent of the transaction, or between $150 and $400 for a $5,000 transaction, whereas a discount brokerage firm will likely charge you between $8 and $60 for the same transaction. Investors who only need the brokerage firm to execute transactions typically use discount brokers, while investors who want advice rely on full-service brokerage firms. Many

12.2   Financial Planning Online: Reviews of Full-Service Brokers

Go to:
http://www.gomez.com

Click on:
Finance, then Brokers (Full-Service)

This Web site provides:
reviews and ratings of various brokers and describes the services offered by each broker.

full-service brokerage firms have recently reorganized so that they can satisfy both types of investors. They may charge higher commissions when they provide advice and lower commissions for investors who simply want their transactions executed.

Buying or Selling Stock Online

Individuals who wish to buy or sell stocks are increasingly using online brokerage services such as Ameritrade and E*Trade. One advantage of placing orders online is that the commission charged per transaction is very low, such as $8 or $20, regardless of the size of the transaction (up to a specified maximum level). A second advantage is the convenience. In addition to accepting orders, online brokers provide real-time stock quotes and financial information about firms. To establish an account with an online brokerage service, you go to its Web site and follow the instructions to set up an account. Then you send the online broker a check, and once the check has cleared, your account will show that you have funds that you can use to invest online.

Recall from Chapter 5 that many online brokerage firms have a money market fund where your cash is deposited until it is used to make transactions. Consequently, you can earn some interest on your funds until you use them to purchase securities. Once you place an order, the online brokerage firm will use the money in your money market fund to pay for the transaction. You may even receive blank checks so that you can write checks against your money market account.

As many investors have shifted to online brokerage, traditional brokerage firms (such as Quick & Reilly and Merrill Lynch) have begun to offer online services. You can place an order in less than a minute from your computer, and the order will be executed within a minute.

Placing an Order

Whenever you place an order to buy or sell a stock, you must specify the following:

- Name of the stock

- Buy or sell

- Number of shares

- Market order or limit order

ticker symbol
The abbreviated term that is used to identify a stock for trading purposes.

Name of the Stock. It is important to know the **ticker symbol** for your stock. The ticker symbol is the abbreviated term that is used to identify a stock for trading purposes. For example, Microsoft's symbol is MSFT, and Nike's symbol is NKE. A symbol is shorter and simpler than the formal name of a firm and easily distinguishes between different firms with similar names.

12.3   Financial Planning Online: Trading Stocks Online

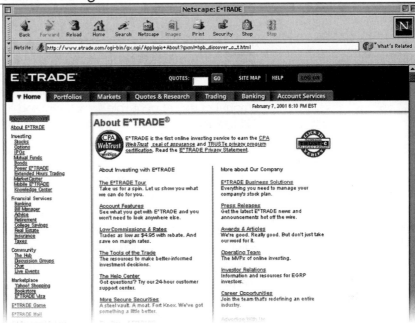

Go to:
http://www.etrade.com

Click on:
About E*Trade

This Web site provides:
information that you can use when making investment decisions. It also illustrates how you can trade stocks online. You can typically reduce your transaction costs by purchasing stocks online.

Buy or Sell. Brokerage firms execute buy and sell transactions. Therefore, it is necessary to specify whether you are buying or selling a security at the time you place the order. Once you place your order and it is executed, you are bound by the instructions you gave.

round lot
Shares bought or sold in multiples of 100.

Number of Shares. Shares are typically sold in multiples of 100, referred to as **round-lot** transactions. An order to buy or sell less than 100 shares is referred to as an **odd-lot** transaction.

odd lot
Less than 100 shares of stock.

market order
An order to execute a transaction to buy or sell a stock at its prevailing market price.

Market Order or Limit Order. You can buy or sell a stock by placing a **market order,** which is an order to execute the transaction at the stock's prevailing market price. The advantage of a market order is that you are assured that your order will be executed quickly. A disadvantage is that the stock price could change abruptly just before you place your order, causing you to pay much more for the stock than you expected.

Example

Last night you checked a Web site that provides financial information and learned that Trendy Computer Company will be offering a new line of computers. You expect that these computers will be very popular and that Trendy will experience high performance as a result. Yesterday's closing market price of Trendy stock was $40 per share. Your valuation indicates that Trendy stock is really worth about $42 per share. This morning, you place a market order to buy 100 shares of Trendy stock. You assume that you will pay about $40 per share, or $4,000 ($40 × 100 shares) for the shares ignoring the commission. However, your order is executed at $43, which means that you pay $4,300 ($43 × 100 shares). Unfortunately for you, many other investors also saw the favorable news and wanted to buy Trendy stock this morning, creating increased demand for the stock. The strong demand relative to the small amount of shares available for sale caused the stock price to increase to $43 before your broker could find a willing seller of Trendy stock. Thus, you actually paid more for the stock than you thought it was worth.

limit order
An order to execute a transaction to buy or sell a stock only if the price is within the limits that you specify.

Alternatively, you can buy or sell stock by placing a **limit order,** which is an order to execute the transaction only if the price is within the limits that you specify. Thus, a limit order sets a maximum price at which the stock can be purchased. A limit order can be for the day or good until canceled (normally canceled in six months if a transaction has not been executed by then). Your limit order will specify whether you are willing to accept a portion of the shares desired (normally, in round lots of 100); alternatively, you can specify that you want the full number of shares to be traded or none at all.

Example

Using the information in the previous example, you place a limit order on Trendy stock, with a maximum limit of $41, good for the day. When the stock opens at $43 this morning, your order is not executed because the market price exceeds your limit price. Later in the day, the stock price declines to $41, at which time your order is executed.

The example above illustrates the advantage of a limit order. However, the disadvantage is that you may miss out on a transaction that you desired. If the price of Trendy stock had continued to rise throughout the day after opening at $43, your order would not have been executed at all.

Limit orders can also be used to sell stocks. In this case, a limit order specifies a minimum price at which the stock should be sold.

Example

You own 100 shares of Zina stock, which is currently worth $18 per share. You would be willing to sell it at $20 per share. You do not have time to monitor the market price so that you can sell the stock when its price is at least $20 per share. So you place a limit order to sell 100 shares of Zina stock at a minimum price of $20, good until canceled. A few months later, Zina's price rises to $20 per share. You soon receive confirmation from your brokerage firm that the transaction has been executed.

stop order
An order to execute a transaction when the stock price reaches a specified level; a special form of limit order.

By using a limit order instead of a market order, you were able to sell your stock at a higher price. But the disadvantage of a limit order is that if Zina's price had not reached $20, you would not have sold the stock. If the price declined to $12 over the next few months, you would regret not placing a market order when Zina's price was $18 per share.

buy stop order
An order for a brokerage firm to buy a stock when the price rises to a specified level.

sell stop order
An order for a brokerage firm to sell a stock when the price falls to a specified level.

Stop Orders. A **stop order** is a special form of limit order; it is an order to execute a transaction when the stock price reaches a specified level. A **buy stop order** is an order for the brokerage firm to buy a stock for the investor when the price rises to a specified level. Conversely, a **sell stop order** is an order for the brokerage firm to sell a stock when the price falls to a specified level. It enables you to sell the stock at the specified level before the price declines further.

BUYING STOCK ON MARGIN

on margin
Purchasing a stock with a portion of the funds borrowed from a brokerage firm.

Some investors choose to purchase stock **on margin,** meaning that a portion of their purchase is funded with money borrowed from their brokerage firm. Buying a stock on margin enables investors to purchase stocks without having the full amount of cash necessary. Interest rates are sufficiently high so that brokerages earn a decent return on their loans.

The Federal Reserve limits the margin to 50 percent, so a maximum of 50 percent of the investment can be borrowed from the brokerage firm. For example, for a $1,500 purchase of stock, you and the brokerage firm would each pay $750. If the value of investments made with partially borrowed funds declines, investors may receive a **margin call** from their brokerage firm, meaning that they have to increase the cash in their account to bring the margin back up to the minimum level.

margin call
A request from a brokerage firm for the investor to increase the cash in the account in order to bring the margin back up to the minimum level.

Impact of Margin on Returns

When you buy a specific stock on margin, the return on your investment is magnified. This effect is favorable if the stock's price increases over the period you hold the stock.

Example

You want to buy 100 shares of Lynde stock, which would require $50 per share, or $5,000. You purchase the 100 shares of Lynde stock on margin by paying $3,000 in cash and borrowing $2,000 from the brokerage firm at an annual interest rate of 12 percent. After one year, you sell the stock for $60 per share, or $6,000, and repay the brokerage firm the amount borrowed plus interest. Lynde stock paid dividends of $1 per share, or $100 over the year. The return from buying a stock on margin is:

Return = $(SP + D - I - LP)/I$

where SP is the proceeds from selling the stock, D is the dividends received over the investment period, I is the initial cash investment, and LP is the amount paid to the broker to repay the loan after selling the stock at the end of the investment period.

You borrowed $2,000, so your loan repayment is:

$LP = \$2,000 \times (1 + .12)$
$= \$2,240.$

Thus, the return on your investment is:

Return = $(SP + D - I - LP)/I$
$= (\$6,000 + \$100 - \$3,000 - \$2,240)/\$3,000$
$= .2867,$ or 28.67%.

If you had invested $5,000 cash to purchase the Lynde stock instead of relying on borrowed funds, there would have been no loan repayment. Your return would have been:

Return = $(SP + D - I)/I$
$= (\$6,000 + \$100 - \$5,000)/\$5,000$
$= .22,$ or 22%.

Notice that the return from buying on margin was 6.67 percentage points higher than when using cash to make the investment.

Impact of Margin on Risk

Margin purchases can amplify stock price movements in a negative way as well. If the price of the stock you buy on margin declines, the negative return from buying on margin is magnified and will be worse than the return from using all cash.

Example

Suppose that Lynde stock declines to $40 per share (instead of increasing to $60 per share) by the end of the year, so you receive $4,000 when you sell the stock. Your return is:

Return = $(SP + D - I - LP)/I$
$= (\$4,000 + \$100 - \$3,000 - \$2,240)/\$3,000$
$= -.38,$ or -38%.

If you had used all cash and no borrowed funds to buy Lynde stock, however, your return would be:

Return = $(SP + D - I)/I$
$= (\$4,000 + \$100 - \$5,000)/\$5,000$
$= -.18,$ or -18%.

Thus, your return in this case is 20 percentage points worse when buying on margin.

"Do you have one that says sorry for your recent losses in the stock market?"

In summary, buying on margin not only increases your potential return when the stock price rises, but also increases the size of your loss when the stock declines. In this way, buying on margin changes the risk-return trade-off. The higher the proportion of funds borrowed to buy on margin, the higher your potential return and the higher your risk.

ASSESSING PERFORMANCE OF STOCK INVESTMENTS

When investing in a stock, how can you measure the performance of your stock? How can you distinguish between performance due to general market conditions and performance due to the firm itself? A convenient and effective method of measuring performance is to compare the return on your stock (or stock portfolio) to the return of a stock index. Stock index returns are provided in most business periodicals and on numerous Web sites such as Yahoo!'s site.

Example

Stephanie Spratt invested in one stock about one year (or four quarters) ago. The returns on her stock are shown in column 2 in Exhibit 12.1. Her return was lowest in the first quarter, but increased in the next three quarters. Stephanie wants to compare her stock's return to the market in general to get a true assessment of its performance. This comparison will indicate whether her specific selection generated a higher return than she could have earned by simply investing in a stock index. In Exhibit 12.1, the return on a market index over the same quarters is shown in column 3. Given the information in columns 2 and 3, Stephanie can determine the excess return on her stock as:

$$ER = R_p - R_i$$

where *ER* is excess return, R_p is the return of her stock portfolio, and R_i is the return of the stock index.

Exhibit 12.1   Stock Performance Evaluation

	Return on Stephanie's Stock	Return on a U.S. Stock Index	Excess Return of Stephanie's Stock (above the market)
Quarter 1	−1%	3%	−4%
Quarter 2	2%	3%	−1%
Quarter 3	5%	7%	−2%
Quarter 4	6%	9%	−3%

The excess return of the stock was negative in each of the four quarters she has held it. Stephanie is disappointed in the performance of the stock, and decides to sell it in the near future if its performance does not improve.

12.4   Financial Planning Online: Assessing Your Investment Performance

Go to:
http://finance.yahoo.com/?u

This Web site provides:
a comparison of the price of a stock you specify to the general market. Insert your stock's symbol. Next, click on "Charts," and then click on the box next to the stock index that you wish to use as a benchmark.

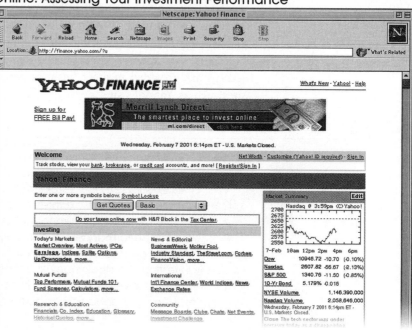

Market Indexes Used to Measure Performance

The most popular market indexes that investors use to assess the performance of their stock portfolios or to monitor the general performance of the stock market are summarized in Exhibit 12.2.

Investors may wish to use a stock index to compare the return on a particular stock with the performance of the stock's sector. This comparison is useful because the index used for comparison more closely matches the stock being evaluated. For example, to assess the performance of a bank stock, you could compare the return with that of a financial sector index. In some periods, the financial sector may experience performance swings that deviate from the market as a whole; these fluctuations may explain movements in your stock's price. Thus, stock price movements can best be evaluated by comparison with stock returns of an index representing other firms in its industry.

The most useful performance evaluation compares a firm's stock return with the returns of other firms of similar size in the same sector. Thus, the stock of a very large firm would be best compared with the NYSE index that represents other large stocks in the same sector, while the stock of a smaller firm would be compared with the Nasdaq index that represents smaller firms in the same sector.

Exhibit 12.2   Indexes Used to Measure Market Performance

- **Dow Jones Industrial Average (DJIA):** represents stocks of 30 large U.S. companies, including General Motors, IBM, and Wal-Mart. It is closely monitored by investors who want to determine how larger stocks are performing in general. When the media report that "the market was up" or "the market was down" for the day, they are commonly referring to the DJIA.

- **Standard and Poor's 500:** represents stocks of 500 large U.S. firms. Its movements tend to be highly correlated with the DJIA because the prices of stocks represented by the index are influenced by the same factors that influence the DJIA stocks.

- **New York Stock Exchange (NYSE) Composite:** represents all stocks traded on the NYSE. This index represents about 3,000 stocks, many of which are smaller than the stocks represented by the DJIA and the S&P 500. The movements in this index are also correlated with those of the DJIA and the S&P 500.

- **Standard & Poor's MidCap 400:** represents stocks of 400 medium-size firms. The firms in this index are smaller than those included in the S&P 500.

- **Russell Index:** represents 2,000 large stocks, but does not include the largest 1,000 stocks.

- **Nasdaq Composite:** represents the stocks that are traded on the Nasdaq. Since the stocks traded on the Nasdaq tend to be from smaller firms than those traded on the NYSE, this index is a more appropriate indicator of performance of smaller publicly traded stocks. However, some Nasdaq stocks represent very large firms (such as Microsoft).

- **Wilshire Index:** The Wilshire index is made up of more than 7,000 stocks traded on the NYSE, American Stock Exchange, and Nasdaq. It is the broadest index available. There are also some other Wilshire indexes that focus on stocks within specific size ranges.

Comparative Performance of Stock Indexes

Exhibit 12.3 shows the performance of several major stock indexes over several different periods. Notice that returns can vary substantially among stock indexes, regardless of the holding period. Exhibit 12.3 also shows that the performance of any given stock index is dependent on the holding period assessed. Some stocks may experience strong performance in a particular year, but cannot sustain the performance over a long-term holding period.

Exhibit 12.3   Comparison of Returns among Types of Stocks

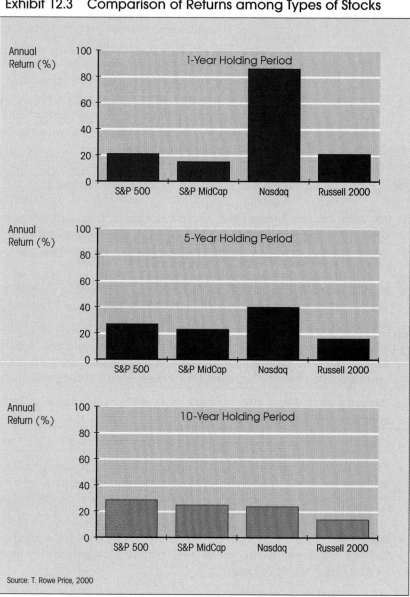

Source: T. Rowe Price, 2000

Price Quotations for Indexes Used to Measure Stock Performance

Quotations of levels for market and sector indexes are reported in financial newspapers. For example, the *Wall Street Journal* provides a Stock Market Data Bank, as shown in Exhibit 12.4. The Data Bank shows the range of index levels during the previous day. It also provides the percentage change in each stock index over the previous day, the last 12 months, and since the start of the calendar year. Thus, it serves as a useful indicator of the general short-term stock market performance.

Consider the Standard & Poor's MidCap 400 index highlighted in Exhibit 12.4. The index level reached a high of 503.56 and a low of 492.88 for the day. When the market closed for the day, the index level was 497.26, which was down .88 percent from the previous day. The index was up 6.09 percent over the previous 12 months and down 3.77 percent since the end of the previous year. Notice how easily you can compare this index with an

Exhibit 12.4   An Example of Stock Index Information

STOCK MARKET DATA BANK   2/28/01

MAJOR INDEXES

†12-MO HIGH	LOW		DAILY HIGH	LOW	CLOSE	NET CHG	% CHG	†12-MO CHG	% CHG	FROM 12/31	% CHG
DOW JONES AVERAGES											
11310.64	9796.03	30 Industrials	10684.77	10423.50	10495.28	− 141.60	− 1.33	+ 357.35	+ 3.52	− 291.57	− 2.70
3145.65	2263.59	20 Transportation	2969.04	2913.95	x2925.04	− 45.97	− 1.55	+ 527.27	+ 21.99	− 21.56	− 0.73
416.11	274.12	15 Utilities	388.45	382.67	x386.22	− 1.25	− 0.32	+ 98.84	+ 34.39	− 25.94	− 6.29
3323.74	2751.55	65 Composite	3255.67	3195.74	x3211.18	− 37.47	− 1.15	+ 356.40	+ 12.48	− 106.23	− 3.20
364.71	287.04	DJ US Total Mkt	292.60	284.69	287.04	− 4.24	− 1.46	− 48.11	− 14.35	− 19.84	− 6.47
STANDARD & POOR'S INDEXES											
1527.46	1239.94	500 Index	1263.47	1229.65	1239.94	− 18.00	− 1.43	− 139.25	− 10.10	− 80.34	− 6.09
1917.64	1438.05	Industrials	1467.43	1425.74	1438.05	− 19.51	− 1.34	− 305.93	− 17.54	− 89.81	− 5.88
353.03	224.61	Utilities	329.22	325.15	326.38	− 2.63	− 0.80	+ 91.46	+ 38.93	− 24.23	− 6.91
548.60	430.94	400 MidCap	503.56	492.88	497.26	− 4.44	− 0.88	+ 28.55	+ 6.09	− 19.50	− 3.77
232.63	185.34	600 SmallCap	218.07	214.17	214.77	− 3.06	− 1.40	− 4.80	− 2.19	− 4.82	− 2.19
324.40	267.56	1500 Index	272.47	265.39	267.56	− 3.77	− 1.39	− 26.24	− 8.93	− 16.54	− 5.82
NASDAQ STOCK MARKET											
5048.62	2151.83	Composite	2238.06	2127.50	2151.83	− 55.99	− 2.54	−2632.25	− 55.02	− 318.69	− 12.90
4704.73	1908.32	Nasdaq 100	2010.32	1880.47	1908.32	− 56.20	− 2.86	−2400.69	− 55.71	− 433.38	− 18.51
2841.00	1352.59	Industrials	1413.18	1356.40	1368.06	− 38.86	− 2.76	−1287.70	− 48.49	− 114.93	− 7.75
2222.68	1602.08	Insurance	2026.49	1995.26	2012.80	− 4.96	− 0.25	+ 278.09	+ 16.03	− 180.57	− 8.23
1984.37	1340.36	Banks	1934.32	1901.35	1915.73	− 12.42	− 0.64	+ 479.87	+ 33.42	− 23.72	− 1.22
2964.66	1075.16	Computer	1132.35	1062.45	1075.16	− 35.39	− 3.19	−1639.43	− 60.39	− 219.81	− 16.97
1230.06	394.47	Telecommunications	409.49	387.10	394.47	− 9.78	− 2.42	− 778.84	− 66.38	− 68.97	− 14.88
NEW YORK STOCK EXCHANGE											
677.58	588.43	Composite	635.55	622.63	626.94	− 6.52	− 1.03	+ 27.46	+ 4.58	− 29.93	− 4.56
851.94	747.89	Industrials	784.90	769.60	775.21	− 5.86	− 0.75	+ 13.34	+ 1.75	− 28.08	− 3.50
519.96	406.01	Utilities	414.39	404.04	406.01	− 6.49	− 1.57	− 95.57	− 19.05	− 34.53	− 7.84
489.85	353.51	Transportation	481.74	475.75	476.61	− 3.75	− 0.78	+ 100.91	+ 26.86	+ 13.85	+ 2.99
657.52	443.87	Finance	615.69	599.40	603.76	− 10.34	− 1.68	+ 140.34	+ 30.28	− 43.19	− 6.68
OTHERS											
1036.40	846.59	Amex Composite	911.62	904.10	907.72	− 0.28	− 0.03	− 94.23	− 9.40	+ 9.97	+ 1.11
813.71	654.25	Russell 1000	666.98	648.94	654.25	− 9.67	− 1.46	− 86.08	− 11.63	− 45.84	− 6.55
606.12	443.80	Russell 2000	479.58	471.28	474.37	− 4.38	− 0.91	− 113.98	− 19.37	− 9.16	− 1.89
844.78	680.52	Russell 3000	693.28	675.08	680.52	− 9.79	− 1.42	− 95.37	− 12.29	− 45.23	− 6.23
439.78	368.19	Value-Line	400.96	393.73	395.97	− 4.02	− 1.01	− 8.82	− 2.18	+ 2.50	+ 0.64
14751.64	11425.29	Wilshire 5000	....	....	11425.29	− 166.82	− 1.44	−2268.01	− 16.56	− 750.59	− 6.16

†-Based on comparable trading day in preceding year.

12.5   Financial Planning Online: Stock Index Quotations

Go to:
http://finance.yahoo.com/m1?u

This Web site provides:
recent quotations of indexes that can be used as benchmarks when assessing your investment portfolio's performance. Click on "Charts" to review historical movements in any specific index so that you can assess the general trend in the performance of this index.

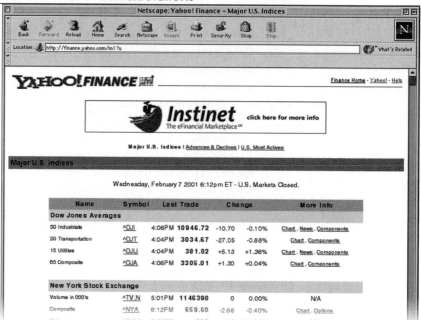

index of smaller firms or an index of much larger firms to determine the relative performance of other firms.

HOW STOCK INVESTMENT METHODS FIT WITHIN YOUR FINANCIAL PLAN

Recall that the following are the key decisions about investing in common stock that should be included within your financial plan:

1. Should you consider buying stock?

2. How should you value stocks when determining whether to buy them?

3. What methods should you use for investing in stocks?

The first decision was discussed in Chapter 10, while the second decision was considered in Chapter 11. The third decision about how to conduct stock transactions has been examined here. Exhibit 12.5 provides an example of how this decision applies to Stephanie Spratt's financial plan.

Exhibit 12.5   How Stock Investment Methods Fit within Stephanie Spratt's Financial Plan

Goals for Investing in Stock

1. Determine if I could benefit from investing in common stock (discussed in Chapter 10).
2. If I decide to invest in common stock, determine how to value a stock (discussed in Chapter 11).
3. Determine the method I should use for investing in stocks.

Analysis

Investment Methods	Comments
Rely on my valuation methods	Simple to use, but they have limitations and could result in poor investment decisions.
Invest in mutual funds	Diversification benefits; rely on mutual fund manager's expertise rather than my own.
Invest in publicly traded indexes	Diversification benefits; not focused on particular stocks.
Rely on investments advisers	Will not necessarily lead to higher performance; may incur additional costs.

Decision

Decision on Stock Investment Methods:

I may use valuation methods to consider individual stocks, but I should focus on mutual funds and publicly traded indexes when I want to invest in stocks. I will also use an established online brokerage service with a user-friendly Web site that offers substantial investment information and charges low transaction fees. I will not buy stocks on margin because the risk is too high and I cannot afford to take such risks at this time.

DISCUSSION QUESTIONS

1. How would Stephanie's decisions concerning conducting stock transactions be different if she were a single mother of two children?

2. How would Stephanie's decisions concerning conducting stock transactions be affected if she were 35 years old? If she were 50 years old?

SUMMARY

Your valuations of stocks can help you identify stocks that are undervalued and therefore should be purchased. A second method of investing is to simply decide which mutual funds to purchase and leave the stock selection to the mutual funds' portfolio managers. Third, if you want to buy shares that mirror a specific market or sector, you can invest in publicly traded stock indexes. Fourth, you can rely on advisers to determine which stocks to purchase.

Once you have decided which stocks to buy or sell, you contact a brokerage firm. You can use an online brokerage firm, which can be more convenient and also less costly than a traditional full-service brokerage firm. Upon receiving your order, the brokerage firm sends your order to the stock exchange where the trade is executed.

When buying a stock on margin, you fund part of the purchase with money borrowed from the brokerage firm. This approach can magnify the returns that you earn from investing in the stock. However, it also magnifies losses and therefore increases your risk.

You can assess the performance of an investment in a particular stock by comparing the return on that stock with an index of stocks that represents similar firms. Several stock market indexes and sector indexes are available to use as benchmarks when assessing a stock's performance.

Integrating the Key Concepts

This chapter emphasizes the performance of your stock investments, which is related to other parts of your financial plan. First, your statements affect your liquidity decisions (Part 2) because some stocks may provide you with periodic income that can serve as a source of liquidity. The more income you expect to receive from dividends, the less liquidity you need from other sources. Second, the performance of your stocks can affect your financing situation (Part 3) because you may be able to sell the stocks after their strong performance and pay off an existing loan. Third, the performance of your stocks can affect the size of your estate and the amount of additional wealth you will need from retirement planning (Part 5).

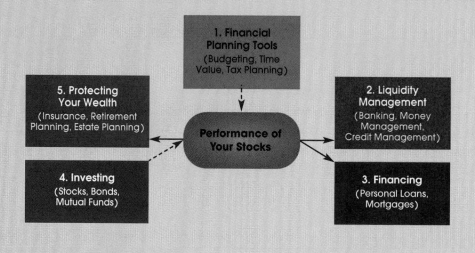

REVIEW QUESTIONS

1. What four strategies might investors use to decide which stocks to purchase?

2. What information does an investor seek through stock valuation? Describe two popular stock valuation methods.

3. List some of the benefits of investing in stock mutual funds.

4. What are publicly traded stock indexes? How do they work? What are Spiders and Diamonds?

5. List some reasons an investor should be cautious about using an adviser's recommendations when purchasing stock. Will investing according to an adviser's recommendations bring a higher return? Why or why not?

6. How is the market for a stock created? How do brokerage firms expedite this process? Compare the two types of brokerage services.

7. What are some advantages of using online brokerage services? Describe how an investor would set up and use an online account.

8. What information must you provide when placing an order to buy or sell stock? What is a ticker symbol, and why is it important?

9. What do the terms *round lot* and *odd lot* refer to in stock transactions?

10. Discuss the differences between a market order, a limit order, and a stop order.

11. What is meant by buying a stock on margin? What happens if the value of the stock bought on margin declines? What are the advantages to investors and brokerages when stocks are bought on margin?

12. Discuss the impact of margin on risk and return.

13. Describe an effective method of measuring the performance of a stock.

14. How can market indexes be used to make excess return comparisons? Give an example.

FINANCIAL PLANNING PROBLEMS

1. Dana invested in Standard and Poor's Depository Receipts (Spiders) when the S&P 500 was at 1320. The S&P 500 is now valued at 1550. What would her return be if she sold today?

2. Richard purchased 40 shares of the Dow Jones Industrial Average Index when the DJIA was 11,420. Today, the DJIA is at 10,434. What would Richard's return be in percentage terms if he were to sell his shares today?

3. Trey wants to buy 200 shares of Turner stock that is selling for $40 per share. Trey pays $4,000 in cash and borrows $4,000 from his broker at 11 percent interest. One year later Turner stock has paid no dividends, and Trey sells the stock for $50 per share. What is Trey's return?

4. What would Trey's return be if he had paid the entire $8,000 for the stock himself?

5. Ryan purchased 200 shares of Neptune stock on margin. The stock sold for $7,000. Ryan paid $5,000 and borrowed $2,000 from his broker at 13 percent interest. The stock paid $2 per share in dividends for the year, and Ryan sold the stock for $9,000 after one year. What is Ryan's return?

6. What would Ryan's return have been if he had sold the stock for $6,500?

FINANCIAL PLANNING ONLINE EXERCISES

Go to http://finance.yahoo.com/?u to review analysts' stock recommendations.

1. Under Yahoo! Finance, enter the stock symbol NOK, for Nokia Corporation, and click on "Get Quotes." Under More Info, click on "Research." Information on analysts' recommendations and forecasts will be provided, as well as earnings per share forecasts, earnings estimates, and earnings history. What is the average broker recommendation? What is your opinion of Nokia after reviewing the analysts' comments and estimates?

2. Use the Back option in your browser to return to http://finance.yahoo.com/?u. Under Yahoo! Finance, enter the symbol XRX, for Xerox. Click on "Get Quotes." Under More Info, click on "Research." What is the average broker recommendation? What is your opinion of Xerox after reviewing the analysts' comments and estimates?

3. What are the major differences between Nokia and Xerox, based on the information on each company provided by analysts?

4. Use the Back option in your browser to return to http://finance.yahoo.com/?u. Under Yahoo! Finance, enter the symbol T, for AT&T. Click on "Get Quotes." Under More Info, click on "Research." What is the average broker recommendation? What is your opinion of AT&T after reviewing the analysts' comments and estimates?

The purpose of the following four exercises is to review market indexes.

1. Go to http://www.bloomberg.com/markets/sp500.html, which provides a snapshot of the S&P 500 stock index. The best and worst performing stocks for the trading session are provided. A full listing of all 500 stocks in the index can be obtained by clicking at the bottom of the page. What categories of stocks did well, and what categories did poorly during this trading session?

2. Review the graphs that show the change in the index for the day and for the year. What does the trend in the yearly graph indicate about the performance of the stock market during the past 12 months?

3. Go to http://finance.yahoo.com/m1?u. This Web site provides recent quotations of indexes such as the Dow Jones Averages, New York Stock Exchange, Nasdaq, and S&P 500. Click on "Charts" to review historical movements in any specific index. Compare the percentage change in the NYSE Composite and the Nasdaq Composite for today's trading session. Comment on the reasons for any difference in the performance of the indexes.

4. Compare the major U.S. indexes. Which index, in your opinion, most closely reflects the U.S. stock market currently? Why? Click on "Charts" for each index and review the performance for the last 12 months. How does this information correspond to your choice for the best index?

Building Your Own Financial Plan

Selecting the right stock investment method is an important decision for any investor. The template for this chapter in the *Financial Planning Workbook* and on the CD-ROM walks you through a list of questions designed to assist you in making this important decision. Carefully consider the types of investments you will be making, how frequently you will have transactions, and how important one-on-one advice from a broker is to you. When comparing brokerage firms' offerings, be sure to consider at least one online or discount broker.

As you get older and your portfolio grows in size and possibly in complexity, you need to periodically review the suitability of your broker just as you do your tax preparer, as we discussed in Chapter 4.

The Sampsons—A Continuing Case

Recall that one of the Sampsons' goals is to invest for their children's future college education. To become more educated investors, they have been reviewing analyst and brokerage firm recommendations on the Web site http://biz.yahoo.com/c/u.html. Dave and Sharon are ready to invest in several firms that this Web site identifies as having BUY recommendations. Before they purchase the stock, they ask you to weigh in with an opinion.

1. Offer advice to the Sampsons on whether they should buy these stocks based on the information on the Web site.

2. Other Web sites identify firms that were top performers the previous day. Should the Sampsons buy these stocks? Explain.

IN-TEXT STUDY GUIDE

True/False:

1. When making investment decisions, investors normally use either fundamental analysis or technical analysis to conduct valuations of specific stocks.

2. Fundamental analysis is the valuation of stocks based on historical price patterns.

3. Technical analysis is the valuation of stocks primarily based on revenue and earnings.

4. Research has shown that sophisticated investors are able to consistently achieve returns on their stock portfolios that exceed the average returns among all stocks.

5. Since indexes represent several stocks, an investor achieves some degree of diversification by investing in an index.

6. Financial advisers tend to be overly optimistic about stocks.

7. The ticker symbol of a stock is the abbreviated term that is used to identify a stock for trading purposes.

8. A buy stop order is an order for a brokerage firm to sell a stock when the price falls below the prevailing price and reaches a specified level.

9. The Standard and Poor's 500 index represents stocks of 500 large U.S. firms.

10. Usually, various industry sectors perform very similarly to the stock market as a whole.

Multiple Choice:

1. _____ analysis is the valuation of stocks based on characteristics such as a firm's revenue or earnings.
   a. Technical
   b. Fundamental
   c. Gamma
   d. IPO

2. Which of the following is not an example of a decision based on technical analysis?
   a. Purchasing a stock that has risen for two consecutive days
   b. Selling a stock that has risen for two consecutive days
   c. Purchasing a stock with strong earnings potential
   d. Selling a stock that has declined for three consecutive days

3. Which of the following is not a method investors use when deciding to purchase a stock?
   a. invest based on valuation methods
   b. invest in publicly traded indexes
   c. rely on advisers to make investment decisions
   d. All of the above are methods used by investors when deciding to purchase a stock.

4. A(n) _____ is a basket of stocks matched to the S&P 500 index. It can be purchased through brokers.
   a. money market mutual fund
   b. bond fund
   c. Spider
   d. open-end mutual fund

5. A Diamond trades at _____ of the S&P 500 value.
   a. one-tenth
   b. one one-hundredth
   c. one one-thousandth
   d. none of the above

6. Which of the following statements is not correct?
   a. Frequent trading may cause you to hold on to stocks less than one year, resulting in short-term capital gains.
   b. All brokerage firms generally recommend the same stocks for investment by their clients.
   c. Investing according to broker recommendations may not lead to unusually high investment performance.
   d. Some advisers have very limited experience in analyzing and valuing securities.

7. A _____ broker offers advice to investors.
   a. full-service
   b. discount
   c. frequency
   d. regular

8. Which of the following is not true regarding online brokers?
   a. The commission charged per transaction is usually very low.
   b. Online brokers are very convenient for investors.
   c. Online brokerage firms do not have a money market fund where your cash is deposited until it is used to make transactions.
   d. All of the above are true.

9. When placing an order to buy or sell a stock, you do not have to provide
   a. the name of the stock.
   b. the industry the firm is in.
   c. the number of shares.
   d. the type of order.

10. You just purchased 70 shares of XYZ Corporation. Your order is referred to as _____ transaction.
    a. a round-lot
    b. a limit lot
    c. a multiple-lot
    d. an odd lot

11. When you place a(n) _____ order to buy or sell a stock, your transaction will be executed only if the price is within the limits that you specify.
    a. market
    b. limit
    c. odd-lot
    d. ticker

12. A _____ order is an order to execute a transaction when the stock price reaches a specified level.
    a. stop
    b. buy stop
    c. sell stop
    d. all of the above

13. A _____ means that investors have to increase the cash in their account.
    a. market call
    b. limit call
    c. margin call
    d. sell stop call

14. Today, you placed a limit order to sell Quontos Corporation stock with a limit of $35 per share. When you placed the order, the stock was trading for $30 per share. Tomorrow, the stock price is $25 per share. Your order
    a. will be executed.
    b. will not be executed.
    c. will be partially executed.
    d. none of the above

15. Which of the following is not a market index?
    a. S&P 500
    b. NYSE Composite
    c. Wilshire
    d. All of the above are market indexes.

The following information applies to questions 16 through 19.

One year ago, Warren Cuffett purchased 200 shares of Bingo Corporation stock for $30 per share by paying $5,000 in cash and borrowing $1,000 from a brokerage firm at an annual interest rate of 15 percent. Today, Warren sold the stock for $45 per share. Bingo Corporation stock paid no dividends last year.

16. Warren's return from this investment is _____ percent.
    a. 50.00
    b. 30.83
    c. 57.00
    d. 47.50

17. If Warren had paid the entire $6,000 in cash one year ago, his return would be _____ percent.
    a. 50.00
    b. 30.83
    c. 57.00
    d. 47.50

18. Now assume Bingo Corporation stock had declined from $30 per share to $25 per share when Warren sold it. His return (assuming he borrowed $1,000 on margin) would be _____ percent.
    a. −20.00
    b. −23.00
    c. −19.17
    d. −16.67

19. If Bingo Corporation stock had declined from $30 per share to $25 per share and Warren had purchased the stock with all cash, his return would be _____ percent.
    a. −20.00
    b. −23.00
    c. −19.17
    d. −16.67

20. The _____ represents stocks of 30 large U.S. companies and is closely monitored by investors who want to determine how larger stocks are performing in general.
    a. Dow Jones Industrial Average
    b. Standard and Poor's 500 index
    c. Russell index
    d. Wilshire index

Chapter 13

Investing in Bonds

Many investors choose to invest in bonds to diversify their portfolio. As with stocks, you need to understand the characteristics of bonds before investing in them. Your bond investment strategies can increase your interest income (cash inflows) and the value of your assets (bond holdings) over time, thereby enhancing your wealth.

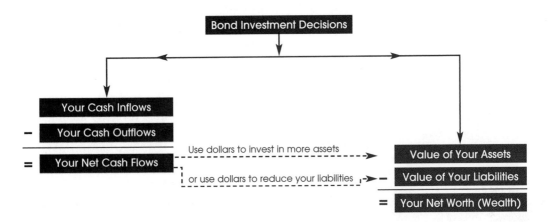

The objectives of this chapter are to:

- identify the different types of bonds,

- explain what affects the return from investing in a bond,

- describe why some bonds are risky, and

- identify common bond investment strategies.

BACKGROUND ON BONDS

bonds
Long-term debt securities issued by government agencies or corporations.

par value
For a bond, its face value, or the amount returned to the investor at the maturity date when the bond is due.

Recall from Chapter 2 that investors commonly invest some of their funds in **bonds,** which are long-term debt securities issued by government agencies or corporations. Bonds are attractive investments for many investors because they often offer more favorable returns than bank deposits. In addition, they typically provide fixed interest payments that represent additional income each year. The **par value** of a bond is its face value, or the amount returned to the investor at the maturity date when the bond is due.

Most bonds have maturities between 10 and 30 years, although some bonds have longer maturities. Investors provide the issuers of bonds with funds (credit). In return, the issuers are obligated to make interest (or coupon) payments and to pay the par value at maturity. When a bond has a par value of $1,000, a coupon rate of 6 percent means that $60 (.06 × $1,000) is paid annually to investors. The coupon payments are normally paid semiannually (in this example, $30 every six months). Some bonds are

sold at a price below par value; in this case, investors who hold the bonds until maturity will earn a return from the difference between par value and what they paid. This income is in addition to the coupon payments earned.

You should consider investing in bonds rather than stock if you wish to receive periodic income from your investments. In general, bonds are a less risky investment than stocks because their future cash flows (coupon payments) are known. For this reason, the return on bonds is normally less than the expected return on stocks. As explained in Chapter 15, many investors diversify among stocks and bonds to achieve their desired return and risk preferences.

Bond Characteristics

Bonds that are issued by a particular type of issuer can offer various features such as a call feature or convertibility.

Call Feature. A **call feature** on a bond allows the issuer to buy back the bond from the investor before maturity. This feature is desirable for issuers because it allows them to retire existing bonds with coupon rates that are higher than the prevailing interest rates.

Example

call feature
A feature on a bond that allows the issuer to repurchase the bond from the investor before maturity.

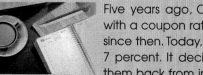

Five years ago, Cieplak, Inc., issued 15-year callable bonds with a coupon rate of 9 percent. Interest rates have declined since then. Today, Cieplak could issue new bonds at a rate of 7 percent. It decides to retire the existing bonds by buying them back from investors and to issue new bonds at a 7 percent coupon rate. By calling the old bonds, Cieplak has reduced its cost of financing.

Investors are willing to purchase bonds with a call feature only if the bonds offer a slightly higher return than similar bonds without a call feature. This premium compensates the investors for the possibility that the bonds may be called before maturity.

convertible bond
A bond that can be converted into a stated number of shares of the issuer's stock if the stock price reaches a specified price.

Convertible Feature. A **convertible bond** allows the investor to convert the bond into a stated number of shares of the issuer's stock if the stock price reaches a specified price. This feature enables bond investors to benefit when the issuer's stock price rises. Because convertibility is a desirable feature for investors, convertible bonds tend to offer a lower return than nonconvertible bonds. Consequently, if the stock price does not rise to the specified trigger price, the convertible bond provides a lower return to investors than alternative bonds without a convertible feature. If the stock price does reach the trigger price, however, investors can convert their bonds into shares of the issuer's stock, thereby earning a higher return than they would have earned on alternative nonconvertible bonds.

A Bond's Yield to Maturity

yield to maturity
The annualized return on a bond if it is held until maturity.

A bond's **yield to maturity** is the annualized return on the bond if it is held until maturity. Consider a bond that is priced at $1,000 and has a par value of $1,000 and a coupon rate of 10 percent. This bond has a yield to maturity of 10 percent, which is the same as its coupon rate, because the price paid for the bond equals the principal.

As an alternative example, if this bond's price were lower than the principal amount, its yield to maturity would exceed the coupon rate of 10 percent. The bond would generate income in the form of coupon payments and would also generate a capital gain, because the purchase price would be less than the principal amount to be received at maturity. Conversely, if this bond's price were higher than the principal amount, its yield to maturity would be less than 10 percent, because the amount paid for the bond would exceed the principal amount to be received at maturity.

Bond Trading in the Secondary Market

Investors can sell their bonds to other investors in the secondary market before the bonds reach maturity. The price at which you can sell a bond in

13.1   Financial Planning Online: Your Bond's Yield

Go to:
http://www.financenter.com/
products/analyzers/bond.fcs

Click on:
"What is my yield to maturity?"

This Web site provides:
an estimate of the yield to maturity of your bond based on its present price, its coupon rate, and its maturity. Thus, you can determine the rate of return that the bond will generate for you from today until it matures.

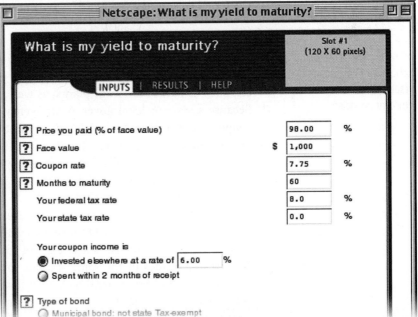

the secondary market changes over time, as bond prices change in response to interest rate movements and other factors. Some bonds are traded on stock exchanges such as the New York Stock Exchange. Other bonds are traded in the over-the-counter market. Many investors sell their bonds in the secondary market to raise funds to cover upcoming expenses or to invest in other more attractive types of securities. Brokerage firms take orders from investors to buy or sell bonds.

TYPES OF BONDS

Bonds can be classified according to the type of issuer as follows:

- Treasury bonds
- Municipal bonds
- Federal agency bonds
- Corporate bonds

Each type is described here.

Treasury Bonds

Treasury bonds
Long-term debt securities issued by the U.S. Treasury.

Treasury bonds are long-term debt securities issued by the U.S. Treasury, a branch of the federal government. Because the payments are guaranteed by the federal government, they are not exposed to the risk of default by the issuer. The interest on Treasury bonds is subject to federal income tax, but it is exempt from state and local taxes. Treasury bonds are very liquid because they can easily be sold in the secondary market.

Municipal Bonds

municipal bonds
Long-term debt securities issued by state and local government agencies.

Municipal bonds are long-term debt securities issued by state and local government agencies; they are funded with proceeds from municipal projects such as parks or sewage plants, as well as tax revenues, in some cases. Because a state or local government agency might possibly default on its coupon payments, municipal bonds are not free from the risk of default. Nevertheless, most municipal bonds have a very low default risk. To entice investors, municipal bonds that are issued by a local government with a relatively high level of risk will have to offer a higher yield than other municipal bonds with a lower level of risk.

The interest on municipal bonds is exempt from federal income tax, which is especially beneficial to investors who are in tax brackets of 30 percent or more. The interest is also exempt from state and local taxes when the investor resides in the same state as the municipality that issued the bonds. Municipal bonds tend to have a lower coupon rate than Treasury bonds issued at the same time. However, the municipal bonds may offer a higher after-tax return to investors.

Example

Mike Lucas lives in Florida, where there is no state tax on income. For federal income tax, however, he faces a 40 percent marginal rate, meaning that he will pay a tax of 40 percent on any additional income that he earns this year. Last year, Mike invested $100,000 in Treasury bonds with a coupon rate of 8 percent and $100,000 in municipal bonds with a coupon rate of 6 percent. His annual earnings from these two investments are shown here:

	Treasury Bonds	Municipal Bonds
Interest income before taxes	$8,000 (computed as .08 × $100,000)	$6,000 (computed as .06 × $100,000)
Federal taxes owed	3,200 (computed as .40 × $8,000)	0
Interest income after taxes	$4,800	$6,000

Notice that even though Mike received more interest income from the Treasury bonds, he must pay 40 percent of that income to the federal government. Therefore, he keeps only 60 percent of that income, or a total of $4,800. In contrast, none of the interest income of $6,000 from the municipal bonds is taxed. Consequently, every year Mike receives $1,200

13.2 Financial Planning Online: Municipal Bond Quotations

Go to:
http://www.bloomberg.com/
markets/psamuni.html

This Web site provides:
quotations of yields offered by municipal bonds with various terms to maturity. Review this information when considering purchasing municipal bonds.

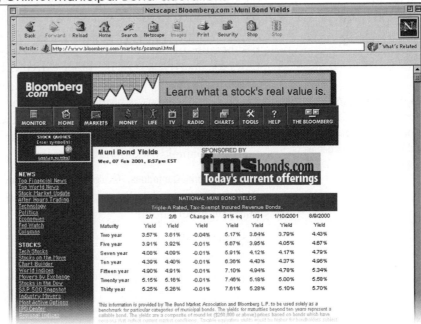

more in after-tax interest income from the municipal bonds with the 6 percent coupon rate than from the Treasury bonds with the 8 percent coupon rate.

Federal Agency Bonds

federal agency bonds
Long-term debt securities issued by federal agencies.

Federal agency bonds are long-term debt securities issued by federal agencies. The Government National Mortgage Association (called Ginnie Mae or abbreviated as GNMA), for example, issues bonds so that it can invest in mortgages that are insured by the Federal Housing Administration (FHA) and by the Veteran's Administration (VA). The Federal Home Loan Mortgage Association (called Freddie Mac) also commonly issues bonds and uses the proceeds to purchase conventional mortgages. A third government agency that commonly issues bonds is the Federal National Mortgage Association (Fannie Mae). Though federally chartered, it is owned by individual shareholders rather than the government. It uses the proceeds from the bonds to purchase residential mortgages.

The bonds issued by these three federal agencies are backed by the mortgages in which the agencies invest. Thus, the bonds have a very low degree of default risk. The income provided by these bonds is subject to state and federal taxes.

Corporate Bonds

corporate bonds
Long-term debt securities issued by large firms.

Corporate bonds are long-term debt securities issued by large firms. The repayment of debt by corporations is not backed by the federal government, so corporate bonds are subject to default risk. At one extreme, bonds issued by corporations such as Coca-Cola and IBM have very low default risk because of the companies' proven ability to generate sufficient cash flows for many years. At the other extreme, bonds issued by smaller, less stable corporations are subject to a higher degree of default risk. These bonds are referred to as **high-yield bonds** or **junk bonds**. Many investors are willing to invest in junk bonds because they offer a relatively high rate of return. However, they are more likely to default than other bonds, especially if economic conditions deteriorate.

high-yield (junk) bonds
Bonds issued by smaller, less stable corporations that are subject to a higher degree of default risk.

Corporate Bond Quotations. Corporate bond quotations are provided in the *Wall Street Journal,* as shown in Exhibit 13.1. The quotations include the following information:

- Coupon rate
- Maturity
- Current yield
- Volume
- Closing price
- Net change in the price from the previous trading day

Exhibit 13.1 An Example of Corporate Bond Quotations

U.S. EXCHANGE BONDS

Friday, March 2, 2001
Quotations as of 4 p.m. Eastern Time

DOW JONES BOND AVERAGES

2000 HIGH	2000 LOW	2001 HIGH	2001 LOW		2001 CLOSE	2001 CHG.	2001 %YLD	2000 CLOSE	2000 CHG.
97.41	93.23	101.51	97.85	20 Bonds	101.51	+ 0.23	7.48	95.65	– 0.86
96.99	90.69	99.43	96.85	10 Utilities	99.43	+ 0.29	7.28	93.94	+ 0.20
99.86	95.53	103.58	98.86	10 Industrials	103.58	+ 0.16	7.68	97.35	– 1.92

VOLUME

Total New York $11,925,000
Corporation Bonds.............$11,746,000
Foreign Bonds $179,000
Amex Bonds...........................$369,000

SALES SINCE JAN. 1

New York
2001 ....$494,071,000
2000 ....$438,094,000
1999 ....$597,303,000

AMEX
2001 ....$69,500,000
2000 ....$29,931,000
1999 ....$28,889,000

DIARIES

New York	DOMESTIC FRI.	DOMESTIC THU.	ALL ISSUES FRI.	ALL ISSUES THU.
Issues Traded	140	151	146	158
Advances	72	79	77	81
Declines	47	45	47	48
Unchanged	21	27	22	29
New highs	16	23	16	23
New lows	1	2	1	2

AMEX	ALL ISSUES FRI.	THU.	WED.	TUE.
Issues Traded	7	13	9	7
Advances	1	6	2	2
Declines	3	6	6	2
Unchanged	3	1	1	3
New highs	0	2	1	0
New lows	3	2	4	1

NEW YORK BONDS

Corporation Bonds

BONDS	CUR YLD.	VOL.	CLOSE	NET CHG.
AES Cp 4½05	cv	30	205	+ 12
ATT 5⅛01	5.1	1	99 17/32	...
ATT 7⅛02	7.1	5	100 1/16	– 9/16
ATT 6½02	6.5	4	100⅝	– ⅜
ATT 6¾04	6.6	15	101½	– ¼
ATT 5⅝04	5.7	254	98⅛	– ⅝
ATT 7½06	7.2	15	104	– 1
ATT 7¾07	7.4	15	105⅛	+ ⅜
ATT 6s09	6.4	215	93¼	– ¾
ATT 8⅛22	8.0	70	101¾	+ ¼
ATT 6½29	7.7	87	84⅞	+ ¼
ATT 8⅝31	8.2	41	104¾	+ ⅜
Aames 10½02	10.9	2	96	...
BkrHgh zr08	...	66	84	– ½
BkOne 8.1s02	7.9	10	103	+ 3
BauschL 7⅛28	9.3	300	76⅝	– 1
BayView 9s07	12.7	2	71	– ¾
BellPa 7⅛12	7.0	5	101½	+ 1⅛
Bellso 6⅜28	7.0	100	91	– ⅜
BellsoT 6¼03	6.2	35	100⅝	– ¾
BellsoT 6⅜04	6.3	23	102	+ 2⅞
BellsoT 6½05	6.4	50	101⅞	+ ⅜
BellsoT 5⅞09	5.9	11	99½	– ⅜
BellsoT 8¼32	7.9	8	104⅝	+ ¼
BellsoT 7⅞32	7.7	5	102	– ¼
BellsoT 6¾33	7.2	110	93¾	+ ¾
BellsoT 7⅝35	7.5	46	101¼	– ¾
BethSt 8.45s05	12.0	116	70½	+ 1
Bluegrn 8¼12	cv	15	59½	+ 1⅜
BurNo 3.80s20	6.4	7	59	+ 2
Case 7¼16	9.4	20	77	+ ¾
ChespkE 9⅛06	8.8	90	104⅛	+ ½
ChespkE 8½12	8.9	20	96	– 1
vjClardg 11¾02f	...	175	80½	...
ClrkOil 9½04	10.6	133	89¼	+ ¼
CoeurDA 7¼05	cv	192	36½	– ½
Coeur 6⅜04	cv	13	37	+ ½
CmclFd 7.95s06	8.1	10	97½	+ ⅛
Consec 8⅛03	8.3	58	97½	...
Conseco 10½04	10.3	69	101¾	– ¾
Conseco 10¼02	11.1	165	92⅜	+ ⅜
CrownC 7⅛02	8.3	55	85⅞	+ 1
CypSemi 4s05	cv	20	83	– 1
DevonE 4.9s08	cv	7	99½	...
DevonE 4.95s08	cv	7	100	+ ½
Dole 7⅞13	7.9	65	99½	+ ¼
DukeEn 6⅞23	7.0	6	98	...
DukeEn 7⅞24	7.5	1	104½	+ 1⅞
FedDS 8⅛02	7.9	5	103	– ⅛
Finova 9⅛02f	...	15	80	+ 1
FstRep 8s09	9.1	5	88	...
Florsh 12¾02	29.6	90	43	+ 1
FordCr 6⅜08	6.5	207	98½	– 1
GBCB 8⅜07	9.4	23	89	– ½
GE Glob 7s26	7.0	5	100¼	+ 1⅛
GMA 5½01	5.5	43	99⅝	...
GMA 7s02	6.9	15	101¼	+ ⅛
GMA dc6s11	6.4	22	94	+ 3
GMA zr12	...	80	425	...
GMA zr15	...	26	346	– 3
vjGenesH 9¾05f	...	44	16¾	+ ⅝
GoldmS 7.35s09	7.1	5	104	– ⅛
Hallwd 10s05	10.1	24	98½	+ 1
HlthcrR 6.55s02	cv	15	97⅝	...
Hilton 5s06	cv	10	86⅛	– ⅜
HuntPly 11¾04	14.5	26	81	...
IBM 7½13	6.8	23	110½	...
IBM 8⅜19	...	10	113⅛	+ ⅛
IPap dc5⅛12	6.6	1	78	+ ½
IntShip 9s03	8.9	11	101⅛	+ 1⅛
JPMChse 6⅛08	6.1	30	100¾	+ ¾
JPMChse 6¾08	6.6	4	102½	– ⅛
JCPL 7⅛04	7.1	38	101	...
JCPL 7½23	7.5	24	100	+ ¼
vjKCS En 8⅞06f	...	123	81½	– ¼
K&B Hm 9⅜03	9.3	85	101	+ ⅜
K&B Hm 7¾04	7.9	35	98¾	...
K&B Hm 9⅝06	9.3	136	103⅞	+ ⅜
KerrM 7½14	cv	80	100	+ 1
Leucadia 7¾13	7.8	56	99⅞	+ ⅜
Loews 3⅛07	cv	344	92½	+ 1
Lucent 6.9s01	6.9	260	99 25/32	– 3/32
Lucent 7¼06	7.8	1364	92⅝	+ 2¼
Lucent 5½08	6.8	115	80½	+ ⅜
Lucent 6½28	9.0	174	72⅝	+ ¼
Lucent 6.45s29	9.0	160	72	+ ⅛
MBNA 8.28s26	8.7	50	95¼	– 3
MSC Sf 7⅞04	cv	5	95	– 2
MailWell 5s02	cv	205	88⅛	+ ⅛
Malan 9½04	cv	469	86½	+ ½
MarO 7s02	7.0	23	100	– ¼
Mascotch 03	cv	10	77½	+ ½
MKT 5½33f	...	12	94⅞	+ 1⅛
Motrla zr09	...	15	78	– 3½
NatData 5s03	cv	25	94	+ 1
NtEdu 6½11	cv	20	90	+ 1
NRurU 6.75s01	6.8	50	99 21/32	+ 1 15/32
NStl 8⅜06	26.0	273	32¼	+ 4¼
NETelTel 6⅛06	6.2	31	98¼	– ⅞
NETelTel 6⅜08	6.4	5	99½	...
NETelTel 6⅞23	7.2	12	95⅜	...
NYTel 4⅝04	4.8	10	96	+ ⅜
NYTel 4⅞06	5.2	6	93⅛	+ ⅛
NYTel 7s25	7.3	32	95⅞	– ⅛
OcciP 10⅛01	9.9	7	102 1/16	– 1/16
OreStl 11s03	13.1	99	83¾	– ¾
PepBoys zr11	...	20	59¼	– ½
PhilPt 6.65s03	6.5	235	101⅝	...
PhilPt 7.92s23	7.8	130	101⅜	+ ¼
PhilPt 7.2s23	7.4	30	98	+ 3
Polaroid 11½06	18.0	155	64	– ⅛
PSvEG 7s24	7.3	4	95¾	+ ¼
Quanx 6.88s07	cv	151	86	...
ReynTob 7⅝03	7.6	190	99⅞	+ ¼
ReynTob 8¾04	8.5	40	103	...
ReynTob 8¾05	8.5	25	102¾	+ ⅜
RobMyr 63	cv	15	101½	– 2
Safwy 9.65s04	8.9	17	108⅝	– 1⅜
SallM zr14	...	120	33⅞	+ ⅜
SilicnGr 5¼04	cv	45	60½	+ ⅛
Sizeler 8s03	cv	30	93⅛	+ ⅛
SouBell 4⅜03	4.5	10	96¼	+ 1⅞
StdCmcl 07	cv	96	79	...
TVA 6⅛03	6.1	147	100⅜	– ⅛
TVA 6⅞43	6.9	10	100	+ ¼
TVA 7.85s44	7.4	26	106	+ ¾
Tenet 7⅞03	7.8	15	101¼	+ 1¼
Tenet 8s05	7.8	70	102⅜	– ⅛
Tenet 8⅝07	8.4	7	102½	– 1
TmeWar 9⅛13	7.7	50	118	+ 1½
TmeWar 9.15s23	7.8	270	118	– 1
US Timb 9⅝07	11.3	18	85	...
WsteM 4s02	cv	19	97½	+ ½
Webb 9¾03	9.7	35	100½	– ⅜
Webb 9¾08	10.0	168	97¾	– ⅞
Webb 10¼10	10.3	270	100	– ⅛
WebbDel 9⅜09	10.0	59	94	– 1
Weirton 11⅜04	30.0	10	37⅞	+ 3⅞
XeroxCr 7.2s12	10.8	70	66⅝	+ 5⅝

Foreign Bonds

BONDS	CUR YLD.	VOL.	CLOSE	NET CHG.
Inco cv04	cv	127	97¼	+ ½
Inco 7¾16	cv	187	97	+ ¼
SeaCnt 12½04A	14.0	59	89	+ ⅛
SeaCnt 12½04B	14.2	7	88	
SeaCnt 9½03	10.6	40	89⅜	+ ⅜
TelArg 11⅞04	11.2	73	106	+ ⅜

EXPLANATORY NOTES

(For New York and American Bonds)

Yield is Current yield.

cv-Convertible bond. **cf**-Certificates. **cld**-Called. **dc**-Deep discount. **ec**-European currency units. **f**-Dealt in flat. **il**-Italian lire. **kd**-Danish kroner. **m**-Matured bonds, negotiability impaired by maturity. **na**-No accrual. **r**-Registered. **rp**-Reduced principal. **st, sd**-Stamped. **t**-Floating rate. **wd**-When distributed. **ww**-With warrants. **x**-Ex interest. **xw**-Without warrants. **zr**-Zero coupon.

vj-In bankruptcy or receivership or being reorganized under the Bankruptcy Act, or securities assumed by such companies.

AMEX BONDS

BONDS	CUR YLD.	VOL.	CLOSE	NET CHG.
AdvMd 7¼02	cv	162	30	...
AltLiv 5¼02	cv	40	14	...
Chandler 8¾14	8.9	3	98½	...
FriedeGld 4½04	cv	40	25	– 5
Simula 8s04	cv	14	53	+ 1
UBS CSCO 02	cv	60	91	– ¼
UBS WCOM02	cv	50	89¼	– 1½

NASDAQ BONDS

BONDS	CUR YLD.	VOL.	CLOSE	NET CHG.
Agnico 3½04	cv	5	73	– 2
Avatar05	cv	10	94	+ 1¾
BankAtl07	cv	7	78	...
HMT Tch 5¾04	cv	10	28½	...
Kaman 6s12	cv	10	82⅛	+ ⅛
Telxon 7½12	cv	10	101	+ 2½

Consider bonds issued by IBM, which are highlighted in Exhibit 13.1. The coupon rate on these bonds is 8 1/8 percent, listed next to the name of the firm. Thus, the annual coupon payment is $81.25 per $1,000 bond. The bonds mature in 2019 (listed as 19). The trading volume on this day was 1,000 bonds. The closing price was 113 1/8, or 1131.25 per $1,000 of par value. The net change from the previous trading day was +1/8, which represents an increase of $1.25 (1/8 of 1%) per $1,000 of par value.

RETURN FROM INVESTING IN BONDS

If you purchase a bond and hold it until maturity, you will earn the yield to maturity specified when you purchased the bond. As mentioned earlier, however, many investors sell bonds in the secondary market before they reach maturity. Since a bond's price changes over time, your return from investing in a bond is dependent on the price at the time you sell it.

Impact of Interest Rate Movements on Bond Returns

Your return from investing in a bond can be highly influenced by the interest rate movements over the period you hold the bond. To illustrate, suppose that you purchase a bond at par value that has a coupon rate of 8 percent. After one year, you decide to sell the bond. At this time, new bonds being sold at par value are offering a coupon rate of 9 percent. Since investors can purchase a new bond that offers coupon payments of 9 percent, they will not be willing to buy your bond unless you sell it to them for less than par value. In other words, you must offer a discount on the price to compensate for the bond's lower coupon rate.

If interest rates had declined over the year rather than increased, the opposite effects would have occurred. You could sell your bond for a premium above par value, because the coupon rate of your bond would be higher than the coupon rate offered on newly issued bonds. Thus, interest rate movements and bond prices are inversely related. This means that your return from investing in bonds will be more favorable if interest rates decline over the period you hold the bonds.

Comparison of Actual Returns among Bonds

The actual return generated varies among types of bonds, as shown in Exhibit 13.2. Notice that high-yield bonds performed better than the other types of bonds, regardless of the holding period assessed. Remember, though, that high-yield bonds could perform relatively poorly if economic conditions weaken and bond defaults increase. The annualized return for any specific type of bonds shown in Exhibit 13.2 varies among the holding periods, because interest rate conditions and other conditions vary across holding periods.

Exhibit 13.2   Comparison of Returns among Types of Bonds

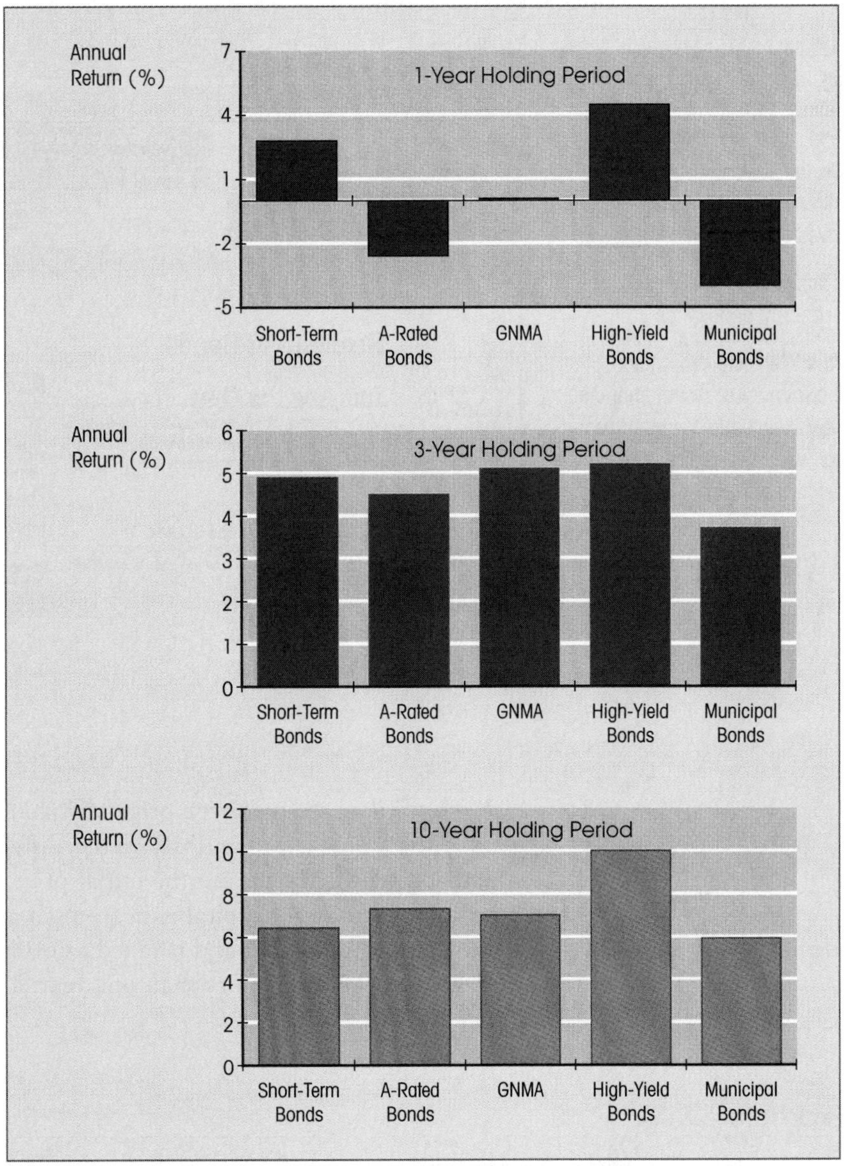

T. Rowe Price, 2000.

Tax Implications of Investing in Bonds

When determining the return from investing in a bond, you need to account for tax effects. The interest income that you receive from a bond is taxed as ordinary income for federal income tax purposes (except for tax-exempt bonds as explained earlier). Selling bonds in the secondary market at a

13.3 Financial Planning Online: Today's Events That Could Affect Bond Prices

Go to:
http://www.businessweek.com/
investor/index.html

Click on:
Economy and Bonds

This Web site provides:
a summary of recent financial
news related to the bond market, which you may consider
before selling or buying bonds.

higher price than the price you originally paid for them results in a capital
gain. The capital gain (or loss) is the difference between the price at
which you sell the bond and the initial price that you paid for it. Recall
from Chapter 4 that a capital gain from an asset held one year or less is
a short-term capital gain and is taxed as ordinary income. A capital gain
from an asset held for more than one year is subject to a long-term capital gains tax.

Example

You purchase 10 newly issued bonds for $9,700. The bonds
have a total par value of $10,000 and a maturity of 10 years.
The bonds pay a coupon rate of 8 percent, or $800 (com-
puted as .08 × $10,000) per year. The coupon payments are
made every six months, so each payment is $400. Exhibit 13.3
shows your return and the tax implications for four different scenarios.
Notice how taxes incurred from the investment in bonds are dependent
on the change in the bond price over time and the length of time the
bonds are held.

Exhibit 13.3   Potential Tax Implications from Investing in Bonds

Scenario	Implication
1. You sell the bonds after 8 months at a price of $9,800.	You receive one $400 coupon payment 6 months after buying the bond, which is taxed at your ordinary income tax rate; you also earn a short-term capital gain of $100, which is taxed at your ordinary income tax rate.
2. You sell the bonds after 2 years at a price of $10,200.	You receive coupon payments (taxed at your ordinary income tax rate) of $800 in the first year and in the second year; you also earn a long-term capital gain of $500 in the second year, which is subject to the long-term capital gains tax in that year.
3. You sell the bonds after 2 years at a price of $9,500.	You receive coupon payments (taxed at your ordinary income tax rate) of $800 in the first year and in the second year; you also incur a long-term capital loss of $200 in the second year.
4. You hold the bonds until maturity.	You receive coupon payments (taxed at your ordinary income tax rate) in each year over the 10-year life of the bond. You also receive the bond's principal of $10,000 at the end of the 10-year period. This reflects a long-term capital gain of $300, which is subject to a long-term capital gains tax in the year you receive the gain.

RISK FROM INVESTING IN BONDS

Bond investors are exposed to the risk that the bonds may not provide the return that was expected. The main sources of risk are default risk, call risk, and interest rate risk.

Default Risk

If the issuer of the bond (a government agency or a firm) defaults on its payments, investors do not receive all of the coupon payments that they are owed and do not receive the principal. Investors will invest in a risky bond only if it offers a higher yield than other bonds to compensate for its risk. The extra yield required by investors to compensate for the risk of default is referred to as a **risk premium**. Treasury bonds do not contain a risk premium because they are free from default risk.

risk premium
The extra yield required by investors to compensate for the risk of default.

Use of Risk Ratings to Measure the Default Risk. Investors can use ratings (provided by agencies such as Moody's Investor Service or Standard and Poor's) to assess the risk of bonds issued by corporations. The ratings reflect the likelihood that the issuers will repay their debt over time. The ratings are classified as shown in Exhibit 13.4. Investors can select the corporate bonds that fit their degree of risk tolerance by weighing the higher potential return against the higher default risk of lower-grade debt securities.

Exhibit 13.4   Bond Rating Classes

Risk Class	Standard & Poor's	Moody's
Highest quality (least risk)	AAA	Aaa
High quality	AA	Aa
High-medium quality	A	A
Medium quality	BBB	Baa
Medium-low quality	BB	Ba
Low quality	B	B
Poor quality	CCC	Caa
Very poor quality	CC	Ca
Lowest quality	DDD	C

Relationship of Risk Rating to Risk Premium. The lower (weaker) the risk rating, the higher the risk premium offered on a bond.

Example

As of today, the bond yields quoted in financial newspapers for bonds with a 10-year maturity are as shown in the second column:

Type of Bond	Bond Yield Offered	Risk Premium Contained within Bond Yield
Treasury bonds	7.0%	0.0%
AAA-rated corporate bonds	7.5	0.5
A-rated corporate bonds	7.8	0.8
BB-rated corporate bonds	8.8	1.8
CCC-rated corporate bonds	9.5	2.5

In the third column, notice that since the Treasury bonds are risk-free, they have no risk premium. However, the other bonds have a risk premium, which is the amount by which their annualized yield exceeds the Treasury bond yield. The premium can change over time.

Based on the yields shown, investors who have no tolerance for risk would invest in Treasury bonds even though the return is lower. Other investors would prefer the AAA-rated corporate bonds because they offer a yield 0.5 percentage point above the Treasury yield and have very low default risk. Other investors would select specific CCC-rated corporate bonds that they believe will not default. If these bonds do not default, they will provide a yield that is 2.0 percentage points above the yield offered on AAA-rated bonds and 2.5 percentage points above the yield offered on Treasury bonds.

Impact of Economic Conditions. Bonds with a high degree of default risk are most susceptible to default when economic conditions are weak. Investors may lose all or most of their initial investment when a bond defaults. They can avoid default risk by investing in Treasury bonds or can at least keep the default risk to a minimum by investing in government agency bonds or AAA-rated corporate bonds. However, they will receive a lower yield on these bonds than investors who are willing to accept a higher degree of default risk.

Call Risk

call (prepayment) risk
The risk that a callable bond will be called.

Bonds with a call feature are subject to **call risk** (also called **prepayment risk**), which is the risk that the bond will be called. If issuers of callable bonds call these bonds, the bondholders must sell them back to the issuer.

13.4   Financial Planning Online: Upcoming Economic Announcements Related to Bonds

Go to:
http://www.businessweek.com/
investor/index.html

Click on:
Economy and Bonds

Click on:
Calendar of Events

This Web site provides:
information on economic announcements that could affect the bond market. You may want to consider how these announcements might affect the prices of bonds that you own or plan to purchase in the future.

Example

Two years ago, Christine Smart purchased 10-year bonds that offered a yield to maturity of 9 percent. She planned to hold the bonds until maturity. Recently, interest rates declined and the issuer called the bonds. Christine could use the proceeds to buy other bonds, but the yield to maturity offered on new bonds is lower because interest rates have declined. The return that Christine will earn from investing in bonds is likely to be less than the return that she would have earned if she could have retained the 10-year bonds until maturity.

Interest Rate Risk

interest rate risk
The risk that a bond's price will decline in response to an increase in interest rates.

All bonds are subject to **interest rate risk,** which is the risk that the bond's price will decline in response to an increase in interest rates. A bond is valued as the present value of its future expected cash flows. Most bonds pay fixed coupon payments. If interest rates rise, investors will require a higher return on a bond. Consequently, the discount rate applied to value the bond is increased, and the market price of the bond will decline.

Example

Three months ago, Rob Suerth paid $10,000 for a 20-year Treasury bond that has a par value of $10,000 and a 7 percent coupon rate. Since then, interest rates have increased. New 20-year Treasury bonds with a par value of $10,000 are priced at $10,000 and offer a coupon rate of 9 percent. Thus, Rob would earn 2 percentage points more in coupon payments from a new bond than from the bond he purchased three months ago. He decides to sell his Treasury bond and use the proceeds to invest in the new bonds. He quickly learns that no one in the secondary market is willing to purchase his bond for the price he paid. These investors avoid his bond for the same reason that he wants to sell it; they would prefer to earn 9 percent on the new bonds rather than earn 7 percent on his bond. The only way that Rob can sell his bond is by lowering the price to compensate for the bond's lower coupon rate (compared to new bonds). Thus, the market price of his bond is related to the yield offered on new bonds, which in turn is tied to prevailing interest rate levels.

The chapter appendix explains how bonds are valued and offers more insight into the relationship between interest rate movements and bond prices (and therefore bond returns).

Impact of a Bond's Maturity on Its Interest Rate Risk. Bonds with longer terms to maturity are more sensitive to interest rate movements than bonds that have short terms remaining until maturity. To understand why, consider two bonds. Each has a par value of $1,000 and offers a 9 percent coupon rate, but one bond has 20 years remaining until maturity while the other has only 1 year remaining until maturity. If market interest rates suddenly decline from 9 to 7 percent, which bond would you prefer to own? The bond with 20 years until maturity becomes very attractive because you would be able to receive coupon payments reflecting a 9 percent return for the next 20 years. Conversely, the bond with one year remaining until maturity will provide the 9 percent payment only over the next year. Thus, investors will increase their demand for the bond that provides a 9 percent payment over the next 20 years. Although the market price of both bonds increases in response to the decline in interest rates, it increases more for the bond with the longer term to maturity.

Now assume that, instead of declining, interest rates have risen from their initial level of 9 percent to 11 percent. Which bond would you prefer? Each bond provides a 9 percent coupon rate, which is less than the prevailing interest rate. The bond with one year until maturity will mature soon, however, so you can reinvest the proceeds at the higher interest rates at that time (assuming the rates are still high). Conversely, you are stuck with the other bond for 20 more years. Although neither bond would be very desirable under these conditions, the bond with the longer term to maturity is less desirable. Therefore, its price in the secondary market will decline more than the price of the bond with a short term to maturity.

Since bond prices change in response to interest rate movements, you may wish to choose maturities on bonds that reflect your expectations of future interest rates. If you prefer to reduce your exposure to interest rate risk, you may consider investing in bonds that have a maturity that matches the time when you will need the funds. If you expect that interest rates will decline over time, you may consider investing in bonds with longer maturities

"Interest rates gyrated wildly today, on rumors that the Federal Reserve Board would be replaced by the cast of 'Saturday Night Live.'"

than the time when you will need the funds. In this way, you can sell the bonds in the secondary market at a relatively high price, assuming that your expectations were correct. If interest rates increase instead of declining over this period, however, your holding period return will be reduced.

BOND INVESTMENT STRATEGIES

If you decide to invest in bonds, you need to determine a strategy for selecting them. Most strategies involve investing in a diversified portfolio of bonds rather than in one bond. Diversification reduces the exposure to possible default by a single issuer. If you cannot afford to invest in a diversified portfolio of bonds, you may consider investing in a bond mutual fund with a small minimum investment (such as $1,000). Additional information on bond mutual funds is provided in Chapter 14. Whether you focus on individual bonds or bond mutual funds, the bond investment strategies summarized here are applicable.

Interest Rate Strategy

interest rate strategy
Selecting bonds for investment based on interest rate expectations.

With an **interest rate strategy,** the investor selects bonds based on interest rate expectations. When you expect interest rates to decline, you invest heavily in long-term bonds whose prices will increase the most if interest rates fall. Conversely, when you expect interest rates to increase, you shift most of your money to bonds with short terms to maturity in order to minimize the adverse impact of the higher interest rates on your bond portfolio.

Investors who attempt the interest rate strategy may experience poor performance if their guesses about the future direction of interest rate movements are incorrect. In addition, this strategy requires frequent trading to capitalize on shifts in expectations of interest rates. Some investors who follow this strategy frequently sell their entire portfolio of bonds so that they can shift to bonds with different maturities in response to shifts in interest rate expectations. The frequent trading results in high transaction costs (in the form of commissions to brokerage firms). In addition, the high turnover of bonds may generate more short-term capital gains, which are taxed at the ordinary federal income tax rate. This rate is higher for most investors than the tax on long-term capital gains.

Passive Strategy

passive strategy
Investing in a diversified portfolio of bonds that are held for a long period of time.

With a **passive strategy,** the investor invests in a diversified portfolio of bonds that are held for a long period of time. The portfolio is simply intended to generate periodic interest income in the form of coupon payments. The passive strategy is especially valuable for investors who want to generate stable interest income over time and do not want to incur costs associated with relying on portfolio managers or engaging in frequent buy and sell transactions.

A passive strategy does not have to focus on very safe bonds that offer low returns; it may reflect a portfolio of bonds with diversified risk levels. The diversification is intended to reduce the exposure to default from a single issuer of bonds. To reduce exposure to interest rate risk, a portfolio may even attempt to diversify across a wide range of bond maturities.

One disadvantage of this strategy is that it does not capitalize on expectations of interest rate movements. Investors who use a passive strategy, however, are more comfortable matching general bond market movements than trying to beat the bond market and possibly failing.

Maturity Matching Strategy

matching strategy
Investing in bonds that will generate payments to match future expenses.

The **matching strategy** involves selecting bonds that will generate payments to match future expenses. For example, parents of an 8-year-old child may consider investing in a 10-year bond so that the principal can be used to pay for the child's college education. Alternatively, they may invest in a bond portfolio just before retirement so that they will receive annual income (coupon payments) to cover periodic expenses after retirement. The matching strategy is conservative, in that it is simply intended to cover future expenses, rather than to beat the bond market in general. It requires investors to invest in a portfolio of bonds that will provide the income needed in future years.

HOW BOND DECISIONS FIT WITHIN YOUR FINANCIAL PLAN

The following are the key decisions about bonds that should be included within your financial plan:

1. Should you consider buying bonds?

2. What strategy should you use for investing in bonds?

Stephanie's first concern should be maintaining adequate liquidity and making her existing loan payments. She is not in a position to buy bonds right now, but will consider bonds once her financial position improves. Exhibit 13.5 provides an example of how bond decisions apply to her financial plan.

Exhibit 13.5   How Bonds Fit within Stephanie Spratt's Financial Plan

> ## Goals for Investing in Bonds
>
> 1. Determine if I could benefit from investing in bonds.
> 2. If I decide to invest in bonds, determine what strategy to use to invest in bonds.

Analysis

Strategy to Invest in Bonds	Opinion
Interest rate strategy	I cannot forecast the direction of interest rates (even experts are commonly wrong on their interest rate forecasts), so this strategy could backfire. This strategy would also complicate my tax return.
Passive strategy	May be appropriate for me in many situations, and the low transaction costs are appealing.
Maturity matching strategy	Not applicable to my situation, since I am not trying to match coupon payments to future expenses.

Decisions

Decision on Whether to Invest in Bonds:
I cannot afford to buy bonds right now, but I will consider purchasing them in the future when my financial position improves. Bonds can generate a decent return, and some bonds are free from default risk.

Decision on the Strategy to Use for Investing in Bonds:
I am not attempting to match coupon payments with future anticipated expenses. I may consider expected interest rate movements according to financial experts when I decide which bond fund to invest in, but I will not shift in and out of bond funds frequently to capitalize on expected interest rate movements. I will likely use a passive strategy of investing in bonds and will retain bond investments for a long period of time.

DISCUSSION QUESTIONS

1. How would Stephanie's bond investing decisions be different if she were a single mother of two children?

2. How would Stephanie's bond investing decisions be affected if she were 35 years old? If she were 50 years old?

SUMMARY

Bonds are long-term debt securities. Bonds can be classified by their issuer. The common issuers are the U.S. Treasury, municipalities, federal government agencies, and corporations.

A bond's yield to maturity is the annualized return that is earned by an investor who holds the bond until maturity. This yield is composed of interest (coupon) payments and the difference between the principal value and the price at which the bond was originally purchased.

Bonds can be exposed to default risk, which reflects the possibility that the issuer will default on the bond payments. Some bonds are exposed to call risk, or the risk that the bond will be called before maturity. Bonds are also subject to interest rate risk, or the risk of a decline in price in response to rising interest rates.

A popular bond strategy is the interest rate strategy, where the selection of which bonds to buy is dependent on the expectation of future interest rates. An alternative strategy is a passive strategy, in which a diversified portfolio of bonds is maintained. A third bond strategy is the maturity matching strategy, in which the investor selects bonds that will mature on future dates when funds will be needed.

Integrating the Key Concepts

Your decision to invest in bonds is not only related to your other investment decisions, but affects other parts of your financial plan. Before investing in bonds, you should reassess your liquidity (Part 2). Bonds that provide periodic coupon payments offer some liquidity. However, the value of a bond is subject to an abrupt decline, and you may not want to sell the bond when its price is temporarily depressed.

The bond decision is related to financing (Part 3) because you should consider paying off any personal loans before you invest in bonds. If after considering your liquidity and your financing situation, you still decide to invest in bonds, you need to decide whether the investment should be for your retirement account (Part 5). There are some tax advantages to that choice, but also some restrictions on when you have access to those funds (as explained in more detail in Chapter 18).

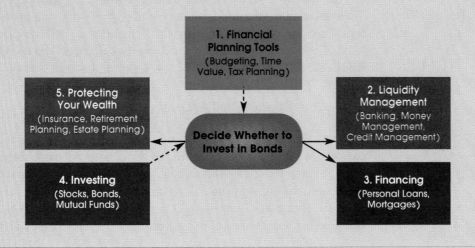

Appendix **13A**

Valuing a Bond

Before investing in a bond, you may wish to determine its value. This process uses the time value of money analysis. A bond's value is determined as the present value of the future cash flows to be received by the investor, which are the periodic coupon payments and the principal payment at maturity. The present value of a bond can be computed by discounting the future cash flows (coupon payments and principal payment) to be received from the bond. The discount rate used to discount the cash flows should reflect your required rate of return. The value of a bond can be expressed as:

$$\text{Value of Bond} = \sum_{t=1}^{n}[C_t/(1 + k)^t] + Prin/(1 + k)^n$$

where C_t represents the coupon payments in year t, *Prin* is the principal payment at the end of year n when the bond matures, and k is the required rate of return. Thus, the value of a bond is composed of the present value of the future coupon payments, along with the present value of the principal payment. If you pay the price that is obtained by this valuation approach and hold the bond to maturity, you will earn the return that you require.

Example

 Victor Kalafa is planning to purchase a bond that has seven years remaining until maturity, a par value of $1,000, and a coupon rate of 6 percent (let's assume the coupon payments are paid once annually at the end of the year). He is willing to purchase this bond only if he can earn a return of 8 percent, because he knows that he can earn 8 percent on alternative bonds that are available.

The first step in valuing a bond is to identify the coupon payments, principal payment, and required rate of return:

■ Future cash flows:

Coupon payment $(C) = .06 \times \$1,000 = \$60$
Principal payment $(PRIN) = \$1,000$

396

■ Discount rate:

Required rate of return = 8 percent.

The next step is to use this information to discount the future cash flows of the bond with the help of the present value tables in the appendix at the end of the book:

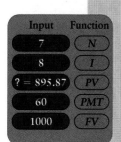

Input	Function
7	N
8	I
? = 895.87	PV
60	PMT
1000	FV

Value of Bond = Present Value of Coupon Payments + Present Value of Principal
= [$C \times$ (PVIFA, 8%, 7 yrs)] + [$Prin \times$ (PVIF, 8%, 7 yrs)]
= [$60 × 5.2064] + [$1,000 × .5835]
= $312.38 + $583.50
= $895.88.

When using a financial calculator to determine the value of the bond, the future value will be 1,000 because this is the amount the bondholder will receive at maturity.

Based on this analysis, Victor is willing to pay $895.88 for this bond, which will provide his annualized return of 8 percent. If he can obtain the bond for a lower price, his return will exceed 8 percent. If the price exceeds $895.88, his return would be less than 8 percent, so he would not buy the bond.

The market price of any bond is based on investors' required rate of return, which is influenced by the interest rates that are available on alternative investments at the time. If bond investors require a rate of return of 8 percent as Victor does, the bond will be priced in the bond market at the value derived by Victor. However, if the bond market participants use a different required rate of return than Victor, the market price of the bond will be different. For example, if most investors require a 9 percent return on this bond, the bond will have a market price below the value derived by Victor (conduct your own valuation using a 9 percent discount rate to verify this).

REVIEW QUESTIONS

1. What is a bond? What is meant by a bond's par value? What are coupon payments, and how are they normally paid? What happens when investors buy a bond below par value? When should you consider investing in bonds?

2. What is a call feature on a bond? How will a call feature affect investor interest in the bond?

3. What is a convertible bond? How does a bond's convertible feature affect its return?

4. What is meant by a bond's yield to maturity? How does the price paid for a bond affect its yield to maturity?

5. Discuss how bonds are sold on the secondary market.

6. What are Treasury bonds? Describe their key characteristics.

7. What are municipal bonds? Why are they issued? Are all municipal bonds free from default risk? What makes municipal bonds especially attractive to high-income investors?

8. What are federal agency bonds? Compare and contrast the three most common federal agency bonds.

9. What are corporate bonds? How much default risk do they exhibit? What are junk bonds? What type of investor should invest in them?

10. What information is provided in corporate bond quotations?

11. When an investor sells a bond on the secondary market before the bond reaches maturity, what determines the return on the bond? How do interest rate movements affect bond returns?

12. Discuss the effect of taxes on your returns from bonds.

13. Discuss default risk as it relates to bonds. How may investors use risk ratings? What is the relationship between the risk rating and the risk premium? How do economic conditions affect default risk?

14. What is the risk to investors on bonds that have a call feature?

15. What is interest rate risk? How does a rise in interest rates affect a bond's price?

16. Bonds come in varying maturities. How is interest rate risk affected by a bond's maturity? How can investors use knowledge of interest rate movements to their advantage?

17. Describe how the interest rate strategy for bond investment works. What are some of the problems with this strategy?

18. How does the passive strategy for bond investment work? What is the main disadvantage of this strategy?

19. Describe the matching strategy when investing in bonds. Give an example. Why is this strategy considered conservative?

20. How is the value of a bond determined? What information is needed to perform the calculation?*

FINANCIAL PLANNING PROBLEMS

1. Bernie purchased 20 bonds with par values of $1,000 each. The bonds carry a coupon rate of 9 percent payable semiannually. How much will Bernie receive for his first interest payment?

2. Michael has $10,000 that he wishes to invest in bonds. He can purchase Treasury bonds with a coupon rate of 7.0 percent or municipal bonds with a coupon rate of 5.5 percent. Michael lives in a state with no state income tax and has a marginal tax rate of 28 percent. Which investment will give Michael the higher dollar return after taxes are considered?

3. Sandy has a choice between purchasing $5,000 in Treasury bonds paying 7.0 percent interest or purchasing $5,000 in BB-rated corporate bonds with a coupon rate of 9.2 percent. What is the risk premium on the BB-rated corporate bonds?

4. Bonnie paid $9,500 for corporate bonds that have a par value of $10,000 and a coupon rate of 9 percent paid annually. Bonnie received her first interest payment after holding the bonds for 12 months, and then sold the bonds for $9,700. If Bonnie is in a 36 percent marginal tax bracket for federal income tax purposes, what are the tax consequences of her ownership and sale of the bonds?

5. Katie paid $9,400 for a Ginnie Mae bond with a par value of $10,000 and a coupon rate of 6.5 percent. Two years later, after having received the annual interest payments on the bond, Katie sold the bond for $9,700. What are her total tax consequences if she is in a 28 percent marginal tax bracket?

6. Timothy has an opportunity to buy a $1,000 par value municipal bond with a coupon rate of 7 percent and a maturity of five years. The bond pays interest annually. If Timothy requires a return of 8 percent, what should he pay for the bond?*

7. Molly wants to invest in Treasury bonds that have a par value of $20,000 and a coupon rate of 4.5 percent. Molly wants bonds with a 10-year maturity, and she requires a 6.0 percent return. How much should Molly pay for her bonds?*

8. Emma is considering purchasing bonds with a par value of $10,000. The bonds have a coupon rate of 8 percent and six years to maturity. The bonds are priced at $9,550. If Emma requires a 10 percent return, should she buy these bonds?*

9. Mark has a Treasury bond that has a par value of $30,000 and a coupon rate of 6 percent. The bond has 15 years to maturity. Mark needs to sell the bond, and new bonds currently are carrying coupon rates of 8 percent. What price should Mark put on the bond?*

10. What if Mark's Treasury bond in the previous question had a coupon rate of 9 percent and new bonds still had interest rates of 8 percent? What price should Mark put on the bond in this situation?*

* Question based on chapter appendix.

FINANCIAL PLANNING ONLINE EXERCISES

Go to http://www.financenter.com/products/analyzers/bond.fcs and click on: "What is my yield to maturity?"

1. This Web site provides an estimate of the yield to maturity of a bond based on its present price, coupon rate, and maturity. On the Inputs page, enter 98 for the percent of face value paid as price of the bond. Enter $1,000 as the Face Value, a Coupon Rate of 7.75 percent, 120 Months to Maturity, 15 percent Federal Tax Rate, 8 percent State Tax Rate, indicate that Your Coupon Income is Invested Elsewhere at a Rate of 4 percent, and that the Type of Bond is a Treasury Security. Click on "Results" to obtain the yield to maturity and the return on the investment. Click on the Graphs tab and the Help tab for additional information.

2. Click on the input tab to return to the Inputs page. Change Price You Paid to 105 percent of face value and keep other values the same as in the previous example. Click on "Results." Compare the yield to maturity to the yield from the previous example. What is the reason for the differences? Click on the Graphs tab and the Explanation tab for additional information.

3. Click on the input tab to return to the Inputs page. Change the Price You Paid as percent of face value, to 100 percent and keep the other values the same as in the previous example. Click on "Results." How does the yield to maturity compare with the coupon rate? How does this result differ from the previous two examples? Click on the Graphs tab and the Explanation tab for more information.

4. Click on the input tab to return to the Inputs page. Enter 98 under Price You Paid as percent of face value, and under Type of Bond, choose Municipal Bond: State Tax Exempt. Keep other values the same as in the previous example. Click on "Results." Note the yield to maturity and the return.

5. Click on the input tab to return to the Inputs page. Keeping the values the same as in the previous example, change the Type of Bond to Corporate Bond. Click on "Results." Compare the yield to maturity and the return to those from the municipal bond example. Why is the Return After Taxes different?

Go to http://cnnfn.com/markets/bondcenter, which allows you to monitor the performance of the bond market.

1. Click on "Latest Rates" and you will get a listing of the current yield to maturity for several types of fixed-income securities, including Treasury bonds, municipal bonds, and corporate bonds. Can you explain the difference in rates within each category and between categories?

2. Use the Back option in your browser to return to http://cnnfn.com/markets/bondcenter. Click on "Short Term Rates." You will receive information on the prime rate, discount rate, and the federal funds rate. What is the significance of each rate, and how are they affected by each other?

3. Go to http://www.bloomberg.com/markets/psamuni.html. You will see information on municipal bond yields for various maturities. The yields observed during the last two trading days will be shown along with the percentage change in yields. The yields from a week ago and six months ago will also be provided. The equivalent yield on a taxable bond for an investor with a federal marginal tax rate of 31 percent will be shown for comparison, as the interest received on municipal bonds is exempt from federal income taxes. Why are the yields different for the various maturities?

Building Your Own Financial Plan

Based on an investor's risk tolerance and/or timeline for goal achievement, bonds may prove to be a useful investment instrument. Referring back to the risk tolerance test that you took in Chapter 10 and the goals that you established in Chapter 1, consider the extent to which bonds may play a role in your overall financial planning. The Web sites mentioned in the template provided with this chapter in the *Financial Planning Workbook* and on the CD-ROM will assist you in the decision.

Bonds, like stocks, need to be reviewed as market conditions change, although bonds are far less volatile than stocks and, therefore, do not require daily monitoring.

The Sampsons—A Continuing Case

 The Sampsons are considering investing in bonds as a way of saving for their children's college education. They learn that there are bonds with maturities between 12 and 16 years from now, which is exactly when they would need the funds for college expenses. Next, Dave and Sharon notice that some highly rated municipal bonds offer a coupon rate of 5 percent, while some highly rated corporate bonds offer a coupon rate of 8 percent. The Sampsons could purchase either type of bond at its par value. The income from the corporate bonds would be subject to tax at their marginal rate of 28 percent. The income on the municipal bonds would not be subject to federal income tax. Dave and Sharon are looking to you for advice on whether bonds are a sound investment and, if so, what type they should purchase.

1. Should the Sampsons consider investing a portion of their savings in bonds to save for their children's education? Why or why not?

2. If the Sampsons should purchase bonds, what maturities should they consider, keeping in mind their investment goal?

3. If the Sampsons should consider bonds, should they invest in corporate bonds or municipal bonds? Factor the return they would receive after tax liabilities into your analysis, based on the bonds having a $1,000 par value and the Sampsons being in a 28 percent marginal tax bracket.

IN-TEXT STUDY GUIDE

True/False:

1. Bonds are short-term debt securities that are issued by government agencies or corporations.

2. Bonds typically provide fixed dividend payments that represent additional income each year.

3. A call feature attached to a bond allows the issuer to buy back the bond before maturity.

4. Investors can sell bonds before maturity to other investors in the secondary market.

5. Treasury bonds are subject to default risk.

6. Federal agency bonds are long-term debt securities issued by federal agencies such as the Government National Mortgage Association.

7. Bonds issued by some smaller, less stable corporations are subject to a higher degree of default risk. They are referred to as trash bonds.

8. When determining the price of a bond, cash flows are discounted at a rate that reflects the investor's required rate of return.*

9. Most strategies for selecting bonds involve investing in a diversified portfolio of bonds rather than in one bond.

10. The matching strategy for selecting bonds involves frequent trading to capitalize on shifts in expectations of interest rate fluctuations.

11. Each bond has a par value (or face value) that is paid by the issuer to the investor holding the bond until maturity.

* Question based on chapter appendix.

Multiple Choice:

1. Typical maturities for bonds are
   a. 1 to 2 years.
   b. 2 to 5 years.
   c. 5 to 10 years.
   d. 10 to 30 years.

2. Bond coupon payments are usually made
   a. annually.
   b. semiannually.
   c. quarterly.
   d. monthly.

3. _____ risk is the possibility that the bond's price will decline in response to an increase in interest rates.
   a. Interest rate
   b. Call
   c. Reinvestment rate
   d. Default

4. _____ bonds allow investors to exchange the bonds for a specified number of shares of the issuer's stock.
   a. Registered
   b. Bearer
   c. Callable
   d. Convertible

5. _____ bonds can be bought back by the issuer before maturity.
   a. Registered
   b. Bearer
   c. Callable
   d. Convertible

6. The _____ is the annualized yield if the bond is held until maturity.
   a. coupon rate
   b. yield to maturity
   c. yield to call
   d. call rate

7. If a bond's price _____ its par value, the yield to maturity _____ the coupon rate.
   a. exceeds; is less than
   b. exceeds; exceeds
   c. is less than; is less than
   d. none of the above

8. _____ bonds are bonds issued by state and local government agencies.
   a. Treasury
   b. Municipal
   c. Government agency
   d. Corporate

9. Grant Gable lives in a state without state income taxes. Grant is in the 28 percent tax bracket for federal income tax purposes. This year, he generated $7,000 in interest from a municipal bond. Grant has to pay federal taxes in the amount of
   a. $0.
   b. $7,000.
   c. $1,960.
   d. none of the above

10. Which of the following bonds are not exposed to default risk?
   a. A-rated corporate bonds
   b. C-rated corporate bonds
   c. municipal bonds
   d. Treasury bonds

11. Your return from a bond is not dependent on
   a. the coupon rate.
   b. the yield to maturity.
   c. the price of the bond.
   d. Your return from a bond is dependent on all of the above.

12. Which of the following ratings indicates the highest degree of default risk?
   a. AA
   b. B
   c. CCC
   d. DDD

13. Investors who own callable bonds are subject to _____ risk.
   a. default
   b. prepayment
   c. interest rate
   d. exchange rate

14. The _____ the risk of a bond, the _____ the yield to maturity.
   a. higher; lower
   b. lower; higher
   c. higher; higher
   d. Answers (a) and (b) are correct.

15. Bonds with _____ terms to maturity are _____ sensitive to interest rate movements.
   a. long; more
   b. short; less
   c. long; not
   d. Answers (a) and (b) are correct.

The following information applies to questions 16 and 17.

Peter Mangler would like to purchase a bond that has nine years remaining until maturity, has a par value of $1,000, and has an annual coupon rate of 11 percent.

16. If Peter requires a return of 12 percent on the bond, he should be willing to pay _____ for this bond.*
   a. $946.72
   b. $1,000.00
   c. $1,055.37
   d. None of the above

17. If Peter requires a return of 10 percent on the bond, he should be willing to pay _____ for this bond.*
   a. $944.63
   b. $1,057.59
   c. $1,000.00
   d. none of the above

18. A(n) _____ strategy involves investing in a diversified portfolio of bonds that are held for a long period of time.
   a. interest rate
   b. passive
   c. matching
   d. none of the above

19. A(n) _____ strategy involves selecting bonds that will generate payments that equal future expenses.
    a. interest rate
    b. passive
    c. matching
    d. none of the above

20. The _____ a bond provides credit.
    a. issuer of
    b. investor in
    c. shareholder of
    d. none of the above

* Question based on chapter appendix.

Investing in Mutual Funds

Mutual funds pool money from you and other investors to purchase portfolios of securities. Recall that money market mutual funds (described in Chapter 6) focus on investing in very liquid investments. This chapter explains how to invest in stock mutual funds and bond mutual funds. Investing in mutual funds may increase your cash inflows received in the form of dividend cash distributions from the mutual funds, while providing an easy means of diversifying your investments. Your decisions to invest in mutual funds will ultimately affect the value of your assets over time, thereby enhancing your wealth.

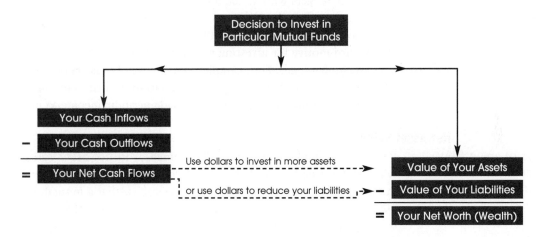

The objectives of this chapter are to:

- identify the types of stock funds,
- present the types of bond funds,
- explain how to choose among mutual funds,
- describe quotations of mutual funds, and
- explain how to diversify among mutual funds.

BACKGROUND ON MUTUAL FUNDS

stock mutual funds
Funds that sell shares to individuals and invest the proceeds in stocks.

bond mutual funds
Funds that sell shares to individuals and invest the proceeds in bonds.

Mutual funds can be broadly distinguished according to the securities in which they invest. **Stock mutual funds** sell shares to individuals and invest the proceeds in stocks. **Bond mutual funds** sell shares to individuals and invest the proceeds in bonds. All types of mutual funds employ portfolio managers who decide what securities to purchase; thus, the individual investors do not have to select stocks themselves. The minimum investment in a mutual fund is usually between $500 and $3,000, depending on the fund. Many mutual funds are subsidiaries of other types of financial institutions.

Motives for Investing in Mutual Funds

A primary reason for investing in mutual funds is the small amount of funds needed. By investing in a mutual fund, you can invest in a broadly diversified portfolio with a small initial investment. If you have $1,000 to invest, you (along with other investors) can own a portfolio of 100 or more stocks through a mutual fund. Yet, if you had attempted to buy stocks directly with your $1,000, you might not have enough money to buy even 100 shares of a single stock.

A second motive for investing in mutual funds is the expertise of the portfolio managers who decide how to invest the money you provide. Your investments reflect the decisions of experienced professionals who have access to the best research available.

A third motive for investing in mutual funds is that they can meet specific investment goals. For example, some mutual funds are designed to satisfy investors who desire potential appreciation in their investments, while other mutual funds are designed to provide periodic income to investors.

Net Asset Value

net asset value (NAV)
The market value of the securities that a mutual fund has purchased minus any liabilities owed.

Each mutual fund's value can be determined by its **net asset value (NAV),** which represents the market value of the securities that it has purchased minus any liabilities owed. For example, suppose that a mutual fund owns 100 different stocks including 10,000 shares of Nike that are currently worth $60 per share. This mutual fund's holdings of Nike are worth $600,000 (computed as $60 × 10,000 shares) as of today. The value of the other 99 stocks owned by the fund is determined in the same manner, and all the values are summed. Then, any liabilities such as expenses owed to the mutual fund's managers are subtracted to determine the NAV.

The NAV is commonly reported on a per-share basis by dividing the NAV by the number of shares in the fund. Each day, the market value of all the mutual fund's assets is determined. Any interest or dividends earned by the fund are added to the market value of the assets, and any expenses (such as mailing, marketing, and portfolio management) that are charged to the fund or any dividends distributed to the fund's shareholders (investors) are deducted. As the value of the mutual fund's portfolio increases, so does the fund's NAV.

Open-End versus Closed-End Funds

Mutual funds are classified as either open-end funds or closed-end funds.

open-end mutual funds
Funds that sell shares directly to investors and repurchase those shares whenever investors wish to sell them.

Open-End Funds. **Open-end mutual funds** sell shares directly to investors and repurchase those shares whenever investors wish to sell them. The funds are managed by investment companies that are commonly subsidiaries of a larger financial conglomerate. Merrill Lynch, Citigroup, First Union, and many other financial institutions have investment company subsidiaries that operate open-end mutual funds. Many investment companies operate

family
A group of separately managed open-end mutual funds held by one investment company.

a **family,** or group of separately managed open-end mutual funds. For example, Fidelity, T. Rowe Price, and Vanguard manage several different open-end funds, each of which has its own investment objective. By offering a diverse set of mutual funds, these investment companies satisfy investors with many different investment preferences.

Consider an open-end stock mutual fund that receives $10 million today as new investors purchase shares of the fund. In addition, today some investors who had previously purchased shares decide to sell those shares back to the fund, resulting in $6 million in redemptions in the fund. In this example, the stock mutual fund has a net difference of $4 million of new money that its portfolio managers will invest.

On some days, the value of redemptions may exceed the value of new shares purchased. Mutual fund managers typically maintain a small portion of the fund's portfolio in the form of cash or marketable securities so that they have sufficient liquidity when redemptions exceed new share purchases. Otherwise, they could sell some stocks in their portfolio to obtain the necessary money for redemptions.

closed-end funds
Mutual funds that sell shares to investors but do not repurchase them; instead fund shares are purchased and sold on stock exchanges.

premium
The amount by which a closed-end fund's share price in the secondary market is above the fund's NAV.

discount
The amount by which a closed-end fund's share price in the secondary market is below the fund's NAV.

Closed-end funds issue shares to investors when the funds are first created, but do not repurchase shares from investors. Unlike an open-end fund, shares of a closed-end fund are purchased and sold on stock exchanges. Thus, the fund does not sell new shares upon demand to investors and does not allow investors to redeem shares. The market price per share is determined by the demand for shares versus the supply of shares that are being sold. The price per share of a closed-end fund can differ from the fund's NAV per share. A closed-end fund's share price may exhibit a **premium** (above the NAV) in some periods and a **discount** (below the NAV) in other periods.

Load versus No-Load Funds

no-load mutual funds
Funds that sell directly to investors and do not charge a fee.

load mutual funds
Funds whose shares are sold by a stockbroker who charges a fee (or load) for the transaction.

Open-end mutual funds can be either load funds or no-load funds. **No-load mutual funds** sell directly to investors and do not charge a fee. Conversely, **load mutual funds** charge a fee (or load) when you purchase them. In most cases, the fee goes to stockbrokers who execute transactions for investors in load mutual funds. Since no-load funds do not pay a fee to brokers, brokers are less likely to recommend them to investors.

Investors should recognize the impact of loads on their investment performance. In some cases, the difference in loads is the reason one mutual fund outperforms another.

Example

You have $5,000 to invest in a mutual fund. You have a choice of investing in a no-load fund by sending your investment directly to the fund or purchasing a mutual fund that has an 8 percent load and has been recommended by a broker. Each fund has an NAV of $20 per share, and their stock portfolios are very similar. You expect each fund's NAV will be $22 at the end of the year, which would represent a 10 percent return from the prevailing NAV of $20 per share (assuming there are no dividends or capital gain distributions over the year). You plan to sell the mutual fund in one year. If the NAVs change as expected, your return for each fund will be as shown in Exhibit 14.1.

Exhibit 14.1   Comparison of Returns from a No-Load Fund and a Load Fund

No-Load Fund

Invest $5,000 in the mutual fund.	$5,000
Your investment converts to 250 shares.	− __ $0__
	$5,000
	÷ __ $20__
$5,000/$20 per share = 250 shares.	250 shares
End of Year 1: You redeem shares for $22 per share.	× __ $22__
Amount received = 250 shares × $22 = $5,500.	$5,500
	− $5,000
	$500
	÷ $5,000
Return = ($5,500 − $5,000)/$5,000 = 10%	= 10%

Load Fund

Invest $5,000; 8% of $5,000 (or $400) goes to the broker.	$5,000 − __ $400__
The remaining 92% of $5,000 (or $4,600) is used to purchase 230 shares.	$4,600 ÷ __ $20__
$4,600/$20 per share = 230 shares.	230 shares
You redeem shares for $22 per share.	× __ $22__
Amount received = 230 shares × $22 = $5,060.	$5,060
	− $5,000
	$60
	÷ $5,000
Return = ($5,060 − $5,000)/$5,000 = 1.2%	= 1.2%

Notice that you would earn a return of 10 percent on the no-load fund versus only 1.2 percent on the load fund. While the load fund's portfolio generated a 10 percent return, you would earn only a small return because of the substantial $400 load fee: the portfolio would earn slightly more than the fee charged to buy the fund.

Based on this analysis, you decide to purchase shares of the no-load fund. If you invest funds for a longer period of time, the fee may not seem so significant. However your funds will need to remain in the fund, meaning you have less liquidity.

Studies on mutual funds have found that no-load funds perform at least as well as load funds on average, even when ignoring the fees paid on a load fund. When considering the fee paid on load funds, no-load funds have outperformed load funds, on average.

So why do some investors purchase load funds? They may believe that specific load funds will generate high returns and outperform other no-load funds, even after considering the fee that is charged. Or perhaps some investors who rely on their brokers for advice do not consider no-load funds. Some investors may purchase load funds because they do not realize that there are no-load funds or do not know how to invest in them. To invest in no-load funds, you can simply call an 800 number for an application or print it off a fund's Web site.

Expense Ratios

expense ratio
The annual expenses per share divided by the net asset value of a mutual fund.

As mentioned earlier in this chapter, mutual funds incur expenses, including administrative, legal, and clerical expenses and portfolio management fees. Some mutual funds have much higher expenses than others. These expenses are incurred by the fund's shareholders because the fund's NAV (which is what investors receive when redeeming their shares) accounts for the expenses incurred. Investors should review the annual expenses of any mutual funds in which they invest. In particular, they should focus on the fund's **expense ratio**, which measures the annual expenses per share divided by the NAV of the fund. An expense ratio of 1 percent means that shareholders incur annual expenses amounting to 1 percent of the value of the fund. The higher the expense ratio, the lower the return for a given level of portfolio performance. Mutual funds that incur more expenses are worthwhile only if they offer a high enough return to offset the extra expenses.

On average, mutual funds have an expense ratio of about 1.5 percent. The expense ratios of mutual funds can be found in various financial newspapers and on many financial Web sites.

Research has shown that mutual funds with similar objectives that incur lower expenses tend to outperform others. This finding suggests that the mutual funds with higher expenses cannot justify them.

TYPES OF MUTUAL FUNDS

Investors can select from a wide array of mutual funds, including both stock mutual funds and bond mutual funds. Each category includes many types of funds to suit the preferences of individual investors.

Types of Stock Mutual Funds

Open-end stock mutual funds are commonly classified according to their investment objectives. If you consider investing in a stock mutual fund, you must decide on the type of fund in which you wish to invest. Some of the more common investment objectives are described here.

growth funds
Mutual funds that focus on stocks that have potential for above-average growth.

Growth Funds. **Growth funds** focus on stocks that have potential for above-average growth.

capital appreciation funds
Mutual funds that focus on stocks that are expected to grow at a very high rate.

Capital Appreciation Funds. **Capital appreciation funds** focus on stocks that are expected to grow at a very high rate. These firms tend to pay low or no dividends so that they can reinvest all of their earnings to expand.

small capitalization (small-cap) funds
Mutual funds that focus on firms that are relatively small.

Small Capitalization (Small-Cap) Funds. **Small capitalization (small-cap) funds** focus on firms that are relatively small. Small-cap funds and capital appreciation funds overlap somewhat because smaller firms tend to have more potential for growth than larger firms.

mid-size capitalization (mid-cap) funds
Mutual funds that focus on medium-size firms.

Mid-Size Capitalization (Mid-Cap) Funds. **Mid-size capitalization (mid-cap) funds** focus on medium-size firms. These firms tend to be more established than small-cap firms, but may have less growth potential.

equity income funds
Mutual funds that focus on firms that pay a high level of dividends.

Equity Income Funds. **Equity income funds** focus on firms that pay a high level of dividends. These firms tend to exhibit less growth because they use a relatively large portion of their earnings to pay dividends rather than reinvesting earnings for expansion. The firms normally have less potential for high returns and exhibit less risk.

balanced growth and income funds
Mutual funds that contain both growth stocks and stocks that pay high dividends.

Balanced Growth and Income Funds. **Balanced growth and income funds** contain both growth stocks and stocks that pay high dividends. This type of fund distributes dividends periodically, while offering more potential for an increase in the fund's value than an equity income fund.

sector funds
Mutual funds that focus on a specific industry or sector, such as technology stocks.

Sector Funds. **Sector funds** focus on stocks in a specific industry or sector, such as technology stocks. Investors who expect a specific industry to perform well may invest in a sector fund. Sector funds enable investors with a small amount of funds to invest in a diversified portfolio of stocks within a particular sector.

Internet funds
Mutual funds that focus on stocks of Internet-based firms and therefore represent a particular type of sector fund.

index funds
Mutual funds that attempt to mirror the movements of an existing stock index.

Internet Funds. **Internet funds** focus on stocks of Internet-based firms and therefore represent a particular type of sector fund. Most of these firms are relatively young. They have potential for very high returns, but also exhibit a high degree of risk because they do not have a consistent record of strong performance.

Index Funds. **Index funds** are mutual funds that attempt to mirror the movements of an existing stock index. Investors who invest in an index fund should earn returns similar to what they would receive if they actually invested in the index. For example, Vanguard offers a mutual fund containing a set of stocks that moves in the same manner as the S&P 500 index. It may not contain every stock in the index, but it is still able to mimic the index's movement. Since the S&P 500 index includes only very large stocks, an S&P 500 index fund does not necessarily move in tandem with the entire stock market.

Other index funds mimic broader indexes such as the Wilshire 5000 for investors who want an index that represents the entire stock market. In addition, there are small capitalization index funds that are intended to mirror movements in the small-cap index. Other index funds mimic foreign stock indexes, such as a European index and a Pacific Basin index. Thus, investors who want to invest in a particular country, but do not want to incur excessive expenses associated with foreign stock exchanges, can invest in an index fund targeted to that country.

Index funds have become very popular because of their performance relative to other mutual funds. They incur less expenses than a typical mutual fund because they are not actively managed. The index fund does not incur expenses for researching various stocks because it is intended simply to mimic an index. In addition, the fund's portfolio is not frequently revised because its goal is to invest in a stock portfolio that mimics a specific stock index. Consequently, index funds incur very low transaction costs, which can enhance performance. Some index funds have expense ratios of between 0.20 and 0.30 percent, which is substantially lower than the expense ratios of most other mutual funds.

Index funds can also offer tax advantages because they do not engage in much trading and therefore do not generate capital gains. Mutual funds that frequently revise their portfolios create capital gains on the stocks that have appreciated in value. They must distribute their capital gains to shareholders in the year that the gains occur. Since index funds do not experience such capital gains or losses, investors are not subject to capital gains taxes until they sell their shares of the index fund. Thus, any appreciation in the stock prices can benefit investors because it increases the NAV of the fund without subjecting the investors to taxes.

Much research has found that the performance of portfolios managed by portfolio managers is frequently lower than the performance of an exist-

ing stock index. Thus, investors may be better off investing in an index fund
rather than investing in an actively managed portfolio.

Example

You consider investing in either a no-load mutual fund that
focuses on growth stocks or an index mutual fund. When ignoring expenses incurred by the mutual funds, you expect that
the growth fund will generate an annual return of 9 percent
versus an annual return of 8 percent for the index fund. The
growth fund has an expense ratio of 1.5 percent, versus an expense ratio
of 0.2 percent for the index fund. Based on your expectations about the
portfolio returns, your returns would be:

	Growth Fund	Index Fund
Fund's portfolio return (excludes expenses)	9.0%	8.0%
Expense ratio	1.5%	0.2%
Your annual return	7.5%	7.8%

The comparison shows that the index fund can generate a higher return
for you than the other fund even if its portfolio return is lower. Based on this
analysis, you should invest in the index fund.

14.1   Financial Planning Online: Index Mutual Funds

Go to:
http://www.indexfunds.com/

This Web site provides:
news and other information
about index mutual funds that
can guide your investment
decisions.

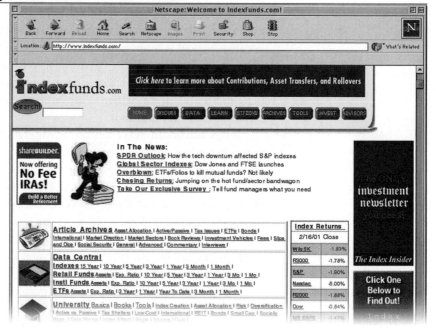

Some index funds have expense ratios that are 1.25 percent or higher, even though their portfolio management expenses are low. Therefore, investors who invest in index funds because of their low expense ratios should ensure that the expense ratio is low before selecting a fund.

international stock funds
Mutual funds that focus on firms that are based outside the United States.

International Stock Funds. **International stock funds** focus on firms that are based outside the United States. Some of these funds focus on firms in a specific country, while others focus on a specific region or continent. Many of these funds require a minimum investment of $1,000 to $2,500, but a few require only $500. Funds with a country or regional concentration are attractive to investors who want to invest in a specific country, but prefer to rely on an experienced portfolio manager to select the stocks. The expenses associated with managing a portfolio are higher for international mutual funds than for other mutual funds, because monitoring foreign firms from the United States is expensive. In addition, transaction costs from buying and selling stocks of foreign firms are higher. Nevertheless, many international stock funds have expense ratios that are less than 1.8 percent.

Some mutual funds invest in stocks of both foreign firms and U.S. firms. These are called "global mutual funds" to distinguish them from international mutual funds.

socially responsible stock funds
Mutual funds that screen out firms viewed as offensive by some.

Socially Responsible Stock Funds. **Socially responsible stock funds** screen out firms viewed as offensive by some investors. For example, they may not invest in firms that produce cigarettes or guns or that pollute the environment.

Other Types of Stock Funds. The types of mutual funds described here can be further subdivided, as funds have proliferated to satisfy the preferences of investors. As an example, some growth stock funds focus on small firms while others concentrate on large firms. Investors who desire large firms that are expected to grow would consider investing in large-cap growth funds. Investors who desire small firms that are expected to grow would consider investing in small-cap growth funds.

Treasury bond funds
Mutual funds that focus on investments in Treasury bonds.

Types of Bond Mutual Funds

Investors can also select a bond fund that satisfies their investment objectives. The more popular types of bond funds are identified here.

Treasury Bond Funds. **Treasury bond funds** focus on investments in Treasury bonds. Recall that these bonds are backed by the federal government, so they are free from default risk.

Ginnie Mae funds
Mutual funds that invest in bonds issued by the Government National Mortgage Association.

Ginnie Mae Funds. **Ginnie Mae funds** invest in bonds issued by the Government National Mortgage Association. These bonds have a low degree of default risk because they are issued by a government agency.

corporate bond funds
Mutual funds that focus on bonds issued by high-quality firms that tend to have a low degree of default risk.

Corporate Bond Funds. **Corporate bond funds** focus on bonds issued by high-quality firms. Thus, they tend to have a low degree of default risk.

high-yield (junk) bond funds
Mutual funds that focus on relatively risky bonds issued by firms that are subject to default risk.

municipal bond funds
Mutual funds that invest in municipal bonds.

index bond funds
Mutual funds that are intended to mimic the performance of a specified bond index.

international bond funds
Mutual funds that focus on bonds issued by non-U.S. firms or governments.

global bond funds
Mutual funds that invest in foreign bonds as well as U.S. bonds.

High-Yield (Junk) Bond Funds. **High-yield (junk) bond funds** focus on relatively risky bonds issued by firms that are subject to default risk. These bond funds tend to offer a higher expected return than corporate bond funds, however, because of the high yields offered to compensate for the high default risk.

Municipal Bond Funds. **Municipal bond funds** invest in municipal bonds. Recall from Chapter 13 that the interest income on these bonds is exempt from federal taxes. Consequently, municipal bond funds are attractive to investors who are in high income tax brackets.

Index Bond Funds. **Index bond funds** are intended to mimic the performance of a specified bond index. For example, Vanguard offers four different bond index funds:

- A total bond index fund that tracks an aggregate (broad) bond index.

- A short-term bond index fund that tracks an index representing bonds with one to five years until maturity.

- An intermediate bond index fund that tracks an index representing bonds with 5 to 10 years to maturity.

- A long-term bond fund that tracks an index representing bonds with 15 to 25 years until maturity.

International Bond Funds. **International bond funds** focus on bonds issued by non-U.S. firms or governments. Some international bonds are attractive to U.S. investors because they offer a higher yield than is offered on U.S. bonds. They are subject to exchange rate risk. If the currency denominating foreign bonds weakens against the dollar, the value of foreign bonds is reduced, and the international bond fund's performance is adversely affected. Also, expenses incurred by international bond funds tend to be higher than those of domestic bond funds because of costs associated with international transactions.

Some bond funds focus on investments within a specific country or region. These funds are attractive to investors who want to invest in a foreign country but do not want to select the bonds themselves. Some bond funds invest in both foreign bonds and U.S. bonds. They are referred to as **global bond funds** to distinguish them from the international bond funds that concentrate solely on non-U.S. bonds.

Like other bond funds, international and global bond funds are exposed to interest rate risk. Foreign bond prices are influenced by the interest rate of the currency denominating the bond in the same way that U.S. bond prices are influenced by U.S. interest rate movements. When the interest rate of the currency denominating the bonds increases, bond prices decline. Conversely, when the interest rate of the currency decreases, prices of bonds denominated in that currency increase.

Maturity Classifications. Each type of bond fund can be segmented further by the range of maturities. For example, some Treasury bond funds are classified as medium term (8–12 years) or long term (20–30 years). Other bond funds are also segmented in this manner.

RETURN AND RISK OF A MUTUAL FUND

Investors purchase shares of a mutual fund so that they can receive a reasonable return on their investment. However, they must balance the expected return with the fund's risk, which reflects the uncertainty surrounding the expected return. Before you purchase a mutual fund, you should set your objectives in terms of expected return and the risk you can tolerate.

Return from Investing in a Mutual Fund

A mutual fund can generate returns for its investors (shareholders) in three different ways: dividend distributions, capital gain distributions, and capital gain distributions from redeeming shares.

Dividend Distributions. A mutual fund that receives dividend payments must distribute those dividends to its investors in the same year. Mutual funds normally allow their investors to choose whether to receive dividends in the form of a cash payment or as additional shares (which means the dividends are reinvested to buy more shares of the fund). Regardless of the form of the distribution, the investors who receive these dividends are taxed at their respective ordinary income tax rates.

Capital Gain Distributions. A mutual fund that realizes capital gains as a result of selling shares of stocks or bonds must distribute those capital gains to its investors in the same year. As with dividend distributions, mutual funds normally allow investors to choose whether to receive capital gains in the form of a cash payment or as additional shares (which means the amount of the capital gains is reinvested to buy more shares of the fund). Distributions of long-term capital gains are taxed at the long-term capital gains rate.

Given the differences in tax rates for dividends and long-term capital gains, investors in high tax brackets will normally achieve higher performance by selecting mutual funds that generate long-term capital gains rather than dividends.

Example

You invest in an equity income mutual fund focused on large, well-established stocks that pay high dividends. You also invest in a growth mutual fund focused on young firms that are attempting to expand and therefore do not pay any dividends.

You are curious about your tax liabilities on distributions from these two investments. The equity income mutual fund distributes $1,000 of dividends over the year, while the growth mutual fund distributes $1,000 of long-term capital gains. Your marginal tax rate on ordinary income is about 40 percent. The prevailing capital gains tax rate is 20 percent.

Given this information, the taxes on the distributions are as follows:

Tax on Dividend Distribution = Amount of Dividend Distribution
    × Marginal Income Tax Rate
    = $1,000 × .40
    = $400.

Tax on Long-Term Capital Gain Distribution = Amount of Capital Gain Distribution
    × Long-Term Capital Gains Tax Rate
    = $1,000 × .20
    = $200.

Even though the funds distributed the same amount to you, your taxes on the long-term capital gains distribution are $200 lower. Thus, your after-tax income from that fund is $200 higher than your income from the other fund, as shown in Exhibit 14.2.

Exhibit 14.2   Potential Tax Implications from Investing in Mutual Funds

	Mutual Fund Focused on Large Stocks	Mutual Fund Focused on Small Stocks
Dividends	$1,000	$0
Capital gains	0	1,000
Total income	$1,000	$1,000
Tax on dividends (40%)	$400	$0
Tax on capital gains (20%)	0	200
Total taxes	$400	$200
After-tax income	$600	$800

As the above example illustrates, individuals in higher tax brackets can reduce their tax liability by investing in mutual funds with low dividend distributions.

Capital Gain from Redeeming Shares. You earn a capital gain if you redeem shares of a mutual fund when the share price exceeds the price at which you purchased the shares. For example, if you purchase 200 shares of a stock mutual fund at a price of $25 per share and sell the shares for $30, your capital gain will be:

interest rate risk
For a bond mutual fund, its susceptibility to interest rate movements.

Internet fund) has potential for a very high return, but also exhibits high risk. A fund that invests in growth stocks of small firms in a small foreign country has even more potential return and risk.

Risk from Investing in a Bond Mutual Fund

Although different types of bond mutual funds will experience different performance levels in a given time period, they are all influenced by general bond market conditions. The performance of a bond mutual fund is dependent on the general movements in interest rates. When interest rates rise, prices of bonds held by a bond fund decrease, and the NAV of the fund declines. This susceptibility to interest rate movements is often referred to as **interest rate risk.**

The prices of all bonds change in response to interest rate movements, but the prices of longer-term bonds are the most sensitive, as discussed in Chapter 13. Thus, investors who want to reduce exposure to interest rate movements can select a bond fund focusing on bonds with short terms to maturity. Conversely, investors who want to capitalize on an expected decline in interest rate movements can select a bond fund that focuses on long-term bonds.

The performance of many bond mutual funds is also dependent on the default risk of the individual bond holdings. Bond funds that invest most of their money in bonds with a high degree of default risk tend to offer a

Exhibit 14.4   Tradeoff between Expected Return and Risk

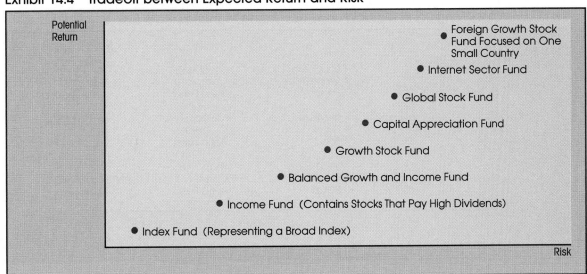

higher potential return to investors, but also exhibit a high degree of risk. Under favorable economic conditions, the issuers of those bonds may be able to cover their payments, and these bond funds will consequently perform very well. If economic conditions are weak, however, some of the bond issuers may default on their payments, and these bond funds will provide relatively low or even negative returns to their shareholders.

The exposure of a bond fund to default risk is independent of its exposure to interest rate risk, as illustrated in Exhibit 14.5. Some bond funds, such as long-term Treasury bond funds and long-term Ginnie Mae bond funds, have no (or low) default risk and a high level of interest rate risk. Other bond funds, such as short-term high-yield bond funds, have a low level of interest rate risk and a high level of default risk. Some bond funds, such as long-term high-yield bond funds, are highly exposed to both default risk and interest rate risk.

Tradeoff between Expected Return and Risk of Bond Funds

The tradeoff between the expected return and the risk of a bond mutual fund is shown in Exhibit 14.6. On the conservative side, a Treasury bond fund that holds Treasury bonds with a short term remaining until maturity has no exposure to default risk and limited exposure to interest rate risk. Thus, the prices of the bonds it holds are not very sensitive to external forces, so the NAV of the fund will not be very sensitive to these forces. The expected return on this fund is relatively low, however. An intermediate-term Ginnie Mae bond fund offers the potential for a higher return. Its bonds have a slight degree of default risk, however, and the intermediate

Exhibit 14.5   Classifying Bond Mutual Funds according to Interest Rate Risk and Default Risk

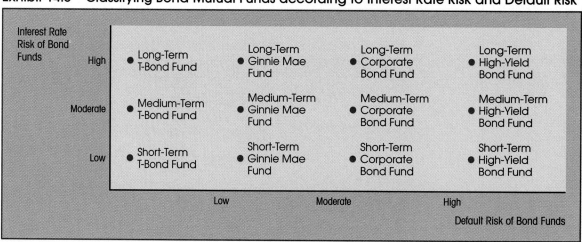

14.3 Financial Planning Online: High-Performing Bond Mutual Funds

Go to:
http://biz.yahoo.com/p/tops/
fixed.html

This Web site provides:
a list of the bond mutual funds
that achieved the highest performance recently. You can
click on "Profile" next to the
bond mutual fund for which
you want more information, or
click on "Chart" to review the
recent trend in its NAV, or click
on "News" to review updated
articles about that fund. You
may want to consider this
information when you are
ready to invest in a bond
mutual fund.

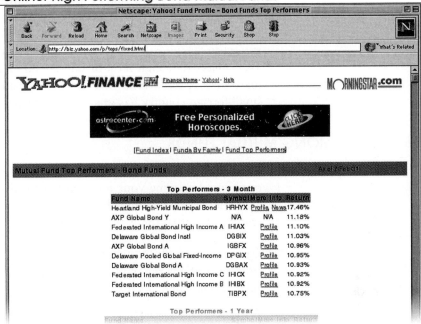

Top Performers - 3 Month

Fund Name	Symbol	More Info	Return
Heartland High-Yield Municipal Bond	HRHYX	Profile, News	17.46%
AXP Global Bond Y	N/A	N/A	11.18%
Federated International High Income A	IHIAX	Profile	11.10%
Delaware Global Bond Instl	DGBIX	Profile	11.03%
AXP Global Bond A	IGBFX	Profile	10.96%
Delaware Pooled Global Fixed-Income	DPGIX	Profile	10.95%
Delaware Global Bond A	DGBAX	Profile	10.93%
Federated International High Income C	IHICX	Profile	10.92%
Federated International High Income B	IHIBX	Profile	10.92%
Target International Bond	TIBPX	Profile	10.75%

Top Performers - 1 Year

Exhibit 14.6 Tradeoff between Expected Return and Risk of Bond Mutual Funds

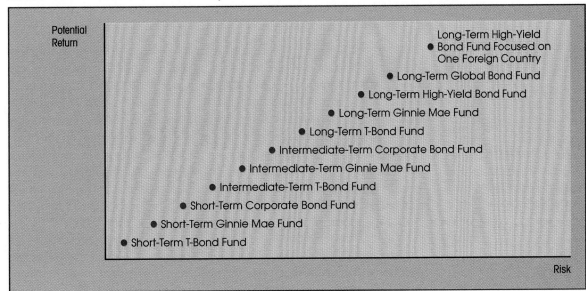

Potential Return

Long-Term High-Yield
● Bond Fund Focused on
One Foreign Country

● Long-Term Global Bond Fund

● Long-Term High-Yield Bond Fund

● Long-Term Ginnie Mae Fund

● Long-Term T-Bond Fund

● Intermediate-Term Corporate Bond Fund

● Intermediate-Term Ginnie Mae Fund

● Intermediate-Term T-Bond Fund

● Short-Term Corporate Bond Fund

● Short-Term Ginnie Mae Fund

● Short-Term T-Bond Fund

Risk

term to maturity causes more exposure to interest rate risk than short terms to maturity. A high-yield bond fund that invests only in junk bonds with long terms to maturity has the potential for a very high return. Its value is subject to default risk, however, because the junk bonds could default. It is also subject to a high level of interest rate risk because of the long-term maturities. A bond fund that invests in bonds issued by risky firms in a small foreign country has even more potential return and risk.

DECIDING AMONG MUTUAL FUNDS

Your decision to purchase shares of a specific mutual fund should be made once you determine your investment objectives, evaluate your risk toler-ance, and decide the fund characteristics that you want. The final step is to search for mutual funds that exhibit those desired characteristics.

Determining Your Preferred Characteristics of a Mutual Fund

When identifying the type of mutual fund you want, you will want to con-sider various fund characteristics.

Minimum Initial Investment. If you have a relatively small amount to invest (such as $1,000), you should limit your choices to mutual funds whose ini-tial investment is equal to or below that level.

Investment Objective (Type of Fund). You must identify your investment goals. First, determine whether you are interested in a stock mutual fund or a bond mutual fund. If you want your investment to have high potential for increasing in value over time, you should consider capital appreciation funds. If you want periodic income, you should consider bond funds. Once you select a stock fund or a bond fund, you should select the particular type of fund that will match your investment objective. Funds vary according to their potential return and their risk, as mentioned earlier.

prospectus
A document that provides finan-cial information about a mutual fund, including expenses and past performance.

Investment Company. Whatever your investment objective, there are probably many investment companies that offer a suitable fund. One way to choose an investment company is by assessing the past performance of the type of mutual funds you are considering. Past performance is not necessarily a good indicator of future performance, however. A better approach may be to compare fees and expenses charged by investment companies on the funds you are considering. You may want to screen your list of funds by removing the load funds from consideration. In addition, you should compare the funds' expense ratios, since some investment companies charge much lower expenses than others.

Reviewing a Mutual Fund's Prospectus

For any mutual fund that you consider, you should obtain a **prospectus**, which is a document that provides financial information about the fund, including expenses and past performance. You can order the prospectus from the mutual fund company over the phone, by e-mail, or over the Internet in some cases. In fact, you may be able to download the prospectus from the Internet. The prospectus contains considerable information, as described in the next paragraphs.

investment objective
In a prospectus, a brief statement about the general goal of the mutual fund.

Investment Objective. The **investment objective** is a brief statement about the general goal of the fund, such as capital appreciation (increase in value) of stocks or achieving returns that exceed that of the S&P 500 or some other index.

investment strategy
In a prospectus, a summary of the types of securities that are purchased by the mutual fund in order to achieve its objective.

Investment Strategy. The **investment strategy** (also called investment policy) summarizes the types of securities that are purchased by the mutual fund in order to achieve its objective. For example, a fund's investment strategy may be to focus on large stocks, technology stocks, stocks that have a high level of growth, foreign stocks, Treasury bonds, corporate bonds, or other securities.

Past Performance. The prospectus will include the return on the fund over recent periods (such as the last year, the last three years, and the last five years). The performance is normally compared to a corresponding stock index (such as the S&P 500) or bond index, which is important since performance should be based on a comparison to general market movements. A stock mutual fund that earned a 15 percent annual return would normally be rated as a high performer, but during the late 1990s such a return would have been relatively low when compared to the stock market in general. Although the past performance offers some insight into the ability of the fund's managers to select stocks, it will not necessarily persist in the future. Thus, investors should be cautious when investing in a mutual fund just because it experienced higher performance than other funds in past periods.

Fees and Expenses. The prospectus will provide a breakdown of the following fees and expenses:

- The maximum load imposed on purchases of the fund's shares.

- The redemption fee or *back-end load* (if any) imposed when investors redeem their shares.

- Expenses incurred by the fund, including management fees resulting from monitoring the fund's portfolio, distribution fees resulting from the fund's advertising costs, and marketing costs that are paid to brokers who recommend the fund to investors. A fund can be classified as a no-load fund and yet still have substantial advertising and marketing fees.

The most important expense statistic mentioned in the prospectus is the expense ratio. Since it adjusts for the size of the fund, you can compare the efficiency of various mutual funds. The expense ratio may also be converted into the actual expenses that you would be charged if you had invested a specified amount in the fund (such as $1,000). The expense ratio may be as low as 0.1 percent for some funds and more than 4.0 percent for others.

Expense ratios can change over time, so you should monitor them over time when investing in a mutual fund.

Risk. The prospectus of a stock fund typically states that the fund is subject to market risk, or the possibility of a general decline in the stock market, which can cause a decline in the value of the mutual fund. In addition, the prices of individual stocks within the fund may experience substantial declines in response to firm-specific problems. Bond funds normally mention their exposure to interest rate risk and default risk. These risks are stated so that investors understand that there is some uncertainty surrounding the future performance of the mutual fund and that the value of the mutual fund can decline over time.

Distribution of Dividends and Capital Gains. The prospectus explains how frequently the mutual fund makes distributions to investors. Most funds distribute their dividends to their shareholders on a quarterly basis and distribute their capital gains once a year (usually in December). The prospectus also describes the means by which dividends and capital gains are distributed.

14.4 Financial Planning Online: Mutual Fund Reports

Go to:
http://www.fundinfo.com

This Web site provides:
a report for a mutual fund that you specify. This report allows you to review key characteristics about the fund, including its performance and expenses.

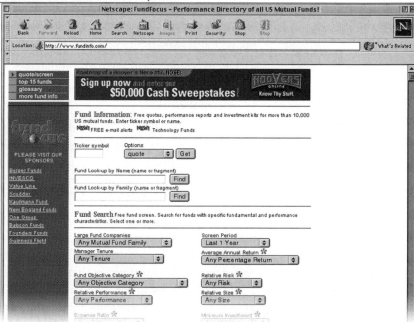

Minimum Investment and Minimum Balance. The prospectus states the minimum investment that can be made in the fund. In addition, it may require that you maintain a minimum balance, as it is costly for a fund to maintain an account that has a very small balance.

How to Buy or Redeem Shares. The prospectus explains how you can invest in the fund by sending in a check along with a completed application form (which is normally attached to the prospectus). If the mutual fund is part of a family of funds operated by a single investment company, the prospectus also explains how you can call the investment company to transfer money from one fund to another within the family. The prospectus also explains how you can sell your shares back to the mutual fund, which normally involves sending a letter asking the fund to redeem your shares.

Making the Decision

Once you have screened your list down to a small number of possible mutual funds, you can create a table to compare the important characteristics. This process will help you select the mutual fund that will best satisfy your preferences.

Example

Stephanie Spratt has $2,000 to invest. She is interested in investing in both stocks and bonds. Since she has limited funds to invest at this time, a mutual fund is an attractive option. She wants to invest in Internet stocks, but also wants to keep her expenses low. She creates a list of possible mutual funds with a minimum investment of $1,000 that would satisfy her preferences. Using a prospectus for each fund that she downloaded online, she assesses the load fee, expense ratio, and past performance, as shown here:

Internet Fund	Load Status	Expense Ratio	Recent Annual Performance
#1	No-load	1.5%	13%
#2	No-load	0.8%	12%
#3	No-load	2.0%	14%
#4	3% load	1.7%	11%

Stephanie immediately eliminates #4 because of its load and high expense ratio. She then removes #1 and #3 from consideration because of their high expense ratios. She selects #2 because it is a no-load fund and has a relatively low expense ratio. She does not place much weight on past performance in her assessment.

Stephanie also wants to invest $1,000 in a bond mutual fund. She is considering high-yield bond funds because she would like a relatively high return. Since she expects the economy to be relatively strong in the future, she believes the risk of default on high-yield bonds will be rather low. However, she is concerned about interest rate risk because she expects that interest rates may rise. She creates a list of possible high-yield bond funds that allow a very small minimum investment and evaluates information from the prospectuses:

High-Yield Bond Funds	Load Status	Expense Ratio	Typical Terms to Maturity
#1	4% load	1.0%	6–8 years
#2	No-load	0.9%	15–20 years
#3	No-load	0.8%	5–7 years
#4	No-load	1.2%	5–7 years

Stephanie eliminates #1 because it has a load. She eliminates #2 because it focuses on bonds with long terms to maturity. She removes #4 from consideration because it has a relatively high expense ratio in comparison with #3. She decides to invest in #3 because it is a no-load fund, has a low expense ratio, and its bonds have a relatively short term to maturity, which reduces the amount of interest rate risk. She also prefers bond fund #3 because it is in the same family of mutual funds as the stock mutual fund that she just selected. Thus, she can easily transfer money between these two mutual funds. Stephanie sends her completed application and a $2,000 check to the mutual fund company.

14.5   Financial Planning Online: Online Services by Mutual Funds

Go to:
http://www.vanguard.com

This Web site provides:
an example of what an investment company that manages mutual funds can provide online to its customers. You can monitor your account online and transfer money from one fund to another within the same family.

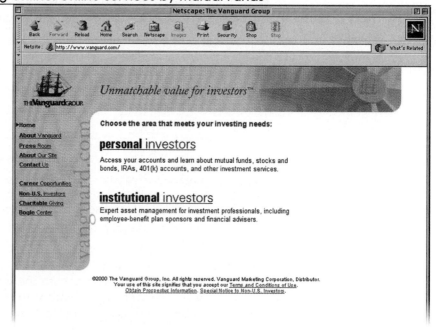

QUOTATIONS OF MUTUAL FUNDS

Financial newspapers such as the *Wall Street Journal* publish price quotations of open-end mutual funds, as shown in Exhibit 14.7. When an investment company offers several different mutual funds, its name is printed in bold, and the funds are listed below. For example, Fidelity is an investment company that offers growth funds, income funds, balance funds, international funds, and other types of funds. Each fund's NAV is shown in the second column, the net change in the NAV is shown in the third column, and the return over the year to date (YTD) is shown in the fourth column. For example, the Large Cap mutual fund highlighted in Exhibit 14.7 is within the Conseco family of funds, and its NAV is quoted as $7.93 per share, which is down by −$.50 per share from the previous trading day. This mutual fund has provided a return of −5.9 percent since the beginning of the year.

Price quotations of closed-end funds are also provided in the *Wall Street Journal*, as shown in Exhibit 14.8. These closed-end funds are listed on the exchanges where they are traded. The special listing in the *Wall Street Journal* discloses the stock exchange where the fund is traded in the second column,

Exhibit 14.7   Open-End Mutual Fund Price Quotations

NAME	NAV	NET CHG	YTD %RET	NAME	NAV	NET CHG	YTD %RET
CitGblSt	22.29	−0.59 −	2.6	**Conseco Fund Group**			
CitInc	10.34	+0.08 +	0.8	20A p	10.67	−1.09 −	9.3
Clipper	78.91	−0.34 −	0.4	20B p	10.42	−1.06 −	9.2
Clover Funds				20C p	10.46	−1.06 −	9.2
Equity	14.38	−0.40 −	2.7	20Y	10.62	−1.08 −	9.2
FixInc	9.98	+0.08 +	0.8	BalancedA p	10.88	−0.20 −	1.8
SmCpVal	15.08	−0.31 −	2.0	ConvSecA p.	11.14	−0.66 −	5.6
Cohen & Steers				ConvSecB r..	11.09	−0.65 −	5.5
♣EqIncA p	10.67	−0.05 −	0.5	ConvSecY	11.15	−0.66 −	5.6
EqIncB †	10.54	−0.05 −	0.5	EquityA p	9.36	−0.50 −	5.1
EqIncC †	10.54	−0.06 −	0.6	EquityY	9.64	−0.52 −	5.1
InstlRlty	30.68	−0.21 −	0.7	FixIncA p	10.02	+0.08 +	0.8
♣RltyShrs	43.96	−0.30 −	0.7	FixIncY	10.05	+0.07 +	0.7
SpecEqty	26.80	+0.20 +	0.8	HiYldA p	8.21	+0.01 +	0.1
Colo Bonds ..	9.38	+0.01 +	0.1	HiYldB p	8.17	+0.01 +	0.1
Columbia Funds				HiYldY	8.25	+0.01 +	0.1
Balance	22.56	−0.40 −	1.7	LargeCapA t.	7.93	−0.50 −	5.9
ComStk	23.52	−0.82 −	3.4	SciTechA p..	6.23	−0.71 −	10.2
Fixed	13.07	+0.10 +	0.8	**Copley**	41.77	−0.49 −	1.2
Grth	37.94	−2.13 −	5.3	CorePlusFxdInc	10.35	+0.08 +	0.8
HiYld	9.00	+0.02 +	0.2	**Cornerstone Funds**			
IntlStk	14.71	−0.06 −	0.4	NYMun p	0.65	+0.01 +	1.6
Muni	12.16	+0.03 +	0.2	**Country Mutual Funds**			
ReEEq	17.74	−0.15 −	0.8	Grth	23.15	−0.43 −	1.8
SmlCap	24.36	−1.51 −	5.8	LgTmBd	10.29	+0.09 +	0.9
Specl	24.41	−1.58 −	6.1	ShTmGvBd ...	10.12	+0.03 +	0.3
STBond	8.39	+0.03 +	0.4	**Credit Suisse Inst**			
ColumbPartEq	10.80	−0.52 −	4.6	IntlEq	10.85	−0.05 −	0.5
Commerce Funds				IntlGr	14.61	−0.10 −	0.7
Balanced	22.25	−0.57 −	2.5	SmCoGr	10.77	−0.92 −	7.9
Bond	18.90	+0.17 +	0.9	USCorEq	13.13	−0.38 −	2.8
Growth	26.31	−1.01 −	3.7	USCorFx	15.16	+0.10 +	0.7
IntlEq	23.03	−0.21 −	0.9	Value p	0.90	−0.02 −	2.2
MidCapGr	30.91	−2.04 −	6.2	CSI Equity r.	17.06	−0.34 −	2.0
MOTFBd	18.94	+0.05 +	0.3	CuFd Adj	9.97	+0.01 +	0.1
NatTFBd	19.15	+0.06 +	0.3	CuFdST	9.97	+0.02 +	0.2
STGovt	18.45	+0.09 +	0.5	CutlerCore	10.65	−0.21 −	1.9
Value	23.63	−0.41 −	1.7	CutlerValue	10.40	−0.08 −	0.8
Comstock Funds							
CapVal p	3.13	+0.13 +	4.3	**-D-D-D-**			
CapValB †	3.13	+0.12 +	4.0	DEM Equity .. ♣	20.07	−1.84 −	8.4
StrategyA p..	4.18	+0.10 +	2.5	DEM EqutyI p	20.35	−1.86 −	8.4
StrategyO	4.18	+0.10 +	2.5				

Exhibit 14.8   Closed-End Fund Price Quotations

Friday, March 2, 2001

Closed-end funds sell a limited number of shares and invest the proceeds in securities. Unlike open-end funds, closed-ends generally do not buy their shares back from investors who wish to cash in their holdings. Instead, fund shares trade on a stock exchange. The following list, provided by Lipper, shows the ticker symbol and exchange where each fund trades (A: American; C: Chicago; N: NYSE; O: Nasdaq; T: Toronto; z: does not trade on an exchange). The data also include the fund's most recent net asset value, share price and the percentage difference between the market price and the NAV (often called the premium or discount). For equity funds, the final column provides 52-week returns based on market prices plus dividends. For bond funds, the final column shows the past 12 months' income distributions as a percentage of the current market price. Footnotes appear after a fund's name. a: the NAV and market price are ex dividend. b: the NAV is fully diluted. c: NAV is as of Thursday's close. d: NAV is as of Wednesday's close. e: NAV assumes rights offering is fully subscribed. v: NAV is converted at the commercial Rand rate. w: Convertible Note-NAV (not market) conversion value. y: NAV and market price are in Canadian dollars. All other footnotes refer to unusual circumstances; explanations for those that appear can be found at the bottom of this list. N/A signifies that the information is not available or not applicable.

FUND NAME (SYMBOL)	STOCK EXCH	NAV	MARKET PRICE	PREM /DISC	52 WEEK MARKET RETURN
General Equity Funds					
Adams Express (ADX)	♣ N	21.11	19.40	− 8.1	−8.1
Alliance All-Mkt (AMO)	N	25.90	30.83	19.0	0.7
Avalon Capital (MIST)	O	16.85	16.37	− 2.8	6.3
Bergstrom Cap (BEM)	A	205.77	202.00	− 1.8	−5.9
Blue Chip Value Fd (BLU)	♣ N	8.16	7.77	− 4.8	11.4
Boulder Tot Rtn (BTF)	N	16.88	14.40	−14.7	63.5
Brantley Cap Corp (BBDC)	O	NA	7.93	NA	−16.5
Central Secs (CET)	A	32.30	30.21	− 6.5	12.5
Engex (EGX)	A	15.41	17.96	16.5	−58.2
Equus II (EQS)	♣ N	15.50	9.05	− 41.6	−7.3
Gabelli Equity Tr (GAB)-h	N	10.46	10.67	2.0	8.9
General American (GAM)	♣ N	36.33	35.81	− 1.4	18.3
Lbrty AllStr Eq (USA)-a	♣ N	12.33	12.90	4.6	37.0
Lbrty AllStr Gr (ASG)-a	♣ N	9.33	9.68	3.8	3.8
MFS Special Value (MFV)	N	11.00	15.25	38.6	25.5
Morgan FunShares (MFUN)-c	O	8.18	7.50	− 8.3	11.1
NAIC Growth (GRF)-c	C	11.36	11.00	− 3.2	50.9
Royce Focus Trust (FUND)	O	6.92	6.25	− 9.7	36.9
Royce Micro-Cap Tr (OTCM)	O	10.80	9.69	−10.3	14.3
Royce Value Trust (RVT)-a	N	16.87	15.75	− 6.6	27.2
SMALLCap (MGC)	♣ N	12.98	11.62	−10.5	−5.4
Salomon Brothers (SBF)-j	N	15.30	14.70	− 3.9	−10.2
Source Capital (SOR)	N	47.69	53.16	11.5	27.6
Tri-Continental (TY)	♣ N	24.59	21.68	−11.8	4.2
Zweig (ZF)	♣ N	9.28	10.09	8.7	21.5
Specialized Equity Funds					
ASA Limited (ASA)-c	N	22.48	18.20	− 19.0	2.7
C&S Realty Inc (RIF)	♣ A	7.87	7.45	− 5.3	37.2
Centrl Fd Canada (CEF)-cl	♣ A	3.40	3.10	− 8.8	−9.5
Cohen&Steers TotRet (RFI)	♣ N	12.70	12.58	− 0.9	32.5
Dundee Prec Mtls (DPM.A)-cy	T	12.45	NA	NA	NA
First Financial (FF)	N	12.91	10.90	− 15.6	50.6
Gabelli Gl MltiMed (GGT)	N	12.31	10.54	−14.4	−29.7
Gabelli Utility (GUT)	N	7.92	8.94	12.9	33.8
H&Q Health Inv (HQH)	♣ N	29.22	23.62	− 19.2	−29.4
H&Q Life Sci Inv (HQL)	♣ N	24.83	20.15	− 18.8	−39.4
INVESCO GloblHlth (GHS)	♣ N	15.72	14.65	− 6.8	−8.0
J Han Bank (BTO)	♣ N	10.07	8.14	−19.2	39.6

FUND NAME (SYMBOL)	STOCK EXCH	NAV	MARKET PRICE	PREM /DISC	52 WEEK MARKET RETURN
LCM Internet Gro (FND)	A	4.80	4.40	− 8.3	−67.3
Munder @Vantage	z	12.57	NA	NA	NS
Petroleum & Res (PEO)	♣ N	31.93	28.85	− 9.6	40.5
Seligman New Tech (N/A)	z	21.44	NA	NA	NA
Seligman New Tech II (N/A)	z	15.98	NA	NA	NS
SthEastrn Thrift (STBF)	♣ O	17.43	14.25	− 18.2	36.2
Tuxis Corp (TUX)	♣ A	13.09	12.35	− 5.7	19.3
meVC DFJ Fd I (MVC)	N	18.41	11.07	− 39.9	NS
Income & Preferred Stock Funds					
Chartwell Div&Inc (CWF)	♣ N	11.41	11.88	4.1	26.0
Delaware Div&Inc (DDF)	N	12.76	13.80	8.2	49.9
Delaware Gl Div (DGF)	N	12.78	12.95	1.3	31.4
Duff&Ph Util Inc (DNP)-a	N	10.06	10.58	5.2	32.3
J Han Pat Globl (PGD)	♣ N	13.93	12.36	− 11.3	33.1
J Han Pat Pref (PPF)	♣ N	12.95	11.80	− 8.9	25.6
J Han Pat Prm (PDF)	♣ N	10.09	9.40	− 6.8	30.1
J Han Pat Prm II (PDT)	♣ N	12.51	10.80	− 13.7	27.1
J Han Pat Sel (DIV)	♣ N	15.46	14.80	− 4.3	32.9
Preferred Inc Op (PFO)	♣ N	11.00	10.88	− 1.1	24.5
Preferred Income (PFD)	♣ N	13.81	13.82	0.1	18.5
Putnam Divd Inc (PDI)	N	10.09	9.85	− 2.4	13.6
Convertible Sec's. Funds					
Bancroft Conv (BCV)	♣ A	22.22	20.65	− 7.1	16.8
Castle Conv (CVF)	A	27.93	23.75	− 15.0	26.7
Ellsworth Conv (ECF)	♣ A	9.37	8.74	− 6.7	16.5
Gabelli Conv Sec (GCV)	N	10.45	10.25	− 1.9	27.4
Lincoln Conv (LNV)-c	♣ N	17.42	15.75	− 9.6	−11.4
Putnam Conv Opp (PCV)	N	19.78	18.95	− 4.2	10.7
Putnam Hi Inc Cv (PCF)	N	7.69	8.21	6.8	32.7
Ren Cap G&I III (RENN)	O	11.06	9.88	− 10.7	−6.5
TCW Conv Secs (CVT)	♣ N	8.07	10.60	31.3	31.6
World Equity Funds					
Argentina (AF)	N	13.82	10.70	− 22.6	−11.8
Asia Pacific (APB)	N	10.83	8.57	− 20.9	−19.8
Asia Tigers (GRR)	N	8.99	7.25	− 19.4	−28.0
Austria (OST)	♣ N	8.63	7.48	− 13.3	−47.8
Brazil (BZF)	N	22.71	17.21	− 24.2	−0.2
Brazilian Equity (BZL)	♣ N	7.61	5.88	− 22.7	−6.8
Cdn Genl Inv (CGI)-ay	♣ T	13.29	8.76	− 34.1	−13.9
Cdn Wrld Fd Ltd (CWF)-cy	♣ T	5.60	3.50	− 37.5	−41.1
Central Eur Eqty (CEE)	♣ N	15.84	12.80	− 19.2	−24.9
Chile (CH)	♣ N	11.42	8.89	− 22.2	−17.2
China (CHN)	N	12.91	10.42	− 19.3	2.8
Clemente Str Val (CLM)	N	9.93	9.15	− 7.9	−19.5
Cornerstone Strat Rtn (CRF)	N	10.99	8.50	− 22.7	−29.8
Economic Inv Tr (EVT)-cy	T	139.35	81.50	− 41.5	39.8
Emer Mkts Grow (N/A)	z	49.51	NA	NA	NA
Emer Mkts Tel (ETF)	♣ N	10.72	8.52	− 20.5	−41.0
Europe Fd (EF)	♣ N	15.60	13.74	− 11.9	−13.9
European Warrant (EWF)-c	N	9.04	8.50	− 6.0	−48.3
First Australia (IAF)	A	7.04	5.92	− 15.9	−3.6
First Israel (ISL)	♣ N	15.25	12.25	− 19.7	−18.9
First Philippine (FPF)	N	4.56	3.46	− 24.1	−29.1
France Growth (FRF)	N	10.84	9.70	− 10.5	−23.8
Germany Fund (GER)	♣ N	10.22	9.72	− 4.9	−29.2
Greater China (GCH)	♣ N	11.24	9.11	− 19.0	8.4
Herzfeld Caribb (CUBA)	O	5.08	4.13	− 18.7	−19.4
India Fund (IFN)	N	15.40	12.05	− 21.8	−37.8
India Growth (IGF)-d	N	13.91	9.79	− 29.6	−48.2
Indonesia (IF)	♣ N	1.82	2.03	11.5	−51.5
Irish Inv (IRL)	N	17.08	14.12	− 17.3	7.1
Italy (ITA)	N	11.23	10.42	− 7.2	−14.9

the NAV in the third column, and the price per share in the fourth column. The premium or discount of the closed-end fund (relative to the price) is reported in the fifth column. Consider the Royce Value Trust closed-end fund highlighted in Exhibit 14.8. Shares of this closed-end fund are traded on the New York Stock Exchange. Its NAV is quoted as $16.87 per share, while its market price is $15.75 per share. Its price has a discount of 6.6 percent relative to its NAV. It has achieved a return of 27.2 percent over the last year.

When investors want to review the performance of mutual funds for a specific investment objective, they monitor the Lipper indexes. Lipper indexes are published in the *Wall Street Journal*, as shown in Exhibit 14.9. The Lipper indexes are especially useful for assessing the recent performance of a

Exhibit 14.9   The Lipper Indexes of Mutual Funds

LIPPER INDEXES

Friday, March 2, 2001

Equity Indexes	PRELIM. CLOSE	% CHANGE PREV.		WK. AGO		SINCE Dec. 31	
Large-Cap Growth	3695.56	−	1.47	−	2.69	−	13.76
Large-Cap Core	2362.25	−	0.71	−	0.89	−	7.24
Large-Cap Value	9619.30	+	0.29	+	0.42	−	3.76
Multi-Cap Growth	3108.17	−	1.05	−	2.62	−	13.43
Multi-Cap Core	6920.46	−	0.33	−	1.16	−	6.14
Multi-Cap Value	3669.78	+	0.63	+	1.48	+	1.36
Mid-Cap Growth	695.41	−	0.59	−	3.13	−	14.36
Mid-Cap Core	551.95	+	0.34	−	0.56	−	4.95
Mid-Cap Value	737.22	+	0.80	+	0.54	+	0.32
Small-Cap Growth	511.26	+	0.00	−	2.18	−	10.31
Small-Cap Core	298.47	+	0.70	−	0.07	−	2.53
Small-Cap Value	405.52	+	0.96	+	1.22	+	4.39
Equity Income Fd	3981.49	+	0.51	+	1.12	−	2.11
Science and Tech Fd	886.42	−	2.80	−	7.20	−	19.25
Gold Fund	62.89	−	0.79	+	1.36	+	2.61
International Fund	746.96	−	0.35	+	0.22	−	6.94
Emerging Markets	72.28	−	0.58	+	0.77	+	1.99
Balanced Fund	4641.02	−	0.22	+	0.20	+	2.00
Bond Indexes							
Short Inv Grade	224.80	−	0.10	+	0.27	+	2.08
Intmdt Inv Grade	249.22	−	0.39	+	0.72	+	2.56
US Government	338.71	−	0.44	+	0.71	+	1.88
GNMA	369.62	−	0.22	+	0.39	+	1.83
Corp A-Rated Debt	891.74	−	0.39	+	0.76	+	2.61
High Current Yield	774.10	−	0.18	+	0.07	+	6.68
Global Income	218.15	−	0.08	+	1.05	+	1.38
International Income	139.88	+	0.00	+	1.45	+	0.88
Short Municipal	131.63	+	0.02	+	0.11	+	1.25
General Muni Debt	620.83	+	0.00	+	0.33	+	1.37
High Yield Municipal	285.06	+	0.03	+	0.32	+	1.40

Indexes are based on the largest funds within the same investment objective and do not include multiple share classes of similar funds. The Yardsticks table, appearing with Friday's listings, includes all funds with the same objective.
Source: Lipper Inc. The Lipper Funds Inc. are not affiliated with Lipper Inc.

Ranges for investment companies, with daily price data supplied by the National Association of Securities Dealers and performance and cost calculations by Lipper Inc. The NASD requires a mutual fund to have at least 1,000 shareholders or net assets of $25 million before being listed. NAV-Net Asset Value Detailed explanatory notes appear elsewhere on this page.

particular mutual fund. For example, consider the index of small-cap growth funds highlighted in Exhibit 14.9. The closing index level is based on the closing NAVs of the small-cap growth funds that make up the index. The index is the same since the previous day, down 2.18 percent since the previous week, and down 10.31 percent since the end of the previous year.

An investor in a small-cap growth fund may compare that fund's performance to the Lipper index of small-cap growth funds. Comparison to the proper Lipper index is more accurate than comparison to the market in general, because some differences in fund performance are attributed to characteristics of the fund. Small-cap growth funds may perform much better in one period, while income funds may perform better in another period. If a specific small-cap growth fund experiences a 6 percent annual return, its performance should still be judged favorably, if other small-cap growth funds experienced only a 2 percent annual return.

14.6   Financial Planning Online: Diversifying among Mutual Funds

Go to:

http://www.mfea.com

This Web site provides:
a recommended portfolio of different types of mutual funds that fit your financial situation and your degree of risk tolerance.

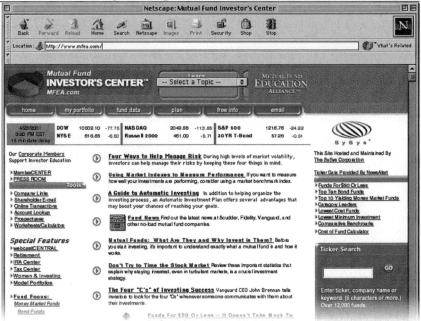

Investors also review the Lipper index quotations to compare the performance of different types of mutual funds over time. For example, you may want to compare small-cap growth funds and large-cap growth funds to determine which type of fund has been performing better lately.

DIVERSIFICATION AMONG MUTUAL FUNDS

If you plan to invest in more than one mutual fund, you may want to consider diversifying across several types of mutual funds to achieve a lower level of risk. When a stock mutual fund that contains large stocks is performing poorly, another stock mutual fund that contains small stocks may be performing well. Diversification benefits can be limited, though, since the returns of most mutual funds move in the same direction as the market. Consequently, when the stock market declines, the values of most stock mutual funds decline as well. Therefore, diversifying among stock mutual funds that invest in U.S. stocks has only limited effectiveness in reducing risk.

Diversification across bond mutual funds may result in less risk than investing in a bond fund that focuses only on long-term bonds. Virtually all bond funds are adversely affected by an increase in interest rates, however, so diversification among bond funds is not an effective means of reducing exposure to interest rate risk.

A more effective diversification strategy is to diversify across stock and bond mutual funds, as Stephanie Spratt chose to do earlier in the chapter.

Exhibit 14.10   Diversifying among Mutual Funds That Are Primarily Affected by Different Factors

Your Return from Investing in:	Is Primarily Affected by:
U.S. growth stock fund	U.S. stock market
U.S. corporate bond fund	U.S. interest rates
European stock fund	European stock markets and the value of the euro
Latin American stock fund	Latin American stock markets and the values of Latin American currencies
Australian bond fund	Australian interest rates and the value of the Australian dollar
Canadian bond fund	Canadian interest rates and the value of the Canadian dollar

mutual fund supermarket

An arrangement offered by some brokerage firms that enables investors to diversify among various mutual funds (from different mutual fund families) and to receive a summary statement for these funds on a consolidated basis.

The returns of stock mutual funds and bond mutual funds are not highly correlated, so diversifying among stock and bond funds can be effective. When U.S. stock market conditions are poor, stock funds focused on U.S. stocks will perform poorly, but the bond funds may still perform well. If U.S. interest rates rise, the bond funds may perform poorly, but the stock funds may still perform well.

You may be able to further reduce your overall risk by diversifying among mutual funds that represent different countries. International stock funds tend to be susceptible to the market conditions of the countries (or regions) where the stocks are based and to the exchange rate movements of the currencies denominating those stocks against the dollar. Thus, the returns of international stock funds are less susceptible to U.S. stock market conditions. International bonds are primarily influenced by the interest rates of their respective countries, so they are also less susceptible to U.S. interest rate movements.

Consider a strategy of investing in the portfolio of mutual funds listed in the first column of Exhibit 14.10. The primary factor that affects each mutual fund's return is shown in the second column. Notice that each fund is primarily affected by a different factor, so one adverse condition (such as a weak U.S. market) will have only a limited adverse effect on your overall portfolio of mutual funds. Any adverse conditions in a single country should affect only a mutual fund focused on that country.

Diversification through Mutual Fund Supermarkets

A **mutual fund supermarket** enables investors to diversify among various mutual funds (from different mutual fund families) and receive summary statement information for these funds on a consolidated basis. Charles Schwab created the first mutual fund supermarket. Many other brokerage firms also offer them, including National Discount Brokers and DLJdirect. One disadvantage of some mutual fund supermarkets is that they charge high fees.

You can also achieve consolidated summary statements of all of your mutual funds by selecting all of your funds from a single family. To the extent that you select funds from a fund family that has low expenses and wide offerings (such as Vanguard), you can probably invest in all of the types of mutual funds you desire and reduce the expenses that you are indirectly charged.

HOW MUTUAL FUNDS FIT WITHIN YOUR FINANCIAL PLAN

The following are the key decisions about mutual funds that should be included within your financial plan:

1. Should you consider investing in mutual funds?

2. What types of mutual funds would you invest in?

Stephanie Spratt's first concern should be maintaining adequate liquidity and being able to make her existing loan payments. As she accumulates money, however, she plans to invest in mutual funds. Exhibit 14.11 provides an example of how mutual fund decisions apply to Stephanie's financial plan.

Exhibit 14.11   How Mutual Funds Fit within Stephanie Spratt's Financial Plan

Goals for Investing in Mutual Funds

1. Determine if and how I could benefit from investing in mutual funds.
2. If I decide to invest in mutual funds, determine what types of mutual funds to invest in.

Analysis

Characteristics of Mutual Funds	Opinion
■ I can invest small amounts over time.	Necessary for me
■ Each fund focuses on a specific type of investment (growth stocks versus dividend-paying stocks, etc.).	Desirable
■ I can rely on a mutual fund manager to decide how the money should be invested.	Desirable
■ Investment is well diversified.	Desirable
■ I can withdraw money if I need to.	Necessary for me

Type of Stock Mutual Fund	Opinion
Growth	Some potential for an increase in value.
Capital appreciation	Much potential for an increase in value, but may have high risk.
Equity income	Provides dividend income, but my objective is appreciation in value.
Balanced growth and income	Not as much potential for an increase in value as some other types of funds.
Sector	May consider in some periods if I believe one sector will perform well.
Internet	Much potential for an increase in value, but may have high risk.
Index	U.S. index funds should have less risk than many other types of funds.
International	Too risky for me at this time.

Type of Bond Mutual Fund	Opinion
Treasury	Low risk, low return.
Ginnie Mae	Low risk, low return.
Corporate bond	Moderate risk, moderate return.
High-yield bond	Higher risk, higher potential return.
Municipal bond	Offers tax advantages, but my tax rate is still relatively low.
Index bond	Low risk, low return.
International bond	Higher risk, higher potential return.

Decisions

Decision on Whether to Invest in Mutual Funds:

Mutual funds would allow me to invest small amounts of money at a time, and I could rely on the fund managers to make the investment decisions. I will likely invest most of my excess money in mutual funds.

Decision of Which Mutual Funds to Consider:

At this time, I would prefer stock mutual funds that offer much potential for capital appreciation. In particular, I believe that Internet stocks should perform well because the prices of many Internet stocks have declined lately and may be bargains. However, I am

> not confident about selecting any particular Internet stocks myself and prefer to rely on a stock mutual fund manager who specializes in these stocks.
>
> I prefer the high-yield bond funds to the other bond mutual funds at this time, because they offer higher returns, and I think the risk is tolerable given the strong economy right now. My financial situation and my preferences may change, so I may switch to other types of mutual funds. I will always select a specific mutual fund that not only achieves my investment objective, but is a no-load fund and has a relatively low expense ratio.

DISCUSSION QUESTIONS

1. How would Stephanie's mutual fund investing decisions be different if she were a single mother of two children?

2. How would Stephanie's mutual fund investing decisions be affected if she were 35 years old? If she were 50 years old?

SUMMARY

The common types of stock mutual funds include growth funds, capital appreciation funds, income funds, sector funds, and index funds. The income funds typically have a lower expected return than the other funds and a lower level of risk. The capital appreciation funds tend to have a higher potential return than the other funds and a higher level of risk.

The common types of bond mutual funds are Treasury bond funds, Ginnie Mae funds, corporate bond funds, high-yield bond funds, and index bond funds. Treasury bond funds with short maturities have low potential return and low risk. High-yield bond funds have higher potential return and high risk (because some of their bonds may default). Any bond funds that invest in long-term bonds are subject to a high level of interest rate risk.

When choosing among stock mutual funds, you should select a fund with a required initial investment that you can afford, an investment objective that satisfies your needs, and a relatively low expense ratio. The prospectus of each fund provides information on these characteristics. When choosing among bond mutual funds, you should select a fund with a required initial investment that you can afford, an investment objective that satisfies your needs, and a relatively low expense ratio.

Mutual fund quotations are provided in the *Wall Street Journal* and other business periodicals. These quotations can be used to review the prevailing prices, net asset values (NAVs), expense ratios, and other characteristics. The quotations can also be used to assess recent performance.

When diversifying among mutual funds, recognize that most stock funds are affected by general stock market conditions, while most bond funds are affected by bond market (interest rate) conditions. You can achieve more effective diversification by investing across stock and bond mutual funds. You may also consider including international stock and bond funds to achieve a greater degree of diversification.

Integrating the Key Concepts

Your decision to invest in mutual funds is not only related to your other investment decisions, but affects other parts of your financial plan. Before investing in mutual funds, you should consider your liquidity situation (Part 2), as you can sell a mutual fund when you need money. However, the value of a mutual fund may decline in some periods, and you may prefer to avoid selling the mutual fund during those periods.

The decision to invest in mutual funds should take into account your financing situation (Part 3). Pay off any personal loans before you invest in mutual funds, unless the return on the fund will exceed the interest rate incurred on the loans. If after considering your liquidity and your financing situation you still decide to invest in mutual funds, you need to decide whether the investment should be for your retirement account (Part 5). There are some tax advantages to that choice, but also some restrictions on when you have access to the money.

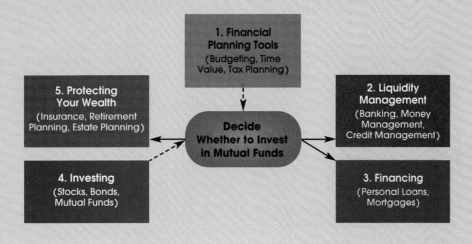

REVIEW QUESTIONS

1. What are mutual funds? What two broad categories of mutual funds exist, and how are they different? What do all mutual funds have in common?

2. List three reasons investors invest in mutual funds.

3. What is a firm's net asset value (NAV)? How is the NAV calculated and reported?

4. What is an open-end mutual fund? What types of companies usually manage open-end funds? Describe how these funds work on a day-to-day basis.

5. What is a closed-end fund? Describe how close-end funds function.

6. What is the difference between no-load mutual funds and load mutual funds? How do loads affect a fund's return? Why do some investors purchase load funds? How does an investor purchase a no-load fund?

7. Explain expense ratios for mutual funds. What kinds of expenses do mutual funds incur? How are expense ratios calculated? Why should investors pay attention to expense ratios?

8. List and briefly describe the different types of stock mutual funds.

9. Why do investors invest in index funds? Discuss the popularity of index fund investment as it relates to expenses. What tax advantage do index funds offer?

10. List and briefly describe the types of bond mutual funds.

11. Why are some U.S. investors attracted to international and global bond funds? What risk is associated with these funds that investors are not subject to when investing strictly in U.S. bond

funds? Discuss the expenses associated with international and global bond funds.

12. Describe the three ways a mutual fund can generate returns for investors.

13. Discuss risk and return as they relate to stock mutual funds. Is a fund's past performance necessarily an indicator of future performance? What type of risk affects all stock mutual funds? Describe the tradeoff between the expected return and risk of stock funds.

14. Discuss return and risk as they relate to bond mutual funds. What type of risk are all bond funds subject to? What other risk is associated with some bond funds? Describe the tradeoff between risk and the expected return from bond mutual funds.

15. What should investors consider when deciding whether to purchase shares of a mutual fund? What characteristics of a mutual fund should be considered? Briefly discuss each characteristic.

16. What is a prospectus? How does an investor obtain one? What information does a prospectus provide?

17. Once an investor has narrowed the list of possible mutual funds, what are the important characteristics to consider?

18. Where can an investor find price quotations for closed-end and open-end funds? What information will be provided in a quotation for open-end funds? What information will be provided in a quotation for closed-end funds?

19. Explain how Lipper indexes are used.

20. Discuss diversification among mutual funds. Why are the benefits of diversification sometimes limited? Describe some strategies that make diversification more effective. What is a mutual fund supermarket?

FINANCIAL PLANNING PROBLEMS

1. Hope invested $9,000 in a mutual fund at a time when the price per share was $30. The fund has a load fee of $300. How many shares did she purchase?

2. If Hope had invested the same amount of money in a no-load fund with the same price per share, how many shares could she have purchased?

3. Hope later sells her shares in the mutual fund for $37 per share. What would her return be in each of the above cases (problems 1 and 2)?

4. Mark owns a mutual fund that has an NAV of $45.00 per share and expenses of $1.45 per share. What is the expense ratio for Mark's mutual fund?

5. Rena purchased 200 shares of a no-load stock mutual fund. During the year, she received $3 per share in dividend distributions, $200 in long-term capital gains distributions, and capital gains of $1,100 when she sold the stock after owning it eight months. What are the tax consequences of Rena's ownership of this stock fund? Rena is in a 36 percent marginal tax bracket.

6. Ronnie owns 600 shares of a stock mutual fund. This year he received dividend distributions of 60 stock mutual fund shares ($40 per share) and long-term capital gains distributions of 45 stock mutual fund shares (also $40 per share). What are the tax consequences of Ronnie's stock mutual fund ownership if he is in a 28 percent marginal tax bracket?

FINANCIAL PLANNING ONLINE EXERCISES

1. Go to http://www.indexfunds.com/. Information on returns for various indexes for the previous trading session will be displayed. The information will show an increase or decrease in percentage terms of the return for the index for that trading session. To learn more about each index, click on its symbol (for example, click on 'Wils 5K,' which is the Wilshire 5000). The display will provide information on the composition of the index and its returns over various time periods.

2. Click on the Home tab on the top of the page to return to the homepage. Click on "S&P" to review information on the S&P 500 index. How do the returns for the S&P 500 compare with those for the Wilshire 5000 for corresponding periods? What is the reason for any differences?

3. Go to http://biz.yahoo.com/p/tops/usstk.html. This Web site provides a list of the stock mutual funds that achieved the highest performance over various time periods. Examine the names under each time period and see if any names appear under more than one. Why do you think the same names do not appear on all the lists? Which time period would give you more confidence in the managers of the fund? Why?

4. Scroll down the list of top-performing funds to "Top Performers—5 Year." For the first name on this list, click under "Profile." You will obtain information on the returns for this fund for various time periods, the minimum initial investment, fees and expenses, Morningstar rating, NAV, and the lead fund manager. Click on the second name on the 5-Year list by using the Back option in your browser. Compare the information on this fund with the earlier one.

5. Go to http://screen.yahoo.com/funds.html. Under Category, select Any; for Morningstar Rating, choose 4 Stars; for Minimum Initial Investment, select $1,001–2,500; for Total Expense Ratio, select 1.01% to 2%; for Net Assets, choose Any; for Turnover, choose Any; for 1 Yr Performance,

choose increased 0–25%, and for Rank in Category, select 0–10%. Click on "Find Funds." What funds meet your criteria?

6. Click on the "Profiles" of the top two funds on the list. Based on the information provided, which one would you choose? Why?

7. Go to http://www.fundclub.com. This Web site provides a listing of mutual funds that can be directly accessed to download the prospectus. Select "American Century Inv" from the Fund Family list. Download the American Century Balanced Fund prospectus. You will have to register prior to downloading. If you do not have Adobe Acrobat software, you can download this from the site. If you prefer, the fund will mail you the prospectus.

8. Use the Back option in your browser to return to the Mutual Funds Prospectuses Online page. If you prefer to use an investment objective to select a mutual fund, choose an objective, say, Capital Appreciation, under "Select Investment Objective." A list of mutual funds will be displayed. You can select one or more funds in this category for downloading.

Building Your Own Financial Plan

Mutual funds provide a relatively inexpensive investment medium for meeting many financial goals. With a relatively small investment, you can obtain diversification and receive professional management of your portfolio.

There are thousands of individual mutual funds that invest in a wide variety of portfolios ranging from very conservative bond portfolios to very aggressive options. Fortunately, various Web sites provide information free of charge to help you sort out this complex question and select mutual funds that will best meet your individual financial goals.

In this exercise, you will explore one of these Web sites and begin the process of selecting some mutual funds that will help you reach the goals you established in Chapter 1.

The Web site that we will use for this exercise is www.smartmoney.com. When you visit this Web

site, double-click on the tab marked "Funds." When the funds page comes up, note on the left a list under the heading "Tools and Research." First, go to the "Fund Portfolio Builder." You will see a list of funds below a graph covering several years. By moving the tab over each category of funds, you can see how your portfolio would have performed if you had invested in that category for the time period covered. You can also see the volatility of that category of funds. Do this for several of the categories and find two or three funds whose growth and volatility will meet the investment needs of some of your intermediate- or long-term goals, while staying within your acceptable risk tolerance limits.

Now, return to the "Main Fund" page. You will see a "Best-Worst" top 25 section. Under the "Top 25 Funds," use the pull-down menu and select the category of funds that you previously identified as meeting one or more of your intermediate- or long-term goals within your risk tolerance limits. Click on that category and hit "go." This will give you a list of the top 25 funds for the past year in that category. Select one of the funds and click on it. This will take you to a page specific to that fund. By going through the various tabs for the fund you have selected, answer the following questions and also note the other information available about your fund:

1. On the "snap-shot" tab, what is the risk-versus-return relationship for your fund?

2. On the "return" tab, how does your fund's return compare to the return for its category over various time spans?

3. On the "expense" tab, what are the expenses for your fund?

4. How do your fund's expenses compare to the expenses for this category?

5. Under the "purchase" tab, is this fund open to new investors?

6. If so, what is the minimum purchase?

7. What is the minimum subsequent purchase?

8. Under the "portfolio" tab, how long has the fund manager been in place?

After reviewing the data, does this fund appear to be one that you wish to utilize to meet one of your intermediate- or long-term goals? If so, enter it in the template provided with this chapter in the *Financial Planning Workbook* and on the CD-ROM. Continue to perform this analysis until you have found two or three funds that you can utilize to meet some of your goals.

One of the "Tools and Research" items is entitled "Fund Analyzer." This function allows you to enter your specific requirements for a fund and then produces a list of funds meeting your requirements. You may find this tool useful in your search.

The Sampsons—A Continuing Case

 Over the last month, the Sampsons have been struggling with how to invest their savings to support their children's college education. They previously considered stocks and bonds and are now being exposed to mutual funds. Dave and Sharon are now seriously considering investing their money in mutual funds. They find the prospect of relying on an investment professional's advice without having to pay for one-on-one service from a brokerage firm appealing. They are now looking to you for advice on what type of funds would be appropriate and whether they should invest their savings in one mutual fund or in several.

1. Why might mutual funds be more appropriate investments for the Sampsons than individual stocks or bonds?

2. Should the Sampsons invest their savings in mutual funds?

3. What types of mutual funds should the Sampsons consider, given their investment objective?

IN-TEXT STUDY GUIDE

True/False:

1. Mutual funds are a very popular means for investors to invest in stocks, but they are not available for bonds.

2. Portfolio managers of mutual funds typically maintain a small portion of the stock portfolios in the form of cash or marketable securities so that they have sufficient liquidity when redemptions exceed new share purchases.

3. Interest or dividends earned by an open-end mutual fund are not included in the fund's net asset value (NAV).

4. Some investors may prefer load funds to no-load funds because they believe that specific load funds will generate high returns and outperform no-load funds.

5. Research has shown that mutual funds with similar objectives that incur higher expenses tend to outperform others.

6. Ginnie Mae funds have no default risk.

7. When a mutual fund receives a capital gain as a result of selling shares of stocks or bonds whose prices have increased, it must distribute those capital gains to its investors in the same year.

8. The most important expense statistic mentioned in a mutual fund prospectus is the expense ratio, which measures all expenses as a percentage of the fund's NAV.

9. Diversification among mutual funds can achieve lower risk than investing in a single mutual fund because returns of mutual funds are perfectly correlated.

10. A mutual fund prospectus usually does not include the fund's investment strategy.

11. The NAV represents the market value of the securities in a mutual fund minus any liabilities owed by the fund.

Multiple Choice:

1. _____ mutual funds sell shares directly to investors and repurchase those shares whenever investors wish to sell them.
   a. Open-end
   b. Closed-end
   c. Discount
   d. Premium

2. The minimum investment in a mutual fund is usually between
   a. $100 and $200.
   b. $500 and $3,000.
   c. $1,000 and $5,000.
   d. $5,000 and $10,000.

3. The value of a(n) _____ fund is usually not measured by its net asset value (NAV).
   a. closed-end
   b. open-end
   c. load
   d. no-load

4. Which of the following types of mutual funds is least likely to be recommended by a broker?
   a. closed-end
   b. open-end
   c. load
   d. no-load

The following information applies to questions 5 and 6.

You just invested $10,000 in an open-end mutual fund. The NAV at the time of purchase is $30 per share. Assume the fund is available as a load fund and as a no-load fund. For the load fund, your broker charges a load of 6 percent. When you sell the fund, the NAV is $35 per share.

5. What is your return if you invested in the load fund?
   a. 9.67 percent
   b. 6.00 percent
   c. 16.67 percent
   d. none of the above

6. What is your return if you invested in the no-load fund?
   a. 9.67 percent
   b. 6.00 percent
   c. 16.67 percent
   d. none of the above

7. _____ funds focus on firms that pay a high level of dividends.
   a. Growth
   b. Equity income
   c. Balanced growth and income
   d. Sector

8. _____ funds focus on firms that are expected to grow at a very high rate.
   a. Capital appreciation
   b. Income
   c. Balanced growth and income
   d. Mid-size capitalization

9. Which of the following is not a type of bond mutual fund?
   a. Treasury bond fund
   b. Ginnie Mae fund
   c. capital appreciation fund
   d. municipal bond fund

10. _____ funds focus on relatively risky bonds issued by firms.
   a. Ginnie Mae
   b. Corporate bond
   c. High-yield (junk) bond
   d. Treasury bond

11. _____ bond funds are subject to exchange rate risk.
   a. Capital appreciation
   b. Treasury
   c. International
   d. Corporate

12. Which of the following is not a way a mutual fund can generate returns for its investors?
   a. dividend distributions
   b. capital gain distributions
   c. capital gain from redeeming shares
   d. All of the above are ways mutual funds can generate returns.

13. When a mutual fund receives dividend payments from the firms in which it invested, it must distribute those dividends to its investors
   a. in the next six months.
   b. in the same year.
   c. in the next two years.
   d. in the next three years.

14. Stock mutual funds are subject to _____ risk.
   a. market
   b. exchange rate
   c. repayment rate
   d. prepayment

15. Which of the following types of mutual funds is least susceptible to interest rate risk?
   a. Treasury bond fund
   b. municipal bond fund
   c. growth fund
   d. corporate bond fund

16. If you want your investment to have high potential for an increase in value over time, you should consider
   a. corporate bond funds.
   b. capital appreciation funds.
   c. municipal bond funds.
   d. zero-coupon bond funds.

17. The _____ is a document that provides financial information about a mutual fund.
   a. indenture
   b. debenture
   c. subordinated debenture
   d. prospectus

18. Most funds distribute their dividends to their shareholders
   a. annually.
   b. semiannually.
   c. quarterly.
   d. monthly.

19. A _____ enables investors to diversify among various mutual funds from different mutual fund families and receive summary statement information for these funds on a consolidated basis.
   a. mutual fund combination
   b. mutual fund wholesaler
   c. mutual fund supermarket
   d. mutual fund retailer

20. Typically, investors in mutual funds that engage in frequent trading will be subject to _____ if they had invested in mutual funds that do not engage in such frequent trading.
    a. higher taxes than
    b. lower taxes than
    c. the same taxes as
    d. none of the above

21. Which of the following is not a motive for investing in mutual funds?
    a. investing in a broadly diversified portfolio with a small initial investment
    b. the expertise of the portfolio managers who decide how to invest the money you provide
    c. mutual funds designed to meet specific investment goals
    d. All of the above are motives for investing in mutual funds.

Chapter # 15

Asset Allocation

Prior chapters in this part of the text focused on building your wealth by investing in stocks, bonds, and mutual funds. Now that you are familiar with each of these types of investments, you can determine how to distribute your money across financial assets. Although there is no universally applicable formula for allocating your money among investments, some general guidelines are available. Effective asset allocation can enhance your interest income and dividend income (cash inflows) and increase the value of your assets (stock and bond holdings) over time, thereby enhancing your wealth.

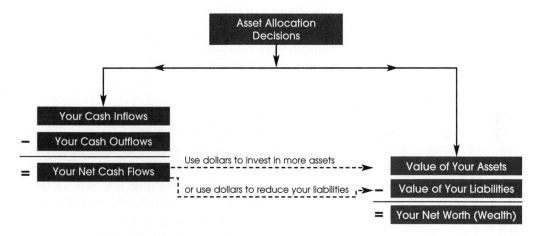

The objectives of this chapter are to:

- explain how diversification among assets can reduce risk,
- describe strategies that can be used to diversify among stocks,
- explain asset allocation strategies, and
- identify factors that affect your asset allocation decisions.

HOW DIVERSIFICATION REDUCES RISK

If you knew which investment would definitely provide the highest return for a specific investment period, investment decisions would be easy: you would invest all of your money in that particular investment. In the real world, there is a tradeoff between risk and return when investing. Although the return on some investments (such as a Treasury security or a bank CD) is known for a specific investment period, these investments offer a relatively low rate of return. Many investments such as stocks and some types of bonds offer the prospect of high rates of return, but their future return is uncertain.

As discussed in Chapter 10, the value of a stock varies over time in response to the issuing firm's performance. Since the firm's future performance

business risk
The risk that a stock invest-ment will perform poorly due to the issuing firm's management decisions.

is uncertain, so are the stock's value and the return that you will earn from investing in the stock. An individual stock is subject to **business risk,** or the risk of poor performance due to the firm's management decisions. When investors holding a firm's stock anticipate that its value will decline, they may attempt to sell the stock. Their desire to sell the stock places down-ward pressure on the price of the stock and causes a loss on investments in the stock. While some stocks are less risky than others, an investment in any individual stock is subject to the risk of a loss of 30 percent or more within a single year. Some stocks have declined more than 30 percent in value over a single day. Recall from Chapter 10 that the stocks of smaller firms are more exposed to large losses. However, even the stocks of very large and well-established firms such as Anheuser Busch, Compaq Com-puter, Rubbermaid, Hilton Hotels, Dillard Department Stores, and Eastman Kodak have experienced losses of at least 10 percent in a single day.

Benefits of Portfolio Diversification

asset allocation
The process of allocating money across financial assets (such as stocks, bonds, and mutual funds) with the objec-tive of achieving a desired return while maintaining risk at a tolerable level.

portfolio
A set of multiple investments in different assets.

Because the returns from many types of investments are uncertain, it is wise to allocate your money across various types of investments so that you are not completely dependent on any one type. **Asset allocation** is the process of allocating money across financial assets (such as stocks, bonds, and mutual funds). The objective of asset allocation is to achieve your desired return on investments while maintaining your risk at a tolerable level.

You can reduce your risk by investing in a **portfolio,** which is a set of multiple investments in different assets. By constructing a portfolio, you diversify across several investments rather than focus on a single invest-ment. A stock portfolio can reduce risk when the stocks in the portfolio do not move in perfect tandem. Even if one stock experiences very poor per-formance, the other stocks may be performing well, so there is some off-setting effect.

Example

You are considering investing in a portfolio consisting of stock A and stock B. Exhibit 15.1 illustrates the portfolio diversification effect using these two stocks. The exhibit shows the return per year for stock A and stock B, as well as for a portfolio with 50 percent of the investment allocated to stock A and 50 per-cent to stock B. The portfolio return in each year is simply the average return of stocks A and B. Notice how the portfolio's range of returns is less than the range of returns of either stock. Also, notice that the port-folio's returns are less volatile over time than the returns of the individual stocks. Since the portfolio return is an average of stocks A and B, it has a smoother trend than either individual stock. The smoother trend demon-strates that investing in the portfolio is less risky than investing in either indi-vidual stock. You decide to invest in a diversified portfolio of both stocks to reduce your risk.

Exhibit 15.1   Example of Portfolio Diversification Effects

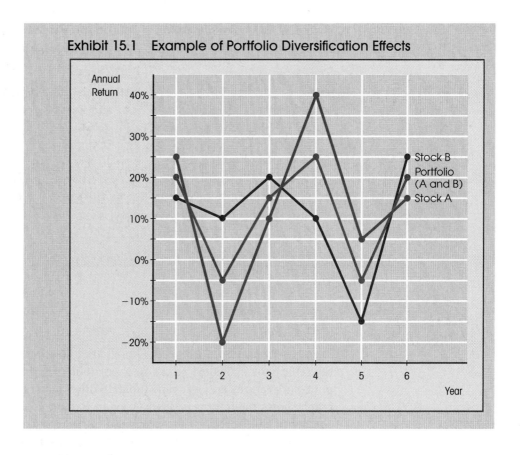

As the previous example illustrates, the main benefit of diversification is that it reduces the exposure of your investments to the adverse effects of any individual stock. In Exhibit 15.1, notice that when stock A experienced a return of −20 percent in year 2, the portfolio return was −5 percent. The adverse effects on the portfolio were limited because stock B's return was 10 percent during that year. Stock A's poor performance still affected the portfolio's performance, but less than if it had been the only stock. When stock B experienced a weak return (such as −15 percent in year 5), its poor performance was partially offset because stock A's performance was 5 percent in that year.

Factors That Influence Diversification Benefits

A portfolio's risk is often measured by its degree of volatility because the more volatile the returns are, the more uncertain the future return on the portfolio is. Some portfolios are more effective at reducing risk than others. By recognizing the factors that affect a portfolio's risk, you can ensure that your portfolio exhibits these characteristics. The volatility of a portfolio's returns is influenced by the volatility of returns on each individual stock within the portfolio and by how similar the returns are among stocks.

Exhibit 15.2   Impact of a Stock's Volatility on Portfolio Diversification Effects

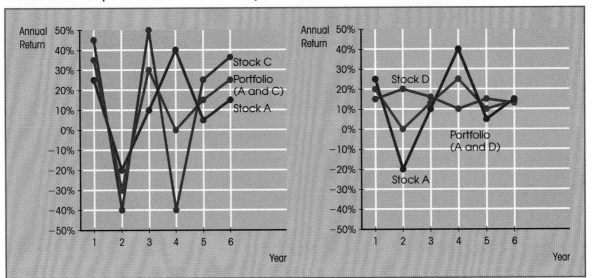

Volatility of Each Individual Stock. As Exhibit 15.2 illustrates, the more volatile the returns of individual stocks in a portfolio are, the more volatile the portfolio's returns are over time (holding other factors constant). The left graph shows the returns of stock A (as in Exhibit 15.1), stock C, and an equal-weighted portfolio of stocks A and C; the right graph shows the individual returns of stocks A and D along with the return of an equal-weighted portfolio of stocks A and D. Comparing the returns of stock C on the left with the returns of stock D on the right, it is clear that stock C is much more volatile. For this reason, the portfolio of stocks A and C (on the left) is more volatile than the portfolio of stocks A and D (on the right).

Impact of Correlations among Stocks. The more similar the returns of individual stocks in a portfolio are, the more volatile the portfolio's returns are over time. This point is illustrated in Exhibit 15.3. The left graph shows the returns of stock A, stock E, and an equal-weighted portfolio of the two stocks. Notice that the stocks have very similar return patterns. When stock A performs well, so does stock E. When stock A performs poorly, so does stock E. Consequently, the equal-weighted portfolio of stocks A and E has a return pattern that is almost identical to that of either stock A or stock E. Thus, this portfolio exhibits few diversification benefits because the returns of the two stocks in the portfolio are highly positively correlated.

The middle graph in Exhibit 15.3 shows the returns of stock A, stock F, and an equal-weighted portfolio of the two stocks. Notice that the return patterns of the stocks are opposite one another. When stock A performs well, stock F performs relatively poorly. When stock A performs poorly, stock F performs well. The returns of stocks A and F are therefore negatively correlated. Consequently, the equal-weighted portfolio of stocks A and F

Exhibit 15.3   Impact of Stock Correlations on Portfolio Diversification Effects

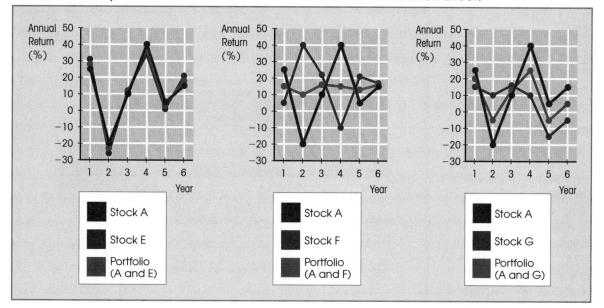

has a very stable return pattern because the returns of the stocks moved in opposite directions and therefore exhibit negative correlation. Consequently, this portfolio offers substantial diversification benefits.

The right graph in Exhibit 15.3 shows the returns of stock A, stock G, and an equal-weighted portfolio of the two stocks. Notice that the return patterns of the two stocks are independent of each other. That is, stock A's performance is not related to stock G's performance. The return pattern of the equal-weighted portfolio of stocks A and G is more volatile than the returns of the portfolio of stocks A and F (middle graph), but less volatile than the returns of the portfolio of stocks A and E (left graph). Thus, the portfolio of stocks A and G exhibits more diversification benefits than a portfolio of two stocks that are positively related, but fewer diversification benefits than a portfolio of negatively correlated stocks.

This discussion of Exhibit 15.3 suggests that when you compile a portfolio of stocks, you should avoid including stocks that exhibit a high positive correlation. Although finding stocks that are as negatively correlated as stocks A and F may be difficult, you should at least consider stocks that are somewhat independent of each other. Thus, you should consider stocks whose values are not influenced by the same conditions (such as stocks of firms in different industries).

In reality, many stocks are influenced by the same conditions as the stock market overall. For example, if economic conditions deteriorate, most stocks' performance will decline. Nevertheless, some stocks are influenced to a higher degree than others. To reduce your risk, you should select stocks whose returns exhibit a low positive correlation rather than a high positive correlation.

15.1   Financial Planning Online: Correlations among Stock Returns

Go to:
http://finance.yahoo.com/?u

This Web site provides:
a graph that shows the returns
on two stocks so that you can
determine their degree of correlation. To perform your own
comparison, insert a stock
symbol, and then click on
"Charts." Next, enter the symbol for another stock in the box
just below the chart where it
says "Compare." The returns of
the two stocks you specify will
be graphed.

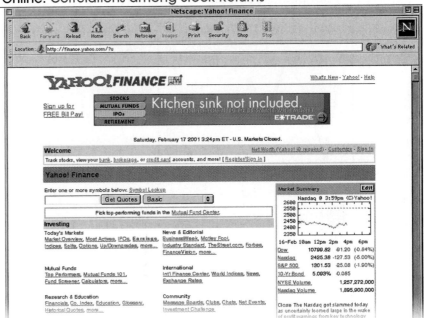

STRATEGIES FOR DIVERSIFYING AMONG STOCKS

There are many different strategies for diversifying among stocks. The most
common strategies are diversifying across industries and across countries.

Diversification of Stocks across Industries

When you diversify your investments among stocks in different industries,
you reduce your exposure to one particular industry. For example, you may
invest in the stock of a firm in the publishing and music industry, the stock
of a firm in the banking industry, the stock of a firm in the health care industry, and so on. When you diversify your investments across firms in different industries, your portfolio performance is less susceptible to the conditions within one industry. When demand for books declines, conditions
may still be favorable in the health care industry. Therefore, a portfolio of
stocks diversified across industries is less risky than a portfolio of stocks
that are all from the same industry.

The left graph in Exhibit 15.4 illustrates the diversification benefits of
a portfolio consisting of three equally weighted stocks: Amazon.com, Dell
Computer, and Disney. Each of these firms is in a different industry and
therefore is subjected to different industry conditions. Notice that Ama-
zon.com experienced very poor performance in January 1999, July 1999,
and October 1999. At least one of the other two stocks, however, did not

Exhibit 15.4   Benefits of Portfolio Diversification

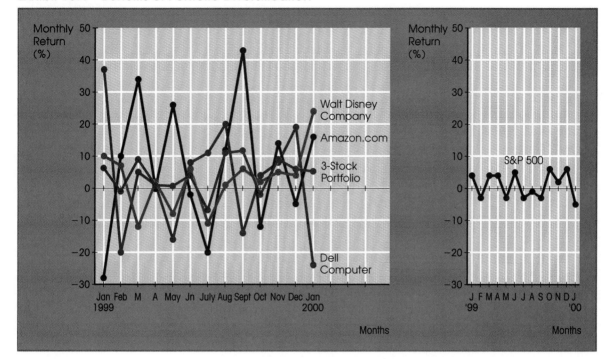

experience such poor performance in those months. Therefore, the poor performance of Amazon.com in those specific months was partially offset by the other stocks within the portfolio.

Dell Computer performed poorly in February 1999, May 1999, September 1999, and January 2000. Yet at least one of the other two stocks typically did not experience such poor performance in those months and therefore had offsetting effects. Disney experienced poor performance in March 1999, May 1999, and July 1999, but those adverse effects were offset by at least one of the other stocks in those same months.

For any single month, each stock's worst return was −28 percent for Amazon.com, −24 percent for Dell Computer, and −12 percent for Disney. Yet the worst monthly return for the portfolio was −6.7 percent (in July 1999, when two of the three stocks had poor returns). The trend of the portfolio returns, which is much more stable than the trend of any individual stocks, illustrates the diversification effects.

The diversification benefits would be even stronger for a more diversified portfolio. For example, the monthly returns from investing in 500 large U.S. stocks (the S&P 500) are illustrated in the right graph of Exhibit 15.4. This trend is more stable than the trend of returns for the three-stock portfolio in the left graph. In general, a very diversified portfolio can reduce the potential for very large losses, but can also reduce the potential for very large gains. Just as diversification buffers the large losses of a single stock, it buffers the large gains of a single stock. For example, if you had invested all of your money in Dell Computer, your return in August 1999 would have been 20 percent. Yet the return on the three-stock portfolio was only 11 percent in that month.

Although diversification among stocks in different industries is more effective than diversification within an industry, the portfolio can still be highly susceptible to general economic conditions. Stocks exhibit **market risk**, or susceptibility to poor performance because of weak stock market conditions. A stock portfolio composed of stocks of U.S. firms based in different industries may perform poorly when economic conditions in the United States are weak. Nevertheless, if stock prices overall decline by 10 percent in a given month, a well-diversified portfolio will likely not experience such a dramatic loss, whereas an individual stock may easily experience such a loss even when general stock market conditions are favorable.

market risk
A stock's susceptibility to poor performance due to weak stock market conditions.

Diversification of Stocks across Countries

Because economic conditions (and therefore stock market conditions) vary among countries, you may achieve more favorable returns by diversifying your stock investments across countries. For example, you may wish to invest in a variety of U.S. stocks across different industries, European stocks, and Asian and Latin American stocks. Many investment advisers recommend that you invest about 80 percent of your money in U.S. stocks and allocate 20 percent to foreign countries.

Diversifying among stocks based in different countries makes you less vulnerable to conditions in any one country. Economic conditions in countries can be interrelated, however. In some periods, all countries may simultaneously experience weak economic conditions, causing stocks in all countries to perform poorly at the same time. Nevertheless, this situation is less likely than the possibility of a single country experiencing weak economic conditions.

When investing in stocks outside the United States, recognize that they are typically even more volatile than U.S.-based stocks, as they are subject to more volatile economic conditions. Therefore, you should diversify among stocks within each foreign country rather than rely on a single stock in any foreign country.

Exhibit 15.5 illustrates the gains from a diversified international portfolio, with an equal weight allocated to three countries (Mexico, China, and the United States), versus the returns from country-specific portfolios. Notice that the international portfolio generates more stable returns than the U.S. portfolio. In some periods (such as May 1999), when the U.S. stock market was weak, the other markets experienced better performance, thereby offsetting the U.S. market's weak returns. In some periods (such as February 1999 and July 1999), all three markets were somewhat weak, reflecting general worldwide pessimism about stocks. In such periods, diversification benefits are limited. The potential benefits from international diversification

Exhibit 15.5   Benefits from International Stock Diversification

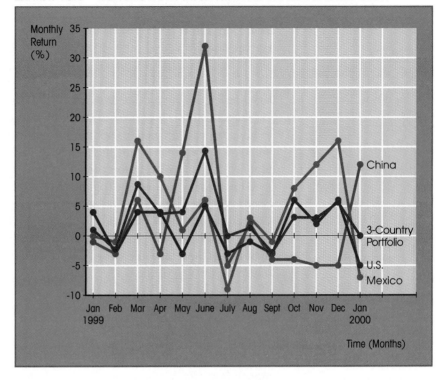

are even greater when you include more than three countries in your stock portfolio. If you want to reduce risk, though, you should not concentrate too heavily on stock markets of developing countries because they commonly exhibit very volatile returns.

ASSET ALLOCATION STRATEGIES

When investors make asset allocation decisions, they should not restrict their choices to stocks. Greater diversification benefits can be achieved by including other financial assets, such as bonds, real estate investment trusts (REITs), and stock options.

Including Bonds in the Portfolio

The returns from investing in stocks and from investing in bonds are not highly correlated. Stock prices are influenced by each firm's expected future performance and general stock market conditions. Bond prices are inversely related to interest rates and are not directly influenced by stock market conditions. Therefore, by including bonds within your portfolio, you can reduce your susceptibility to stock market conditions. The expected return on bonds is usually less than the return on stocks, however.

As you allocate more of your investment portfolio to bonds, you reduce your exposure to market risk, but increase your exposure to interest rate risk. Your portfolio is more susceptible to a decline in value when interest rates rise because the market values of your bonds will decline. Recall from Chapter 13 that you can limit your exposure to interest rate risk by investing in bonds with relatively short maturities because the prices of those bonds are less affected by interest rate movements than the prices of long-term bonds.

In general, the larger the proportion of your portfolio that is allocated to bonds, the lower will be your portfolio's overall risk (as measured by the volatility of returns). Thus, the portfolio's value will be more stable over time, and it is less likely to generate a loss in any given period. Investors who are close to retirement commonly allocate much of their portfolio to bonds because they are relying on it to provide them with periodic income. Conversely, investors who are 30 to 50 years old tend to focus their allocation on stocks. They recognize that stocks offer more upside potential than bonds, and they can afford to take risks in order to strive for a high return on their portfolio.

Real Estate Investments

real estate investment trusts (REITs)
Trusts that pool investments from individuals and use the proceeds to invest in real estate.

Many individuals include real estate investments in their portfolio. One method of investing in real estate is to purchase a home or condominium and rent it out. Doing this requires a substantial investment of time and money, however. You must conduct credit checks on prospective renters and maintain the property in good condition. An alternative is to invest in **real estate investment trusts (REITs)**, which pool investments from individuals and use the proceeds to invest in real estate. REITs commonly invest in commercial real estate such as office buildings and shopping centers.

REITs are similar to closed-end mutual funds in that their shares are traded on stock exchanges; the value of the shares is based on the interplay between the supply of shares for sale (by investors) and investor demand for the shares. REITs are popular among individual investors because the shares can be purchased with a small amount of money. For example, an investor could purchase 100 shares of a REIT priced at $30 per share for a total of $3,000 (computed as 30×100 shares). Another desirable characteristic of REITs is that they are managed by skilled real estate professionals, who decide what properties to purchase and manage the maintenance of the properties.

equity REITs
REITs that invest money directly in properties.

mortgage REITs
REITs that invest in mortgage loans that help to finance the development of properties.

Types of REITs. REITs are classified according to how they invest their money. **Equity REITs** invest money directly in properties, while **mortgage REITs** invest in mortgage loans that help to finance the development of properties. The performance of an equity REIT is based on changes in the value of its property over time, so returns are influenced by general real estate conditions. The performance of a mortgage REIT is based on the interest payments it receives from the loans it provided.

Role of REITs in Asset Allocation. Individual investors may invest in REITs to further diversify their investment portfolios. When stock market and/or bond market conditions are poor, real estate conditions may still be favorable. Thus, REITs could perform well in a period when stocks or bonds are performing poorly. Consequently, a portfolio that contains stocks, bonds, and REITs may be less susceptible to major declines because it is unlikely that all three types of investments will simultaneously perform poorly.

Stock Options

stock option
An option to purchase or sell stocks under specified conditions.

When making your asset allocation decisions, you may want to consider **stock options**, which are options to purchase or sell stocks under specified conditions. Like stocks, stock options are traded on exchanges. Stock options are a popular—and relatively complex—type of investment. Realize that an investment in stock options can be very risky. Therefore, it is important to understand them fully, so that you can invest in them wisely (if at all). Some employers include stock options in compensation packages, so you should be aware of them. Stock options are explained in detail in the appendix to this chapter.

An Affordable Way to Conduct Asset Allocation

When allocating money across a set of financial assets, you are subject to transaction fees on each investment that you make. Thus, it can be costly to invest in a wide variety of investments. You can reduce your diversification costs by investing in mutual funds. Since a typical stock mutual fund contains more than 50 stocks, you can broadly diversify by investing in a few stock mutual funds.

For example, you could invest in a mutual fund focusing on stocks of large U.S. firms, another stock mutual fund that focuses on stocks of small U.S. firms, and a third stock mutual fund that focuses on a foreign region. You could also invest in a bond mutual fund that contains the types of bonds and maturities that you desire. You may also consider investing in a REIT to diversify your portfolio even further. With this type of portfolio, you can limit your exposure to adverse conditions such as weak performance by a single firm, a single industry, a single country, or an increase in interest rates.

FACTORS THAT AFFECT THE ASSET ALLOCATION DECISION

Your ideal asset allocation will likely not be appropriate for someone else because of differences in your personal characteristics and investment goals. The asset allocation decision hinges on several factors, including your stage in life and your risk tolerance.

Your Stage in Life

Investors who are early in their career path will need easy access to funds, so they should invest in relatively safe and liquid securities, such as money

"Gee, thanks! What rate of interest does it pay?"

market investments. If you do not expect to need the invested funds in the near future, you may want to consider investing in a diversified portfolio of individual stocks, individual bonds, stock mutual funds, and bond mutual funds. Investors who expect to be working for many more years may invest in stocks of smaller firms and growth stock mutual funds, which have high growth potential. Conversely, investors nearing retirement age may allocate a larger proportion of money toward investments that will generate a fixed income, such as individual bonds, stock mutual funds containing high-dividend stocks, bond mutual funds, and some types of REITs.

Although no single asset allocation formula is suitable for everyone, the common trends in asset allocation over a lifetime are shown in Exhibit 15.6. Notice the heavy emphasis on stocks at an early stage of life, as individuals take some risk in the hope that they can increase their wealth. Over time, they gradually shift toward bonds or to stocks of stable firms that pay high dividends. The portfolio becomes less risky as it is changed to contain a higher proportion of bonds and stocks of stable firms. This portfolio is less likely to generate large returns, but it will

Exhibit 15.6   Asset Allocation over Time

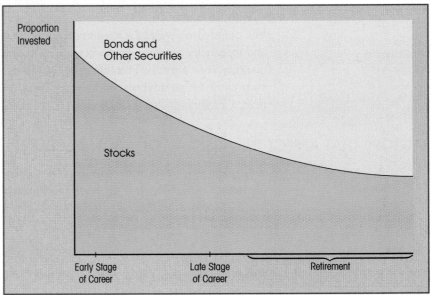

provide periodic income upon retirement. In fact, your portfolio will likely be your main source of income after you retire. (Chapter 18 discusses the role of savings in retirement planning in detail.)

Your Degree of Risk Tolerance

Investors also vary in their degree of risk tolerance. If you are unwilling to take much risk, you should focus on safe investments. For example, you might invest in Treasury bonds with relatively short maturities. Since the bonds are issued by the Treasury, they have no default risk; the focus on short maturities limits your exposure to interest rate risk.

If you are willing to accept a moderate level of risk, you may consider a stock mutual fund that represents the S&P 500 stock index and large-cap stock mutual funds that invest in stocks of very large and stable firms. These investments offer more potential return than an investment in Treasury bonds, but they may also result in losses in some periods.

If you are willing to tolerate a higher degree of risk in order to strive for higher returns, you may consider individual stocks. Smaller stocks that are focused on technology tend to have potential for high returns, but they are also very risky. Even if you can tolerate a high level of risk, you should still diversify your investments. You might consider various mutual funds that have the potential of achieving a high return, but contain a diversified set of stocks, so you are not overly exposed to a single stock. Recall from Chapter 14 that you can choose among various growth funds, capital appreciation funds, and even funds focused on Internet companies. You may also consider bond mutual funds that invest in corporate bonds. You can increase your potential return (and therefore your risk) by focusing on high-yield (junk) bond mutual funds with long terms to maturity.

Your Expectations about Economic Conditions

Your expectations about economic conditions also influence your asset allocation. If you expect strong stock market conditions, you may shift a larger proportion of your money into your stock mutual funds. Conversely, if you expect a temporary weakness in the stock market, you may shift a larger proportion of your money to your bond mutual funds. If you expect interest rates to decrease, you may consider shifting money from a bond mutual fund containing bonds with short maturities to one containing bonds with long maturities. You can easily shift money among mutual funds if the funds are part of the same family; simply call the investment company that sponsors the mutual funds, provide your account number, and request a transfer of money out of one fund and into another. You can make your request online at many of the larger investment companies.

If you anticipate favorable real estate conditions, you may allocate some of your money to REITs. As time passes, your expectations may change, causing some types of financial assets to become more desirable than others.

15.2   Financial Planning Online: Advice on Your Asset Allocation

Go to:
http://moneycentral.msn.com/
investor/calcs/assetall/main.
asp

This Web site provides:
a personal recommended
asset allocation considering
your income, your stage in life,
and other characteristics once
you input some basic information regarding your desired
return and your degree of risk
tolerance.

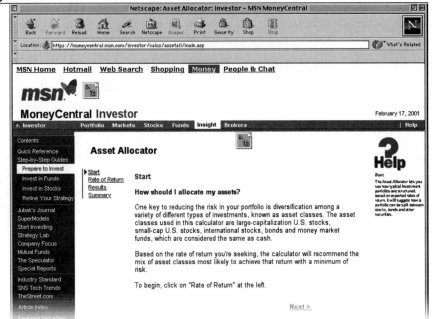

Over time, you should change the composition of your investment portfolio in response to changes in your market expectations, investment goals,
and life circumstances.

Example

Stephanie Spratt wants to develop a long-term financial plan
for allocating money to various financial assets. Specifically,
she wants to set rough goals for the proportion of money that
she will invest in stocks, bonds, and REITs over the next 10 years.
Since she just recently started her career and may be working
for another 30 years, she does not feel it is necessary to allocate a large
proportion of her money to bonds at this time. She recognizes that bonds
are typically safer than stocks, but she plans to invest in bonds only when
she believes that market conditions will cause bond prices to increase.
She decides not to impose any minimum limit on the proportion of money
allocated to bonds at this time. She recognizes that stocks are risky, but is
comfortable taking some risk at this stage in her life. She plans to consider
small stocks, some international stocks, growth stock mutual funds, and
international mutual funds.

As Stephanie accumulates more funds for investing over the next five
years, she plans to invest in various stocks or stock mutual funds. She will
invest in REITs only if her view of the real estate market throughout the
United States becomes more favorable.

In 20 years, as she nears retirement, she will still consider market conditions, but will take a more conservative investment approach that reduces

risk (and offers a lower potential return). Thus, throughout her life, Stephanie's asset allocation will be shaped by her stage in life and by her expectations about the market conditions that influence the prices of various securities.

Because it is nearly impossible to predict economic conditions, it is difficult to determine which types of investments will perform best in a given period. Consequently, you may be better off basing your asset allocation decisions completely on your stage in life and degree of risk tolerance. Then, once you establish a diversified portfolio of investments, you will need to revise the portfolio only when you enter a different stage in life or change your degree of risk tolerance.

HOW ASSET ALLOCATION FITS WITHIN YOUR FINANCIAL PLAN

The following are the key asset allocation decisions that should be included within your financial plan:

1. Is your present asset allocation of investments appropriate?

2. How will you apply asset allocation in the future?

Exhibit 15.7 provides an example of how asset allocation decisions apply to Stephanie Spratt's financial plan. Stephanie's first concern is maintaining adequate liquidity and being able to make her existing loan payments. As she accumulates more money beyond what she needs for these purposes, she will allocate money to various investments.

Exhibit 15.7   How Asset Allocation Fits within Stephanie Spratt's Financial Plan

Goals for Asset Allocation

1. Ensure that my present asset allocation is appropriate.
2. Determine a plan for asset allocation in the future as I accumulate more money.

Analysis

Present Asset Allocation of Investments

Investment	Market Value of Investment	Proportion of Invested Funds Allocated to This Investment
Common stock	$3,000	$3,000/$5,000 = 60%
Stock mutual fund	1,000	$1,000/$5,000 = 20%
Bond mutual fund	1,000	$1,000/$5,000 = 20%
Total	$5,000	

Decisions

Decision on Whether My Present Asset Allocation Is Appropriate:

My present asset allocation is too heavily concentrated on one stock. With just $5,000 in investments, I should probably have all of my money invested in mutual funds so that my investments are more diversified. I should consider selling the stock and investing the proceeds in a stock mutual fund. I already own shares of a mutual fund focused on Internet firms. I will invest the proceeds from selling my stock in a different type of stock mutual fund so that I can achieve more diversification.

Decision on Asset Allocation in the Future:

Once I revise my asset allocation as described above, I will have $4,000 invested in stock mutual funds and $1,000 in bond mutual funds. This revision will result in a balance of 80 percent invested in stock funds and 20 percent invested in bond funds. The stock funds have a higher potential return than the bond funds. During the next few years, I will invest any extra money I have in stock or bond mutual funds, maintaining the same 80/20 ratio.

DISCUSSION QUESTIONS

1. How would Stephanie's asset allocation decisions be different if she were a single mother of two children?

2. How would Stephanie's asset allocation decisions be affected if she were 35 years old? If she were 50 years old?

SUMMARY

Asset allocation uses diversification to reduce your risk from investing. In general, a portfolio achieves more benefits when it is diversified among assets whose returns are less volatile and are not highly correlated with each other over time.

Common stock diversification strategies include diversifying among stocks across industries and among stocks across countries. You should consider using these two types of diversification so that you limit the exposure of your stock investments to any external forces that could affect their value.

Your asset allocation decision should not be restricted to stocks. Because bond returns are primarily influenced by interest rate movements rather than stock market conditions, they are not highly positively correlated with stock returns over time. Therefore, bonds can reduce the risk of an investment portfolio. Real estate investment trusts (REITs) are primarily influenced by real estate conditions and can also be useful for diversifying an investment portfolio.

Your asset allocation decision should consider your stage in life, your degree of risk tolerance, and your expectations of economic conditions. If you are young, you may be more willing to invest in riskier securities to build wealth. If you are near retirement, you should consider investing more of your money in investments that can provide you with a stable income (dividends and interest payments) over time. If you are more willing to tolerate risk, you would invest in riskier stocks and bonds. Your asset allocation is also influenced by your expectations about future economic conditions. These expectations affect the expected performance of stocks, bonds, and REITs and therefore should shape your decision of how to allocate your money across these financial assets.

Integrating the Key Concepts

Your asset allocation decision is central to your other investment decisions and also affects other parts of your financial plan. Asset allocation affects your liquidity situation (Part 2) because some securities are more liquid than others. Even if you own some money market instruments to maintain liquidity, your asset allocation decision can achieve additional liquidity. For example, bonds and dividend-paying stocks provide periodic income. Some securities such as small stocks are subject to larger losses, and you may be less willing to sell those stocks when they perform poorly; consequently, small stocks are not liquid.

The asset allocation decision is related to financing (Part 3) because you should consider paying off any personal loans before you invest in some other assets. If, after considering your liquidity and financing situation, you still decide to invest in securities or mutual funds, you need to decide whether the investment should be for your retirement account (Part 5). An asset allocation decision for retirement purposes is likely to be more conservative than short-term asset allocation decisions.

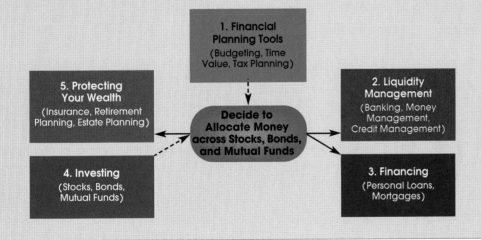

Appendix **15A**

Including Stock Options in Your Asset Allocation

Exchanges facilitate the trading of options by ensuring that buyers or sellers of options fulfill their obligations. The exchange does not take positions in options, however. A popular exchange for trading options is the Chicago Board of Options Exchange (CBOE). Stock options should be considered only by investors who are willing to tolerate a high level of risk or who know how to use them in a manner that can reduce risk.

CALL OPTIONS

call option
An option on a specified stock that provides the right to purchase 100 shares at a specified price by a specified expiration date.

exercise (strike) price
The price specified for exercising a stock option.

A **call option** on a stock provides the right to purchase 100 shares of a specified stock at a specified price (called the **exercise price** or **strike price**) by a specified expiration date. The advantage of a call option is that it locks in the price you have to pay to purchase the stock and also gives you the flexibility to let the option expire if you wish. The price that you pay when purchasing a call option is referred to as a **premium**. The premium of a call option is influenced by the number of investors who wish to buy call options on that particular stock. Investors can purchase call options through their brokerage firm, which charges a commission for executing the transaction.

Example

premium
The price that you pay when purchasing a stock option.

On September 10, you pay a premium of $2 per share, or $200, to purchase a call option on Gamma stock. The stock price is currently $28. The call option gives you the right to buy 100 shares of Gamma stock at the exercise price of $30 at any time up until the end of November. Thus, no matter how much Gamma's stock price rises before the end of November, you can still buy the stock at $30 per share.

Selling a Call Option

For every buyer of a call option, there must be a seller who is willing to sell the call option. The seller of a call option is obligated to sell the shares of the specified stock to the buyer for the exercise price if and when the buyer exercises the option.

Example

Joan Montana sold you the call option on Gamma stock. Joan receives the $200 premium that you paid to buy the call option. She is obligated to sell 100 shares of stock to you for $30 per share if and when you exercise the call option.

Gain or Loss from Trading Call Options

Your net gain or loss from buying a call option can be determined by considering the amount received when you sell the stock, the amount you paid for the stock when exercising the option, and the amount you paid for the premium.

Example

Recall that you paid a premium of $2 per share, or $200, to purchase the call option on Gamma stock. The price of Gamma stock increases from $28 to $35 per share by the end of November. You can exercise the option and then sell the stock in the market at its prevailing price of $35. Your gain is:

Amount Received from Selling the Stock ($35 × 100 shares)	$3,500
Amount Paid for Gamma Stock ($30 × 100 shares)	− $3,000
Amount Paid for the Premium ($2 × 100 shares)	− $200
Net Gain	= $300

Since you paid $200 for the call option and your net gain was $300, your return can be derived as your net gain divided by the amount of your investment:

$$\text{Return} = \text{Net Gain/Amount of Investment}$$
$$= \$300/\$200$$
$$= 1.50, \text{ or } 150\%.$$

Joan Montana does not own shares of Gamma stock, so she has to buy it in the market at $35 per share before selling it to you at $30 per share. Thus, her net gain (or loss) is:

Amount Received from Selling the Stock ($30 × 100 shares)	$3,000
Amount Paid for Gamma Stock ($35 × 100 shares)	−$3,500
Amount Received from the Premium ($2 × 100 shares)	+$200
Net Gain/Loss	= −$300

Notice that the dollar amount of your gain is equal to the dollar amount of Joan's loss.

When investing in a call option on a stock rather than the stock itself, you can magnify your return. If you had purchased Gamma stock on September 10 at a price of $28 per share, your gain would have been $7 per share. The return from investing in the call option (150 percent) is much higher. However, the risk from investing in the call option is higher than the risk from investing in the stock itself.

Example

Suppose Gamma's stock price had remained at $28 until the expiration date. Since the price stayed below the exercise price, you let the option expire. Thus, you lost the $200 premium that you paid for the call option. Your loss was 100 percent of your investment. Compare this return with what would have happened if you had invested in the stock itself when it was initially priced at $28. Since the price did not change, you could have sold the stock for $28, so your return would have been zero percent, which is much better than −100 percent.

Since you did not exercise your call option, Joan Montana (the seller of the call option) would have earned a net gain of $200. That is, she received your premium of $200 and did not sell you shares of Gamma stock because you let the option expire.

As these examples illustrate, you can benefit from holding a call option when the value of the stock rises. Some employers provide their employees with call options on the firm's stock as an incentive to perform well and to stay with the company. Employee stock options are usually issued at the prevailing market price at that time. If the stock price should rise, the employees with stock options will benefit.

PUT OPTIONS

put option
An option on a specified stock that provides the right to sell 100 shares at a specified price by a specified expiration date.

A **put option** on a stock provides the right to sell 100 shares of a specified stock at a specified exercise price by a specified expiration date. You place an order for a put option in the same way that you place an order for a call option. The put option locks in the price at which you can sell the stock and also gives you the flexibility to let the option expire if you wish. You buy a put option when you expect the stock's price to decline.

Example

On January 18, you pay a $300 premium to purchase a put option on Winger stock with an exercise price of $50 and that expires at the end of March. The stock price is currently $51 per share. The put option gives you the right to sell 100 shares of Winger stock at the exercise price of $50 at any time up until the end of March. Thus, no matter how much Winger's stock price decreases before the end of March, you can still sell the stock at $50 per share.

Selling a Put Option

For every buyer of a put option, there must be a seller who is willing to sell the put option. The seller of a put option is obligated to buy the shares of the specified stock from the buyer of the put option for the exercise price if and when the buyer exercises the option.

Example

Kevin Warner sold you the put option on Winger stock. Kevin receives the $300 premium that you paid. He is obligated to buy 100 shares of stock from you for $50 per share if and when you exercise the put option.

Gain or Loss from Trading Put Options

Your net gain or loss from buying a put option can be determined by considering the amount received when you sell the stock by exercising the put option, the amount you paid for the stock, and the amount you paid for the premium.

Example

The price of Winger stock decreases to $46 by the end of March. You decide to buy the stock at its prevailing market price and then exercise your put option by selling the stock at the option's exercise price. Your gain can be determined as follows:

Amount Received from Exercising the Put Option ($50 × 100 shares)	$5,000
Amount Paid for Winger Stock ($46 × 100 shares)	− $4,600
Amount Paid for the Premium ($3 × 100 shares)	− $300
Net Gain	= $100

Since you paid $300 for the put option and your net gain was $100, your return can be derived as your net gain divided by the amount of your investment:

$$\text{Return} = \text{Net Gain/Amount of Investment}$$
$$= \$100/\$300$$
$$= .333, \text{ or } 33.3\%.$$

Kevin Warner is obligated to purchase the stock from you at $50 per share. He sells the stock at its prevailing price right after you exercise the put option, so his net gain (or loss) is:

Amount Received from Selling the Stock ($46 × 100 shares)	$4,600
Amount Paid for Winger Stock ($50 × 100 shares)	− $5,000
Amount Received from the Premium ($3 × 100 shares)	+ $300
Net Gain/Loss	= − $100

Notice that the dollar amount of your gain is equal to the dollar amount of Kevin's loss.

To recognize the risk of buying a put option, consider what would have happened if the stock price of Winger had remained above $50. Under these conditions, you would have let your option expire. Thus, you would have lost 100 percent of the $300 premium that you paid for the call option. And Kevin Warner would have earned a net gain of $300.

QUOTATIONS OF STOCK OPTIONS

Stock option quotations are provided in many financial newspapers. An example from the *Wall Street Journal* is shown in Exhibit 15.A1. The stock option quotations are organized according to the stocks (identified in bold print) that they represent. A call option's exercise price is in the second column, and its expiration date is listed in the third column. The volume of contracts traded for the specified call option is shown in the fourth column, while the latest ("last") quoted premium of the call option is shown in the fifth column. The volume of put options with the specified exercise price and maturity is shown in the sixth column, while the latest ("last") quoted premium of the put option appears in the seventh column.

Exhibit 15.A1   An Example of Stock Option Quotations

OPTION/STRIKE	EXP.	CALL VOL.	CALL LAST	PUT VOL.	PUT LAST	OPTION/STRIKE	EXP.	CALL VOL.	CALL LAST	PUT VOL.	PUT LAST
ADC Tel	12^{50}	Feb	16	3^{38}	588	0^{56}	Abgenix	45	Feb	27	4^{63}	500	4^{50}
15^{06}	15	Feb	1557	1^{69}	503	1^{63}	About.cm	45	Feb	...	...	961	17^{25}
15^{06}	15	May	150	3^{88}	856	3^{25}	Activisn	17^{50}	May	503	3	...	...
15^{06}	17^{50}	Feb	1066	0^{88}	121	3^{13}	Acxiom	30	Feb	98	4^{50}	1171	1^{31}
15^{06}	17^{50}	May	778	2^{81}	16	4^{88}	33^{06}	30	Mar	...	...	500	2^{88}
15^{06}	20	Feb	702	0^{44}	12	5^{38}	AdvFibCm	20	Feb	480	3^{63}	248	1^{75}
A M R	40	Feb	746	1^{19}	10	3^{13}	22^{25}	22^{50}	Feb	517	2^{38}	38	3
AmOnline	35	Feb	1150	19^{50}	216	0^{10}	22^{25}	25	Feb	637	1^{69}	...	...
54^{15}	40	Apr	1011	15^{70}	32	1^{10}	22^{25}	25	Jun	1381	4^{75}	...	...
54^{15}	45	Feb	378	9^{80}	734	0^{65}	22^{25}	45	Mar	4020	0^{19}	...	...
54^{15}	45	Jul	1015	13^{50}	136	3^{30}	A M D	20	Feb	576	3^{25}	1959	0^{63}
54^{15}	50	Feb	57783	5^{80}	60936	1^{50}	22^{31}	20	Apr	84	5	5202	1^{88}
54^{15}	50	Mar	856	6^{90}	358	2^{40}	22^{31}	20	Jul	1179	6	114	3^{13}
54^{15}	50	Jul	34	10^{40}	4956	4^{70}	22^{31}	22^{50}	Feb	1401	1^{63}	171	1^{75}
54^{15}	55	Feb	2691	2^{55}	1473	3^{30}	22^{31}	25	Feb	556	0^{88}	33	3^{25}
54^{15}	55	Mar	701	4	292	4^{40}	22^{31}	25	Apr	5158	2^{50}	11	5
54^{15}	55	Apr	420	5^{20}	1623	5^{40}	22^{31}	25	Jul	498	4	44	5^{88}
54^{15}	60	Feb	3636	0^{95}	84	6^{70}	Agnico	7^{50}	Mar	500	0^{38}	...	...
54^{15}	60	Mar	1405	1^{90}	5	7^{50}	AkamaiT	30	Mar	531	7^{50}	...	...
54^{15}	60	Apr	991	3	27	8^{40}	Alcoa	30	Jul	15	6^{50}	500	2^{13}
54^{15}	60	Jul	2238	5^{30}	60	10	33^{94}	35	Feb	3951	1	109	2^{25}
54^{15}	65	Feb	751	0^{30}	160	11^{50}	33^{94}	35	Apr	572	2^{63}	2	3^{75}
54^{15}	65	Apr	1341	1^{65}	6	12^{10}	AlexionPh	65	Feb	567	9^{63}	105	4^{75}
54^{15}	70	Apr	1668	0^{90}	...	...	71^{38}	70	Feb	518	8	...	...
54^{15}	70	Jul	1465	2^{35}	...	...	Allaire	7^{50}	Jul	...	...	600	1^{19}
54^{15}	75	Jul	693	1^{65}	...	...	Allste	30	Mar	...	...	800	0^{50}
54^{15}	80	Jul	3609	1	...	...	37^{69}	35	Apr	5	4^{25}	1000	2^{25}
AT&T Cda	30	Mar	3000	0^{75}	...	...	Amazon	20	Feb	2456	1^{75}	110	3^{38}
29^{88}	30	Apr	1005	1^{25}	5	1^{06}	18^{95}	20	Mar	1157	2^{75}	1752	3^{63}
AT&T	20	Feb	361	3^{63}	832	0^{31}	A Hess	60	Feb	...	...	10000	0^{88}
23^{31}	22^{50}	Feb	1043	1^{69}	307	0^{75}	68^{31}	75	Feb	10000	1^{13}	...	...
23^{31}	25	Feb	1383	0^{63}	220	2^{13}	AmExpr	45	Feb	582	2^{88}	583	1^{25}
Abbt L	40	Mar	10	5^{38}	1026	1^{13}	46^{50}	47^{50}	Feb	554	1^{75}	78	2^{31}
44	45	Feb	799	1^{56}	80	2^{38}	46^{50}	50	Feb	2773	0^{75}	75	4
44	45	May	543	3^{75}	510	4^{13}	46^{50}	50	Jul	762	4^{25}	10	7
AberFitch	17^{50}	May	10	10^{25}	700	0^{94}	Am Hom	50	Mar	...	...	1056	2

Consider the stock options on Amazon.com stock with a strike price of $20 per share and February expiration date, which are highlighted in Exhibit 15.A1. The call options on Amazon.com stock with a strike price of $20 and expiration date of February have a premium of $1.75 per share. The put options on Amazon stock with the same strike price and expiration date have a premium of $3.38 per share.

For a given stock, there are usually several different call options and put options. You may have a choice of options that have different exercise prices. Notice in Exhibit 15.A1 that there are several rows of information for Amazon stock. Each row provides quotations for a different strike price or expiration date.

When the exercise price of a call or put option may be exercised profitably, the option is referred to as **in the money**. Conversely, when the exercise price of a call or put option cannot be exercised profitably, the option is said to be **out of the money**. A call or put option is said to be **at the money** when the prevailing stock price is equal to the option's exercise price. At a given point in time, some options for a given stock may be in the money, while others are out of the money or at the money.

You may also have a choice of options with different expiration dates. Some options may expire within a month, while others may expire as far into the future as nine months.

in the money
A stock option that can be exercised profitably.

out of the money
A stock option that cannot be exercised profitably.

at the money
An option on a stock whose prevailing price is equal to the option's exercise price.

15.3 Financial Planning Online: Stock Option Quotations

Go to:
http://biz.yahoo.com/opt/

This Web site provides:
quotations of premiums for call and put options. You can review the option premiums for any firm by entering its stock symbol into the space in the left frame and clicking, "Get Options." Consider this information before deciding whether to invest in options.

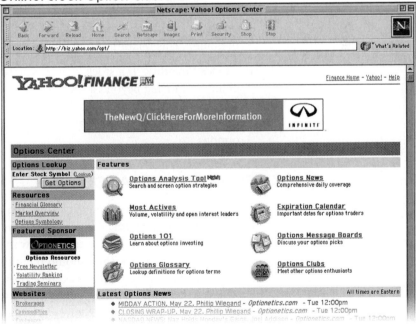

FACTORS THAT AFFECT THE OPTION PREMIUM

The premium charged on a call option is influenced by the following factors:

■ **Stock Price Relative to Exercise Price.** The premium on a call option is influenced by the relationship between the option's exercise price and the stock's price.

When a call option is in the money, it is already in a position to be exercised. Thus, the premium charged for such an option will be relatively high. Conversely, when a call option is out of the money, the premium will be lower because the price would have to increase before the option could be exercised. If the stock price is lower than the exercise price, there is less chance that the call option will be exercised. In Exhibit 15.A1, compare the premiums among call options for a given stock and given expiration date but different exercise prices to confirm the relationships suggested here.

When a put option is in the money, it is already in a position to be exercised. Thus, the premium charged for such an option will be relatively high. Conversely, when a put option is out of the money, the premium will be lower because the price would have to decrease before the option could be exercised. If the stock price is higher than the exercise price, there is less chance that the put option will be exercised. Compare the premiums among put options in Exhibit 15.A1 for a given stock and given expiration date but different exercise prices to confirm the relationships suggested here.

■ **Option's Time to Expiration.** The longer the period until expiration for a given stock option, the longer the period that you have to exercise the option. Thus, a stock option with a longer maturity will have a higher premium. This relationship holds for both call and put options.

■ **Stock's Volatility.** If a stock is more volatile, its price has a higher probability of moving beyond a specified exercise price before the expiration date. Thus, investors are willing to pay more for options on volatile stocks, other things being equal. This relationship holds for both call and put options.

THE ROLE OF STOCK OPTIONS IN ASSET ALLOCATION

There are many stories about investors who earned a hefty return from investing in stock options. Although stock options have become a popular investment for individual investors who want to achieve very high returns, options are still very risky and should therefore play only a minimal role (if any) in asset allocation. Since asset allocation is normally intended to limit exposure to any one type of investment, any allocation to stock options should be made with caution. Many stock options are never exercised, which means that the investment generates a return of −100 percent.

Nevertheless, there are some ways of using stock options to reduce the risk of your portfolio. Two of the more common methods are discussed next.

Buying Put Options on Stocks You Own

You can limit the risk of stocks you are holding by purchasing put options on them.

Example

You invested in 100 shares of Dragon.com stock a year ago. Although the stock has performed well, you think it may perform poorly in the near future. The present price of the stock is $40 per share. You decide to pay a premium of $3 per share, or $300, for a put option on Dragon.com stock with an exercise price of $38. If the stock price stays above $38 per share, you will not exercise the put option. Conversely, if the stock price falls below $38 per share, you can exercise the put option by selling the shares you are holding for $38 per share.

In this example, your purchase of a put option locked in a minimum price at which you could sell a stock you were holding, no matter how much that stock's price declined. Thus, you were able to reduce your portfolio's risk by limiting your potential loss on this stock.

covered call strategy
Selling call options on stock that you own.

Selling Call Options on Stocks You Own

You can also reduce your risk by selling call options on a stock you hold. Doing so is referred to as a **covered call strategy** because the call option you purchase is covered by the stock you already own.

Example

Assume once again that you are concerned that the price of Dragon. com stock may decline in the near future. There is a call option available with an exercise price of $42 and a premium of $2. You decide to sell a call option on Dragon.com stock and receive a premium of $200 (computed as $2 × 100 shares). If the price of Dragon.com stock rises above $42 per share, the call option will be exercised, and you will have to sell the stock to fulfill your obligation. Yet you at least will sell the stock for a gain. Conversely, if the stock price remains below $42, the call option will not be exercised. In this case, the $200 that you earned from selling the call option can help offset the stock's poor performance, thereby reducing your potential losses from holding it.

REVIEW QUESTIONS

1. Why is it important to diversify your financial holdings across financial assets? How does asset allocation enable you to accomplish diversification?

2. What is a portfolio? How does a diverse portfolio help reduce risk?

3. What factors influence a portfolio's risk? Explain.

4. Describe two strategies for diversifying a portfolio among stocks.

5. How can allocating some of your assets to bonds reduce the level of risk in your portfolio?

6. What are real estate investment trusts (REITs)? How are they classified? What are some attractive characteristics of REITs? How can REITs help diversify a portfolio?

7. Why is it important for an investor to understand how stock options function?

8. What makes asset allocation expensive? How can you reduce the costs?

9. Discuss the role that your stage in life plays in your asset allocation decisions.

10. How does your risk tolerance affect your asset allocation?

11. How might your expectation of economic conditions influence your asset allocation? Why is this strategy risky?

12. What is a stock option? How are stock options traded? What is the exchange's role in the trade?*

13. What is a call option? How does it work?*

14. How is a gain or loss calculated from the trading of call options?*

15. What is a put option? How does it work?*

16. How is a gain or loss calculated from the trading of put options?*

17. What information is provided in quotations of stock options?*

18. Discuss the terms *in the money, out of the money,* and *at the money* as they relate to call and put options.*

19. List and briefly discuss some of the factors that affect the premium paid on a stock option.*

20. "There is a right way and a wrong way to use stock options in asset allocation." Evaluate this statement.

FINANCIAL PLANNING PROBLEMS

1. Maryanne paid $300 for a call option on a stock. The option gives her the right to buy the stock for $27 per share until March 1. On February 15, the stock price rises to $32 per share, and Maryanne exercises her option. What is Maryanne's return on this transaction?*

2. Chris purchased a call option on a stock for $200. The option gave him the right to purchase the stock at $30 per share until May 1. On May 1 the price of the stock was $28 per share. What was Chris's return on the stock option?*

3. Teresa purchased a call option on a stock for $250. The option allowed her to purchase the stock for $40 per share if she exercised the option by December 31. On December 15, the stock went to $60 per share and Teresa exercised the option. What was Teresa's return on the stock option?*

4. Last year Bill purchased 100 shares of stock for $35 per share. The price of the stock rose to $37 per share, but Bill was not convinced that the price would continue to rise and sold a call option on the stock for $300 with an exercise price of $39 per share. The day that the stock price rose to $42 per share the call option was exercised, and Bill sold his stock. What was Bill's return on this transaction?*

5. Dara paid a premium of $225 for a put option to sell a stock for $40 per share. At the time, the stock price was $42 per share. Prior to the expiration date of the option, the stock's price fell to $35 per share, and Dara exercised her option. What was Dara's return on this transaction?*

* Question based on chapter appendix.

FINANCIAL PLANNING ONLINE EXERCISES

1. Go to http://finance.yahoo.com/?u to determine how stocks are correlated with various indexes. Under Yahoo! Finance, enter GE, the symbol for General Electric. Click on "Get Quotes." Under More Info, click on "Charts." Scroll down to the bottom of the page and check S&P to compare S&P returns with the returns on GE for the past year. Click on "Compare." What can you discern from this chart? You can choose various time periods from one day to five years by choosing the period at the bottom of the page.

2. You can add the Nasdaq and Dow indexes to the chart by checking these at the bottom of the page. Click on "Compare." Interpret the results and comment on GE's performance relative to the performances of the major indexes.

3. At the bottom of the page, click on the tab for "Moving Averages." The 200-day and 50-day moving averages are shown along with the closing price chart for GE. Interpret the current price of GE with respect to the 200-day and 50-day moving averages.

4. At the bottom of the page, click on "Basic." Scroll to the bottom of the page and in the box next to "Compare GE to," enter IBM and click on "Compare." The new chart will show a comparison of the returns on GE and IBM. Comment on the performance of GE and IBM and any interrelationship.

5. Go to http://www.ihatefinancialplanning.com. Scroll down and click on "Online Advice." Submit a question on finances and receive an answer by e-mail. The question can be on any area of finance such as mutual funds, stocks, insurance, or budgeting.

6. Go to http://finance.yahoo.com/?u. Enter "NKE" under Yahoo! Finance and choose "Options" from the pull-down menu to the right of "Get Quotes." Then click on "Get Quotes." Call and put options at various strike prices and expiration dates for Nike will be displayed. What is the pattern in premium costs for calls as the strike price increases? Why is this so?

7. Using the previous screen, review the premiums for put options as the strike price increases. Can you explain the relationship? How does this compare with what you observed with call premiums?

8. As the expiration period of put and call options increases, what is the effect on premiums? Why is this so?

Building Your Own Financial Plan

Achieving the proper asset allocation balance in a portfolio is a significant part of any financial plan. Reviewing the selections you have made to meet your goals in Chapters 11 and 14, prepare an analysis on the template provided with this chapter in the *Financial Planning Workbook* and on the CD-ROM as to what percentage of your goals is being met by various types of investments. For example, if 2 of your 10 goals (intermediate and long term) are met by investing in large-cap stocks and mutual funds, for this category you would enter 20 percent as your answer for the percentage of your portfolio invested in large-cap stocks and mutual funds.

You also need to consider diversification by sector, which is also addressed in the template. After completing the template, look for any imbalance, such as one particular sector being 50 percent or more of your portfolio. Because some goals may be repeated in different categories, the total percentages on the template will not equal 100 percent (for example, you may be invested in a large-cap tech fund, which is addressed in both the large-cap and the technology sections of the template).

Asset allocation is an area of your personal financial plan that will change significantly as you get older and many of your goals have a shortened time horizon. Therefore, an annual review of your asset allocation is imperative.

The Sampsons—A Continuing Case

The Sampsons have been evaluating methods for investing money that will ultimately be used to support their children's college education. They have concluded that a mutual fund is better suited to their needs than investing in individual stocks or individual bonds. They are now seriously considering a biotechnology fund, which is composed of numerous biotechnology stocks. They have heard that biotechnology stocks can experience very high returns in some periods. They are not concerned about some biotechnology stocks performing poorly in any period because they have a mutual fund (rather than a single stock) and are therefore diversified.

1. Advise the Sampsons regarding the soundness of their tentative decision to invest all of their children's college education money in a biotechnology mutual fund.

2. The Sampsons are aware that diversification is important. Therefore, they have decided that they will initially invest in one biotechnology mutual fund and then invest in three other biotechnology mutual funds as they accumulate more money. In this way, even if one mutual fund performs poorly, they expect that the other biotechnology mutual funds will perform well. How can the Sampsons diversify their investments more effectively?

IN-TEXT STUDY GUIDE

True/False:

1. Asset allocation refers to the distribution of your money across financial assets.

2. A portfolio is a set of multiple investments in different assets.

3. When you compose a portfolio of stocks, you should avoid including stocks that exhibit a high negative correlation.

4. In general, diversifying your investments among stocks within an industry yields no diversification benefits.

5. Since economic conditions vary among countries, you may achieve more favorable benefits by diversifying your stock investments across countries.

6. A real estate investment trust (REIT) pools investments from individuals and uses the proceeds to invest in real estate.

7. The value of equity REITs is primarily influenced by general stock market conditions.

8. Smaller stocks that are focused on technology tend to have potentially high returns, but they are also very risky.

9. Stock options are usually agreements by the firms to repurchase their stock.*

10. A covered call strategy involves the sale of put options on stock you already own.*

Multiple Choice:

1. Proper asset allocation can
   a. enhance your interest income and dividend income.
   b. increase the value of your assets.
   c. enhance your wealth.
   d. Proper asset allocation can accomplish all of the above.

2. An individual stock is subject to _____ risk, or the risk of poor performance due to the firm's management decisions.
   a. business
   b. market
   c. leverage
   d. interest rate

3. The _____ highly correlated the returns of individual stocks in a portfolio are, the _____ volatile the portfolio's return is over time.
   a. less; more
   b. more; less
   c. more; more
   d. Answers (a) and (b) are correct.

4. The _____ volatile the returns of individual stocks in a portfolio are, the _____ volatile the portfolio's return is over time.
   a. more; more
   b. less; less
   c. more; less
   d. Answers (a) and (b) are correct.

5. Diversification among stock in different industries is _____ than diversification within an industry.
   a. less effective
   b. more effective
   c. as effective as
   d. none of the above

6. Many investment advisers recommend that you invest about _____ percent of your portfolio in stocks of foreign countries.
   a. 90
   b. 60
   c. 20
   d. 0

7. The prices of foreign stocks are _____ volatile than those in the United States. A portfolio consisting of U.S. and foreign stocks is more _____ than a portfolio consisting of U.S. stocks only.
   a. more; stable
   b. more; volatile
   c. less; stable
   d. less; volatile

8. As you increase the proportion of your investment allocated to bonds, you _____ your exposure to market risk and _____ your exposure to interest rate risk.
   a. increase; increase
   b. reduce; reduce
   c. increase; reduce
   d. reduce; increase

9. In general, the _____ the proportion of your portfolio that is allocated to bonds, the _____ will be your portfolio's overall risk.
   a. smaller; lower
   b. larger; lower
   c. smaller; higher
   d. Answers (a) and (c) are correct.

10. _____ REITs invest money directly in properties.
    a. Mortgage
    b. Equity
    c. Asset
    d. Bond

11. Your asset allocation decision is not dependent on
    a. your stage in life.
    b. your degree of risk tolerance.
    c. your expectations about financial market conditions.
    d. Your asset allocation decision is dependent on all of the above.

12. A portfolio invested in _____ is probably most successful in achieving maximum diversification benefits.
    a. domestic stocks, bonds, foreign stocks, and REITs
    b. domestic stocks only
    c. domestic and foreign stocks
    d. bonds, foreign stocks, and REITs

13. The price at which an option can be exercised is the _____ *
    a. premium.
    b. exercise price.
    c. put add-on.
    d. call price.

The following information applies to questions 14 and 15.

You just purchased a call option for Z Corporation for $2.50 per share ($250 total). The price of Z Corporation stock increases from $50 to $76. The strike price of the option is $55.

14. Your gain (loss) when exercising the option is _____ *
    a. $2,600.
    b. $2,350.
    c. $2,100.
    d. $1,850.

15. The gain (loss) for the writer of this option is _____ *
    a. $2,100.
    b. −$2,100.
    c. $1,850.
    d. −$1,850.

16. A _____ option is an option providing the right to sell shares of a specified stock at a specified price.*
    a. call
    b. put
    c. covered call
    d. straddle

The following information applies to questions 17 and 18.

Hubert Porter just purchased a put option to buy 100 shares of Polar, Inc., for a premium of $3.50 per share. When Hubert purchased the option, the stock was trading for $50 per share. At the time the option matures, the stock is trading for $56 per share. The exercise price of the option is $45.

17. Based on this information, what is Hubert's gain (loss) from this option, assuming he pursues the most profitable course of action when the option matures?*
    a. $750
    b. −$750
    c. $350
    d. −$350

18. What is the gain (loss) accruing to the writer of this option?*
    a. $750
    b. −$750
    c. $350
    d. −$350

19. When the exercise price of a call option is below the stock's price, the call option is said to be _____ *
    a. in the money.
    b. at the money.
    c. out of the money.
    d. none of the above

20. Which of the following does not directly influence the premium on a put option?*
    a. stock price relative to exercise price
    b. the option's time to expiration
    c. the stock's volatility
    d. the stock's price-earnings ratio

*Question based on chapter appendix.

Part 4: Brad Brooks—A Continuing Case

Between watching a financial news network on cable, reading articles in some business magazines, and listening to a co-worker recount his story of doubling his portfolio in six months, Brad is now convinced that his financial future lies in the stock market. His co-worker's windfall was in Internet stocks, so Brad has focused his portfolio on three highly speculative Internet stocks. He believes that the three stocks will give him adequate diversification with maximum growth potential.

Although he has heard that it might be a good time to buy bonds due to possible declines in interest rates, he finds bonds boring and their returns too low. Brad read an article on how trading online with a margin account can increase his return, and he's interested in your opinion. Brad admits that he has virtually no knowledge of investing or time to do research, but a friend whose brother-in-law plays golf with a broker gives him lots of "hot tips." He believes that is all he really needs.

With "hot tips" and an online margin account, Brad believes he is prepared to make his first million on the Internet technology explosion, but, just to be safe, he would like to hear what you think of his plan.

1. Comment on each of the following elements of Brad's plan:
   a. Level of diversification with three Internet stocks
   b. Views on bonds and decision not to include them in his portfolio
   c. Trading online
   d. Margin trading
   e. Source of information ("hot tips")

2. Given Brad's lack of knowledge of investing and limited time to learn or do research, what might be the best option for him to pursue and still get the benefit of the growth of the Internet?

3. What factors will influence Brad's asset allocation? Based on these factors, what might be a suitable sample portfolio for Brad?

4. How would your answer to the sample portfolio part of question 3 be affected if Brad were:
   a. 45 years old?
   b. 60 years old?

5. Prepare a written or oral report on your findings and recommendations to Brad.

PART 5

Protecting Your Wealth

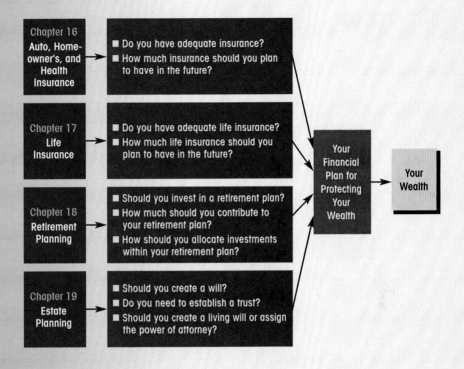

Chapter 16 Auto, Homeowner's, and Health Insurance	■ Do you have adequate insurance? ■ How much insurance should you plan to have in the future?
Chapter 17 Life Insurance	■ Do you have adequate life insurance? ■ How much life insurance should you plan to have in the future?
Chapter 18 Retirement Planning	■ Should you invest in a retirement plan? ■ How much should you contribute to your retirement plan? ■ How should you allocate investments within your retirement plan?
Chapter 19 Estate Planning	■ Should you create a will? ■ Do you need to establish a trust? ■ Should you create a living will or assign the power of attorney?

Your Financial Plan for Protecting Your Wealth → **Your Wealth**

The chapters in this part explain how you can protect the wealth that you accumulate over time through effective financial planning. Chapter 16 focuses on the decisions that must be made regarding auto insurance, homeowner's insurance, health insurance, and disability insurance, and Chapter 17 describes similar types of decisions regarding life insurance. Chapter 18 explains how to plan effectively for your retirement so that you can maintain your wealth and live comfortably. Chapter 19 explains how you can pass on as much of your estate as possible to your heirs.

Chapter 16

Auto, Homeowner's, and Health Insurance

Evaluating your insurance needs is necessary to protect the assets you purchase and the wealth you build through the financial planning process. Insurance shields your assets and income from specific unexpected events. In this way, your decision to purchase insurance protects your assets and income while limiting your liabilities, thereby affecting your wealth.

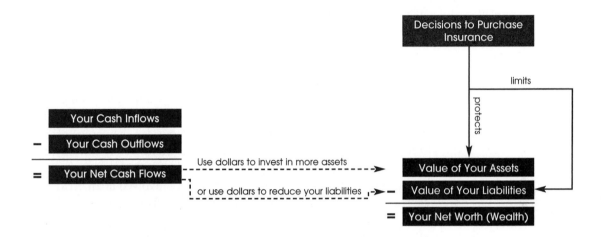

The objectives of this chapter are to:

- describe automobile insurance,

- explain homeowner's insurance,

- describe health insurance, and

- discuss disability insurance.

BACKGROUND ON INSURANCE

Insurance protects you against potential financial losses or liability as a result of unexpected events. It can ensure that your income continues if an accident or illness prevents you from working, or it can prevent others from taking away your personal assets. Thus, its primary function is to maintain your existing level of wealth. Insurance can ensure that your family can continue their lifestyle, that your medical bills will be covered, that any damages to your home and vehicle will be covered, and that your personal assets are protected from any liability. When discussing insurance, the term *liability* is used to mean that you may be required to pay someone for damages that you caused.

Individuals benefit from having insurance even when they do not receive any payments from the insurance company. For example, if you have auto insurance but did not file any claims over the last year, you are relieved that you were not involved in any accidents, and you also have the peace of mind of knowing that your assets were protected if you had been in a collision. Insurance may seem costly, but it is well worth the cost to ensure that your wealth will not be taken away from you.

How Insurance Relates to Risk

When you invest money, your investment decision affects your future wealth and your degree of risk tolerance. Assume you are considering two choices for using all of your personal assets. The first choice is to buy a diversified portfolio of mutual funds. The second choice is to invest all of your money in lottery tickets. The second choice may make you very rich, but it may also cause you to lose all of your personal assets (if you do not win the lottery).

The decision of whether to purchase insurance also affects your future wealth and your degree of risk tolerance. Consider the choice of buying auto, homeowner's, health, and disability insurance versus not buying any insurance and gambling with your personal assets. Without insurance, you risk losing all of your personal assets if you are involved in an accident that causes lost income, health problems, or liability. For example, if you are in a car accident, you could incur major expenses to repair your car and may also be liable for others who are injured in the accident, which could cost hundreds of thousands or even millions of dollars. By purchasing insurance, you remove the risk that your personal assets will be taken away and therefore protect your wealth.

One alternative to insuring your assets is to avoid risk. You could invest your money in bank deposits and not purchase assets that require insurance, such as a car and a home. This strategy would be very inconvenient, however. Besides, you would still be subject to the possible loss of income due to an event that makes you disabled and to major medical expenses due to an illness. Thus, even though your bank deposit accounts would be safe, you would need to withdraw money from them to cover major expenses. If your funds were insufficient to cover your expenses, you would have a major problem.

Types of Insurance

Since you are exposed to many different types of risk, it follows that there are many types of insurance. This chapter covers auto insurance, homeowner's insurance, health insurance, and disability insurance. Chapter 17 focuses on life insurance.

Most types of insurance can be purchased from an insurance company by contacting an insurance agent. Some insurance companies focus on one type of insurance (such as life), while many others offer a variety of insurance. Because the premiums charged and the specific coverage offered vary among insurance companies, you should shop around before buying insurance.

16.1 Financial Planning Online: Reviews of Insurance Companies

Go to:
http://www.gomez.com

Click on:
Finance, then on Insurance
Carriers

This Web site provides:
reviews and ratings of various
insurance companies and
descriptions of services offered
by each insurance company.

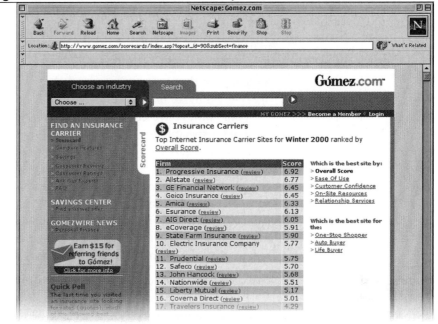

AUTO INSURANCE

Auto insurance insures against damage to an automobile and expenses associated with accidents. In this way, it protects one of your main assets (your car) and also limits your potential liabilities (expenses due to an accident). If you own or drive a car, you need auto insurance. Policies are purchased for a year or six months at property and casualty insurance companies. Your policy specifies the amount of coverage if you are legally liable for bodily injury, if you and your passengers incur medical bills, and if your car is damaged as the result of an accident or some other event (such as a tree falling on the car).

Auto Insurance Policy Provisions

When you purchase auto insurance, you set the terms for coverage with the insurer. You pay a premium based on the coverage you select. Most of the terms are standard. For example, liability for a single accident normally is subject to specific monetary limits on the coverage of bodily injury per person, bodily injury for all people who are injured, and property damage. Commonly, the maximum for bodily injury to others is $100,000 per person or a total of $300,000 for all persons in an accident. A typical limit for property damage is $50,000.

The policy limits are often described as 100/300/50, which means that the coverage is limited to $100,000 per person injured in an accident, $300,000 for all people combined, and $50,000 to cover damage to the car or other property. If one person suffers bodily injury that results in a liability of $80,000, the entire amount of the liability is covered. If one person's bodily injury results in a liability of $120,000, the coverage is limited to $100,000. If four people suffer bodily injuries amounting to a total of $400,000, $300,000 of that amount is covered. Auto insurance may also cover damages caused by an uninsured driver who is at fault in an accident.

Some states have implemented no-fault insurance programs, which do not hold a specific driver liable for causing the accident. The intent is to avoid costly court battles in which each driver in an accident attempts to blame the other driver.

Most states require that you maintain a minimum amount of auto insurance. However, the minimum amount may not be sufficient to cover your liability. Therefore, you should consider obtaining more insurance than the minimum. In addition, when you purchase a car with a loan, the lender may require that you maintain a certain coverage level.

deductible

A set dollar amount that you are responsible for paying before any coverage is provided by your insurer.

Deductible. The **deductible** is the amount of damage that you are responsible for paying before any coverage is provided by the insurance company. For example, with a deductible of $250, you must pay the first $250 in damages due to an accident; the insurance company pays any additional expenses.

Medical Payment Insurance. The medical coverage applies only to the insured automobile. Therefore, if you are in an accident while driving someone else's car, your insurance policy does not provide medical coverage for passengers in that car. Instead, the owner of that car is responsible for the medical coverage of the passengers. You can obtain medical insurance that covers you if you ride in another car driven by an uninsured driver.

Factors That Affect Auto Insurance Premiums

Your insurance premium can change from one year to the next in response to various factors.

Value of the Insured Vehicle. The higher the value of the vehicle, the higher the potential damage to the vehicle, and the higher the insurance premium. The potential for loss is greater on a new Mercedes than on a Saturn, so the insurance premium on the Mercedes will be higher. Before buying a car, you should always get an insurance estimate.

Amount of Coverage. The larger the amount of coverage for liability (such as a total of $500,000 for all passengers instead of $300,000), the greater the potential amount that your insurance company will have to pay in response to a claim. Therefore, your insurance premium will be higher if you want more coverage. If your net worth and income are high, however, you should have sufficient coverage to protect your assets.

16.2 Financial Planning Online: How Much Car Insurance Coverage Do You Need?

Go to:
http://insurance.yahoo.com/
auto.html

Click on:
Auto Coverage Analyzer

This Web site provides:
a recommendation on the
amount of car insurance coverage that is appropriate for you.

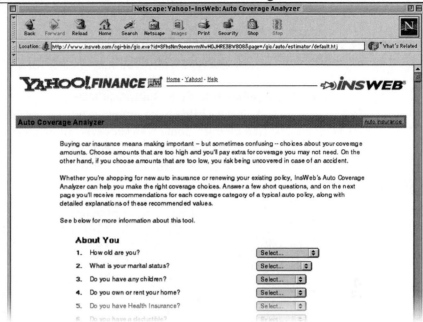

Amount of Deductible. With a higher deductible, fewer claims are made against the insurance policy because some accidents involve damages that are less than the deductible. If the damage is less than the deductible, the vehicle owner pays for car repairs as an out-of-pocket expense. If you are willing to accept a higher deductible, such as paying the first $500 on any damages, you can reduce your premium.

Your Age. Your insurance premium is dependent on your age. Drivers aged 16 to 25 tend to get in more accidents than drivers aged 25 to 50. Therefore, you pay a higher insurance premium if you are younger.

Your Driving Record. Insurance companies recognize that your previous driving record is a reasonable indicator of your future driving record. Therefore, they charge higher insurance premiums to individuals with poor records. Traffic tickets and other infractions (such as drunk driving charges) also result in higher premiums.

Potential Damage to Insured Vehicle. Your insurance premium may depend on the car itself (beyond its value). Some cars experience more severe damage than others in accidents or are more costly to repair. These types of cars will have higher insurance premiums, everything else being equal.

Location. Auto insurance is more expensive in large cities, where the probability of being involved in an accident or theft is higher.

Discounts. For a given type of car, discounts may be available if the car has antilock brakes, airbags, alarms, or other features that may prevent or reduce damage in an accident or deter theft. If you have high grades, have completed a driver training program, or have not been in an accident for the last several years, you may qualify for a discount.

Using the Internet to Price Auto Insurance

You can easily obtain estimates on auto insurance and comparison shop on the Internet. Some Web sites even allow you to buy cars online and provide estimates for insurance. Several Web sites (such as Ins Web, eCoverage, and Esurance, Inc.) provide auto insurance quotes online.

Example

Stephanie Spratt needs to renew her car insurance. Her policy is 100/300/40, which means that the coverage is limited to $100,000 per person injured in an accident, $300,000 for all people combined, and $40,000 to cover damage to the car or other property. She has a $400 deductible. Her insurance premium of $1,400 per year is lower than her friends' premiums because she has an excellent driving record. She also received discounts because her car has an alarm system, antilock brakes, and airbags. Stephanie is comfortable with her level of coverage, but she is considering a deductible of $500 if it will reduce her auto insurance premium.

HOMEOWNER'S INSURANCE

homeowner's insurance
A type of insurance policy that protects you in the event of property damage, theft, or personal liability relating to your home.

Homeowner's insurance provides insurance in the event of property damage, theft, or personal liability relating to your home. It not only protects the most valuable asset for many individuals, but also limits their potential liabilities (expenses) associated with the home. Premiums on homeowner's insurance are commonly paid yearly or may be included in your mortgage payment.

Homeowner's Insurance Policy Provisions

A homeowner's insurance policy specifies coverage on property damage and on protection from personal liability.

Types of Events Covered. The standard homeowner's insurance policy specifies the types of events that are covered, such as fire, burglary, lightning, and tornadoes. The policy may also specify events that are not covered, such as war and floods. It may also limit the amount of coverage for cash, jewelry, checks, or other items that are lost due to an event.

To broaden the standard homeowner's insurance, you can obtain supplemental insurance. For example, you may purchase insurance to cover your home against floods or to provide additional coverage for a particular piece of jewelry.

Personal Liability Coverage. A homeowner's insurance policy can protect you against personal liability if someone is injured on your property as a result of your actions. For example, it could provide coverage if your neighbor sues you after falling on your driveway.

Factors That Affect Homeowner's Insurance Premiums

The premium you pay for homeowner's insurance is primarily dependent on the following factors:

- **Value of Insured Home.** Insurance premiums reflect the value of the insured home and therefore are higher for more expensive homes.

- **Deductible.** If you are willing to pay the first $2,000 of any damage, your insurance premium will be lower than if you choose to have no deductible.

- **Location.** The potential for damage is greater in some areas, and therefore the premiums are higher as well. For example, homes along the southeastern Florida coast are more likely to be damaged by a hurricane than homes located 40 miles inland. Home insurance rates are therefore much higher along the coast. Similarly, premiums will be higher for homes in locations prone to tornadoes, floods, or earthquakes.

- **Degree of Protection.** If you want protection against an earthquake on a home in California, you must pay a higher premium. If you want protection against a flood, you may need to buy an additional insurance policy.

16.3 Financial Planning Online: Purchasing Homeowner's Insurance

Go to:
http://moneycentral.msn.com/articles/insure/home/contents.asp

This Web site provides:
step-by-step instructions for purchasing homeowner's insurance.

"Would you mind giving me a receipt for what you're stealing? If I don't have one I know I'm going to have a big hassle with my insurance company."

- **Discounts.** You may obtain discounts on your insurance by maintaining a smoke detector system in your house, paying for your insurance in one lump sum, or purchasing multiple types of insurance (such as auto, health, and life) from the same insurer.

Pricing Homeowner's Insurance on the Internet

You can easily obtain estimates for homeowner's insurance on the Internet from various Web sites (such as http://insurance.yahoo.com/h1.html). The Internet also allows you to easily compare premiums among insurance companies.

Filing a Claim

You should maintain a list of all your valuables so that you can fully account for your property in the event of a fire or other catastrophe. Keep the list and a copy of your homeowner's policy in a safety deposit box at a bank. If your property is damaged, you should contact your insurance company immediately. A claims adjuster from your insurance company will come to estimate the damage. This estimate will include the cost of repairing the damage done to your home and compensation for damaged property. The company may be willing to issue a check so that you can hire someone to do the repairs. You should consider obtaining an independent estimate on the repairs to ensure that the amount the insurance company offers you is sufficient. If the insurance company's estimate is too low, you can appeal it.

renter's insurance
An insurance policy that protects your possessions within a house, condominium, or apartment that you are renting.

Renter's Insurance

Renter's insurance insures your possessions within a house, condominium, or apartment that you are renting. It does not insure the structure itself because the insurance is for the renter only, not the owner of the property. It covers personal assets such as furniture, a television, computer equipment, and stereo equipment. The insurance protects against damage due to weather or the loss of personal assets due to burglary.

Renters whose personal assets have little market value do not need renter's insurance. Anyone whose personal assets have substantial market value, however, should seriously consider renter's insurance, as the policies are relatively inexpensive.

Renter's Insurance Policy Provisions. Renter's insurance specifies the maximum amount of coverage for your personal assets. It may also specify maximum coverage for specific items such as jewelry. The insurance premium is dependent on the amount of coverage you desire. Your renter's insurance may also cover liability resulting from damages to a person while on your premises. For example, if your pet injures a neighbor in your yard, your renter's insurance may cover your liability up to a limit. Because renter's insurance policies vary, you should closely review any policy to ensure that the insurance coverage is appropriate.

Deciding on Homeowner's (or Renter's) Insurance

Anyone who owns a home needs homeowner's insurance, and a mortgage lender typically requires it. Homeowners need to determine whether to purchase extra insurance to cover against floods and other events not covered in the standard homeowner's insurance policy. Renters with substantial household assets (such as furniture or computer equipment) need to determine whether to purchase renter's insurance.

16.4   Financial Planning Online: Renter's Insurance Quotation

Go to:
http://insurance.yahoo.com/r1.html

This Web site provides:
a customized renter's insurance quotation based on information about your personal property.

Netscape: Yahoo! Insweb: Renters Insurance Estimate

Location: http://insurance.yahoo.com/r1.htm

YAHOO!FINANCE Finance Home · Yahoo! · Help   **INSWEB**

INSWEB Enter **ASAP** click here

Renters Insurance Quick Estimate   Home & Renters Insurance

For an estimate of your renters insurance costs, please complete the brief form below. **To then receive a full customized quote, click on the [Get Quotes From InsWeb] button that will appear.**

1. Street Address:
2. City:
3. State: Select...
4. What is the ZIP Code of your home?
5. Is your home located within 1000 feet of a fire hydrant? ○ Yes ○ No
6. Is your home located within 5 miles of a fire station? ○ Yes ○ No
7. What is the value of your personal property? (Include furniture, clothing, electronics, collectibles, etc.) If you know this amount, you can choose it from a list. If you are unsure, use the tool to calculate it for you.
   ○ I know the value of my personal property. (Select from list) $ Select...
   ○ I would like to calculate the value of my personal property.

Umbrella Personal Liability Policy

umbrella personal liability policy
A supplement to auto and homeowner's insurance that provides additional personal liability coverage.

Individuals can supplement their auto and homeowner's insurance with an **umbrella personal liability policy,** which provides additional personal liability coverage. This type of policy is intended to provide additional insurance, not to replace the other policies. In fact, the insurance will not be provided unless individuals show proof of existing insurance coverage. Umbrella policies are especially useful for wealthy individuals who want to ensure that their personal assets are protected against possible liability.

HEALTH INSURANCE

health insurance
A type of insurance offered by private insurance companies or the government that covers health care expenses incurred by policyholders for necessary medical care.

Health insurance covers health care expenses incurred by policyholders; thus, it limits their potential liabilities and ensures that they will receive necessary medical care. Many more options are available for health insurance than for auto or homeowner's insurance. Health insurance is offered by private insurance companies and by the government. Our discussion of health insurance begins with private insurance.

Some private insurance companies provide only health insurance, while other companies offer it along with other types of insurance. Most large employers offer their employees the opportunity to participate in a health insurance plan as part of their benefits package. The employer and employee typically share the cost of the health insurance. The employees' portion of the premium is deducted from their pay, and the employer pays the remainder. Some employers pay a large portion of the premium in order to attract and retain good employees. Employers tend to obtain all their health insurance from one company. Individuals who are self-employed or unemployed can purchase a private health insurance plan. Private insurance is usually more expensive than insurance provided under an employer's plan. Information about health insurance premiums is available at insuremarket.com and quotesmith.com.

Private Health Care Plans

Private health care plans are commonly classified as indemnity plans or managed health care plans.

indemnity plan
Health insurance that reimburses individuals for part or all of the expenses they incur from health care providers; individuals are free to decide whether to seek care from a primary care physician or a specialist.

Indemnity Plans. An **indemnity plan** reimburses individuals for part or all of the health care expenses they incur from health care providers (such as doctors or hospitals). Individuals have the freedom to decide whether to seek care from a primary care physician or a specialist. They are billed directly by the health care providers and then must complete and submit forms to request reimbursement for the services rendered and prescriptions.

The advantage of an indemnity plan is that you can choose your own health care provider. The disadvantage is that you must deal with a bureaucracy to get reimbursement for your health care bills. Although indemnity plans offer more flexibility than managed care plans, they also charge higher premiums. Furthermore, you normally must pay a deductible, although most of the bill will be reimbursed by the insurer.

managed health care plan
A health insurance policy under which individuals receive services from specific doctors or hospitals that are part of the plan.

Managed Health Care Plans. Managed health care plans allow individuals to receive health care services only from specific doctors or hospitals that are part of the plan. When you receive services, you are billed only for any amounts not covered by your insurance. Therefore, you do not have to pay the full cost and then wait to be reimbursed, as is typically the process for indemnity plans. Managed health care plans charge lower premiums than indemnity plans, but impose more restrictions on the specific health care providers (doctors, hospitals) that individuals can use. Managed health care plans are normally classified as health maintenance organizations or preferred provider organizations.

health maintenance organization (HMO)
A health insurance plan that covers health care services approved by doctors; a primary care physician provides general health services and refers patients to a specialist as necessary.

Health Maintenance Organizations. A **health maintenance organization (HMO)** provides insurance for health care services approved by doctors. Individuals choose a primary care physician who is part of the HMO. The primary care physician provides general health services, such as checkups and treatment of minor illnesses, and refers patients to a specialist as necessary. In this way, individuals are directed to the appropriate specialist, rather than deciding on their own which type of specialist they need. By restricting access to specialists, HMOs also seek to control costs.

An advantage of HMOs is that they offer health care services at a low cost. The premiums charged are relatively low. Individuals also typically pay a small fee (such as $10) for a visit to a physician who participates in an HMO or for a prescription. A disadvantage, however, is that individuals must choose among the primary care physicians and specialists who participate in the plan. Thus, they cannot select a physician who is not approved by the HMO. HMO members pay lower premiums in exchange for less flexibility.

preferred provider organization (PPO)
A health insurance plan that allows individuals to select a health care provider and covers most of the fees for services; a referral from a doctor is not required to visit a specialist.

Preferred Provider Organizations. A **preferred provider organization (PPO)** allows individuals to select their health care providers and have most of the fee covered. In a PPO, referrals from a doctor are not required to visit a specialist. In addition, more physicians are avaialble for each area of specialization than in an HMO. Thus, individuals have more choice. The premiums and fees for health care services are higher in a PPO, however. For example, individuals may be charged 20 percent of the bill for certain health care services provided by a PPO versus a small flat fee such as $15 for the same services provided by an HMO.

Insurance Provided by Private Insurance Companies. Many insurance companies offer private health care insurance. The individual pays a premium and a deductible, and the company pays the bill charged by the doctor or hospital (beyond the deductible) up to the allowable limit for each health care service covered.

16.5   Financial Planning Online: Should You Enroll in an HMO or a PPO?

Go to:
http://insurance.yahoo.com/lh/
health.html

Click on:
Individual and Family Quotes

This Web site provides:
an opinion on whether an HMO
or a PPO would be better for
you, based on your situation.

The largest health care insurer, Blue Cross and Blue Shield, serves many employers with a group participation plan. Blue Cross and Blue Shield makes agreements with doctors and hospitals on the types of services it will cover and the amount it will pay for each service. Individuals insured by Blue Cross and Blue Shield are then covered up to the agreed-on specific dollar amount for each service. Policyholders are responsible for any additional costs beyond the set limit.

Government Health Care Plans

The government-sponsored health care plans are Medicare and Medicaid.

Medicare. Recall from Chapter 4 that the Medicare program provides health insurance to individuals who are 65 years of age or older and qualify for Social Security benefits, or who are disabled. Medicare also provides payments to health care providers in the case of illness. It provides basic coverage (including hospital expenses, surgeries, some nursing home care, home health services, and some prescriptions) for all individuals who qualify. Individuals who qualify for Medicare can also pay a monthly premium to receive supplemental insurance that covers additional health services not covered under the standard policy.

Medicaid
A federal program that provides health care to the aged, blind, disabled, and needy families with dependent children.

Medicaid. The **Medicaid** program provides health insurance for individuals with low incomes and those in need of public assistance. It is intended to provide health care to the aged, blind, disabled, and needy families with depend-

16.6   Financial Planning Online: Medicare Coverage

Go to:
http://www.medicare.gov/
Basics/overview.asp

This Web site provides:
an overview of services offered
by Medicare, including the specific benefits that are available.

ent children. To qualify, individuals must meet some federal guidelines, but
the program is administered on a state-by-state basis. Individuals who qualify for Medicare may also be eligible for Medicaid if they need public assistance; in this case, they will receive more health benefits.

Other Health Care Plans

Other types of health insurance commonly offered through employers include
dental and vision insurance. You should consider participating in these plans
if your employer offers them as part of your benefits package.

Dental Insurance. Dental insurance covers part or all of the fees imposed for
dental services, including annual checkups, orthodontics, and oral surgery.
Dental insurance, like other types of private insurance, can be offered as an
indemnity or a managed care plan.

Vision Insurance. Vision insurance covers part or all of the fees imposed for
optician and optometrist services, including annual checkups, glasses, contact lenses, and surgery. The specific premiums and benefits of vision insurance vary among plans.

Deciding on Health Insurance

The high expenses of health care could quickly eliminate most of your wealth
if you did not have insurance. Therefore, health insurance is essential to your
physical and financial health. The health insurance decision is not whether to

16.7   Financial Planning Online: Health Insurance Information

Go to:
http://www.hiaa.org

This Web site provides:
information about all aspects
of health insurance.

obtain it, but how much and what kind you need. This decision is largely
based on what your employer offers. If you have a choice between different types of indemnity and managed care plans, you will need to weigh the
tradeoff between the plans' flexibility and costs to make your choice.

Example

**disability
income
insurance**
Insurance that pro-
vides income to poli-
cyholders in the
event that they
become disabled.

When Stephanie Spratt started working for her present employer, she was offered the opportunity to purchase employer-
provided health insurance. She opted for an HMO, as she
expected her health care needs would be met by a primary
care physician. Plus, her monthly payment for this insurance
was only $20 per month. She also had the option of paying for dental
insurance and vision insurance. The premium she would have to pay per
year for the dental and vision insurance was substantially more than the
amount she anticipated that she would pay for her annual checkups.
Therefore, she decided to decline the dental insurance and vision insurance.

DISABILITY INSURANCE

Disability income insurance provides income to policyholders in the event
that they become disabled. Individuals typically purchase enough disability
insurance to ensure that they can support their lifestyle if they are disabled.

Because disability income is normally tax-free, the insurance coverage should cover an individual's disposable (after-tax) income or, alternatively, should at least cover the individual's typical expenses over time. Anyone who relies on income from a job should have disability insurance. If you have dependents, disability insurance can ensure that they will receive financial support even if you become disabled.

Sources of Disability Income Insurance

Some of the more common sources of disability income insurance are discussed here.

Individual Disability Insurance. You can purchase individual disability insurance and specify the amount of coverage that you desire. The insurance premium varies with your type of job. For example, workers in a steel plant are more at risk than workers in an office building.

Employer Disability Insurance. Many employers provide some disability insurance for their employees or charge low premiums for this insurance as part of the employee benefits package. For example, professors may be able to apply for disability insurance through their university. Group plans commonly provide benefits to policyholders who become disabled. The benefits provided represent a percentage of the policyholder's current salary.

Insurance from Social Security. Individuals who are disabled may receive some income from the Social Security Administration. The income is influenced by the amount of Social Security contributions you have made over time. The guidelines to qualify for disability benefits from Social Security are strict, meaning that you may not necessarily receive benefits even if you believe that you are disabled. In addition, the income provided by Social Security may not be sufficient to maintain your lifestyle. Therefore, you will probably need disability income insurance to supplement the possible disability benefits that you would receive from Social Security.

Insurance from Worker's Compensation. If you become disabled at your workplace, you may receive some income through worker's compensation from the state where you reside. The income you receive is influenced by your prevailing salary level. Disability income insurance may supplement any benefits that you would receive from worker's compensation.

Disability Insurance Provisions

The specific characteristics of disability insurance vary among insurance contracts, as explained here.

Amount of Coverage. The disability insurance contract specifies the amount of income that will be provided if you become disabled. The amount may be specified as a maximum dollar amount or as a percentage of the income that you were earning before being disabled. The higher your coverage, the more you will pay for disability insurance.

probationary period
The period extending from the time your disability income application is approved until your coverage goes into effect.

waiting period
The period from the time you are disabled until you begin to receive disability income benefits.

Probationary Period. You may be subject to a **probationary period,** which extends from the time your application is approved until your coverage goes into effect. A common probationary period is one month.

Waiting Period. The disability insurance contract should specify if there is a **waiting period** (such as three months or six months) before you would begin to receive any income benefits. You would have to cover your expenses during the waiting period. For example, if you become disabled today, and your policy specifies a three-month waiting period, you will receive benefits only if your disability lasts beyond the three-month period. One reason for having a waiting period is that it eliminates many claims that would occur if people could receive benefits when they were disabled for just a few days or weeks because of a sore neck or back. The premiums for disability insurance would be higher if there was no waiting period or a very short waiting period.

Length of Time for Disability Benefits. Disability benefits may be limited to a few years or may last for the policyholder's lifetime. The longer the period in which your policy provides disability income, the more you will pay for disability insurance.

Deciding on Disability Insurance

You can contact insurance companies about disability insurance rates or ask your employer's benefits department whether the insurance is available.

Example

When Stephanie Spratt was hired by her employer, she had the opportunity to purchase disability insurance, but she declined. She now recognizes the potential benefits of disability insurance and has called her benefits department to obtain more information. She learns that she can purchase disability insurance that will provide her with 70 percent of her income if she becomes disabled. Although she does not believe that she is likely to become disabled, she still decides to consider disability insurance. Since her employer would cover part of the insurance premium, her payment would be $10 per month. She decides that the disability insurance is worth the small monthly insurance payment.

HOW INSURANCE FITS WITHIN YOUR FINANCIAL PLAN

The following are the key decisions about car, homeowner's, health, and disability insurance that should be included within your financial plan:

1. Do you have adequate insurance to protect your wealth?

2. How much insurance should you plan to have in the future?

Exhibit 16.1 provides an example of how insurance decisions apply to Stephanie Spratt's financial plan.

Exhibit 16.1   How Insurance Planning Fits within Stephanie Spratt's Financial Plan

---

Goals for Insurance Planning

1. Ensure that my property and health are covered by insurance.
2. Determine whether I should increase my insurance levels in the future.

Analysis

Type of Insurance	Protection	Status
Auto	Protects one of my main assets and limits my potential liabilities.	Already have sufficient insurance.
Homeowner's	Protects my largest asset and limits my potential liabilities.	Recently purchased home insurance as a result of buying a home.
Health	Limits my potential liabilities associated with health care.	Good health insurance plan through work.
Disability	Protects my income if I become disabled.	Did not have disability insurance until now; have just signed a disability insurance policy.

Decisions

Decision on Whether My Present Insurance Coverage Is Adequate:
My car, home, health, and disability insurance policies are adequate for protecting my main assets, protecting my income, and limiting my liabilities.

Decision on Insurance Coverage in the Future:
In the future, I need to ensure that I have proper insurance coverage if I buy a car or a home with a larger market value. I may also consider obtaining more disability income insurance if I want more income protection. I will explore ways of lowering my insurance premiums (such as increasing deductibles).

DISCUSSION QUESTIONS

1. How would Stephanie's insurance purchasing decisions be different if she were a single mother of two children?

2. How would Stephanie's insurance purchasing decisions be affected if she were 35 years old? If she were 50 years old?

SUMMARY

Automobile insurance insures against damage to your automobile and expenses associated with an accident. The premium paid for auto insurance is dependent on the automobile's value and type, as well as the insurance deductible.

Homeowner's insurance provides insurance in the event of property damage or personal liability. The premium paid for homeowner's insurance is dependent on the home's value, the deductible, and the likelihood of damage to the home.

Health insurance covers health care expenses incurred by policyholders. Health care plans can be classified as private plans or managed care plans. Private plans allow much flexibility in your choice of the health care provider, but require a reimbursement process. Managed care plans include health maintenance organizations (HMOs) and preferred provider organizations (PPOs), which bill only the amount that is not covered by the plan. This avoids the reimbursement process. HMOs require the use of a specified primary care physician who refers the individual to a specialist when necessary; PPOs allow more flexibility in the choice of the health care provider, but require much higher premiums. There are also government health plans. The Medicare program provides health insurance to individuals who are over 65 years of age and qualify for Social Security, or are disabled. The Medicaid program provides health insurance to individuals with low incomes.

Disability insurance provides income to you if you become disabled. It can replace a portion of the income that you would have received had you been able to continue working.

Integrating the Key Concepts

Your decisions regarding auto, homeowner's, health, and disability insurance affect other parts of your financial plan. Insurance not only protects specific assets, but also limits your liability. Such protection gives you more flexibility on your other financial planning decisions. For example, it allows you to maintain a smaller amount of liquidity (Part 2) because you do not have to accumulate the large amount of funds that would be needed to insure yourself. Insurance makes purchasing a home possible because financing (Part 3) is available only if you insure your home. It also allows you to maintain a smaller amount of investments (Part 4) because you do not have to accumulate a large amount of investments to insure yourself. Finally, it allows you to contribute extra savings toward retirement (Part 5) rather than maintain the funds to cover any liability due to an accident or other unexpected event.

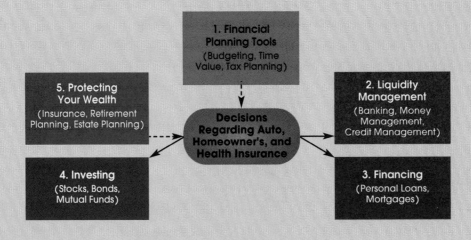

REVIEW QUESTIONS

1. What is the purpose of insurance? What is meant by the term *liability*? How can individuals benefit from insurance?

2. How does the decision to purchase insurance affect your future wealth and risk tolerance? What is an alternative to purchasing insurance? What is the problem with this alternative?

3. What four types of insurance should individuals be aware of? Who provides insurance, and how is it purchased? Why should you shop around for insurance?

4. What do policy limits of 25/50/25 mean? If these were the minimum amounts of liability insurance required by your state, would these amounts be suitable for all drivers? Explain your answer.

5. What is a deductible? How does medical payment coverage under an auto insurance policy work?

6. List and briefly discuss factors that will affect your auto insurance premium.

7. What is the purpose of homeowner's insurance? How are the premiums normally paid?

8. Describe the two main provisions of a homeowner's insurance policy.

9. List and briefly describe some of the factors that affect homeowner's insurance premiums.

10. Describe the steps you would take to file a claim on your homeowner's insurance.

11. How is renter's insurance different from homeowner's insurance? Who should consider purchasing renter's insurance? Briefly describe some of the provisions of a renter's insurance policy.

12. What should an individual consider when purchasing homeowner's or renter's insurance?

13. What is the purpose of an umbrella personal liability policy? Who might need one?

14. How do individuals benefit from having health insurance? Who offers health insurance? Can self-employed or unemployed people have health insurance?

15. Compare and contrast private health care indemnity plans and managed health care plans.

16. Describe how an HMO works. What are the advantages and disadvantages of this type of health care coverage?

17. How does a PPO operate?

18. Describe the two government-sponsored insurance plans.

19. Describe other types of insurance that might be offered by an employer.

20. Discuss the considerations involved in purchasing health insurance.

21. What is the purpose of disability income insurance? How can individuals determine how much disability insurance they might need? Who needs disability income insurance?

22. Briefly describe the sources of disability income insurance.

23. List and briefly describe some of the characteristics of disability income insurance.

24. What key decisions should individuals consider when deciding about insurance?

FINANCIAL PLANNING ONLINE EXERCISES

1. Go to http://insurance.yahoo.com/auto.html. Click on Coverage Analyzer and enter the requested information. Click on See Your Results. The screen will display recommendations for coverage under an auto insurance plan. You will also be able to proceed further to get an insurance quote, if you would like.

2. Go to http://insurance.yahoo.com/h1.html. Obtain an estimate for homeowner's insurance by entering the requested information. You will receive high and low estimates and a replacement cost for the home.

3. Go to http://insurance.yahoo.com/r1.html. To obtain a Renter's Insurance Estimate, input the requested information. Click on Get Estimate to view the results. Then increase the value of your personal property by $10,000. How much higher is the premium?

4. Go to http://insurance.yahoo.com/hs.html. To obtain an Individual Health Quote, input the requested information with a $250 deductible. Click on View Results. Now change the deductible to $1,000. How much lower is the policy premium?

5. Go to http://insurance.yahoo.com/life.html. Click on Personalized Quote and input the requested data. Is there a relationship between each insurance company's S&P ratings and the payment amount?

Building Your Own Financial Plan

Referring to the balance sheet that you prepared in Chapter 2, identify assets that you believe require insurance coverage. In your analysis, many of the assets (such as a house and automobile) will be obvious. But do not overlook risk exposures that can be covered by insurance for items not found on your personal balance sheet, such as health and disability income insurance for you and your spouse or significant other.

 In the template provided for this chapter in the *Financial Planning Workbook* and on the CD-ROM, list those assets and liabilities for which you wish to seek insurance coverage. At www.worldinsurance.com, follow the instructions to obtain premium quotes for the insurance protection that you seek. When you have obtained the quotes, total them up and refer back to the personal cash flow statement that you prepared in Chapter 2 to determine if you over- or underbudgeted for your insurance needs. Make changes to your personal cash flow statement as needed.

Your needs for insurance coverage will change significantly as you proceed along life's journey. When you move from an apartment to your own home, you will need homeowner's insurance; trading in your "old clunker" for your first shiny new car will change your car insurance needs. You should therefore review your insurance coverage as major milestones occur in your life. Keep in mind that while insurance is mandatory in some cases (such as for a car and home), in other cases it is a matter of personal choice closely tied to your risk tolerance. No law requires that a person have disability income insurance. Also remember that some risk exposures will be covered by insurance provided by your employer and, in some rare cases, by a governmental unit.

The Sampsons—A Continuing Case

 As the next step in reviewing their finances, the Sampsons are taking stock of their insurance needs related to their vehicles, home, and health. They indicated the amount of money they spend on insurance on their personal balance sheet in Chapter 2.

They currently have auto insurance on their two cars. Each insurance policy has a $1,000 deductible and specifies limits of 100/200/20 ($100,000 per person injured in an accident, $200,000 for all people combined, and $20,000 to cover other damage to the car or to other property).

Their homeowner's insurance covers the market value of their home and has a deductible of $3,000. Their policy does not cover floods, which periodically occur in their area. Their house has never been flooded, though, so Dave and Sharon are not concerned.

The Sampsons' health insurance is provided by a health maintenance organization (HMO). They do not have disability income insurance because they both have office jobs and do not believe that they are at risk.

1. Advise the Sampsons regarding their car insurance. Do they have enough insurance? Do they have too much insurance? How might they be able to reduce their premium?

2. Consider the Sampsons' homeowner's insurance. Do they have enough insurance? Do they have too much insurance? Is increasing their deductible well advised?

3. Make suggestions to the Sampsons regarding their health insurance. Do they have enough insurance? Do they have too much insurance?

4. Should the Sampsons have disability insurance? Why or why not?

IN-TEXT STUDY GUIDE

True/False:

1. The primary function of insurance is to maintain your existing level of wealth.

2. Auto insurance does not provide coverage if you are legally liable.

3. The deductible is the amount you must pay before any coverage is provided by the insurance company.

4. For a given type of car, insurance discounts may be available for persons who achieved high grades in school recently.

5. Homeowner's insurance premiums are commonly paid on a monthly basis.

6. A health maintenance organization (HMO) allows individuals to select their health care providers and have most of the fee covered.

7. The largest health care insurer is Blue Cross and Blue Shield.

8. Disability income insurance usually covers an individual's before-tax income.

9. Indemnity plans allow much flexibility in the choice of health care provider but require a reimbursement process.

10. Renter's insurance may provide coverage for specific items such as jewelry.

Multiple Choice:

1. Instead of purchasing insurance, you could try to avoid risk by not acquiring assets that require insurance, but you probably would not pursue this strategy because
   a. it is very inconvenient.
   b. you would still be subject to the possible loss of income due to an event that makes you disabled.
   c. you would still be subject to major medical expenses due to an illness.
   d. All of the above are true.

The following information applies to questions 2 and 3.

You review an auto insurance quotation that reads 100/200/30.

2. The maximum amount of coverage for all people combined is
   a. $30,000.
   b. $100,000.
   c. $200,000.
   d. none of the above.

3. The maximum coverage for damage to the car or other property is
   a. $30,000.
   b. $100,000.
   c. $200,000.
   d. none of the above.

4. With no-fault auto insurance, blame is not attached to
   a. the insured driver.
   b. the uninsured driver.
   c. a specific driver.
   d. none of the above.

5. The basic medical coverage of auto insurance covers you when you are driving
   a. your insured car.
   b. someone else's car.
   c. Both (a) and (b) are correct.
   d. none of the above.

6. If you are willing to use a _____ deductible, your premium will be _____.
   a. higher; increased
   b. higher; reduced
   c. lower; reduced
   d. Answers (a) and (c) are correct.

7. Homeowner's insurance premiums are commonly paid on a(n) _____ basis.
   a. weekly
   b. quarterly
   c. semiannual
   d. annual

8. The _____ the value of the home, the _____ is the insurance premium.
   a. higher; higher
   b. lower; lower
   c. higher; lower
   d. Answers (a) and (b) are correct.

9. _____ insurance insures your personal assets within a house, condominium, or apartment that you are renting.
   a. Lessee's
   b. Lessor's
   c. Renter's
   d. Homeowner's

10. You can supplement your insurance with a(n) _____ policy, which provides additional personal liability coverage.
    a. umbrella personal liability
    b. balloon personal liability
    c. overall personal liability
    d. specific personal liability

11. _____ are not examples of private health care plans.
    a. Indemnity plans
    b. Managed health care plans
    c. Health maintenance organizations
    d. Medicare plans

12. A(n) _____ gives you the freedom to seek care from a primary care physician or a specialist.
    a. indemnity plan
    b. HMO
    c. PPO
    d. none of the above

13. The _____ program provides health insurance to individuals who are 65 years of age or older and qualify for Social Security benefits.
    a. government health care
    b. Medicare
    c. Medicaid
    d. HMO

14. The _____ program provides health insurance to individuals with low incomes in need of public assistance.
    a. government health care
    b. Medicare
    c. Medicaid
    d. HMO

15. Which of the following is not a common source of disability income insurance?
    a. individual disability insurance
    b. employer disability insurance
    c. insurance from Social Security
    d. insurance from the IRS

16. Worker's compensation is paid by
    a. the state you were born in.
    b. the state where you reside.
    c. the federal government.
    d. none of the above.

17. The _____ period for disability income insurance extends from the time your application is approved until your coverage goes into effect.
    a. probationary
    b. waiting
    c. holding
    d. none of the above

18. The _____ the period in which you want to receive disability income, the _____ you will pay for disability insurance.
    a. longer; less
    b. longer; more
    c. shorter; more
    d. Answers (a) and (c) are correct.

19. Auto insurance is provided by
    a. investment banks.
    b. commercial banks.
    c. property and casualty insurance companies.
    d. savings institutions.

20. A deductible of $500 requires
    a. the insurance company to pay the first $500 in damages.
    b. you to pay the first $500 in damages.
    c. the party at fault to pay the first $500 in damages.
    d. none of the above.

Chapter 17

Life Insurance

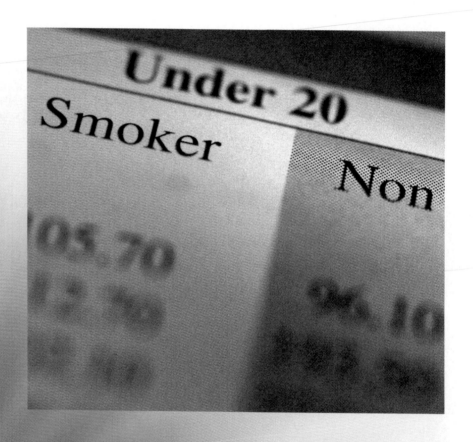

Life insurance is intended to provide financial support to those you designate in the event of your death. Your decision to purchase life insurance can ensure that your family members will be financially secure; thus, having life insurance can give you peace of mind. Your decisions about life insurance also affect the amount of wealth that you can pass on to your family members.

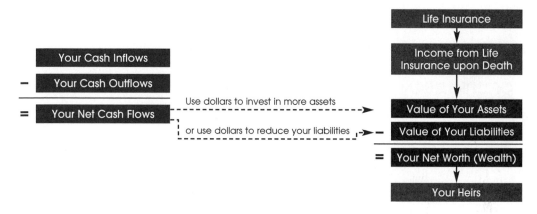

The objectives of this chapter are to:

- describe the types of life insurance that are available,

- identify the factors that influence the amount of insurance needed,

- identify the factors that affect the size of the life insurance premium,

- examine the decision of whether to purchase life insurance, and

- explain the possible settlement options that are available when payments are made to a beneficiary.

BACKGROUND ON LIFE INSURANCE

life insurance
Insurance that provides a payment to a specified beneficiary when the policyholder dies.

Life insurance provides a payment to a specified beneficiary when the policyholder dies. Therefore, it allows you to eliminate or at least substantially reduce the financial consequences of your death on dependents. A $100,000 policy means that in the event the policyholder dies, the beneficiary named in the policy will receive $100,000. Life insurance is provided by life insurance companies, which may be independent firms or subsidiaries of financial conglomerates. Many financial institutions that provide banking and brokerage services also have a subsidiary that provides life insurance. You pay a premium on a periodic (such as quarterly) basis for life insurance.

Life insurance is critical to protect a family's financial situation in the event that a breadwinner dies. Life insurance provides the family with financial support to cover burial expenses or medical expenses not covered by health insurance. Life insurance can also maintain the family's future lifestyle even without the breadwinner's income. If you are the breadwinner and have a spouse and children who rely on your income, you should have life insurance.

If no one else relies on your income, life insurance may not be necessary. For example, if you and your spouse both work full-time and your spouse could be self-sufficient without your income, life insurance is not as important. If you are single and are not providing financial support to anyone, life insurance is typically not needed.

TYPES OF LIFE INSURANCE

The following are the most popular types of life insurance.

- Term insurance

- Whole life insurance

- Universal life insurance

Each type is described in turn.

Term Insurance

term insurance
Life insurance that is provided over a specified time period and does not build a cash value.

Term insurance is life insurance provided over a specified time period. The premium that you pay for term insurance is dependent on the likelihood of death during that period. This likelihood is affected by your health, age, gender, and the length of the term in which insurance is desired. Term insurance does not build a cash value, meaning that the policy does not serve as an investment. It is intended strictly to provide insurance to a beneficiary in the event of death. If the insured person remains alive over the term, the policy expires at the end of the term and has no value. Nevertheless, the insurance was still valuable over the term in that the insured person knew that if she died, her beneficiaries would receive financial support.

Term insurance is cheaper for younger individuals, for women (because they tend to live longer than men), and for shorter time periods. Term insurance is usually renewable, which means that you can renew the insurance at the end of the term. You will have to pay higher premiums, however, to reflect your age at the time of renewal.

decreasing-term insurance
A form of term insurance in which the benefits that will be paid to the beneficiary are reduced over time and the premium remains constant.

Decreasing-Term Insurance. A common type of term insurance is **decreasing-term insurance**, in which the insurance benefits to the beneficiary are reduced over time. The premium paid for the insurance remains constant over the term. This type of insurance is popular for families because it provides a relatively high level of insurance in the earlier years when it is most needed. As time passes, a family can accumulate savings, pay off part of a mortgage, and increase their investments. Therefore, the family could survive with smaller life insurance benefits. Several forms of decreasing-term insur-

17.1   Financial Planning Online: How to Buy Term Life Insurance

Go to:
http://moneycentral.msn.com/
insure/lifelp.asp

This Web site provides:
step-by-step instructions
on shopping for term life
insurance.

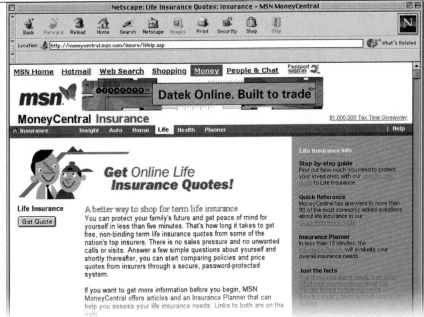

ance are available, with different terms and different degrees to which the insurance benefits decrease over the term. The same factors that affect the premium of term insurance also affect the premium of decreasing-term insurance.

mortgage life insurance
Life insurance that pays off a
mortgage in the event of the
policyholder's death.

Mortgage Life Insurance. **Mortgage life insurance** pays off a policyholder's mortgage in the event of his death. It is commonly purchased to ensure that a family can afford to continue living in their home even if the breadwinner dies. Mortgage insurance is a special form of decreasing-term insurance. In fact, individuals can achieve the same goal by purchasing a term insurance policy that provides benefits large enough to pay off the mortgage. This alternative may be cheaper than having mortgage life insurance.

Whole Life Insurance

whole life insurance
Life insurance that continues to
provide insurance as long as
premiums are paid; not only
provides benefits to the beneficiary but also has a cash value.

Whole life insurance continues to provide insurance as long as premiums are paid; the policy accumulates savings for the policyholder over time. In this way, it not only provides benefits to a beneficiary if the policyholder dies, but also creates a form of savings that has a cash value. For this reason, whole life insurance is sometimes referred to as a cash-value life insurance policy. A whole life insurance policy offers a lower return than many other investments, but may still be desirable because it also provides life insurance. If policyholders decide to terminate their whole life insurance policy, they can withdraw the cash value of the savings that have accumulated over time. The amount by which the cash value exceeds the premiums paid is subject to taxes. If the policyholder dies, the beneficiary receives the cash value and the policy death benefit.

The premium on whole life insurance is constant for the duration of the policy. In the earlier years, a portion of the premium paid for the insurance reflects the potential payout to a beneficiary someday, and the remainder is invested by the insurance company as a form of savings. The portion of the premium dedicated to savings is high in the earlier years when the policyholder is young because the portion of the premium needed to insure against the possibility of death is relatively low. In the later years, the premium required to insure against possible death is relatively high, as the likelihood of death is greater. Because the insurance premium is constant, it is not sufficient to cover the amount needed to insure against possible death in the later years. Thus, a portion of the policy's cash value is used to supplement the premium paid in these years.

Many alternative forms of whole life insurance are available, so policyholders can structure the premium payments in a manner that fits their needs. Some forms also specify higher insurance benefits for the beneficiary in the earlier years and lower benefits in the later years.

The premium for whole life insurance is higher than the premium for term insurance. The advantage of whole life insurance over term insurance is that it not only provides insurance against possible death, but also accumulates savings over time. However, individuals could accumulate savings

17.2   Financial Planning Online: Should You Buy Whole Life or Term Insurance?

Go to:
http://www.financenter.com/
products/analyzers/lifeins.fcs

Click on:
"Which is better: Term or
Whole Life?"

This Web site provides:
an opinion on whether you
should purchase whole life
insurance or term insurance
based on the premiums that
exist and other information.

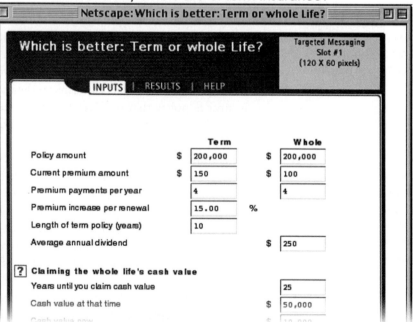

17.3   Financial Planning Online: Return on Your Whole Life Insurance Policy

Go to:

http://www.financenter.com/
products/analyzers/lifeins.fcs

Click on:

"What is my return on a whole
life policy?"

This Web site provides:

an estimate of the return that
you would earn on your whole
life insurance policy, based on
information about that policy.

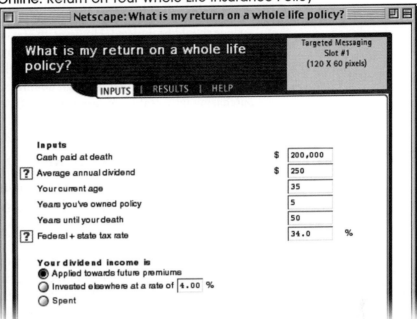

on their own by purchasing term insurance with lower premiums and then investing the remainder in investments of their own choice.

Universal Life Insurance

universal life insurance

Life insurance that provides insurance over a specified term and accumulates savings for the policyholder over this time.

Universal life insurance provides insurance over a specified term and accumulates savings for policyholders over this time. It is a combination term insurance and a savings plan. Because it allows policyholders to build savings, it is classified as a cash-value life insurance policy.

Universal life insurance allows policyholders to alter their payments over time. It specifies the premium needed to cover the term insurance portion. When policyholders pay more than that amount, the extra amount is invested in savings on which policyholders earn interest. Unlike whole life insurance policies where the insurance company makes the investment decisions, policyholders are given a set of alternative investments and can decide how the funds allocated toward the savings plan are to be invested. Policyholders may skip premium payments, and the amount needed to cover the term insurance portion or any administrative expenses will be withdrawn from their savings plan.

variable life insurance

Life insurance that provides insurance over a specified term and allows policyholders to invest residual funds, after the premium on the term portion is paid, in various types of investments.

A related type of insurance called **variable life insurance** allows policyholders to invest the residual funds, after the premium payment on the term portion is paid, in various types of investments, including mutual funds. Variable life insurance differs from whole life and universal life insurance in that it allows policyholders to make their own investment decisions.

An advantage of universal life insurance is that it provides policyholders with some flexibility in making their payments and in deciding how the savings should be invested. However, the fees on universal life insurance can be high. You can achieve the benefits of universal life insurance by simply purchasing term insurance and investing other money in the manner you prefer—without incurring the high administrative fees that you pay when purchasing universal life insurance.

DETERMINING THE AMOUNT OF LIFE INSURANCE NEEDED

You can determine the amount of life insurance you need by applying the income method or the budget method, as explained next.

Income Method

income method
A method that determines how much life insurance is needed based on the policyholder's annual income.

Financial planners who utilize the **income method** use a general formula to determine how much life insurance you should maintain based on your income. This method normally specifies the life insurance amount as a multiple of your annual income, such as 10 times your annual income. For example, if you have an annual income of $40,000, this formula would suggest that you need $400,000 in life insurance. This method is very easy to use. The disadvantage is that it does not consider your age and your household situation (including your annual household expenses). Thus, it does not differentiate between a household that has no children and one with four children. A household with four children will likely need more life insurance because its expenses will be higher.

Budget Method

budget method
A method that determines how much life insurance is needed based on the household's future expected expenses.

An alternative method is the **budget method,** which determines your life insurance needs by considering your future budget based on your household's future expected expenses and your current financial situation. This method takes factors such as the following into account:

- **Annual Living Expenses.** You should have sufficient insurance so that your family can live comfortably without your income. The family's future expenses will be higher if you have children. Younger children will need financial support for a longer period of time.

- **Special Future Expenses.** If you want to ensure a college education for your children, you need adequate life insurance to cover the expected future expenses.

- **Debt.** You may want to ensure that your life insurance can pay off any debt such as credit card bills and even a mortgage. If your family relies on your income to cover this debt, it may not be able to pay off that debt over time if you die.

- **Job Marketability of Spouse.** If your spouse has very limited job marketability, you may need more life insurance so that your spouse can receive some specialized training.

- **Value of Existing Savings.** If you have a large amount of savings accumulated, your family may possibly draw interest or dividends from these savings to cover a portion of their periodic expenses. Thus, the more savings your household has accumulated, the less life insurance you need.

Example

You wish to purchase a life insurance policy that generates a pre-tax income of at least $30,000 per year for the next 20 years to cover living expenses (excluding the mortgage payment) for your spouse and two children in the event that you die. You have just enough savings to cover burial expenses, and you anticipate no unusual expenses for the household in the future.

To determine your insurance needs, you must estimate the amount of insurance today that will cover your household's future living expenses. You can use the time value of money concepts from Chapter 3 to determine the amount of funds today that can provide an annuity equal to $30,000 over each of the next 20 years. First, assume that you expect that your spouse will be able to earn at least 6 percent annually by investing the money received from the life insurance policy. Next, estimate the present value of an annuity (see the Present Value of an Annuity Table in the appendix) that can provide your household with a $30,000 annuity over 20 years if it generates an annual return of 6 percent:

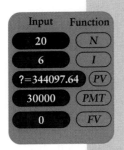

Input	Function
20	N
6	I
?=344097.64	PV
30000	PMT
0	FV

Amount of Insurance Needed = Annuity Amount × PVIFA ($i = 6\%$, $n = 20$)

= $30,000 × 11.47

= $344,100.

Based on the following additional information about your household, you then adjust the amount of insurance needed:

- **Other Special Future Expenses.** You also want to set aside a total of $50,000 to pay for your two children's college expenses. Although college expenses will rise in the future, the money set aside will accumulate interest over time, so it should be sufficient to provide a college education. You decide to allocate an extra $50,000 in life insurance.

- **Job Training.** You want to have additional insurance of $20,000 to ensure that your spouse can pay for job training in the event of your death.

- **Debt.** You have a $60,000 mortgage and no other loans or credit card debt outstanding. You decide to increase the life insurance amount so that the mortgage can be paid off in the event that you die. Therefore, you specify an extra $60,000 in life insurance.

By summing up your preferences, you determine you need a total of $474,100 in life insurance.

17.4   Financial Planning Online: How Much Life Insurance Do You Need?

Go to:

http://moneycentral.msn.com/
investor/calcs/n_life/main.asp

This Web site provides:
a recommendation for the amount of life insurance that you should have, based on your financial situation.

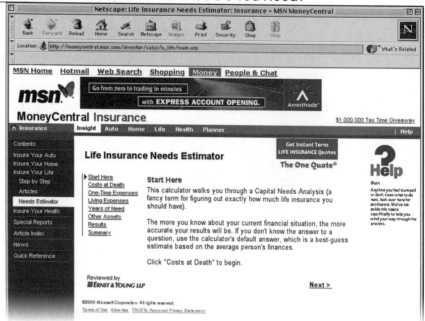

LIFE INSURANCE PREMIUMS

Now that you have determined how much life insurance you need, the next step is to determine your premiums to purchase life insurance. Recall that term insurance is pure insurance in the sense that the premiums are insuring against the possible death of the policyholder, as the policy does not build a cash value.

Factors That Affect Your Insurance Premiums

The premium you pay for life insurance is dependent on the following factors:

- **Amount of Insurance.** The larger the amount that a life insurance company must pay your beneficiary in the event that you die, the higher the premium the company will charge you.

- **Cash Value.** A life insurance policy that has a cash value requires a higher premium than a policy that does not have a cash value. As mentioned earlier, whole life and universal life insurance can build a cash value, while term insurance does not. If you terminate a policy with a cash value, you receive the cash value.

- **Personal Characteristics.** The premium charged on insurance is higher for individuals who are more likely to die in the near future. Thus, it is higher for older persons than for very young persons. The premium is also higher for individuals who smoke because statistics show that, on average, smokers do not live as long as nonsmokers. The premium is also higher for males than females because males do not live as long as females, on average.

"It covers you for everything except fire, accident, illness, loss, personal injury or death."

Using the Internet to Price Term Insurance

Many life insurance companies have Web sites where you can obtain quotes on term insurance. The Internet is a very efficient means of purchasing insurance if you know what you want. Information on life insurance premiums is available on Web sites such as insweb.com, insuremarket .com, and quotesmith.com. Web sites quickly provide a quote based on your age, gender, and other information. You may obtain insurance at a lower price because you do not require personal attention; at the same time, you can avoid sales pressure from an insurance agent.

Example of Term Insurance Quotations. Term insurance premiums vary among insurers. Exhibit 17.1 shows annual premiums that might be charged for a 10-year term (actual quotes vary among companies). For a given age level, the insurance premium increases with the amount of term insurance desired. If you are 25 years old, your annual premium is only $97 for a $250,000 policy versus $300 for a $1 million policy.

Exhibit 17.1   Example of Quoted Term Life Insurance Premiums Offered over the Internet

	Amount of Insurance Desired		
Age	$250,000	$500,000	$1,000,000
25	$97	$160	$300
30	110	185	315
35	128	201	328
40	155	242	414
45	231	404	745
50	339	645	1,245
55	506	970	1,884
60	789	1,536	3,031
65	1,340	2,629	5,222

www.cartoonstock.com

Notice that for a given amount of term insurance, the premium is higher if you are older. For a $250,000 policy, the annual premium is less than $130 if you are younger than 35 years old, but more than $500 if you are at least 55.

The premiums shown here are for males. For relatively young ages, the annual premiums of females are slightly lower. For relatively old ages, the annual premiums of females are substantially lower.

THE DECISION TO PURCHASE LIFE INSURANCE

Some people definitely need life insurance as a form of protection in the event of their death, because they have a family that relies on them for income. Those without a spouse or dependents may not necessarily need life insurance.

Using Life Insurance Company Ratings

When you purchase life insurance from an insurance company, you rely on that company to provide the insurance benefits that your policy specifies. If the life insurance company goes bankrupt, it may not be able to provide the benefits. To assess the possibility that an insurance company will go bankrupt, you can review its ratings. Insurance companies are assigned ratings by agencies (including A. M. Best, Standard & Poor's, and Moody's) that indicate the insurance company's risk.

settlement options
The alternative ways a beneficiary can receive life insurance benefits in the event that the insured person dies.

You should purchase life insurance (or any other insurance) only from insurance companies that receive high ratings and therefore have a relatively low likelihood of experiencing bankruptcy in the future. You can review ratings of insurance companies in libraries or on the Internet. If you are considering a specific insurance company, you can ask what its rating is.

SETTLEMENT OPTIONS ON A LIFE INSURANCE POLICY

Settlement options are the alternative ways a beneficiary can receive life insurance benefits in the event that the insured person dies. Normally, the benefits are not taxed, although there are some exceptions that are beyond the scope of this text. When individuals purchase a life insurance policy, they select the settlement option that is most appropriate for their respective beneficiary. The appropriate option is dependent on the needs and other characteristics of the beneficiaries. Some of the common options are identified next.

lump-sum settlement
A single payment of all the benefits owed to a beneficiary under a life insurance policy.

Lump Sum

A **lump-sum settlement** provides all the benefits to the beneficiary in a single payment upon the death of the insured. Thus, a $250,000 life insurance policy would provide $250,000 to the beneficiary in a lump sum. This settlement is often used if the beneficiary is disciplined and will use the proceeds wisely. If the beneficiary does not have sufficient discipline, however, an alternative settlement option may be more appropriate.

Installment Payments

installment payments settlement

The payment of the benefits owed to a beneficiary under a life insurance policy as a stream of equal payments over a specified number of years.

The policyholder can elect to use an **installment payments settlement,** which means that the beneficiary will receive a stream of equal payments over a specified number of years. For example, instead of paying $300,000 to the beneficiary in a lump sum, the policy may specify that the beneficiary will receive annual payments starting at the time of the policyholder's death and lasting for 10 years. By spreading the amount over time, this settlement option ensures that the beneficiary will not immediately spend the total amount to be received.

Interest Payments

interest payments settlement

A method of paying the benefits owed under a life insurance policy in which the company retains the amount owed for a specified number of years and pays interest to the beneficiary.

The policyholder can also elect to use an **interest payments settlement,** which means that the amount owed to the beneficiary will be held by the life insurance company for a specified number of years. Until the amount is distributed, the beneficiary will receive periodic interest payments on the amount. Like the installment payments option, this settlement option prevents the beneficiary from quickly spending all of the proceeds from the life insurance policy.

HOW LIFE INSURANCE FITS WITHIN YOUR FINANCIAL PLAN

The following are the key decisions about life insurance that should be included within your financial plan:

1. Do you need life insurance?

2. How much life insurance should you plan for in the future?

Exhibit 17.2 provides an example of how life insurance decisions apply to Stephanie Spratt's financial plan.

Exhibit 17.2 How Life Insurance Fits within Stephanie Spratt's Financial Plan

Goals for Life Insurance Planning

1. Determine whether I need to purchase life insurance.
2. Determine whether I should purchase or add to my life insurance in the future.

Analysis

Type of Insurance Plan	Benefits	Status
Term insurance	Insurance benefits provided to beneficiary.	Not needed at this time, since I do not have a spouse or dependents.
Whole life insurance	Insurance benefits provided to beneficiary, and policy builds a cash value over time.	Not needed at this time.
Universal life insurance	Insurance benefits provided to beneficiary, and policy builds a cash value over time.	Not needed at this time.

Decisions

Decision on Whether I Need Life Insurance:

Life insurance could be beneficial if I need to ensure that a specific beneficiary is provided with financial support in the event that I die. I do not have a beneficiary, so this reasoning is not a consideration. The whole life and universal life insurance policies build a cash value over time and therefore can be useful to build my savings. However, I can build savings on my own, so I will not buy a life insurance policy for this reason. At this time, I do not need a life insurance policy.

Decision on Insurance Coverage in the Future:

In the future, I will need to ensure proper life insurance coverage if I have a family. I would want to ensure that my children have sufficient funds to support them and possibly even pay for their college education if I die. I plan to obtain a term life insurance policy of $300,000 for any child I have. I will reassess this plan if and when I have children.

DISCUSSION QUESTIONS

1. How would Stephanie's decisions regarding purchasing life insurance be different if she were a single mother of two children?

2. How would Stephanie's decisions regarding purchasing life insurance be affected if she were 35 years old? If she were 50 years old?

SUMMARY

Life insurance provides payments to a specified beneficiary if the policyholder dies. Term insurance is strictly intended to provide insurance in the event of the possible death of the policyholder, while whole life insurance and universal life insurance use a portion of the premium to build a cash value. The premiums for whole life and universal life insurance are higher to account for the portion distributed into a savings plan and for the administrative fees.

The amount of life insurance that you need can be measured by the income method, in which you attempt to replace the income that would be discontinued due to death. The amount of life insurance can be more precisely measured by the budget method, which considers factors such as the household's future annual living expenses and existing debt.

The life insurance premium is dependent on the amount of life insurance coverage, on whether the life insurance policy has a cash value, and on personal characteristics such as age.

The decision to purchase life insurance is partially dependent on whether family members are currently relying on your income. If you decide to purchase insurance, a related decision is the choice of the insurance company. Since the payment from the insurance company to your beneficiaries may not occur until the distant future, you should select an insurance company that you believe will definitely be in service at that time. You can review life insurance company ratings to assess their financial condition, which may indicate whether they will survive over time.

A life insurance policy can be set up to pay the beneficiary a lump-sum payment, installment payments over a specified period, or interest payments over a specified period with a lump sum at the end of the period. The installment option or interest payment option may be most appropriate for ensuring that beneficiaries do not squander the entire life insurance coverage.

Integrating the Key Concepts

Your decisions regarding life insurance affect other parts of your financial plan. Because life insurance provides income to beneficiaries in the event of your death, you are not forced to achieve a level of wealth that will provide sufficient support for your dependents in the event of your death. Without life insurance, you may take excessive risk in your efforts to achieve substantial wealth for your family in the event of your death. For example, you might decide to ignore the need for liquidity (Part 2), so that you could focus on investments that are expected to offer a high rate of return. This strategy could cause you to experience cash shortages in some periods. You might also take excessive risk to achieve extremely high returns when making your investment decisions (Part 4), which could backfire. Moreover, you may be unable to finance a car or a home (Part 3) because you would need to avoid incurring loan payments, so that you could accumulate much wealth quickly. The advantage of life insurance is that it allows you more time to build wealth for yourself and for your family so that you can make financing and investment decisions that are based on a long-term perspective.

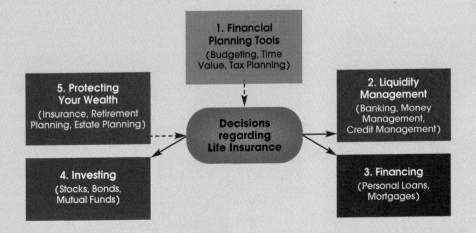

REVIEW QUESTIONS

1. What is the purpose of life insurance? Does everyone need life insurance? Explain.

2. What is term insurance? What determines the premium for term insurance? What is meant by decreasing-term insurance? Is mortgage life insurance a good buy? Why or why not?

3. What is whole life insurance? What benefit does it provide that term life insurance does not? Why is the premium paid for whole life higher than the premium for term life? What alternative approach to purchasing life insurance might provide the same benefits as whole life?

4. What is universal life insurance? How does it differ from term life and whole life?

5. What is variable life insurance? What are the advantages and disadvantages of variable or universal life policies? How else might an individual achieve these benefits?

6. Describe the income method of determining the amount of life insurance needed. What is the disadvantage of this method?

7. Describe the budget method of determining the amount of life insurance needed. What must be considered in making this calculation? Briefly discuss each element.

8. List and briefly discuss the factors that will affect an individual's life insurance premium.

9. Explain how the Web can expedite the purchase of life insurance. Why do many customers prefer this method?

10. What is the determining factor in the decision to purchase life insurance?

11. Why are life insurance company ratings important to those who purchase life insurance?

12. What are settlement options? What determines the option chosen?

13. What is a lump-sum settlement? What kind of beneficiary would benefit from this option?

14. What is an installment payments settlement? When would an insured choose this option?

15. What is the interest payments option? How does it differ from the installment payments option?

FINANCIAL PLANNING PROBLEMS

1. Nancy is a widow with two teenage children. Nancy's gross income is $3,000 per month, and taxes take about 30 percent of her income. Using the income method, Nancy calculates she will need to purchase about eight times her disposable income in life insurance to meet her needs. How much insurance should Nancy purchase?

2. Nancy's employer provides her with two times her annual gross salary in life insurance. How much additional insurance should Nancy purchase based on the information in the previous problem?

3. Peter is married and has two children. He wants to be sure that he has sufficient life insurance to take care of his family if he dies. Peter's wife is a homemaker but attends college part-time pursuing a law degree. It will cost approximately $40,000 for her to finish her education. Since the children are teenagers, Peter feels he will only need to provide the family with income for the next 10 years. He further calculates that the household expenses run approximately $35,000 per year. The balance on the home mortgage is $30,000. Peter set up a college fund for his children when they were babies, and it currently contains sufficient funds for them to attend college. Assuming that Peter's wife can invest the insurance proceeds at 8 percent, calculate the amount of insurance Peter needs to purchase.

4. Marty and Mary both have jobs and contribute to the household expenses according to their income. Marty contributes 75 percent of the expenses and Mary contributes 25 percent. Currently, their household expenses are $30,000 annually. Marty and Mary have three children, and the youngest is 12, so they would like to ensure that they could maintain their current standard of living for at least the next 8 years. They feel that the insurance proceeds could be invested at 6 percent. In addition to covering the annual expenses, they would like to make sure that each of their children has $25,000 available for college. If Marty were to die, Mary would go back to school part-time to upgrade her training as a nurse. This would cost $20,000. They have a mortgage on their home with a balance of $55,000. How much life insurance should they purchase for Marty?

5. Considering the information in the previous problem, how much life insurance should they carry on Mary?

FINANCIAL PLANNING ONLINE EXERCISES

1. Go to http://www.financenter.com/products/ analyzers/lifeins.fcs and click on: "Which is better: Term or Whole Life?" To answer this question, click on Results to view the findings based on the default information. Click on Graphs to see a graphical presentation of the results. By clicking on the Explanation tab, you will get additional information on the calculations.

2. Click on the input tab to return to the Input page. Change the Policy Amount to $500,000 for Term and $250,000 for Whole Life. Change the premium to $500 in each case. Keeping other values the same, check the Results, Graph, and Explanation.

3. Go to http://moneycentral.msn.com/investor/ calcs/n_life/main.asp. The Life Insurance Needs Estimator walks you through a series of steps to determine your insurance requirements. After you input amounts in each step, the Estimator will provide you with the results.

4. Go to http://moneycentral.msn.com/insure/lifelp. asp. Click on Get Quote and then Begin. Enter personal data to request a quote for $100,000 of term life insurance.

5. Use the Back option in your browser to return to the Start page and request a quote for $500,000 of Term Life; do not change any other information. Review the quote and discuss the reasons for the difference in premium pricing for the $100,000 and $500,000 policies.

6. Use the Back option in your browser to return to the Start page. Click on Get Quote and then click on Begin. Use the same information as in question 4, including the amount of insurance as $100,000. Change only the gender. Review the difference in rates for the change in gender and discuss the reason for the difference.

7. Go to http://insurance.yahoo.com/life.html. Use the Back option in your browser to return to the Yahoo! page and click on Life Insurance FAQ. Review the section on the amount of insurance required and comment on this information. Is it good advice? On the same page, read about the differences between whole and term life insurance. What are the pros and cons? How would you integrate these two options?

Building Your Own Financial Plan

Life insurance is the most controversial and hard-to-select form of insurance. It is controversial because opinions vary greatly on whether a person should even have life insurance. No external source requires that you have life insurance in the way that you are required to insure an automobile or home. It is also the one form of insurance for which you, the policyholder, will not be the one to file the claim.

Selection is difficult because the insurance industry has numerous policy options. On the one hand, there is term insurance, and on the other, whole life, both of which were thoroughly discussed in the chapter.

In this experiential exercise, you will first have to decide whether you need life insurance. Next, you will attach a dollar amount to any needs. Finally, you will be directed to a Web site where you can obtain quotes for the amount of insurance you have deemed necessary. A template

 is provided in the *Financial Planning Workbook* and on the CD-ROM to assist you with your research. You can obtain insurance premium data from numerous Web sites, as mentioned in the chapter. If you have not previously visited such a Web site, then go to www.selectquote .com. Once you determine your insurance needs, if any, you need to choose between term and whole life. The Web site in Financial Planning Online 17.2 will be of assistance.

Insurance needs should be reviewed when major changes occur in your life. Specifically, this review should be done if you marry, divorce, or become a parent. If you believe that you do not need life insurance at this point in your life, you need not complete this exercise. It is, however, to your benefit to consider what kinds of policies may suit your future needs.

The Sampsons—A Continuing Case

The Sampsons have one remaining insurance need: life insurance. They have decided to purchase term life insurance. They want a life insurance policy that will provide for the family in the event of Dave's death, as he is the breadwinner. The Sampsons do not know how much insurance to purchase, but their goal is to have enough money for general expenses over the next 15 years.

Recall that Dave's salary after taxes is about $40,000. He wants to ensure that the family would have insurance benefits that could provide $40,000 for the next 15 years. By the end of this period, the children would have completed college. Dave also wants to add an additional $300,000 of insurance coverage to provide support for Sharon through her retirement years, since they have not saved much money for retirement.

1. Determine the present value of the insurance benefits that could provide $40,000 over the next 15 years for the Sampson family. Assume that the insurance payment could be invested to earn 6 percent interest over time.

2. Considering the insurance benefits needed to provide $40,000 over the next 15 years, plus the additional $300,000 of insurance coverage, what amount of insurance coverage is needed?

3. Given the amount of insurance coverage needed and Dave's present age (30 years old), estimate the premium that the Sampsons would pay using one of the insurance Web sites mentioned in the chapter (such as insweb.com).

IN-TEXT STUDY GUIDE

True/False:

1. Life insurance is intended to provide financial support for your beneficiaries after you die.

2. Whole life insurance provides insurance over a specified term and accumulates savings for policyholders over this time.

3. Since the insurance premium in whole life insurance is constant, it is sufficient to cover the amount needed to insure against possible death in the later years.

4. An advantage of whole life insurance over term insurance is that it not only provides insurance against possible death, but also accumulates savings over time.

5. If your spouse has very limited job marketability, you need less life insurance.

6. If you terminate a life insurance policy with a cash value, you forfeit the cash value.

7. Life insurance premiums are higher for older persons than for younger persons.

8. In general, you should purchase life insurance from insurance companies that receive high ratings.

9. Settlement options are the alternative ways in which beneficiaries can pay their premiums.

10. In decreasing term insurance, the insurance premiums paid by the beneficiary are reduced over time.

11. If the insured person remains alive over the term specified in term insurance, the policy expires at the end of the term and has no value.

Multiple Choice:

1. Which of the following institutions are unlikely to offer life insurance policies?
   a. subsidiaries of financial conglomerates
   b. independent firms
   c. financial institutions providing banking and brokerage services
   d. All of the above may offer life insurance policies.

2. _____ insurance is not a type of life insurance.
   a. Term
   b. Wholesale
   c. Universal life
   d. Mortgage

3. In _____ insurance, the insurance benefits to the beneficiary are reduced over time.
   a. decreasing-term
   b. whole life
   c. universal life
   d. mortgage

4. In decreasing-term insurance, the premiums paid _____ over time.
   a. increase
   b. decrease
   c. remain constant
   d. none of the above

5. The premium paid for whole life insurance is _____ the premium paid for term insurance.
   a. higher than
   b. lower than
   c. equal to
   d. none of the above

6. _____ life insurance allows policyholders to alter their payments over time.
   a. Term
   b. Whole
   c. Universal
   d. Mortgage

7. _____ life insurance pays off a policyholder's mortgage in the event of the person's death.
   a. Term
   b. Whole
   c. Universal
   d. Mortgage

8. In the _____ method, the life insurance amount is determined as a multiple of your annual income.
   a. income
   b. budget
   c. asset allocation
   d. none of the above

9. The _____ savings your household has accumulated, the _____ life insurance will be needed.
   a. more; less
   b. less; more
   c. more; more
   d. Answers (a) and (b) are correct.

The following information applies to questions 10 and 11.

Otto Klein would like to purchase a life insurance policy that generates an income of at least $40,000 per year for the next 15 years to cover various expenses for his household in the event that he dies. Otto believes that his wife Emma could earn a return of about 7 percent annually.

10. How much insurance does Otto need?
    a. $14,497.84
    b. $144,978.41
    c. $364,316.56
    d. $82,770.95

11. Now assume that Otto would like to set aside $70,000 to pay off his mortgage in the event that he dies. How much insurance does Otto need?
    a. $84,497.84
    b. $434,316.56
    c. $389,687.78
    d. $1,001,870.54

12. The premium you pay for life insurance does not depend on which of the following?
    a. amount of insurance
    b. cash value
    c. personal characteristics, such as age
    d. The premium depends on all of the above.

13. In general, life insurance premiums for males are _____ those for females.
    a. higher than
    b. lower than
    c. the same as
    d. None of the above

14. The _____ the amount that a life insurance company must pay your beneficiary in the event that you die, the _____ the premium that the company will charge you.
    a. larger; lower
    b. smaller; higher
    c. larger; higher
    d. Answers (a) and (b) are correct.

15. The premium for a life insurance policy that has a cash value is _____ the premium for a policy that does not have a cash value.
    a. the same as
    b. lower than
    c. higher than
    d. none of the above

16. You would like to purchase life insurance that will provide your beneficiaries with $20,000 annually for 25 years. You expect your beneficiaries will invest the money at an interest rate of 9 percent. You should purchase _____ in life insurance.
    a. $231,935.67
    b. $172,461.61
    c. $196,451.59
    d. none of the above

17. Which of the following agencies does not assign ratings to insurance companies?
    a. A. M. Best
    b. Standard & Poor's
    c. Moody's
    d. Dow Jones Company

18. The _____ settlement option is appropriate only if the beneficiary has sufficient discipline to use the proceeds wisely.
    a. lump-sum
    b. installment payments
    c. interest payments
    d. none of the above

19. In the _____ settlement option, the beneficiary receives a stream of equal payments over a specified number of years.
    a. lump-sum
    b. installment payments
    c. interest payments
    d. none of the above

20. The insurance premium is _____ related to one's age.
    a. never
    b. rarely
    c. inversely
    d. positively.

21. Mortgage insurance is a form of _____ insurance.
    a. increasing-term
    b. decreasing-term
    c. whole life
    d. universal life

Chapter 18

Retirement Planning

Your retirement may seem far off, but it is never too early to start planning. The sooner you start saving for retirement, the more you can benefit from the potential growth in your retirement account. Planning for retirement will increase the amount of savings you will have in your retirement account by the time you retire and will therefore enhance your wealth. Retirement planning also offers tax-saving benefits.

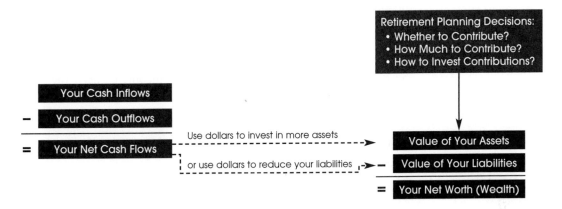

The objectives of this chapter are to:

- describe the role of Social Security,

- explain the difference between defined-benefit and defined-contribution retirement plans,

- present the key decisions you must make regarding retirement plans,

- introduce the retirement plans offered by employers,

- outline the retirement plans available for self-employed individuals,

- describe types of individual retirement accounts,

- illustrate how to estimate the savings you will have in your retirement account at the time you retire, and

- show how to measure the tax benefits from contributing to a retirement account.

SOCIAL SECURITY

Recall from Chapter 4 that Social Security is a federal program that taxes you during your working years and uses the funds to make payments to you upon retirement (subject to age and other requirements). It is intended to ensure that you receive some income once you retire and therefore is an important part of retirement planning. However, Social Security does not provide sufficient income to support the lifestyles of most individuals. Therefore, additional retirement planning is necessary to ensure that you can live comfortably when you retire. Before discussing other means of retirement planning, we will describe how Social Security functions.

Qualifying for Social Security

To qualify for Social Security benefits, you need to build up a total of 40 credits from contributing to Social Security over time through payroll taxes. You receive one credit for every $780 in income per year, but you can earn no more than four credits per year. In addition to receiving income at retirement, you will also receive Social Security benefits if you become disabled and are unable to work for at least one year, or if you are the survivor when the breadwinner of the household dies. If the person who qualified for Social Security dies (the household's main income earner), the following benefits are provided to the survivors:

- A one-time income payment to the spouse.

- Monthly income payments if the spouse is older than age 60 or has a child under the age of 16.

- Monthly income payments to children under the age of 18.

Social Security Taxes

As discussed in Chapter 4, the federal government taxes both you and your employer 7.65 percent of your gross income each pay period. Recall that this tax is referred to as FICA (Federal Insurance Contributions Act) on your paycheck. Your FICA taxes are used to support Social Security and Medicare, the federal government's health insurance program. The Social Security tax is 6.2 percent of your gross income up to $80,400 in 2001 (this amount is adjusted periodically). The maximum that you pay per year for Social Security taxes is $4,984.80 (6.2 percent of $80,400). The Medicare tax of 1.45 percent of gross income is also included in FICA. There is no cap on the income level, however, so you and your employer must pay this tax on your gross income beyond $80,400. The FICA tax rates applied to various levels of gross income are shown in Exhibit 18.1.

The taxes received by the Social Security program are distributed to current retirees. Thus, your payments to the Social Security program are not invested for your retirement. When you retire, you will receive Social Security payments provided by individuals and their employers at that time.

Retirement Benefits

The amount of income that you receive from Social Security when you retire is dependent on the number of years you earned income and your average level of income. Social Security provides you with about 42 percent of your average annual income during your working years. Due to adjustments, however, this proportion is higher for individuals who had low-income levels and lower for those who had high-income levels.

Exhibit 18.1 FICA Taxes on Various Income Levels

Gross Income Level	FICA Tax Rate Imposed on You	FICA Tax Imposed on You	FICA Tax Rate Imposed on Your Employer	FICA Tax Imposed on Your Employer
$20,000	7.65%	$1,530	7.65%	$1,530
30,000	7.65	2,295	7.65	2,295
40,000	7.65	3,060	7.65	3,060
50,000	7.65	3,825	7.65	3,825
60,000	7.65	4,590	7.65	4,590
70,000	7.65	5,355	7.65	5,355
80,000	7.65	6,120	7.65	6,120
90,000	7.65% of the first $80,400; 1.45% of the remainder	$6,290 [computed as $(.0765 \times \$80,400) + (.0145 \times \$9,600)$]	7.65% of the first $80,400; 1.45% of the remainder	$6,290 [computed as $(.0765 \times \$80,400) + (.0145 \times \$9,600)$]
100,000	7.65% of the first $80,400; 1.45% of the remainder	$6,435 [computed as $(.0765 \times \$80,400) + (.0145 \times \$19,600)$]	7.65% of the first $80,400; 1.45% of the remainder	$6,435 [computed as $(.0765 \times \$80,400) + (.0145 \times \$19,600)$]

18.1 Financial Planning Online: Request a Social Security Statement

Go to:
http://www.ssa.gov/top10.html

This Web site provides:
a form that you can use to request that a statement of your lifetime earnings and an estimate of your benefits be mailed to you.

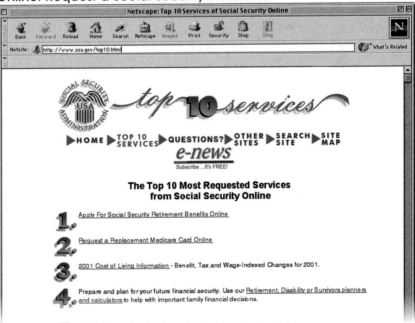

"Winning is crucial to my retirement plans."

At the age of 65, you can qualify for full retirement benefits. Starting in 2003, the eligibility age will gradually increase until it reaches age 67. You can receive retirement benefits at age 62, but the benefits will be lower than if you wait until you are 65 years old. As a general rule, though, early retirement will give you about the same total Social Security benefits over your lifetime as full retirement benefits.

You can earn other income while receiving Social Security benefits. If your income exceeds a specified limit (which is adjusted over time), however, a portion of your Social Security benefits will be taxed; the amount that is subject to taxes is dependent on how much other income you earn. The Social Security Administration estimates each individual's retirement benefits and sends this information annually to all individuals who will be receiving benefits.

Concern about Retirement Benefits in the Future

There is some concern about whether the Social Security program will be able to support retirees in the future. Today's retirees are now living longer, which means that the program must provide income over a longer period to individuals on average. In addition, there will be more retirees in the future and fewer workers to support them. When the generation of baby boomers begins retiring in the year 2011, much more funding will be needed to provide Social Security payments to all the retirees. Therefore, given the program's uncertain future, many individuals are relying less on Social Security income in their retirement planning.

Even if the Social Security program continues, many individuals will want more income after retirement than it provides. In 2000, the average monthly Social Security payment was about $800. Thus, even if the Social Security program continues in its current form, its benefits are unlikely to be sufficient to provide a comfortable lifestyle for most people. For this reason, many individuals establish their own retirement programs.

EMPLOYER-SPONSORED RETIREMENT PLANS

Employer-sponsored retirement plans are designed to help you save for retirement. Each pay period, you and/or your employer contribute money to a retirement account. If you withdraw money from the account before you reach a specific age, you will be subject to a penalty tax. The money in most of these accounts can be invested in a manner that you specify (within the range of possibilities offered by your specific plan). The money you contribute to the retirement plan is not taxed until you withdraw it from the account. Any money you withdraw from the retirement account after you retire is taxed as ordinary income.

Employer-sponsored retirement plans are classified as defined-benefit or defined-contribution plans.

Defined-Benefit Plans

defined-benefit plan
An employer-sponsored retirement plan that guarantees you a specific amount of income when you retire based on your salary and years of employment.

vested
Having a claim to a portion of the money in an employer-sponsored retirement account that has been reserved for you upon your retirement even if you leave the company.

Defined-benefit plans guarantee you a specific amount of income when you retire, based on factors such as your salary and years of employment. Your employer makes all the contributions to the plan. The specific formula varies among employers. Guidelines also determine when employees are **vested**, which means that they have a claim to a portion of the retirement money that has been reserved for them upon retirement. For example, a firm may allow you to be 20 percent vested after two years, which means that 20 percent of the amount reserved for you through employer contributions will be maintained in your retirement account even if you leave the company. The percentage increases with the number of years with the employer, so you may be fully vested (able to retain 100 percent of your retirement account) after six years based on the guidelines of some retirement plans. Once you are fully vested, all money that is reserved for you each year will be maintained in your retirement account. These vesting rules encourage employees to stay at one firm for several years.

Defined-Contribution Plans

defined-contribution plan
An employer-sponsored retirement plan that specifies guidelines under which you and/or your employer can contribute to your retirement account and that allows you to invest the funds as you wish.

Defined-contribution plans specify guidelines under which you and/or your employer can contribute to your retirement account. The benefits that you ultimately receive are determined by the performance of the money invested in your account. You can decide how you want the money to be invested. You can also change your investments over time.

As a result of their flexibility, defined-contribution plans have become very popular. In the last 10 years, many employers have shifted from defined-benefit to defined-contribution plans. This places more responsibility on the employees to contribute money and to decide how the contributions should be invested until their retirement. Therefore, individuals need to understand the potential benefits of a defined-contribution plan and how to estimate the potential retirement savings that can be accumulated under this plan.

Benefits of a Defined-Contribution Plan. A defined-contribution plan provides you with many benefits. Any money contributed by your employer is like extra income paid to you beyond your salary. In addition, having a retirement account can encourage you to save money each pay period by directing a portion of your income to the account before you receive your paycheck.

Investing in a defined-contribution plan also offers tax benefits. The retirement account allows you to defer taxes on income paid by your employer because your contribution to your account is deducted from your pay before taxes are taken out. Also note that the income generated by your investments in a retirement account is not taxed until you withdraw the money after you retire. This tax benefit is very valuable because it provides you with more money that can be invested and accumulate. In addition, by the time you are taxed on the investments (at retirement), you will likely be in a lower tax bracket because you will have less income. Consequently, you not only defer taxes, but incur lower taxes by contributing to your retirement plan.

Investing Funds in Your Retirement Account. Most defined-contribution plans sponsored by employers allow some flexibility on how your retirement funds can be invested. You can typically select from a variety of stock mutual funds, bond mutual funds, or even money market funds. The amount of funds you accumulate will depend on how your investment in the retirement account performs.

YOUR RETIREMENT PLANNING DECISIONS

Your key retirement planning decisions involve choosing a retirement plan, determining how much to contribute, and allocating your contributions. Each of these decisions is discussed next.

Which Retirement Plan Should You Pursue?

The retirement benefits resulting from an employer-sponsored retirement plan vary among employers. Some employer-sponsored plans allow you to invest more money than others. If your employer offers a retirement plan, that should be the first plan that you consider because your employer will likely contribute to it.

How Much to Contribute?

Some retirement plans allow individuals to determine how much money (up to some specified maximum level) to contribute to their retirement account. Although some individuals like this freedom, others are not comfortable making this decision. You do not need to know how much money you will require at retirement to measure your potential savings from contributing to your retirement plan, as the following example shows.

Example

Stephanie Spratt is considering whether she should start saving toward her retirement. Although her retirement is 40 years away, she wants to ensure that she can live comfortably at that time. She can contribute $5,000 per year to her retirement through her employer's defined-contribution plan. Her employer will match whatever contribution she makes up to a maximum of $5,000 per year. Therefore, her actual contribution to her retirement account will be $10,000 per year. Contributing $5,000 per year means Stephanie will have less spending money and will not have access to these savings until she retires in about 40 years. However, her $5,000 annual contribution would help reduce her taxes now because the money she contributes would not be subject to income taxes until she withdraws it at retirement.

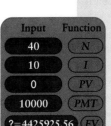

Stephanie wants to determine how much money she will have in 40 years based on the total contribution of $10,000 per year. She expects to earn a return of 10 percent on her investment. She can use the future value of annuity tables (in Appendix A) to estimate the value of this annuity in 40 years. Her estimate of her savings at the time of her retirement is:

Savings in Retirement Account = Annual Contribution × FVIFA (*i* = 10%, *n* = 40)

$$= \$10,000 \times 442.59$$
$$= \$4,425,900.$$

Stephanie realizes that she may be overestimating her return, so she re-estimates her savings based on a 6 percent return:

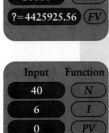

Savings in Retirement Account = Annual Contribution × FVIFA (*i* = 6%, *n* = 40)

$$= \$10,000 \times 154.76$$
$$= \$1,547,600.$$

Even with this more conservative estimate, Stephanie realizes that she will be able to accumulate more than $1.5 million by contributing $10,000 per year. Therefore, she decides to start contributing to her employer's retirement plan immediately.

How Much to Save? The amount that you try to save by the time you retire is partially dependent on the retirement income that you will need to live comfortably. There are various methods of determining the amount that you should save for your retirement. Among the important variables to consider are whether you will be supporting anyone besides yourself at retirement, your personal needs, the expected price level of products at the time of your retirement, and the number of years you will live while retired. Various online calculators based on these factors are available.

Given the difficulty of estimating how much income you will need at retirement, a safe approach is to recognize that Social Security will not provide sufficient funds and to invest as much as you can on a consistent basis in your retirement plan. After maintaining enough funds for liquidity purposes, you should invest as much as possible in retirement accounts, especially when the contribution is matched by the employer.

How to Invest Your Contributions?

When considering investment alternatives within a defined-contribution retirement plan, you do not have to worry about tax effects. All the money

18.2   Financial Planning Online: Retirement Expense Calculator

Go to:
http://moneycentral.msn.com
/investor/calcs/n_retireq/main.
asp

This Web site provides:
an estimate of your expenses
at retirement based on your
current salary and expenses.

you withdraw from your retirement account at the time you retire will be
taxed at your ordinary income tax rate, regardless of how it was earned.
Most financial advisers suggest a diversified set of investments, such as investing most of the money in one or more stock mutual funds and investing the
remainder in one or more bond mutual funds. In general, stocks generate
higher long-term returns than bonds, but bonds provide some balance in
case stocks perform poorly.

Your retirement plan investment decision should consider the number
of years until your retirement, as shown in Exhibit 18.2. If you are far from
retirement, you might consider mutual funds that invest in stocks with high
potential for growth (such as a capital appreciation fund, an Internet fund,
and maybe an international stock or bond fund). If you are close to retirement, you might consider Ginnie Mae bond funds, Treasury bond funds,
and a stock mutual fund that focuses on stocks of very large firms that pay
high dividends. Remember, however, that any investment is subject to a
possible decline in value. Some investments (such as a money market fund
focused on Treasury bills or on bank certificates of deposits) are less risky,
but also offer less potential return. Most retirement plans allow a wide variety of investment alternatives to suit various risk tolerances.

If you are young and far from retirement, you are in a position to take
more risk with your investments. As you approach retirement, however, your
investments should be more conservative. For example, you may shift some
of your investment to Treasury bonds so that your retirement fund is less
exposed to risk.

Exhibit 18.2   Typical Composition of a Retirement Account Portfolio

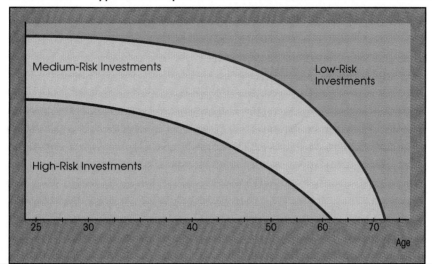

	Common High-Risk Investments	**Common Medium-Risk Investments**	**Common Low-Risk Investments**
Stock Mutual Funds	Growth stock funds Capital appreciation funds Small-cap funds International stock funds Sector stock funds	High-dividend stock funds S&P 500 index funds	
Bond Mutual Funds	Junk bond funds International bond funds	Medium-rated corporate bond funds	Treasury bond funds Ginnie Mae funds High-rated corporate funds
Hybrid Mutual Funds		Balanced (stock and bond) funds	
Money Market Funds			Treasury money market funds Money market funds that contain commercial paper and CDs

RETIREMENT PLANS OFFERED BY EMPLOYERS

The following are some of the more popular defined-contribution retirement plans offered by employers:

- 401(k) plan.

- 403-b plan.

- Simplified Employee Plan (SEP).

- Savings Incentive Match Plan for Employees (SIMPLE).
- Profit sharing.
- Employee stock ownership plan (ESOP).

401(k) Plan

401(k) plan

A defined-contribution plan that allows employees to contribute a maximum of $10,500 per year or 15 percent of their salary on a pre-tax basis.

A **401(k) plan** is a defined-contribution plan established by firms for their employees. Under federal guidelines, the maximum amount that employees can contribute is 15 percent of their salary up to a maximum of $10,500 per year (as of the year 2001). As a result of the Tax Relief Act of 2001, the maximum annual contribution allowed for the 401(k) plan will increase gradually until it reaches $15,000 in 2006. It may also be adjusted beyond that time for inflation. Individuals over age 50 will be able to make additional yearly contributions of up to $5,000. You can usually start contributing after one year of employment. The money you contribute is deducted from your paycheck before taxes are assessed. When you participate in a 401(k) plan, you are automatically vested. Thus, the money you contribute to the plan is yours, regardless of when you leave the firm.

Each firm offers a set of investment alternatives for the money contributed to a 401(k). For example, you may be able to invest in one or more mutual funds. The mutual funds are not necessarily part of a single family, as many firms allow their employees to choose among mutual funds sponsored by many different investment companies.

Matching Contributions by Employers. Some firms' 401(k) plans require the entire contribution to come from the employee with no matching contribution from the employer. Other firms match the employee's contribution. This means that if an employee contributes $400 per month, the employer will provide an additional $400 per month to the employee's retirement account. Or the firm may match a percentage of the employee's contribution. For example, if the employee contributes $400, the employer may contribute 50 percent of that amount, or an additional $200, to the employee's retirement account. The amount of matching (if any) provided by the employer has a large impact on the savings that the employee will have at retirement. More than 80 percent of all firms offering 401(k) plans match a portion or all of an employee's contributions.

Tax on Money Withdrawn from the Account. If you withdraw money from your 401(k) account before age 59 1/2, you will be subject to a penalty equal to 10 percent of the amount withdrawn. Your withdrawal will also be taxed as regular income at your marginal income tax rate. However, if you are retired and over age 59 1/2 when you withdraw the money, you may not have much other income and therefore will be in a very low marginal income tax bracket. Thus, the 401(k) plan allows you to defer paying taxes on the income you contributed for several years and may also allow you to pay a lower tax rate on the money once you withdraw it.

403-b Plan

403-b plan
A defined-contribution plan allowing employees of non-profit organizations to invest up to $10,000 of their income on a tax-deferred basis.

Nonprofit organizations such as educational institutions and charitable organizations offer **403-b plans**, which are very similar to 401(k) plans in that they allow you to invest a portion of your income on a tax-deferred basis. The maximum amount that you can contribute is dependent on your compensation and years of service, up to a limit of $10,500. As a result of the Tax Relief Act of 2001, the maximum annual contribution allowed for the 403-b plan will increase gradually until it reaches $15,000 in 2006.

A 403-b plan allows you to choose investment alternatives. You will be penalized for withdrawals before age 59 1/2, and when you withdraw the money at retirement, you will be taxed at your marginal tax rate.

Simplified Employee Plan (SEP)

Simplified Employee Plan (SEP)
A defined-contribution plan commonly offered by firms with 1 to 10 employees or used by self-employed people.

A **Simplified Employee Plan (SEP)** is commonly offered by firms with 1 to 10 employees. The employee is not allowed to make contributions. The employer can contribute up to 15 percent of the employee's annual income, up to a maximum annual contribution of $25,500. SEPs give an employer much flexibility in determining how much money to contribute. The employer may establish your SEP account at an investment company, depository institution, or brokerage firm of your choice. If it is established at an investment company, you will be able to invest the money in a set of mutual funds that the company offers. If the account is established at a depository institution, you will be able to invest the money in CDs issued by the institution. If it is established at a brokerage firm, you may be able to invest in some individual stocks or mutual funds that you choose. Withdrawals should occur only after age 59 1/2 to avoid a penalty, and the withdrawals are taxed at your marginal income tax rate at that time.

SIMPLE Plan

SIMPLE (Savings Incentive Match Plan for Employees) Plan
A defined-contribution plan intended for firms with 100 or fewer employees.

The **SIMPLE (Savings Incentive Match Plan for Employees) plan** is intended for firms with 100 or fewer employees. A SIMPLE account can be established at investment companies, depository institutions, or brokerage firms.

The employee can contribute up to $6,000 per year; due to the Tax Relief Act of 2001, this maxiumum amount will be raised gradually until it reaches $10,000 in 2005. It may also be adjusted beyond that time for inflation. As with the other retirement plans mentioned so far, this contribution is not taxed until the money is withdrawn from the account. Thus, a SIMPLE account is an effective means of deferring tax on income. In addition, the employer can match a portion of the employee's contribution.

profit sharing
A defined-contribution plan in which the employer makes contributions to employee retirement accounts based on a specified profit formula.

Profit Sharing

Some firms provide **profit sharing,** in which the employer makes contributions to employee retirement accounts based on a specified profit formula.

The employer can contribute up to 15 percent of an employee's salary each year, up to a maximum annual amount of $25,500.

Employee Stock Ownership Plan (ESOP)

employee stock ownership plan (ESOP)
A retirement plan in which the employer contributes some of its own stock to the employee's retirement account.

With an **employee stock ownership plan (ESOP),** the employer contributes some of its own stock to the employee's retirement account. A disadvantage of this plan is that it is focused on one stock; if this stock performs poorly, your retirement account will not be able to support your retirement. A recent survey by the John Hancock Insurance Company found that many individuals believe an individual stock is less risky than a diversified stock mutual fund. Recall from Chapter 15, however, that a diversified mutual fund is less susceptible to wide swings in value because it contains various stocks that are not likely to experience large downturns simultaneously. An ESOP is generally more risky than retirement plans invested in diversified mutual funds.

Managing Your Retirement Account after Leaving Your Employer

When you leave an employer, you may be able to retain your retirement account there if you have at least $5,000 in it. Another option is to transfer your assets tax-free into your new employer's retirement account, assuming that your new employer allows such transfers (most employers do). However, some employers charge high annual fees to manage transferred retirement plans.

rollover IRA
An individual retirement account (IRA) into which you can transfer your assets from your company retirement plan tax-free while avoiding early withdrawal penalties.

You can also create a **rollover IRA** by transferring your assets tax-free from your company retirement plan to an individual retirement account (IRA). You can initiate a rollover IRA by completing an application provided by various investment companies that sponsor mutual funds or by various brokerage firms. By transferring your retirement account into a rollover IRA, you can avoid cashing in your retirement account and therefore can continue to defer taxes and avoid the early withdrawal penalty.

RETIREMENT PLANS FOR SELF-EMPLOYED INDIVIDUALS

Two popular retirement plans for self-employed individuals are the Keogh Plan and the Simplified Employee Plan (SEP).

Keogh Plan

Keogh Plan
A retirement plan that enables self-employed individuals to contribute part of their pre-tax income to a retirement account.

The **Keogh plan** enables self-employed individuals to contribute part of their pre-tax income to a retirement account. An individual can contribute up to 25 percent of net income, up to a maximum annual contribution of $35,000. As with other retirement accounts, contributions are not taxed until they are withdrawn at the time of retirement. You can establish a Keogh plan by completing an application form provided by investment companies and some brokerage firms. Withdrawals can begin at age 59 1/2, and you are responsible for determining how the plan's funds are invested.

Simplified Employee Plan (SEP)

The Simplified Employee Plan (SEP) is also available for self-employed individuals. If you are self-employed, you can contribute up to 15 percent of your annual income, up to a maximum annual contribution of $25,500. You can establish your SEP account at an investment company, depository institution, or brokerage firm of your choice. A SEP is easier to set up than a Keogh Plan, but the maximum contribution is less.

INDIVIDUAL RETIREMENT ACCOUNTS

You should also consider opening an individual retirement account (IRA). There are two main types of IRAs: the traditional IRA and the Roth IRA.

Traditional IRA

traditional individual retirement account (IRA)
A retirement plan that enables individuals to invest $2,000 per year ($4,000 per year for married couples).

The **traditional individual retirement account (IRA)** enables you to save for your retirement, separate from any retirement plan provided by your employer. You can invest $2,000 per year ($4,000 per year for a married couple) in an IRA. As a result of the Tax Relief Act of 2001, the maximum annual contribution limit will increase gradually until it reaches $5,000 in 2008. The $5,000 level will be adjusted periodically for inflation. Individuals over age 50 will also be able to make higher contributions. If you are covered by an employer-sponsored plan, and your gross income is above limits specified by the Internal Revenue Service, your IRA contribution is not tax-deductible. However, the income earned on your investments within the IRA is not taxed until you withdraw your money at retirement. You will not be taxed again on the initial investment when you withdraw that money at retirement. (If you are not covered by an employer-sponsored plan, your IRA contribution is tax-deductible unless your income is very high.)

When you contribute to an IRA, your investment choices will depend on the retirement plan sponsor. If you set up your IRA at Vanguard, you can select among more than 60 mutual funds for your account.

You can withdraw funds from an IRA at age 59 1/2 or later. You are taxed on the income earned by your investments at your ordinary income tax rate at the time you withdraw funds. If you withdraw the funds before age 59 1/2, you are not only taxed at your ordinary income tax rate, but are typically charged a penalty equal to 10 percent of the withdrawn funds.

Roth IRA
A retirement plan that enables individuals who are under specific income limits to invest $2,000 per year ($4,000 per year for married couples).

Roth IRA

The **Roth IRA** allows individuals who are under specific income limits to invest $2,000 per year ($4,000 per year for married couples). Due to the Tax Relief Act of 2001, the maximum annual contribution limit will be increased gradually until it reaches $5,000 in 2008. Individuals over age 50 have higher contribution limits. You can withdraw funds from the Roth IRA at age 59 1/2 or later. You are taxed on money invested in the Roth IRA at the time of the contribution. However, you are not taxed when you withdraw the money, as long as you withdraw the money after age 59 1/2 and the Roth IRA has been in existence for at least five years. These tax characteristics differ from the traditional IRA, in which you are not taxed when contributing (if you are under specific income limits), but are taxed when you withdraw the money after retirement. You can invest in both a Roth IRA and a traditional IRA, but you are limited to a total IRA contribution. For example, if you are single and invest the maximum amount in a Roth IRA this year, you cannot invest in a traditional IRA. If you invest $1,000 less than the maximum amount in a Roth IRA this year, you can also invest $1,000 in a traditional IRA. You need not maintain a specific allocation between the two types of IRAs each year, but you are subject to the maximum total contribution.

Individuals who earn high income are not eligible for the Roth IRA. For married taxpayers filing jointly, the Roth IRA begins to phase out at $150,000 of adjusted gross income. For single taxpayers, the Roth IRA begins to phase out at $95,000.

Comparison of the Roth IRA and Traditional IRA. To illustrate the difference between the Roth IRA and the traditional IRA, we will consider the effects of investing $2,000 in each type of IRA.

Advantage of the Traditional IRA over the Roth IRA. The $2,000 that you contribute to a traditional IRA is sheltered from taxes until you withdraw money from your account. Conversely, you pay taxes on your income before you contribute $2,000 to a Roth IRA so that $2,000 is subject to taxes immediately. Assuming that you are in a 30 percent tax bracket, you would incur a tax of $600 now (computed as $2,000 × 30%) on the income contributed to a Roth IRA. Had you invested that income in a traditional IRA instead of a Roth IRA, you would not incur taxes on that income at this time.

Advantage of the Roth IRA over the Traditional IRA. IRA contributions should grow over time, assuming that you invest each year and that you earn a reasonable return. Assume that you are retired and withdraw $10,000 after several years of investing in your IRA. If you withdraw $10,000 from your Roth IRA, you will not pay any taxes on the amount withdrawn. Conversely, if you withdraw $10,000 from your traditional IRA, you will pay taxes on the amount withdrawn, based on your marginal income tax bracket. If your marginal tax bracket at that time is 20 percent, you will incur a tax of $2,000 (computed as $10,000 × 20%). Thus, you would incur a tax of $2,000 more than if you had withdrawn the money from a Roth IRA. Investment income accumulates on a tax-free basis in a Roth IRA, whereas money withdrawn from a traditional IRA is taxable.

18.3   Financial Planning Online: Traditional IRA or Roth IRA?

Go to:

http://www.financenter.com/
products/analyzers/rothira.fcs

Click on:

"Which will provide the most
retirement income?"

This Web site provides:

an analysis of whether a traditional IRA or a Roth IRA is better suited to you based on your
input about your financial situation.

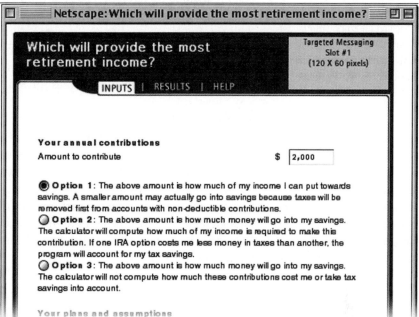

Factors That Affect Your Choice. So which IRA is better? The answer depends on many factors, including what your marginal income tax rate is at the time you contribute money to your IRA and at the time that you withdraw money from your IRA. If you are in a high tax bracket now and expect to be in a very low tax bracket (since you may be retired) when you withdraw money from the IRA, you may be better off with the traditional IRA. Because you are not taxed on the initial contribution, you will receive your tax benefit when you are working and subject to a high tax rate. If you withdraw money from the IRA after you retire, and you do not have much other income, the money withdrawn from the IRA will be taxed at a low tax rate.

A counterargument is that if you save a substantial amount of money in your employer-sponsored account and your IRA, you will be withdrawing a large amount of money from your accounts every year after you retire, so you will likely be in a high tax bracket. In this case, you may be better off paying taxes on the income now with a Roth IRA (as you contribute to your retirement account) rather than later.

ANNUITIES

annuity

A financial contract that provides annual payments over a
specified period.

An **annuity** is a financial contract that provides annual payments until a specified year or for one's lifetime. The minimum investment in an annuity is usually $5,000. The investment in an annuity is not sheltered from income taxes. Thus, if you invest $5,000 in an annuity, you cannot reduce your

fixed annuity
An annuity that provides a specified return on your investment, so you know exactly how much money you will receive at a future point in time (such as retirement).

taxable income by $5,000. The return on the investment in an annuity is tax-deferred, however, so any gains generated by the annuity are not taxed until the funds are paid to the investor. Although there are benefits from being able to defer the tax on your investment, they are smaller than the benefits from sheltering income by using a retirement account. Therefore, annuities are not suitable substitutes for retirement plans.

Fixed versus Variable Annuities

variable annuity
An annuity in which the return is based on the performance of the selected investment vehicles.

Annuities are classified as fixed or variable. **Fixed annuities** provide a specified return on your investment, so you know exactly how much money you will receive at a future point in time. **Variable annuities** allow you to choose among various investments (specific stock and bond portfolios), so the return is dependent on the performance of those investments. You may even change the investments (within the list of those allowed) over time. You can withdraw your investment as a lump sum or as a series of payments over time.

Annuity Fees

surrender charge
A fee that may be imposed on any money withdrawn from an annuity.

The main disadvantage of annuities is the high fees charged by the financial institutions (primarily insurance companies) that sell and manage annuities. These fees include management fees that are charged every year (similar to those for a mutual fund) and a so-called **surrender charge** that may be imposed on any money withdrawn in the first eight years or so. The sur-

---

18.4   Financial Planning Online: Comparison of Fixed Annuity Products

Go to:
http://www.nationwide.com/
learn_about/annuities.htm

This Web site provides:
more information concerning annuities.

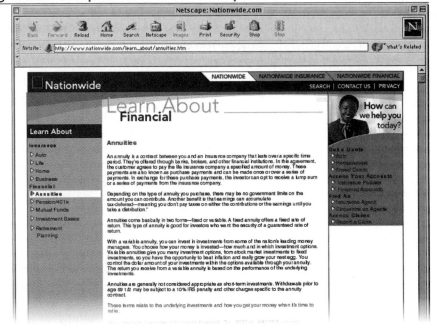

render charge is intended to discourage withdrawals. In addition, there may be so-called insurance fees that are essentially commissions to salespeople for selling the annuities to you. These commissions commonly range from 5.75 to 8.25 percent of your investment.

Some financial institutions now offer no-load annuities that do not charge commissions and also charge relatively low management fees. For example, Vanguard's variable annuity plan has total expenses between 0.58 and 0.86 percent of the investment per year, which are lower than what many mutual funds charge.

ESTIMATING YOUR FUTURE RETIREMENT SAVINGS

To determine how much you will have accumulated by retirement, you can calculate the future value of the amount of money you save.

Estimating the Future Value of One Investment

Recall from Chapter 3 that the future value of an investment today can be computed by using the future value interest factor (*FVIF*) table in Appendix A. You need the following information:

- The amount of the investment.

- The annual return that you expect on the investment.

- The time when the investment will end.

Example

You consider investing $5,000 this year, and this investment will remain in your account until 40 years from now when you retire. You believe that you can earn a return of 10 percent per year on your investment. Based on this information, you expect the value of your investment in 40 years to be:

Value in 40 Years = Investment × *FVIF* (*i* = 10%, *n* = 40)

$$= \$5,000 \times 45.259$$
$$= \$226,295.$$

It may surprise you that $5,000 can grow into more than a quarter of a million dollars if it is invested over a 40-year period. This should motivate you to consider saving for your retirement as soon as possible.

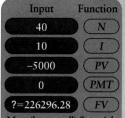

Input	Function
40	N
10	I
−5000	PV
0	PMT
?=226296.28	FV

Most (but not all) financial calculators, such as the Texas Instruments BAII PLUS, require a negative present value (*PV*) input. You should consult your manual to determine the requirements of your financial calculator.

Relationship between Amount Saved Now and Retirement Savings. Consider how the amount you save now can affect your future savings. As Exhibit 18.3 shows, if you invested $10,000 instead of $5,000 for 40 years, your savings would grow to $452,590 by retirement. The more you save today, the more money you will have at the time of your retirement.

Exhibit 18.3   Relationship between Savings Today and Amount of Money at Retirement (in 40 years, assuming a 10% annual return)

Amount Saved Today	Savings at Retirement
$1,000	$45,259
$2,000	$90,578
$3,000	$135,777
$4,000	$181,036
$5,000	$226,295
$6,000	$271,554
$7,000	$316,813
$8,000	$362,072
$9,000	$407,331
$10,000	$452,590

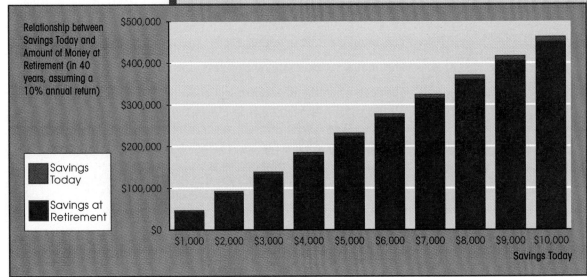

Relationship between Savings Today and Amount of Money at Retirement (in 40 years, assuming a 10% annual return)

Relationship between Years of Saving and Your Retirement Savings. The amount of money you accumulate by the time you retire is also dependent on the number of years your savings are invested. As Exhibit 18.4 shows, the longer your savings are invested, the more they will be worth (assuming a positive rate of return) at retirement. If you invest $5,000 for 25 years instead of 40 years, it will be worth only $54,175.

Exhibit 18.4 Relationship between the Investment Period and Your Savings at Retirement (assuming a $5,000 investment and a 10% annual return)

Number of Years	Savings at Retirement
1	$5,500
5	$8,053
10	$12,969
15	$20,886
20	$33,638
25	$54,175
30	$87,245
35	$140,510
40	$226,295

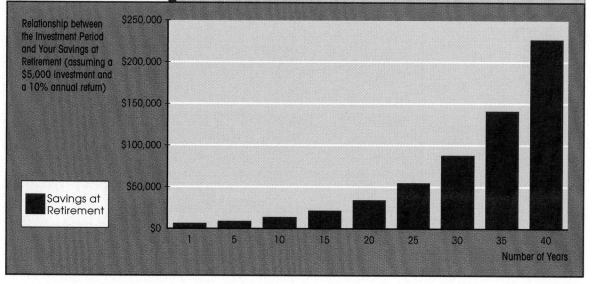

Relationship between the Investment Period and Your Savings at Retirement (assuming a $5,000 investment and a 10% annual return)

Relationship between Your Annual Return and Your Retirement Savings. The amount of money you will accumulate by the time you retire is also dependent on your annual return, as shown in Exhibit 18.5. Notice the sensitivity of your savings at retirement to the annual return. Two extra percentage points on the annual return can increase the savings from a single $5,000 investment by hundreds of thousands of dollars. With a 14 percent return instead of 10 percent, your $5,000 would be worth $944,400 in 40 years when you retire.

Exhibit 18.5   Relationship between the Annual Return on Your Investment and Your Savings at Retirement (in 40 years, assuming a $5,000 initial investment)

Annual Return	Savings at Retirement
0%	$5,000
2	$11,040
4	$24,005
6	$51,430
8	$108,625
10	$226,295
12	$465,255
14	$944,400

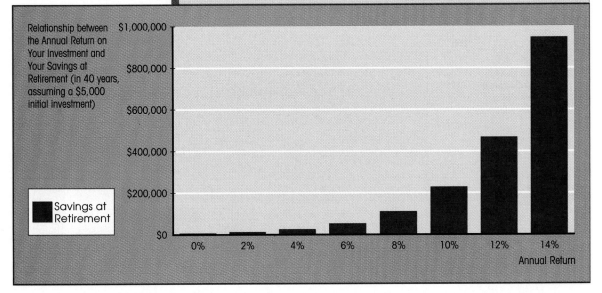

Relationship between the Annual Return on Your Investment and Your Savings at Retirement (in 40 years, assuming a $5,000 initial investment)

Estimating the Future Value of a Set of Annual Investments

If you plan to save a specified amount of money every year for retirement, you can easily determine the value of your savings by the time you retire. Remember that a set of annual payments is an annuity. The future value of an annuity can be computed by using the future value interest factor of an annuity (*FVIFA*) table in Appendix A. You need the following information:

- The amount of the annual payment (investment).
- The annual return that you expect on the investments.
- The time when the investments will end.

Example

You consider investing $5,000 at the end of each of the next 40 years to accumulate retirement savings. You anticipate that you can earn a return of 10 percent per year on your investments. Based on this information, you expect the value of your investments in 40 years to be:

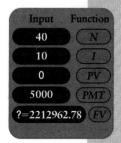

Input	Function
40	N
10	I
0	PV
5000	PMT
?=2212962.78	FV

Value in 40 Years = Annual Investment × FVIFA (i = 10%, n = 40)

= $5,000 × 442.59

= $2,212,950.

This is not a misprint. You will have more than $2 million in 40 years if you invest $5,000 each year for the next 40 years. The compounding of interest is very powerful and allows you to accumulate a large amount of funds over time with relatively small investments. Set aside income for your retirement as soon as possible so that you can benefit from the power of compounding.

Relationship between Size of Annuity and Retirement Savings. Consider how the amount of your savings at retirement is affected by the amount that you save each year. As Exhibit 18.6 shows, for every extra $1,000 that you can save by the end of each year, you will accumulate an additional $442,590 at retirement.

Relationship between Years of Saving and Retirement Savings. The amount of money you will accumulate when saving money on a yearly basis is also dependent on the number of years your investment remains in your retirement account. As Exhibit 18.7 shows, the longer your annual savings are invested, the more they will be worth at retirement. If you plan to retire at age 65, notice that if you start saving $5,000 per year at age 25 (and therefore save for 40 years until retirement), you will save $857,850 more than if you wait until age 30 to start saving (and therefore save for 35 years until retirement).

Relationship between Your Annual Return and Your Savings at Retirement. The amount you will have at retirement is also dependent on the return you earn on your annual savings, as shown in Exhibit 18.8. Notice how sensitive your savings are to the annual return. Almost $1 million more is accumulated from an annual return of 10 percent than from an annual return of 8 percent. An annual return of 12 percent produces about $1.6 million more in accumulated savings than an annual return of 10 percent.

Exhibit 18.6   Relationship between Amount Saved per Year and Amount of Savings at Retirement (in 40 years, assuming a 10% annual return)

Amount Saved per Year	Savings at Retirement
$1,000	$442,590
$2,000	$885,180
$3,000	$1,327,770
$4,000	$1,770,360
$5,000	$2,212,950
$6,000	$2,655,540
$7,000	$3,098,130
$8,000	$3,540,720
$9,000	$3,983,310
$10,000	$4,425,900

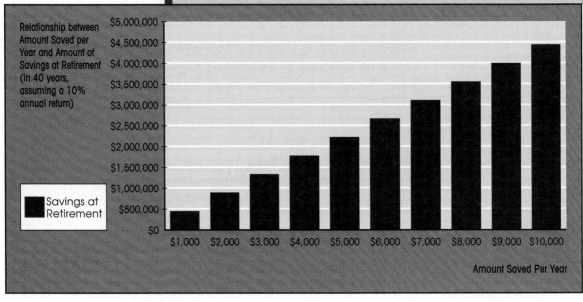

Relationship between Amount Saved per Year and Amount of Savings at Retirement (in 40 years, assuming a 10% annual return)

Savings at Retirement

Amount Saved Per Year

Exhibit 18.7   Relationship between the Number of Years You Invest Annual Savings and Your Savings at Retirement (assuming a $5,000 investment and a 10% annual return)

Number of Consecutive Years You Invest $5,000 at the End of Each Year	Savings at Retirement
1	$5,000
5	$30,255
10	$79,685
15	$158,860
20	$286,375
25	$491,735
30	$822,450
35	$1,355,100
40	$2,212,950

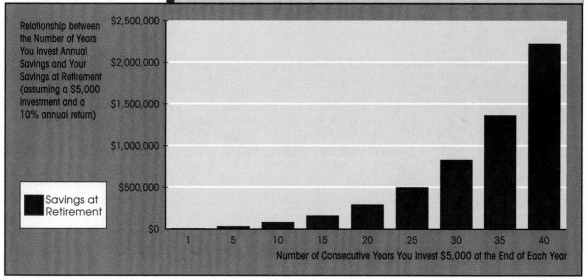

Relationship between the Number of Years You Invest Annual Savings and Your Savings at Retirement (assuming a $5,000 investment and a 10% annual return)

Number of Consecutive Years You Invest $5,000 at the End of Each Year

Exhibit 18.8   Relationship between the Annual Return on Your Annual Savings and Your Savings at Retirement (in 40 years, assuming a $5,000 annual investment)

Annual Return	Savings at Retirement
0%	$200,000
2	$302,010
4	$475,130
6	$773,800
8	$1,295,300
10	$2,212,950
12	$3,835,450
14	$6,710,000

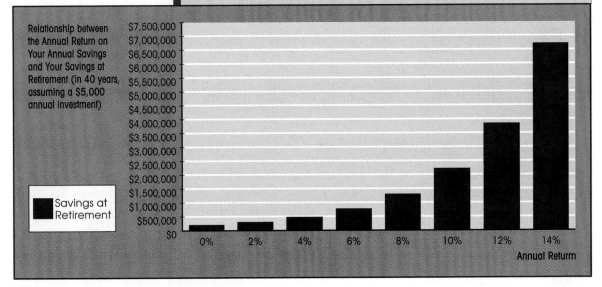

Relationship between the Annual Return on Your Annual Savings and Your Savings at Retirement (in 40 years, assuming a $5,000 annual investment)

MEASURING THE TAX BENEFITS FROM A RETIREMENT ACCOUNT

The potential tax benefits of investing in a retirement account are illustrated in the following example.

Example

You wish to invest $5,000 per year in a retirement account for the next 40 years when you plan to retire. You expect to earn a return of 10 percent per year. Using the future value of an annuity (*FVIFA*) table in Appendix A, your savings at retirement would be:

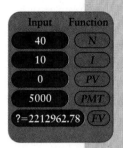

Savings at retirement = Annual Investment $\times$ FVIFA (i = 10%, n = 40)

$$= \$5,000 \times 442.59$$
$$= \$2,212,950.$$

As you withdraw the money from your account after you retire, you will be taxed at your ordinary income tax rate, even though the investment appreciated over time due to capital gains. If you withdraw all of your money in one year, and are taxed at a 25 percent rate, your tax will be:

Tax = Income $\times$ Tax Rate

$$= \$2,212,950 \times .25$$
$$= \$553,238.$$

You probably would not withdraw all your funds in one year, but this lump-sum withdrawal simplifies the example. Your income after taxes in this example would be:

Income after Taxes = Taxable Income – Income Tax

$$= \$2,212,950 - \$553,238$$
$$= \$1,659,712.$$

To compare the return from investing $5,000 in the retirement account to the return from investing $5,000 elsewhere, consider first that if you invest elsewhere, you will have an additional amount of taxable income of $5,000 each year. Assuming that your prevailing marginal income tax rate is 30 percent, you are subject to a tax of $1,500 each year. That leaves you with $3,500 that you can invest each year. Assume that you earn 10 percent on those annual savings invested over the next 40 years. Referring to the future value of annuity (FVIFA) table in Appendix A, you will receive:

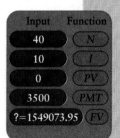

Savings at Retirement = Annual Investment $\times$ FVIFA (i = 10%, n = 40)

$$= \$3,500 \times 442.59$$
$$= \$1,549,065.$$

Next, consider that you will have to pay taxes when you cash in this investment. For many investments such as bonds or dividend-paying stocks, you would have been paying taxes every year over this 40-year period. Even if you had minimized taxes by choosing a stock that does not pay dividends, you would still pay a capital gains tax when you cash in the investment. Since you invested $3,500 per year, or a total of $140,000 over 40 years, your capital gain is:

Capital Gain = Selling Price of Stock – Purchase Price of Stock

$$= \$1,549,065 - \$140,000$$
$$= \$1,409,065.$$

Assuming a capital gains tax rate of 20 percent, your capital gains tax would be:

Capital Gains Tax = Capital Gain $\times$ Capital Gains Tax Rate

$$= \$1,409,065 \times .20$$
$$= \$281,813.$$

18.5 Financial Planning Online: How to Build Your Retirement Plan

Go to:
http://www.quicken.com/
retirement/planner/personal

This Web site provides:
a framework for building a
retirement plan based on your
financial situation.

Therefore, after 40 years, you have:

Value of Investment = Value of Investment before Taxes − Capital Gains Tax

$$= \$1,549,065 - \$281,813$$

$$= \$1,267,252.$$

Overall, investing $5,000 per year for the next 40 years in your retirement account will be worth over $390,000 more than if you invest $5,000 per year on your own. If you withdraw funds gradually from your retirement plan, the benefits of the retirement plan will be even greater because you will defer taxes longer. If you use a different annual return, you will get different results, but the advantage of the retirement account will remain. If you invest in something other than non-dividend-paying stocks on your own, the advantage of the retirement account will be even greater. Any investments on your own are subject to annual taxes on any ordinary income (dividend or interest payments), while income generated in the retirement account is not taxed until you withdraw the funds.

HOW RETIREMENT PLANNING FITS WITHIN YOUR FINANCIAL PLAN

The following are the key retirement planning decisions that should be included within your financial plan:

1. Should you invest in a retirement plan?

2. How much should you invest in a retirement plan?

3. How should you allocate investments within your retirement plan?

Exhibit 18.9 provides an example of how the retirement planning decisions apply to Stephanie Spratt's financial plan.

Exhibit 18.9   How Retirement Planning Fits within Stephanie Spratt's Financial Plan

Goals for Retirement Planning

1. Ensure an adequate financial position at the time I retire.
2. Reduce the tax liability on my present income.

Analysis

Type of Retirement Plan	Benefits
Employer's retirement plan	I can contribute up to $5,000 of my income (tax-deferred) per year to my retirement plan. In addition, my employer will contribute the same amount to my plan each year.
Traditional IRA or Roth IRA	I can contribute up to $2,000 of income per year (tax-deferred) to a traditional IRA. Alternatively, I could contribute up to $2,000 annually to a Roth IRA; in that case, the contribution occurs after taxes, but the withdrawal after retirement will not be taxed.
Annuities	I can contribute money to annuities to supplement any other retirement plan. The only tax advantage is that any income earned on the money invested is not taxed until I withdraw the money after retirement.

Decisions

Decision on Whether I Should Engage in Retirement Planning:

There is no guarantee that Social Security benefits will exist when I retire. Even if the benefits are available, they will not be sufficient to provide the amount of financial support that I desire. Given the substantial tax benefits of a retirement plan, I should engage in retirement planning. I should attempt to take full advantage of my employer's retirement plan. The benefits of traditional and Roth IRAs are also substantial. Although I have not contributed to these retirement accounts in the past, I hope to do so in the future. Annuities are not attractive to me at this point.

Decision on How Much to Contribute to Retirement:

I should attempt to contribute the maximum allowed to my employer's retirement plan and to a traditional or Roth IRA. These contributions will reduce the amount of money that I can dedicate toward savings and investments, but the tradeoff favors retirement contributions because of the tax advantages.

Decision on Asset Allocation within the Retirement Account:

I plan to invest the money slated for retirement in stock and bond mutual funds. I will invest about 70 or 80 percent of the money in a few diversified stock mutual funds and the remainder in a diversified corporate bond mutual fund.

DISCUSSION QUESTIONS

1. How would Stephanie's retirement planning decisions be different if she were a single mother of two children?

2. How would Stephanie's retirement planning decisions be affected if she were 35 years old? If she were 50 years old?

SUMMARY

Social Security provides income to qualified individuals to support them during their retirement. However, the income provided normally is not sufficient for most individuals to live comfortably. Therefore, individuals engage in retirement planning so that they will have additional sources of income when they retire.

Retirement plans sponsored by employers are normally classified as defined-benefit plans or defined-contribution plans. Defined-benefit plans guarantee a specific amount of income to employees upon retirement, based on factors such as their salary and number of years of service. Defined-contribution plans provide guidelines on the maximum amount that can be contributed to a retirement account. Individuals have the freedom to make decisions about how much to invest and how to invest for their retirement.

Two key retirement planning decisions are how much to contribute to your retirement plan and how to invest your contributions. When an employer is willing to match your retirement contribution, you should always contribute enough to take full advantage of the match. In addition, you should also try to contribute the maximum amount allowed, even if doing so means you will have less funds to invest in other ways. Most

financial advisers suggest investing most of your contribution in one or more diversified stock mutual funds and putting the remainder in a diversified bond mutual fund. The specific allocation depends on your willingness to tolerate risk.

Retirement plans offered by employers include the 401(k) plan, 403-b plan, Simplified Employee Plan (SEP), SIMPLE, profit sharing, and ESOP. They offer similar types of benefits in that they encourage you to save for retirement and can defer your income from taxes. The specific eligibility requirements and other characteristics vary among retirement plans.

Self-employed individuals can use a Keogh plan, which allows them to contribute up to 25 percent of their net income, up to a maximum of $35,500. Alternatively, they can use a SEP, which allows them to contribute up to $25,500.

In addition to retirement accounts offered by employers, individuals can also establish an individual retirement account (IRA), such as a traditional IRA or a Roth IRA.

Your future savings from investing in a retirement account can easily be measured based on information regarding the amount you plan to invest each year, the annual return you expect, and the number of years until retirement. The future savings reflect the future value of an annuity.

The tax benefits from investing in a retirement account can be estimated by measuring the amount of retirement savings once they are converted to cash (and the income taxes are paid) versus the amount of savings if you had simply made investments without a retirement account. The tax benefits arise from deferring tax on income received from your employer until retirement and deferring tax on income earned from your contributions until retirement. Retirement accounts are the preferred investment in any comparison because of the tax advantages.

Integrating the Key Concepts

Your retirement planning affects other parts of your financial plan. If you build your retirement account when you are young, any funds that you invest in a retirement plan cannot be used for maintaining your liquidity (Part 2) or other investments (Part 4). Yet, by contributing to a retirement plan consistently over time, you are not forced to quickly build wealth shortly before you retire and are able to benefit from the power of compounding.

If you start saving for retirement at age 50 or later, you may take excessive risk in your efforts to quickly amass substantial wealth for your retirement. For example, you may decide to ignore the need for liquidity (Part 2) so that you can focus on investments that are expected to offer a high rate of return. This strategy could cause you to experience cash shortages in some periods. You may not be able to finance a car or a home (Part 3) because you would need to avoid interest payments and focus on accumulating a lot of money quickly. You may also take excessive risk when making your investment decisions (Part 4), which could backfire. The advantage of retirement planning is that it allows you more time to build wealth for your retirement, so that you can make financing and investment decisions that are based on a long-term perspective.

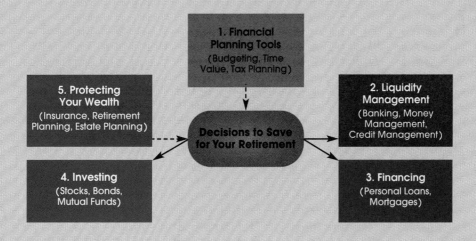

REVIEW QUESTIONS

1. How does Social Security fit into retirement planning? How does an individual qualify for Social Security benefits? When do you receive benefits? How is Social Security funded?

2. How are the retirement benefits under Social Security calculated? Describe some factors that might affect the amount of your benefits.

3. Discuss some of the concerns about the future of Social Security.

4. Briefly describe how employer-sponsored retirement plans work in general.

5. What is a defined-benefit plan? How is the amount of retirement income you receive calculated?

6. What is a defined-contribution plan? Why are some employers switching to this type of plan? List some of the benefits of a defined-contribution plan.

7. What are the key retirement planning decisions an individual must make? Discuss each briefly.

8. Discuss the characteristics of a 401(k) plan. What is a 403-b plan?

9. Compare and contrast a Simplified Employee Plan (SEP) and a SIMPLE.

10. Discuss profit-sharing and employee stock ownership (ESOP) plans.

11. Discuss the choices for managing a retirement account upon leaving an employer.

12. Briefly describe the two popular retirement plans for self-employed individuals.

13. Compare and contrast a traditional IRA with a Roth IRA. Discuss the advantages of each. What factors will affect your choice of IRAs?

14. What is an annuity? What is the difference between a fixed annuity and a variable annuity? What is the main disadvantage of annuities?

15. Why are retirement accounts more beneficial than other investments? Describe an effective strategy for retirement planning.

16. When estimating the future value of one retirement investment, what factors will affect the amount of funds available to you at retirement? Explain.

17. When estimating the future value of a set of annual investments, what factors will affect the amount of funds available to you at retirement?

18. Explain the tax benefits of investing within a retirement account versus investing outside a retirement account.

19. What is the main advantage of retirement planning?

FINANCIAL PLANNING PROBLEMS

1. Barry has just become eligible for his employer-sponsored retirement plan. Barry is 35 and plans to retire at 65. Barry calculates that he can contribute $3,600 per year to his plan. Barry's employer will match this amount. If Barry can earn an 8 percent return on his investment, how much will he have at retirement?

2. How much would Barry have at retirement if he had started this plan at age 25?

3. How much would Barry have if at age 35 he could earn a 10 percent return on his investment?

4. How much would Barry have if at age 35 he could invest an additional $1,000 per year that his employer would match?

5. Thomas is an attorney who earns $45,000 per year. What retirement plan should Thomas consider under the following circumstances?
   a. He works for a large private firm.
   b. He works at a university.
   c. He owns a small firm with employees.

6. How much will Marie have in her retirement account in 10 years if her contribution is $7,000 per year and the annual return on the account is 6 percent?

7. Lloyd and his wife Jean contribute $4,000 each year to a traditional IRA. They are in a 28 percent marginal tax bracket. What tax savings will they realize for these contributions?

8. In need of extra cash, Troy and Lilly decide to withdraw $8,000 from their IRA. They are both 40 years old. They are in a 28 percent marginal tax bracket. What will be the tax consequences of this withdrawal?

9. Noel and Brady married at age 22. Each year until their thirtieth birthdays, they put $4,000 into their IRAs. By age 30 they had bought a home and started a family. Although they continued to make contributions to their employer-sponsored retirement plans, they made no more contributions to their IRAs. If they receive an average annual return of 8 percent, how much will they have in their IRAs by age 60? What was their total investment?

10. Ricky and Sharon married at age 22, started a family, and bought a house. At age 30, they began making a contribution of $4,000 to an IRA. They continued making these contributions annually until age 60. If the average return on their investment was 8 percent, how much was in their IRA at age 60? What was their total investment?

FINANCIAL PLANNING ONLINE EXERCISES

1. Go to http://www.quicken.com/retirement/ planner/personal. Click on IRAs and then on Roth IRA Planner. Next, click on Launch Planner. Enter information on a series of screen displays. Review the results and graphs to determine which IRA is better for you, your eligibility, and how much your contributions will grow to by retirement. You can register with Quicken to save the results.

2. Go to http://www.ssa.gov/retire2/calculators. htm. Click on Quick Calculator. Enter your age in years and current total earnings for the year. Then select your benefit in today's dollars or inflated future dollars. Click on Submit Request. What are your monthly Social Security benefits at age 62, 65, and 70?

3. Go to http://www.thirdage.com/cgi-bin/calcs/ RET1.cgi/thirdagemedia. To determine what your expenses will be after you retire, fill in the information on current and retirement expenses. The results will show the income required with and without an inflation adjustment.

4. Go to http://www.thirdage.com/cgi-bin/calcs/ SAV2.cgi/thirdagemedia. To determine how much your savings will be worth, say, 30 years from now, enter data on initial investment, monthly deposits, rate of return expected, tax rates, and inflation rate. The results will be shown before and after taxes.

5. Use the Back option in your browser to return to the input page. Increase the monthly deposit by $300 and check the results.

Building Your Own Financial Plan

Difficult as it may be to visualize, retirement really is "right around the corner." The reality is that the earlier you begin dealing with the issues of retirement, the more successful and enjoyable retirement will be.

You will very likely change jobs, if not careers, numerous times in your working life. Most of your employers will offer a defined-contribution plan, such as a 401(k), rather than a defined-benefit plan. It is therefore to your benefit to begin planning and executing a plan for your retirement as soon as possible. The tax benefits of retirement planning should serve as an additional motivator. The key decisions you need to make are how much to save each month, what type of plan(s) to contribute to, and how to allocate various retirement investments.

A number of Web sites can assist you in this planning. Find a Web site that you can navigate comfortably and utilize it. To help you get started, this exercise will utilize the MSN Web site mentioned in Financial Planning Online 18.2 in the chap-

ter. Use the template provided with this chapter in the *Financial Planning Workbook* and on the CD-ROM to make additional calculations, and enter your findings and decisions.

Your first step is to go to www.msn.com. Click on the tab "money." This will bring up a page entitled "money central." Scroll to the bottom of the page and click on the "site map." When the site map comes up, go to the area marked "retirement and wills." Under this category, begin surfing the retirement topics. Be sure to use the cal-

culator to determine how much you will need in retirement. Two other Web sites that provide excellent retirement planning facilities are "smartmoney.com" and "money.com." Next, determine how much money you must save per year, the return, and savings period to amass the needed savings. Review the various retirement plans available from your employer, as well as IRAs and annuities. Keep in mind that present-day tax savings are an added benefit.

A retirement plan, like a portfolio, should be reviewed annually. You will probably not make major changes to your plan, but an annual review will help you to see whether you are on target to achieve your goals and retirement needs. For example, if you are earning a smaller than expected return, you may consider increasing your contributions so that you can still meet your goals.

The Sampsons—A Continuing Case

Next on the Sampsons' financial planning checklist is saving for retirement. Dave's employer offers a 401(k) plan, but he has not participated in it up to this point. He now wants to seriously consider contributing. His employer will allow him to invest about $7,000 of his salary per year and match his contribution up to $3,000, for a total contribution of $10,000 per year.

The retirement funds will be invested in one or more mutual funds. Dave's best guess is that the retirement fund investments will earn a return of 7 percent a year.

1. If Dave and his employer contribute a total of $10,000, how much will that amount accumulate to over the next 30 years when Dave and his wife Sharon hope to retire?

2. Assuming that Dave 's marginal tax rate is 28 percent, by how much should his federal

taxes decline this year if he contributes $7,000 to his retirement account?

3. Assuming that Dave contributes $7,000 to his retirement account and that his taxes are lower as a result, by how much are Dave's cash flows reduced over one year? (Refer to your answer in question 2 when solving this problem.)

4. If Dave contributes $7,000 to his retirement account, he will have less cash inflows as a

result. How can the Sampsons afford to make this contribution? Suggest some ways that they may be able to offset the reduction in cash inflows by reexamining the cash flow statement you created for them in Chapter 2.

IN-TEXT STUDY GUIDE

True/False:

1. Social Security is a federal program that taxes individuals while they are working and after they retire.

2. The Medicare tax of 1.45 percent of gross income is included in FICA and is capped at a specific income level.

3. Retirement plans are programs designed to help you build your pension for your retirement.

4. In a defined-contribution plan, you can change your investments over time.

5. All retirement plans require individuals to contribute a fixed amount toward their retirement.

6. A 401(k) plan is a defined-benefit plan.

7. The traditional individual retirement account (IRA) enables you to save for your retirement separate from any retirement plan provided by your employer.

8. Even if you do not withdraw money from your retirement account, you will pay taxes on the interest generated by bonds every year.

9. The higher the annual return, the lower the savings at retirement.

10. The main disadvantage of annuities is the high fees that are charged by the financial institutions that sell and manage them.

Multiple Choice:

1. In the Social Security program, you receive one credit for every _____ in income per year, and you must earn _____ credits to qualify for Social Security retirement benefits.
   a. $320; 40
   b. $780; 20
   c. $320; 30
   d. $780; 40

2. Which of the following is not a benefit provided to the survivors of someone who qualified for Social Security?
   a. yearly income payment to the spouse
   b. monthly income payments if the spouse is younger than age 60 or has a child under the age of 16
   c. monthly income payments to children under the age of 18
   d. All of the above are benefits provided to the survivors.

3. If your gross income level is $90,000, the amount of FICA tax you must pay is
   a. $5,760.30
   b. $5,553.
   c. $6,290.
   d. $1,305.

4. The Social Security program provides you with an annual income equal to about _____ percent of your average annual income during the years that you worked.
   a. 10
   b. 27
   c. 42
   d. 68

5. Individuals who defer their retirement are eligible to receive _____ level of annual income from the Social Security program.
   a. the same
   b. a lower
   c. a higher
   d. none of the above

6. In a _____ plan, the benefits that you ultimately receive are determined by the performance of the money invested in your retirement account.
   a. defined-benefit
   b. defined-contribution
   c. Social Security
   d. none of the above

7. Which of the following is not an advantage of a defined-contribution plan?
   a. It can direct a portion of the income to a retirement account before you receive your paycheck.
   b. It allows you to defer the income taxes on income paid by your employer.
   c. The income generated by your investments in a retirement account is taxed when you withdraw the money before you retire.
   d. Any money provided by your employer constitutes additional compensation beyond your salary.

The following information applies to questions 8 and 9.

Walter Plateau is allowed to contribute $6,000 per year toward his retirement. Walter's employer matches this contribution. Walter intends to retire in 30 years. He has chosen investments that will generate a return of 10 percent annually.

8. Based on this information, Walter should have savings at the time of retirement in the amount of
   a. $986,964.14.
   b. $493,482.07.
   c. $104,696.41.
   d. none of the above

9. If Walter can earn only an 8 percent return annually, he will have _____ when he retires in 30 years.
   a. $60,375.94
   b. $339,849.63
   c. $679,699.27
   d. none of the above

10. A _____ is commonly used by small firms with 1 to 10 employees.
    a. 401(k) plan
    b. 403-b plan
    c. Simplified Employee Plan (SEP)
    d. employee stock ownership plan (ESOP)

11. A popular retirement plan offered by nonprofit organizations is the
    a. 401(k) plan.
    b. 403-b plan.
    c. SEP.
    d. Savings Incentive Match Plan for Employees (SIMPLE).

12. The _____ is intended for firms with 100 or fewer employees and is similar to a SEP.
    a. profit-sharing plan
    b. ESOP
    c. 403-b plan
    d. SIMPLE

13. A _____ is established to transfer assets tax-free from a company retirement plan.
    a. Keogh plan
    b. rollover IRA
    c. Roth IRA
    d. SEP

14. The _____ enables self-employed individuals to contribute part of their income to a retirement account.
    a. Keogh plan
    b. disability IRA
    c. Roth IRA
    d. 403-b plan

15. A(n) _____ allows you to choose among various investments and provides a return that will depend on the performance of those investments.
    a. fixed annuity
    b. variable annuity
    c. ordinary annuity
    d. annuity due

16. You would like to invest $3,000 this year for your retirement in 35 years. You put your money into a bond fund that you expect will pay 7 percent annually. In 35 years, you will have
    a. $414,710.64.
    b. $61,475.58.
    c. $32,029.74.
    d. $24,516.45.

17. If you invest an amount today for your retirement, the amount you will have at the time you retire does not depend on
    a. the amount of the annual payment.
    b. the annual return that you expect on the investments.
    c. the time at which the investment will end.
    d. the amount of the investment.

The following information applies to questions 18 and 19.

You consider saving $500 at the end of each of the next 35 years for your retirement. You believe that you can earn a return of 9 percent per year on your investments.

18. Based on this information, the value of your investments in 35 years is expected to be
    a. $10,206.98.
    b. $24,493.03.
    c. $5,307.90.
    d. $107,855.38.

19. If you could instead save $700 a year, you would have _____ by the time you retire in 35 years.
    a. $14,289.78
    b. $150,997.53
    c. $73,967.75
    d. $34,290.25

20. You just retired and are thinking about withdrawing the $200,000 in your retirement account. Your entire retirement savings were invested in stock for the last 20 years with a total purchase price of $180,000. You are in the 28 percent tax bracket. Your capital gains taxes are
    a. $0.
    b. $40,000.
    c. $4,000.
    d. $5,600.

Chapter 19

Estate Planning

Estate planning involves the planning and documentation of how your assets will be distributed when you die. One of the key goals of estate planning is to minimize the taxes on assets you ultimately transfer to your beneficiaries. Estate planning is necessary not just for rich people. It is important for all individuals who want to ensure that their assets are distributed in the manner that they desire. Throughout this chapter, there are references to the Tax Relief Act of 2001 and to methods for reducing estate taxes.

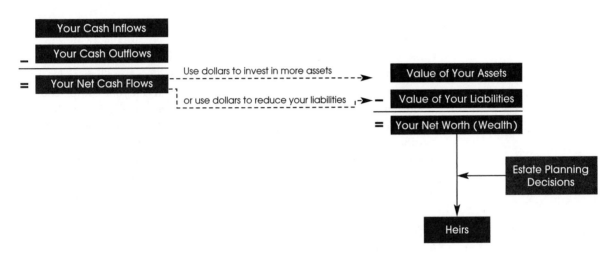

The objectives of this chapter are to:

- explain the use of a will,
- describe estate taxes,
- explain the use of trusts, gifts, and contributions, and
- introduce other aspects of estate planning.

USE OF A WILL

estate
The assets of a deceased person after all debts are paid.

estate planning
The act of planning for how your wealth will be allocated on or before your death.

will
A legal request for how your estate should be distributed upon your death. It can also identify a preferred guardian for any surviving children.

An **estate** represents a deceased person's assets after all debts are paid. At the time of a person's death, the estate is distributed according to that person's wishes. **Estate planning** is the act of planning how your wealth will be allocated on or before your death. One of the most important tasks in estate planning is the creation of a **will**, which is a legal request for how your estate should be distributed upon your death. It can also identify a preferred guardian for any surviving children.

Reasons for Having a Will

A will is critical to ensure that your estate is distributed in the manner that you desire. Once you have a positive net worth to be distributed upon your death,

557

beneficiaries (heirs)
The persons specified in a will to receive a part of an estate.

intestate
The condition of dying without a will.

you should consider creating a will. In your will, you can specify the persons you want to receive your estate—referred to as your **beneficiaries** (or **heirs**). If you die **intestate** (without a will), the court will appoint a person (called an administrator) to distribute your estate according to the laws of your state. In that case, one family member may receive more than you intended, while others receive less. If there is no surviving spouse, the administrator would also decide who would assume responsibility for any children. Having an administrator also results in additional costs being imposed on the estate.

Creating a Valid Will

To create a valid will, you must be a minimum age, usually 18 or 21, that varies by state. You must also be mentally competent and should not be subject to undue influence (threats) from others. A will is more likely to be challenged by potential heirs if there is some question about your competence or whether you were forced to designate one or more beneficiaries in the will. Some states require that the will be typed, although handwriting is accepted in other states. To be valid, a will must be dated and signed. Two or three witnesses who are not inheriting anything under the will must also witness the signing of the will. Although you are not required to hire a lawyer, you should still consider doing so to ensure that the will is created properly.

Common Types of Wills

A **simple will** specifies that the entire estate be distributed to a person's spouse. It may be sufficient for many married couples. If the estate is large

19.1   Financial Planning Online: Quiz for Preparing Your Own Will

Go to:
http://moneycentral.msn.com/articles/retire/will/tlwillq.asp

This Web site provides:
a quiz that indicates your ability to create your own will.

simple will
A will suitable for smaller estates that specifies that the entire estate be distributed to the person's spouse.

traditional marital share will
A will suitable for larger estates that distributes half of the estate to the spouse and the other half to any children or to a trust.

executor (personal representative)
The person designated in a will to execute your instructions regarding the distribution of your assets.

(valued at \$675,000 or more), however, a simple will may not be appropriate because the estate will be subject to a high level of taxes. A more appropriate will for large estates is the **traditional marital share will,** which distributes half of the estate to the spouse and the other half to any children or to a trust (to be discussed later in the chapter). This type of will is useful for minimizing taxes on the estate.

Key Components of a Will

A sample of a will is provided in Exhibit 19.1. The key components of a will are described next.

Distribution of the Estate. The will details how the estate should be distributed among the beneficiaries. Since you do not know what your estate will be worth, you may specify your desired distribution according to percentages of the estate. For example, you could specify that two people each receive 50 percent of the estate. Alternatively, you could specify that one person receive a specific dollar amount and that the other person receive the remainder of the estate.

Executor. In your will, you name an **executor** (also called a **personal representative**) to carry out your instructions regarding how your assets will be distributed. An executor may be required to collect any money owed to the estate, pay off any debts owed by the estate, sell specific assets (such as a home) that are part of the estate, and then distribute the proceeds as specified in the will.

19.2   Financial Planning Online: How to Prepare Your Own Will

Go to:
http://moneycentral.msn.com/retire/home.asp

Click on:
Wills

Click on:
Prepare a Will

This Web site provides:
step-by-step instructions for creating your will.

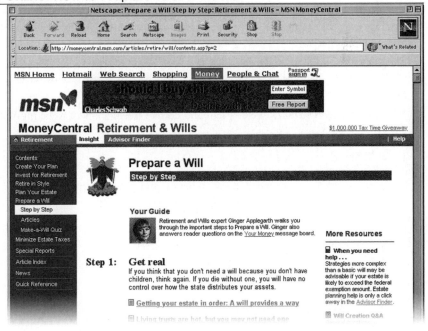

Exhibit 19.1 A Sample Will

WILL of James T. Smith

I, James T. Smith of the City of Denver, Colorado, declare this to be my will.

ARTICLE 1

My wife, Karen A. Smith, and I have one child, Cheryl D. Smith.

ARTICLE 2 Payment of Debt and Taxes

I direct my Executor to pay my funeral expenses, my medical expenses, the costs of administration, and my debts.

ARTICLE 3 Distribution of the Estate

I direct that my estate be distributed to my wife, Karen A. Smith. If my wife predeceases me, my estate shall be distributed to my Trustee, to be managed as explained in Article 4.

ARTICLE 4 Trust for Children

4A. *Purpose.* This trust provides for the support of my daughter, Cheryl D. Smith, and any other children born to me.

4B. *Use of Funds.* The Trustee shall use as much of the trust income and principal as necessary to care for my child (or children). When the youngest of my children reaches the age of 25, the assets of this trust shall be split equally among the children.

4C. *No Survivors.* If no child of mine survives until age 25, assets of the trust shall be liquidated and 100 percent of the proceeds shall be donated to the San Diego Humane Society.

4D. *Nomination of Trustee.* I appoint my brother, Edward J. Smith, to serve as Trustee. If he is unable or unwilling to serve, I appoint my sister, Marie S. Smith, to serve as Trustee.

ARTICLE 5 Executor

I appoint my wife, Karen A. Smith, to serve as Executor. If she is unable or unwilling to serve, I appoint my brother, Edward J. Smith, to serve as Executor.

ARTICLE 6 Guardian

If my spouse does not survive me, I appoint my brother, Edward J. Smith, to serve as Guardian of my children. If he is unable to serve as Guardian, I appoint my sister, Marie S. Smith, to serve as Guardian.

ARTICLE 7 Power of Executor

My Executor has the right to receive payments, reinvest payments received, pay debts owed, pay taxes owed, and liquidate assets.

ARTICLE 8 Power of Trustee

My Trustee has the right to receive income generated by the trust, reinvest income received by the trust, sell assets in the trust, and use the proceeds to invest in other assets.

IN WITNESS WHEREOF, I hereby sign and declare this document to be my Will.

_____   _____

James T. Smith   Date

The above-named person signed in our presence, and in our opinion is mentally competent.

Signatures of Witnesses   Addresses of Witnesses

_____

Kenneth Tagan   44241 Lemon Street
                                   Denver, Colorado 80208

_____

Barbara Russell   101 Courtney Street
                                   Denver, Colorado 80208

The executor must be a U.S. citizen, may not be a minor or convicted felon, and, under some states' laws, must reside in the same state as the person creating the will. The executor is entitled to be paid by the estate for services provided, but some executors elect not to charge the estate.

Guardian. If you are a parent, you should name a guardian, who will be assigned the responsibility of caring for the children and managing any estate left to the children. You should ensure that the person you select as guardian is willing to serve in this capacity. Your will may specify an amount of money to be distributed to the guardian to care for the children.

letter of last instruction
A supplement to a will that can describe your preferences regarding funeral arrangements and indicate where you have stored any key financial documents.

codicil
A document that specifies changes in an existing will.

Signature. Your signature is needed to validate the will and ensure that someone else does not create a fake will.

Letter of Last Instruction. You may also wish to prepare a **letter of last instruction**. This describes your preferences regarding funeral arrangements and indicates where you have stored any key financial documents such as mortgage and insurance contracts.

Changing Your Will

You may need to change your will if you move to a different state because state laws regarding wills vary. If you get married or divorced after creating your will, you may also need to change it.

probate
A legal process that declares a will valid and ensures the orderly distribution of assets.

If you wish to make major changes to your will, you will probably need to create a new will. The new will must specify that you are revoking your previous will, so that you do not have multiple wills with conflicting instructions. When you wish to make only minor revisions to your will, you can add a **codicil**, which is a document that specifies changes in your existing will.

Executing the Will during Probate

Probate is a legal process that ensures that when people die, their assets are distributed as they wish, and the guardianship of any children is assigned as they wish. The purpose of the probate process is for the court to declare a will valid and ensure the orderly distribution of assets. To start the probate process, the executor files forms in a local probate court, provides a copy of the will, provides a list of the assets and debts of the deceased person, pays debts, and sells any assets that need to be liquidated. The executor typically opens a bank account for the estate that is used to pay the debts of the deceased and to deposit proceeds from liquidating the assets. If the executor does not have time or is otherwise unable to perform these tasks, an attorney can be hired to complete them.

"...And I, Arthur Boggins being of sound mind, hereby authorise that my entire stock of kryptonite be distributed amongst the good citizens of the planet Zug..."

www.cartoonstock.com

ESTATE TAXES

An estate may be subject to taxes before it is distributed to the beneficiaries. When a person dies and has a surviving spouse who jointly owned all the assets, the spouse becomes sole owner of the estate. In this case, the estate is not subject to taxes. If there is not a surviving spouse and the estate is to be distributed to the children or other beneficiaries, the estate is subject to taxes. The estate taxes are assessed after the value of the estate is determined during the probate process. You should estimate the estate taxes based on your net worth, however, so that you can take steps to minimize the tax liability upon your death.

Determining Estate Taxes

The estate's value is equal to the value of all the assets minus any existing liabilities (including a mortgage) and minus the funeral and administrative expenses. Any funds that are provided as a result of a life insurance policy are included in the estate.

A specified portion of an estate is exempt from estate taxes. During 2001, the first $675,000 of an estate could be distributed to children or others tax-free. The Tax Relief Act of 2001 increased the tax-exempt level to $1 million for 2002-2003, $1.5 million for 2004-2005, $2 million for 2006-2008, and $3.5 million in 2009.

Beyond the specific limit, federal estate taxes are imposed. The federal estate tax rates on the taxable part of the estate range from 37 to 50 percent. The Tax Relief Act of 2001 gradually reduces the maximum rate to 45 percent. In 2010, the estate tax will be repealed, but it could reappear in 2001 due to a sunset provision in the Tax Relief Act of 2001. There are several ways of reducing your exposure to high estate taxes, as explained later in the chapter.

Other Related Taxes

Several states impose inheritance taxes or state excise taxes on an estate, although these taxes are being phased out in some states. To avoid state taxes on an estate, residents of such states sometimes retire in other states that do not impose them.

Valuing Your Estate to Assess Potential Estate Taxes

Since the potential estate tax you could incur someday is dependent on the value of your estate, you should periodically calculate the value of your estate. Anyone who saves a relatively small amount of money every year can easily become a millionaire later in life due to the power of compounded interest. Therefore, many people will be millionaires in the future and may need estate planning to ensure that they can pass as much of their wealth as possible on to their beneficiaries. Once your net worth exceeds the tax-free limit, you should carefully plan your estate to minimize any potential tax liability.

TRUSTS, GIFTS, AND CONTRIBUTIONS

Estate planning commonly involves trusts, gifts, and contributions for the purpose of avoiding estate taxes. You may consider hiring an attorney to complete the proper documents.

Trusts

trust
A legal document in which one person (the grantor) transfers assets to another (the trustee) who manages them for designated beneficiaries.

grantor
The person who creates a trust.

trustee
The person or institution named in a trust to manage the trust assets for the beneficiaries.

living trusts
A trust in which you assign the management of your assets to a trustee while you are living.

revocable living trust
A living trust that can be dissolved.

irrevocable living trust
A living trust that cannot be changed, although it can provide income to the grantor.

standard family trust (credit-shelter trust)
A trust established for children in a family.

testamentary trust
A trust created by a will.

A **trust** is a legal document in which one person (called a **grantor**) transfers assets to another person (called a **trustee**), who manages the assets for designated beneficiaries. The grantor must select a trustee who is capable of managing the assets being transferred. Various types of investment firms can be hired to serve as trustees.

Living Trusts. A **living trust** is a trust in which you assign the management of your assets to a trustee while you are living. You identify a trustee that you want to manage the assets (which includes making decisions on how to invest cash until it is needed or how to spend cash).

Revocable Living Trust. With a **revocable living trust**, you can dissolve or revoke the trust at any time because you are still the legal owner of the assets. For example, you may revoke a living trust if you decide that you want to manage the assets yourself. Alternatively, you may revoke a living trust so that you can replace the trustee. In this case, you would create a new living trust with a newly identified trustee.

By using a revocable living trust, you can avoid the probate process. You are still the legal owner of the assets, however, so you do not avoid estate taxes. The assets are still considered part of your estate.

Irrevocable Living Trust. An **irrevocable living trust** is a living trust that cannot be changed. This type of trust is a separate entity. It can provide income for you, but the assets in the trust are no longer legally yours. The assets are not considered part of your estate and therefore are not subject to estate taxes upon your death.

Standard Family Trust. A **standard family trust** (also called a **credit-shelter trust**) is a trust established for children in a family. The standard family trust is just one of many types of **testamentary trusts**, or trusts created by wills. It is a popular type of trust because it can be used to avoid estate taxes in a manner somewhat similar to the irrevocable living trust, except that it is not structured as a living trust. Consider the following example.

Example

Stephanie Spratt's parents earned a modest income before retiring. As a result of their diligent saving and the strong performance of their stock investments, they have about $1.2 million in assets and no will. If the estate is worth $1.2 million at the time it is passed on to Stephanie and her sister, the portion of the estate over the current $675,000 limit will be taxed at a high tax rate. Stephanie explains to her parents that these high taxes can be avoided. The Spratt family decides to meet with a financial planner.

With the financial planner's help, Mr. and Mrs. Spratt create a will declaring that they are each sole owners of specific assets. Mr. Spratt declares he is the owner of assets worth $600,000, and Mrs. Spratt declares she is the owner of the other assets, which are worth $600,000. Mr. Spratt specifies in the will that if he dies first, his assets are to be distributed to a standard family trust for the children.

The trust will be managed by a trustee and will provide Mrs. Spratt with income while she is alive, and ultimately it will provide income for her children. The assets in the trust will no longer be legally owned by Mrs. Spratt. These assets will ultimately be distributed to the children when they reach an age specified in the trust document. Therefore, Mrs. Spratt now legally owns $600,000 in assets, rather than $1.2 million in assets. Upon her death, her estate will be less than the maximum that can be passed on tax-free to her children.

The will could also state that if Mrs. Spratt dies first, her assets are to be distributed to a standard family trust. Since the Tax Relief Act of 2001 increases the estate tax exemption over time, the Spratts may not require the trust in the future.

Gifts

gift
A tax-free distribution of up to $10,000 per year from one person to another.

From an estate planning perspective, a **gift** is a tax-free distribution of funds from one person to another. The law currently allows up to $10,000 to pass by gift per year. The maximum amount of the gift allowed will increase in increments of $1,000 over time with inflation.

If your goal is to ultimately pass on your estate to your children, but you are concerned about estate taxes, you can reduce the size of your estate by giving $10,000 tax-free to each of your children each year. The recipient does not have to report the gift as income, and therefore it is not subject to taxes. If you are married, you and your spouse can each give $10,000 to each of your children and to others. Thus, a married couple with three children may give $60,000 in gifts to their children every year. Over a five-year period, the couple could give $300,000 to their three children without any tax consequences to the parents or the children. Such gifts are especially important for people whose estate value exceeds the tax-free limit. Frequent gifts may enable the parents to ensure that their estate is under the tax-free limit by the time of their death.

Contributions to Charitable Organizations

Many individuals wish to leave a portion of their estate to charitable organizations. Any money donated from an estate to charitable organizations is

19.3   Financial Planning Online: How to Build Your Estate Plan

Go to:
http://moneycentral.msn.com/
retire/home.asp

Click on:
Estate Planning

Click on:
Plan Your Estate

This Web site provides:
step-by-step instructions for
estate planning.

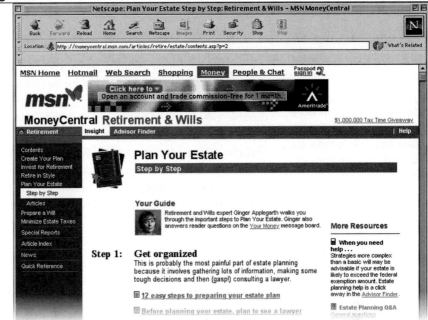

not subject to estate taxes. Consider an estate worth $200,000 more than the prevailing tax-free limit. If this entire estate is passed on to family members or other individuals, $200,000 of the estate will be subject to estate taxes. If $200,000 is donated to charitable organizations, however, none of the estate will be subject to estate taxes. Many individuals plan to leave donations for charitable organizations regardless of the tax implications, but it is nonetheless important to recognize the tax benefits.

OTHER ASPECTS OF ESTATE PLANNING

In addition to wills and trusts, estate planning also involves some other key decisions regarding a living will and power of attorney.

Living Will

living will
A legal document in which individuals specify their preferences if they become mentally or physically disabled.

A **living will** is a simple legal document in which individuals specify their preferences if they become mentally or physically disabled. For example, many individuals have a living will that expresses their desire not to be placed on life support if they become terminally ill. In this case, a living will also has financial implications because an estate could be charged with large medical bills resulting from life support. In this way, those who do not want to be kept alive by life support can ensure that their estate is used in the way that they prefer.

Power of Attorney

power of attorney
A legal document granting a person the power to make specific decisions for you in the event that you are incapable.

durable power of attorney for health care
A legal document granting a person the power to make specific health care decisions for you.

A **power of attorney** is a legal document granting a person the power to make specific decisions for you in the event that you are incapacitated. For example, you may name a family member or a close friend to make your investment and housing decisions if you become ill.

A **durable power of attorney for health care** is a legal document granting a person the power to make specific health care decisions for you. A durable power of attorney ensures that the person you identify has the power to make specific decisions regarding your health care in the event that you become incapacitated. While a living will states many of your preferences, a situation may arise that is not covered by your living will. A durable power of attorney for health care means that the necessary decisions will be made by someone who knows your preferences, rather than by a health care facility.

Maintaining Estate Plan Documents

Key documents such as your will, living will, and power of attorney should be kept in a safe, accessible place. You should tell the person (or people) you named as executor and granted power of attorney where you keep these documents so that they can be retrieved if and when they are needed.

19.4   Financial Planning Online: Legal Advice on Estate Planning

Go to:
http://www.nolo.com

Click on:
Estate Planning

This Web site provides:
a background on estate planning decisions and the terminology used in estate planning.

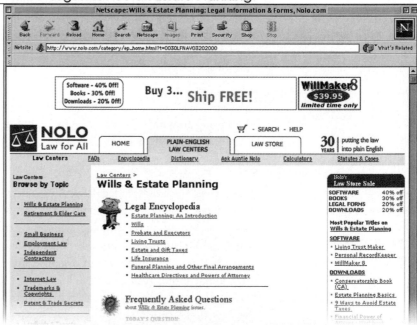

HOW ESTATE PLANNING FITS WITHIN YOUR FINANCIAL PLAN

The following are the key decisions about estate planning that should be included within your financial plan:

1. Should you create a will?

2. How can you limit your estate taxes?

3. Should you create a living will or designate an individual to have power of attorney?

Exhibit 19.2 provides an example of how estate planning decisions apply to Stephanie Spratt's financial plan.

Exhibit 19.2   How Estate Planning Fits within Stephanie Spratt's Financial Plan

Goals for Estate Planning

1. Create a will.
2. Establish a plan for trusts or gifts if my estate is subject to high taxes.
3. Decide whether I need to create a living will or assign power of attorney.

Analysis

Estate Planning and Related Issues

Issue	Status
Possible heirs to my estate?	My sister and parents.
Tax implications for estate?	Small estate at this point; exempt from taxes.
Power of attorney necessary?	Yes; I want someone to make decisions for me if I am unable.
Living will necessary?	Yes; I do not want to be placed on life support.

Decisions

Decision regarding a Will:

I will create a will that stipulates a contribution of $5,000 to the local humane society. I plan to make my parents my heirs if they are alive; otherwise, I will name my sister as the heir. I will designate my sister to be executor.

Decision regarding Trusts and Gifts:

My estate is easily under the limit at which taxes are imposed, so it would not be subject to taxes at this point. Therefore, I do not need to consider establishing trusts or gifts at this time.

Decision on a Power of Attorney and Durable Power of Attorney:

I will assign my mother the power of attorney and the durable power of attorney. I will hire an attorney who can complete these documents along with my will within a period of about one or two hours.

DISCUSSION QUESTIONS

1. How would Stephanie's estate planning decisions be different if she were a single mother of two children?

2. How would Stephanie's estate planning decisions be affected if she were 35 years old? If she were 50 years old?

SUMMARY

A will is intended to make sure that your preferences are carried out after your death. It allows you to distribute your estate, select a guardian for your children, and select an executor to ensure that the will is executed properly.

Estate taxes are imposed on estates that exceed a tax-free limit. The limit will gradually increase over time, until it reaches $3.5 million in 2009.

Estate planning involves the use of trusts, gifts, and charitable contributions. Trusts can be structured so that a larger estate can be passed on to the beneficiaries without being subjected to estate taxes. Gifts are tax-free payments that can be made on an annualized basis; they allow parents to pass on part of their wealth to their children every year. By making annual gifts,

parents may reduce their wealth so that when they die, their estate will not be subject to estate taxes. An estate's contributions to charity are not subject to estate taxes.

In the event that you someday might be incapable of making decisions relating to your health and financial situation, you should consider creating a living will and power of attorney now. A living will is a legal document that allows you to specify your health treatment preferences, such as that you do not want to be placed on life support. The power of attorney is a legal document that allows you to assign a person the power to make specific decisions for you if and when you are no longer capable of making these decisions.

Integrating the Key Concepts

Your estate planning decisions are related to other parts of your financial plan. For example, your estate planning decision to make $10,000 gifts to various family members each year reduces your liquidity. It also reduces the amount of funds available to pay off personal loans or a mortgage (Part 3) or to invest (Part 4). Yet making gifts may be more appropriate than paying off loans early or making more investments because it can help reduce the taxes on your estate. If you use the funds in some other way, the before-tax value of your estate may be larger, but your heirs will receive less due to the taxes imposed on the estate.

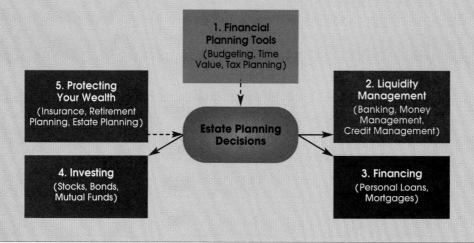

REVIEW QUESTIONS

1. What is an estate? What is estate planning? What is the main goal of estate planning?

2. What is a will? Why is a will important? What happens if a person dies without a will?

3. List the requirements for a valid will.

4. Describe the two common types of wills.

5. List and briefly discuss the key components of a will.

6. When might you need to change your will? How can your will be changed?

7. What is probate? Describe the probate process.

8. Discuss estate taxes. When is an estate not subject to estate taxes? When is an estate subject to estate taxes? What is the range of federal estate tax rates? What other taxes may be levied against an estate?

9. Why is it important to periodically calculate the value of your estate?

10. Beyond the will, what does estate planning involve?

11. What is a trust? What is the difference between a living trust and a testamentary trust?

12. What is a revocable living trust? How can a revocable living trust be used to help your estate? How does a revocable living trust affect estate taxes?

13. What is an irrevocable living trust?

14. What is a standard family trust? Give an illustration.

15. How do gifts fit into estate planning?

16. How do contributions to charitable organizations help in estate planning?

17. What is a living will? What are its implications for estate planning?

18. What is a power of attorney?

19. What is a durable power of attorney for health care? Why is it needed even if you have a living will?

20. How should estate plan documents be maintained?

FINANCIAL PLANNING ONLINE EXERCISES

Go to http://moneycentral.msn.com/retire/home.asp.

1. Click on Step-by-Step Guides and then click on Prepare a Will. Then scroll down to Step 2 and click on Make-a-Will Quiz. Taking this quiz will enable you to gauge your level of preparedness.

2. Use the Back option in your browser to return to the home page. Under Quick Reference, click on Living Trusts. Scroll down to Questions and click on What Is a Living Trust? Read the answer and then click on Return to Questions. Click on What Is a Revocable Living Trust? Report on the pros and cons of a revocable living trust.

3. Use the Back option in your browser to return to the home page. Under More Tools, click on Retirement IQ Test. Take the test to determine your understanding of retirement issues. The quiz will grade your score.

4. Use the Back option in your browser to return to the home page. Under More Tools, click on Expense Calculator. Click on Work and enter data for various current and anticipated expenses. The calculator will provide you with the difference between expenses while working and in retirement; more detail is available under the summary tab.

5. Use the Back option in your browser to return to the home page. Under More Tools, click on Income Calculator. Choose a goal (e.g., preserving capital, spending capital, or growing capital). Then follow the steps and enter the requested data. Results, Details, and a Summary will provide you with information on income flows and the estate that will remain for your heirs.

6. Use the Back option in your browser to return to the home page. Under Quick Reference, click on Estate Planning. Then click on Plan Your Estate. Under Step 1, click on 12 Steps to Preparing Your Estate Plan. Review the 12 steps and report on how you would apply them in your own plan.

Building Your Own Financial Plan

Like life insurance, wills are something that many people mistakenly believe are necessary only if one is "wealthy." For today's college graduate, the accumulation of a $1 million estate is possible with disciplined savings. A will is necessary for anyone with positive net worth, and, as the chapter indicated, it is also necessary if you care about how and to whom your assets are distributed and to whom the guardianship of any children is assigned. Your key goals for estate planning are to create a will, establish a plan for trusts or gifts if your estate is subject to high taxes, and decide whether you need to create a living will

or assign power of attorney. Use the template provided with this chapter in the *Financial Planning Workbook* and on the CD-ROM to enter your findings and decisions.

We will once again utilize the "msn.com" Web site for this chapter. Go to www.msn.com, click on the tab marked "money," and then go to the "site map." Under the column in the site map headed "retirement and wills," go down and click on the "Make-a-Will Quiz" if you have not already done so in Financial Planning Online Exercise 1 in this chapter. Look carefully at your results to gain insight into your need for a will and the assistance of a good attorney to prepare it. Review the other information found at this site dealing with wills and estate planning.

To determine your need for a will, examine the personal balance sheet you created in Chapter 2. After you have visited the msn.com Web site and thoroughly reviewed the materials, consider visiting an attorney to find out the cost of preparing a will. You should also consider the need for a living will and assigning power of attorney and at what point in your life various types of trusts or gifts may be useful.

The key events that necessitate the review and/or change of your will are marriage, divorce, widowhood, parenthood, and grandparenthood. Significant changes in your assets (such as the receipt of a significant bequest from a friend or relative's will) may also necessitate a review and/or change of your will.

The Sampsons—A Continuing Case

Dave and Sharon Sampson want to make sure that their family is properly cared for in the event of their death. They recently purchased term life insurance and want to make sure that the funds are allocated to best serve the children in the long run. Specifically, they have set the following goals. First, they want to make sure that a portion of the insurance proceeds is set aside for the children's education.

Second, they want to make sure that the insurance proceeds are distributed evenly over several years, so that the children do not spend the money too quickly.

1. Advise the Sampsons on how they can plan their estate to achieve their financial goals.

2. What important consideration are the Sampsons overlooking in their estate planning goals?

IN-TEXT STUDY GUIDE

True/False:

1. An estate represents a person's assets before any existing liabilities are paid.

2. If you die without a will, the court will appoint an administrator to distribute your estate according to the laws of your state.

3. The executor carries out the instructions specified in your will regarding how your assets will be distributed.

4. If you make changes to your will, you must create a new will.

5. The letter of last instruction can describe your preferences regarding funeral arrangements.

6. A trust is a legal document in which one person (called the trustee) transfers assets to another person (called a grantor), who manages the assets for designated beneficiaries.

7. You should periodically attempt to calculate the value of your estate.

8. The family trust can be used to avoid estate taxes in a manner somewhat similar to the irrevocable living trust.

9. From an estate planning perspective, a gift is a taxable distribution of funds from one person to another.

10. The family trust is just one of many types of testamentary trusts.

Multiple Choice:

1. A(n) _____ is a legal request for how one's estate should be distributed upon death.
   a. letter of last instruction
   b. asset distribution
   c. will
   d. none of the above

2. If you die _____, you die without a will.
   a. intrastate
   b. interstate
   c. intestate
   d. none of the above

3. Which of the following is not a requirement for creating a valid will?
   a. You must be of a minimum age, usually 30.
   b. You must be mentally competent.
   c. A will must be dated and signed.
   d. A will must have two or three witnesses who are not inheriting anything under the will.

4. A(n) _____ will specifies that the entire estate is to be distributed to a person's spouse.
   a. traditional marital share
   b. simple
   c. executorial
   d. intestate

5. A traditional marital share will distributes _____ of the estate to the spouse.
   a. none
   b. one-quarter
   c. one-half
   d. all

6. The _____ is assigned the responsibility of caring for the children and managing any estate left to the children.
   a. executor
   b. guardian
   c. codicil
   d. grantor

7. A(n) _____ is a document that specifies changes in an existing will.
   a. codicil
   b. intestate
   c. indenture
   d. probate

8. _____ is a legal process that ensures that when people die, their assets are distributed as they wish.
   a. Intestate
   b. Codicil
   c. Probate
   d. Will court

9. The estate's value is equal to the value of all the _____ minus any existing _____.
   a. assets; expenses
   b. assets; liabilities
   c. income; expenses
   d. liabilities; assets

10. The maximum federal estate tax rate will eventually be reduced to _____ percent, until it is eliminated in 2010.
    a. 25
    b. 45
    c. 90
    d. 67

11. The person transferring assets to another person in a trust is called the
    a. grantor.
    b. trustee.
    c. executor.
    d. none of the above

12. The person receiving assets in a trust is called the
    a. grantor.
    b. trustee.
    c. executor.
    d. none of the above

13. A(n) _____ is a trust in which you assign the management of your assets to a trustee while you are living.
    a. living trust
    b. revocable living trust
    c. irrevocable living trust
    d. all of the above

14. In a(n) _____ trust, the grantor is no longer the owner of the assets in the trust.
    a. living
    b. revocable living
    c. irrevocable living
    d. none of the above

15. A(n) _____ trust is a trust established for the children in a family.
    a. standard family
    b. credit-shelter
    c. testamentary
    d. all of the above

16. A _____ is a legal document created by individuals to specify their preferences if they become mentally or physically disabled.
    a. living will
    b. power of attorney
    c. living trust
    d. codicil

17. A _____ is a legal document naming a person with the power to make specific decisions for an individual in the event that the individual is no longer capable of making these decisions.
    a. living will
    b. power of attorney
    c. living trust
    d. codicil

18. Which of the following is not true regarding estate taxes?
    a. They are dependent on the value of an estate.
    b. Any funds that are provided as a result of a life insurance policy are counted as part of the estate for tax purposes.
    c. All the assets in an estate can be distributed tax-free to children or others.
    d. All of the above are true.

19. The executor of a will is also referred to as the
    a. grantor.
    b. trustee.
    c. personal representative.
    d. guardian.

20. Which of the following is not true regarding a guardian?
    a. If you have children, you should name a guardian.
    b. You should ensure that the person you select as guardian is willing to serve as the guardian.
    c. You may specify an amount of money to be distributed to the guardian to care for your children.
    d. All of the above are true.

Part 5: Brad Brooks—A Continuing Case

 Brad has taken you out to dinner as a "thank you" for all your help in getting control of his personal finances. During the course of the meal, he brings up several more issues on which he wishes your advice.

During the appetizer, he tells you that he is shopping for a whole life insurance policy. He believes that the loan feature will give him an option for meeting his liquidity needs.

During the main course, Brad tells you that he has revised his retirement plans. He would like to retire in 20 years instead of the original 30. His goal is to save $500,000 by that time. He admits that he would rather spend than save, which is evidenced by the fact that he is not taking advantage of his employer's retirement match; his employer will match retirement plan contributions up to $300 per month. Factoring in the employer match, Brad could have a possible total annual retirement contribution of $7,200.

Just as dessert arrives, Brad unveils his plan to provide for his two nephews' college education in the event of his death. He does not have a will and wonders if one is necessary.

1. Concerning Brad's insurance plan, comment on:

   a. His plan to use the whole life policy's loan feature as a means of maintaining liquidity

   b. His need for life insurance

   c. If you see any reasons for life insurance in (b), is whole life the best way to meet it?

2. With regard to Brad's revised retirement plans:

   a. How much will he have in 30 years if he invests $300 per month at 8 percent?

   b. How much will he have to save per month at 8 percent to reach his $500,000 goal in 20 years? In 30 years?

   c. What impact could retiring 10 years earlier have on Brad's current standard of living?

   d. If Brad takes advantage of his employer's match, what will be the impact on his retirement savings (assume an 8 percent return) in 20 years? In 30 years?

   e. What other options are available to Brad to save for his retirement? Give the pros and cons of each.

3. If Brad really wishes to provide for his nephews' college education, how can a will help him achieve that goal? What else might Brad consider to pay for his nephews' college education?

4. Would your advice in questions 1–3 change if Brad were:

   a. 45 years old?

   b. 60 years old?

5. Prepare a written or oral report on your findings and recommendations to Brad.

PART 6

Synthesis of Financial Planning

Chapter 20 Integrating the Components of a
Financial Plan

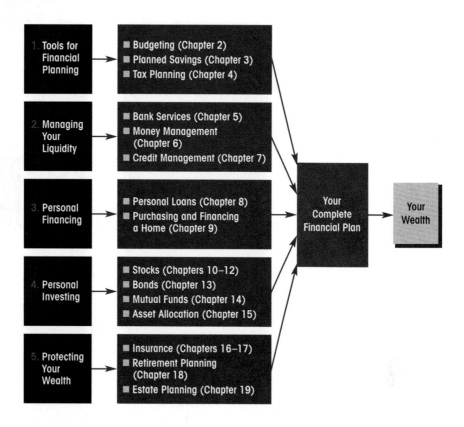

1. Tools for Financial Planning	■ Budgeting (Chapter 2) ■ Planned Savings (Chapter 3) ■ Tax Planning (Chapter 4)
2. Managing Your Liquidity	■ Bank Services (Chapter 5) ■ Money Management (Chapter 6) ■ Credit Management (Chapter 7)
3. Personal Financing	■ Personal Loans (Chapter 8) ■ Purchasing and Financing a Home (Chapter 9)
4. Personal Investing	■ Stocks (Chapters 10–12) ■ Bonds (Chapter 13) ■ Mutual Funds (Chapter 14) ■ Asset Allocation (Chapter 15)
5. Protecting Your Wealth	■ Insurance (Chapters 16–17) ■ Retirement Planning (Chapter 18) ■ Estate Planning (Chapter 19)

Your Complete Financial Plan → Your Wealth

This part serves as a capstone by summarizing the key components of a financial plan. It also illustrates the interrelationships among the segments of a financial plan by highlighting how decisions regarding each component affect the other components.

Chapter **20**

Integrating the Components of a Financial Plan

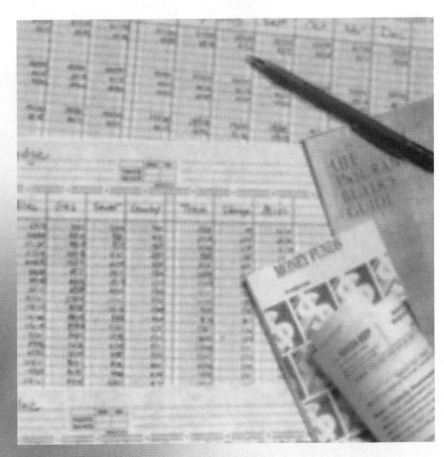

As explained throughout this text, each component of a financial plan allows you to build your wealth and achieve the various financial goals that you set. You have now mastered the key decisions related to the five components of your financial plan: budgeting and tax planning, managing your liquidity, financing large purchases, investing, and protecting your wealth.

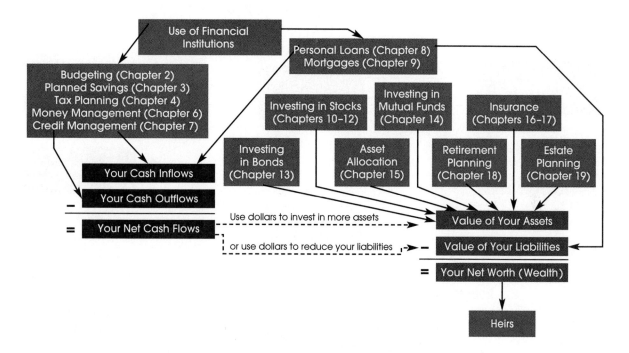

The objectives of this chapter are to:

- review the components of a financial plan,
- illustrate how a financial plan's components are integrated, and
- provide an example of a financial plan.

INTEGRATION OF COMPONENTS WITHIN A FINANCIAL PLAN

A key to financial planning is recognizing how the components of your financial plan are related. Each part of this text has focused on one of the five main components of your financial plan, which are illustrated once again in Exhibit 20.1. The decisions that you make regarding each component of your financial plan affect your cash flows and your wealth. The five components are summarized next, with information on how they are interrelated.

Exhibit 20.1   Your Personal Cash Flow Chart

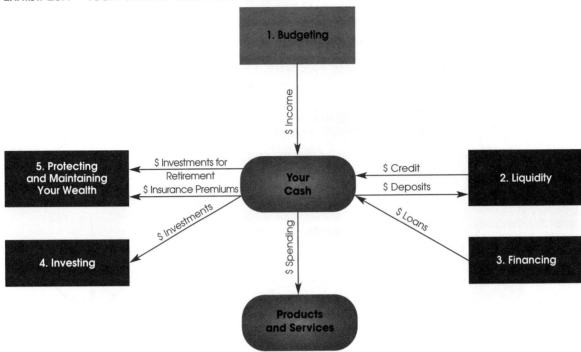

Budgeting

Recall that budgeting allows you to forecast how much money you will have at the end of each month so that you can determine how much you will be able to invest in assets. Most importantly, budgeting allows you to determine whether your cash outflows will exceed your cash inflows so that you can forecast any shortages in that month. Your spending decisions affect your budget, which affects every other component of your financial plan. Careful budgeting can prevent excessive spending and therefore help you achieve financial goals.

Budgeting Tradeoff. The more you spend, the less money you will have available for liquidity purposes, or to make investments, or to save for retirement. Thus, your budgeting decisions involve a tradeoff between spending today and allocating funds for the future. Your budget should attempt to ensure that you have net cash flows every month for investments or for retirement. The more funds you can allocate for the future, the more you will be able to benefit from compounded interest, and the more you will be able to spend in the future. In addition, the means by which you spend may have tax implications.

Managing Liquidity

You can prepare for anticipated cash shortages in any future month by ensuring that you have enough liquid assets to cover the deficiency. Some of the more liquid assets include a checking account, a savings account, a money market deposit account, and money market funds. The more funds you maintain in these types of assets, the more liquidity you will have to cover cash shortages. Even if you do not have sufficient liquid assets, you can cover a cash deficiency by obtaining short-term financing (such as using a credit card). If you maintain adequate liquidity, you will not need to borrow every time you need money. In this way, you can avoid major financial problems and therefore be more likely to achieve your financial goals.

Liquidity Tradeoff. Since liquid assets generate relatively low returns, you forgo earning a higher return. A checking account does not earn interest, and the other types of liquid assets have relatively low interest rates. If you choose to earn higher returns by investing all of your money in stocks or bonds, however, you may not have sufficient liquidity. Therefore, you should maintain just enough money in liquid assets to satisfy your liquidity needs; then you can earn a higher return on your other assets.

Personal Financing

Personal financing allows you to make purchases now without having the full amount of cash on hand. Thus, financing can increase the amount of your assets. Financing is especially useful for large purchases such as a car or a home.

Personal Financing Tradeoff. One advantage of personal financing with a mortgage or home equity loan is that the interest payments are tax-deductible.

20.1   Financial Planning Online: Links to Facilitate Your Financial Planning Decisions

Go to:
http://www.superstarinvestor.
com

This Web site provides:
links to learn more about all the components of a personal financial plan.

A disadvantage is that financing can cause budgeting problems. When you borrow to pay for a car, to purchase a home, or even to pay off a credit card balance, you affect your future budget, because the monthly loan payment means that you will have less cash available at the end of each month. Although a loan allows you to make purchases now, it restricts your spending or saving in future months while you are paying off the loan. Therefore, an excessive amount of financing can prevent you from achieving your financial goals.

It is easier to cover the monthly loan payment if you select financing with a relatively long maturity. But the longer the maturity, the longer the loan will be outstanding, and the more interest you will pay.

You may want to consider paying off a loan before its maturity so that you can avoid incurring any more interest expenses, especially when the interest rate charged is relatively high. You should not use all of your liquid funds to pay off a loan, however, because you will still need to maintain liquidity. Paying off loans rather than making additional investments is appropriate when the expected after-tax return on the investments you could make is lower than the interest rate you are paying on the loan.

Managing Investments

When making investments, recall that your main choices are stocks, bonds, and mutual funds. If you want your investments to provide periodic income, you may consider investing in stocks that pay dividends. The stocks of large, well-known firms tend to pay relatively high dividends, as these firms are not growing as fast as smaller firms and can afford to pay out more of their earnings as dividends. Bonds also provide periodic income. If you do not need periodic income, you may consider investing in stocks of firms that do not pay dividends. These firms often are growing at a fast pace and therefore offer the potential for a large increase in the stock value over time.

Investment Tradeoff. By investing in the stocks of large, well-known firms, you may enhance your liquidity because you will receive dividend income and can easily sell the stocks if you need money. You can also enhance your liquidity by investing in Treasury bonds or highly rated corporate bonds because these bonds provide periodic income and can easily be sold if you need money. However, these investments typically do not generate as high a return as investments in stocks of smaller firms.

If you try to earn high returns by investing all of your money in stocks of smaller firms, you forgo some liquidity because the prices of these stocks are volatile, and you may want to avoid selling them when prices are relatively low. If you have sufficient liquid assets such as checking and savings accounts, however, you do not need additional liquidity from your investments in stocks.

Another concern about the stocks of smaller firms is that they can be very risky and are more likely to result in large losses than investments in stocks of large, well-known firms. You can invest in small stocks without being exposed to the specific risk of any individual stock by investing in a mutual fund that focuses on small stocks. When market conditions are weak, however, such funds can experience large losses, although not as much as a single stock of a small firm.

Whenever you use money for investments, you forgo the use of that money for some other purpose, such as investing in more liquid assets, paying off existing debt, investing in your retirement, or buying insurance. You should make investments only after you have sufficient liquidity and sufficient insurance to protect your existing assets. Investments are the key to building your wealth over time. By investing a portion of your income consistently over time, you are more likely to achieve your financial goals.

Protecting Your Wealth

You can protect your assets by purchasing insurance. Recall from Chapter 16 that property and casualty insurance insures your assets (such as your car and home), health insurance covers health expenses, and disability insurance provides financial support if you become disabled. Life insurance provides your family members or other named beneficiaries with financial support in the event of your death. Thus, insurance protects against events that could reduce your income or your wealth. You can also maintain your wealth by setting aside funds for your retirement. These funds can provide you with the support to continue your lifestyle after you retire. Finally, proper estate planning can ensure that your assets are distributed to your heirs in the manner that you desire.

Insurance Tradeoff. Any money that is used to buy insurance or that is set aside for retirement cannot be used for other purposes such as investing in liquid assets, paying off loans, and making investments. You need to have insurance to cover your car and your home. If you have a family, you may also need life insurance. Take care that you do not have excessive insurance, however, because it may be costly relative to the potential extra benefits you receive.

Retirement Account Tradeoff. The more money you contribute to your retirement account now, the more money you will have at retirement. However, you should make sure you can afford whatever you decide to contribute. You need to have enough money to maintain sufficient liquidity so that you can afford any monthly loan payments before you contribute to your retirement.

When deciding whether to invest your money in current investments or in your retirement account, consider your goals. If you plan to use the investments for tuition or some other purpose in the near future, then you should not put this money in your retirement account. Funds invested in a retirement account are not liquid. Any money withdrawn early from the account is subject to a penalty. If your goal is to save for retirement, though, you should allocate money to a retirement account. Although you will not have access to these funds, you are typically not taxed on contributions to your retirement account until the funds are withdrawn at the time of retirement. This deferral of taxes is very beneficial. In addition, some employers match part or all of your contribution to a retirement account.

Maintaining Your Financial Documents

As you monitor your financial plan over time, you should store all financial-related documents in one place, such as a safe at home or a safety deposit box. The key documents are identified in Exhibit 20.2.

Exhibit 20.2 Documents Used for Financial Planning

Monitoring Liquidity

- Certificates of deposit
- Bank account balances
- Any other money market securities owned

Monitoring Financing

- Credit card account numbers
- Credit card balances
- Personal loan (such as car loan) agreements
- Mortgage loan agreement

Monitoring Investments

- Stock certificates
- Bonds
- Account balance showing the market value of stocks
- Account balance showing the market value of bonds
- Account balance showing the market value of mutual funds
- Retirement plan balances

Protecting and Maintaining Wealth

- Insurance policies
- Retirement plan balances
- Will
- Trust agreements

20.2 Financial Planning Online: Insight about Financial Planning Concepts

Go to:
http://www.kiplinger.com

This Web site provides:
useful information about retirement planning and other concepts that may help you complete your financial plan.

EXAMPLE OF HOW THE COMPONENTS ARE INTEGRATED

At this point, you have sufficient background to complete all the components of your financial plan. As time passes, however, your financial position will change, and your financial goals will change as well. You will need to revise your financial plan periodically in order to meet your financial goals. The following example for Stephanie Spratt illustrates how an individual's financial positions can change over time, how a financial plan may need to be revised as a result, and how the components of the financial plan are integrated.

EXAMPLE

Recall from Chapter 1 that Stephanie Spratt established the following goals:

- Purchase a new car within a year.

- Buy a home within a year.

- Make investments that will allow her wealth to grow over time.

- Build a large amount of savings by the time of her retirement in 20 to 40 years.

Stephanie purchased a new car and a new home this year. She also made some small investments. She has clearly made progress toward her goal of building a large amount of savings by the time she retires.

Recall from Chapter 2 that Stephanie originally had a relatively simple personal balance sheet. Her assets amounted to $9,000, and she had credit card debt of $2,000 as her only liability. Thus, her net worth was $7,000 at that time. Since she created the balance sheet shown in Chapter 2, her assets, liabilities, and net worth have changed substantially.

Stephanie's current personal balance sheet is compared to her personal balance sheet from Chapter 2 in Exhibit 20.3. Notice how her personal balance sheet has changed. These are the main changes in her assets:

1. She purchased a home for $80,000 that still has a market value of $80,000.

2. She purchased a new car for $18,000 that currently has a market value of $15,000.

3. She recently used $2,000 income to invest in two mutual funds, which are now valued at $2,100.

4. She recently started investing in her retirement account and has $800 in it.

The main changes in her liabilities are as follows:

1. Her purchase of a home required her to obtain a mortgage loan, which now has a balance of $71,000.

2. Her purchase of a car required her to obtain a car loan (she made a down payment of $1,000, has paid $2,000 of principal on the loan, and still owes $15,000).

3. She has a $1,000 credit card bill that she will pay off soon.

As Exhibit 20.3 shows, Stephanie's total assets are now $105,000. She increased her assets primarily by making financing decisions that also increased her liabilities. Exhibit 20.3 shows that her liabilities are now $87,000. Thus, her net worth is:

Net Worth = Total Assets − Total Liabilities

$$= \$105,000 - \$87,000$$

$$= \$18,000.$$

The increase in her net worth since the beginning of the year is mainly attributable to her saving a portion of her income over time. She received a bonus from her employer this year, which helped her cover the down payment on her house. Yet, even without the bonus, she was saving a portion of her income each month. Now that she has a car loan and a mortgage, she uses a large portion of her income to cover loan payments and will not be able to save as much money.

As time passes, Stephanie hopes to invest in more stocks or other investments to increase her net worth. If the value of her home increases over time, her net worth will also grow. However, her car will likely decline in value over time, which will reduce the value of her assets and therefore reduce her net worth.

Exhibit 20.3   Update on Stephanie Spratt's Personal Balance Sheet

	As of the Beginning of Your School Term	As of Today
Assets		
Liquid Assets		
Cash	$500	$200
Checking account	3,500	200
Money market deposit account	0	2,600
Total liquid assets	**$4,000**	**$3,000**
Household Assets		
Home	$0	$80,000
Car	1,000	15,000
Furniture	1,000	1,000
Total household assets	**$2,000**	**$96,000**
Investment Assets		
Stocks	$3,000	$3,100
Mutual funds	0	2,100
Investment in retirement account	0	800
Total investment assets	**$3,000**	**$6,000**
TOTAL ASSETS	**$9,000**	**$105,000**
Liabilities and Net Worth		
Current Liabilities		
Credit card balance	$2,000	$1,000
Total current liabilities	**$2,000**	**$1,000**
Long-Term Liabilities		
Car loan	$0	$15,000
Mortgage	0	71,000
Total long-term liabilities	**$0**	**$86,000**
TOTAL LIABILITIES	**$2,000**	**$87,000**
Net Worth	**$7,000**	**$18,000**

Budgeting

Stephanie's recent cash flow statement is shown in Exhibit 20.4. The major change in her cash inflows from Chapter 2 is that her disposable income is now higher as a result of a promotion and salary increase at work. The major changes in her cash outflows are as follows:

1. She no longer has a rent payment.

2. As a result of buying a new car, she now saves about $100 per month on car maintenance because the car dealer will do all maintenance at no charge for the next two years.

3. Primarily by discontinuing her health club membership and exercising at home, she has reduced her recreation expenses to about $400 per month (a reduction of $200 per month).

4. She now has a car loan payment of $412 each month.

5. She now has a mortgage loan payment of $688; with her property tax and her homeowner's insurance, her total payment for her home is $848 per month.

6. She just started contributing $400 per month to her retirement account.

Budgeting Dilemma. While Stephanie's monthly cash inflows are now $500 higher than they were initially, her monthly cash outflows are $800 higher. Thus, her monthly net cash flows have declined from $400 to $100. This means that even though her salary (and therefore her cash inflows) increased, she has less money to allocate toward investments.

Budgeting Decision. Stephanie reviews her personal cash flow statement to determine how she is spending her money. Some of her cash flows are currently being invested in assets. Even if she does not invest any of her net cash flows now, her net worth will grow over time because she is paying down the debt on her home and on her car each month and is contributing to her retirement account.

Furthermore, she will now receive a tax refund from the IRS each year because she can itemize her mortgage expense. Overall, she decides that she is pleased with her cash flow situation. However, she decides to reassess the other components of her financial plan (as discussed below), which could affect her budget.

Long-Term Strategy for Budgeting. Some of Stephanie's budgeting is based on the bills that she incurs as a result of her car and home. Other parts of the budget are determined by the other components of her financial plan:

- The amount of cash (if any) allocated to liquid assets is dependent on her plan for managing liquidity.

- The amount of cash allocated to pay off existing loans is dependent on her plan for personal financing.

- The amount of cash allocated to investments is dependent on her plan for investing.

Exhibit 20.4   Update on Stephanie Spratt's Cash Flow Statement

	First Month at Beginning of Your School Term (from Chapter 2)	Last Month	Change since Beginning of Your School Term
Cash Inflows			
Disposable (after-tax) income	$2,500	$3,000	+$500
Interest on deposits	0	0	No change
Dividend payments	0	0	No change
Total cash inflows	$2,500	$3,000	+$500
Cash Outflows			
Rent	$600	$0	−$600
Cable TV	50	50	No change
Electricity and water	60	90	+30
Telephone	60	60	No change
Groceries	300	300	No change
Health and disability insurance and expenses	130	140	+10
Clothing	100	100	No change
Car insurance and maintenance	200	100	−100
Recreation	600	400	−200
Car loan payment	0	412	+412
Mortgage payment (includes property taxes and insurance)	0	848	+848
Contribution to retirement plan	0	400	+400
Total cash outflows	$2,100	$2,900	+$800
Net cash flows	$400	$100	−$300

- The amount of cash allocated to insurance payments and to her retirement account is dependent on her plan for protecting and maintaining her wealth in the future.

Managing Liquidity

Every two weeks, Stephanie's paycheck is direct deposited to her checking account. She writes checks to pay all her bills and to cover the other cash outflows specified in Exhibit 20.4; she also pays her credit card bill each month. Her credit card balance is high right now, but she can use her next paycheck to cover most of it, as she has already paid her other bills for this month. She normally has about $100 at the end of the month after paying her recreation expenses.

Stephanie wants to ensure that she has sufficient liquidity. Her most convenient source of funds is her checking account; since her paycheck is deposited there, she knows she will have enough funds every month to pay her bills. If she had any other short-term debt, she would use her net cash flows to pay it off. She recently set up a money market deposit account (MMDA) and invested $2,600 in it. This account is her second most convenient source of funds; it allows her to write a limited number of checks in the event that unanticipated expenses occur.

Liquidity Dilemma. Stephanie must decide whether she should change her liquidity position. She considers these options.

Stephanie's Options If She Changes Her Liquidity	Advantage	Disadvantage
1. Reduce liquidity position by transferring money from MMDA to mutual fund	May earn a higher rate of return on her assets	Will have a smaller amount of liquid funds to cover unanticipated expenses
2. Increase liquidity position by transferring money from mutual fund to MMDA	May earn a lower rate of return on her assets	Will have a larger amount of liquid funds to cover unanticipated expenses

Liquidity Decision. Stephanie determines that she has access to sufficient funds to cover her liquidity needs. If she has any major unanticipated expenses beyond the funds in her MMDA, she could sell shares of the stock or the mutual funds that she owns. She decides to leave her liquidity position as is.

Long-Term Strategy for Managing Liquidity. Stephanie's plan for managing liquidity is to continue using her checking account to cover bills and to use funds from the MMDA to cover any unanticipated expenses. She prefers not to invest any more funds in the MMDA because the interest rate is low. Thus, she will use any net cash flows she has at the end of the month for some other purpose. If she ever needs to withdraw funds from her MMDA, she will likely attempt to replenish that account once she has new net cash flows that can be invested in it.

Personal Financing

Stephanie has a car loan balance of $15,000 and a mortgage loan balance of $71,000. She has no need for any additional loans. The interest expenses on the mortgage are tax-deductible, but the interest expenses on the car loan are not. She considers paying off her car loan before it is due (about three years from now).

Financing Dilemma. Stephanie wants to pay off the car loan as soon as she has saved a sufficient amount of money. She realizes that to pay off this liability, she will need to reduce some of her assets. She outlines the following options for paying off her car loan early:

Stephanie's Options for Paying Off Her Car Loan Early	Advantage	Disadvantage
1. Withdraw funds from MMDA	Would be able to reduce or eliminate monthly car loan payment	Will no longer have adequate liquidity
2. Withdraw funds from retirement account	Would be able to reduce or eliminate monthly car loan payment	Will be charged a penalty and will no longer have funds set aside for retirement
3. Sell stock	Would be able to reduce or eliminate monthly car loan payment	Would forgo the potential to earn high returns on stock
4. Sell mutual funds	Would be able to reduce or eliminate monthly car loan payment	Would forgo the potential to earn high returns on a mutual fund

Financing Decision. Stephanie needs to maintain liquidity, so she eliminates the first option. She also eliminates the second option because she does not want to pay a penalty for early withdrawal and believes those funds should be reserved for retirement purposes.

The remaining options deserve more consideration. Stephanie's annual interest rate on the car loan is 7.60 percent. Once she has a large enough investment in stocks and mutual funds that she can pay off the car loan (perhaps a year from now), she will decide how to use that money as follows:

- If she thinks that the investments will earn an annual after-tax return of less than 7.60 percent, she will sell them and use the money to pay off the car loan. In this way, she will essentially earn a return of 7.60 percent with that money because she will be paying off debt for which she was being charged 7.60 percent.

- If she thinks that the investments will earn an annual after-tax return greater than 7.60 percent, she will keep them. She will not pay off the car loan because her investments are providing her with a higher return than the cost of the car loan.

Long-Term Strategy for Financing. Once Stephanie pays off her car loan, she will have an extra $412 per month (the amount of her car loan payment) that can be used to make more investments. She does not plan to buy another car until she can pay for it with cash. Her only other loan is her mortgage, which has a 15-year life. If she stays in the same home over the next 15 years, she will have paid off her mortgage by that time. In this case, she will have no debt after 15 years. She may consider buying a more expensive home in the near future and would likely obtain another 15-year mortgage. She does not mind having a mortgage because the interest payments are tax-deductible.

Managing Investments

Stephanie currently has an investment in one stock worth $3,100 and an investment in two mutual funds worth $2,100.

Investing Dilemma. If the one stock that Stephanie owns performs poorly in the future, the value of her investments (and therefore her net worth) could decline substantially. She expects the stock market to do well but is uncomfortable having an investment in a single stock whose market value could easily decline by 30 percent or more in a month.

She considers the following options:

Stephanie's Options If She Changes Her Investments	Advantage	Disadvantage
1. Sell stock; invest the proceeds in bonds	Lower risk	Lower expected return than from her stock
2. Sell stock; invest the proceeds in her MMDA	Lower risk and improved liquidity	Lower expected return than from her stock
3. Sell stock; invest the proceeds in a stock mutual fund	Lower risk	Lower expected return than from her stock

Investing Decision. All three possibilities offer lower risk than the stock, but given that Stephanie expects the stock market to perform well, she prefers a stock mutual fund. She is not relying on the investment to provide periodic income at this time and wants an investment that could increase in value over time. She decides to sell her 100 shares of stock at the prevailing market value of $3,100 and to invest the proceeds in her stock mutual fund to achieve greater diversification. This transaction reflects a shift of $3,100 on her personal balance sheet from stocks to mutual funds. Her total amount of investment assets does not change.

Long-Term Strategy for Investing. Stephanie hopes to use most of her $100 in net cash flows each month to purchase additional shares of the stock mutual fund in which she recently invested. She does not specify the amount she will invest because she recognizes that in some months she may face unanticipated expenses that will need to be covered. Once her car loan is paid off, she will have an additional $412 in net cash flows per month that she can invest in the stock mutual fund or in other investments.

Protecting and Maintaining Wealth

Stephanie pays for car insurance, participates in a health insurance plan through her employer, pays for disability insurance, and pays for home-owner's insurance. She does not have any life insurance.

Stephanie recently started to contribute to a retirement account. This account is beneficial because her contributions will not be taxed until the funds are withdrawn during retirement. In addition, this account should grow in value if she consistently contributes to it each month and selects investments that appreciate in value over time.

Insurance Dilemma. An insurance agent recently recommended that Stephanie purchase a life insurance policy that would provide $500,000 to a beneficiary of her choice at the time of her death.

Insurance Decision. Stephanie decided that she does not need life insurance at this time because she does not have any children.

Long-Term Strategy for Insurance. Stephanie will purchase life insurance if and when she has children. She will always maintain enough insurance to cover the replacement of her home and car. She will always maintain a high level of car insurance to limit her liability in the event of an accident.

Retirement Contribution Dilemma. Last month, Stephanie started contributing $400 per month to her retirement account, which is matched by a con-tribution from her employer. As her salary increases in the future, she will have the option of contributing an additional $100 per month (which will not be matched by her employer) to her retirement account. However, she cannot use any of the contributed funds until she retires.

She considers the following options:

Stephanie's Options regarding Her Retirement Account	Advantage	Disadvantage
1. Do not contribute any funds to her retirement account	Can use all net cash flows for other purposes	Forgo tax benefits and matching contribution from employer; will have no money set aside for retirement
2. Continue to contribute $400 per month	Benefit from matching contribution, and achieve some tax benefits	Could use the $400 for other purposes
3. Contribute $500 per month	Benefit from $400 matching contribution and increased tax benefits	Could use the $500 for other purposes

Retirement Contribution Decision. Stephanie wants to know how much more she will have in 40 years (when she hopes to retire) if she saves an additional $100 per month ($1,200 per year). She expects to earn an annual return of 10 percent per year on the money in her retirement account. She can use the future value annuity table in Appendix A to determine the future value of her extra contribution. The *FVIFA* for a 10 percent interest rate and a period of 40 years is 442.59. In 40 years, her extra contribution of $1,200 per year would accumulate to be worth:

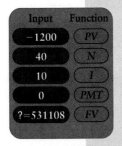

Input	Function
– 1200	PV
40	N
10	I
0	PMT
? = 531108	FV

$$\text{Extra Savings at Retirement} = \text{Extra Amount Invested} \times FVIFA_{i,n}$$
$$= \$1,200 \times 442.59$$
$$= \$531,108.$$

She decides to save the additional $100 per month since it will result in $531,108 more at retirement. She also realizes that contributing the extra amount will provide present-day tax benefits. Contributing the extra $100 will reduce her net cash flows, however, so she may have more difficulty meeting her liquidity needs, will be less likely to pay off her existing car loan quickly, will have less money to invest, and will have less money to spend on recreation. Yet, by accepting these disadvantages in the short run, she can receive major tax benefits and ensure a high level of wealth when she retires. Stephanie's view is that any dollar invested in a retirement account is more valuable than a dollar invested in a nonretirement account because of the tax advantages.

Long-Term Strategy for Retirement Contributions. Stephanie plans to invest the maximum allowed in her retirement account so that she can take full advantage of the tax benefits. The maximum annual limit on her retirement contribution is dependent on her income. As her income increases over time, she will be able to increase her monthly contribution up to the maximum limit. If she decides to raise a family or if her net worth increases dramatically, she will develop an estate plan to specify how her estate should be distributed upon her death.

FINANCIAL PLAN

Stephanie Spratt's financial plan is illustrated in Exhibit 20.5. It incorporates her most recent decisions (discussed earlier in this chapter). Her budget plan determines how she will use her cash inflows. Notice how she adjusts her budget plan in response to decisions regarding other components of her financial plan.

A review of Stephanie's financial plan shows that she is building her wealth over time in four ways:

1. She is increasing her equity investment in her car as she makes monthly payments on her car loan.

2. She is increasing her equity investment in her home as she makes monthly payments on her mortgage loan.

3. She is increasing her investment in a mutual fund as she uses the net cash flows each month to buy more shares.

4. She is increasing her retirement account assets as she makes monthly contributions.

If Stephanie follows the financial plan she has created, she will pay off her car loan within a year or two. She will also pay off her mortgage loan in 15 years and then will not have any remaining debt. In addition, she will continue to use her net cash flows to make investments in either stock or bond mutual funds. Her retirement account contributions ensure that she will have substantial wealth by the time she retires.

Stephanie's wealth may also increase for other reasons. The value of her home, mutual fund, and any investments she makes for her retirement account may increase over time. Overall, Stephanie's financial plan should provide her with sufficient wealth so that she can afford a very comfortable lifestyle in the future.

Exhibit 20.5   Stephanie Spratt's Financial Plan

Budget Plan

My monthly salary of $3,000 after taxes is direct deposited to my checking account. I will use this account to cover all bills and other expenses. My total expenses (including recreation) should be about $2,900 per month. This leaves me with net cash flows of $100. I will also receive an annual tax refund of about $3,000. The taxes I pay during the year will exceed my tax liability, as the interest payments on my mortgage will reduce my taxable income.

I will use the net cash flows each month to cover any unanticipated expenses that occurred during the month. My second priority is to use the net cash flows to keep about $2,600 in my money market deposit account (MMDA) to ensure liquidity. If this account is already at that level, I will use the net cash flows to purchase additional shares of the stock mutual fund in which I have invested.

Plan for Managing Liquidity

Since my salary is direct deposited to my checking account, I have a convenient means of covering my expenses. My backup source of liquidity is my MMDA, which currently contains $2,600; I will maintain the account balance at about that level to ensure liquidity. If I ever need more money than is in this account, I could rely on my net cash flows. In addition, I could sell some shares of my mutual fund, or I could cover some expenses with a credit card; that way I will have an extra month before the credit card bill arrives.

Plan for Financing

I have two finance payments: a monthly car loan payment of $412, and a monthly mortgage payment of $848 (including property taxes and homeowner's insurance). I would like to pay off the car loan early if possible. The interest rate on that loan is 7.60 percent, and the interest is not tax-deductible. I will invest money in the stock mutual fund over time, and the value of that fund may increase. Meanwhile, the principal remaining on the car loan will decrease over time as I pay down the debt with my monthly payments.

Once I have more money invested in the mutual fund than I owe on the car loan, I will consider selling my shares of the mutual fund and using the proceeds to pay off the car loan. Whether I do this will depend on whether I believe the mutual fund can provide a higher return to me than the cost of the car loan.

When I pay off the car loan, my cash outflows will be reduced by $412 per month. Thus, I should have more net cash flows that I can use to make investments or spend in other ways.

Investment Plan

I currently have $6,000 in investments. This amount should increase over time as I use my net cash flows of about $100 each month to buy more shares of the mutual fund. I may sell my shares of the mutual fund someday when I have accumulated enough money to pay off my car loan. Once I pay off the car loan, I will have an additional $412 per month that I can use to make investments. My net cash flows should also increase over time as my salary increases, and most of the net cash flows will be directed toward investments over time.

When I make additional investments, I will consider those that have tax advantages. Since I am not relying on investments to provide me with income at this point, I will only consider investing in mutual funds that do not pay out high dividend and capital gain distributions. A stock index mutual fund that focuses on small stocks may be ideal for me because these types of stocks typically do not pay dividends. In addition, an index fund does not trade stocks frequently and therefore does not generate large capital gain distributions. This type of mutual fund provides most of its potential return in the form of an increase in the fund's value over time. I would not pay taxes on this type of capital gain until I sell the mutual fund.

I will focus on mutual funds rather than stocks to achieve diversification. If I invest in any individual stocks in the future, I will only consider stocks that pay no dividends and have more potential to increase in value.

If I consider investing in bonds in the future, I may invest in a Treasury bond fund or a municipal bond fund. Before selecting a bond fund, I will determine whether municipal bonds would offer me a higher after-tax yield (because of their tax advantage) than other types of bonds.

Retirement Plan

I just recently began to contribute $400 per month to my retirement account; my contribution is matched by my employer. I will soon increase my contribution by $100 (which will not be matched by my employer), for a total of $900 every month ($10,800 per year). If I work over the next 40 years and earn 10 percent a year on this investment, the future value of my contributions will be:

Savings at Retirement = Amount Invested × $FVIFA_{i,n}$

$$= \$10,800 \times 442.59$$
$$= \$4,779,972.$$

If I have children, I may not work full-time for the next 40 years, so I may not be able to invest $10,800 per year for 40 years. In addition, the return on the retirement fund may be less than 10 percent a year. Therefore, I may be overestimating my future savings. Consequently, I should maximize my contributions now while I am working full-time.

Insurance Plan

I have car insurance that covers the car and limits my liability. I have homeowner's insurance that covers the full market value of my home. I have disability insurance that will provide financial support if I become disabled. I do not need life insurance at this time, but will purchase it if I have children.

20.3 Financial Planning Online: A Synthesized Financial Plan

Go to:
http://quicken.com/saving/
checkup/

Click on:
Start the Checkup

This Web site provides:
a synthesized financial planning assessment for you, including tax planning, money management, insuring your assets, retirement planning, and estate planning.

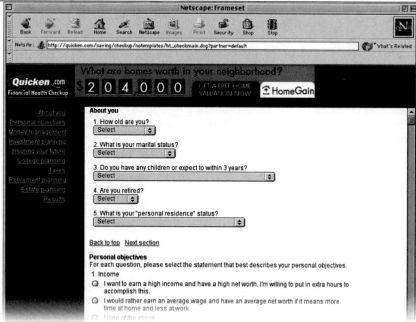

SUMMARY

The financial plan consists of a budget (covered in Part 1 of this text), a plan for managing liquidity (covered in Part 2), a financing plan (covered in Part 3), an investment plan (covered in Part 4), and a plan for protecting and maintaining wealth (covered in Part 5). The budget determines how you will spend or invest your money. Your plan for managing liquidity will ensure that you can cover any unanticipated expenses. Your financing plan is used to finance large purchases. Financing also involves decisions that affect the interest rate you are charged and the duration of any loans. Your investment plan determines how much you allocate toward investments and how you allocate money across different types of investments. Your plan for protecting and maintaining your wealth involves decisions as to what types of insurance to purchase, how much insurance to buy, how much to periodically invest in your retirement account, and how to distribute your estate to your heirs.

The components of a financial plan are integrated in that they depend on each other. The budget plan is dependent on the other components of the financial plan. The amount of money available for any part of the plan is dependent on how much money is used for liquidity purposes, to make loan (financing) payments, to make investments, to buy insurance, or to contribute to retirement accounts. The more money you allocate toward any part of the financial plan, the less money you have for the other parts. Thus, a key aspect of financial planning is to decide which components of the financial plan deserve the highest priority, because the decisions made about those components will influence the decisions for the others.

The example featuring Stephanie Spratt's financial plan shows how the plan can be segmented into the five components. The example also illustrates how the components are integrated so that a decision about any one component can only be made after considering the others. As time passes and financial conditions change, you should continuously reevaluate your financial plan.

Integrating the Key Concepts

As this chapter showed, all five parts of the financial plan are related. The financial planning tools (Part 1) allow you to budget, apply time value calculations (measure how money grows over time), and assess the tax effects of various planning decisions. Your money and credit management (Part 2) allows you to establish liquidity as a cushion in case your cash outflows exceed your cash inflows in a particular month. This cushion should always be maintained before you consider any other financial planning decisions. Your financing decisions (Part 3) deter-mine how much you will borrow and dictate what you can afford to purchase. Your investment decisions (Part 4) are related to the financing decisions in Part 3, as you should first consider whether the money to be invested could be put to better use by paying off any personal loans. Your financing decisions determine your large purchases such as a home or car and therefore prompt decisions about insurance (Part 5). Your investment decisions in Part 4 should consider whether the money you have to invest should be used for your retirement account (Part 5).

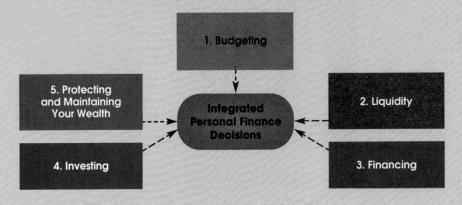

REVIEW QUESTIONS

1. Why is it important to integrate the components of your financial plan?

2. How does budgeting fit into a financial plan? How is your financial plan affected by your spending? What is the budgeting tradeoff?

3. Discuss how managing liquidity fits into your financial plan. What is the liquidity tradeoff?

4. Describe some advantages and disadvantages of using personal financing to achieve your financial goals. What is the personal financing tradeoff?

5. How does managing your investments fit into your financial plan? What is the investment tradeoff?

6. Discuss some methods for maintaining and protecting your wealth. What is the insurance tradeoff? What is the retirement account tradeoff?

7. What will time do to your financial plan?

8. What happens to your budget when your financial position changes?

9. You have a $7,000 balance on your car loan at 11 percent interest. Your favorite aunt has just left you $10,000 in her will. You can put the money in a money market account at your bank and pay off your car loan, or you can invest the money in mutual funds. What factors must you consider in making your decision?

10. In the previous question, you decide to pay off the car loan and invest the difference. Now you no longer have a $350 per month car payment. Suggest some ways you might use these additional funds.

11. You have some extra cash in your budget that you wish to invest. You have narrowed your choices to a single stock, treasury bonds, or stock mutual funds. What characteristics of each option should you consider in making your decision?

12. How does purchasing car insurance and homeowner's insurance help in protecting and maintaining your wealth?

13. How does purchasing sufficient health insurance and disability insurance help in protecting and maintaining your wealth?

14. How does life insurance protect your wealth? Who needs life insurance?

FINANCIAL PLANNING PROBLEMS

1. Judy has just received $12,500 as an inheritance from her uncle. She is considering ways to use her money. Judy's car is one year old, and her monthly payment is $304. She owes 48 more payments. The amount to pay off the loan is $12,460. How much will Judy save in interest if she pays off her car loan now?

2. Judy is also considering investing the $12,500 in a certificate of deposit (CD). She is guaranteed a return of 4 percent on a four-year CD. How much would Judy earn from the CD? Which of the two options offers the better return?

3. Judy pays off her car loan and now must decide how she wants to invest the extra $3,648 per year that she budgeted for car payments. She decides to invest this additional amount in her employer-sponsored retirement plan. Currently, the plan is averaging a 12 percent annual return. Judy has 15 years until retirement. How much more money will she have at retirement if she invests this additional amount?

4. Judy believes that another benefit of investing the extra $3,648 in her employer-sponsored retirement plan is the tax savings. Judy is in a 28 percent marginal tax bracket. How much will investing in this manner save her in taxes annually? Assuming she remains in a 28 percent marginal tax bracket until she retires, how much will it save her in total over the next 15 years?

FINANCIAL PLANNING ONLINE EXERCISES

1. Go to http://quicken.com/saving/checkup. Gather your financial information and Click on Start the Checkup Now. The Financial Health Checkup is a unique way to check on your financial fitness. The session takes about 20 minutes. You will have to answer several questions dealing with your finances (taxes, insurance, investments, personal information). At the end, click Done to get your results.

2. Use the Back option in your browser to go to the Bills and Banking page. Under Tools, click on Debt Reduction Planner. Next click on Build Your Plan Now. Enter information on your debts as you are led through each step. The Planner will work out a debt reduction plan for you based on several components of your financial plan.

Building Your Own Financial Plan

Congratulations. By completing the preceding 19 *Building Your Own Financial Plan* exercises, you have created a comprehensive financial plan. At this point, using the Excel-based software that accompanies your book, you should print out your completed plan and store it in a safe place.

As with any plan, periodic review and modification of your financial plan are essential. Many of the exercises have included prompts for when decisions should be reviewed or modified. The template provided with this chapter in the *Financial Planning Workbook* and on the CD-ROM will assist you in establishing your own timing for this review and tracking your progress toward meeting your goals. Setting a specific time to do this review is helpful in preventing procrastination. For example, while watching bowl games on New Year's Day, review your portfolio using your laptop. Establish a time that is practical and comfortable for you. The important thing is that you do the review on schedule and then follow up by making any necessary

changes indicated by your review. Use the Excel spreadsheets that accompany the *Building Your Own Financial Plan* exercises to change your financial plan as needed.

Remember that good financial planning is the result of informed decisions rather than luck.

The Sampsons—A Continuing Case

With your help, Dave and Sharon Sampson have now established a financial plan. Among their key financial planning decisions are the following:

- **Budgeting.** They decided to revise their budget to make it possible to start amassing savings. By reducing their spending on recreation and other programs, they freed up funds to be saved for a down payment on Sharon's new car and the children's college education.

- **Liquidity.** They paid off the credit card balance to avoid the high interest charges they were accumulating by carrying their balance from month to month.

- **Financing.** They obtained a four-year car loan to finance Sharon's new car. In addition, they considered refinancing their mortgage, but it was not feasible to do so. They may refinance the mortgage if they decide to live in their home for a long period of time or if interest rates decline further.

- **Investments.** They decided not to buy individual stocks for now, because of the risk involved. They decided that they will invest their savings for their children's education in mutual funds. They will not invest all the money in one mutual fund or one type of fund, but will diversify among several types of mutual funds.

- **Protecting Their Wealth.** They decided to increase their car insurance, reduce the deductible on their homeowner's insurance, and buy disability insurance. They also purchased a life insurance policy for Dave. They decided that Dave should invest at least $3,000 per year in his retirement account since his employer matches the contribution up to that amount. They made a will that designates a trustee who can allocate the estate to ensure that the children's college education is covered and that the children receive the benefits in small amounts (so they do not spend their inheritance too quickly).

Now that Dave and Sharon have completed their financial plan, they are relieved that they have a plan to deal with their budget, liquidity, financing, investing, and retirement.

1. Explain how the Sampsons' budgeting affects all of their other financial planning decisions.

2. How are the Sampsons' liquidity and investment decisions related?

3. In what ways are the Sampsons' financing and investing decisions related?

4. Explain how the Sampsons' retirement planning decisions are related to their investing decisions.

5. How likely is it that the Sampsons will achieve their financial goals, now that they have captured them in a financial plan? What activity must they periodically undertake?

IN-TEXT STUDY GUIDE

True/False:

1. A decision you make about one component of your personal financial plan may affect the other components of the plan.

2. You can prepare for anticipated cash shortages in any future month by ensuring that you have enough illiquid assets that cannot be converted to cash to cover the deficiency.

3. One advantage of personal financing with a mortgage or home equity loan is that the interest payments are tax-deductible.

4. You should pay off a loan before maturity if the interest rate is low.

5. One way to invest in small stocks without being exposed to the specific risk of any individual stock is to invest in a mutual fund that focuses on small stocks.

6. Funds in a retirement account are taxed annually.

7. The financing plan is used to finance purchases that you cannot pay for with cash.

8. The components of a financial plan are independent of each other.

9. A key part of the financial planning process is deciding which components of the financial plan deserve the highest priority.

10. Your budget should attempt to ensure that there are some net cash flows every month for investments or for retirement.

Multiple Choice:

1. The _____ funds you can allocate for the future, the _____ you will be able to spend in the future.
   a. more; more
   b. less; less
   c. more; less
   d. Answers (a) and (b) are correct.

2. In general, liquid assets generate _____ illiquid assets.
   a. higher returns than
   b. lower returns than
   c. the same returns as
   d. none of the above

3. It is easier to cover monthly loan payments if you select financing with a _____ maturity.
   a. relatively short
   b. relatively long
   c. medium
   d. none of the above

4. The stocks of large, well-known firms tend to pay _____ dividends.
   a. relatively high
   b. relatively low
   c. no
   d. none of the above

5. Melanie Treynor has assets worth $15,000 and credit card debt of $5,000. Her net worth is
   a. $20,000.
   b. $15,000.
   c. $10,000.
   d. $5,000.

6. In general, to reduce your liabilities, you have to
   a. increase your assets.
   b. decrease your assets.
   c. leave your assets unchanged.
   d. none of the above

7. Peter Boiler would like to maintain liquidity but at the same time would like to pay off a bank loan. Which of the following options is Peter least likely to pursue?
   a. withdraw funds from his money market deposit account
   b. withdraw funds from his retirement account
   c. sell his investments in stock
   d. sell his investments in mutual funds

8. You should sell some of your investments and pay off a loan with the proceeds if the return on those investments _____ the interest rate charged on the loan.
   a. is less than
   b. is equal to
   c. exceeds
   d. none of the above

9. Which of the following investments achieves the greatest degree of diversification?
   a. a single stock
   b. a single bond
   c. Treasury bonds
   d. a growth and income mutual fund

10. You consider shifting some of your stock invest-
    ments to bonds. Based on this information, you
    probably believe the stocks are
    a. fairly priced.
    b. undervalued.
    c. overvalued.
    d. none of the above

11. Andre Bagassi would like to ask his employer to
    deduct an additional $50 per month from his
    paycheck to be invested in his retirement
    account. Andre thinks he can earn a return of 7
    percent annually for the next 45 years. By the
    time Andre retires in 45 years, an extra _____
    will be in his retirement account.
    a. $14,287.47
    b. $171,449.59
    c. $81,633.13
    d. $342,899.17

12. Which of the following are not documents used
    to monitor financing?
    a. certificates of deposit
    b. credit card account numbers
    c. personal loan agreements
    d. mortgage loan agreements

13. Which of the following are not documents used
    to protect and maintain wealth, according to
    your text?
    a. insurance policies
    b. retirement plan balances
    c. wills
    d. loan certificates

14. Which of the following does not indicate a build-
    ing of wealth over time?
    a. an increase in equity investment by making
       monthly mortgage payments
    b. an increase in equity investment by making
       monthly car loan payments
    c. an increase in a retirement account by mak-
       ing monthly contributions
    d. All of the above indicate a building of
       wealth over time.

15. The _____ is not a part of the financial
    plan.
    a. budget
    b. plan for managing liquidity
    c. personal bank statement
    d. financing plan

16. The interest payments from a _____ are
    tax-deductible.
    a. mortgage
    b. home equity loan
    c. retirement account
    d. Answers (a) and (b) are correct.

17. In general, firms that do not pay dividends
    a. grow slowly.
    b. grow fast.
    c. do not grow.
    d. none of the above

18. The _____ allows you to forecast how
    much money you will have at the end of each
    month.
    a. financing plan
    b. investment plan
    c. budget
    d. plan for the protection and maintenance of
       wealth

19. Everything else being equal, your total interest
    payments for long-maturity loans will be
    _____ the total interest payments on short-
    maturity loans.
    a. higher than
    b. lower than
    c. the same as
    d. none of the above

20. If you want your investments to provide periodic
    income, you should probably not invest in
    a. the stock of large, well-known firms.
    b. bonds.
    c. the stock of small, fast-growing firms.
    d. a bond mutual fund.

Financial Tables

Table A-1 Future Value Interest Factors for One Dollar Compounded at i Percent for n Periods:

$$FV = PV \times FVIF_{i,n}$$

Table A-2 Present Value Interest Factors for One Dollar Discounted at i Percent for n Periods:

$$PV = FV \times PVIF_{i,n}$$

Table A-3 Future Value Interest Factors for a One-Dollar Annuity Compounded at i Percent for n Periods:

$$FVA = PMT \times FVIFA_{i,n}$$

Table A-4 Present Value Interest Factors for a One-Dollar Annuity Discounted at i Percent for n Periods:

$$PVA = PMT \times PVIFA_{i,n}$$

Table A-1   Future Value Interest Factors for One Dollar Compounded at *i* Percent for *n* Periods: $FV = PV \times FVIF_{i,n}$

Period	1%	2%	3%	4%	5%	6%	7%	8%	9%	10%	11%	12%	13%	14%	15%	16%	17%	18%	19%	20%
1	1.010	1.020	1.030	1.040	1.050	1.060	1.070	1.080	1.090	1.100	1.110	1.120	1.130	1.140	1.150	1.160	1.170	1.180	1.190	1.200
2	1.020	1.040	1.061	1.082	1.102	1.124	1.145	1.166	1.188	1.210	1.232	1.254	1.277	1.300	1.322	1.346	1.369	1.392	1.416	1.440
3	1.030	1.061	1.093	1.125	1.158	1.191	1.225	1.260	1.295	1.331	1.368	1.405	1.443	1.482	1.521	1.561	1.602	1.643	1.685	1.728
4	1.041	1.082	1.126	1.170	1.216	1.262	1.311	1.360	1.412	1.464	1.518	1.574	1.630	1.689	1.749	1.811	1.874	1.939	2.005	2.074
5	1.051	1.104	1.159	1.217	1.276	1.338	1.403	1.469	1.539	1.611	1.685	1.762	1.842	1.925	2.011	2.100	2.192	2.288	2.386	2.488
6	1.062	1.126	1.194	1.265	1.340	1.419	1.501	1.587	1.677	1.772	1.870	1.974	2.082	2.195	2.313	2.436	2.565	2.700	2.840	2.986
7	1.072	1.149	1.230	1.316	1.407	1.504	1.606	1.714	1.828	1.949	2.076	2.211	2.353	2.502	2.660	2.826	3.001	3.185	3.379	3.583
8	1.083	1.172	1.267	1.369	1.477	1.594	1.718	1.851	1.993	2.144	2.305	2.476	2.658	2.853	3.059	3.278	3.511	3.759	4.021	4.300
9	1.094	1.195	1.305	1.423	1.551	1.689	1.838	1.999	2.172	2.358	2.558	2.773	3.004	3.252	3.518	3.803	4.108	4.435	4.785	5.160
10	1.105	1.219	1.344	1.480	1.629	1.791	1.967	2.159	2.367	2.594	2.839	3.106	3.395	3.707	4.046	4.411	4.807	5.234	5.695	6.192
11	1.116	1.243	1.384	1.539	1.710	1.898	2.105	2.332	2.580	2.853	3.152	3.479	3.836	4.226	4.652	5.117	5.624	6.176	6.777	7.430
12	1.127	1.268	1.426	1.601	1.796	2.012	2.252	2.518	2.813	3.138	3.498	3.896	4.334	4.818	5.350	5.936	6.580	7.288	8.064	8.916
13	1.138	1.294	1.469	1.665	1.886	2.133	2.410	2.720	3.066	3.452	3.883	4.363	4.898	5.492	6.153	6.886	7.699	8.599	9.596	10.699
14	1.149	1.319	1.513	1.732	1.980	2.261	2.579	2.937	3.342	3.797	4.310	4.887	5.535	6.261	7.076	7.987	9.007	10.147	11.420	12.839
15	1.161	1.346	1.558	1.801	2.079	2.397	2.759	3.172	3.642	4.177	4.785	5.474	6.254	7.138	8.137	9.265	10.539	11.974	13.589	15.407
16	1.173	1.373	1.605	1.873	2.183	2.540	2.952	3.426	3.970	4.595	5.311	6.130	7.067	8.137	9.358	10.748	12.330	14.129	16.171	18.488
17	1.184	1.400	1.653	1.948	2.292	2.693	3.159	3.700	4.328	5.054	5.895	6.866	7.986	9.276	10.761	12.468	14.426	16.672	19.244	22.186
18	1.196	1.428	1.702	2.026	2.407	2.854	3.380	3.996	4.717	5.560	6.543	7.690	9.024	10.575	12.375	14.462	16.879	19.673	22.900	26.623
19	1.208	1.457	1.753	2.107	2.527	3.026	3.616	4.316	5.142	6.116	7.263	8.613	10.197	12.055	14.232	16.776	19.748	23.214	27.251	31.948
20	1.220	1.486	1.806	2.191	2.653	3.207	3.870	4.661	5.604	6.727	8.062	9.646	11.523	13.743	16.366	19.461	23.105	27.393	32.429	38.337
21	1.232	1.516	1.860	2.279	2.786	3.399	4.140	5.034	6.109	7.400	8.949	10.804	13.021	15.667	18.821	22.574	27.033	32.323	38.591	46.005
22	1.245	1.546	1.916	2.370	2.925	3.603	4.430	5.436	6.658	8.140	9.933	12.100	14.713	17.861	21.644	26.186	31.629	38.141	45.923	55.205
23	1.257	1.577	1.974	2.465	3.071	3.820	4.740	5.871	7.258	8.954	11.026	13.552	16.626	20.361	24.891	30.376	37.005	45.007	54.648	66.247
24	1.270	1.608	2.033	2.563	3.225	4.049	5.072	6.341	7.911	9.850	12.239	15.178	18.788	23.212	28.625	35.236	43.296	53.108	65.031	79.496
25	1.282	1.641	2.094	2.666	3.386	4.292	5.427	6.848	8.623	10.834	13.585	17.000	21.230	26.461	32.918	40.874	50.656	62.667	77.387	95.395
30	1.348	1.811	2.427	3.243	4.322	5.743	7.612	10.062	13.267	17.449	22.892	29.960	39.115	50.949	66.210	85.849	111.061	143.367	184.672	237.373
35	1.417	2.000	2.814	3.946	5.516	7.686	10.676	14.785	20.413	28.102	38.574	52.799	72.066	98.097	133.172	180.311	243.495	327.988	440.691	590.657
40	1.489	2.208	3.262	4.801	7.040	10.285	14.974	21.724	31.408	45.258	64.999	93.049	132.776	188.876	267.856	378.715	533.846	750.353	1051.642	1469.740
45	1.565	2.438	3.781	5.841	8.985	13.764	21.002	31.920	48.325	72.888	109.527	163.985	244.629	363.662	538.752	795.429	1170.425	1716.619	2509.583	3657.176
50	1.645	2.691	4.384	7.106	11.467	18.419	29.456	46.900	74.354	117.386	184.559	288.996	450.711	700.197	1083.619	1670.669	2566.080	3927.189	5988.730	9100.191

Table A-1 (Continued)

Period	21%	22%	23%	24%	25%	26%	27%	28%	29%	30%	31%	32%	33%	34%	35%	40%	45%	50%
1	1.210	1.220	1.230	1.240	1.250	1.260	1.270	1.280	1.290	1.300	1.310	1.320	1.330	1.340	1.350	1.400	1.450	1.500
2	1.464	1.488	1.513	1.538	1.562	1.588	1.613	1.638	1.664	1.690	1.716	1.742	1.769	1.796	1.822	1.960	2.102	2.250
3	1.772	1.816	1.861	1.907	1.953	2.000	2.048	2.097	2.147	2.197	2.248	2.300	2.353	2.406	2.460	2.744	3.049	3.375
4	2.144	2.215	2.289	2.364	2.441	2.520	2.601	2.684	2.769	2.856	2.945	3.036	3.129	3.224	3.321	3.842	4.421	5.063
5	2.594	2.703	2.815	2.932	3.052	3.176	3.304	3.436	3.572	3.713	3.858	4.007	4.162	4.320	4.484	5.378	6.410	7.594
6	3.138	3.297	3.463	3.635	3.815	4.001	4.196	4.398	4.608	4.827	5.054	5.290	5.535	5.789	6.053	7.530	9.294	11.391
7	3.797	4.023	4.259	4.508	4.768	5.042	5.329	5.629	5.945	6.275	6.621	6.983	7.361	7.758	8.172	10.541	13.476	17.086
8	4.595	4.908	5.239	5.589	5.960	6.353	6.767	7.206	7.669	8.157	8.673	9.217	9.791	10.395	11.032	14.758	19.541	25.629
9	5.560	5.987	6.444	6.931	7.451	8.004	8.595	9.223	9.893	10.604	11.362	12.166	13.022	13.930	14.894	20.661	28.334	38.443
10	6.727	7.305	7.926	8.594	9.313	10.086	10.915	11.806	12.761	13.786	14.884	16.060	17.319	18.666	20.106	28.925	41.085	57.665
11	8.140	8.912	9.749	10.657	11.642	12.708	13.862	15.112	16.462	17.921	19.498	21.199	23.034	25.012	27.144	40.495	59.573	86.498
12	9.850	10.872	11.991	13.215	14.552	16.012	17.605	19.343	21.236	23.298	25.542	27.982	30.635	33.516	36.644	56.694	86.380	129.746
13	11.918	13.264	14.749	16.386	18.190	20.175	22.359	24.759	27.395	30.287	33.460	36.937	40.745	44.912	49.469	79.371	125.251	194.620
14	14.421	16.182	18.141	20.319	22.737	25.420	28.395	31.691	35.339	39.373	43.832	48.756	54.190	60.181	66.784	111.119	181.614	291.929
15	17.449	19.742	22.314	25.195	28.422	32.030	36.062	40.565	45.587	51.185	57.420	64.358	72.073	80.643	90.158	155.567	263.341	437.894
16	21.113	24.085	27.446	31.242	35.527	40.357	45.799	51.923	58.808	66.541	75.220	84.953	95.857	108.061	121.713	217.793	381.844	656.841
17	25.547	29.384	33.758	38.740	44.409	50.850	58.165	66.461	75.862	86.503	98.539	112.138	127.490	144.802	164.312	304.911	553.674	985.261
18	30.912	35.848	41.523	48.038	55.511	64.071	73.869	85.070	97.862	112.454	129.086	148.022	169.561	194.035	221.822	426.875	802.826	1477.892
19	37.404	43.735	51.073	59.567	69.389	80.730	93.813	108.890	126.242	146.190	169.102	195.389	225.517	260.006	299.459	597.625	1164.098	2216.838
20	45.258	53.357	62.820	73.863	86.736	101.720	119.143	139.379	162.852	190.047	221.523	257.913	299.937	348.408	404.270	836.674	1687.942	3325.257
21	54.762	65.095	77.268	91.591	108.420	128.167	151.312	178.405	210.079	247.061	290.196	340.446	398.916	466.867	545.764	1171.343	2447.515	4987.883
22	66.262	79.416	95.040	113.572	135.525	161.490	192.165	228.358	271.002	321.178	380.156	449.388	530.558	625.601	736.781	1639.878	3548.896	7481.824
23	80.178	96.887	116.899	140.829	169.407	203.477	244.050	292.298	349.592	417.531	498.004	593.192	705.642	838.305	994.653	2295.829	5145.898	11222.738
24	97.015	118.203	143.786	174.628	211.758	256.381	309.943	374.141	450.974	542.791	652.385	783.013	938.504	1123.328	1342.781	3214.158	7461.547	16834.109
25	117.388	144.207	176.857	216.539	264.698	323.040	393.628	478.901	581.756	705.627	854.623	1033.577	1248.210	1505.258	1812.754	4499.816	10819.242	25251.164
30	304.471	389.748	497.904	634.810	807.793	1025.904	1300.477	1645.488	2078.208	2619.936	3297.081	4142.008	5194.516	6503.285	8128.426	24201.043	69348.375	191751.000
35	789.716	1053.370	1401.749	1861.020	2465.189	3258.053	4296.547	5653.840	7423.988	9727.598	12719.918	16698.906	21617.363	28096.695	36448.051	130158.687	*	*
40	2048.309	2846.941	3946.340	5455.797	7523.156	10346.879	14195.051	19426.418	26520.723	36117.754	49072.621	66519.313	89962.188	121388.437	163433.875	700022.688	*	*
45	5312.758	7694.418	11110.121	15994.316	22958.844	32859.457	46897.973	66748.500	94739.937	134102.187	*	*	*	*	*	*	*	*
50	13779.844	20795.680	31278.301	46889.207	70064.812	104354.562	154942.687	229345.875	338440.000	497910.125	*	*	*	*	*	*	*	*

*Not shown because of space limitations.

Table A-2 Present Value Interest Factors for One Dollar Discounted at *i* Percent for *n* Periods: $PV = FV \times PVIF_{i,n}$

Period	1%	2%	3%	4%	5%	6%	7%	8%	9%	10%	11%	12%	13%	14%	15%	16%	17%	18%	19%	20%
1	.990	.980	.971	.962	.952	.943	.935	.926	.917	.909	.901	.893	.885	.877	.870	.862	.855	.847	.840	.833
2	.980	.961	.943	.925	.907	.890	.873	.857	.842	.826	.812	.797	.783	.769	.756	.743	.731	.718	.706	.694
3	.971	.942	.915	.889	.864	.840	.816	.794	.772	.751	.731	.712	.693	.675	.658	.641	.624	.609	.593	.579
4	.961	.924	.888	.855	.823	.792	.763	.735	.708	.683	.659	.636	.613	.592	.572	.552	.534	.516	.499	.482
5	.951	.906	.863	.822	.784	.747	.713	.681	.650	.621	.593	.567	.543	.519	.497	.476	.456	.437	.419	.402
6	.942	.888	.837	.790	.746	.705	.666	.630	.596	.564	.535	.507	.480	.456	.432	.410	.390	.370	.352	.335
7	.933	.871	.813	.760	.711	.665	.623	.583	.547	.513	.482	.452	.425	.400	.376	.354	.333	.314	.296	.279
8	.923	.853	.789	.731	.677	.627	.582	.540	.502	.467	.434	.404	.376	.351	.327	.305	.285	.266	.249	.233
9	.914	.837	.766	.703	.645	.592	.544	.500	.460	.424	.391	.361	.333	.308	.284	.263	.243	.225	.209	.194
10	.905	.820	.744	.676	.614	.558	.508	.463	.422	.386	.352	.322	.295	.270	.247	.227	.208	.191	.176	.162
11	.896	.804	.722	.650	.585	.527	.475	.429	.388	.350	.317	.287	.261	.237	.215	.195	.178	.162	.148	.135
12	.887	.789	.701	.625	.557	.497	.444	.397	.356	.319	.286	.257	.231	.208	.187	.168	.152	.137	.124	.112
13	.879	.773	.681	.601	.530	.469	.415	.368	.326	.290	.258	.229	.204	.182	.163	.145	.130	.116	.104	.093
14	.870	.758	.661	.577	.505	.442	.388	.340	.299	.263	.232	.205	.181	.160	.141	.125	.111	.099	.088	.078
15	.861	.743	.642	.555	.481	.417	.362	.315	.275	.239	.209	.183	.160	.140	.123	.108	.095	.084	.074	.065
16	.853	.728	.623	.534	.458	.394	.339	.292	.252	.218	.188	.163	.141	.123	.107	.093	.081	.071	.062	.054
17	.844	.714	.605	.513	.436	.371	.317	.270	.231	.198	.170	.146	.125	.108	.093	.080	.069	.060	.052	.045
18	.836	.700	.587	.494	.416	.350	.296	.250	.212	.180	.153	.130	.111	.095	.081	.069	.059	.051	.044	.038
19	.828	.686	.570	.475	.396	.331	.277	.232	.194	.164	.138	.116	.098	.083	.070	.060	.051	.043	.037	.031
20	.820	.673	.554	.456	.377	.312	.258	.215	.178	.149	.124	.104	.087	.073	.061	.051	.043	.037	.031	.026
21	.811	.660	.538	.439	.359	.294	.242	.199	.164	.135	.112	.093	.077	.064	.053	.044	.037	.031	.026	.022
22	.803	.647	.522	.422	.342	.278	.226	.184	.150	.123	.101	.083	.068	.056	.046	.038	.032	.026	.022	.018
23	.795	.634	.507	.406	.326	.262	.211	.170	.138	.112	.091	.074	.060	.049	.040	.033	.027	.022	.018	.015
24	.788	.622	.492	.390	.310	.247	.197	.158	.126	.102	.082	.066	.053	.043	.035	.028	.023	.019	.015	.013
25	.780	.610	.478	.375	.295	.233	.184	.146	.116	.092	.074	.059	.047	.038	.030	.024	.020	.016	.013	.010
30	.742	.552	.412	.308	.231	.174	.131	.099	.075	.057	.044	.033	.026	.020	.015	.012	.009	.007	.005	.004
35	.706	.500	.355	.253	.181	.130	.094	.068	.049	.036	.026	.019	.014	.010	.008	.006	.004	.003	.002	.002
40	.672	.453	.307	.208	.142	.097	.067	.046	.032	.022	.015	.011	.008	.005	.004	.003	.002	.001	.001	.001
45	.639	.410	.264	.171	.111	.073	.048	.031	.021	.014	.009	.006	.004	.003	.002	.001	.001	.001	*	*
50	.608	.372	.228	.141	.087	.054	.034	.021	.013	.009	.005	.003	.002	.001	.001	.001	*	*	*	*

*PVIF is zero to three decimal places.

Table A-2 (Continued)

Period	21%	22%	23%	24%	25%	26%	27%	28%	29%	30%	31%	32%	33%	34%	35%	40%	45%	50%
1	.826	.820	.813	.806	.800	.794	.787	.781	.775	.769	.763	.758	.752	.746	.741	.714	.690	.667
2	.683	.672	.661	.650	.640	.630	.620	.610	.601	.592	.583	.574	.565	.557	.549	.510	.476	.444
3	.564	.551	.537	.524	.512	.500	.488	.477	.466	.455	.445	.435	.425	.416	.406	.364	.328	.296
4	.467	.451	.437	.423	.410	.397	.384	.373	.361	.350	.340	.329	.320	.310	.301	.260	.226	.198
5	.386	.370	.355	.341	.328	.315	.303	.291	.280	.269	.259	.250	.240	.231	.223	.186	.156	.132
6	.319	.303	.289	.275	.262	.250	.238	.227	.217	.207	.198	.189	.181	.173	.165	.133	.108	.088
7	.263	.249	.235	.222	.210	.198	.188	.178	.168	.159	.151	.143	.136	.129	.122	.095	.074	.059
8	.218	.204	.191	.179	.168	.157	.148	.139	.130	.123	.115	.108	.102	.096	.091	.068	.051	.039
9	.180	.167	.155	.144	.134	.125	.116	.108	.101	.094	.088	.082	.077	.072	.067	.048	.035	.026
10	.149	.137	.126	.116	.107	.099	.092	.085	.078	.073	.067	.062	.058	.054	.050	.035	.024	.017
11	.123	.112	.103	.094	.086	.079	.072	.066	.061	.056	.051	.047	.043	.040	.037	.025	.017	.012
12	.102	.092	.083	.076	.069	.062	.057	.052	.047	.043	.039	.036	.033	.030	.027	.018	.012	.008
13	.084	.075	.068	.061	.055	.050	.045	.040	.037	.033	.030	.027	.025	.022	.020	.013	.008	.005
14	.069	.062	.055	.049	.044	.039	.035	.032	.028	.025	.023	.021	.018	.017	.015	.009	.006	.003
15	.057	.051	.045	.040	.035	.031	.028	.025	.022	.020	.017	.016	.014	.012	.011	.006	.004	.002
16	.047	.042	.036	.032	.028	.025	.022	.019	.017	.015	.013	.012	.010	.009	.008	.005	.003	.002
17	.039	.034	.030	.026	.023	.020	.017	.015	.013	.012	.010	.009	.008	.007	.006	.003	.002	.001
18	.032	.028	.024	.021	.018	.016	.014	.012	.010	.009	.008	.007	.006	.005	.005	.002	.001	.001
19	.027	.023	.020	.017	.014	.012	.011	.009	.008	.007	.006	.005	.004	.004	.003	.002	.001	.001
20	.022	.019	.016	.014	.012	.010	.008	.007	.006	.005	.005	.004	.003	.003	.002	.001	.001	*
21	.018	.015	.013	.011	.009	.008	.007	.006	.005	.004	.003	.003	.003	.002	.002	.001	*	*
22	.015	.013	.011	.009	.007	.006	.005	.004	.004	.003	.003	.002	.002	.002	.001	.001	*	*
23	.012	.010	.009	.007	.006	.005	.004	.003	.003	.002	.002	.002	.001	.001	.001	*	*	*
24	.010	.008	.007	.006	.005	.004	.003	.003	.002	.002	.002	.001	.001	.001	.001	*	*	*
25	.009	.007	.006	.005	.004	.003	.003	.002	.002	.001	.001	.001	.001	.001	.001	*	*	*
30	.003	.003	.002	.002	.001	.001	.001	*	*	*	*	*	*	*	*	*	*	*
35	.001	.001	.001	.001	*	*	*	*	*	*	*	*	*	*	*	*	*	*
40	*	*	*	*	*	*	*	*	*	*	*	*	*	*	*	*	*	*
45	*	*	*	*	*	*	*	*	*	*	*	*	*	*	*	*	*	*
50	*	*	*	*	*	*	*	*	*	*	*	*	*	*	*	*	*	*

*PVIF is zero to three decimal places.

Table A-3 Future Value Interest Factors for a One-Dollar Annuity Compounded at *i* Percent for *n* Periods: $FVA = PMT \times FVIFA_{i,n}$

Period	1%	2%	3%	4%	5%	6%	7%	8%	9%	10%	11%	12%	13%	14%	15%	16%	17%	18%	19%	20%
1	1.000	1.000	1.000	1.000	1.000	1.000	1.000	1.000	1.000	1.000	1.000	1.000	1.000	1.000	1.000	1.000	1.000	1.000	1.000	1.000
2	2.010	2.020	2.030	2.040	2.050	2.060	2.070	2.080	2.090	2.100	2.110	2.120	2.130	2.140	2.150	2.160	2.170	2.180	2.190	2.200
3	3.030	3.060	3.091	3.122	3.152	3.184	3.215	3.246	3.278	3.310	3.342	3.374	3.407	3.440	3.472	3.506	3.539	3.572	3.606	3.640
4	4.060	4.122	4.184	4.246	4.310	4.375	4.440	4.506	4.573	4.641	4.710	4.779	4.850	4.921	4.993	5.066	5.141	5.215	5.291	5.368
5	5.101	5.204	5.309	5.416	5.526	5.637	5.751	5.867	5.985	6.105	6.228	6.353	6.480	6.610	6.742	6.877	7.014	7.154	7.297	7.442
6	6.152	6.308	6.468	6.633	6.802	6.975	7.153	7.336	7.523	7.716	7.913	8.115	8.323	8.535	8.754	8.977	9.207	9.442	9.683	9.930
7	7.214	7.434	7.662	7.898	8.142	8.394	8.654	8.923	9.200	9.487	9.783	10.089	10.405	10.730	11.067	11.414	11.772	12.141	12.523	12.916
8	8.286	8.583	8.892	9.214	9.549	9.897	10.260	10.637	11.028	11.436	11.859	12.300	12.757	13.233	13.727	14.240	14.773	15.327	15.902	16.499
9	9.368	9.755	10.159	10.583	11.027	11.491	11.978	12.488	13.021	13.579	14.164	14.776	15.416	16.085	16.786	17.518	18.285	19.086	19.923	20.799
10	10.462	10.950	11.464	12.006	12.578	13.181	13.816	14.487	15.193	15.937	16.722	17.549	18.420	19.337	20.304	21.321	22.393	23.521	24.709	25.959
11	11.567	12.169	12.808	13.486	14.207	14.972	15.784	16.645	17.560	18.531	19.561	20.655	21.814	23.044	24.349	25.733	27.200	28.755	30.403	32.150
12	12.682	13.412	14.192	15.026	15.917	16.870	17.888	18.977	20.141	21.384	22.713	24.133	25.650	27.271	29.001	30.850	32.824	34.931	37.180	39.580
13	13.809	14.680	15.618	16.627	17.713	18.882	20.141	21.495	22.953	24.523	26.211	28.029	29.984	32.088	34.352	36.786	39.404	42.218	45.244	48.496
14	14.947	15.974	17.086	18.292	19.598	21.015	22.550	24.215	26.019	27.975	30.095	32.392	34.882	37.581	40.504	43.672	47.102	50.818	54.841	59.196
15	16.097	17.293	18.599	20.023	21.578	23.276	25.129	27.152	29.361	31.772	34.405	37.280	40.417	43.842	47.580	51.659	56.109	60.965	66.260	72.035
16	17.258	18.639	20.157	21.824	23.657	25.672	27.888	30.324	33.003	35.949	39.190	42.753	46.671	50.980	55.717	60.925	66.648	72.938	79.850	87.442
17	18.430	20.012	21.761	23.697	25.840	28.213	30.840	33.750	36.973	40.544	44.500	48.883	53.738	59.117	65.075	71.673	78.978	87.067	96.021	105.930
18	19.614	21.412	23.414	25.645	28.132	30.905	33.999	37.450	41.301	45.599	50.396	55.749	61.724	68.393	75.836	84.140	93.404	103.739	115.265	128.116
19	20.811	22.840	25.117	27.671	30.539	33.760	37.379	41.446	46.018	51.158	56.939	63.439	70.748	78.968	88.211	98.603	110.283	123.412	138.165	154.739
20	22.019	24.297	26.870	29.778	33.066	36.785	40.995	45.762	51.159	57.274	64.202	72.052	80.946	91.024	102.443	115.379	130.031	146.626	165.417	186.687
21	23.239	25.783	28.676	31.969	35.719	39.992	44.865	50.422	56.764	64.002	72.264	81.698	92.468	104.767	118.809	134.840	153.136	174.019	197.846	225.024
22	24.471	27.299	30.536	34.248	38.505	43.392	49.005	55.456	62.872	71.402	81.213	92.502	105.489	120.434	137.630	157.414	180.169	206.342	236.436	271.028
23	25.716	28.845	32.452	36.618	41.430	46.995	53.435	60.893	69.531	79.542	91.147	104.602	120.203	138.295	159.274	183.600	211.798	244.483	282.359	326.234
24	26.973	30.421	34.426	39.082	44.501	50.815	58.176	66.764	76.789	88.496	102.173	118.154	136.829	158.656	184.166	213.976	248.803	289.490	337.007	392.480
25	28.243	32.030	36.459	41.645	47.726	54.864	63.248	73.105	84.699	98.346	114.412	133.333	155.616	181.867	212.790	249.212	292.099	342.598	402.038	471.976
30	34.784	40.567	47.575	56.084	66.438	79.057	94.459	113.282	136.305	164.491	199.018	241.330	293.192	356.778	434.738	530.306	647.423	790.932	966.698	1181.865
35	41.659	49.994	60.461	73.651	90.318	111.432	138.234	172.314	215.705	271.018	341.583	431.658	546.663	693.552	881.152	1120.699	1426.448	1816.607	2314.173	2948.294
40	48.885	60.401	75.400	95.024	120.797	154.758	199.630	259.052	337.872	442.580	581.812	767.080	1013.667	1341.979	1779.048	2360.724	3134.412	4163.094	5529.711	7343.715
45	56.479	71.891	92.718	121.027	159.695	212.737	285.741	386.497	525.840	718.881	986.613	1358.208	1874.086	2590.464	3585.031	4965.191	6879.008	9531.258	13203.105	18280.914
50	64.461	84.577	112.794	152.664	209.341	290.325	406.516	573.756	815.051	1163.865	1668.723	2399.975	3459.344	4994.301	7217.488	10435.449	15088.805	21812.273	31514.492	45496.094

Table A-3   (Continued)

Period	21%	22%	23%	24%	25%	26%	27%	28%	29%	30%	31%	32%	33%	34%	35%	40%	45%	50%
1	1.000	1.000	1.000	1.000	1.000	1.000	1.000	1.000	1.000	1.000	1.000	1.000	1.000	1.000	1.000	1.000	1.000	1.000
2	2.210	2.220	2.230	2.240	2.250	2.260	2.270	2.280	2.290	2.300	2.310	2.320	2.330	2.340	2.350	2.400	2.450	2.500
3	3.674	3.708	3.743	3.778	3.813	3.848	3.883	3.918	3.954	3.990	4.026	4.062	4.099	4.136	4.172	4.360	4.552	4.750
4	5.446	5.524	5.604	5.684	5.766	5.848	5.931	6.016	6.101	6.187	6.274	6.362	6.452	6.542	6.633	7.104	7.601	8.125
5	7.589	7.740	7.893	8.048	8.207	8.368	8.533	8.700	8.870	9.043	9.219	9.398	9.581	9.766	9.954	10.946	12.022	13.188
6	10.183	10.442	10.708	10.980	11.259	11.544	11.837	12.136	12.442	12.756	13.077	13.406	13.742	14.086	14.438	16.324	18.431	20.781
7	13.321	13.740	14.171	14.615	15.073	15.546	16.032	16.534	17.051	17.583	18.131	18.696	19.277	19.876	20.492	23.853	27.725	32.172
8	17.119	17.762	18.430	19.123	19.842	20.588	21.361	22.163	22.995	23.858	24.752	25.678	26.638	27.633	28.664	34.395	41.202	49.258
9	21.714	22.670	23.669	24.712	25.802	26.940	28.129	29.369	30.664	32.015	33.425	34.895	36.429	38.028	39.696	49.152	60.743	74.887
10	27.274	28.657	30.113	31.643	33.253	34.945	36.723	38.592	40.556	42.619	44.786	47.062	49.451	51.958	54.590	69.813	89.077	113.330
11	34.001	35.962	38.039	40.238	42.566	45.030	47.639	50.398	53.318	56.405	59.670	63.121	66.769	70.624	74.696	98.739	130.161	170.995
12	42.141	44.873	47.787	50.895	54.208	57.738	61.501	65.510	69.780	74.326	79.167	84.320	89.803	95.636	101.840	139.234	189.734	257.493
13	51.991	55.745	59.778	64.109	68.760	73.750	79.106	84.853	91.016	97.624	104.709	112.302	120.438	129.152	138.484	195.928	276.114	387.239
14	63.909	69.009	74.528	80.496	86.949	93.925	101.465	109.611	118.411	127.912	138.169	149.239	161.183	174.063	187.953	275.299	401.365	581.858
15	78.330	85.191	92.669	100.815	109.687	119.346	129.860	141.302	153.750	167.285	182.001	197.996	215.373	234.245	254.737	386.418	582.980	873.788
16	95.779	104.933	114.983	126.010	138.109	151.375	165.922	181.867	199.337	218.470	239.421	262.354	287.446	314.888	344.895	541.985	846.321	1311.681
17	116.892	129.019	142.428	157.252	173.636	191.733	211.721	233.790	258.145	285.011	314.642	347.307	383.303	422.949	466.608	759.778	1228.165	1968.522
18	142.439	158.403	176.187	195.993	218.045	242.583	269.885	300.250	334.006	371.514	413.180	459.445	510.792	567.751	630.920	1064.689	1781.838	2953.783
19	173.351	194.251	217.710	244.031	273.556	306.654	343.754	385.321	431.868	483.968	542.266	607.467	680.354	761.786	852.741	1491.563	2584.665	4431.672
20	210.755	237.986	268.783	303.598	342.945	387.384	437.568	494.210	558.110	630.157	711.368	802.856	905.870	1021.792	1152.200	2089.188	3748.763	6648.508
21	256.013	291.343	331.603	377.461	429.681	489.104	556.710	633.589	720.962	820.204	932.891	1060.769	1205.807	1370.201	1556.470	2925.862	5436.703	9973.762
22	310.775	356.438	408.871	469.052	538.101	617.270	708.022	811.993	931.040	1067.265	1223.087	1401.215	1604.724	1837.068	2102.234	4097.203	7884.215	14961.645
23	377.038	435.854	503.911	582.624	673.626	778.760	900.187	1040.351	1202.042	1388.443	1603.243	1850.603	2135.282	2462.669	2839.014	5737.078	11433.109	22443.469
24	457.215	532.741	620.810	723.453	843.032	982.237	1144.237	1332.649	1551.634	1805.975	2101.247	2443.795	2840.924	3300.974	3833.667	8032.906	16579.008	33666.207
25	554.230	650.944	764.596	898.082	1054.791	1238.617	1454.180	1706.790	2002.608	2348.765	2753.631	3226.808	3779.428	4424.301	5176.445	11247.062	24040.555	50500.316
30	1445.111	1767.044	2160.459	2640.881	3227.172	3941.953	4812.891	5873.172	7162.785	8729.805	10632.543	12940.672	15737.945	19124.434	23221.258	60500.207	154105.313	383500.000
35	3755.814	4783.520	6090.227	7750.094	9856.746	12527.160	15909.480	20188.742	25596.512	32422.090	41028.887	51868.563	65504.199	82634.625	104134.500	325394.688	*	*
40	9749.141	12936.141	17153.691	22728.367	30088.621	39791.957	52570.707	69376.562	91447.375	120389.375	*	*	*	*	*	*	*	*
45	25294.223	34970.230	48300.660	66638.937	91831.312	126378.937	173692.875	238384.312	326686.375	447005.062	*	*	*	*	*	*	*	*

*Not shown because of space limitations.

Table A-4 Present Value Interest Factors for a One-Dollar Annuity Discounted at i Percent for n Periods: $PVA = PMT \times PVIFA_{i,n}$

Period	1%	2%	3%	4%	5%	6%	7%	8%	9%	10%	11%	12%	13%	14%	15%	16%	17%	18%	19%	20%
1	.990	.980	.971	.962	.952	.943	.935	.926	.917	.909	.901	.893	.885	.877	.870	.862	.855	.847	.840	.833
2	1.970	1.942	1.913	1.886	1.859	1.833	1.808	1.783	1.759	1.736	1.713	1.690	1.668	1.647	1.626	1.605	1.585	1.566	1.547	1.528
3	2.941	2.884	2.829	2.775	2.723	2.673	2.624	2.577	2.531	2.487	2.444	2.402	2.361	2.322	2.283	2.246	2.210	2.174	2.140	2.106
4	3.902	3.808	3.717	3.630	3.546	3.465	3.387	3.312	3.240	3.170	3.102	3.037	2.974	2.914	2.855	2.798	2.743	2.690	2.639	2.589
5	4.853	4.713	4.580	4.452	4.329	4.212	4.100	3.993	3.890	3.791	3.696	3.605	3.517	3.433	3.352	3.274	3.199	3.127	3.058	2.991
6	5.795	5.601	5.417	5.242	5.076	4.917	4.767	4.623	4.486	4.355	4.231	4.111	3.998	3.889	3.784	3.685	3.589	3.498	3.410	3.326
7	6.728	6.472	6.230	6.002	5.786	5.582	5.389	5.206	5.033	4.868	4.712	4.564	4.423	4.288	4.160	4.039	3.922	3.812	3.706	3.605
8	7.652	7.326	7.020	6.733	6.463	6.210	5.971	5.747	5.535	5.335	5.146	4.968	4.799	4.639	4.487	4.344	4.207	4.078	3.954	3.837
9	8.566	8.162	7.786	7.435	7.108	6.802	6.515	6.247	5.995	5.759	5.537	5.328	5.132	4.946	4.772	4.607	4.451	4.303	4.163	4.031
10	9.471	8.983	8.530	8.111	7.722	7.360	7.024	6.710	6.418	6.145	5.889	5.650	5.426	5.216	5.019	4.833	4.659	4.494	4.339	4.192
11	10.368	9.787	9.253	8.760	8.306	7.887	7.499	7.139	6.805	6.495	6.207	5.938	5.687	5.453	5.234	5.029	4.836	4.656	4.486	4.327
12	11.255	10.575	9.954	9.385	8.863	8.384	7.943	7.536	7.161	6.814	6.492	6.194	5.918	5.660	5.421	5.197	4.988	4.793	4.611	4.439
13	12.134	11.348	10.635	9.986	9.394	8.853	8.358	7.904	7.487	7.013	6.750	6.424	6.122	5.842	5.583	5.342	5.118	4.910	4.715	4.533
14	13.004	12.106	11.296	10.563	9.899	9.295	8.745	8.244	7.786	7.367	6.982	6.628	6.302	6.002	5.724	5.468	5.229	5.008	4.802	4.611
15	13.865	12.849	11.938	11.118	10.380	9.712	9.108	8.560	8.061	7.606	7.191	6.811	6.462	6.142	5.847	5.575	5.324	5.092	4.876	4.675
16	14.718	13.578	12.561	11.652	10.838	10.106	9.447	8.851	8.313	7.824	7.379	6.974	6.604	6.265	5.954	5.668	5.405	5.162	4.938	4.730
17	15.562	14.292	13.166	12.166	11.274	10.477	9.763	9.122	8.544	8.022	7.549	7.120	6.729	6.373	6.047	5.749	5.475	5.222	4.990	4.775
18	16.398	14.992	13.754	12.659	11.690	10.828	10.059	9.372	8.756	8.201	7.702	7.250	6.840	6.467	6.128	5.818	5.534	5.273	5.033	4.812
19	17.226	15.679	14.324	13.134	12.085	11.158	10.336	9.604	8.950	8.365	7.839	7.366	6.938	6.550	6.198	5.877	5.584	5.316	5.070	4.843
20	18.046	16.352	14.878	13.590	12.462	11.470	10.594	9.818	9.129	8.514	7.963	7.469	7.025	6.623	6.259	5.929	5.628	5.353	5.101	4.870
21	18.857	17.011	15.415	14.029	12.821	11.764	10.836	10.017	9.292	8.649	8.075	7.562	7.102	6.687	6.312	5.973	5.665	5.384	5.127	4.891
22	19.661	17.658	15.937	14.451	13.163	12.042	11.061	10.201	9.442	8.772	8.176	7.645	7.170	6.743	6.359	6.011	5.696	5.410	5.149	4.909
23	20.456	18.292	16.444	14.857	13.489	12.303	11.272	10.371	9.580	8.883	8.266	7.718	7.230	6.792	6.399	6.044	5.723	5.432	5.167	4.925
24	21.244	18.914	16.936	15.247	13.799	12.550	11.469	10.529	9.707	8.985	8.348	7.784	7.283	6.835	6.434	6.073	5.746	5.451	5.182	4.937
25	22.023	19.524	17.413	15.622	14.094	12.783	11.654	10.675	9.823	9.077	8.422	7.843	7.330	6.873	6.464	6.097	5.766	5.467	5.195	4.948
30	25.808	22.396	19.601	17.292	15.373	13.765	12.409	11.258	10.274	9.427	8.694	8.055	7.496	7.003	6.566	6.177	5.829	5.517	5.235	4.979
35	29.409	24.999	21.487	18.665	16.374	14.498	12.948	11.655	10.567	9.644	8.855	8.176	7.586	7.070	6.617	6.215	5.858	5.539	5.251	4.992
40	32.835	27.356	23.115	19.793	17.159	15.046	13.332	11.925	10.757	9.779	8.951	8.244	7.634	7.105	6.642	6.233	5.871	5.548	5.258	4.997
45	36.095	29.490	24.519	20.720	17.774	15.456	13.606	12.108	10.881	9.863	9.008	8.283	7.661	7.123	6.654	6.242	5.877	5.552	5.261	4.999
50	39.196	31.424	25.730	21.482	18.256	15.762	13.801	12.233	10.962	9.915	9.042	8.304	7.675	7.133	6.661	6.246	5.880	5.554	5.262	4.999

Table A-4 (Continued)

Period	21%	22%	23%	24%	25%	26%	27%	28%	29%	30%	31%	32%	33%	34%	35%	40%	45%	50%
1	.826	.820	.813	.806	.800	.794	.787	.781	.775	.769	.763	.758	.752	.746	.741	.714	.690	.667
2	1.509	1.492	1.474	1.457	1.440	1.424	1.407	1.392	1.376	1.361	1.346	1.331	1.317	1.303	1.289	1.224	1.165	1.111
3	2.074	2.042	2.011	1.981	1.952	1.923	1.896	1.868	1.842	1.816	1.791	1.766	1.742	1.719	1.696	1.589	1.493	1.407
4	2.540	2.494	2.448	2.404	2.362	2.320	2.280	2.241	2.203	2.166	2.130	2.096	2.062	2.029	1.997	1.849	1.720	1.605
5	2.926	2.864	2.803	2.745	2.689	2.635	2.583	2.532	2.483	2.436	2.390	2.345	2.302	2.260	2.220	2.035	1.876	1.737
6	3.245	3.167	3.092	3.020	2.951	2.885	2.821	2.759	2.700	2.643	2.588	2.534	2.483	2.433	2.385	2.168	1.983	1.824
7	3.508	3.416	3.327	3.242	3.161	3.083	3.009	2.937	2.868	2.802	2.739	2.677	2.619	2.562	2.508	2.263	2.057	1.883
8	3.726	3.619	3.518	3.421	3.329	3.241	3.156	3.076	2.999	2.925	2.854	2.786	2.721	2.658	2.598	2.331	2.109	1.922
9	3.905	3.786	3.673	3.566	3.463	3.366	3.273	3.184	3.100	3.019	2.942	2.868	2.798	2.730	2.665	2.379	2.144	1.948
10	4.054	3.923	3.799	3.682	3.570	3.465	3.364	3.269	3.178	3.092	3.009	2.930	2.855	2.784	2.715	2.414	2.168	1.965
11	4.177	4.035	3.902	3.776	3.656	3.544	3.437	3.335	3.239	3.147	3.060	2.978	2.899	2.824	2.752	2.438	2.185	1.977
12	4.278	4.127	3.985	3.851	3.725	3.606	3.493	3.387	3.286	3.190	3.100	3.013	2.931	2.853	2.779	2.456	2.196	1.985
13	4.362	4.203	4.053	3.912	3.780	3.656	3.538	3.427	3.322	3.223	3.129	3.040	2.956	2.876	2.799	2.469	2.204	1.990
14	4.432	4.265	4.108	3.962	3.824	3.695	3.573	3.459	3.351	3.249	3.152	3.061	2.974	2.892	2.814	2.478	2.210	1.993
15	4.489	4.315	4.153	4.001	3.859	3.726	3.601	3.483	3.373	3.268	3.170	3.076	2.988	2.905	2.825	2.484	2.214	1.995
16	4.536	4.357	4.189	4.033	3.887	3.751	3.623	3.503	3.390	3.283	3.183	3.088	2.999	2.914	2.834	2.489	2.216	1.997
17	4.576	4.391	4.219	4.059	3.910	3.771	3.640	3.518	3.403	3.295	3.193	3.097	3.007	2.921	2.840	2.492	2.218	1.998
18	4.608	4.419	4.243	4.080	3.928	3.786	3.654	3.529	3.413	3.304	3.201	3.104	3.012	2.926	2.844	2.494	2.219	1.999
19	4.635	4.442	4.263	4.097	3.942	3.799	3.664	3.539	3.421	3.311	3.207	3.109	3.017	2.930	2.848	2.496	2.220	1.999
20	4.657	4.460	4.279	4.110	3.954	3.808	3.673	3.546	3.427	3.316	3.211	3.113	3.020	2.933	2.850	2.497	2.221	1.999
21	4.675	4.476	4.292	4.121	3.963	3.816	3.679	3.551	3.432	3.320	3.215	3.116	3.023	2.935	2.852	2.498	2.221	2.000
22	4.690	4.488	4.302	4.130	3.970	3.822	3.684	3.556	3.436	3.323	3.217	3.118	3.025	2.936	2.853	2.498	2.222	2.000
23	4.703	4.499	4.311	4.137	3.976	3.827	3.689	3.559	3.438	3.325	3.219	3.120	3.026	2.938	2.854	2.499	2.222	2.000
24	4.713	4.507	4.318	4.143	3.981	3.831	3.692	3.562	3.441	3.327	3.221	3.121	3.027	2.939	2.855	2.499	2.222	2.000
25	4.721	4.514	4.323	4.147	3.985	3.834	3.694	3.564	3.442	3.329	3.222	3.122	3.028	2.939	2.856	2.499	2.222	2.000
30	4.746	4.534	4.339	4.160	3.995	3.842	3.701	3.569	3.447	3.332	3.225	3.124	3.030	2.941	2.857	2.500	2.222	2.000
35	4.756	4.541	4.345	4.164	3.998	3.845	3.703	3.571	3.448	3.333	3.226	3.125	3.030	2.941	2.857	2.500	2.222	2.000
40	4.760	4.544	4.347	4.166	3.999	3.846	3.703	3.571	3.448	3.333	3.226	3.125	3.030	2.941	2.857	2.500	2.222	2.000
45	4.761	4.545	4.347	4.166	4.000	3.846	3.704	3.571	3.448	3.333	3.226	3.125	3.030	2.941	2.857	2.500	2.222	2.000
50	4.762	4.545	4.348	4.167	4.000	3.846	3.704	3.571	3.448	3.333	3.226	3.125	3.030	2.941	2.857	2.500	2.222	2.000

Solutions to In-Text
Study Guide Questions

In-Text Study Guide Solutions

CHAPTER 1

TRUE/FALSE

1. T
2. F
3. F
4. F
5. T
6. T
7. F
8. F
9. T
10. T
11. T

MULTIPLE-CHOICE

1. c
2. a
3. b
4. d
5. a
6. b
7. c
8. c
9. d
10. a
11. b
12. c
13. c
14. d
15. c
16. d
17. b
18. a
19. c
20. d
21. b

CHAPTER 2

TRUE/FALSE

1. F
2. T
3. F
4. F
5. T
6. T
7. F
8. T
9. T
10. F
11. F
12. T
13. T

MULTIPLE-CHOICE

1. b
2. a

   $4,300 - $1,200 = $3,100

3. d

   $3,100 - $1,000 - ($40 + $30 + $80 + $200 + $30 + $50) - ($50 + $400 + $500) = $720

4. a

   $720 - $1,000 = -$280

5. c
6. b
7. d
8. b
9. c
10. a

    -$100 + $50 = -$50

11. a
12. d

    ($2,200 - $1,500) × 12 = $8,400

13. b
14. c
15. a
16. d
17. b

    $10,000 - $5,000 = $5,000

18. c

    $5,000 + $25,000 - $1,500 - $5,000 - $18,500 = $5,000

19. c
20. b
21. a

CHAPTER 3

TRUE/FALSE

1. F
2. F
3. T
4. F
5. T
6. F
7. T
8. F
9. T
10. T

MULTIPLE-CHOICE

1. b
2. c
3. a
4. b
5. d

   $FV = $5,000 × 1.4641 = $7,320.50

6. c
7. c

   $PV = $30,000 × 0.7084 = $21,252.76

8. a

   Calculator Input:
   N = 22
   I = 7
   PMT = 0
   FV = 1,000,000
   CPT PV = 225,713.17

9. a
10. c

    $FV = $20,000 × 164.4940 = $3,289,880.45

11. b

    $PV = $20,000 × 11.2578 = $225,155.67

12. d

    Calculator Input:
    N = 60
    I = 8
    PMT = 10,000
    FV = 0
    CPT PV = 123,765.52

13. a

    $PV = $30,000 × 10.5753 = $317,260.24

14. b
15. d

    $FV = $30,000 × 13.4121 = $402,362.69

16. c

    Calculator Input:
    N = 36
    I = 1
    PMT = 0
    PV = -2,500
    CPT FV = 3,576.92

17. b
18. a

    Calculator Input:
    N = 10
    I = 6.5
    PMT = 5,000
    FV = 0
    CPT PV = 35,944.15

In-Text Study Guide Solutions

19. b

20. c

Calculator Input:
N = 5
I = 11
PMT = 0
FV = 50,000
CPT PV = 29,672.57

CHAPTER 4

TRUE/FALSE

1. T
2. F
3. T
4. T
5. T
6. F
7. F
8. T
9. F
10. T
11. F
12. T

MULTIPLE-CHOICE

1. d
2. b
3. a

$52,000 \times 6.20\% =$
$3,224.00

4. c

$52,000 \times 1.45\% =$
$754.00

5. c
6. c
7. a
8. b

$35,000 \times 20\% =$
$7,000

9. c

Gross Income =
$70,000 + $1,000 +
$2,000 + $5,000 =
$78,000

10. d

Taxable Income =
$78,000 − $6,450 −
(2×$2,800) =
$65,950

11. b

12. a

13. d

Itemized
Deductions =
$8,000 + 1,000 +
$500 = $9,500

14. b

Taxable Income =
$90,000 − $8,100 =
$81,900

15. c

16. a

17. c

18. b

$3,675 + $850
(Additional
Deduction) =
$4,525

19. b

$80,000 × 6.20% =
$4,960

20. a

$80,000 × 7.65% =
$6,120

21. a

CHAPTER 5

TRUE/FALSE

1. T
2. F
3. F
4. T
5. T
6. F
7. T
8. F
9. F

10. T

11. F

MULTIPLE-CHOICE

1. b
2. c
3. c
4. a
5. a
6. d
7. c

8.0% − 4.5% = 3.5%

8. a

9. c

10. d

4.63% + 4.50% =
9.13%

11. b

$1,500 × 1.05 =
$1,575

12. c

$1,500 × 1.04 =
$1,560

13. b

$1,500 × 1.08 =
$1,620

14. a
15. c
16. c
17. d
18. c
19. c
20. c
21. b

CHAPTER 6

TRUE/FALSE

1. F
2. T
3. T
4. F

5. T
6. F
7. F
8. F
9. T
10. T
11. T

MULTIPLE-CHOICE

1. b

2. c

$1,300 × 2.5% =
$32.50

3. a

$3,200 × 5.7% ×
31/365 = $15.49

4. b
5. a
6. d
7. b
8. a

$$\frac{\$10,000 - \$9,500}{\$9,500}$$
$$= 5.26\%$$

9. c

$$\frac{\$10,000 - \$9,650}{\$9,650}$$
$$\times 365/182 = 7.27\%$$

10. d

$$\frac{\$9,870 - \$9,650}{\$9,650}$$
$$\times 365/90 = 9.25\%$$

11. b
12. b
13. c
14. c
15. a
16. d

$$\frac{\$10,000 - \$9,875}{\$9,875}$$
$$\times 365/91 = 5.08\%$$

In-Text Study Guide Solutions

17. a

$$\frac{\$9,950 - \$9,875}{\$9,875}$$

$$\times\ 365/45 = 6.16\%$$

18. c

19. b

20. b

CHAPTER 7

TRUE/FALSE

1. F
2. T
3. F
4. T
5. T
6. T
7. F
8. F
9. F
10. T
11. F

MULTIPLE-CHOICE

1. b

$\$45,000 \times 11\% =$
$\$4,950$

2. a

$(\$45,000 \times 11\%) \times 5$
$= \$24,750.00$

3. a
4. d
5. c
6. b
7. a
8. c
9. d
10. a
11. c
12. a

$\$2,100 \times 1.5\% =$
$\$31.50$

13. b

$\$1,600 \times 1.5\% =$
$\$24.00$

14. c

$\$1,100 \times 1.5\% =$
$\$16.50$

15. c

16. d

17. b

$(\$1,000 \times 20\%) -$
$(\$1,000 \times 4\%) =$
$\$160$

18. a

19. b

20. c

21. b

CHAPTER 8

TRUE/FALSE

1. T
2. F
3. T
4. T
5. F
6. F
7. T
8. T
9. F
10. T

MULTIPLE-CHOICE

1. d
2. c
3. b
4. a
5. b
6. c

$((\$5,000 \times 6\%) +$
$\$150)/\$5,000 =$
9.00%

7. d

$((\$5,000 \times 8\%) +$
$\$100)/\$5,000 =$
10.00%

8. b

9. d

$\$3,500 \times 10\%/12 =$
$\$29.17$

10. c

$\$3,500 - (\$307.71 -$
$\$29.17) = \$3,221.46$

11. b

$\$3,221.46 \times 10\%/12$
$= \$26.85$

12. b

$(\$3,500 \times 1.10)/12 =$
$\$320.83$

13. b

14. c

15. a

$(\$30,000 + \$15,000)$
$\times 70\% = \$31,500$

16. c

$(\$175,000 -$
$\$105,000) \times 70\% =$
$\$49,000$

17. d

$\$2,000 \times 28\% =$
$\$560$

18. d

19. a

20. d

CHAPTER 9

TRUE/FALSE

1. F
2. T
3. F
4. T
5. F
6. F
7. F

8. T
9. T
10. F

MULTIPLE-CHOICE

1. d
2. b
3. a
4. d
5. c
6. d

$(2\% \times \$90,000) +$
$(1\% \times \$90,000) +$
$\$250 + \$500 =$
$\$3,450$

7. d

$(10\% \times \$100,000) +$
$\$3,450 = \$13,450$

8. b
9. a
10. a
11. c
12. d
13. c
14. d

$(\$1,000 \times 12 \times 4) +$
$(\$500 \times 5\% \times 4) =$
$\$48,100$

15. a

$\$800 \times 12 \times 4 =$
$\$38,400$

16. c

$(\$800 \times 12 \times 4) +$
$\$20,000 + (\$1,500 \times$
$4) + \$650 + (\$1,200$
$\times 4) - (\$28,000 \times$
$28\%) + (\$20,000 \times$
$5\% \times 4) = \$66,010$

17. c
18. d
19. b
20. c
21. a

In-Text Study Guide Solutions

CHAPTER 10

TRUE/FALSE

1. T
2. F
3. F
4. F
5. T
6. T
7. F
8. T
9. F
10. T
11. T
12. F

MULTIPLE-CHOICE

1. b
2. d
3. b
4. a
5. c

   $1,000,000,000/
   20,000,000 = $50.00

6. d
7. c

   30 × $0.50 = $15.00

8. a

   $R =$

   $$\frac{(\$19 - \$20) + \$0.50}{\$20}$$

   $= -2.50\%$

9. b

   ($15.00 + $570) −
   $600 = −$15.00

10. b

    (($65 − $50) × $50)
    × 28% = $210.00

11. d

    (($65 − $50) × $50)
    × 20% = $150.00

12. c

($5,000 − $3,500) ×
20% = $300.00

13. a
14. a

$5,000 × 1.5386 =
$7,693.12

15. b
16. c

15% × 1.5 = 22.50%

17. b
18. d
19. a
20. c

CHAPTER 11

TRUE/FALSE

1. T
2. F
3. T
4. F
5. T
6. F
7. F
8. T
9. F
10. T

MULTIPLE-CHOICE

1. b
2. d
3. d

$60 + (2 × $2) =
$64.00

4. a

$$\frac{\$2}{(1.1)^1} + \frac{\$62}{(1.1)^2}$$

$= $53.06

5. d

$$3.12 \times \left(\frac{\$15 + \$20}{2}\right)$$

$= $54.60

6. b
7. d
8. c
9. c

$25 × 3.0 = $75.00

10. a
11. d
12. b
13. a
14. d
15. c
16. a
17. b
18. c
19. a
20. d

CHAPTER 12

TRUE/FALSE

1. T
2. F
3. F
4. F
5. T
6. T
7. T
8. F
9. T
10. F

MULTIPLE-CHOICE

1. b
2. c
3. d
4. c
5. d
6. b
7. a
8. c
9. b
10. d

11. b
12. d
13. c
14. b
15. d
16. c

$R =$

$$\frac{\$9,000 - \$5,000 - \$1,150}{\$5,000}$$

$= 57.00\%$

17. a

$R =$

$$\frac{\$9,000 - \$6,000}{\$6,000}$$

$= 50.00\%$

18. b

$R =$

$$\frac{\$5,000 - \$5,000 - \$1,150}{\$5,000}$$

$= -23.00\%$

19. d

$R =$

$$\frac{\$5,000 - \$6,000}{\$6,000}$$

$= -16.67\%$

20. a

CHAPTER 13

TRUE/FALSE

1. F
2. F
3. T
4. T
5. F
6. T
7. F
8. T
9. T
10. F
11. T

In-Text Study Guide Solutions

MULTIPLE-CHOICE

1. d
2. b
3. a
4. d
5. c
6. b
7. a
8. b
9. a
10. d
11. d
12. d
13. b
14. c
15. d
16. a

$$(\$110 \times 5.3282) + (\$1,000 \times 0.3606) = \$946.72$$

17. b

$$(\$110 \times 5.7590) + (\$1,000 \times 0.4241) = \$1,057.59$$

18. b
19. c
20. b

CHAPTER 14

TRUE/FALSE

1. F
2. T
3. F
4. T
5. F
6. F
7. T
8. T
9. F
10. F
11. T

MULTIPLE-CHOICE

1. a
2. b
3. a
4. d
5. a

$$\frac{[(\$10,000 \times 0.94)/\$30 \times \$35] - \$10,000}{\$10,000}$$
$$= 9.67\%$$

6. c

$$\frac{(\$10,000/\$30 \times \$35) - \$10,000}{\$10,000}$$
$$= 16.67\%$$

7. b
8. a
9. c
10. c
11. c
12. d
13. b
14. a
15. c
16. b
17. d
18. c
19. c
20. a
21. d

CHAPTER 15

TRUE/FALSE

1. T
2. T
3. F
4. F
5. T
6. T
7. F
8. T
9. F
10. F

MULTIPLE-CHOICE

1. d
2. a
3. c
4. d
5. b
6. c
7. a
8. d
9. b
10. b
11. d
12. a
13. b
14. d

$$(\$76 \times 100) - (\$55 \times 100) - \$250.00 = \$1,850.00$$

15. d

The buyer's gain (loss) is the writer's loss (gain).

16. b
17. d

The option would not be exercised.

18. c

The buyer's gain (loss) is the writer's loss (gain).

19. a
20. d

CHAPTER 16

TRUE/FALSE

1. T
2. F
3. T
4. T
5. F
6. F
7. T

8. F
9. T
10. T

MULTIPLE-CHOICE

1. d
2. c
3. a
4. c
5. a
6. b
7. d
8. d
9. c
10. a
11. d
12. a
13. b
14. c
15. d
16. b
17. a
18. b
19. c
20. b

CHAPTER 17

TRUE/FALSE

1. T
2. F
3. F
4. T
5. F
6. F
7. T
8. T
9. F
10. F
11. T

MULTIPLE-CHOICE

1. d
2. b

In-Text Study Guide Solutions

3. a

4. c

5. a

6. c

7. d

8. a

9. d

10. c

$40,000 × 9.1079 = $364,316.56

11. b

$364,316.56 + $70,000 = $434,316.56

12. d

13. a

14. c

15. c

16. c

$20,000 × 9.8226 = $196,451.59

17. d

18. a

19. b

20. d

21. b

Chapter 18

True/False

1. F

2. F

3. T

4. T

5. F

6. F

7. T

8. F

9. F

10. T

Multiple-Choice

1. d

2. b

3. c

($80,400 × 7.65%) + ($9,600 × 1.45%) = $6,290

4. c

5. c

6. b

7. c

8. a

$6,000 × 164.4940 = $986,964.14

9. c

$6,000 × 113.2832 = $679,699.27

10. c

11. b

12. d

13. b

14. a

15. b

16. c

Calculator Input:
N = 35
I = 7
PMT = 3,000
PV = 0
CPT FV = 32,029.74

17. a

18. d

Calculator Input:
N = 35
I = 9
PMT = 500
PV = 0
CPT FV = 107,855.38

19. b

Calculator Input:
N = 35
I = 9
PMT = 700
PV = 0
CPT FV = 150,997.53

20. c

($200,000 − $180,000) × 20% = $4,000

Chapter 19

True/False

1. F

2. T

3. T

4. F

5. T

6. F

7. T

8. T

9. F

10. T

Multiple-Choice

1. c

2. c

3. a

4. b

5. c

6. b

7. a

8. c

9. b

10. b

11. a

12. b

13. d

14. c

15. d

16. a

17. b

18. c

19. c

20. d

Chapter 20

True/False

1. T

2. F

3. T

4. F

5. T

6. F

7. T

8. F

9. T

10. T

Multiple-Choice

1. d

2. b

3. b

4. a

5. c

$15,000 − $5,000 = $10,000

6. b

7. a

8. a

9. d

10. c

11. b

Calculator Input:
N = 45
I = 7
PMT = 50 × 12 = 600
PV = 0
CPT FV = 171,449.59

12. a

13. d

14. d

15. c

16. d

17. b

18. c

19. a

20. c

Index

Credits

CHAPTER 1: FPG International; p.3: Courtesy of careers-in- finance.com; p.7: Courtesy of careers-in-finance.com; p.11: CartoonStock; p.15: Reproduced with permission of Yahoo! Inc. © 2000 by Yahoo! Inc. YAHOO! and the YAHOO! logo are trademarks of Yahoo! Inc.

CHAPTER 2: p.24: FPG International; p.26: Screen shot reprinted by permission from Microsoft Corporation; p.33: CartoonStock; p.37: Screen shot reprinted by permission from FinanCenter, Inc.; p.38: Screen shot reprinted by permission from FinanCenter, Inc.

CHAPTER 3: p.56: Tony Stone; p.67: Screen shot reprinted by permission from Microsoft Corporation; p.74: Screen shot reprinted by permission from Microsoft Corporation.

CHAPTER 4: p.84: FPG International; p.86: Courtesy of irs.gov; p.93: Reproduced with permission of Yahoo! Inc. © 2000 by Yahoo! Inc. YAHOO! and the YAHOO! logo are trademarks of Yahoo! Inc.; p.98: Reproduced with permission of Yahoo! Inc. © 2000 by Yahoo! Inc. YAHOO! and the YAHOO! logo are trademarks of Yahoo! Inc.; p.99: CartoonStock; p.104: Reproduced with permission of Yahoo! Inc. © 2000 by Yahoo! Inc. YAHOO! and the YAHOO! logo are trademarks of Yahoo! Inc.; p.108: Reproduced with permission of Yahoo! Inc. © 2000 by Yahoo! Inc. YAHOO! and the YAHOO! logo are trademarks of Yahoo! Inc.

CHAPTER 5: p.122: © PhotoDisc, Inc., 2002; p.129 top: Courtesy of Gomez, Inc.; p.129 bottom: CartoonStock; p.130: Reproduced with permission of Yahoo! Inc. © 2000 by Yahoo! Inc. YAHOO! and the YAHOO! logo are trademarks of Yahoo! Inc.; p.132: © 2001 Bloomberg L.P. All Rights Reserved. Reprinted with permission. Visit www.Bloomberg.com; p.136 top: © 2001 Dow Jones & Company, Inc. All Rights Reserved; p.136 bottom: © 2001 Bloomberg L.P. All Rights Reserved. Reprinted with permission. Visit www.Bloomberg.com; p.144: © 2001 Bloomberg L.P. All Rights Reserved. Reprinted with permission. Visit www.Bloomberg.com.

CHAPTER 6: p.154: Chuck Savage, The Stock Market; p.157: Screen shot reprinted by permission from FinanCenter, Inc.; p.159: © 2001 The New Yorker Collection from Cartoonbank.com. All Rights Reserved; p.162: Source: Bankrate.com, © 2001; p.165: © 2001 Dow Jones & Company, Inc. All Rights Reserved; p.167: Screen shot reprinted by permission from FinanCenter, Inc.

CHAPTER 7: p.182: Tony Stone; p.185: Reproduced with permission of Yahoo! Inc. © 2000 by Yahoo! Inc. YAHOO! and the YAHOO! logo are trademarks of Yahoo! Inc.; p.188 top: © 2001 The New Yorker Collection from Cartoonbank.com. All Rights Reserved; p.188 bottom: Reproduced with permission of Yahoo! Inc. © 2000 by Yahoo! Inc. YAHOO! and the YAHOO! logo are trademarks of Yahoo! Inc.; p.191: Screen shot reprinted by permission from FinanCenter, Inc.; p.192: Courtesy of Gomez, Inc.; p.193: FPG International; p.195: Source: Bankrate.com, © 2001; p.198: Screen shot reprinted by permission from FinanCenter, Inc.; p.199: Screen shot reprinted by permission from FinanCenter, Inc.

CHAPTER 8: p.214: The Image Bank, Inc.; p.216: Digital Federal Credit Union; p.218 top: CartoonStock; p.218 bottom: courtesy of LendingTree, Inc.; p.225: Reproduced with permission of Yahoo! Inc. © 2000 by Yahoo! Inc. YAHOO! and the YAHOO! logo are trademarks of Yahoo! Inc.; p.226: courtesy of kbb.com; p.227: Reproduced with permission of Yahoo! Inc. © 2000 by Yahoo! Inc. YAHOO! and the YAHOO! logo are trademarks of Yahoo! Inc.; p.228: Reproduced with permission of Yahoo! Inc. © 2000 by Yahoo! Inc. YAHOO! and the YAHOO! logo are trademarks of Yahoo! Inc.; p.231: Reproduced with permission of Yahoo! Inc. © 2000 by Yahoo! Inc. YAHOO! and the YAHOO! logo are trademarks of Yahoo! Inc.; p.232: Screen shot reprinted by permission from FinanCenter, Inc.; p.233: Reproduced with permission of Yahoo! Inc. © 2000 by Yahoo! Inc. YAHOO! and the YAHOO! logo are trademarks of Yahoo! Inc.

CHAPTER 9: p.244: Tony Stone; p.248: CartoonStock; p.247: Screen shot reprinted by permission from FinanCenter, Inc.; p.249: Reproduced with permission of Yahoo! Inc. © 2000 by Yahoo! Inc. YAHOO! and the YAHOO! logo are trademarks of Yahoo! Inc.; 250: courtesy of Homestore.com, Inc. and the National Association of REALTORS®; p.256: Reproduced with permission of Yahoo! Inc. © 2000 by Yahoo! Inc. YAHOO! and the YAHOO! logo are trademarks of Yahoo! Inc.; p.260: Reproduced with permission of Yahoo! Inc. © 2000 by Yahoo! Inc. YAHOO! and the YAHOO! logo are trademarks of Yahoo! Inc.; p.261: Screen shot reprinted by permission from FinanCenter, Inc.; p.264: Reproduced with permission of Yahoo! Inc. © 2000 by Yahoo! Inc. YAHOO! and the YAHOO! logo are trademarks of Yahoo! Inc.; p.267: Screen shot reprinted by

continued from inside front cover